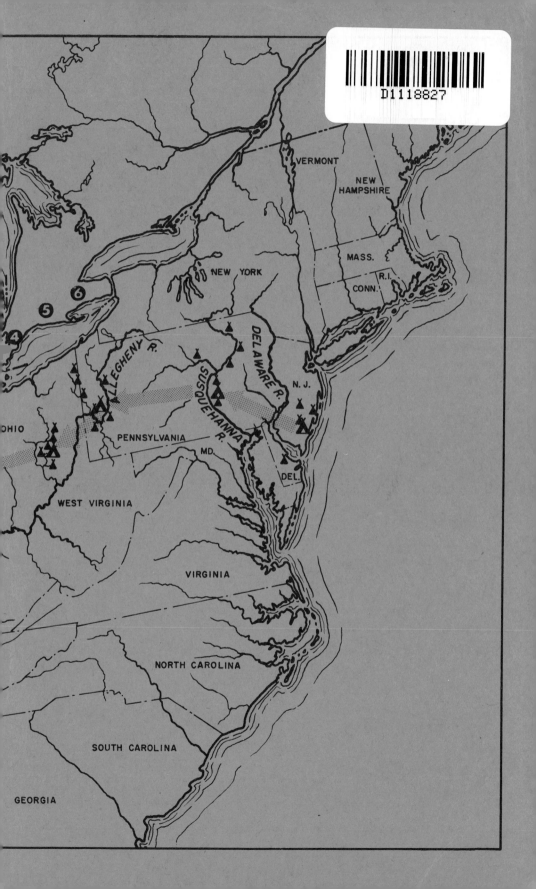

THE DELAWARE INDIANS

NOTE ON ENDPAPER MAP

The map on the endpapers shows the migration route of the main body
of the Delaware Indians from the time they left the Delaware River and
its tributaries until they settled in Indian Territory (Oklahoma) three
centuries later. Teepees show locations of major settlements enroute.
Locations of surviving groups of Delawares today are indicated by numbers: (1) The main body in northeastern Oklahoma; splinter groups at
(2) Anadarko, Oklahoma (3) Shawano County, Wisconsin (4) Moraviantown, Ontario (5) Muncy Town, Ontario (6) Six Nations Reserve, Ontario.
(Map by Charlotte Carlson)

The Delaware Indians *A History*

C. A. Weslager

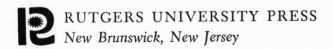

RUTGERS UNIVERSITY PRESS
New Brunswick, New Jersey

Library of Congress Cataloging in Publication Data

Weslager, Clinton Alfred, 1909–
  The Delaware Indians.

  Includes bibliographical references.
  1. Delaware Indians—History. I. Title.
E99.D2W39   970.3   78–185397
ISBN 0-8135-0702-2

To Clint and Elizabeth

Contents

Illustrations

Preface

One of the important uses of a preface is to enable the author to explain what he has tried to achieve in his book. This clarification is often necessary because readers frequently look in vain for something the author did not intend to include; and then they unjustly censure him for supposed sins of omission.

When I made up my mind to write a book about the Delaware Indians, my daughter, a voracious reader, suggested that I focus on an imaginary Indian family and, through the lives of several generations, tell the story of the family's trials and tribulations against the changing historic backdrop of the American scene. Although this would have been a worthy undertaking, it would have required the talents of one proficient in writing fiction, and I quickly disqualified myself. Conversely, one of my faculty associates suggested that I produce a work of two or three volumes, encyclopedic in concept, that would be a magnum opus on the Delaware Indians. Such a ponderous work, if I were ever capable of completing it, would be limited in its readership to a few scholars, and it would not fill the need that now exists for a comprehensive account in a single volume. What I have tried to do is to write a book that can be enjoyed by the general reader, including intelligent young adults. Yet I am also hopeful that the historian and anthropologist will find it a worthwhile contribution to the literature.

Obviously it has been necessary for me to synthesize some material already in print and familiar to scholars; for example, I felt it desirable to discuss the story of the Walam Olum, because no history of the Delawares would be complete without it. The chapters dealing with William Penn and the Indians, Pennsylvania's Indian policy, the infamous Walking Purchase, and the part played by the Delawares during the French and Indian War represent condensations of material covered in greater detail in papers and monographs. But it would be an oversight not to bring these events into their proper historical context. On the other hand, I have made use of primary source material not previously tapped. One example is the John G. Pratt Papers in the collections of the Kansas Historical Society (an estimated 10,000 raw documents), containing letters, notes, account records, vouchers, annuity and roll lists that crossed Pratt's desk during the years he served the Delawares as a minister and later as their Indian Agent. These—and other manuscript sources which I consulted in a number of institutions—broaden our knowledge of the Delawares after they left their native hearths. In his monograph on the Delaware Indian Big House, Frank G. Speck wrote of the Delaware wanderings that we know "almost nothing covering the century of migration from Pennsylvania to Kansas and Indian Territory." If Speck were living, I think he would be glad to see that this gap in our knowledge of Delaware Indian history has now been filled.

One difficulty in undertaking a book like this is that there is such a tremendous amount of data scattered through printed and manuscript sources that one can be avalanched by its magnitude. The Delaware Indian deeds on record covering lands sold to settlers in Pennsylvania, New Jersey, and Delaware during the seventeenth century would fill a volume larger than this one. Moreover, to synopsize all of the conferences between the Delawares and governmental agencies as recorded in the *Pennsylvania Archives* and the *Pennsylvania Colonial Records* (to say nothing of the archival records of Maryland, Delaware, New York, and New Jersey) would probably fill another volume.

The Dutch explorer David Pietersz De Vries, who met the Indians in the Delaware Bay area as early as 1632, and the Englishman Thomas Yong, who explored the Delaware River in 1634 seeking the Northwest Passage, both left journals which contain valuable information. Swedish officials such as Governor Johan Printz, the Reverend Johan Companius Holm, Governor Johan Rising, the young engineer Peter Lindeström, the Reverend Andreas Hesselius, and others who lived in New Sweden in the seventeenth century wrote about the natives in their letters and journals. William Penn, Thomas Paschall, Francis Daniel Pastorius, Gabriel Thomas, and others associated with the Province of Pennsylvania left accounts of the Indians also written at a very early date. The Moravian missionaries John Heckewelder, David Zeisberger, George Henry Loskiel, John Christian Frederick

Cammerhoff, John Peter Kluge, Abraham Luckenbach, and others; missionaries of other denominations, such as David and John Brainerd, Isaac McCoy, David Jones, and Charles Beatty; and diarists like Christian Frederick Post, George Croghan, and Conrad Weiser came into contact with the Delawares in the eighteenth and early nineteenth centuries, and their writings are equally valuable.

I will not attempt any listing of manuscript sources except to point out that *A Guide to the Manuscripts Relating to the American Indian in the Library of the American Philosophical Society* (1966) contains no less than twenty-eight pages devoted to a listing of manuscripts relating to the Delawares held by this single institution. A bibliography of the printed and manuscript material pertaining in whole, or in part, to the Delawares would constitute a small volume of its own. In the chapter notes, I have cited only selected references where I feel that specific authority is needed to validate a quotation or statement of fact. From my citations, I'm sure the reader will get a feeling of the depth of the literature—and yet is it not ironical that up to the present time there has not been available an inclusive history of the tribe?

In an important paper published in 1957, "American Indian And White Relations to 1830," William N. Fenton pointed out that despite efforts among historians to bridge the gap between history and ethnology no one up to that time had "yet succeeded in producing a book which is securely footed in both disciplines." What Dr. Fenton meant was that the danger of the direct historical approach is in believing everything that comes through the eyes and pens of white men whose interests and values were entirely different from the Indians. Many contemporary writers were biased by commercial, political, or religious motives, and none of them had formal ethnological training. Most of them were not conversant in the Indian tongues; and, conditioned to European society, they did not understand all of the incidents they witnessed. Although there is reality in personal narrative and diary entries, the early writers were subjective and often too close to the events for a proper understanding of them.

As a student of history, I don't wish to degrade contemporary writings, which are the essence of history. Despite bias, inaccuracies, and omissions, they constitute a rich source of information, provided one examines them critically as a corpus of data, not as isolated pieces of intelligence on which conclusions would not be warranted.

Moreover, a student who has kept abreast of archeological work and has participated in some of it, augmented by ethnographic study among living Delawares, should be able to look at the recorded data critically. Thus, although this book is rooted in documentary sources, much of it has been written from the broader dimension of the discipline known as ethno-history. Lest there be any misunderstanding, this book is not intended as a discussion and analysis of Delaware culture—it is an account of *what* took place and an attempt to analyze and understand *why* the events occurred; in short, it is history. For that reason, I have tried to provide in brief, the historical background at different points in time that will enable the reader to fit Delawares into the particular events of the period. Where there were conflicting issues, I've done my best to present both sides, without prejudice.

A few words of explanation about points of style are in order: I prefer the spelling Munsie (pl. Munsies), instead of Munsi, Munsee, Muncy, or Moncy. There is a precedent for this form as early as 1756 in the *Pennsylvania Colonial Records* (vol. 7, pp. 146, 726). I have also chosen to pluralize Delaware, which is an English word, by adding the English *s*, whereas, following the practice of anthropologists, I use the same form for both singular and plural of all other tribal names, e.g., Cherokee, Shawnee, and Wyandot. Where it is possible to do so, I have given English translations of Indian personal names in a quotation in parentheses, usually, but not always, following the first citation of the name, e.g., Pisquetomen ("he that keeps on though it is getting dark"). I have reviewed the majority of the Indian names cited in the text with Mrs. Nora Thompson Dean (Touching Leaves), a fluent Delaware speaker, and have had the benefit of her interpretations in those instances where English meanings are apparent to her. In other instances, I have relied on documentary sources where both the Indian name and its English translation were given, although these occurrences are relatively few. If there is any doubt about a translation of a personal name, I have offered none, and this unfortunately is true of the majority of names found in seventeenth-century records, whose meanings have been lost. With a few exceptions, I have not attempted to give English translations of Indian geographical names. Each of these names once had its own meaning, but this is a complex subject, and I refer the reader to the place-name

literature of the respective areas where the Delawares lived. Finally,
I admit to using the term *tribe* very loosely as applied to the Delawares and other Indian groups, but when one is writing about Indians
it is difficult to find another descriptive term.

C.A.W.

March 15, 1971

Acknowledgments

I owe a great debt to Mrs. Nora Thompson Dean (Touching Leaves) for translating numerous Indian personal names for me, for critically reading portions of two chapters in my original manuscript, for supplying me with important items about her people during my visits to Oklahoma, and for assisting me in many ways through subsequent correspondence. Others having Delaware Indian ancestry to whom I am also indebted for information or assistance are Mrs. Mary Townsend Crow, Fred Falleaf, Earl Frenchman, Mrs. Annie Parks, James (Lone Bear) Revey, Henry A. Secondine, Bruce Miller Townsend, Mrs. Elizabeth West, and Mrs. Mary Smith Witcher. Mrs. Witcher, a direct descendant of Chief Ketchum, not only loaned me documentary and microfilm data which were new to me but graciously went to the trouble of finding answers to a number of my questions. Belva Secondine, who has been gathering information about Chief William Anderson and his Indian contemporaries, was also very kind in making information available to me, for which I am extremely grateful.

James A. Rementer, a member of the Dean household and a student of Delaware language and culture who has been under Mrs. Dean's tutelage since 1961, was of invaluable aid in a hundred different ways. I owe more to him than words can repay for his guidance, companionship, and assistance.

My introduction to Delaware Indian informants in Washington County, Oklahoma, was through Paul Endacott as a result of our fortuitous exchange of correspondence in 1962. I learned from him that a portion of the centerpost from the last Delaware Big House had been installed by a contractor as a supporting beam in his ranch house near Copan. It was he who later introduced me to Horace L. McCracken, former Chairman of the Delaware Tribal Business Committee, who invited me to his home in Bartlesville and made available the briefs and other legal documents pertaining to the several suits pending before the Indian Claims Commission. Mr. McCracken, also of Delaware heritage, had been a tax expert employed by a large oil company prior to his retirement in 1965, and his keen mind absorbed the legal technicalities of this documentation, which he explained to me and interpreted.

Other Oklahomans whose kindnesses I want to acknowledge are Joe Barber III, Mrs. Harold J. Hepp, George R. Kennedy, M.D., and Elmer J. Sark. I also received the utmost cooperation from Gene Winn, Director of the Bartlesville Public Library, and Mrs. Wilma M. Berry, Curator of the History Room. They not only provided me with photocopies of reference material during my visits, but Mrs. Berry continued to send pertinent material to me by mail, at my request, while this book was being written.

Among other persons associated with libraries and institutions who were especially helpful to me I would like to acknowledge the assistance of the following: Mrs. Margaret Blaker, Anthropology Archives, Smithsonian Institution; Marc T. Campbell, Forsyth Library, Fort Hays Kansas State College; Mrs. Hilda M. Carpenter, Carnegie Library, Ottawa, Kansas; D. R. Cassie, District Supervisor, Brantford (Ontario) District, Department of Indian Affairs and Northern Development; Frederick J. Dockstader, Museum of the American Indian; Caroline Dunn and Mrs. Leona T. Alig, William Henry Smith Memorial Library, Indiana Historical Society; G. N. Faulkner, District Supervisor, London District (Ontario), Department of Indian Affairs and Northern Development; Magdalena Houlroyd, Savitz Library, Glassboro State College; James H. Howard, Oklahoma State University; Donald G. Humphrey, Philbrook Art Center; William A. Hunter, Pennsylvania Historical and Museum Commission; Mrs. Jane Hukill, Brandywine College Library; Donald and Jean Hutslar, the Ohio Historical Society; John E. Kilbourne, Historical Society of Pennsylvania; Herbert C. Kraft, Seton Hall University Museum; Thaddeus J. Krom, New Jersey Historical Society; Mrs. Rella Looney, Oklahoma Historical Society; Mrs. David N. Low and Mrs. Donald W. Hallman, Eleutherian Mills Historical Library; Miss Dorothy Lapp, Chester County Historical Society; Nyle Miller, Kansas State Historical Society; William W. Newcomb, Jr., Texas Memorial Museum; Ernest Root, Fairfield Village and Museum; Laura L. Reid, Department of Records, Philadelphia Friends Yearly Meeting; Kenneth W. Richards, Archives and History Bureau, State of New Jersey; Mrs. H. Hadley Sleight, the State Historical Society of Missouri; Murphy D. Smith, American Philosophical Society; Mrs. Bernice C. Sprenger, Burton Historical Collections, Detroit Public Library; and Mrs. Frances H. Stadler, Missouri Historical Society.

The staffs of the following institutions also provided me with information, and I want to acknowledge their cooperation: Great Lakes Agency, Bureau of Indian Affairs; William L. Clements Library, University of Michigan; Carnegie Library of Pittsburgh; Historical Society of Delaware; Morris Library of the University of Delaware; New York Public Library; Library of Congress; Peabody Museum Library; University of Pennsylvania Museum Library; Wilmington Institute Free Library; Woolaroc Museum.

I also want to express my appreciation to the following individuals: William Baldwin, Herbert Bernstein, Senator J. Caleb Boggs, W. Albert Caleb, Mrs. Minnie Chamberlin, Arthur R. Dunlap, Ives Goddard, Mrs. Elma E. Gray, Leslie R. Gray, Nathaniel Claiborne Hale, Jasper Hill (Big White Owl), Mrs. Georgia W. Hyatt, C. L. Hudiburg, M.D., Francis P. Jennings, Hugh Johns, Charles F. Kier, Jr., Wm B. Marye, Mrs. Irene Montour, Olof Norbeck of Djursholm, Sweden, Howard Piepenbrink, Guy W. Lovell, Louis L. Rochmes, Walter D. Rutherford, Ronald A. Thomas, Arthur G. Volkman, and Albright Zimmerman.

Needless to say, none of the persons or institutions I have named are answerable for anything appearing in this volume. Their assistance, or encouragement, in no way relieves me of the full responsibility for the contents of the work.

THE DELAWARE INDIANS

1

The Delawares Today

During the weekend of June 5, 6, 7, 1970, I attended a powwow as the guest of a Delaware Indian family. It was the sixth annual Delaware powwow, an event that had its origin in June of 1965 when a number of persons of Delaware Indian descent in Oklahoma decided to celebrate their Indianism in a weekend of fun and relaxation.

The site of the powwow was a grove shaded by post oak trees on property owned by a Delaware named George Falleaf, about two miles north and three miles east of the rural town of Copan in Washington County, Oklahoma. A narrow, unpaved secondary road brought the participants to the grove; they turned in at right angles to the road, bumped across a meadow, and backed their cars into the places under the trees they had selected for their camps. I watched as several hundred men, women, and children, mostly in cars with Oklahoma license plates, although there were a few from other states, including one car from Ohio and another from Arizona, converged on the grove. Having been absorbed into Oklahoma's social and economic system, the Delawares today may be found competing with success in industry, the trades, and professions in Bartlesville, Dewey, Copan, Lenapah, Delaware, Nowata, Alluewe, Tahlequah, Tulsa, and elsewhere in Oklahoma. The powwow provides an exciting weekend having nativistic overtones and is a change of pace from the Delawares' normal pattern of living.

Each family group set up its own camp, and the aggregation of camps formed a semicircle around the dance area, a level clearing of hard-packed earth about half the size of a baseball infield. Some families slept in trailers or campers, others pitched canvas tents purchased from a mail-order house or a home-and-auto store, and still others erected nondescript shelters of tree limbs, blankets, and awning material. Those with small children or babies strung clotheslines from tentpoles to nearby trees on which they hung their wash. Each family prepared its own food and did its own cooking, usually over kerosene stoves, and there was much visiting back and forth. The basic rations allocated each individual by those in charge of the affair consisted of bread, potatoes, and meat, made available once a day, free of charge. The families provided their own vegetables, desserts, breakfast foods, and coffee.

The main activity during the weekend was the dancing, which usually began each day in the middle of the afternoon and continued until it was time for the campers to prepare their evening meals. The dancing was informal, often improvised, and one danced or stopped dancing at his own discretion; no questions were asked, no credentials were required, and there were no rehearsals. Those who chose not to dance, or who rested between dances, sat on plank benches on the perimeter of the dance ground or on folding chairs, some of the elderly women shielding their heads from the hot sun with parasols. Dancing was resumed at sundown, after the supper dishes had been cleared away, and continued well beyond midnight. Anyone who felt like it—from wrinkled grandparents to toddlers—took part in the dancing, which consisted mainly of shuffling clockwise around the dance area. As the evening wore on, the very old and the very young left to go to bed, so fatigued that they fell asleep despite the hubbub. The others continued the festivities until the early hours of the morning, and they slept late the next day, when the very old and the very young were stirring again.

Music for the dancing was supplied by a group of ten male singers and drummers under the direction of a patriarch known as the Head Singer. They were all mature men, wearing colorful sport shirts, slacks, and felt cowboy hats, and they huddled together on folding chairs around a large cowhide drum that was set up at the edge of the dance area so they would not interfere with the dancers. Each drummer had one drumstick, and they all beat in the same rhythm, blending their voices in a sort of chant that had no identifiable lyrics. The tempo was slowed down or speeded up as the various dances were performed—the Round Dance, War Dance, Snake Dance, Buffalo Dance, Stomp Dance, Turkey Dance, and others.[1] The participants did not seem to touch each other's bodies as they danced, except during the Two Step, when the men danced with the women, each couple holding hands as they moved around the ground. In some dances the drum was silent, the singers providing a rhythmic chant to accompany the performers, and there were other dances, especially late at night, when the drummers used a water drum. Everyone seemed to enjoy himself in the carnival-like atmosphere, and I saw no rowdyism.

There were two Head Dancers, a male and female, both handsome youngsters in their late teens, and since Head Dancers (like Indian princesses) were alien to traditional Delaware ceremonies, the notion must have been borrowed from one of the other acculturated tribes who also stage powwows. The male Head Dancer was decked out in a colorful costume of his own creation that would have made him the outstanding contender for first prize at a masquerade ball. He wore red briefs with a covering black breechclout, his thighs were bare, and bells were tied to each knee with orange ribbons; tufted white feathers reached from his knees all the way down to his white chamois moccasins. His close-fitting red tunic, with long sleeves, was constricted at the waist with a white sash ornamented with multicolored beadwork. He wore a beaded band around his forehead and a roach of animal hair on his head, with two clusters of red and white feathers like sunbursts fastened to his back. When I met and talked with him, I found that he was not the belligerent savage chief his costume might have suggested, but an intelligent college boy who probably would not have been recognized as an Indian descendant in his street clothes.

The female Head Dancer was more conservative in her leggings, white moccasins, and beaded, fringed dress. She, too, wore a forehead band in which multicolored beads were strung in a fancy pattern. The two young people were supposed to start the dancing, although one of the men, acting as a master of ceremonies, prompted the dancers over a microphone and loudspeaker. The microphone was also used when the powwow was officially opened by an old Indian reciting a long prayer in the Delaware tongue. Although only a few of the elderly people understood it, both young and old sat quietly with heads bowed as the speaker asked the Creator's blessing.

A number of special dances were held in honor of individuals whose names were called out over the loudspeaker, and there was also a special dance dedicated to each of the Head Dancers. At one stage in the performance, the Head Dancers distributed gifts in special wrappings to close friends of their families, and I had the impression that considerable expense had been incurred in buying these presents. As the recipients' names were called, they came forward to receive their presents, and they reciprocated by tendering a present to the Head Dancer, usually money. During one of the sessions held for the female Head Dancer, she received a number of one-dollar bills—perhaps fifteen or twenty—which she carried to the singers and placed on the drum to be divided among them.

Most of the men dancers were in slacks, or blue denims, and short-sleeved sport shirts of bright hues—yellows, pinks, blues, and greens. Although a few wore feather headdresses, ranging from one or two feathers to ornate bonnets, most of them danced bareheaded. Some, like myself, removed their coats and ties and shuffled along with the others in ordinary street clothes and shoes, and I saw one dancer wearing blue tennis shoes with crepe soles. The typical garment worn by the women was a fringed scarf draped over their shoulders and arms, like a shawl, practically covering their dresses, and extending to the knees and even below. These shawls were gayly colored, with purples, reds, and greens predominant, and some of the women wore beaded bands on their foreheads and carried feather fans. A handsome brunette of Delaware descent, who was accompanied by her non-Indian husband, carried a red fringed shawl folded over her left forearm as she danced. She wore cloth leggings, a belted, blue overblouse with long sleeves, and a black skirt trimmed with red ribbonwork. Like many of the others she also wore a bead pendant around her neck to which a medallion was fastened, and she carried a long buckskin bag, beaded and fringed. The latter was definitely part of the traditional Delaware costume. Nevertheless, I gathered that the dancers wearing clothing known to be traditional with the Delaware tribe were in the minority, and that the costuming was either nontribal or that it combined articles of dress copied from other tribes.

During the day, when some of the singers and dancers were resting, chatting, or visiting each other's camps, males and females of all ages played an Indian football game in a field adjacent to the dance ground. Apparently any number of players could participate in this game known to the Delawares as paw-sah-hum-mon. Two goalposts made of saplings about fifteen feet high with the limbs cut off, spaced about six feet apart, but without crosspieces, were set up on each end of the playing field. The ball, called a paw-saw-hee-kun, made of deerskin stuffed with deer hair, was not spherical but oblong like a small pillow about nine or ten inches long. The game began when the ball was thrown into the air, as in basketball, and two of the players, a male and female, jumped to try and knock it toward their own goal-posts.

From then on the game was, or, to one unfamiliar with the rules, seemed to be a disorganized scramble. The men and boys were not permitted to run with the ball in their hands, nor could they throw it, but, as in soccer, they had to kick it toward the goal or in the direction of another member of their team. The women and girls were permitted to throw the ball and also to pick it up and run with it, as the males tried to knock it from their hands or prevent their passing it. The females were allowed to grab or tackle a male who had the ball, as they tried to take it away from him, but the males were not supposed to grab the females, although some did, which caused much giggling. The women players could throw the ball between the goal-posts, or run through with it, whereas the men had to kick it across their goal.

An old man kept score by removing one of the twelve small sticks about two or three inches long that lay in a little pile on the ground before him. Each time the ball was kicked or carried between the goalposts, a twig was placed in a row for either the men or the women. When the twelve twigs were used up, the game was over, and the side having the most twigs was the winner. In case of a tie, a play-off took place to make the deciding point.

I was told that this is an ancient Delaware game that was once played every spring in all Delaware communities. The people considered it wrong to continue playing after the middle of June. At the close of the final game, an old lady cut open the ball and allowed the deer hair to fall to the ground while she prayed, thanking the Creator for allowing the people to live and play, and asking that He permit them to live and play in the future. The deerhide cover was then given to someone to be kept until the next season, when it was stuffed and used again.

Saturday evening was the gala night at the powwow, and a large number of visitors, both whites and Indians, came by car in clouds of dust to watch the performers; and some of the newcomers also joined in the dancing. An enterprising dealer, who sold a variety of commercially made Indian trinkets from an aluminum trailer lettered with the word SOUVENIRS, the letters alternately painted red and blue, enjoyed his best business from these visitors. A second hawker vending hot dogs, barbecues, pop, and coffee from an adjacent trailer parked on the powwow grounds did a land-office business; he ran out of sandwich buns before the evening festivities ended. A third vendor sold floss candy and candy apples from another trailer.

After the dancing was over, there was a tangle of traffic on the country roads as the visitors tried to get back to the main highway, which was swollen with Saturday night traffic. The police had to be called out to clear the congestion. "We've got to do something about that next year," I heard someone say, "because every year we get more and more visitors." On Sunday morning the campers started taking down their tents and packing up, preparing to return home, where they would resume their respective trades and professions on Monday morning. The majority of them would not have occasion to wear Indian dress, nor to participate in an Indian dance, until the next Delaware powwow, although a few would probably take their families to attend powwows held by other Oklahoma tribes. By nightfall the grove was practically deserted.

Despite the good time that everyone had at the powwow, the years have not been kind to the once-great Delaware Nation, venerated by their Algonkian neighbors as "the grandfather tribe" among the American Indians. Today, the Delawares and their tribal affiliates, the Munsies, are divided and scattered. The white man's blood is in their veins; they speak his language and compete in his busy world.

In 1907 ethnologist James Mooney accepted a commission to write an entry summing up information about the Delawares for publication in a bulletin sponsored by the Bureau of American Ethnology. One of his most difficult problems was to find where the fragmented and scattered groups were then living. After completing his investigations, he estimated that the Delaware population in the United States and Canada had declined to a pathetic total of 1,900 men, women, and children. He enumerated as follows the approximate number of Delaware descendants at the principal places where they were then living:

Incorporated with the Cherokee Nation, Indian Territory, 870; Wichita Reserve, Oklahoma, 95; Munsies with Stockbridges in Wisconsin, perhaps 260; Munsies with Chippewa in Kansas, perhaps 45; "Moravians of the Thames," Ontario, 347; "Munsies of the Thames," Ontario, 122; with the Six Nations on the Grand River, Ontario, 150.[2]

Mooney did not take into account the scattered individuals of Delaware stock who had intermarried with the High Plains and Plateau tribes, nor the families among the wandering Texas bands having Delaware blood, and he elected not to include the Eastern mixed-bloods having Delaware ancestry. His principal concern was in trying to account for the major communities that formed recognizable units; and the first group he cited, numbering 870 persons, represented all that was left of the main body of the Delawares. Members of this group, who had merged with the civilized Cherokee, were living in the northeastern part of Oklahoma, where their children and grandchildren may still be found. Mooney's second group was a small band of ninety-five persons who had split from the main body to join remnants of the Caddo tribe, and whose descendants are living today in the environs of Anadarko, Oklahoma, formerly the Wichita Caddo Reservation.

There are no Indian reservations in Oklahoma, and these Oklahoma-Delawares no longer exist as a self-contained tribal group, as do some 400,000 other American Indians living on government reservations in 26 states. In 1907, along with other Indians settled in former Indian Territory, the Delawares became American citizens in the newly formed state of Oklahoma.

Delaware chiefs and councilors are now a thing of the past, but the main body is represented by a Delaware Tribal Business Committee, consisting of five active, well-educated Indian descendants who serve without remuneration, and whose prime function is to handle business relations with the United States government. The members of the committee, a chairman, vice-chairman, secretary, and two members at large are elected by ballot for four-year terms at open meetings usually held in the Dewey High School to which all persons claiming Delaware blood are invited. Detailed minutes are kept of each meeting, as stipulated under bylaws adopted on September 7, 1958, and approved by the Commissioner of Indian Affairs in Washington, D.C.

The former president of the committee, Horace L. McCracken, who died on December 28, 1970, had held office since 1951, and although he was never called a chief, he was, in fact, the titular leader of the Oklahoma Delawares during his term in office (see Fig. 1). The last time I saw Mr. McCracken was at the 1970 powwow, and it was immediately apparent that he was much loved and admired by the Delaware people. His death seven months later was considered a real loss.

The small splinter group at Anadarko, sometimes called Absentee Delawares, indicating their voluntary separation from the main body, now officially call themselves the Delaware Tribe of Western Oklahoma. They are also represented by a Business Committee whose present members are Arthur L. Thomas, president; Alene Martinez,

Figure 1. Delaware Tribal Business Committee: seated, Horace L. Mc-Cracken, former Chairman, who died Dec. 28, 1970; and Bruce Miller Townsend, present Chairman. Standing: Nathan H. Young; Mary Townsend (Mrs. Joe) Crow, Secretary-Treasurer; and Henry A. Secondine. Absent, Y. A. "Zeke" Scott, who was elected a member of the committee Mar. 20, 1971.

secretary; Myrtle Holder, treasurer; and Tommy Holder, Lawrence Snake, and Charles Taylor, members at large.

Full-blooded Delawares are extremely rare in Oklahoma, due to intermarriage with white persons; nevertheless, there are excellent Indian physical types to be found in both groups, as I observed at the 1970 powwow. In the absence of genealogical data, who can say with certainty that this or that person is not a full-blood, especially if his straight, jet-black hair, high cheekbones, squinted eyes, and skin color seem to lend credence to that claim? On the other hand, some individuals have such a small amount of Indian blood that I have been astonished to meet fair-haired, blue-eyed men and women who can honestly claim having Delaware ancestors in their family trees. In the absence of reservations in Oklahoma on which Indians can be confined and counted, the problem in arriving at an accurate estimate of the number of Delewares now living in the state becomes a question of who is Indian and who is not. If a Delaware Indian is defined as a person whose parents were *both* Delawares, neither having white increments, then the total number would indeed be minimal. On the other hand, if one is willing to define a Delaware Indian as a person who had at least one Delaware grandparent, i.e., one-quarter Indian blood (which, incidentally, satisfies the United States government that an individual may be classed as an Indian), then there are several hundred Delawares in Oklahoma. Some of these, however, prefer to classify themselves as white because of their dominant three-quarters white blood. Persons who have lesser amounts of Delaware blood than one-quarter are in the thousands, and some of these also lay claim to Osage, Pawnee, Cherokee, Kiowa, Choctaw, and other tribal ancestry, as well as Delaware. About twenty-nine different tribes retained their identities in Oklahoma, and members of these groups have been widely assimilated in Oklahoma's general population.

There is an Indian Women's Club in Bartlesville, a social group whose members represent a number of these tribes, and at special meetings, fashion shows, and the like they wear Indian costume. Traditional Delaware costume, as a form of daily dress, is no longer seen except on such special occasions. There are still a few adults capable of speaking the Delaware language fluently, although none of them habitually speaks Delaware, nor have I ever heard any of the children speaking any language other than English. The Indian speakers complain that there are too few opportunities to engage in

Figure 2. Rare photo of last Delaware Indian Big House near Copan, Okla. (c. 1916), where last ceremony was held in 1924. Deer and other game were hung on trimmed tree or "meat pole" in foreground; log mortar in front of east doorway used for pounding corn to make hominy, cooked in iron kettles by the ash-ka-suk (ceremonial attendants) and served to participants. (Courtesy the late Fred Falleaf)

conversation in their native tongue because so few remain who understand the language. Even those speakers who are trying to keep alive the language and other elements in Indian tradition own automobiles, radios, telephones, and television sets, and have taken up other conveniences of modern living.

Christianity has replaced the native religions, and parishioners of Delaware descent who have completely given up their non-Christian rituals attend Catholic and Protestant churches along with whites and descendants of other tribes. The so-called Big House Ceremony, formerly held each fall during a twelve-day period and whose origin lies in the dim, distant past, was conducted annually by the Delawares until 1924. That year the recitative singing was led by a traditionalist, since deceased, named Frank Wilson (his Delaware name was Em-mah).

Built of rough logs laid horizontally and corner-notched, having an earthen floor, and a roof of hand-split shingles pierced by two gaping smokeholes, the Big House measured approximately 24½ feet by 40 feet. It stood 400 feet southwest of the center of Section 18, 28 North,

13 East, Washington County, on a high tract on the west side of the
Little Caney River, south of "the old Indian ford," and about 4½
miles west of Copan (see Fig. 2). Of ceremonial significance was the
oaken centerpost which supported the ridgepole, and which bore two
large carvings of the human face—one facing east, the other west,
each painted half black, half red, their foreheads incised with wrinkles
to simulate age and wisdom. After the 1924 ceremony, the Big House
began to rot away, and in time it fell apart from disuse, some of the
wood carried away by looters. A section of the centerpost containing
two bas-relief faces found its way to the collections of the Philbrook
Art Center in Tulsa where it has been preserved (see Fig. 3). The
Woolaroc Museum near Bartlesville also has in its collections a carved
face from one of the six sideposts, each of which bore similar carvings,
as did the four interior doorposts.[3]

Figure 3. Carved faces, originally painted half red, half black, from centerpost of the last Delaware Big House. Face on the left was carved on the
east side of post, and the face to right on the west side. The faces were
not worshipped as idols but represented the M'sing (the Masked Spirit),
who was Keeper of the Game in the Delaware pantheon. Participants recited and sang their visions as they danced around the centerpost, which
symbolized the tie between the Creator and the Earth. The post measured
13½" by 11" at the base. (Courtesy Donald G. Humphrey, Philbrook
Art Center, Tulsa, Okla.)

During the Second World War an improvised Big House Ceremony was held three times; in the spring and fall of 1944, and again in the spring of 1945. Anciently the Delawares were taught that there would be disastrous earthquakes, and the world might come to an end if their annual ceremony was discontinued. Some of the old-timers brooded over the sacrilege that had been committed in terminating the rite, and were anxious to have it resumed. Second, some of the old-timers wanted to exemplify the solemn rite in order to entreat the Creator to give the United States a speedy victory and thus permit the return of American fighting men, including Delaware youths, to their families. The ceremony was held in a makeshift structure of bark and canvas thrown up on property owned by one of the Indians and located north of Dewey. There were no carved faces to look down upon the celebrants, and the other paraphernalia was also missing, such as the white wampum beads so essential to the rite, which someone had collected and sold to museums.[4] Despite the devout efforts of a handful of older people, including Reuben Wilson, whose Delaware name was Week-peh-kee-xeeng ("he who is like receding water"), and James H. Thompson, whose Indian name was Oh-huh-lum-mee-tahk-see ("the one who can be heard from afar"), it was a pitiful attempt, and unsatisfying to those who attended. The younger people didn't come, either because they considered it superstitious nonsense or because they didn't understand the Delaware language. Week-peh-kee-xeeng, a fluent speaker who has since died, was the only one who made an effort to sing, but he was handicapped due to the lack of ceremonial properties.

The discontinuance of the Big House and other traditional Indian ceremonies has, to some extent, been filled by Peyotism, through which the Indian participants seek spiritual independence. The peyote plant (*Lophophora williamsii*) is a grayish green, spineless cactus, whose rounded top is cut off and eaten in a ceremony long practiced by natives of Mexico and southwestern Indian tribes. The peyote button contains both stimulants and sedatives, but since proof is lacking that it is habit-forming, it is not classified as a true narcotic. The use of peyote spread northward, and its ritualistic use, as practiced by a number of Indian tribes and bands, has been organized into a full-fledged religion, Christian in orientation. During the peyote meetings, a tea made by boiling the dried peyotes is sipped by the participants, and the peyote buttons, both green and dried, are eaten the same way that Christians partake of bread and wine during the communion sacrament.

About 1885, John Wilson, a Caddo-Delaware, who had become a peyotist, began to convert some of the Delawares, as well as other Oklahoma Indians, to the cult. His version of Peyotism, termed Big Moon or Moonhead, is the most popular form in northeastern Oklahoma, although a less Christianized ritual called Little Moon was introduced some time later. Anthropologists who have attended peyote meetings held by Delaware Indians have described the expressions of emotion and reverence that are present, and the interested reader will find full details in their accounts.[5]

As the old Indian culture crumbled away, the void was partly bridged by such things as Peyotism (which actually is now practiced by only a small number of Delawares), and by participation in other activities that fall under the broad classification of Pan-Indianism. This is one of the final stages of acculturation, a process by which native Indians who have lost, or are losing, their tribal distinctiveness, substitute nonspecific cultural elements in an almost futile struggle to keep Indianism alive. The substitutions may be modifications of old customs; whereas others, like the powwow, may be peculiar to Pan-Indianism.[6]

The Delawares living in Oklahoma have little or no contact with the four communities of Delawares existing elsewhere as tribal groups on lands reserved for their occupancy. The first of these, the Stockbridge-Munsie Community of Wisconsin, which included 260 Munsies in 1907 according to Mooney's estimate, is officially recognized as an Indian tribe by the United States government. The group is organized under a constitution and bylaws ratified by members of the community on October 30, 1937, and subsequently approved by the Secretary of the Interior. When the corporation was formed, membership was limited to those persons whose names appeared on a Stockbridge Indian Allotment Roll of 1910 "who are residing within the original confines of the Stockbridge Reservation in Shawano County, State of Wisconsin, on the date of the adoption of this Constitution and By-Laws."[7] The Tribal Council, consisting of a president, vice-president, treasurer, and four councilmen elected by popular vote, constitutes the administrative body, and the incumbent president is Mr. Aught Coyhis of Bowler, Wisconsin.

There are approximately 1,424 enrolled members of the community, and the area of their occupancy comprises 2,249 acres of tribal property in Shawano County, about 55 miles west of Green Bay, and 13,000 acres of federal lands which, at this writing, have been promised them by the government but have not yet been transferred to them.[8] The Indians earn their livelihood as loggers, farmers, federal employees, and craftsmen (welders, machinists, and carpenters, for example), or are in the professions. The families are mostly Presbyterians and Lutherans; they attend church on the reservation, but there are no schools in the reserved area, and the children are sent to public schools in Bowler and Gresham.

The Indian language is extinct among the Stockbridge-Munsies, and today only English is spoken. No separate identifiable Delaware Indian culture survives, and there is no certain way of knowing how many residents on the reserve have Delaware blood. This is due to the admixture, because most of the group came from New York and New England originally; they were joined by some Delaware and Munsie families (some calling themselves Brotherton Indians), and intermarriage resulted. There has been, and continues to be, intermarriage with white persons, and a recent investigator wrote that due to miscegenation it was difficult to distinguish many of the Indians from their rural non-Indian neighbors.[9] Nevertheless, it should be said that there are excellent Indian physical types to be found on the reservation if one is able to meet a sufficient number of residents. At the town of Stockbridge, Wisconsin, on the eastern shore of Lake Winnebago, some miles southeast of the reserved lands, there is a small group of Indian descendants (some, perhaps having Delaware ancestry), who also call themselves Brothertons.

In addition to the Munsies on the Stockbridge Reservation, Mooney noted that in 1907 there were 45 Munsies living with the Chippewa in Kansas. The Swan Creek and Black River bands of the Chippewa settled in Kansas in 1836, on lands set aside for them by the government, after ceding their lands in Michigan. About 1859 some Munsie families joined them on the reserve, which originally lay southwest of the present town of Ottawa in Franklin County. A visitor in 1859 said there were then about 40 Munsies and 40 Chippewa on the reserve, each group clinging to its own language and nationality.[10] Today in the general area of Ottawa may be found 60 or 70 persons who have varying amounts of Munsie increments, although the native language is no longer spoken. Like the Oklahoma Delawares, they no longer live on reservation, but have been absorbed into the general population.

In Ontario, Canada, there are approximately 251 persons registered as Delaware Indians on the Six Nations Reserve in Brant County (a small section of the reserve is in Haldimand County), in the environs of Ohsweken, Hagersville, and what was formerly called Smoothtown on the south side of the Grand River. The Delawares constitute a minority group among the 5,312 Indians living on this reserve who are mostly Mohawk, Onondaga, Tuscarora, Seneca, Cayuga, and Mississauga (Chippewa). The reserved land, originally consisting of a tract six miles wide on each side of the Grand from its mouth to its source, was granted in 1784 by General Frederick Haldimand to his Mohawk allies to compensate them for land in the Mohawk Valley lost to the Americans during the Revolution. As time went on, other members of the Six Nations joined the Mohawk, and, as a result of the demand for food, the animal population was so greatly reduced that the reserved lands did not afford the Indians a dependable means of support. The Six Nations Council appointed Mohawk chief Captain Joseph Brant to negotiate with the English; he sold over 300,000 acres to raise money to help support his people.

Today the reserved lands have shrunk to 44,900 acres, or 70 square miles, mostly farm land, and there are stores, churches, a post office, library, nursing home, and 14 schools on the reserve.[11] The houses are small, mostly frame, and there are also a number of old log dwellings occupied by Indian families. The 251 Delawares are descended from Indian migrants from the United States who first settled at Dunnville at the mouth of the Grand under the protective wing of the Cayuga. The Cayuga said later that the Delawares stopped and asked permission to stay overnight, which was granted; they were there at breakfast, and they never left. Dr. Frank G. Speck, a University of Pennsylvania ethnologist who studied these Delawares intermittently during a ten-year period beginning in 1930, was fortunate to become acquainted with a number of old-timers who were then alive.[12] Although these Delawares did not have a separate political identity on the reservation, they continued to speak their own language, and they kept alive those elements in their culture that differed from those of their Cayuga hosts. They built a ceremonial Big House near Dunnville that had a dirt floor, two open fires, and no benches. Later when they moved farther up the Grand, they rebuilt

Figure 4. Artist's conception of the last Big House of the Canadian Delawares, still standing in 1850 on the east bank of Boston Creek near
Hagersville, Ontario. Logs were later hauled away and used for farm
building. From Frank G. Speck, *The Celestial Bear Comes Down to
Earth*. (Courtesy Reading (Pa.) Public Museum and Art Gallery)

their Big House at a new location near Hagersville. In 1934 Speck was
shown the site of this structure, which was no longer standing, and
informants gave him a good description of it (see Fig. 4). The logs that
had formed its walls were moved to a farm in Caledonia for use in a
farm building after the ceremony was discontinued.[13]

As the Delawares were becoming Christianized, the story goes, two
of the Indian converts used axes to destroy all the carved faces in the
last Big House in 1852.[14] This is not strictly true, because a Delaware
descendant, Elliott Moses of Ohsweken, has in his possession an old
wooden mask which tradition says had been salvaged from the Big
House.

Under the influence of Christian teachings, the Indian way of life
disintegrated slowly but surely, and very little remains today that can
be singled out as a specific vestige of Delaware culture. The last of the
traditionalists, Nathan Montour, died suddenly on November 24,
1969, at age seventy-eight, about two months after I visited him and
his wife Irene at their home near Hagersville. At the time of my visit,

he was in excellent health, and I think I may have taken the last photograph that was made of him (see Fig. 5).

Mr. Montour was a gentle, soft-spoken, self-educated man who had taken up wood carving in his later years, and his works were displayed in exhibits in both Canada and the United States. He told me that as a small child he had spoken the Delaware language, but except for a few words he had long since forgotten it. He said that the last fluent Delaware speaker on the reserve was his aunt Jane Montour Battice, who died October 26, 1956, at age eighty-six or eighty-seven. He lamented the fact that the Delaware language had become extinct, and he wrote the following line in a personal letter to me dated July 7, 1969: "I have become convinced that when the older people of this generation pass away there will be no one left that will be able to relate the traditions and cultures of the past, as our culture of today parallels

Figure 5. Nathan Montour, wood carver and last of the Delaware traditionalists on the Six Nations Reservation, Ohsweken, Ontario, who died Nov. 24, 1969, aged seventy-eight, two months after the author visited him and took this picture alongside a cabin that resembled his birthplace

that of the white man, and the younger generation couldn't care less. . . ." Mr. Montour did not live to see the dedication of the Chapel of the Delawares (United Church of Canada) in Ohsweken on June 21, 1970, which would have brought him pleasure and a twinge of sadness. He would have been delighted to welcome Mrs. Nora Thompson Dean, who came on special invitation from far-off Oklahoma to offer a prayer to the Creator in the Delaware language during the services, but he would have been saddened that none of the Indian parishioners could speak or understand their native tongue.

The Six Nations Reserve is divided into six geographical sections, and the Elected Council is composed of two representatives from each section. At present there are two Delawares on the council representing the district where the majority of Delawares live. A chief is elected by popular vote every two years. Mr. Montour told me that the old Delaware families on the reserve were named Anthony, Douglas, Jacobs, Woodruff, Cayuga, John, Moses, Peters, Cornelius, Wampum, Latham, Snake, Wilson, as well as Montour. In recent years there has been considerable intermarriage with both whites and members of other tribes; and many Delawares, as well as those of Iroquois ancestry, have left the reserve to seek more attractive economic opportunities elsewhere. These Indians have become assimilated in the white population of Hamilton and Brantford, as well as smaller towns in Ontario, and in another generation there will probably be little awareness of the native background.

In Kent County, Ontario, about 125 miles west of the Six Nations Reserve, there is another reservation occupied exclusively by Delaware Indians, descendants of the people Mooney referred to as "Moravians of the Thames." The reserve continues to be called Moraviantown, which is a misnomer, because it is not a town but an area containing 3,028 acres, about 6 square miles, lying between the towns of Bothwell and Thamesville on the opposite, or south, side of the Thames River. Approximately 300 Delawares live on this land, reserved for their use by the Canadian government, where they plant and cultivate their small lots. Some of the men work for white farmers whose lands surround the reserve; others are employed in small factories in Kent County.[15] When an Indian woman marries a white, she must leave the reserve and forfeit her rights, and the lands on the reserve cannot be sold to a white or a nonmember of the Delaware tribe.

The majority of inhabitants of the reserve are descended from Christian Indians who, in 1792, under the leadership of the Moravian preacher David Zeisberger broke away from the main body in the United States, and came to Canada to found Fairfield on the north side of the Thames. The town was burned by American soldiers during the War of 1812 and never rebuilt, but in recent years a small museum and historical park have been established on the former town site. Archeological work conducted by the Museum of the University of Western Ontario brought to light evidence of the location of the Indian log houses—as well as representative domestic artifacts, some of which are on display in the museum.[16]

In 1815 the Indians who fled from Fairfield at the approach of the Americans returned and founded a New Fairfield on the south side of the Thames, directly opposite the old town, where a Moravian mission built in 1848 is still standing. There is no longer evidence of a town, and what was formerly called New Fairfield is now part of the reserved Moraviantown area. On November 11, 1902, the Moravians gave up their work among the Canadian Indians and turned over their property on both sides of the Thames to the Canadian Methodist Episcopal Church. In 1925 the Methodists merged with the United Church of Canada, which now owns the historic park and museum and the old Moravian mission across the river. The present pastor, Reverend Ernest Root, who ministers to the Indians, is also curator of the museum and custodian of the park.

The Moraviantown Reservation includes an Indian cemetery, an Indian school, a community hall, the band offices, and three small churches owned by the United Church, the Anglicans, and the Pentecostal denomination. All of these buildings, as well as the bungalows occupied by the Indian families, are built of wood, and many are weather-worn. Some have television aerials on the roofs, and most of the Indian families appear to own cars, many second-hand. As one drives along the unpaved roads on the reservation, he sees nothing that seems different from rural neighborhoods occupied by low-income white families in Canada or the United States. Some of the Indian residents have pronounced white increments, but many excellent Indian physical types can be seen, and when we visited the reserve in August, 1970, I was impressed with the Indian features of the children. They have apparently been taught to avoid strangers —some looked away pretending they did not see us, while others ran and hid when we stopped the car to look at some of the buildings. Among the Indian family names seen on the mailboxes or on the gravestones in the cemetery were Stonefish, White Eye, Snake, Jacobs, Henry, Logan, Tobias, Pheasant, Dolsen, Hill, Peter, and Noah. Once every two years the residents elect a chief and four councilors who represent the group in all business matters and negotiations with the Canadian government. The incumbent chief is Richard Snake, and the councilors are Mrs. Barbara Nash, Harvey Jacobs, Sr., Pliney Stonefish, and Donald White Eye. As in Oklahoma, a few of the traditionalists still speak the Indian language, but tribal and family religious ceremonies have long since been forgotten. These Indians have been exposed to Christian influences for more than two hundred years, and there was never a Big House at this location—the Moravian brethren would never have tolerated pagan devotion at one of their mission towns.

About thirty miles up the Thames River from Moraviantown, south of the city of London, and near the town of Melbourne, there is a third Indian reservation where there are found Mooney's "Munsies of the Thames." Originally the Indian residents were under the jurisdiction of what was called the Caradoc Indian Agency, which was superseded in 1969 by the London district office of the Department of Indian Affairs and Northern Development, which also has jurisdiction over the Moraviantown reserve. There are actually three reserves in the former Caradoc Agency; the Chippewa, who number 500, live on 8,068 acres; the Oneida, with a population of 1,250, have 2,732 acres; and the Munsies, with a population slightly in excess of 100, have 2,732 acres.[17] There are no apparent division lines between these reserves, but Muncy Town (the Canadian spelling) is a small hamlet on a rise of land from which the road dips down to a bridge across the deep, narrow, muddy Thames. The town contains a post office, the band office, and a general store; the homes of the Munsies consist largely of weathered frame bungalows and are scattered in the surrounding farming country, parts of which are still wooded. The children from the three reserves attend a joint kindergarten and primary schools on the reserve, but they must obtain secondary education at public schools off the reserve.

There were Munsies living in this identical area, having wandered into Canada from Pennsylvania, when Mr. Zeisberger brought his

Moravian converts to settle at Fairfield. Unlike the Moravian Indians, the Munsies were unconverted; they were still practicing native religious ceremonies when missionaries John Heckewelder and Benjamin Mortimer crossed the Thames in 1798 en route to Moraviantown. Mortimer wrote deprecatingly of the Munsies, stating that they were *all* heathens.[18] When Reverend James Beaven, an English clergyman, visited Ontario in 1845–46, he saw the remains of a ceremonial Big House built of round logs at Muncy Town. The walls, corner-notched in the mode of a log cabin, were still standing, but the roof was gone (see Fig. 6). Two years before, an Indian who lived nearby had removed the roof to obtain wood to improve his own premises.[19] Mr. Beaven stated that a Methodist mission had been established among the Munsies in 1835, and the first convert was the chieftain, Captain Snake, baptized in 1838.[20] At the time of Beaven's visit, the Munsie population was 230, some living in bark huts, others in log cabins. He added that the "whole of these Indians have disused their heathen customs although a comparatively small portion have become Christians." [21]

During our visit in August, 1970, we learned that some of the older Indians could still speak the Munsie dialect, and doubtless a skilled ethnographer could still obtain information about ancient crafts and customs. Although ethnologist M. R. Harrington visited these Munsies

Figure 6. Remains of the last Big House at Muncy Town on the Thames River, Ontario, sketched in 1846 by James Beaven and reproduced in his *Recreations of a Long Vacation*

briefly in the summer of 1907, noting that the population numbered about 118,[22] he did not write anything separately about this band, who have gone unnoticed in the ethnographic literature. During my short visit we saw a number of excellent Indian types, including two fine-looking young Delaware women dressed like other Canadian housewives, walking home from the general store, their arms bulging with groceries. As at Moraviantown, the children were not friendly; when we stopped several boys and girls to ask directions, they merely stared at us without replying. Nor did any of the adults show any willingness to speak to us.

The Delawares at Muncy Town are formally organized, and they elect a chief and councilors every two years. The last elected chief was Lloyd Nicholas, and the councilors are William Dolson and Franklin Waddilove. At present (February 15, 1971) William Dolson is the Acting Chief.

It would appear that the language spoken at Muncy Town differs in some respects from that spoken at Moraviantown, and probably both differ from the dialect, now obsolete, that was used by the Delawares at Ohsweken. The dialect at Moraviantown is different from that spoken in Oklahoma, because the Delaware language, like other living languages, was a steadily evolving medium that reflected the transitions of the Indian world. As the horizon of Delaware experience widened through contact with other tribes, new words and idioms entered the vocabularies of the different groups. There can be little doubt that by the time the main body arrived in Oklahoma their language contained words and expressions which would have sounded strange to their ancestors. Even the splinter group at Anadarko has a slightly different speech pattern from those living in northeastern Oklahoma. The Anadarko group, I am told by Dr. Ives Goddard, speak more slowly and use certain expressions that a speaker from the main body would consider old-fashioned. The subject of Indian dialects is a highly specialized one that must be left to experienced linguists to study and analyze. From the viewpoint of the historian, it suffices to say that the Delaware language is rapidly dying out in Oklahoma where it is known only to a handful of persons. Those at Moraviantown and Muncy Town who speak the language are also becoming fewer as the older generation passes away. Within another generation the Delaware language will probably be dead in

Oklahoma and along the Thames in Ontario, as it has already faded away in the Delaware community at Ohsweken.[23]

The spring of 1963 marked the 325th anniversary of the founding of New Sweden, and the event was celebrated in the Delaware Valley with special programs in Wilmington and Philadelphia. The Swedes reciprocated by inviting an American delegation to visit Sweden and participate in similar festivities there later. A retired Stockholm banker and amateur ethnographer, Olof Norbeck, on learning what was being planned, asked if any Delaware Indians had taken part in the events in America and wondered if any of them would participate in the celebration in Sweden. I first met Mr. Norbeck in 1949 when he came to Wilmington to learn more about early Swedish settlements on the Delaware and about the Indians who had greeted his countrymen there three centuries before. On that trip—and on later ones in which he combined business and pleasure—he visited Delaware Indian survivors in Oklahoma, Wisconsin, and Canada, and made many friends in the Indian communities.

Mr. Norbeck was dismayed when he learned that no Delaware Indians had been invited to the anniversary celebration on the Delaware River; nor was the committee in charge of the Swedish program planning to include any Indians. To him this seemed a grievous oversight, since he knew that the Delawares owned the land on which the Swedish colony in America was founded in 1638, and that the Indians had befriended the Swedes and Finns when they arrived in this strange land. At Norbeck's insistence the subject was brought before the members of the committee, and after some discussion they agreed to the logic of his argument. It was decided that a delegation of Delaware Indians should be invited to visit Sweden, their expenses paid by their Swedish hosts. Mr. Norbeck was probably the only living Swede who knew exactly to whom to write and what Delawares should be represented, as a result of his several American trips, and he was authorized to make the arrangements.

In June of 1963 three Delaware Indians were met at the Stockholm airport by Mr. Norbeck and his daughter: Cephas Snake (Blackbird) from Moraviantown; Willard Thomas (Little Eagle) from Oklahoma; and Jasper Hill (Big White Owl) from Toronto (see

Figure 7. Jasper Hill (Wapi-Gok-Hos, Big White Owl), Canadian Delaware, born and raised on Moraviantown Reservation, Ontario, wearing a traditional war bonnet of the Plains Indians. He was one of four Delawares selected to go to Sweden in 1963 to celebrate 325th anniversary of the founding of the New Sweden colony on the Delaware River.

Fig. 7). A fourth Indian delegate should have been there, too, Mrs. C. O. Davis of Dewey, Oklahoma, but, as she boarded the plane at Tulsa, she was handed a telegram informing her that her youngest daughter had been killed in an automobile accident.

The Delaware delegation, dressed in Indian costume, remained in Sweden for two weeks, during which time they were escorted from place to place in Stockholm in a chauffeur-driven limousine, and from town to town by train and bus. They attended civic receptions and banquets where they met political figures and educators, as well as industrial leaders. It was ironic that these Delawares, who had been completely overlooked in the festivities held in their homeland, should be fêted in a foreign country and win the hearts of the Swedish people. In a personal letter written to me describing the visit, this is what Mr. Norbeck said:

These Delawares represented their people in a very fine way at the celebrations held in the city of Kalmar, at the city of Jonkoping, from where Governor Johan Printz came, and at several occasions in Stockholm, being also received by King Gustavus VI Adolphus in a private audience. They stole most of the festivities in the different places, dressed in their native costumes.

The most touching part of the whole journey was a visit we made to the old parish church northwest of Stockholm where the Rev. Johan Campanius served as pastor for many years, after his return from the American colony, and where his gravestone (with inscriptions in Latin and the Delaware language) lies in the floor beside the altar. The Indians talked to his memory, and placed a wreath of flowers on the stone marking the grave of the man who had preached to their ancestors in their native tongue.

And then suddenly, Willard Thomas, very moved by his feelings at this solemn occasion, went back to the tomb, and after having raised his arms to heaven and the four points North, South, West, and East, lowered them towards the earth, and then said a long prayer in the Delaware tongue. I can assure you that in the big congregation that had gathered in the church and sung hymns, not one eye was dry when the little Delaware quietly retired to his seat.

I was very happy that I had been able to arrange this visit of the Delaware Indians to Sweden. In Sweden we felt grateful that we could greet as guests these fine representatives of a once great and powerful people, now but scattered splinters, but nevertheless, worthy members in an old covenant of friendship, made more than three hundred years ago with our ancestors, and renewed in a remarkable way.

NOTES—CHAPTER 1

1. In 1859 Lewis Henry Morgan obtained the names of a number of Delaware dances from informants in Kansas, and even at that early date some of them, e.g., Horse Dance and Buffalo Dance, were obviously adopted from other tribes; Lewis Henry Morgan, *The Indian Journals, 1859–62*, ed. Leslie A. White, Ann Arbor, 1959, p. 52.

2. *Handbook of American Indians North of Mexico*, ed. Frederick Webb Hodge, Bureau of American Ethnology Bulletin no. 30, Washington, 1907, vol. 1, p. 386; cf. John Wesley Powell, "Indian Linguistic Families of America North of Mexico," Bureau of American Ethnology, *Seventh Annual Report, 1885–86*, Washington, 1891, p. 49.

3. For details regarding the location of the last Big House and how a portion of the center post was installed as a beam in his ranch house after the carved faces had been sawed off, see "Memorandum Regarding Delaware Big House" written by Paul Endacott on June 19, 1970, on file in the Bartlesville (Oklahoma) Library. There are carved faces from the Big House in the collections of the Museum of the American Indian, New York City.

4. William W. Newcomb, Jr., *The Culture and Acculturation of the Delaware Indians*, Ann Arbor, 1956, pp. 110–11.

5. Vincenzo Petrullo, *The Diabolic Root: A Study of Peyotism*, Philadelphia, 1934; William W. Newcomb, Jr., "The Peyote Cult of the Delaware Indians," *Texas Journal of Science*, vol. 8, no. 2, June 1956, pp. 202–11.

6. James H. Howard, "Pan-Indian Culture of Oklahoma," *Science Monthly*, vol. 81, no. 5, November 1955, pp. 215–20; William W. Newcomb, Jr., "A Note on Cherokee-Delaware Pan-Indianism," *American Anthropologist*, vol. 57, no. 5, October 1955, pp. 1041–45.

7. The constitution and bylaws are reprinted in *Journal of the Wisconsin Indians Research Institute*, Department of Anthropology and Sociology, Colorado State College, vol. 3, no. 1, September 1967, pp. 105–8.

8. Personal letters of Dec. 7 and Dec. 17, 1970, from Edmund Manydeeds, Acting Superintendent, Great Lakes Agency, Bureau of Indian Affairs, Ashland, Wis.; also a letter from Mr. and Mrs. Aught Coyhis, Dec. 28, 1970.

9. Marion Johnson Mochow, "Stockbridge-Munsee Cultural Adaptations: Assimilated Indians," *Proceedings of the American Philosophical Society*, vol. 112, no. 3, 1968, pp. 182–219. An excellent bibliography of the Stockbridges may be found in *Journal of the Wisconsin Indians Research Institute*, vol. 1, no. 1, March, 1965, pp. 125–27.

10. Morgan, *Indian Journals*, p. 84. See also Joseph Romig, "The Chippewa and Munsee (Or Christian) Indians of Franklin County, Kansas," *Kansas Historical Society Collections*, vol. 11, 1909–10, pp. 314–23.

11. These and other figures were sent to me by D. D. Cassie, Superintendent of the Six Nations Agency, Brantford, Ontario, in personal letters dated Aug. 28, 1969, and Nov. 18, 1970. An excellent compilation of documents relating to the reservation is found in Charles M. Johnston, ed., *The Valley of the Six Nations*, Toronto, 1964.

12. Frank G. Speck, *The Celestial Bear Comes Down to Earth*, Scientific Publications, no. 7, Reading, Pa., 1945, pp. 9, 18.

13. Ibid., pp. 11, 31. Nekatcit (Nicodemus Peters) constructed a model of this Big House which Speck deposited in the Reading (Pennsylvania) Public Museum and Art Gallery along with other ceremonial objects from the Canadian-Delawares.

14. Ibid., p. 35. Cf. Speck's *Oklahoma Delaware Ceremonies, Feasts and Dances*, Philadelphia, 1937, fn. p. 13, wherein he stated that an interesting summary of the religious history of the Delawares living on the Six Nations Reserve had been compiled by R. R. Whale of the Brantford (Ontario) Historical Society. This is evidently where the information was obtained about the two Christian Indians destroying the carved faces in the Big House. Walter D. Rutherford of the Ontario Historical Society, who was personally acquainted with R. R. Whale, now deceased, has made every effort on my behalf, but without success, to locate this summary, which was evidently never published, but may still exist in MS. I am indebted to Mr. Rutherford for this assistance, for photocopies of useful reference material, and for his advice and companionship during my trips to Ontario. The information about the existing mask was passed on to me by Mr. Moses in a personal letter dated Feb. 26, 1971.

15. Information supplied me by D. M. Hett, former Superintendent of London district, Department of Indian Affairs and Northern Development, in a letter of Sept. 29, 1969; and also by G. N. Faulkner, District Supervisor, in a letter of Oct. 15, 1970.

16. These excavations, conducted by Mr. Wilfrid Jury, Curator of the Museum of Indian Archeology, University of Western Ontario, are described in two publications: *Report of Excavations Made on the Site of the Early Mission Village, 1942–1943*, Museum of the University of Western Ontario Bulletin no. 3, 1945, and Bulletin no. 5, 1946.

17. Personal letter from G. N. Faulkner, Nov. 6, 1970.

18. Paul A. W. Wallace, *Thirty Thousand Miles with John Heckewelder*, Pittsburgh, Pa., 1958, p. 367.

19. James Beaven, *Recreations of a Long Vacation or a Visit to Indian Missions in Upper Canada*, London-Toronto, 1846, p. 75.

20. Ibid., p. 81.

21. Ibid., p. 76.

22. M. R. Harrington, "Vestiges of Material Culture among the Canadian Delawares," *American Anthropologist*, vol. 10, no. 3, 1908, p. 408.

23. The literature regarding the Moraviantown Delawares is meager, consisting of Jasper Hill (Big White Owl), "My People The Delawares," *Bulletin of the Archeological Society of Delaware*, vol. 4, no. 1, May, 1943, pp. 9–13; Arthur D. Graeff, "Transplants of Pennsylvania Indian Nations

in Ontario," *Pennsylvania History*, vol. 15, no. 3, July 1948, pp. 180–93; Fred Bruemmer, "The Delawares of Moraviantown," *Canadian Geographic*, March 1964, pp. 95–97. I have found nothing in the anthropological literature about Muncy Town, and in a letter to me of Nov. 11, 1970, Professor R. W. Dunning of the Department of Anthropology, University of Toronto, stated that to the best of his knowledge there is no material in print.

2

The Homeland of the Delawares

The home of the Delawares at the time they were first encountered by the white man was far from Oklahoma, Wisconsin, Kansas, and Ontario, where their descendants are found today. Centuries before, they lived along the banks of the Delaware River and in the area drained by its tributaries, but in their native habitat they were not known as Delawares. Their name for themselves was Lenni Lenâpé, which has been given various meanings, such as "original people," "men among men," and "men of our kind." But the element *len*, which is present in both words, means "common," and *âpé* refers to "people." The word *Lenape* standing alone can be translated as "common people," and the addition of *Lenni*, a redundancy, reinforces that meaning.

After the English arrived along the Atlantic seacoast, the Lenape were given their new name, which was derived from the third Lord de la Warr, Sir Thomas West, who was appointed governor of the English colony at Jamestown, Virginia, in 1610. One of his followers, Captain Samuel Argall, seeking provisions for the Virginia colonists, left for a voyage up the Atlantic coast, and on his way back to Jamestown sailed into a majestic bay that he named in honor of the governor. As time went on, the Lenape people living on the shores of the "de la Warr Bay" and along the banks of the river that emptied into it came to be called Delaware Indians.[1] The irony is that Lord de la Warr returned to England without seeing the river or the bay named after him, or any of the Indians who still perpetuate his name.

When the earliest Dutch explorers like Cornelis Hendricksen, who made the first map of the Delaware River, and Cornelis May (sometimes spelled Mey), for whom Cape May is named, sailed up the river they saw some of the homes of the Indians on both sides of the stream. The Delawares also placed their villages along the small, fresh-water tributaries because such locations afforded their families better protection from bad weather than the exposed windswept banks of the Delaware River proper. It also brought them in closer proximity to the animals and birds that sought out the interior streams and marshes for feeding and breeding. Shad, herring, and other fish were more easily netted when they entered the headwaters of the tributary streams to spawn, and the fertile upstream fastlands were also conducive to agriculture.

Not only were the Delawares dispersed into small communities, each located on a suitable waterway, but these groups were separate from and politically independent of each other. Some writers have arbitrarily assigned the Delawares to an extensive geographical area, even going so far as to suggest that the Indians living on Long Island, such as the Montauk and Shinnecock, and those along the upper Hudson, usually classified as Mahicanni or Mahican, should also be included in the Lenape family. Some of these notions had their origin in an appendix that Charles Thomson contributed to Thomas Jefferson's *Notes on the State of Virginia*, first published in 1787. Thomson wrote that the "Lenopi" was a nation or confederacy of five tribes "who all spoke one language." He identified these five tribes and their areas of occupancy as the Chihohocki, who lived on the west side of the Delaware River; the Wanami who inhabited New Jersey; the Munseys on the upper Delaware; the Wabings or Mohickanders between the Delaware and the Hudson; and the Mahiccon, or Manhattan, who occupied Staten Island, Manhattan Island, Long Island, and that part of the states of New York and Connecticut lying between the Hudson and Connecticut rivers. There is no historical evidence for these classifications, which Thomson garbled, and no justification for using the word *Lenape* as a catchall to cover tribes living on Manhattan and adjacent islands.

Another early writer, E. M. Ruttenber, also arbitrarily included a number of tribes of New York state under the broad heading of the term *Lenape*, which has been repeated by later historians, although this assumption is also without historical foundation.[2] Modern ethnologists use the terms *Delaware Indians* and *Lenni Lenape* synonymously, and agree that the homeland of these Indians should be delimited to the states of New Jersey and Delaware, that part of southeastern Pennsylvania lying between the Susquehanna and Delaware rivers, and the southeastern part of New York state west of the Hudson. It should not be inferred, however, that the Indian occupants of this area were closely knit political groups having a head sachem who wielded authority over a host of Indian subjects. This concept is alien to the basic structure of Delaware Indian society, although Europeans never seemed able to divest themselves of the idea that the Delawares had to have an authoritarian chief who ruled all of his people. In actuality, each Delaware village was an independent community, having its own chieftains, and great men, who served the chieftains in the role of councilors, and participated in the decision making. Often the people living in villages along the same stream constituted what can best be described as a band, and the most influential village chief may have functioned as the nominal head of the band. The Indians and the streams on which their villages were situated were often known by the same name. For instance the natives living on Sickoneysinck Creek at Lewes, Delaware, were called Sickoneysinck Indians (also rendered by Europeans in such spellings as Siconese, Sikonesse, and Checonnesseck); those living on Rancocas Creek were called Rancocas Indians; those on the Brandywine, were known as Brandywine Indians, and so forth.

The names of a number of the autonomous native villages in the Delaware Valley, as well as descriptive names for some of the Delaware Indian groups, were recorded by seventeenth-century chroniclers and were also shown on maps made by contemporary cartographers. These words appear in different spellings because scribes of differing nationalities heard different sounds in the strange Indian language, depending upon the individual's ear conditioning. The Swedes alternated the *l* and the *r* sounds and rendered Lenape as Renappi; they also pluralized Indian words by adding the Swedish suffix *er*, which, for example, changed a New Jersey band called the Mantes Indians into Mantesser. Both Dutch and Swedish mapmakers often affixed their word *kil*, meaning stream or river, to an Indian word, and the river where the Mantes Indians lived might appear on a map as the Manteskil. Other liberties were taken with Indian words by writers who did not comprehend the native language, and a word was customarily recorded by the English in a different form from the way the same word was written by a Swede or Dutchman.

In 1654 the young Swedish engineer Peter Lindeström, in addition to keeping a journal, made several maps on which may be found the names of some of the earliest Delaware Indian communities in the environs of present-day Philadelphia, where a relatively large native population was seated. Among the village communities on the Delaware River were Pemickpacka, Poaetquissingh, Wichquaquenscke, and Wickquakonick (later contracted to Wicoa). Along the Schuylkill River, known to the Delawares as the Menejackse, according to Lindeström, were the communities of Nittabakonck and Passajung (now spelled Passayunk). He referred to the Delawares on the Schuylkill River as the Schuylkill Indians and to those at nearby Passayunk as the Passajung Indians, as though they were separate and unrelated. There was a chief in each community, "each one commanding his tribe or people under him . . . several hundred strong under each chief counting women and children, some being stronger, some weaker." Lindeström also describes a treaty Governor Johan Rising held with these Delaware sachems on June 17, 1654.[3]

At a later date, a Delaware Indian village known as Shackamaxon, situated in the outskirts of present Philadelphia, was a community of importance.

In Bucks County, not far from Philadelphia on the headwaters of a tributary to Neshaminy Creek, was a Delaware town called Playwicky, first mentioned by name in a deed dated July 15, 1682.[4]

On Ridley and Crum creeks in Chester County south of Philadelphia lived a band of Delawares called the Ockanickon or Okehocking Indians, although none of the names of their villages have been recorded.[5]

In the Big Bend on Brandywine Creek, Delaware County, Pennsylvania, there was the village of Quineomissinque (also given as Queonemysing).[6]

On White Clay Creek in London Britain Township, Chester County, was another Delaware Indian village called Minguannan (also spelled Minguhanan), and a contemporary reference states that its population numbered fifty warriors.[7]

Downstream at Lewes, Delaware, near Cape Henlopen, where the river widens to form Delaware Bay, were situated the principal villages of the Sickoneysincks. Their area of occupation lay between present-day Bombay Hook, at the mouth of Duck Creek, and Lewes. Lindeström referred to them as a "powerful nation rich in maize plantations." In 1629 a Dutchman who was desirous of purchasing some of their land met in council with the chiefs and great men of the Sickoneysincks. Since this meeting is one of the earliest on record between Europeans and the Indians living on Delaware Bay, it is of interest to note how the Dutch scribe recorded the names of the Indian participants: Aixtamin, Oschoesien, Choqweke, Menatoch, Awijkapoon, Mehatehan, Nehatehan, Atowesen, Ackseso, Maekemen, Queskakons, and Eesanques.[8]

At a later date the Dutch negotiated another land purchase from the Sickoneysincks; in the presence of a large number of Indians, sixteen of the chieftains and great men affixed their marks to the parchment.[9] The document is especially interesting because it refers to Quistin, Tarackus, Peskamohot, Kwickenesse, and Seckatackomeck as places belonging to some of these sachems, probably the names of their hunting territories.[10]

On the opposite side of the Delaware River, in New Jersey, the villages occupied by Delaware Indians were located on all the major streams, and each of these Indian communities had a separate name. Following a visit in 1634 as lieutenant to his explorer uncle Thomas Yong, Robert Evelyn wrote a letter to Sir Edmund Plowden's wife in which he enumerated nine separate Indian communities in present New Jersey. From my interpretation of Evelyn's descriptions, I have associated these groups (in the spellings given by him) with the following streams: [11]

The Kechemeches, according to Evelyn, had fifty men; and from his account I have placed them along the present Maurice River.

The Manteses (listed in other sources as Mantas or Mantaes) had one hundred men, Evelyn said, and his description indicates that they lived along the Salem River. Other early writers noted that the Mantes were a strong and powerful Delaware band, and that their principal village on the Salem River was called Watcessit.

The Assomocches, who had one hundred men, lived along Big Timber Creek.

The Eriwoneck (also listed in other sources as the Armewamese, Armewamex, and Ermamex) had forty men; they lived along Newton Creek, and possibly on Big Timber and Little Timber creeks.

The Ramcock (Remkokes) had one hundred men and occupied the drainage system of Rancocas Creek.

The Axion (given in other contemporary accounts as Atsayonck and Atsayongky) had two hundred men who lived on the banks of Assunpink Creek.

The Calcefar were an inland people who had one hundred fifty men, but Evelyn's description provides no clues to the identity of the waterway where they made their home.

The Mosilian had two hundred men, and the area of their principal occupation was on Crossweeks Creek.

Some of the names cited by Evelyn are also found in contemporary Dutch accounts and on Dutch maps, usually in slightly different forms. For example, Evelyn calls one of the bands the Sikonesses, and from his description I have placed these people along Oldman's Creek and Raccoon Creek. This word is a variant of the form Siconese (the same as Sickoneysincks and Sikonesse), also found on the opposite side of the Delaware. On a map drawn circa 1629, a Dutch cartographer referred to the Indians in Delaware as the Groote [Great] Siconese, and those in New Jersey as the Klyne [Small] Siconese.[12] Evidently the New Jersey Siconese were either less populous or were less important than the Siconese in Delaware. In a legend on his map the same cartographer stated that, "The above written tribes have a friendship all together the one with the other, and are mostly one type of people and of one speech," which suggests that both groups of Siconese spoke the same dialect.

In addition to the native communities cited above, other seventeenth-century accounts refer to the Sankikans, a group of Delawares who occupied the area around Trenton; the Sewapoos, who lived along Cohansey Creek; the Narraticons, who lived on Raccoon Creek; the Rechaweygh (Rockaway), who lived at the confluence of Rockaway Creek and the Passaic River.[13] Another band known as the Matikongh (also spelled Mattikonghy) lived in the environs of Trenton south of the Sankikans, and the Momakarongk dwelt along Pennsauken Creek. In Sussex County, New Jersey, a few miles southeast of Milford, there was an important Indian settlement referred to in contemporary accounts as Minisink. Part of this settlement was on a large island in the Delaware; and within the immediate area there were at least seven Minisink villages, although the word

Minisink came to be applied to an extensive area that went well beyond the villages.[14] The residents of these northernmost communities, who were later called Munsies, spoke a different dialect from those who lived in the area south of them.

Throughout the full extent of the Delaware drainage system, there were probably thirty to forty different Indian communities, some of which are indicated by name on the accompanying map (see Fig. 8). Appendix 1 of this book lists additional maps and drawings relating to Delaware Indian villages and reservations. By checking these sources, the reader will learn that each group had its own chiefs and councilors, and independently exercised authority over recognized territories.

The Delaware concept of land tenure was entirely different from the European traditions of land ownership and sale. To the Delawares, land was like air, sunlight, or the waters of a river—a medium necessary to sustain life. The idea of an individual exclusively owning the life-giving soil was as alien to their thinking as owning the air one breathed, or the water that bubbled forth from a woodland spring. They considered plants, trees, flowers, and other natural things in the same context. An Indian once released his horses overnight in Mr. Heckewelder's meadow on the Muskingum River in Ohio, and next morning Heckewelder criticized him for so doing, to which the Indian replied,

My friend, it seems you lay claim to the grass my horses have eaten because you had enclosed it with a fence: now tell me, who caused the grass to grow? Can *you* make the grass grow? . . . the grass which grows out of the earth is common to all; the game in the woods is common to all. Say, did you ever eat venison and bear's meat?—"Yes, very often"—Well, and did you ever hear me or any other Indian complain about that? No; then be not disturbed at my horse having eaten only once of what you call *your grass*, though the grass my horses did eat, in like manner as the meat you eat, was given to the Indians by the Great Spirit. Besides, if you will but consider, you will find that my horse did not eat all your grass.[15]

Land "ownership" to the Delawares meant the right to use the land, to plant on it, to build wigwams on it, to hunt the animals that lived on it, but not to possess it permanently in the sense that it belonged to one person in perpetuity. One might transfer to another person the hunting, fishing, and trapping rights on a piece of prop-

Figure 8. The heart of the ancient land of the Lenape, showing names of some of the native communities cited in early records. Because of shifting populations, the locations are only approximations. (Map by Charlotte Carlson)

erty, but this did not mean that the "owner" was permanently dis-
possessing himself from the use of the land nor that the lessee could
erect a fence and exclude all others from entry. The concept of
using the land was subtly related to the basic Indian belief in hospitality whereby a stranger's physical needs were fully satisfied by
his host, who didn't hesitate to proffer his wigwam, his food, his
fields, or even his wife to his guest.

Among the Delawares there existed family hunting territories consisting of parcels of wooded land of various sizes, bounded by streams,
the seashore, or other natural landmarks, usually known by designated
names. Individuals and members of their families "owned" the right
of hunting, fishing, and trapping on these particular territories. Other
members of the community, who had their own hunting territories,
respected this right, although in the use of the land none of these
owners conceived of the land itself as a personal possession. From a
careful study of the land transfer records in the Delaware Valley, I
have formed the opinion that in some instances a large hunting territory was used by an entire community of Delawares, the ownership
rights vested communally in the people of that village.

These hunting territories were not necessarily contiguous to the
villages where the owners resided, and in many instances they were
some distance away. This is consistent with the Delawares' custom
of seasonally leaving their villages to hunt, each group of families
pursuing game on their respective territories. Successive generations
of the same family, or of closely related kinship groups, probably
hunted on the same territory, and the use rights were handed down
from one generation to the next. Land was plentiful, game abundant,
and there was no reason for one hunter to trespass on another's territory. If he did so unintentionally, no one considered that any great
harm had been done.

In contrast, the land in Europe had been divided and subdivided
for so many centuries that the idea of vast stretches of unoccupied
forests was completely new to the white man. In his homeland, every
foot of ground belonged to somebody, and fields and woods beyond
the towns and cities were clearly identified as real property and the
owner's rights were protected by law. The common man in rural
parts of Europe lived in a world owned by other people, and he had
no rights to firewood, game, fish, recreation, or even farming privileges
unless granted him by an owner. European town and city life, with

law enforcement officers and courts of justice, had no counterpart in the homeland of the Delawares. In the Indian habitat there were no jails for the confinement of lawbreakers, and, although individual misbehavior may have been subject to criticism, there were no laws in the European sense with prescribed penalties for specific crimes.

European traditions were alien to the Indians and were destined to cause misunderstandings, because essentially the European saw nature as something to be dominated by his superiority. Conversely, the Indian considered himself an integral part of the world of nature, his survival depending upon maintaining his place in the scheme of things, but not necessarily dominating nature or exploiting his fellow man.

There was a wide variety of climates and ecological zones in the area of Delaware occupancy, which included the windswept coastal plain and the flat, marshy lowlands of southern Delaware and New Jersey, the undulating wooded hills of southeastern Pennsylvania, the rocky terrain of northern New Jersey and southeastern New York. Common to the area was the Delaware River, whose numerous tributaries went deep into the interior of the land, branching into scores of lesser streams originating in springheads hundreds of miles distant from the bay that debouched into the Atlantic Ocean. Naturally there were differences among the bands of Delaware Indians who occupied this area—differences in culture and in the way they adapted to their local habitats. Colder climate in the northern areas necessitated a seasonal adjustment in clothing, type of dwelling, and pattern of food gathering. The coastal people were more dependent upon shellfish than those living upstream, and the excessively hot weather of the southern areas, with periodic droughts, also influenced the manner of living. There were also variations in dialect, and although all the Delawares probably could understand each other, there were significant differences in vocabulary and pronunciation between the most northerly and most southerly peoples.

These Delaware dialects all fall within the language group called *Algonkian*, a linguistic term used to classify not only the Delawares but also the Powhatan tribes of Virginia; the Nanticoke, Conoy, and Choptank of Maryland; the Shawnee; the Mahican, and a number of other New England tribes. The same language, with certain differences in dialect, was also spoken by the western tribes of the Blackfoot Confederacy; the Menominee; the Sauk and Fox; Arapaho and

Cheyenne; the Miami; the Chippewa living in the Great Lakes region; by the Montagnais and Abnaki groups of Canada and Maine; and by a number of other tribes, all of which apparently had a common Algonkian ancestry. Although in most instances the dialects were mutually intelligible, in extreme cases the difference between one Algonkian dialect and another was probably comparable to the difference between modern French and Spanish.

On the other hand, the Algonkians could not understand members of the Siouan, Muskogean, and Iroquoian linguistic families, whose lands surrounded the territories of the eastern Algonkians. These Indians, who were also divided into tribes and bands, spoke varying dialects of languages unrelated to the Algonkian tongue. It came as a surprise to the early European explorers that, not only were different languages spoken by the American Indian tribes, but some Indians could not understand others. None of the Indian languages were related in any way to the languages spoken in the European countries, and that made the differences even more perplexing.

The word *Algonkian* as applied to a family of Indian languages was derived from a small tribal division that resided in Canada north of the Ottawa and Saint Lawrence rivers, known to the French as the Algonquin, or Algonkin. The prominence of the tribe was not the result of its size, but of the emphasis given its customs and language in the writings of early French Jesuit missionaries. The Algonquin people were only one among many Indian groups who spoke the same language, and, through the influence of a Swiss student interested in American Indian tongues, Albert Gallatin, their name became used arbitrarily as a generic for the language. When John Wesley Powell of the United States Bureau of American Ethnology published a classification and map of the Indian languages of North America, he employed the same term.[16] Hence, the word *Algonkian*, a modification of *Algonquin*, has come to apply to a family of related dialects. The term is not correctly used to classify Indian cultures or artifacts, because there were substantial cultural differences among many of the tribes who spoke dialects of the Algonkian language.

The question of the size of the Delaware Indian population at the time the Europeans arrived has long been discussed by anthropologists, and a figure of 8,000, suggested by one of the early scholars of the Bureau of American Ethnology, is often given as a conservative estimate. On the basis of Evelyn's estimate of the warrior strength of the nine New Jersey bands he enumerated, which amounted to 890, and recognizing that he overlooked a number of other communities, it would appear that the total Indian population of New Jersey alone could have amounted to 3,000 or 4,000. Taking into consideration the Delawares living in the states of Delaware, Pennsylvania, and New York, perhaps 10,000 to 12,000 would be a better estimate of the total Delaware population, but this, too, is speculative. Students of population statistics have arrived at the opinion that estimates of the aboriginal population of North America were grossly underestimated by contemporary observers.[17]

It is extremely difficult for a modern American living under federal, state, and local governments, and within well-defined political bounds, to understand Delaware Indian society. There was no *tribe* in the modern understanding of the term, which is generally accepted to mean a body of people occupying a definite territory, speaking a common language, having its own social, political and religious organization, and its own leaders. In this context a tribe might be composed of a number of lineages, but possessing a cohesiveness that was conspicuously lacking in the unfederated Delaware communities. To refer to the Delawares at the time of white contact as a *tribe* would seem to be a misapplication of the term, even though I continue to use it in this volume for want of a better word.

One might compare Delaware Indian society to a number of small rural towns in modern America scattered over the landscape, but lacking county, state, or federal affiliation, each responsible for its own government and the welfare of its citizens. The main difference was that in the Delaware Indian towns there was a high percentage of persons related to each other, and the frequent movements of the people and the perambulations of their communities gave the population a group mobility generally lacking in modern American towns. The inhabitants of Delaware Indian towns spoke dialects of the common language and had a sufficient feeling of common identity to call themselves Lenni Lenape, just as modern dwellers in small towns refer to themselves as Americans.

By the time the Christian missionaries began their work of conversion among the Delawares early in the eighteenth century, many changes had taken place in Indian society. As a result of warfare with other Indians, and of contracting European diseases, the Delaware population had been drastically reduced. The former band structures disintegrated, and the surviving Delawares were brought much closer together than they had ever been in their native surroundings. When the missionaries asked questions about how their society was organized by their parents and grandparents before they left the East, the Indians may have conveyed misinformation, or they may have been misinterpreted. In any event, the impression was left that originally there were three tribes of Delawares—not the series of autonomous bands as described in seventeenth-century accounts. The concept of this tripartite division had its origin in David Zeisberger's writings, and it is important to understand precisely what he said:

The Delaware Nation, consisting of three tribes, the Unamis, Wunalachticos and Monsys formerly lived in the region about Philadelphia, also in New Jersey about Trenton, Brunswick, and Amboy. The Unamis are the chief people of the nation; their language, differing but little from that of the Wunalachtico, is the most melodious. The Monsy tongue is quite different, even though the three grew out of one parent language. The last named tribe lived in Minnissing along the Delaware, behind the Blue Mountains.[18]

When he wrote these words, Zeisberger was living among the Delawares at a mission in Ohio in 1779–80, at which time there were no longer any Indians still occupying their native villages in the Delaware Valley. Zeisberger's informants were limited in their geographical knowledge, because, with the exception of a very few old people, none of them had ever lived in the East, and they knew little about where the scattered bands of their ancestors had been located, nor how the bands were anciently organized.

In 1820 John Heckewelder published a history of the Indians, and therein he not only repeated the information that had been recorded by Mr. Zeisberger but also associated the alleged three Delaware tribes with three animal groupings. The following is an exact quotation from his writings.

Those of the Delawares who fixed their abode on the shores of the Atlantic divided themselves into three tribes. Two of them, distinguished by the names of the *Turtle* and the *Turkey*, the former calling themselves *Unamis* and the other *Unalâchtgo* chose those grounds to settle on, which lay nearest to the sea between the coast and the high mountains. As they multiplied their settlements extended from the *Mohicannittuck* (river of the Mohicans, which we call the North or Hudson River) to beyond the Potomack. Many families with their connexions choosing to live by themselves, were scattered not only on the larger, but also on the small streams throughout the country, having towns and villages, where they lived together in separate bodies, in each of which a chief resided; those chiefs, however, were subordinate (by their own free will, the only kind of subordination which the Indians know) to the head chiefs or great council of the nation, whom they officially informed of all events or occurrences affecting the general interest which came to their knowledge. The third tribe, the *Wolf*, commonly called the *Minsi*, which we have corrupted into *Monseys*, had chosen to live back of the other two. tribes, and formed a kind of bulwark for their protection.[19]

In elaborating on Zeisberger's original statement, Heckewelder not only confused the issue by introducing animal names supposedly synonymous with the alleged tribes, but he extended the Delaware territory "to beyond the Potomack," which was the territory occupied by the Powhatan tribes. Furthermore, he referred to a "great council of the nation," consisting of head chiefs to whom the Delaware village chiefs were subordinate, and this, too, is erroneous. While they lived in the Delaware Valley, authority was decentralized among the various bands, and each group acted independently. There was no great council of authoritarian chiefs who were kept posted on political developments of the "Nation."

Laying aside Heckewelder's animal embellishments, which most ethnologists now reject, one cannot discount Zeisberger, who was a conscientious, thorough, and reliable observer, fluent in the Delaware tongue, and a confidant of the Indian leaders. If one carefully rereads what he said, his principal emphasis is on the fact that three different dialects were spoken by the Delawares in their native habitat, and those who spoke these dialects lived in separate but contiguous areas. This is reconcilable with seventeenth-century documentation, and there is no disagreement that the Delaware bands living in one area spoke a different dialect from those occupying other areas. It is Zeisberger's use of the word *tribes*, and the inferences that were later drawn by Heckewelder and others about the tripartite division, which cannot be reconciled with what is known of the atomistic Delaware society at the time of the arrival of the Europeans.

Ethnologists have long puzzled over this question, and some years after Zeisberger's death Dr. Daniel G. Brinton, a physician and student of the American Indian, came to the conclusion that the alleged tribal designations were *wholly* geographical terms, which characterized the areas occupied by what he chose to call the Delaware subtribes. Dr. Brinton's explanation of the terms was as follows:

Minsi [Monseys, Montheys, Munsies, or Minisinks], properly *Minsiu*, and formerly *Minassiniu*, means "people of the stony country" or briefly "mountaineers." It is a synthesis of *minthiu*, "to be scattered," and *achsin*, "stone," according to the best living native authorities.

Unami, or *W'namiu*, means "people down the river," from *naheu*, down-stream.

Unalachtigo, properly *W'nalachtko*, means "people who live near the ocean" from *wunalawat*, to go towards, and *t'kow* or *t'kou*, "wave." [20]

One can readily accept these geographical designations as the Indian way of differentiating between the physical environments of the differents parts of Delaware territory where at least three different dialects were spoken. In this context it would have been logical for the Schuylkill, Ockanickon, and Brandywine Indians, and their neighbors, for example, to be referred to as "people down the river" (Unami). The Groote Siconese living between Bombay Hook and Lewes in Delaware, the Klyne Siconese, the Narraticons, the Kechemekes, and other bands of southern New Jersey could have been called "people who live near the ocean" (Unalachtigo). The Minisinks, Manteses, Sankikans, Axion, and the other bands occupying northern New Jersey in the rugged area along the upper Delaware could have been termed "people of the stony country" (Minsi, i.e., Munsies).

As the remnant bands left their homeland and settled in new locations, the terms *Unami* and *Munsie* clung to them and helped differentiate between their dialects. Since the members of these groups were no longer living in the geographical areas implicit in the original terms, *Unami* and *Munsie* came to be used in a political sense, referring to separate groups having their own chiefs and councilors. The word *Unalachtigo* became obsolete because the handful of survivors of the "people who live near the ocean" merged with the others. Their dialect was similar in pronunciation to the Unami, which facilitated the admixture, and as time went on the term *Unalachtigo* lost its separate meaning. Thus, in Zeisberger's day, two groups,

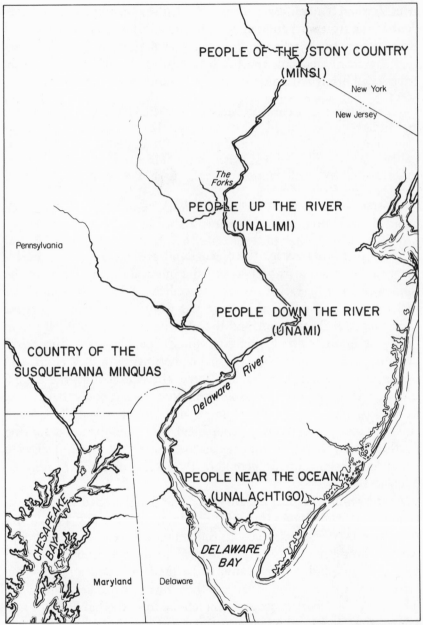

Figure 9. Autonomous Delaware Indian communities were situated in territories to which the natives loosely applied the geographical terms shown. Moravian missionaries erroneously used three of the terms in the sense of tribes, thus giving them political significance which they did not originally have. (Map by Charlotte Carlson)

Munsies and Unami, existed as two political entities speaking different dialects, and there was still a memory of the Unalachtigo group who in bygone days lived in an area different from the other two. His informants led him to believe that these were vestiges of three tribes in the original homeland, a surmise without foundation.

There has since come to light an early manuscript which adds weight to the hypothesis that *Minsi, Unami,* and *Unalachtigo* were originally used as geographical terms. In an undated deposition made by a Delaware named Moses Tatamy having to do with native land ownership on the western side of the Delaware River in the vicinity of present Easton, a creek named Tohiccon was cited as an important boundary. In his deposition Tatamy quoted the Delaware chief Nutimus as saying "that the Land below Tohiccon belonged to the Unami Indians & that they never claimed a Right to any Land over that Creek, but that Tohiccon & upward belonged to the Unalimi or upRiver Indians of which he [Nutimus] was the chief." [21] In the native dialect *Unami,* as previously explained, means "people down the river," and it did not refer to a tribe but to an area wherein there lived autonomous political groups like those previously described. *Unalimi,* on the other hand can be translated as "people up the river," and this term, unknown to Zeisberger and Heckewelder, also was used in a geographical sense to encompass an area wherein were located a number of independent villages, one of which was the home of Nutimus (see Fig. 9).

NOTES—CHAPTER 2

1. John Heckewelder, *An Account of the History, Manners, and Customs of the Indian Nations,* . . . new and revised ed., Philadelphia, 1881,, p. xli, states that "The name 'Delaware' which we give to these people is unknown in their language, and I well remember the time when they thought the whites had given it to them in derision; but they were reconciled to it upon being told it was the name of a great white chief, Lord de la Warr, which had been given to them and their river. As they are fond of being named after distinguished men, they were rather pleased, considering it a compliment."

2. E. M. Ruttenber, *History of the Indian Tribes of Hudson's River,* Albany, 1872.

3. Peter Lindeström, *Geographia Americae,* trans. Amandus Johnson, Philadelphia, 1925, pp. 126–32, 170–71. Lindeström gives the names of the following Delaware chiefs who attended the treaty conference on Tinicum

Island with Rising: from *Passayunk*, Ahopamen and his brother Quirocus, Peminacka, Speck, Weymotto, and Juncker; from *Nittabakonck*, Matta-wiracka and Skalitzi; from *Sipaessingh*, Winangene and Naaman; ibid., p. 128.

4. A transcription of the deed is given in Albert Cook Myers, *William Penn: His Own Account of the Lenni Lenape or Delaware Indians*, Moylan, Pa., 1937 (hereafter cited as Myers, *William Penn*), pp. 76–79. Another contemporary spelling of Playwicky was Plahe Wickon; Penn-Physick Manuscripts, Letter Book 3, 1769–1804, p. 577, Historical Society of Pennsylvania, Philadelphia. Cf. Sarah Gilpin Underhill, *The Indians of Bucks County, Pennsylvania*, . . . , vol. 23, no. 1, *Bulletin of the Friends Historical Society*, Philadelphia, 1934, p. 10.

5. See transcript of 1702 document relating to the Okehocking Indian reservation in C. A. Weslager, *Red Men on the Brandywine*, Wilmington, 1953, pp. 139–41.

6. Ibid., p. 62; see also A. R. Dunlap and C. A. Weslager, "Two Delaware Valley Indian Place Names," *Names*, vol. 15, no. 3, August 1967, pp. 41–46. Whereas we translated *Queonemysing* as "at the place of many fish," Mrs. Nora Thompson Dean believes that a more literal translation is "place where there are long fish."

7. *Maryland Archives* (1697), vol. 16, p. 520. Mrs. Dean translates *Minguannan* as "place on a creek used by the Minquas."

8. See transcript of the 1629 documents in C. A. Weslager, *Dutch Explorers, Traders, and Settlers in the Delaware Valley* (hereafter cited as Weslager, *Dutch Explorers*), Philadelphia, 1961, pp. 258–59.

9. Ibid., pp. 288–89. These chieftains' names all appear to be of Delaware provenience, and Mrs. Dean was readily able to translate a number of them.

10. Ibid., p. 288.

11. See A. R. Dunlap and C. A. Weslager, "Toponymy of the Delaware Valley as Revealed by an Early Seventeenth Century Dutch Map,' *Bulletin of the Archeological Society of New Jersey*, no. 15–16, November 1958, pp. 3–4. The names cited from Evelyn's letter are thoroughly discussed in C. A. Weslager, "Robert Evelyn's Indian Tribes and Place-Names of New Albion," ibid., no. 9, November 1954, pp. 1–4.

12. Dunlap and Weslager, "Toponymy of the Delaware Valley, . . ." p. 12.

13. In 1643, De Vries visited the principal town of the Rechaweygh people called Rechqua-akie, where there were from 200 to 300 Indians living in 30 wigwams; "Extracts from the Voyages of De Vries," New-York Historical Society, *Collections*, 2d series, vol. 1, 1841, p. 270.

14. Charles A. Philhower, "The Historic Minisink Site," *Bulletin of the Archeological Society of New Jersey*, no. 7, November 1953, pp. 1–9.

Ruttenber, *Indian Tribes*, pp. 89–95, lists certain "chieftaincies" as Unami and others as Minsi, which is unjustified.

15. Heckewelder, *History*, p. 102.

16. John Wesley Powell, "Indian Linguistic Families of North America North of Mexico," Bureau of American Ethnology, *Seventh Annual Report*, 1885–86, Washington, 1891.

17. Henry F. Dobyns, "Estimating Aboriginal American Population: An Appraisal of Techniques with a New Hemispheric Estimate," *Current Anthropology*, vol. 7, no. 4, October 1966, pp. 395–416. In view of Dobyns's analysis, the population estimates for the Delawares made by Mooney, Krober, and others now require careful reexamination.

18. Archer B. Hulbert and William N. Schwarze, *David Zeisberger's History of the Northern American Indians, Ohio Archeological and Historical Publications* (hereinafter cited as *Zeisberger's History*), vol. 19, 1910, p. 27. Loskiel, who borrowed considerable material from Zeisberger, elaborated on the tripartite division but added nothing new; George Henry Loskiel, *History of the Mission of the United Brethren*, . . . , trans. by Christian Ignatius La Trobe, London, 1794, pt. 1, pp. 18–19.

19. Heckewelder, *History*, pp. 51–52.

20. D. G. Brinton, *The Lenâpé and Their Legends* . . . (hereinafter cited as Brinton, *Lenâpé Legends*), Philadelphia, 1885, p. 36. Brinton fell into error when he tried to explain Heckewelder's animal eponyms as totemic animals, from which each of the subtribes claimed mythical descent. This is sheer speculation.

21. Papers Relating to the Friendly Association, Department of Records, Philadelphia Yearly Meeting of Friends, 302 Arch Street, Philadelphia, vol. 1, pp. 406–7. Although Anthony F. C. Wallace quotes from this manuscript in *King of the Delawares: Teedyuskung*, 1700–1763, Philadelphia, 1949, pp. 21–22, he did not cite the line I have quoted.

3

How the Delawares Lived

No one knows the name or nationality of the first white man to visit a Delaware village, but to him the Indian way of life must have seemed strangely primitive. His greatest surprise must have been the complete absence of guns and ammunition, swords, steel knives, iron and copper pots, China dishes, and the other metal weapons and domestic utensils commonly used in Europe. The native artifacts were fashioned from stone, bone, wood, shell, and clay, and the principal weapon was a crude bow made of pliable wood fitted with a bowstring of a twisted thong of deerskin. The arrows were reeds tipped with sharp points of flint, bone, or deer antler. There were no wheeled vehicles; no horses; no cotton, wool, silk, or any other kind of cloth; no glass; no gold or silver; no precious stones. To the European, the Delawares must have seemed to be in a stone age.

The first thing the visitor would have seen was the one-room bark huts haphazardly strung along the banks of a creek, with no semblance of streets or a public square. There were three different-shaped huts, which the Indians called wigwams—round with a dome-shaped roof, oblong with an arched roof, and oblong with a ridgepole and pitched roof—but, regardless of shape, each had a gaping hole in the roof that served as a chimney. There were no windows in any of the wigwams, only a single doorway curtained with animal skins. Within each dwelling an open fire smoldered on the earthen floor, and the furniture consisted of tiered platforms of skin-covered tree limbs built along the walls to serve as seats and beds.

Strings of corn held together by their braided husks, strips of dried pumpkin, and clumps of roots, tobacco, red cedar, and medicinal herbs were tied to a pole across the smoky ceiling beyond the reach of the flea-ridden dogs. Pottery vessels blackened by many fires and stone and wood utensils were stored under the platforms to be brought out when needed, then wiped with dried grass and put away for another day.

Except during cold weather or when it rained, members of the family spent most of their time outdoors, using their wigwam as a place to sleep at night. In front of each dwelling, there was a second fireplace where the family gathered to eat during the summer and where silo-shaped pits dug in the earth, each lined with straw and covered with bark lids, were used to store corn, beans, nuts, and other edibles. Stews and soups were prepared in pointed-bottom clay vessels held upright in the fire by supporting stones, and the tableware consisted of wooden bowls, clam shell spoons, and stone knives. Lacking forks, the members of the family ate most solid food with their fingers, all dipping out of the same pot. Pieces of meat and fowl were skewered on sticks and held over the embers; other food was placed in the coals to roast.

A visitor from Sweden or Finland would have understood the purpose of the small sweat lodges along the creek bank, built of stones and earth, but a Dutchman or Englishman would have been puzzled by their use. When the Indians periodically took sweat baths in these lodges, stones were heated and carried inside through the small hole that served as an entrance. Cold water was poured over the stones to make steam, and one by one each member of the family took his turn crawling into the lodge and remaining until his pores were opened and his naked body was glistening with sweat. Then he backed out on all fours and plunged into the cold waters of the creek. Not only was the practice believed to be beneficial as a preventive as well as a cure for ailments, but it also had religious significance as a purification rite.

Regardless of his nationality or skin color, a visitor would have been greeted with warm hospitality. Deeply ingrained in the Delawares' tradition was the obligation they felt to share their food and the comfort of their wigwams with a stranger. It was not uncommon for an Indian host to offer his wife or daughter to a visitor. As the European visitor entered the village and for the first time came face to face with the Indians, he immediately realized that in their size and anatomy they differed little from himself. The average height of males ranged from about five feet seven to five feet ten inches, although there were as many exceptions as there were among Europeans.[1] It did not take long to recognize, however, that the Indians were strong, quick on their feet, capable of long endurance, and certainly better able than a European to survive in a woodland environment. On the other hand, the Indian span of life was probably shorter than that of the average European because of lower resistance to infectious diseases. Nevertheless, blindness, cripples, hunchbacks, and those with physical deformations were rare.

The European visitor would not have noticed anything unusual about the oval-shaped head of the average Delaware, which modern anthropologists classify as *dolicocephalic*, but he would have been impressed with their prominent cheekbones, their small, dark eyes, and their skin color, which ranged from a swarthy *café au lait* to almost black. The contrasting whiteness of their teeth was enhanced by their natural diet, although dental cavities were frequent, as archeological evidence indicates. Indians with beards were rare, because hair grew sparsely on their faces, and it was the custom to use a hinged mussel shell like tweezers to pull the hair out by the roots. Evidently the men thought it unmanly to grow beards, and by removing the hair they had a smoother surface to paint on when they decorated themselves for festivals and ceremonial dances. Painting the face with white, red, and yellow clay, wood ashes, black shale, or the juices of herbs and berries was a custom practiced by both men and women. The colors had a special meaning; white, for example, was a symbol of happiness and peace; black of grief, evil, and death.

At times the Indian males applied paint not only to their faces but to their thighs, legs, or breasts in various designs that probably had some particular ceremonial meaning. Red seems to have been a favorite color with the women; they reddened their eyelids, dabbed circular red spots on their cheeks, and sometimes outlined the rims of their ears in red. Both men and women practiced tattooing, usually in snake, bird, and animal representations, which were accomplished by puncturing the skin with flint or sharp bone, then rubbing powdered tree bark or paint into the abrasions.

The European, surrounded in his homeland by people having a wide range of hair colors and textures, would have taken special note

Figure 10. Three Delaware Indian brothers from Oklahoma photographed about 1906, left to right, John, George, and Sam Anderson. The boy is John's son Andrew. George is wearing the traditional Plains feather bonnet, but the feather fan held by Sam is typically Delaware. (Courtesy Smithsonian Institution National Anthropological Archives)

that the hair of men, women, and children alike was coarse, straight, and black. Older men generally allowed their hair to grow down to their shoulders, whereas boys and young men shaved their heads with a sharp flint or plucked out the hairs, leaving a small cock's comb in the center. This crest, which was later referred to as a scalp lock, was often greased to make it stand erect, and the young brave ornamented it with an eagle feather, because he believed this would confer the courage of the eagle on him. The Delawares did not originally wear the ornate feather war bonnets like those found among the Plains tribes that have come to symbolize American Indian dress. In recent years some of the Delawares borrowed this custom, even though a headdress was not part of the traditional costume (see Fig. 10).

The native clothing was made of animal skins, feathers, and plant fibers. The women sewed the skins together with thread made of sinew, hair, or tough grass. They punched holes in the hide with an awl of deer or turkey bone, and they cut the skin with a stone knife. In the summer the Indian male wore either an apron, or a loin cloth, a breechclout, of soft deerskin, which passed between his legs, and was brought up and folded to hang down from his deerskin belt, front and back. In the winter he wore a robe, usually of bearskin, thrown over one shoulder, leaving free the other arm, on which he sometimes wore a sleeve of animal skin. Leggings of fringed buckskin kept his legs warm during the cold weather, and his moccasins made of deerskin were often decorated with shell beads or dyed porcupine quills.

The European would have found the Indian women very shy, modest, and desirous of pleasing their men. In their knee-length skirts of deerskin, their breasts bare, and long braided tresses setting off their soft features, the young women would have been highly attractive to the white visitor. They used bear grease as a hair dressing, and men as well as women applied it to their bodies as an insect repellant. The women wore bands of wampum beads around their foreheads, and both men and women adorned themselves with stone and shell gorgets, pendants, beads, necklaces, arm bands, and anklets and earrings of stone, shells, animal teeth, and claws. In the winter the women covered their breasts and shoulders with shawls of animal pelts and robes of turkey feathers. The feather robes were so neatly and expertly made that the feathers formed a smooth, downy surface to shed rain and protect the wearer from the cold. In cold weather the women also protected their legs with deerskin leggings and their feet with moccasins.

When a baby was born, the mother tied it to a flat cradle board, which she thought would make the child tall and straight. She carried the infant by fastening the cradle board to her back, and when she worked in the fields she hung it on a tree limb. At night it served as a crib when she laid the baby by her side covered with animal skins. When the child was old enough to walk, he toddled around without any clothing during the summer, and in the winter he was bundled in furs. As the children grew old enough to take care of themselves, the boys dressed like their fathers, the girls like their mothers. Parents were indulgent of their children and rarely punished them for fear that mistreatment might result in the child being taken away from them by the Creator.

On his initial visit to the Indian village, a European would have seen many things that perplexed him but which were explained through later association with the Indians. Today we have the benefit of the diaries, letters, journals, and diplomatic and legal records written by contemporary observers; [2] in addition, ethnologists and archeologists have added to our knowledge of Indian custom. For example, in the summer of 1952, with the assistance of several members of the Archeological Society of Delaware, we located a Delaware Indian grave near Glen Moore, Chester County, Pennsylvania, on the headwaters of the Brandywine. According to local tradition this site was believed to be an Indian cemetery (although there were no surface indications of graves), and, if this was the case, a local historical society wanted to preserve and mark the site.

As we dug a series of test pits, we located the badly disintegrated skeleton of a Delaware Indian. Clustered together in the area of his neck were three clay smoking pipes (made in England between 1700 and 1740), two gun flints, and an embossed brass button, which he must have carried as an amulet. From the position of these objects, it was apparent that they had been buried in a pouch that had long since decayed. This confirmed early accounts that the male Delaware wore a pouch of animal skin on a thong around his neck, and the pouch contained tobacco and good luck charms which he wanted to keep on his person. The grave also contained sixty-one glass beads, which, like the other artifacts, had been obtained from white traders probably in exchange for animal pelts. His mourners must have considered these objects valuable enough to be placed in the grave to accompany him to the next world. Having corroborated that the site was indeed a burial ground, we reburied the bones and appropriately marked the location. [3]

A belief in the survival of a soul or spirit after death was an integral part of Delaware religion, although there was no concept of redemption from sin and salvation in the Christian sense. The Indians were taught that the spirit departed from the body at death but remained in the vicinity for a designated number of days, after which it left the earth, making its way to the highest heaven where it lived on indefinitely in a place where pain, sickness, and sorrow were unknown. Early writers said that it was customary, during the period of mourning, for the widow and other close relatives to blacken their faces, although this practice was discontinued in later years and has not been observed within the memory of living Delawares. The belongings of the deceased were often taken to the burial site; some were put in the grave, others were distributed among members of the family, or, in more recent times, to the "workers" who participated in the graveside ceremony.

Prior to the arrival of Europeans, no coffins were used; the corpse was placed in a shallow hole in the earth, fully dressed and with the face painted. Archeological work in the Delaware Valley on graves presumed to be those of prehistoric Delawares, and on later burials known to have been those of historic Delawares, indicates that funerary customs varied by village and band, and by different time periods. Archeologists believe that burial customs may have changed from generation to generation, and that the Delawares were probably influenced by other Indians. In some instances graves were dug within the occupied area of a village; in others, as with the later Delaware communities in Canada and Oklahoma, there was a cemetery beyond the bounds of the village. Bodies were placed in the graves in both extended and flexed positions, and at some sites disarticulated bones of the deceased were buried in nests or bundles, the remains of a number of individuals placed in the same grave. Pipes, shell beads, pottery, and stone artifacts are often found in some graves, but in others no artifacts are present.

The manner in which a person died was also a factor in the way he was positioned in the grave; some Indian suicides, for example, were buried face down. Once they were thrown in contact with the whites, the Indians began to modify their burial customs, and boxes and coffins soon began to be used in imitation of European practices. Some Delawares cut a hole in each coffin to allow the spirit of the deceased to go in and out at pleasure until it had found the place of its future residence. Food was occasionally placed on the grave by mourners, and annual feasts at the grave have been recorded.[4]

Early observers emphasize that agriculture was the foundation of Delaware economy, which attached the people to the soil during the growing seasons, although the quest for food and clothing necessitated their moving back and forth at certain seasons. The principal crops were corn, beans, pumpkins, squash, and tobacco, but the Indian diet also included fish, flesh, and fowl, which took the men away from their homes periodically on hunting and fishing trips. During the hunting and gathering season, women and children often accompanied the men, leaving the old people in the village. Knowledge of trees and plants, and of the habits of living creatures, was extremely important, because the livelihood of a family depended upon it. The boys were taught woodcraft and hunting at an early age; the girls learned housekeeping, gardening and domestic crafts from their mothers and female relatives. As a peaceful, sedentary folk, their village and local community was the social center, and, for the individual, life revolved around his immediate family.

The Delawares were a cornfed people, and corn was prepared in a variety of ways, some of which were imitated by white settlers and are still in use in our modern society. Corn on the cob was roasted in the hot ashes without removing husks; it was also boiled in water with the husks in place. The kernels, removed from the cob, were mixed with beans to make succotash and boiled to make a popular dish called hominie. The women dried the corn kernels and pounded them into cornmeal in a log mortar, using a wooden or stone pestle, and the meal, or flour, was used to make mush or dumplings. Mixed with water, the meal formed a dough that was molded into small patties, wrapped in husks, and baked in the hot ashes or on a hot stone in front of the fire.

One kind of corn bread became known to the whites as Johnnycake, but there were a number of other recipes, some having dried berries, fruits, or nuts mixed with the dough. Corn meal was also mixed with meat and fish and cooked into a thick, nourishing pottage. A favorite with Indian children was a confection consisting of maple sugar mixed with corn meal. Wild fruit, berries, nuts, and edible roots were all part of the diet, and there were times when the family ate dog meat, animal entrails, eels, certain insects such as wild locusts, and other foods that seem as distasteful to us as some highly seasoned European dishes did to the Indians.

A few of the old recipes have been handed down in Delaware Indian families. For example, in June of 1969 I was a dinner guest at the home of Mrs. Mary Townsend Crow, a well-educated Delaware descendant, who lived with her husband Joe on a ranch near Bartlesville, Oklahoma. Mrs. Crow was secretary-treasurer of the Delaware Tribal Business Committee, and other members of the committee and their families were present at the dinner and assisted in its preparation. The special menu for the occasion inclued pee-too-can-oh-uk, milkweed boiled with dumplings; kaw-ha-pawn, grated corn that had been baked, dried, and then boiled; ta-sa-mannana, cooked dried corn; shoe-k'lee-pe-nah, sweet potatoes; sa-law-pawn, fried corn bread; sulus-see-kon, ground meat with dumplings; a cup-pitch (cabbage) salad; with hot coffee and blackberry cobbler for dessert. Some of these dishes were strange to my taste and lacked the seasoning characteristic of modern American foods, but I found all of them pleasant and satisfying.

To the Delawares tobacco, an indigenous American plant, had an almost sacred character, holding a unique place in their ceremonial life. The men smoked the powdered leaves in clay or stone smoking pipes, sometimes mixing it with other pulverized dried leaves, like sumac, to form a blend called kinnikinnick. The smoking of tobacco was practiced in divination, in the cure of diseases, in treaty councils, in social intercourse with other Indians, and as a personal recreation. When an Indian smoked for recreation, the act also held a meaning in native symbolism, which also survived in modern Delaware life. In 1944 Jesse Moses, an educated Delaware living in Canada, wrote a letter about another Delaware, a traditionalist whose Indian name was Nekatcit ("tame little fellow")—in English he was called Nicodemus Peters—as follows:

He was not a smoker. But when he had come into the house, made the greetings and taken a seat, he would either suggest that we have a smoke, or ask for one. If I made no indication of having a smoke with him, he would say, "Come on! Light up!" We usually spent about ten minutes just sitting and smoking—no conversation whatever—each seeming to be absorbed in his own thoughts.

He explained this period of silence and smoking together as essential, for, said he, "See our smoke has now filled the room, first it was in streaks and your smoke and my smoke moved about that way, but now it is all mixed up into one. That is like our minds and spirits too, when we must talk. We are now ready, for we will understand one another better." [5]

A pinch of dried tobacco was often thrown into the fire, the way incense might be burned, to accompany a prayer asking for special favors, or it might be used to propitiate angry waters, quiet howling winds, appease a destructive storm, or protect a traveler before he set out on a journey. When a Delaware cut down a tree, he sprinkled tobacco at its base as an offering to the Spirit Forces living in the tree, and he used tobacco for other religious purposes.

Clippings from the leaves of the cedar (sometimes called juniper) were also used for purifying purposes because the Delawares believed the Creator endowed the tree with spiritual powers. On one of my visits to Oklahoma, I was privileged when Mrs. Nora Thompson Dean burned the clippings of the awl-shaped red cedar leaves (*Juniperus virginia*) in the embers of an open wood fire. While doing so she offered a prayer in the Delaware tongue to Kee-shay-lum-moo-kawng, the Indian name for the Creator, asking for my safe return home. When she had completed the prayer, those of us gathered around the fire in her yard "bathed" one by one in the smoke of the cedar, each going through the motions of laving his face, head, and body in an act signifying spiritual purification. Using an ancient fan made of the feathers of an eagle (which the Delawares considered a noble bird whose wings were believed capable of sweeping away obstacles and malevolent forces), she made several passes across our outstretched hands, palms up, symbolizing our willingness to seek and receive the Creator's blessing. Meanwhile she fanned the sweet-smelling smoke toward the sky to carry her prayers to Kee-shay-lum-moo-kawng in the twelfth heaven. I felt invigorated by the experience, and it was, of course, a coincidence (or was it?) that the return trip to my home in Delaware, which involved two automobile rides and two plane flights, was pleasant and without accident, with arrivals and departures on schedule, and a pair of loving arms waiting to greet my safe arrival home.

To return to ancient custom, seasonal cycles included a time to plant and hoe, periods when the men hunted, and other periods when they went to the seashore to gather clams and oysters. Nuts and roots were gathered in season; herbs, berries, grapes and wild plums were picked; and sap was collected from the maple trees to be boiled down to sugar. At other times the hunters went into the marshes for ducks, geese, and other wild fowl, or to trap the muskrat, otter, and beaver. The beaver was especially useful because of its soft, thick fur; and its tail cooked in bear grease was considered a delicacy. Smaller animals, including foxes, rabbits, squirrels, chipmunks, groundhogs, raccoons, and opossums were also sought for both their flesh and pelts.

Of all the wild animals, none was more useful than the Virginia white-tailed deer, originally abundant in the Delaware Valley, where it fed on buds and twigs, or wild shrubs. The deer was a source of venison; hides were used for clothing, antler and bone for tools, and sinew and gut for bindings and glue. Deer was taken by stalking the individual animal with bow and arrow, by snares set in the woods where the does browsed for food, or by driving herds into a natural or artificial enclosure—by setting fires or other means—where a party of Indian hunters could close in on them. Also of importance to the Indian economy were the black bear and the brown-pelted member of the species known as the cinnamon bear, some weighing as much as five hundred pounds, which were both native to the Delaware Valley. Their shaggy fur was prized for making winter robes; grease used for cooking and as an ointment was rendered from the fat.

In early fall the families were normally back in their home village for the harvest and the attendant corn festivals and feasts, which were part of the ceremonial life. In late fall the men moved again to their hunting territories, where they remained on and off during the winter. When the Indians were away from their villages, they built crude shelters or lean-tos of tree branches, or, if they could find a suitable overhanging rock ledge, they camped at its mouth. Year after year successive native hunters used the same rock shelters. The Todd Rock Shelter in Sussex County, New Jersey, the Fairy Hole Rock Shelter in Warren County in the same state, the Buckskin Cave in Pike County, Pennsylvania, the Broomall Rock Shelters near Philadelphia, the Dutchess Quarry Cave in Orange County, New York, and the Beaver Valley Rock Shelter in New Castle County, Delaware, are examples of Indian rock shelters where archeologists have unearthed pottery, arrowheads, stone knives, and axes carried by the Indian hunters.

To catch fish the Delawares often built fish weirs, which were stone dams laid across a stream in the shape of a V, with an opening in the center. Men and boys wading in the stream drove the fish to the dam where other Indians speared them or caught them in nets made of vines of plaited grass. Fish was baked or boiled and often used in stews; oysters and clams gathered at the seashore were eaten raw or smoked and stored away for use during the winter.

Along Delaware and Chesapeake bays, and on the New Jersey coast in the salt marshes near Tuckerton and Barnegat, there once were heaps of shells left by Indian fishermen. Stone artifacts and fragments of clay pottery were found in these heaps; shells in quantity are often scattered over sites where the Indians lived or camped in southern Delaware and New Jersey, the remains of oyster feasts and clambakes.

Although the Delawares did not construct birchbark canoes, they navigated the waterways in canoes made of hollowed-out logs. They also followed on foot the trails that ran from one village to another, to their hunting territories, and to the seashore. These paths became an intricate crisscross of travel-ways used by hunters, warriors, messengers, and even family parties. Considerable trading was carried on intertribally, and on archeological sites in the Delaware Valley numerous artifacts have been found which the local Indians obtained from distant tribes and carried over the trails to their home villages. The paths were narrow, about eighteen inches wide, sufficient only for persons moving in single file, although some were wide enough for two people. The Europeans gave them different names, and among the better known ones were the Minisink Trail, Wyalusing Path, Choptank Path, Allegheny Path, Great Minquas Path, and the Warrior's Path, of which there were several bearing the same name.[6]

Early deed records in Delaware, New Jersey, and Pennsylvania refer to Indian trails or "old Indian paths" crossing the properties. These paths led to fording places, where streams could be crossed, and also enabled native travelers to go through the mountains and forests without getting lost. The names of the paths were usually taken from their termini, and these were reversible—what was the Tulpehocken Path at Shamokin was the Shamokin Path at Tulpehocken, and there were as many Shamokin paths as there were paths going to Shamokin. Many of our highways follow the same general course of some of the Indian trails, which successively evolved into bridle paths, wagon roads, and motor highways.

When the Indian family traveled over one of the trails, the squaw usually carried the supplies and fur blankets on her back held by a packstrap across her breast or forehead. This freed her husband's hands and arms if it became necessary to protect the family against wild animals or enemy Indians. The Indian woman was not a slave or beast of burden subservient to her husband, as some European observers concluded. She held a respected position, but like her husband she assumed responsibilities necessary for the survival of the family, some involving physical exertion. A division of labor was well understood, and the woman's duties included planting, harvesting, preparing food, tanning hides, gathering firewood, carrying water, making clothing, weaving baskets, taking care of the children, and carrying the supplies on a journey. The men felled the trees, cleared the land, built the wigwams, constructed dugouts and animal traps, fished and hunted, and bore the responsibility of protecting their families. The old people, who were much respected, knitted nets; made clay bowls, wampum beads, and stone implements; and scraped and dressed the pelts for clothing.

Every member of the Indian family—from the youngest to the oldest—had work to do, and a woman did not feel abused because her tasks included physical labor. Contrary to American folklore, the Delaware Indian female was no drudge but a respected matriarch who had recognized authority within the family and the community. In some respects she held a more privileged position than the women in European society. It may come as a surprise to the reader to learn that white women taken captive by the Delaware Indians in warfare often refused to be rescued after they had become members of an Indian community, because they did not want to return to the subordination accorded women in colonial society.

There were no formal marriage ceremonies or nuptial vows, and, though a union might be arranged by the parents, more often a young couple merely decided that they would live together as man and wife. Courtship was more a matter of giving presents than of romantic love, and when a man selected his marriage partner he usually sent presents of furs, food, or perhaps wampum beads to her parents or nearest relatives. The affection between a husband and wife was never publicly demonstrated, but it was usually strong and enduring. His attachment to her led him to many acts of devotion, and although divorce was easy, depending only upon the expressed wish of one or both parties, couples with children usually remained together. Instances of Delaware Indians having more than one wife were recorded by early white scribes, but this appears to have been an exception rather than the rule.

Although the Delaware chiefs were considered political leaders, they hunted, fished, lived in wigwams, and raised their families like other villagers. The chiefs did not have servants, possessed no more "wealth" than their native associates, and exercised a very limited authority. Some Europeans called the village or band chiefs "kings," which was an exaggeration, because there was no comparison between the functions of a Delaware chief and the king of a European state who wielded vast powers. Even though the position of the chief entailed both executive and ceremonial responsibilities, a strong democratic spirit governed the conduct and that of their people in what was an economic as well as political democracy. William Penn wrote that when presents were given to him, a chief "sub-divideth it in like manner among his Dependents, they hardly leaving themselves an Equal share with one of their Subjects; and be it on such occasions, at Festivals, or at their common Meals, the Kings distribute, and to themselves last." [7] The amassing of worldly goods was not an ambition among the chiefs, and, as with other members of the tribe, their personal property consisted of the clothing they wore, the wigwams they lived in, and their tools, domestic implements, and weapons. In the processe of decision making, the chiefs were advised by a council. Penn wrote that nothing of importance was undertaken by the chiefs without consultation with these councilors. [8]

None of the contemporary visitors to the Delaware villages obtained detailed information as to how the chiefs were selected, and consequently some historians have speculated about this subject without having any facts. Through careful scrutiny of the meager documentary information that has come to light, it appears that when an old chief was nearing death he nominated a successor from among a number of individuals whose lineage qualified them to take his place. The dying words of the old chief, Ockanickon, as recorded by an early scribe, illustrate this practice in the italicized words:

Whereas Sehoppy and Swanpis *were appointed Kings by me in my Stead*, and I understanding by my Doctor that Sehoppy secretly advised him not to Cure me, and they both being with me at John Hollingshead's House, there I my self see by them that they were given more to Drink than to take notice of my last Words . . . therefore I refused them to be kings after me in my stead, *and I have chosen my Brother's Son Jahkursoe in their stead to succeed me.*[9] (Italics added)

Another Delaware chief named Tamanend, also known as Tamany, was quoted in a document dated July 5, 1697, nominating "Weheequeckhon, alias Andrew, who is to be king after my death." [10] It is not clear what Weheequeckhon's relationship was to Tamany, but the likelihood is that they were brothers, or uncle and nephew. The records indicate that Tamany had a brother named Weheeland and at least two sons, Yaqueekhon, alias Nicholas, and Quenameckquid, alias Charles.

The old man did not explain why he selected Weheequeckhon from among the several candidates eligible by heritage to succeed him.

In a later chapter the reader will learn that the Delaware sachem known as Sassoonan, alias Olumapies, also named a nephew to succeed him, although the Pennsylvania authorities had other ideas about who should be elevated to this position. The reader will also find that the chief Custaloga nominated his nephew Captain Pipe as his successor. This does not mean that an aged chief was endowed with autocratic power, or that his selection of a successor was final and irrevocable, because this was not the case. The councilors and other elder members of the band or tribe also had something to say, although the subject is imperfectly understood due to incomplete information. One thing is certain: The Delaware women did not take an active part in choosing a chief as did certain matrons in the Iroquois League of the Five Nations who were known as the chiefmakers, although eligibility as a candidate for chieftaincy was determined by the succession in the female line rather than in the male. This means that the sons of a chief did not inherit his rank; his successor was normally a brother, a son of a sister, or the son of a sister's daughter. In the Delaware matrilineal society at any one time, there were usually a number of individuals possessing the "royal" blood that qualified one to be selected as chief. Once again we find that William Penn, who was curious about Indian customs, has an explanation for this practice:

Their Government is by Kings, which they call *Sachema,* and those by Succession, but always of the Mothers side; for Instance, the Children of him that is now King, will not succeed, but his Brother by the Mother, or the Children of his Sister, whose Sons (and after them the Children of her Daughters) will reign; for no Woman inherits; the Reason they render for this way of Descent, *is that their Issue may not be spurious.*[11]

Another way of clarifying the words I have italicized in this quotation is to understand that one may be sure of the mother who bore him but, as Penn intimates, the identity of the father may be less certain. When the Delawares considered descent through the mother's side of the family, there was no question that all her offspring had "royal" blood. Thus, one's qualification to be elevated to the chieftaincy was gained through inheritance, although obviously not everyone so qualified could become a chief, and this is why the incumbent had to choose his successor. The chiefs represented the lineage in religious ceremonies (the ritualistic paraphernalia were handed down in the female line), in treaties, in land transactions, and in other diplomatic matters involving whites or other Indian groups.

Kinship was a fundamental concept in the Delaware social organization, far more important than in modern American society. The Indian household, or economic family, comprising a man, his wife, and their children—and perhaps other relatives—was the basic social unit. Since the continuum rested in the maternal lineage, the members of each lineage knew their blood relatives by whom they were bound together by kinship ties. As time went on and the population increased, exact kinship relations were not clearly remembered, and other ways had to be found whereby a person knew who was related to him. Although there is no documentary evidence that the early Delawares had clan organizations, it is very probable that they did, and this was the way common ancestries were stressed. A clan was composed of persons who laid claim to a common ancestor, each one usually named after a totemic animal. Among the Indian tribes known to have had clans, there were taboos that discouraged a man from mating with a woman of his own clan—which was supposed to prevent intermarriage between blood relations.

Europeans were confused by the system of matrilineal descent and by kinship terms that differed in meaning from those used in the Old World. An excellent example of the strange use of kinship terms is illustrated in this statement made by a Shawnee informant:

The son of my aunt is my son, the daughter of my aunt is my daughter. My brother's son is my nephew, the son of my nephew is my grandson. My brother's daughter is my niece, and his son is my son, and the daughter of my niece is my daughter, and the children of this son and daughter are your grandchildren.[12]

The religious beliefs and practices of the Delawares were also so different from Christian customs that the Europeans never fully understood the full significance of the ceremonies, feasts, and dances. White observers saw the Indian ceremonies either as childish antics, or pagan rites, instead of a sincere expression of a religious fervor based on deep-seated spiritual convictions. Some of the early writers went so far as to call the Delawares "devil worshipers," an insult to a religion that did not include a Satan or Devil, a concept introduced to the Indians by Christians.

Christians accepted the biblical account that Man was created in the image of one living God, but the Delawares believed that Kee-shay-lum-moo-kawng and his subordinate Spirit Forces were present in all living things. In addition to meaning "Our Creator," Kee-shay-lum-moo-kawng was also freely translated to mean Great Spirit, and sometimes he was referred to as the Great Manito, which also means God or Maker. The lesser spiritual agents, the subordinate Manitowuk (the plural of Manito), were, in effect, the forces present in trees, flowers, grass, rivers, rocks, and other manifestations of nature.

The Delawares felt a special closeness to these Manitowuk, who were an integral part of woodland living. They believed that God was everything and everything was God, a pantheistic concept in which the entire world was under the control of invisible beings. Some were great and powerful; others had lesser influence; in some, good seemed to dominate, in others, evil. The Delawares addressed their prayers to the Great Manito, as well as to the lesser Manitowuk, and the response to their supplications was seen in the sunrise and sunset, the stars, the winds, the snows, and in the spring rains that nourished the corn. Realization of the frailty of human power was deeply imbued in the Indian mind; he believed that without guidance from the Great Manito and the other Spirit Forces life would have been futile.

Although the Delawares had several creation myths (see Trow-bridge's hitherto unpublished report in Appendix 3 containing an account of how one group of Delawares believed they were descended from the Wyandot, who sprang from a hole in the earth), one that was promulgated widely held that the world was created on the back of a giant turtle. This legendary tale taught the Indians that in the beginning there was nothing but water everywhere, and that the Creator brought up a turtle from the depths of the water. As the water fell from his back, a tree took root on it. The tree sent out a sprout, and the sprout grew into a man. A second sprout appeared on the tree, which became a woman, and the Delawares believed they were descended from this first human couple. The turtle became a vener-ated symbol of Mother Earth; in fact it was life itself and its symboli-cal breathing, which caused the surrounding water to ebb and flow, that was the origin of the tides. The twelve plates in its carapace became a sacred number that was incorporated in Delaware cere-monies.

The Great Manito assigned the four quarters of the earth to four powerful Manitowuk, the North, West, and East, known as Grandfathers, whose duty it was to take care of these regions, and the South was under the guardianship of Koo-hum-mun-nah (Our Grandmother). They caused the wind to blow from different directions; they sent the snows from the North, and the balmy winds from the South; and they were custodians for other weather influences that came from the directions under their custody.

The Great Manito gave the duty of providing light to the sun, who traveled by day across the heavens from east to west, and at night went under the earth. The Delawares addressed the sun and the moon, who was delegated the duty of lighting the earth at night, as Elder Brothers. Yet it is incorrect to think of the Delawares as sun worshipers or moon worshipers, as some early white observers may have interpreted the devotions, because deification was not centered on one element in nature but included everything.

Modern ethnologists, denied the privilege given contemporary observers of witnessing the ceremonies while the Delawares were still practicing ancient rites, have done their utmost to reconstruct the native religious patterns. Their principal technique—and in most cases the last method of obtaining information—has been to probe the memories of informants among Delaware descendants. With few exceptions, most of the significant data about Delaware ceremonial life, was obtained through the efforts of two investigators, M. R. Harrington and Frank G. Speck.

Between 1907 and 1910, Harrington made a number of visits to Oklahoma and Ontario, Canada, under the auspices of the Heye Foundation, Museum of the American Indian. He learned to his regret that he was many years too late to witness any of the native religious practices of the Delawares living in Canada. Their conversion to Christianity resulted in a discontinuance of all non-Christian rites, including the Big House Ceremony; however, a few of the older Canadian Indian informants were able to give him details of some of the ancient rites practiced by their ancestors.[13]

Fortunately, the Delawares in Oklahoma were still observing some of their native beliefs, even though many had become Christians, and Harrington was able to obtain information from the traditionalists about the calendar of religious events. The Big House Ceremony was still being held at the time of his visits, and other ceremonies that the Delawares no longer practiced were remembered by the older Indians; Harrington made a record of what they told him.[14]

Between 1928 and 1938 Speck also worked among Delaware descendants in Oklahoma and Canada, under the auspices of the University of Pennsylvania and the Pennsylvania Historical Commission. Through patient and skillful inquiry, taking advantage of his knowledge of the Algonkian language, he was able to supplement and expand Harrington's findings.[15] Discussions with Delaware traditionalists made both ethnologists aware that the most vital and intimate phase of Delaware religion was a belief in dreams and visions, and in the existence of personal guardian spirits. The vision was the point of contact, a line of communication between the supernatural world and the sphere of everyday life. An individual who received his guardian spirit in a vision could always appeal to this spirit as his own special protector for aid or comfort in times of trouble, and sometimes to foretell coming events. This guardian spirit, usually an animal or bird, took a personal interest in his affairs, whereas the Creator and the subordinate Manitowuk were so busy controlling other natural forces that they might not be able to concern themselves with the affairs of one individual. The individual prayed to both the Creator and his guardian spirit, although not every Delaware was endowed with a guardian spirit, because its possession was a special blessing received by chosen boys and girls as part of their initiation into puberty.

Sometimes a vision came later in life when an individual was saddened by the death of a loved one, or as a result of other suffering or trouble. Some persons went through life without ever having experienced a vision, although this did not mean that their associates lost their respect for him. It was just something that didn't happen to them, for unexplained reasons. Those who had visions were called upon to make and keep on their person a symbol in clay, wood, or stone representing their guardian spirit, which was usually regarded as a charm.

Both Speck and Harrington learned that there were individual rites, family rites, and band or tribal rites held for different ceremonial purposes, usually accompanied by feasting and dancing. Some of these had strong social overtones, with minimal religious implication, contrary to the belief of early missionaries who tended to consider all Indian ceremonies designed for worshiping pagan gods. When conducted for religious purposes, most of the ceremonies, if one can generalize about them, were intended to satisfy offended Spirit Forces and seek added blessings from spiritual agents for such things as crop protection, avoidance of sickness, control of bad weather, success in hunting, and the elimination of catastrophe.

The Big House Ceremony, known as Gamwing, was no doubt of ancient origin, and was probably held in an earlier and perhaps simpler form when the Indians lived in the Delaware Valley. As the ceremony was practiced in Oklahoma, the positions occupied by the participants, the role of the ceremonial attendants or ash-kah-suk, and the part played by the leader seem to have been vestiges of the past (see Fig. 11). One assumes that anciently each community of native villages had its own Big House constructed of the same material used in building the wigwams. In Oklahoma the twelve faces carved on posts in the interior were not worshiped as idols; their purpose was to "watch" the ceremony and carry the Indians' prayers to the Creator. The two fires on the earthen floor were lighted by a sacred fire drill to provide light and heat, and the floor was repeatedly swept twelve times by the ash-kah-suk using turkey wings to brush clear the path to heaven. The ash-kah-suk took care of painting the carved faces, passing the twelve prayer sticks, keeping the fires going, and placing hay on the earth where the participants sat. Their tents were at designated places on the Big House grounds (as in Fig. 11).

Men and women in their best clothing, their faces appropriately painted, sat separately in special places around the performance area within the Big House. They maintained silence until they were called upon to perform or join the singing, because it was a solemn occasion, having deep religious significance. During the ceremony, those gifted with a vision or dream, and hence in communication with the supernatural world, were called upon to recite their visions. Shaking a tortoise shell rattle (which was passed from one to the other), each communicant recited an account of how he received his vision in a sort of chant, pausing after each word or phrase to give the singers, who also beat a rolled dry deerskin drum with drumsticks carved with human heads, ample time to repeat his words. The song was interspersed with dancing around the fires, in which every adult was free to join—all following the same peculiar stomp, and moving counterclockwise.

At the conclusion of each night's ceremonies, the women ash-kah-

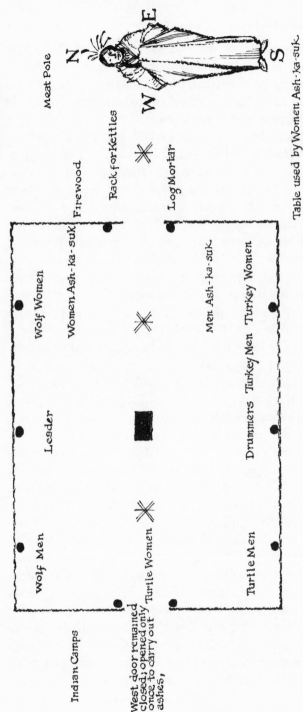

Figure 11. Diagram showing places of participants and some of the ceremonial properties used in Big House Ceremony. Centerpost had two carved faces; two posts at each doorway and six posts along walls each bore a carved face —twelve faces in all. Participants sat on hay strewn on ground. Holes in roof vented smoke from two holy fires. Three male and three female ash-ka-suk (ceremonial attendants) camped as shown and handled important ceremonial duties. The other Indians camped on three sides of structure, and all entered and left by the east doorway. (Drawing by Charles Waterhouse)

suk prepared the hominy or corn mush called sä'pan in a large kettle and served it to all in attendance, which was believed to bring spiritual blessing or strength. The twelfth night, or ah-tay-hoom-ween, was reserved for the women to recite their visions.

During the day, the people rested in their camps, assembling again at dusk. Certain prescribed rituals were observed at each meeting with designated men and women performing special functions. The purpose of the ceremony was outlined by one of the leaders to Harrington as follows:

When we come into this house of ours we are glad and thankful that we are well and for everything that makes us feel good which the Creator has placed here for our use. We come here to pray to Him to have mercy on us for the year to come and to give us everything to make us happy; may we have good crops, and no dangerous storms, floods nor earthquakes . . .

We are thankful to the East because everyone feels good in the morning when they awake, and see the bright light coming from the East, and when the Sun goes down in the West we feel good and are glad that we are well; then we are thankful to the West. And we are thankful to the North, because when the cold winds come we are glad to have lived to see the leaves fall again; and to the South, for when the south wind blows and everything is coming up in the spring, we are glad to live to see the grass growing and everything green again. We thank the Thunders, for they are the manitowuk that bring the rain, which the Creator has given them power to rule over. And we thank our mother, the Earth whom we claim as mother because the Earth carries us and everything we need.[16]

The Big House represented the universe; its floor, the earth; its four walls, the four quarters; its vault, the sky dome where the Creator resided in his supremacy. The centerpost was a staff linking the right hand of the Creator with His chosen people. At the close of the twelfth night, after the ceremony ended, the Delawares believed they had worshiped everything on earth and that, by pleasing the Creator and the Spirit Forces, their prayers would help all of humanity.[17]

Another phase of Delaware religious life was that of name-giving. Names were bestowed on children by parents after experiencing a significant dream or vision or by special visionaries, known as way-huh-wée-huh-lahs ("one who gives names over and over"). Children were not named at birth, because the parents believed that the infant did not obtain a firm hold on this world for some time after its birth, and at any time he might be taken away by the ever-present spirits of those who had died. When a name-giver was called to bestow a name, a ceremony with deep religious connotations was held, and the name created by the name-giver was usually related to the vision he had experienced. Since the Delaware language was polysynthetic, a number of ideas could be covered in one name; for instance, the Indian name bestowed on my friend James A. Rementer is Mooshhah-kwee-nund, which means "he who appears like a clear sky." A person and the real name bestowed upon him became indivisible. When he died, his real name, in effect, died with him and was rarely ever spoken aloud by members of the family.[18]

Because of the esoterism associated with real names, many nicknames were used to avoid saying the real name, and the whites called these aliases. Individuals were hesitant to disclose their real names beyond the family circle because they believed that knowledge of a person's real name by an enemy capable of conjuring evil might be used to that person's detriment. Nicknames, which were not real, were useless in conjuring, and there seems little question that many of the Delaware personal names recorded on early deeds and in other written records were nicknames. At a very early date, the Delawares (as well as members of other eastern tribes) also adopted Christian names and family names of Europeans, which they used in lieu of their real Indian names. Andrew Montour, John Pumpshire, John Peters, Tom Store, Isaas Stille, John Jacob, Cutfinger Peter, and Stephen Calvin—just to cite a few examples—were all Delaware Indians who lived in the early part of the eighteenth century.

In this chapter I have discussed only a few of the Indian customs and religious practices which have been treated in greater detail in the literature cited in the notes. I have not attempted to cover the training of children, puberty rites, games, musical instruments, herbalism and shamanism, storytelling, and other phases of Delaware life.[19] Nor have I discussed the differences in dialects spoken by the Delawares, because this is a highly technical subject, requiring the specialized skill of trained linguists.[20] The customs I have discussed illustrate that much of the daily life of the Indian family was spent satisfying the basic need for food, clothing, and shelter; that hunting and fishing were not sports but necessary methods of obtaining food at the expense of patience and considerable effort. It was not superior weapons that made the Indian a good hunter but his skill in stalking the game.

Primitive in contrast to European civilization, Delaware culture imposed heavy burdens on both husband and wife, since she, too, shared a definite economic responsibility. Yet it would be incorrect to leave the impression that the Indians were unhappy or frustrated because of the economic demands of their society. Seen against the backdrop of rivers, marshes, beaches, and forests, they were, like the animals and birds, products of a sylvan environment, having their place in nature's scheme of things. Considering the Delaware Valley milieu and separation by a vast expanse of ocean from Europe, comparisons with the more technically advanced European civilization become historical embroidery. The Delawares' simple tools, weapons, utensils, and clothing met their economic needs; their religious life gave them spiritual fulfillment; and they lived in peace in the unhurried communal life of their little villages, where they were taught to share with each other, lacking the competition present in European society. According to their own standards, the Delawares satisfied their living requirements through an attunement to their environment; they were content because they had few unfilled wants. Theirs was not a warrior society. Never having been seriously molested, the male population was inexperienced in military matters, unaware that the vulnerable location of their homes along navigable streams made their towns easy prey for pillage by white and Indian enemies.

NOTES—CHAPTER 3

1. The skeleton of an Indian taller than six feet was excavated at the Slaughter Creek site in Delaware; C. A. Weslager, *Delaware's Buried Past*, new and enlarged ed., New Brunswick, N.J., 1968, p. 172.

2. In the notes to chapter 2, reference was made to the accounts of Lindeström, William Penn, and De Vries written in the seventeenth century. Other valuable contemporary descriptions are found in the writings of Thomas Paschall, Thomas Yong, Francis Daniel Pastorius, and Gabriel Thomas in Albert Cook Myers, ed., *Narratives of Early Pennsylvania, West New Jersey, and Delaware, 1630–1707*, New York, 1912 (hereinafter referred to as Myers, *Narratives*). Governor Johan Printz's accounts of the Delaware Indians occur in Amandus Johnson, trans., *The*

Instruction for Johan Printz, Philadelphia, 1930; the notes of the Reverend Johan Campanius are incorporated in a volume written by his grandson Thomas Campanius Holm, *A Short Description of the Province of Pennsylvania*, Memoirs of the Historical Society of Pennsylvania, vol. 3, Philadelphia 1834. Excerpts from two of Governor Johan Rising's accounts are found in Myers, *Narratives*; and Rising also was the author of a journal which has not yet been published in the English language, although Dr. Amandus Johnson has made a translation of it.

3. C. A. Weslager, *Red Men on the Brandywine*, Wilmington, 1953, pp. 113–14.

4. On June 13, 1969, James A. Rementer took me to visit the Delaware Indian cemetery near Dewey, Oklahoma. Having attended Delaware funerals in recent years, he briefly described some of the practices to me, such as the processional to the cemetery; the partaking of food in a prescribed manner beside the grave after the interment; the orientation of the body with the head pointing east; making a hole in the coffin, the edges of which were reddened with paint; and the erection of wooden grave posts known as kee-keen-he-kun. It seemed clear to me that many of these non-European customs must have been handed down from the distant past.

5. Frank G. Speck, *The Celestial Bear Comes Down to Earth*, Scientific Publications, no. 7, Reading, Pa., 1945, p. xiii.

6. See Paul A. W. Wallace, *Indian Paths of Pennsylvania*, Harrisburg, Pa., 1956, for an excellent treatise on Indian trails. For a brief account of Indian trails in New Jersey, see Charles A. Philhower, "The Indians of the Morris County Area," *Proceedings of the New Jersey Historical Society*, vol. 54, no. 4, October, 1936, pp. 249–67; for an account of some of the trails in Delaware, see Wm B. Marye, "Indian Paths of the Delmarva Peninsula," *Bulletin of the Archeological Society of Delaware*, vol. 2, no. 3, March 1936, pp. 5–22; vol. 2, no. 4, October 1936, pp. 4–27.

7. Myers, *Narratives*, p. 233.

8. Ibid., p. 235.

9. *A True Account of the Dying Words of Ockanickon*, . . . , London, 1682. Ockanickon's wife's name is given as Matollionequay. A slightly different version of his dying words is given by Samuel Smith, *The History of the Colony of Nova-Caesaria or New Jersey* (hereafter cited as Smith, *History*), 2d ed., Burlington, N.J., 1877, pp. 148–49.

10. *Pennsylvania Archives*, 1st series, 12 vols., Philadelphia, Pa., 1852–56, vol. 1, ed. Samuel Hazard, pp. 124–25.

11. Myers, *Narratives*, pp. 234–35.

12. Lewis Henry Morgan, *The Indian Journals*, 1859–62, ed. Leslie A. White, Ann Arbor, 1959, p. 45.

13. Harrington's published works relating to the Delawares consist of "Vestiges of Material Culture among the Canadian Delawares," *American Anthropologist*, n.s., vol. 10, no. 3, July–September, 1908, pp. 408–18; "Some Customs of the Delaware Indians," *Museum Journal*, Philadelphia, Pa., vol. 1, no. 3, 1910, pp. 52–60; "A Preliminary Sketch of Lenape Culture," *American Anthropologist*, n.s., vol. 15, no. 2, April–June, 1913, pp. 208–35; *Religion and Ceremonies of the Lenape*, Indian Notes and Monographs, Museum of the American Indian, Heye Foundation, New York, 1921.

14. I have ascertained that none of Harrington's notes are in the files of the University of Pennsylvania Museum, but through correspondence with Frederick J. Dockstader, Director, Museum of the American Indian, Heye Foundation, I learned that this institution has a voluminous collection of Harrington's field notes, although this material is disorganized and requires collation to determine the extent of the Delaware data. Students of Delaware Indian ethnology may find useful information in these notes.

15. In addition to a number of papers, Speck's three principal monographs dealing with the Delawares are *A Study of the Delaware Indian Big House Ceremony* . . . , Harrisburg, Pa., 1931; *Oklahoma Delaware Ceremonies, Feasts and Dances*, Philadelphia, 1937; *The Celestial Bear Comes Down to Earth*, Reading, Pa., 1945.

16. Harrington, *Religion and Ceremonies of the Lenâpé*, 1921, pp. 88–90, quoting Chief Charles Elkhair, who died in 1935. Cf. the Big House oration of Colonel Jackson, another Delaware ceremonial leader, given in November, 1903, Richard C. Adams, *The Ancient Religion of the Delaware Indians*, Washington, D.C., 1904.

17. An article by Horace L. McCracken, former chairman of the Delaware Business Committee, entitled "The Delaware Big House" was published in the *Chronicles of Oklahoma*, vol. 34, no. 2, Summer 1956, pp. 183–92. In 1912 Dr. Truman Michelson of the Smithsonian Institution visited the Delawares in Oklahoma "and was gratified that many of their ancient customs were preserved almost intact. Elaborate notes were taken of several dances and observations on the social organizations were made"; *Smithsonian Miscellaneous Collections*, vol. 60, no. 30, 1913, p. 35. I am indebted to Dr. Ives Goddard for bringing to my attention that Michelson's notes are still available in the Anthropological Archives of the Smithsonian, and with the kind assistance of Mrs. Margaret Blaker I have been able to examine those pertaining to the Delawares. In 1951 and 1952, William W. Newcomb, Jr., conducted an ethnographic study of the Delawares in Oklahoma, and his data were published in a monograph entitled *The Culture and Acculturation of the Delaware Indians*, Ann Arbor, 1956.

18. For detailed information on the naming process and the ceremony, see C. A. Weslager, "Name-Giving among the Delaware Indians," *Names*, vol. 19, no. 4, December 1971, pp. 268–83.

19. Discussions of Delaware herbalism may be found in Gladys Tantaquidgeon, *A Study of Delaware Indian Medicine Practice and Folk Beliefs*, Harrisburg, Pa., 1942; George A. Hill, Jr., "Delaware Ethnobotany," *News Letter*, Oklahoma Anthropological Society, vol. 19, no. 3, March 1971, pp. 3–18. For a detailed listing of Delaware cultural elements, see Regina Flannery, *An Analysis of Coastal Algonquian Culture*, Washington, D.C., 1939. Between May 1932 and May 1939 the Archeological Society of New Jersey published seven popular articles in a series of leaflets relating to Delaware culture; cf. Dorothy Cross, *New Jersey's Indians*, New Jersey State Museum Report 1, Trenton, 1965.

20. A Delaware grammar was published by C. F. Voegelin, "Delaware, An Eastern Algonquian Language," *Linguistic Structures of Native America, Viking Fund Publications in Anthropology*, no. 6, New York, 1946, pp. 130–57. In another paper Voegelin recorded the words of the vision song of his Delaware informant, Willie Longbone, and also the words of a number of other visions sung by Big House participants and recited by his informant; "Word Distortion in Delaware Big House and Walam Olum Songs," *Proceedings of the Indiana Academy of Science*, vol. 51, 1942, pp. 48–54. The Zeisberger and Brinton-Anthony dictionaries are well known to ethnologists, and an extremely interesting paper devoted to an analysis of a list of words recorded in 1684 is J. Dyneley Prince's, "An Ancient New Jersey Indian Jargon," *American Anthropologist*, n.s., vol. 14, no. 3, July–September 1912, pp. 508–24. The collections of the American Philosophical Society in Philadelphia include a Delaware vocabulary of 275 words obtained for Thomas Jefferson from the Indians living at Edgepillock in New Jersey, also a manuscript dictionary compiled by Matthew S. Henry.

Among the modern scholars, Dr. Ives Goddard has studied Delaware dialects extensively in the field. His doctoral dissertation, accepted by Harvard University in 1968, relates to Delaware verbal morphology, and he has evaluated the ethno-historical implications of early Delaware linguistic materials in his paper on this subject read at a meeting of the American Society for Ethnohistory in 1969 and published under the title "The Ethnohistorical Implications of Early Delaware Linguistic Materials," by *Man in the Northeast*, vol. 1, 1971, pp. 14–26. In August of 1970 Dr. Goddard and I spent several days together at Moraviantown, Ontario, Canada, where he played for me representative tapes from a large series he had recorded of the Delaware dialects spoken by the Oklahoma and Canadian groups.

4

The Walam Olum

Talking Wood, an Indian patriarch, went from one Delaware village to another trying to keep alive the story of the ancient tribal migrations by reciting the words of the sacred Walam Olum, or "red score," according to M. R. Harrington's account in his fictional book *Dickon among the Lenape Indians.**

The old man recounted the narrative as his companion Naked Bear handed him, one by one, the flat wooden sticks or tablets that he arranged on matting spread before him carefully on white-tanned deerskin. His dusky-complexioned audience of men, women, and children sitting cross-legged on the earthen floor of the Big House strained their ears to catch every one of the words. Talking Wood recited in a sort of chant, and his words had a rhythm like poetry and were pleasant to the ear, although disconnected and difficult to understand. As he looked fixedly at each tablet, with its stylized picture, he quoted the words he had been taught to recite and then handed the stick back to his companion, who returned it to its proper place. The figures had been scratched on the wood and rubbed with red ochre, although they weren't likenesses of known objects but strange symbols no one could understand unless instructed.

Although Harrington's story was the product of his own imaginative good sense and must not be cast in any other light, there can be no doubt that it has always been natural for man to spin yarns about himself. *The Iliad* and *The Odyssey* came from tales told by

* Reprinted as *The Indians of New Jersey* by Rutgers University Press in 1963.

early Mediterranean sailors that were perpetuated in Greek lore in the form of epic poems. Peoples of all races and of all nationalities have always asked questions about themselves—who they were, where they came from, and how they got to the place they were living—and the Delaware Indians were no exception. One can readily imagine an old Indian hunter, no longer able to pursue the fleet deer, beguiling his younger fellows with tales of the past after they had eaten their fill and were huddled in leisure around the fire. It is also reasonable to suppose that someone intrigued with the narratives of the storytellers tried to make some kind of record so that he could repeat what he had heard. If unable to write, what would be more natural for him than to make scratches on a piece of wood, stone, or bark to aid his memory? And, as the years rolled by, others preserved his handiwork and added to it. Harrington's story was fictional, but his episode describing the contents of the Walam Olum was based on actual copies of pictographs he had seen which were attributed to the Delaware Indians.

The meanings of these mnemonic glyphs, according to Harrington, were passed down orally to a chosen few from one generation to another, and it was their obligation to preserve the sticks and keep repeating the story to the people, lest it be forgotten. Harrington's description was based on a work by Dr. Daniel G. Brinton in which 183 separate glyphs were reproduced, each accompanied by an explanatory verse.[1] The first three glyphs in Book 1 of the Walam Olum look like this:

The Indian verses that accompanied these glyphs, and their translations, are as follows:

1. *Sayewi talli wemiguma wokgetaki*
   "There at the edge of all the water where the land ends . . ."
2. *Hackung kewlik owanaku wak yutali Kitanitowit-essop*
   ". . . the fog over the earth was plentiful, and this was where the Great Spirit stayed."

3. *Sayewis hallemiwis nolemiwi elemamik Kitanitowit-essop*
"It began to be invisible everywhere, even at the place where the Great Spirit stayed." [2]

The above three ideographs and those that follow, and the verses accompanying them, describe how the Great Spirit made the world. The Delawares (or perhaps the whole Algonkian family) are depicted as living in a far distant land, which some anthropologists believe to be Asia. For a long time there were no wars or sicknesses, food was plentiful, and life was pleasant for everyone. Then evil beings possessing strange powers appeared suddenly and interrupted the peaceful life of the people by introducing cold, war, disease, and premature death. The people had to find relief from their woes, and in Book 3 of the Walam Olum there appear these pictographs and verses:

15. *Witehen wemiluen wemaken nihillen*
"All of them said they would go together to the land there, all who were free . . ."
16. *Nguttichin lowaniwi Nguttichin wapaniwi Agamunk topanpek Wulliton epannek*
". . . the Northerners were of one mind and the Easterners were of one mind; it would be good to live on the other side of the frozen water."
17. *Wulelemil w'shakuppek Wemopannek hakhsinipek Kitahikan pokhakhopek*
"Things turned out well for all those who stayed at the shore of water frozen hard as rocks, and for those at the great hollow well."

These three verses have been interpreted to mean that two groups of people decided to leave their homes in Siberia and cross the Bering Strait, which is referred to in the verse as frozen water.[3] As the additional pictures which follow in Book 3 can be interpreted, the migrants crossed the Bering Strait, then proceeded up the Yukon, and made their way to a point between the headwaters of the Columbia and Mackenzie rivers, where one group broke away to become the progenitors of the northern Algonkians. The second group continued in a southeasterly direction across mountains and plains until the Mississippi River was reached, which took several generations. Here they were confronted by a warlike people called the Talligewi, whom they defeated and drove to the south. Then they continued to move farther eastward until, at long last, they arrived on the Atlantic seaboard to become the first human inhabitants there. They split into several groups, each settling in different parts of the land, where they lived in peace until the coming of the white man.

This interpretation of the glyphs is in keeping with another name the Delawares had for themselves, as reported by Zeisberger: "They call themselves Lenni Lenape Indians or *Woapanachke* [Wabanaki], that is people living toward the rising sun . . ." [4] The basic element in this word *waban* means "dawn," which, when conjoined with *aki*, meaning "land," is translatable as "dawn land" or "sunrise land." From it comes the meaning of "people of the sunrise country," or, as one might say in English, "easterners." The prestige invested in this name for a people who lived where the sun arose implies that their forebears were the original inhabitants of the eastern part of the North American continent. Here is the origin of the concept that the term *Wabanaki* carried with it the implication of a venerable grandfather to other tribes. From this kinship a broader relationship was recognized in which the Indian tribes arranged themselves into a huge family identified by kinship terms grading down from grandfather to grandchildren, uncles, nephews, and cousins. As grandfathers, the Delawares addressed other Algonkian tribes as their grandchildren, although some tribes also knew them as nephews or cousins. Since European nations did not possess such a pattern of kinship in their diplomatic relations, the whites were either puzzled or amused when one tribe called another its grandfather, uncle, cousin or nephew, although the Indians fully understood the metaphoric use of the terms and the implied primogeniture of the Delawares. [5]

Some modern anthropologists reject the Walam Olum, as a fake. Another school of thought holds to the view that, although it may be a genuine native production, it is not ancient but came into existence long after the Delawares were in contact with whites and were desperately trying to keep alive some elements of their decaying culture. Having been long exposed to European ways, their basic subsistence patterns and general economy had materially changed, with

the result that old ways of Indian life were rapidly dying out. Some
Delaware sentimentalist then presumably tried to strengthen the
revival of nativism by composing the Walam Olum, making up
glyphs to conform to tales and legends well known in the tribe, and
perhaps inventing other details to describe events that never took
place.[6]

Underlying the doubts as to whether or not the pictures were
fraudulent is the manner in which they were first brought to attention
by a man who many felt was untrustworthy. Constantine S. Rafinesque, professor of botany and natural history at Transylvania
College in Lexington, Kentucky, from 1819 to 1825, an eccentric,
unconventional teacher and a prolific writer, claimed that the original
painted record was obtained in 1820 by a "Dr. Ward of Indiana."
According to Rafinesque, Dr. Ward obtained the Walam Olum
from remnants of the Delaware Indians then living on the White
River in the present state of Indiana,[7] where they had settled after
moving west from their homes in the Delaware Valley to Pennsylvania and Ohio.

Rafinesque said that Dr. Ward was given the "wood" record "as
a reward for a medical cure," and one assumes that it consisted either
of wood tablets or possibly small sheets of bark, on which the crude
pictures were drawn. Rafinesque did not state that this "wood" record
was given to *him* in 1820 but that Dr. Ward obtained it that year,
that it was deemed a curiosity, and that the pictures were then inexplicable. He adds, "In 1822 were obtained from another individual
the songs [i.e., the verses] annexed thereto in the original language,
but no one could be found by me able to translate them." This apparently means that by 1822 Rafinesque had come into possession of
the wood record, or copies of the pictures, and also a manuscript in
the Delaware language that contained the verses explaining the
ideographs. Both were without meaning to him because he couldn't
understand the pictures or read the explanatory text.

In 1826 Rafinesque moved from Lexington to Philadelphia, taking
with him the manuscript text. "I had therefore," he wrote, "to learn
the language, since by the help of Zeisberger, Heckewelder, and a
manuscript dictionary, on purpose to translate them, which I only
accomplished in 1833." [8] Rafinesque could write English, French,
Latin, German, and Italian with ease, and, when he found access in
Philadelphia to manuscript and published material written by the

Moravian missionaries, he evidently did not have any difficulty translating the verses into English. He accomplished this over a seven-year period, interspersed with other projects. He was very prolific during this period, and the American Philosophical Society has in its custody more than 250 manuscripts in his hand. He was the author of other manuscripts which are in the possession of various American institutions. A bibliography of his published works contains 939 items.

After making the English translation of the Indian verses, he copied the pictures in two small paper-covered notebooks of forty pages each. Alongside each picture he wrote the Delaware words for the accompanying verse, and his English translation. On the first page of the first notebook he entered these words, "This Mpt & the wooden original was procured in 1822 in Kentucky but was inexplicable till a deep study of the Linapi enabled me to translate them, with explanations." [9]

On the cover of the first notebook, he wrote, "Value $20—(cost $5)," and on the second "Value $25 (cost $7)," which suggests he did not have any grandiose ideas about the monetary value of his handiwork. If he did anything fraudulent, it was certainly not because of financial motives. The Walam Olum was incidental to his broader interests, for he was preoccupied with a monumental work dealing with the history of the ancient and modern nations of North and South America, initially to be published in six volumes and later to be expanded to twelve. He apparently had no thoughts of getting rich from this effort either, since he planned to sell the books for a dollar each, which would scarcely have covered printing costs.

In 1836, at his own expense, Rafinesque published in Philadelphia the first two-part volume in the contemplated series that has this profound title: *The American Nations; or Outlines of Their General History, Ancient and Modern, including the Whole History of the Earth and Mankind in the Western Hemisphere; the Philosophy of American History; the Annals, Traditions, Civilization, Languages &c, of All the American Nations, Tribes, and States, ...* It was a costly project, paid for from the sale of a secret nostrum he concocted called "pulmel," which he claimed would cure consumption.[10] It was this kind of unusual conduct, added to the negligence of his own person, that brought about his exclusion from the Philadelphia scientific community, which treated him as a sort of outcast.

Chapter 5 of *The American Nations* contains Rafinesque's only printing of his translations of the verses of the Walam Olum, a small part of a ponderous work lavished with his extravagant theories. He did not reproduce any of the glyphs because of the cost, and he did not include any of the verses in the Delaware language. The Walam Olum story was only a minor chapter in the work on which he had labored for years, and if Rafinesque were living today he probably would be amazed at the attention given it, in contrast to the main part of his book, which he believed was his main contribution to science.

In addition to the translations of the verses, he also included in the same chapter—as a sort of afterthought—twenty additional verses written in the English language entitled "Fragment on the History of the Linapis since abt 1600 when the Wallamolum closes." This addendum purported to extend the history of the Delawares from the time the Walam Olum ended until A.D. 1800, when the Delawares were living in Indiana Territory. He did not say where he obtained this additional information except that it was "Translated from the Linapi—By John Burns." Like Dr. Ward and the nameless individual who provided the Delaware text of the verses, John Burns still remains otherwise unidentified.

When Rafinesque died of stomach cancer in a garret in Philadelphia on September 18, 1840, at the age of fifty-seven, his financial affairs were in such a sorry state that there was scarcely enough money to give him a decent burial. (Some years later his remains were removed from the grave and reinterred with honors on the campus of Transylvania College.) His collection of books, minerals, and shells was auctioned off, but it brought only $131.42. His manuscripts were sold for a few dollars. Among those purchased by Professor S. S. Haldeman of the University of Pennsylvania was a survey of the Indian mounds in Kentucky and neighboring states, the draft of a work relating to the ancient monuments of North and South America, and his Walam Olum notebooks. Whether or not a wood or bark record was also preserved is a question that cannot be answered, nor, as I have pointed out, is it certain that he ever had it in his possession. The notebooks and the two manuscripts relating to the Indian mounds were later acquired by Brantz Mayer of Baltimore. Whether Haldeman gave or sold them to Mayer, or whether Mayer obtained them from a third party, was never explained. Mayer was a lawyer, diplomat, historian, Civil War veteran, collector of Americana, and the first secretary—later president —of the Maryland Historical Society, which he helped organize.[11] An entry in the minutes of the society indicates that a bark record of some kind was also acquired by Mayer from an unknown source. At a meeting held Thursday evening, December 5, 1844 (this date coincides with the time Mayer came into possession of the Rafinesque manuscripts), Mayer presented to the society "pieces of birch bark with picture writing and hieroglyphics by northwestern Indians and other curiosities." [12] The "northwestern Indians" were those occupying the old Northwest Territory, of which Indiana Territory was a part before it became a state.

In 1846 Brantz Mayer loaned the Rafinesque manuscripts to E. G. Squier when Squier and his coauthor E. H. Davis were preparing the first volume of the Smithsonian Institution's series *Contributions to Knowledge*, entitled *Ancient Monuments of the Mississippi Valley*, which dealt with prehistoric Indian mounds. Squier made extensive use of Rafinesque's material on the mounds, giving credit to him in the finished work.

In the meantime, Squier became intrigued with the Walam Olum, which he discussed in a paper he read before the New-York Historical Society. The paper was later published, and in an 1877 reprint Squier noted that "there is slight doubt that *the original is what it professes to be, a genuine Indian record.*" [13] Although Squier was of the conviction that Rafinesque's drawings and text were genuine his contemporary Henry R. Schoolcraft, a geologist who became an Indian authority, was unconvinced. Schoolcraft questioned the glyphs themselves, which he believed too closely resembled the characters of archaic Chinese or other Orientals. I have introduced in Appendix 2 a transcript of a hitherto unpublished letter written by Schoolcraft to Squier, probably the first expression of doubt by a qualified scientist about the authenticity of the glyphs.

On September 29, 1875, Brantz Mayer withdrew from the Maryland Historical Society his gift of the "pieces of birch bark with picture writing and hieroglyphics," which had rested in the society's collections for thirty years. Wm B. Marye of Baltimore, one of Mayer's successors as secretary of the Maryland Historical Society, assures me that the manner in which Mayer took back his gift was unprecedented. Mayer merely made a pencil notation in the society's gift book, opposite the recording of the gift, stating: "Withdrawn by him, September 29, 1875. B.M." Mr. Marye tells me the withdrawal of a gift, which is an extremely unusual procedure, normally requires an act of the council of the society. Whether these pieces of bark had any relationship to the Walam Olum has never been made clear.

Squier subsequently returned to Mayer the documents he had borrowed, and, at the time of Mayer's death in Baltimore in 1879, the Rafinesque papers were again in his possession. What happened to the bark records he withdrew from the Maryland Historical Society is not known. By the terms of his will, probated October 29, 1879, he left all his real and personal property to his wife, Cornelia Mayer.[14] Shortly thereafter, 1,300 items of her husband's personal and collected manuscripts, books, drawings, and related materials were sold at auction, although no Rafinesque items were listed in the auctioneer's catalog.

Some time later, Dr. Daniel G. Brinton obtained the Rafinesque manuscripts from the Mayer family, and in 1885 he published his book containing illustrations of the glyphs that he had copied from Rafinesque's notebooks. In addition, he included the Indian words to the verses and a new translation of the verses that he had made with the assistance of native Delaware speakers, who all agreed the glyphs were unquestionably of Indian origin.[15] Brinton concluded that Rafinesque's text was "a genuine native production, which was repeated orally to someone indifferently conversant with the Delaware language, who wrote it down to the best of his ability. In its present form it can, as a whole lay no claim either to antiquity, or to purity of linguistic form. Yet, as an authentic modern version, slightly colored by European teachings, of the ancient tribal traditions, it is well worth preservation, and will repay more study in the future . . ."[16]

Distrust shadowed Rafinesque's scientific reputation during his lifetime, although his genius, which was lost on his contemporaries, has since been recognized by scholars who have taken the time to examine his theories. He enunciated the concept of evolution a generation before Darwin, and he championed a new principle of natural botanical classification that was later adopted widely. He also advanced the theory that one of the routes for the peopling of America was across the Bering Strait. After having spent many years reconstructing the history of the Delawares *after* A.D. 1600, I am much impressed with the content of the twenty additional verses which Rafinesque said were translated by John Burns and which he appended to the Walam Olum text. Brinton did not publish these verses, assuming that they had no historic value, but he was unaware that they included the names of a number of Delaware sachems, all of whom can now be positively identified, and that they describe incidents for which there is now supporting historical documentation. In my judgment, the information in these twenty verses could only have been obtained from native sources.

Rafinesque's failure to identify Dr. Ward, or to name the second individual from whom the text of the Walam Olum verses was obtained, tends to arouse the suspicion that he may have fabricated the whole story. This, however, does not necessarily indict him because the twenty additional verses are patently authentic. Moreover, it was in keeping with Rafinesque's character to handle many details superficially, and, as I have already indicated, he attached less importance and value to the glyphs than we do today. In fact, he stated that he had collected similar glyphs from a number of other tribes.

Another criticism that has been offered is that the Delaware words in the native verses may be found in the spelling books, dictionaries, and other works of the Moravians available to Rafinesque, and that he composed the verses himself by simply copying the words, with their English translations, and stringing them together. This is so obvious that it immediately occurred to Dr. Brinton, who found examples in Rafinesque's text to convince himself, at least, that this was not the case.[17] Moreover, if Rafinesque merely plagiarized the Moravians, it is unlikely that he would have frankly admitted that he learned the Delaware dialect from studying their writings. One must also realize that the Moravians obtained their Delaware vocabularies from the tribe in Ohio, which then moved to Indiana; naturally the words would be similar to those used in the verses.

Brinton died in 1899, when the well-known Algonkianist Dr. Frank G. Speck was only eighteen years of age; and, althought the professional careers of both men were centered at the University of Pennsylvania in Philadelphia, they were of different generations. Speck nevertheless admired and respected Brinton; and Speck's independent research among Delaware descendants in Oklahoma and Canada resulted in his agreement with Brinton, Squier, and Harrington as to the authenticity of the glyphs. Dr. Speck and I were close friends, and during our frequent trips together between 1942 and 1944, when we were studying the community of Nanticoke Indians in Indian River Hundred, Sussex County, Delaware, we often discussed the Walam Olum. During one of our discussions, Speck told me of his interviews, about thirteen years before, with Joseph Montour, hereditary successor in the line of Delaware chiefs then living on the Six Nations Reservation at Ohsweken, Ontario, Canada. Speck recalled that Chief Montour told him about an ancient Delaware custom of keeping records on wood by means of pictures, and how this information had been passed down from preceding generations. In an appendix to a monograph published in 1945, after recounting his interviews with the old chief, he wrote:

I have no hesitation in affirming the authenticity of the Walam Olum, the Red Score, or whatever title such a document of tribal history bears, as a form of native iconography known to the Delawares of historic times, and as being a vivid memory of tradition in the mind of Joseph Montour, an indisputably reliable source of Delaware customs and language.[18]

Although some anthropologists now take a view that is contrary to Speck's, they do not disagree that picture writing was a common technique of communication among the Delawares as a substitute for a written language. Zeisberger put it succinctly when he wrote, "Of writing they know nothing except the painting of hieroglyphics . . . These drawings in red by the warriors may be legible for fifty years. After a hero has died his deeds may, therefore, be kept in mind for many years by these markings." [19]

A young English adventurer, Nicholas Cresswell, visiting the Delawares settled in western Pennsylvania and Ohio in 1775, noted in his journal that their knowledge of past times "is handed down to them by hieroglyphics or tradition." [20] He also learned that as a technique of current communication individual Indians also scratched or painted pictures on wood, bark, leather, or stone surfaces to record memorable events in connection with messages they wanted to transmit. Delaware chief Captain White Eyes explained the crude scratchings on a tree made by a Lenape warrior. These markings communicated the details of a war party, the number of men, the direction they were marching, the number of forts they attacked, the number of scalps taken, and whether the victims were men or women.[21]

In 1954 a new translation of the Walam Olum with faithful reproductions of the Rafinesque drawings was made by C. F. Voegelin and seven coauthors. In this reexamination of the Walam Olum, the authors agreed that they "believe wholeheartedly that some day discovery of additional facts will further vindicate their faith in the genuiness and value of the Walam Olum." [22]

Apart from the meaning of the Walam Olum verses, John Heckewelder related in his *An Account of the History, Manners, and Customs of the Indian Nations* a tradition that the Lenape lived several hundred years earlier in a distant country in the western part of the American continent. This has often been cited, but Heckewelder amplified this story in a manuscript account that has never been published. The excerpt below is quoted in full for the first time from this account entitled, "A short account of the emigration of the Nation of Indians calling themselves Lenni Lennape (since by the whites improperly called Delaware Indians) as related by themselves." [23]

These say that an early Period—many hundred Years ago, they emigrated from a far Country into this—That their number then was very great—a great many thousands—that they were on the Journey into this country a great many Years—that they made many *night* encampments * by the way, in order to rest & provide necessarys for the next days travel **—that at length they reached the Namaessisipu (Mississippi) † followed the same down according to its course, untill they came within an hundred or more Miles from where the Ohio River falls into the same where they made a halt in order to recoynoitre the Country on the East side of the same— That while there they fell in with some of the Menque # Nation, who also had emigrated from a very distant Country into this, & of whom they learnt that *they* had come in more to the North, and were about setting on large Lakes that were in that direction, where they would have not only both Game & Fish in abundance, but would be able to secure themselves against a might People inhabiting the Country to the Southward said to be great Warriors. That on learning this, they (the Lenni Lennape) throught proper before they attempted to cross the *Namaessippi*, to negotiate with this Nation for permission to cross into their Country & travel

* "a nights encampment" (or lodging) is a halt of one Year [These and the other notes are Heckewelder's].
** "a days travel" is one Years travelling.
† Namaessisipu is in English, River of Fish
# Menque is the Name the Iroquois, or all the People belonging to the Six Nations go by, with them (the L. Lennape).

thro the same in search of uninhabited Country towards the rising of the Sun. That they sent negotiators accross & who were well recieved by this Nation, who called themselves *"Talligewi"*—but who, after little better than one half of them (the Lenni Lennape) had crossed, fell upon them, cutting off their retreat, & preventing that body of their People, who had not yet crossed over from coming accross to their assistance. That in this situation they applied to the Menque for assistance & who readily joined them in the conflict; they agreeing with each other, that after they should have conquered the Talligewi, they would divide the Country between themselves—& having after hard struggles, & many bloody battles, fought between them; in which hundreds of the Talligewi were slain, become victorious; by putting what remained of this Nation to flight, & who all went down the Ohio & Mississippi Rivers: they made choice of the Country each Nation should be possessed of; namely, the Menque chose that part including the great Lakes, together with all Streams tributary to the same—& the Lenni Lennape were to take possession of the whole Country to the South of there.

Note, they say that the Talligewi, were a remarkable tall & stout People, & that there had been Giants among them—People of a much larger size than the tallest of them (the Lenni Lennape) that they had built themselves angular fortifications—or entrenched themselves, from which they could sally out, but were generally beaten—Both, of the fortifications & entrenchments, said to be built by them I have seen many, two of which in particular were remarkable, the one being near the Mouth of the River Huron, which emptieth in Lake St. Clair, on the North Side of that Lake, distance about 20 Miles N. East of Detroit—this Spot of Ground was in the Year 1786 owned & occupied by a Mr. Tucker—the other Works or other entrenchments, (since Walls, or banks of Earth had been regularly thrown up with a deep ditch on the outside & were on the Huron River, *East* of the Sandusky, & about from 6 to 8 miles from Lake Erie—at each of these two entrenchments, which lay within a Mile of each other, were outside of the Gateway, a number of large flat Mounds, in which the Indian Pilot said, *hundreds* of the slain Talligewi were buried—Of these last entrenchments a Mr. Abraham Steiner, the Gentleman at that time with me, gave a very accurate description & which was published in a Magazine (I *think* by Matthew Carey *) about the Year 1789 or 1790.

They say that the Talligewi being gone, they settled that Country, & lived there for a great number of Years, when at length their huntsmen having discovered the Country East of the Mountains, & *no* inhabitants on the same; they proceeded on to the rising of the Sun, yet many of their Nation chose to remain in that fine Country still suspecting that *that*

* but it might have been some other publisher of that day, perhaps [Mr. ?]

part of the Nation, which unfortunately durst not venture to cross the Mississippi at the time *they* had crossed; would yet follow them; which however had never taken place. They further say: that as they proceeded on from West to East, so did also the Menque (Mingoes, or Iroquois as they are otherwise called) move on—these however formed their Settlement along the Lakes on both sides while they (the L. Lennape) occupied the Country South of these; & arriving at the Atlantic Shores, they spread over a large range of Country, multiplying & living to a great Age, (as they say they did in those times, & before the white People came among them) they had become a numerous People & so much so, that many then existing Tribes or Nations, since destroyed by Wars with the White People— had sprung from them; but moving at *too* great a distance to partake of their protection, they that escaped, or fled, & incorporated themselves with other Tribes or Nations. [The manuscript continues with a discussion of other phases of Lenape culture.]

In *The American Nations,* Rafinesque maintained that Heckewelder, who had died in 1823, actually "saw the Olumapi or painted sticks of the Linapi, but did not describe them; he merely translated some of their traditional tales: which agree in the main with these historical songs . . ." [24] In none of Heckewelder's published works, nor in the manuscript from which the above passage was taken, is there any specific reference to the Walam Olum by name—but who is to say that Rafinesque may not have had access to some of Heckewelder's writings which to date have escaped modern scholars? There may also be relevant information in the voluminous manuscript records in the Moravian Church Archives at Bethlehem written in the German language, which Rafinesque could have read with ease.

The basic question is whether Rafinesque was a liar who framed the whole Walam Olum story from his own imagination. If so, did he fabricate it to support his theories about the peopling of the North American continent? Or was it a genuine native work, and, as such, one of the most significant contributions ever made to the prehistory of the Delaware Indians? [25] Although these questions still remain unanswered, certain discoveries made in the years following Rafinesque's death are not inconsistent with the story told in the Walam Olum. First of all, the Indians bearing the prestigious name Wabanaki, who lived in the Delaware Valley at the time of the arrival of the Europeans, were not created there in a New World Garden of Eden. Their ancestors came there from some other place, and it has now been well established through archeological findings that America was settled by a primitive, Stone Age people who crossed the Bering Strait from Asia to Alaska, as Rafinesque stated in his *American Nations*. Anthropologists now are reasonably certain that the original home of the forebears of the American Indian was in Asia, as the verses of the Walam Olum have been interpreted.

For hundreds of millions of years there were no human inhabitants on the North American continent, although certain plant and animal life was present. An extensive ice sheet lay over Canada and the northern parts of the United States, and, after the ice started to recede and the land became habitable, the mastodon, mammoth, the cave-dwelling ground sloth, bison, and other animals now extinct roamed the land. When the climate became favorable for human habitation the primitive people, designated by anthropologists as Paleo-Indians, crossed the Bering Strait. They were followed by others in a series of migratory waves that continued for a long period of time.

These Paleo-Indians pursued the mammoth and mastodon, seeking their flesh for food and their skins for clothing. They were in an earlier stage of cultural development than the American Indians who greeted the first Europeans along the Atlantic seaboard several thousand years later, and were probably their direct ancestors, although this still remains to be authenticated. If one views the Walam Olum as a creation-myth and an ancestral tradition, not as a historical document, it can be interpreted to mean that the Asiatic genesis of the American Indian had been preserved in the tribal lore of the Delawares. As in other folk tales, it is embellished with the names of unidentifiable places and mythical heroes, and, as a consequence of its oral transmission, it contains many fanciful details. Yet the story it tells of a movement of humans from west to east across the North American continent is supported by scientific evidence, if it is related to the precursors of the Indians and not taken literally to mean the historic tribes.

It must have required many centuries for the Delawares to perfect the bow and arrow and the techniques of pottery-making unknown to the Paleo-Indians, to develop agriculture, to organize their society into families and villages of kinship groups, and to develop religious rites connected with visions and the Spirit Forces surrounding them. Yet the European explorers and settlers who first encountered the Delawares in the New World considered them illiterate heathens emerging from the Stone Age. When the Delawares addressed them as "brothers," which denoted not only affection but also a common fatherhood, as though a real blood relationship existed, the whites were amused. What made it almost laughable was that these inferior, non-Christian people painted their skins red (and so were called "redskins"), could not read or write, lived in flimsy hutches, and were scarcely worthy of social acceptance as fraternal equals.

In retrospect, it is apparent that in contrast to the primitive life of the Paleo-Indians, the ascendancy of the Delawares to the level of the cultural development they reached when the first Dutch explorers sailed into Delaware Bay was an example of remarkable progress. They had advanced well beyond the savages who came from Asia, but it would appear that in the folk memory there may have still existed faint information from the past. One pertinent example is an unusual piece of Delaware folklore, the legend of the Yah-qua-whee, or mastodon, recorded by an educated Delaware Indian seventy years ago. This legend, which takes on new meaning in light of the Paleo-Indian discoveries, is given below exactly as he wrote it: [26]

Long ago, in time almost forgotten, when the Indians and the Great Spirit knew each other better, when the Great Spirit would appear and talk with the wise men of the Nation, and they would counsel with the people; when every warrior understood the art of nature, and the Great Spirit was pleased with his children; long before the white man came and the Indians turned their ear to the white man's God; when every warrior believed that bravery, truth, honesty, and charity were the virtues necessary to take him to the happy hunting-grounds; when the Indians were obedient and the Great Spirit was interested in their welfare there were mighty beasts that roamed the forests and plains.

The Yah Qua Whee or mastodon that was placed here for the benefit of the Indians was intended as a beast of burden and to make itself generally useful to the Indians. This beast rebelled. It was fierce, powerful and invincible, its skin being so strong and hard that the sharpest spears and arrows could scarcely penetrate it. It made war against all other animals that dwelt in the woods and on the plains which the Great Spirit had created to be used as meat for his children—the Indians.

A final battle was fought and all the beasts of the plains and forests arrayed themselves against the mastodon. The Indians were also to take part in this decisive battle if necessary, as the Great Spirit had told them they must annihilate the mastodon.

The great bear was there and was wounded in the battle.

The battle took place in the Ohio Valley, west of the Alleghanies. The Great Spirit descended and sat on a rock on the top of the Alleghanies to watch the tide of battle. Great numbers of mastodons came, and still greater numbers of the other animals.

The slaughter was terrific. The mastodons were being victorious until at last the valleys ran in blood. The battlefield became a great mire, and many of the mastodons, by their weight, sank in the mire and were drowned.

The Great Spirit became angry at the mastodon and from the top of the mountain hurled bolts of lightning at their sides until he killed them all except one large bull, who cast aside the bolts of lightning with his tusks and defied everything, killing many of the other animals in his rage until at last he was wounded. Then he bounded across the Ohio river over the Mississippi, swam the Great Lakes, and went to the far north where he lives to this day.

Traces of that battle may yet be seen. The marshes and mires are still there, and in them the bones of the mastodon still are found as well as the bones of many other animals.[27]

There was a terrible loss of the animals that were made for food for the Indians in that battle, and the Indians grieved much to see it so the Great Spirit caused in remembrance of that day, the cranberry to come and grow in the marshes to be used as food, its coat always bathed in blood, in remembrance of that awful battle.

One can easily pass over this legend as primitive folklore having no basis in fact—but could it not have been handed down by word of mouth to the Delawares from an early generation of Paleo-Indian ancestors who, in fact, pursued the mammoth and mastodon? [28] Recent archeological discoveries made in New Jersey by Herbert C. Kraft, director of the museum at Seton Hall University and an active field archeologist, cause one to reflect carefully before rejecting this possibility. Working on an archeological site in the upper Delaware Valley, which may eventually be inundated by the Tocks Island reservoir, Kraft has found evidence of a pre-Lenape population, whose presence has been dated by Carbon 14 methods at 1720 B.C. Other artifacts in a deeper stratigraphic context are suggestive of an even earlier occupancy by archaic hunters. On this identical site, European trade goods have been found in more recent Indian graves and refuse pits, indicating that it was still being occupied by a band of Munsie-Delawares at the time of the coming of the white man. This may mean that successive generations of a primitive people had been living on this site for three or four thousand years, or even longer, when they were first encountered by Europeans, their culture having undergone many changes during their long period of occupancy.[29]

But even more significant than this discovery, yet directly related to it, is information obtained by Kraft that points to the existence along the Musconetcong River at Asbury in Warren County, New Jersey, of a Paleo-Indian campsite of an earlier period. Fluted stone points of the unique type known to have been made by Paleo-Indians, as well as distinctively shaped stone knives and scrapers, and the rejectage from their manufacture in the form of flakes and chips, have been recovered in large quantities from this site.[30] Although no bones of prehistoric animals or skeletal remains of Paleo-Indians have been found, the typology of the stone artifacts indicates they were made and used by primitive hunters ten thousand or more years ago, at a time when the mastodon and mammoth ranged in the Delaware Valley. In the state of New Jersey, for example, mastodon or mammoth remains have been found at forty different locations.[31]

Archeologists are now reexamining such discoveries as the famous Lenape Stone found in 1872 near Doylestown, Pennsylvania, and the shell gorget found near Claymont, Delaware, in 1864.[32] Both of these unusual artifacts contain the incised likeness of an elephant-like animal. As archeological work continues in New Jersey and elsewhere on eastern sites, more refined interpretations will be permissible as new data come to light. The future may even permit postulating a cultural evolution from the Paleo-Indians down to the historic Delawares. If so, it will strengthen the hypothesis herein advanced, that the Walam Olum, like the Delaware Indian legend of the mastodon, or Heckewelder's migration story, may be folkloristic explanations of events that occurred on the North American continent in the distant past, culminating in the emergence of the historic Delawares and other American Indian tribes.

Notes—Chapter 4

1. D. G. Brinton, *The Lenâpé and Their Legends*; . . . Philadelphia, 1885.

2. In the translations of the verses, I have used C. F. Voegelin's translations in *Walam Olum, or Red Score*; . . . Indianapolis, 1954.

3. In *Lenâpé Legends* Brinton interpreted the verses to mean that the ancestors of the Delawares lived in Labrador, and from there moved south into New York state, thence into Ohio and Indiana, and at a later date eventually made their way to the Atlantic coast.

4. *David Zeisberger's History*, p. 114.

5. Frank G. Speck discusses the kinship terms among Delaware survivors in Oklahoma and Ontario in "The Wapanachki Delawares and the English: Their Past as Viewed by an Ethnologist," *Pennsylvania Magazine of History and Biography*, vol. 67, 1943, pp. 319–44.

6. William W. Newcomb, Jr., "The Walam Olum of the Delaware Indians in Perspective," *Texas Journal of Science*, vol. 7, no. 1, March 1955, pp. 57–63.

7. Rafinesque's account of how he obtained the ideographs is given in *The American Nations*, . . . , Philadelphia, 1836, p. 122; see also p. 151. For biographical material about Rafinesque, see Charles Boewe, "The Manuscripts of C. S. Rafinesque, 1783–1840," *Proceedings of the American Philosophical Society*, vol. 102, no. 6, December 15, 1958 , pp. 590–95.

8. Ibid., p. 151.

9. The notebooks now rest in the collections of the Museum of the University of Pennsylvania, where they were placed by Brinton.

10. Brinton, *Lenâpé Legends*, p. 155.

11. Paul Weer, "Brantz Mayer and the Walam Olum Manuscript," *Proceedings of the Indiana Academy of Science*, 1945, pp. 44–48.

12. Ibid., p. 45.

13. W. W. Beach, ed., *The Indian Miscellany*, Albany, 1877, note p. 14.

14. I am indebted to Wm B. Marye for locating this will in Will Book 45, Folio 197, Register of Wills, Baltimore, Maryland. This is a source Weer overlooked, but it contained no reference to the bark records, as we hoped it might.

15. Brinton, *Lenâpé Legends*, pp. 88, 156.

16. Ibid., p. 158.

17. Ibid., pp. 154–58.

18. Frank G. Speck, *The Celestial Bear Comes Down to Earth*, Reading, Pa., 1945, pp. 90–91.

19. *Zeisberger's History*, p. 145.

20. *The Journal of Nicholas Cresswell*, 1774–1777, New York, 1924, p. 117.

21. Ibid., p. 110.

22. Voegelin in *Walam Olum*, 1954, p. xiv. See pp. 270–71, ibid., for a list of all the known publications, in whole or part, of the Walam Olum.

23. This twenty-page manuscript is in the collections of the American Philosophical Society, whose permission to quote from it is gratefully

acknowledged. It is listed as item no. 890 in A *Guide to Manuscripts
Relating to the American Indian in the Library of the American Philo-
sophical Society*, compiled by John F. Freeman and Murphy D. Smith,
Philadelphia, 1966, p. 125.

24. Rafinesque, *The American Nations*, p. 123.

25. In his "Ancient Annals of Kentucky," which appears in the second
edition of Humphrey Marshall, *The History of Kentucky*, 2 vols., Frank-
fort, 1824, vol. 1, pp. 31–33, Rafinesque states that the Lenape crossed the
Bering Strait to reach North America, continued to the Mississippi River,
conquered the powerful "Talegans," forcing them to move south, and
then settled on the eastern seaboard. Since these identical details can
also be interpreted from the Walam Olum verses, the question arises
whether Rafinesque fabricated the verses to support a migration theory
that he had previously advanced. This seems to me to be a tenuous argument, and I fail to find evidence in "Ancient Annals," which I have carefully studied, to indict him on this count. Rafinesque himself said that the
contents of the Walam Olum were totally unknown to him in 1824 when
he wrote "Ancient Annals," the inference being that he would have expressed himself differently if he had known the contents of the Walam
Olum; *The American Nations*, p. 151. In fact, he admitted in fn. 22, p.
155, that in "Ancient Annals" he placed the conquest of the Talegans
"about 500 of our era, but these annals [the Walam Olum] are more correct and remove further this event." If he had fabricated the latter to
support the former, he certainly would have made the dates correspond.
Actually, much of what he said in *The American Nations* about the
Lenape migrations, including the confrontation and defeat of the Talligewi, was already published by Heckewelder in his *History* in 1881 and
available to Rafinesque in English, French, and German editions when he
wrote *The American Nations*. Because the text of the Walam Olum has
been interpreted to reinforce a concept he is accused of having borrowed
from Heckewelder, this is not in itself justification for calling him a fake.
If Rafinesque had been intent upon manufacturing evidence to support
his theory that the Lenape crossed the Bering Strait to reach America
(which, incidentally, was not mentioned by Heckewelder) he could easily
have made it less controvertible than verses 15, 16, and 17 which I have
quoted, which presumably described this crossing but which Brinton interpreted to mean that the Lenape came from Labrador.

26. Richard C. Adams, *Legends of the Delaware Indians and Picture
Writing*, Washington, D.C., 1905, pp. 70–71. The word *Ya-qua-whee* is
meaningless today to Delaware speakers in Oklahoma.

27. This might possibly refer to the well-known Big Bone Lick, Boone
County, Kentucky, where George Croghan in 1765 found two mammoth
or mastodon tusks among what were known as "elephant bones"; R. G.

Thwaites, ed., *Early Western Travels*, 1748–1846, Cleveland, 1904, vol. 1, p. 135.

28. W. D. Strong's paper, published in 1934, "North American Indian Traditions Suggesting a Knowledge of the Mammoth," *American Anthropologist*, n.s., vol. 36, pp. 81–88, must also be read in a new light in view of the Paleo-Indian discoveries. Strong pointed out that folklore about the mammoth and mastodon was known to the Naskapi, Penobscot, and other eastern Indians. He said he was inclined to regard some of these tales as historical tradition, which seemed to embody a formal knowledge of the living animals in question.

29. Mr. Kraft is the author of two reports describing this work: *The Miller Field Site, Warren County, New Jersey*, South Orange, N.J., 1970; *Seton Hall University Museum Excavations in the Tocks Island Area, 1968–1969 Season*, South Orange, N.J., September 1970, pp. 2–71.

30. Mr. Kraft reported this discovery at the November 1970 meeting of the Eastern States Archeological Federation, and I am indebted to him for a copy of his report. It should also be noted that archeological discoveries in 1965, in Orange County, N.Y., only ten miles from the New Jersey border, and in the area occupied by the historic Delawares, indicates the presence of Paleo-Indians; Robert E. Funk, George R. Walters, and William F. Ehlers, Jr., "The Archeology of Dutchess Quarry Cave, Orange County, New York," *Pennsylvania Archeologist*, vol. 39, nos. 1–4, 1969, pp. 7–22.

31. *A New Jersey Mastodon*, New Jersey State Museum Bulletin 6, revised 1964, Trenton, New Jersey.

32. H. C. Mercer, *The Lenape Stone*, New York, 1885; C. A. Weslager, "An Incised Fulgur Shell from Holly Oak, Delaware," *Bulletin of the Archeological Society of Delaware*, vol. 3, no. 4, 1941, pp. 10–15.

5

Early Relations with the Dutch

Living in their separate and autonomous communities along the numerous tributaries to the Delaware River, the scattered bands of Delaware Indians apparently had little ambition to expand their territories or to extend their political influence. There was no reason for them to adopt a militant attitude against their Indian neighbors, such as the Mahican living north of them on the Hudson River, or the Nanticoke, Choptank, and Conoy to the south, who occupied the shores of Chesapeake Bay and the banks of its tributaries. This unaggressiveness was consistent with their sedentary pattern of living and their equanimity in the face of a continual struggle for survival. As they desired only to hunt, plant, and fish—and to exist in peace—and presented no threat to other tribes, it is ironical that the unfederated bands of Delawares should have fallen prey to a smaller but more aggressive tribe whose home villages lay along the lower Susquehanna River in Pennsylvania. These Susquehannock Indians, known to the Delawares as Minquas and later to Pennsylvanians as Conestogas, spoke a dialect of the Iroquoian tongue, a language with which the Delaware peoples were not conversant. However, the Susquehannock were not politically affiliated with the Five Nations Iroquois, and the fact that they spoke a related language by no means reflected a unity of purpose or action, or even friendship. Some of the bitterest wars of the Five Nations were fought with their linguistic kinsmen, such as the Huron, the Erie—and finally the Susquehannock.[1]

With their own women and children protected in their palisaded villages in the Susquehanna Valley, the Minquas sent out marauding parties to harass their Algonkian neighbors in Delaware, Pennsylvania, New Jersey, Maryland, and Virginia. Evidently their aim was to bring the coastal bands under subjection, undoubtedly to force them to pay tribute, perhaps to capture and adopt some of their women and children, but certainly to expand Minquas territorial influence. In so doing, they were able to present a more formidable front against encroachment by the Five Nations. The Five Nations were also preoccupied with subduing the neighboring Algonkians and reducing them to tributary people, and their war parties also paddled down the Susquehanna from New York to wage war against the Minquas. There was probably an economic reason why the Delawares were singled out for attack by the Minquas—the Delawares' preferred geographical position when trade was established with the Dutch. Dutch traders were the first Europeans to barter with the Indians along the Delaware River, and it was after the arrival of these traders that the Minquas apparently intensified their attacks on the Delawares. Their obvious motive was to try to eliminate a trade rival and monopolize for themselves the commerce in Dutch merchandise.

As early as 1607, Captain John Smith encountered a party of fifty Minquas warriors in their canoes in Chesapeake Bay while he was exploring its tributaries. He was impressed with their size, dress, deep voices, and the variety of their weaponry. He wrote that their able men numbered six hundred, and this may have been a realistic estimate, even though Smith did not visit any of their villages to make firsthand observations.[2] Later, in 1647, it was recorded that in one of the Minquas villages there were thirteen hundred men able to bear arms, but this figure may have been an exaggeration.[3] There seems little reason to doubt that the total Delaware Indian population well exceeded that of the Minquas, even though accurate statistics are lacking.

Although there are frequent references to the Minquas in contemporary accounts, documented information about the specific locations of their villages is sparse and, since the tribe became extinct at an early date, knowledge of their culture is largely restricted to archeological findings. Numerous sites have been excavated in the Susquehanna Valley, and one of the largest was a Minquas town, on the east bank of the Susquehanna in Lancaster County about three miles south of Columbia, known as the Washington Boro Site. The modern town by that name was built at almost the same location as the Minquas town, which is believed to have covered about forty acres. In the aboriginal cemetery excavated at Washington Boro, a great many Minquas skeletons have been uncovered, as well as the remains of some of their Indian prisoners. Goods buried with some of the dead include brass kettles, glass beads, forks, spoons, axes, hoes, and other European objects dating from the early seventeenth century which the Minquas received from Dutch and other European traders in exchange for their animal pelts.[4]

As the first contenders for the fur trade with the Delawares, the Dutch traders immediately became aware of the enmity existing between the Delaware River Indians and the natives living on the Susquehanna. The first account of this warfare occurs in an entry dated February 11, 1633, in a journal written by David Pietersz. De Vries. It was a cold, blustering winter day, and he brought his little sailing yacht *Little Squirrel* to anchor in the icy waters of the Delaware River opposite present Gloucester, New Jersey. He had only eight men in his party because the rest of his crew were aboard a larger vessel, the *Walvis*, which lay at anchor farther south in Delaware Bay. Their supply of provisions was practically exhausted, and De Vries sailed up the river in the yacht, hopeful of obtaining corn from the Indians. Near the shore he saw fifty Minquas warriors in their canoes who, as he wrote in his journal, "came on a warlike expedition." Because he was greatly outnumbered he did not want to have a confrontation with the Minquas, so he sailed his yacht into the middle of the river. The ice floes discouraged the Minquas from pursuing the Dutchmen.[5]

Two days later, farther upstream, De Vries met three frightened Delaware Indians whom he identified as "Armewamen," who were undoubtedly residents of the Armewamex Indian community living in the vicinity of Newton Creek and Big Timber Creek. "They told us," De Vries wrote, "that they were fugitives—that the Minquas had killed some of their people, and they had escaped. They had been plundered of all their corn, their houses had been burnt, and they escaped in great want, compelled to be content with what they could find in the woods . . . They told us also, that the *Minquas had killed about ninety men of the Sankiekans . . ."* [6] (Italics added)

These Sankiekans (usually spelled Sankikans) were occupants of the Delaware Indian community near Trenton who had fled their villages to escape the Minquas and had hidden their women and children in the woods. Doubtless other New Jersey Delaware bands were similarly harassed; if they had united their forces they might have been able to repulse an enemy they greatly outnumbered. Since the Delawares had not consolidated their men, the Minquas were able to pick them off one by one.

A second reference to the Minquas raids on Delaware villages is found the following year in the journal of Captain Thomas Yong, written during his exploratory trip along the Delaware River in search of the northwest passage. Yong learned from a Delaware Indian refugee who lived on the west side of the river in present Delaware, perhaps one of the Sickoneysincks, that "the people of that River were at warre with a certain Nation called the Minquaos, who had killed many of them, destroyed their corne, and burned their houses; insomuch as that the Inhabitants had wholy left that side of the River, which was next to their enimies, and had retired themselves on the other side farre up into the woods, the better to secure themselves from their enimies." [7]

What Yong meant when he said the western side of the river was "next to their enimies" was that there was no water barrier separating the Delawares living on that side of the river from the Minquas war parties. The natives living in New Jersey were afforded some protection by the broad expanse of the Delaware River, but those on the opposite shore in Delaware were openly exposed to Minquas depredations; they were forced to flee across the river and hide in the New Jersey woods. They did not, however, leave their homes permanently, as Yong implies, because later accounts indicate they returned to their homes on the western side of the river after the Minquas had gone.

The records are clear that the Minquas could come by canoe from their Susquehanna villages via the Elk River, thence up the Bohemia River and, after a short portage over a trail the whites later knew as the Old Man's Path, they could complete their journey to the Delaware down the Appoquinimink. Both the Christina and Appoquinimink rivers came to be called Minquas Kills, not because the Minquas lived on them, but because they were the water routes used by the Minquas warriors to reach the Delaware River. Minquas portage paths also led to the Schuylkill River and to other smaller tributaries of the Delaware.

While Yong was sailing up the Delaware he, too, encountered one small party of Minquas traveling in a single canoe; since his party outnumbered them, he did not hesitate to invite them aboard his vessel. They gave him some fresh corn they had taken from the Delawares, "whome they had overcome and slayne some of them." Yong gave each of them a European hatchet, a white clay pipe, a knife, and a pair of scissors—articles to which the Minquas attached great value. The Minquas war captain indicated that his warriors would go back to their homes and return as soon as possible with beaver and otter pelts to exchange for more European goods. The Minquas then paddled away from Yong's vessel and headed their canoe into one of the tributaries of the Delaware that led in the direction of their homeland.

As Yong continued upstream, he was welcomed at each Delaware village where he dropped anchor, although he found many of the wigwams in ruins, corn fields destroyed or pillaged, beaver pelts con- fiscated, and the inhabitants fearful that the Minquas would return and do further injury to them. The journals of both De Vries and Yong make it clear that the Delawares were not warlike prior to the coming of Europeans; and neither by disposition, experience, nor in military weaponry were they a match for the Minquas attacking parties. They were wholly unprepared for battle, and there is no evidence to suppose that they then had war captains, a concept that characterized their warfare at a later period after they had left the Delaware Valley.

While the occupants of communities along the lower Delaware River lived in fear of Minquas attack, the Algonkian peoples living upriver in present New York state were exposed to the military pres- sures exerted by the Five Nations Iroquois. Despite their many virtues, the Five Nations had a reputation for disrupting other In- dian societies as far south as Virginia and westward beyond the Ohio. The Iroquois made war, prior to the coming of Europeans, to avenge murders done their people and, by taking prisoners, to maintain or increase their own village populations; also to extend their political influence over other tribal groups, thus eliminating potential enemies.

The paradox was that the five tribes, despite their aggressiveness, believed that the most desirable life was a peaceful one, and they devoted time and energy to attempts to maintain peace with their near neighbors, although usually on their own terms. With the arrival of the whites, who brought a demand for animal skins, the domination over other tribes had another purpose, for it gave the Iroquois access, either by trade or hunting, to distant areas rich in peltries.

Perhaps the fiercest member of the Five Nations was the Mohawk tribe (known to the Dutch as Maquaas), who lived along the Hudson; immediately west of it was the Oneida; then came the Onondaga, a relatively peaceful tribe; farther west lived the Cayuga; the most westerly and most numerous was the Seneca. This area between the Hudson and Lake Erie occupied by the five tribes was compared to a longhouse, with the Seneca the keepers of the western door through which Iroquois warriors traditionally went to attack western and southern Indians. The five tribes were allied in what they called the Hodesaunee, or League of the Five Nations; and in the Great Council of the confederacy at Onondaga voting representatives from the five tribes (later nonvoting delegates from affiliated tribes) met annually in the autumn, and at other times if summoned, to discuss issues affecting the welfare of all the member tribes. Some authorities believe the League eventually might have brought most of the Indians living between the Great Lakes and the Atlantic under its control had not the arrival of the English and the French upset the balance of power in native society. When the first Europeans arrived, the Five Nations had already begun to encroach on the territory of the Delaware Indians, and, although the records are incomplete, Dutch accounts written in the early seventeenth century indicate that apparently the Five Nations had already subjugated some of the more northerly Delaware bands. It seems certain that residents of the Minisink community on the upper Delaware had fallen under Five Nations domination. On a visit there in 1694, the Dutch officer Captain Arent Schuyler found the Minisink chiefs fearful that the Seneca (a loose term that might have designated any one of the Five Nations) had attacked and slain some of their hunting parties. Schuyler wrote that "ye Menissink Indians have not been with ye Sinneques as usiall to pay their Dutty . . ."[8] The word *Dutty* no doubt had reference to the wampum beads paid by the tributary Algonkian peoples to the Five Nations, and this notice suggests that the Minisink division of

the Delawares, or at least one or more of its bands, had been subjugated by the Five Nations, and was strongly under Iroquois influence. It was the most northerly of the Delawares, and its vulnerable geographical position exposed it to Iroquois attack first.

The early Dutch explorers found a Delaware Indian society whose
peaceful existence was being disrupted through fear of the incursions
of Iroquoian-speaking enemy tribes. Dutch interest in the New
World was awakened by Henry Hudson's disclosure, following his
voyage in 1609, that the lands he had visited in America abounded in
fur-bearing animals that could be obtained through trade with the
natives. There was immediate action among opportunistic merchants
in Amsterdam and Hoorn to exploit this commerce. They formed a
company having authority from the government to make voyages to
the New World and claim trading rights to lands and places discovered by them between the 40th and 45th degrees of latitude.
This region, which became known as the New Netherland, included
the valleys of the Hudson and Delaware rivers and the heart of Delaware Indian territory.

In the modern world, with the abundance of both natural and
synthetic fabrics, it is difficult to appreciate the obsession for furs that
was manifest throughout Europe in the seventeenth century. No
fabric could equal the warmth, wearability, and glistening beauty of
natural furs that were widely in demand for both men's and women's
clothing. Persons of importance wore furs to display their rank and
wealth, and kings and princes set the style by wearing robes of price-
less white ermine. Fur coats, muffs, wraps, and gloves—and fur-
trimmed garments—were all in vogue, and the consuming demand
was for beaver pelts used in the manufacture of men's hats. The
velvety soft fur of the beaver could be felted to make a smooth surface
that could not be equaled by any type of woven cloth. Fur-bearing
animals were not numerous in most European countries, except those
in the more northerly cold climates, and the dictates of fashion caused
Dutch merchants to seek a source of furs in more distant lands. The
information Hudson brought back from the New World about the
availability of furs proved to be a turning point in history; it started
a movement to America that was to become accelerated as time
passed and have unimagined consequences.

In Delaware Indian folklore, several accounts have been preserved
about the Delawares' original encounter with Dutch fur traders; the

best-known version was related to Heckewelder by aged and respected Delawares.[9] This encounter supposedly occurred on Manhattan Island at a time before the Indians had seen a person with white skin or a sailing vessel. Some coastal Algonkians who were fishing in their canoes saw something on the horizon that appeared to be an uncommonly large fish or a huge canoe. They paddled to shore and reported what they had seen. Runners were sent to carry the news to their scattered chiefs, who came with their warriors to view the approach of the strange object. Meanwhile, as the vessel came closer it appeared to be a large house in which Kee-shay-lum-moo-kawng lived, and they thought he was coming to pay them a visit. Preparations were made to greet the Creator; the women prepared the best of foods, meat was brought for sacrifice, and arrangements were made for a dance and for entertainment.

As the vessel approached the shore, the Indians saw that it was full of strangely dressed men whose faces were of a white color, different from the Indians, and their leader wore a red coat with lace cuffs. They felt certain he was Kee-shay-lum-moo-kawng. Terror seized the Indians. Some wanted to run off and hide in the woods, but their chiefs prevailed on them to stay lest they give offense to their guests.

The vessel finally came to anchor, and a smaller boat was sent ashore with a landing party, including the leader with the red coat. The chiefs and councilors formed a large circle, and the Dutchmen strode into the center; the Indians were lost in admiration. The leader filled a glass of liquor which he drank. Then he refilled the glass and gave it to the chief next to him to drink, but the chief smelled it and passed it to the next chief, who did the same until the glass had been handled by everyone without being tasted. Suddenly one of the Indians, a spirited man and a great warrior, jumped up and harangued the assembly on the impropriety of returning the glass with its contents untasted. He said this would displease the Creator and might be the cause of his destroying all of them. He said if the contents were poisonous it would be better for one man to die than for the whole nation to be destroyed. He then took the glass and, bidding the assembly farewell, drank it. Every eye was fixed on him. Soon he began to stagger around, and then he fell to the ground in a sleep as though dead. The spectators were almost paralyzed with terror, but in a little while the warrior opened his eyes, jumped to his feet, and declared he had never been so happy before as after he had drunk the liquor. He asked for more, and the wish was granted, following which the whole assembly started to drink, and everyone became intoxicated.

The Dutchmen returned to their vessel while the Indians were carousing, and then came ashore again with a quantity of presents including beads, axes, hoes, and stockings which they distributed. This represented untold wealth to the Indians and further convinced them they had been honored by a visit from their deities.

After several encounters, the Indians began to realize that their visitors were not gods but men like themselves from a faraway country, and they called them *Swannakens*.[10] Familiarity increased daily between the Dutch and the Indians, and the former asked for a small piece of land in order to sow some seeds and raise herbs to season their broth. The Dutch said they needed only so much land as the skin of a bull would cover, and they spread the hide on the ground in front of the Indians to show its size. The request was granted, whereupon a Dutchman took a knife and, beginning at one place on the hide, cut it into a rope no thicker than the finger of a little child. When he was done there was a large coil. This hide rope was then drawn out to a great distance and brought around so that both ends would meet, and it encompassed a large piece of land. The Indians were surprised by the superior wit of the Swannakens, but they did not complain about allowing their guests to have this small plot of land since they had more than they needed.

So goes the tradition. In Appendix 3, the reader will find a similar version recorded at a later date by Trowbridge, including the reference to the bull's hide.

The likelihood is that the first Dutchmen to enter the Delaware River brought with them a native from Manhattan Island to act as their interpreter, and during their first encounter there is no doubt that liquor was dispensed to the natives. The Dutch, long practiced in the use of alcohol, offered it as a gesture of conviviality, with no intention of getting the Indians drunk or addicting them to liquor. At a much later date, however, there is no question that on more than one occasion foreign visitors deliberately got Indians drunk to take advantage of them; but the first Dutch traders wanted furs, and a drunken Indian was useless as a trapper or hunter.

Neither the Dutch nor the first English or Swedish trader who proffered a glass to an Indian was aware of the consequences of introducing strong drink to one who had never tasted alcohol before and who had no capacity for it. They knew even less about the psychology of the Delaware Indians, who had been disciplined since childhood not to make a display of emotions in interpersonal relations, especially with strangers. Little did they realize that, not only would a glass of liquor set the Indian's head whirling, but it would suddenly release his inhibitions with unpredictable results.

When a drunken Indian went berserk, he was berated for not being able to hold his liquor and for behaving like a beast. Social drinking in moderation or lifting a glass to seal a bargain or cement bonds of friendship were European customs that were never properly taught the Indians. What made matters worse was that the Indian enjoyed the sensation of excitement, the emotional release followed by numbness, and finally the stupor that resulted from overindulgence of alcohol. It was a new kind of game to play, and after sleeping off a period of intoxication the Indian was not only willing but anxious to try it again. Liquor became a commodity in wide demand, and one for which Indians would readily trade animal pelts or anything else; but it was an expensive product for Dutch traders to supply and heavy to transport, and it took up valuable cargo space in the holds of the small sailing vessels.

Of much less value in terms of Dutch currency, but of inestimable worth to the Indians, was the European merchandise the Dutch traders brought with them. In this area there was also a widely different sense of values between whites and Indians. An unbreakable iron or brass kettle, to an Indian who had only fragile clay pottery, was more precious than a bag of gold coins, that had no utilitarian value to him. The coarsely woven red and blue wool fabric known as duffel cloth, or simply duffels (named for the town of Duffel near Antwerp), was prized more by the natives than bearskin robes or fur muffs, which had much greater financial value to the Dutch. Several yards of the cheap cloth, far less weighty and cumbersome than a bearskin, could be draped on an Indian's shoulders, and another piece wrapped around his thighs as a warmer substitute for a deerskin clout. After a while the Indians found that the red duffel cloth was so conspicuous that it exposed their position when stalking animals. They soon demanded darker colors, and more somber dyes were substituted for red.

The European glass beads, combs, mirrors, Jews' harps, white clay smoking pipes, metal hoes, axes, and knives were all new and useful commodities to the Indian, who attached considerable value to them.

At first, the records tell us, the Indians did not understand the real purpose for certain trade goods; they used the cloth stockings they were given as tobacco pouches and hung metal utensils on their persons as decoration, but it did not take long for the men to learn how to use a metal axe, and the Indian women soon adapted to European hoes instead of using digging sticks and hoes made of stone or the scapula of deer.

Conversely, the furs the traders avidly sought, which were as valuable to them as gold and silver, were commonplace among the Indian tribes. When Indians and Europeans are viewed in terms of their differing cultural backgrounds and the laws of supply and demand in their respective societies, it might be argued that, when an Indian traded a pack of beaver pelts for an iron cooking pot, he got the best of the bargain. Beavers were found everywhere, but an iron pot was such a rarity in America that no Indian artisan anywhere on the vast continent could duplicate it.

There is no reason to accuse the Dutch traders, during the initial period of trading with the Delaware, of deliberately cheating the natives by giving them baubles and cheap utensils in exchange, for furs represented much greater monetary value in the European market. This usual interpretation of what happened is not necessarily correct. The Indian's measure of values was not in Dutch florins, guilders, and stuivers, which were useless to him in a woodland environment and unacceptable as a medium of exchange among his own people or other tribes. The traders supplied the kind of merchandise that the Indians wanted and that was in demand and highly negotiable in intertribal trade. It was not until cultural changes occurred as a result of white influence and until monetary values were superimposed on native society some years later that the negotiations with the Indians became fraudulent and deceptive.

During the early period of trade with the Indians, the Dutch were not interested in acquiring tracts of land along the Delaware River, because settlement in the New World was not then their objective. They periodically sailed in and out of the Delaware, pausing here and there to trade for furs, and, as Yong noted in his journal:

The River aboundeth with beavers, otters, and other meaner furrs, which are not only taken upon the bankes of the mayne River, but likewise in other lesser rivers, which discharge themselves into the greater . . . the Countrey is very well replenished, with deere and in some places store of Elkes.[11]

When Cornelius Hendricksen came into the river, later submitting to his merchant employers in Holland the first known map of the Delaware River, he wrote that he "did there trade with the inhabitants, said trade consisting of Sables, furs, Robes and other skins."

Other Dutch traders came for the same purpose, bringing cargoes of Dutch merchandise and returning to Holland with bundles of pelts, especially the skins of the beaver, to satisfy Europe's voracious appetite for furs. Adriaen Van der Donck, writing in 1656, said that eighty thousand beaver pelts were being shipped *annually* from the New Netherland to Holland.[12] Consistent with their ideologies, the Delawares extended warm hospitality to their Dutch guests, welcoming them to their wigwams and inviting them to share their other domestic resources. Daniel Denton wrote that one could travel from one end of the New Netherland to another in safety, "And if you chance to meet with an Indian-Town, they shall give you the best entertainment they have, and upon your desire, direct you on your way." [13] During the early period, the river of the Sickoneysincks at Lewes, Delaware, received a new and vulgar name—Hoeren Kill (Whore's Creek)—which originated, according to an early Dutch account, "from the liberality of the Indians in generously volunteering their wives or daughters to our Netherlanders at that place." [14] Evidence of miscegenation was soon to be seen in some of the Delaware villages when dusky-skinned females gave birth to lighter-complexioned, blue-eyed infants. The process of Europeanizing the Indians had a subtle beginning, and unplanned cross-breeding preceded the technological changes.

Meanwhile, England was busy colonizing Virginia and New England. From a New World base on Chesapeake Bay, Henry Fleet was trading with local tribes; and William Claiborne had gone up the bay from his headquarters on Kent Island to make contact with the Minquas on the Susquehanna, where he initiated a profitable trade in beaver skins.[15] Claiborne built a trading post on Palmer's Island in the Susquehanna, stocking axes, hoes, duffels, and other merchandise in demand among the Minquas. Beavers were not only vastly more numerous along the Susquehanna and its tributaries than along the

Delaware but the Minquas followed the waterways as far as the Allegheny River in search of game. The Minquas had long been more preoccupied with hunting and trapping than the Delawares, whose coastal environment permitted them to obtain food readily by fishing, crabbing, and oystering. The Minquas became highly skilled trappers, and in their zeal to get their hands on liquor and other European trade goods they concentrated on hunting and trapping from December to June. It was during that period when the animal furs thickened and the pelts were at their best. Because of their hunting and trading activity, the Minquas had less time than in the past to bother the Algonkian bands, and their attacks on the Delawares lessened and finally ceased.

Among the Indians, personal property had always been limited to the things one carried, wore, or used, and prior to the arrival of the Dutch there was no motivation to build up a surplus. Normally, an Indian had one pair of moccasins, one bow, one loincloth, one stone axe, and that was all he felt he needed. The technique used by the Dutch, and later by other white traders, was to increase the Indians' wants, which roused them to hunt for extended periods and bring back more and more furs to the trading posts. For example, once an Indian came into possession of a gun, he was dependent on the white trader to supply him with powder and lead, without which the weapon was useless. The only way he could obtain these products—or replace his gun when it became broken or worn out—was by bartering furs. The Indian women developed a fondness for European cloth to dress themselves and their children, and, when the cloth wore out, the only way it could be replaced was when their husbands accumulated sufficient animal pelts to exchange with the traders. And, of course, the Indian who developed a taste for liquor—or a fondness for European ornaments—had to hunt and trap more than he had ever done in the past to satisfy his needs.

The appearance of English traders resulted in greater pressure being exerted on the Indians as keen trade rivalry to obtain furs developed between England and Holland. As this competition became more heated, Dutch merchants realized they could not conduct a business in the New World from their counting houses in far-off Holland, allowing the English the unchallenged tactical advantage of having permanent settlements in Virginia and Maryland as bases of operation. After the West India Company was organized in 1621, its nineteen-member executive committee, known as the Assembly of XIX, took steps to establish a commercial seat on Manhattan Island in the New Netherland, and it later permitted individual members called patroons to send colonists to the New World as private ventures.

To understand fully the early Dutch relations with the Delaware Indians, it is important to recognize that colonization as an extension of Dutch life and that culture was never the prime aim of the merchants who formed the West India Company.[16] These men were beset with commercial interests, among which the fur trade ranked high, and financial gain for the stockholders and patroons was the sole purpose of colonizing efforts. If they could have controlled the Indian commerce by continuing to send vessels to America from time to time, they would have done so and avoided the expense of colonization, which was a heavy drain on the company's treasury and eventually led to its failure. One of the problems was in mustering colonists to go to America, because the usual causes of group migration, such as overcrowding, soil exhaustion, food shortages, and religious or political persecution, did not prevail in Holland's prosperous seventeenth-century economy.

In this colonizing phase of Dutch exploitation of the New Netherland trade, it was necessary for the merchants to acquire lands on the Hudson and Delaware where houses and trading posts could be built. These fortified settlements would then become the American branch offices, so to speak, of the parent West India Company, having the advantage of being set in the marketplace where the business was to be conducted. In Holland, as in other European countries, when one sought land acquisition, he negotiated a purchase with the owner, and for a stipulated sum of money the title to the land was transferred to the new proprietor. Preconditioned to this kind of commercial environment and legal practice, Dutch agents, not understanding Indian culture and having no concept of the principles underlying native land tenure, sailed to the New Netherland to consummate formal contracts for land from the Indian owners in the legal manner of the Old World.

NOTES—CHAPTER 5

1. The military and diplomatic affairs of the Iroquois constitute a complex series of events that are ably discussed by Anthony F. C. Wallace,

"Origins of Iroquois Neutrality," *Pennsylvania History*, vol. 24, no. 3, July 1957, pp. 223–35; cf. George T. Hunt, *The Wars of the Iroquois*, Madison, Wis., 1967.

2. Edward Arber, ed., *The Travels and Works of Captain John Smith*, A. G. Bradley edition, Edinburgh, 1910, vol. 1, pp. 53–54.

3. Francis P. Jennings, "Glory, Death and Transfiguration: The Susquehannock Indians in the Seventeenth Century," *Proceedings of the American Philosophical Society*, vol. 11, no. 1, Feb. 15, 1968, p. 21.

4. There have been a number of accounts of these excavations, which are listed in the excellent bibliography in John Witthoft and W. Fred Kinsey III, eds., *Susquehannock Miscellany*, Harrisburg, Pa., 1959. *Archeological News Letter*, published September 1969 by Carnegie Museum, Pittsburgh, described recent excavations on the Strickler and Schultz sites in Lancaster County, both occupied by the Susquehanna Minquas.

5. Myers, *Narratives*, p. 22.

6. Ibid., p. 24.

7. Ibid., p. 38.

8. B. Fernow ed., *Documents Relative to the Colonial History of New York*, (hereinafter cited as *NYCD*), vol. 4, Albany, 1877, pp. 98–99.

9. "Indian Tradition &c.," New-York Historical Society, *Collections*, 2d series, vol. 1, 1841, pp. 69–74.

10. In his *History*, Heckewelder states that the word *Schwannack*, used to mean "white man," was a derisive term that signified "salt beings or bitter beings; for in their language the word *Schwan* is in general applied to things that have a salt, sharp, bitter or sour taste"; p. 142. Brinton's *A Lenâpé-English Dictionary*, Philadelphia, 1888, defines *schwon* as "saltish, sour," and, "A white man is called *schwonack* from the salt ocean." The same word, as applied to the Dutch, occurs as early as 1643 in the writings of De Vries as *Swannekins*, and in an entry in 1654 as *Swaneckes*; *NYCD*, vol. 13, p. 47.

11. Myers, *Narratives*, pp. 47, 48.

12. Adriaen Van der Donck, "A Description of New Netherlands," New-York Historical Society, *Collections*, 2d series, vol. 1, 1841, p. 210.

13. Daniel Denton, "A Brief Description of New York, . . . ," *Gowan's Bibliotheca Americana*, New York, 1845, p. 20.

14. C. A. Weslager, *Dutch Explorers*, p. 294.

15. Nathaniel C. Hale, *Virginia Venturer*, Richmond, Va., 1951.

16. The policies that guided the West India Company are discussed by Van Cleaf Bachman, *Peltries or Plantations* . . . , Baltimore, 1969.

6

Rivalry for the Land

From 1609, when Henry Hudson discovered Delaware Bay, to 1638, when the first Swedish settlements were made on the Delaware, the Dutch had the Indian trade along the river practically to themselves. Dutch trading vessels sailed in and out of Delaware Bay conducting trade with the Delawares that was mutually satisfactory, and relations were good. When the West India Company executives decided to compete more aggressively with the English by establishing commercial settlements along the Delaware, they needed only small plots of land, and at the time it did not seem to be necessary to make extensive territorial purchases from the Indians.

To prepare for the handful of Walloon colonists placed in 1624 on Burlington Island (the first Dutch settlement on the Delaware, which was short-lived because the colonists were soon removed to Manhattan Island) and for the building of a trading post called Fort Nassau at Gloucester, New Jersey, the Dutch doubtless gave the Indians European goods for the two parcels of land. The company's instructions to Willem Verhulst, who was named the "provisional director" of the New Netherland, told him not to drive the Indians away by force or threat, but to give them something for their lands and negotiate a written contract to cover any land purchases.[1] Whatever conveyances may have been drawn up to cover these two plots are no longer in existence, but the question is strictly academic because the lands in question were of insignificant proportions, and the Dutch occupation of them proved to be impermanent.

Verhulst's council banished him from the New Netherland for reprehensible conduct in the affairs of the colony, and he and his wife returned in disgrace to Holland in the fall of 1626 on *The Arms of Amsterdam*. In addition to several thousand pelts taken back in the hold of the vessel for the benefit of the West India Company, Verhulst returned with a tabard made of sixteen beaver pelts, and his wife with a jacket sewn from thirty-two otter skins. So prodigal were they with the animal pelts that they selected only the finest black skins for the two garments, cutting and discarding the tails and the lighter portions of the furs.[2]

Transcriptions of two documents covering lands purchased by Dutch patroons on Delaware Bay in 1629 have been preserved, *the first land transfers on record* with the Delaware Indians. The first plot, purchased on June 1, 1629, by Gillis Hossitt on behalf of patroon merchants Samuel Godyn, Kiliaen van Rensselaer, and Samuel Blommaert consisted of a strip of land along the *west* shore of Delaware Bay at present Lewes, Delaware. It was eight Dutch miles long (thirty-two English miles), and one-half Dutch mile wide (two English miles). The Delaware Indian owners of this land were Sawowouwe, Wuoyt, Pemhake, Mekowetick, Techepewoya, Mathemek, Sacook, Anehoopen, Janqueno, and Pokahake—members of the Sickoneysincks. The chief of the band was a "King under years," i.e., a minor (evidently entitled to inherit the chieftancy through matrilineal descent), and the council deputed two of the older councilors, Queskakons (Quesquaekous) and Eesanques, to represent the Indians when the transaction was confirmed on Manhattan Island and there entered in the records of the West India Company by Peter Minuit, who had succeeded Willem Verhulst as the company's ranking official in the New Netherland. The document specifically refers to "cloth [apparently duffels], axes, adzes, and beads" paid the Indians for the land, although the exact quantity is not stated.[3]

The second plot, purchased on May 5, 1631, by Hossitt on behalf of the same three patroons, consisted of sixteen square miles, Dutch measure, on the *east* side of Delaware Bay near Cape May. The owners of this land were the same Sickoneysincks. They were compensated by an indeterminate quantity of trade goods not enumerated in the document and, of course, none of them understood the significance of the complicated legal language in the parchment to which they affixed their marks.

. . . they herewith entirely and absolutely desist from, give up, abandon and renounce it now and forever, promising further not only to keep, fulfill and execute firmly, inviolately and irrevocably in infinitum this, their contract and what might be done hereafter on the authority thereof, but also to deliver the said tract of land and keep it free against everybody, from any claim, challenge or incumbrance which anybody might intend to create; as well as to have the sale and conveyance approved and confirmed by the remainder of the co-owners, for whom they are the trustees; all this under the obligations required by law, in good faith, without evil intent or deceit.[4]

In the spring of 1631, the patroons seated a small colony called Swanendael ("valley of Swans") under Gillis Hossitt's supervision at present Lewes on land previously purchased from the Indians. The settlers, all men, were in the employ of the patroons, and their mission was to carry on whale fishing and cultivate grain and tobacco for export to Holland. The fur trade with the Indians, which the West India Company reserved to itself, was permitted the patroons as long as the company did not place its own agent at Swanendael to handle this activity.

The colony survived less than a year, until the Sickoneysincks burned the buildings and stockade and murdered the entire contingent of thirty-two settlers. No Dutchman was left alive to tell the story of what had prompted such a heinous crime, so alien to the behavior of the Delaware Indians toward strangers. The massacre must have been provoked by unforgivable acts on the part of the Dutch colonists, but the only explanation of what happened is found in De Vries's journal. This was based on information he obtained after questioning the Indians when he arrived at Swanendael after the massacre and found the bones of the colonists strewn on the ground. One wonders if there were not other circumstances unknown to him, but the following is his version:

An Indian remained on board of the yacht at night, whom we asked why they had slain our people, and how it happened. He then showed us the place where our people had set up a column, to which was fastened a piece of tin, whereon the arms of Holland were painted. One of their chiefs took this off for the purpose of making tobacco pipes, not knowing that he was doing amiss. Those in command at the house [Hossitt] made such an ado about it, that the Indians, not knowing how it was, went away and slew the chief who had done it, and brought a token of the dead to the house to those in command, who told him that they wished they had not done it, that they should have brought him to them, as they wished to have forbidden him to do the like again. They then went away, and the friends of the murdered chiefs incited their friends—as they are a people like the Italians, who are very revengeful, to set about the work of vengeance.[5]

Under the guise of friendship, according to De Vries's account, the Indians entered the trading post and killed Hossitt, a watchdog, and one of the colonists who was lying sick. Then they attacked the other settlers, who were at work in the fields, and one by one murdered all of them. The Swanendael massacre deterred the patroons from seating a second commercial colony on the sixteen-square-mile tract at Cape May, as they originally had planned, and Swanendael was not resettled. Thus in 1638 when the Swedes entered the Delaware River to establish a colony, there were no colonists living on the river, although Dutch traders from Manhattan Island continued to sail back and forth to meet the Delaware Indians periodically at Fort Nassau, where the natives came to barter their furs. If the Swanendael colony had prospered, and if women and children had been sent from Holland to increase the population, there would certainly have been an eventual confrontation with the Indians about land ownership. The thirty-two-mile stretch of territory along the bay and river, which the patroons believed they had purchased outright from the Indians, included the hunting territories of the Sickoneysincks. The Indians were unaware that the document they had signed with their marks excluded them from these territories, but the tragedy at Swanendael had the effect of delaying the inevitable confrontation between Dutch and Indians over land tenure.

As a result of several years of contact with Dutch traders, the technology was the first aspect of Delaware Indian culture to undergo change. Their simple gardening-hunting-fishing subsistence pattern became a predominantly hunting-for-barter economy in order to obtain furs to trade for European merchandise. Although the Indian women continued to plant corn, beans, and other crops, the role of the male changed because his former hunting and fishing pursuits for food became of less importance than his activity as a supplier of pelts to Dutch traders.

As friction began to develop between whites and Indians, well illustrated in the hostility that followed the Swanendael massacre, the Delawares began to move in the direction of consolidating their forces. When De Vries sailed up the Delaware in 1633, after finding the Swanendael settlement in ruins, the Indians he encountered were sullen and suspicious, and when he weighed anchor opposite Fort Nassau he found it was crowded with hostile Delawares. A party of chiefs paddled out to his vessel in a dugout canoe, and he noted in his journal that there were "nine chiefs, sachems from nine different places." [6] The reader will recall that Robert Evelyn cited nine different Indian communities in New Jersey, and it would appear from De Vries's account that the sachems of these communities had taken the first step toward unification as a defensive measure against the whites.

Open warfare broke out at an early date between the Dutch and the Indian bands on Manhattan Island and Staten Island, in Westchester County, and along the Hudson. Although the Delawares were not directly involved, the shedding of the blood of their Algonkian neighbors, who lived such a short distance away, made them nervous and apprehensive of the Dutch. The root of the problem seems to have been misunderstandings over lands—the Dutch bought lands from the Indians and looked upon their purchases with finality, whereas the Indians expected to continue to fish, hunt, and plant corn. There were also day-to-day quarrels—Dutch traders adulterated brandy with water to cheat the Indians; the Dutch settlers claimed that Indian dogs worried their poultry and livestock; the Indians complained that cows, goats, and swine owned by Dutch farmers ran unattended through their fields. There were also ill-advised governmental measures, such as the tax which Governor Willem Kieft levied on the Indians, to be paid in skins, corn, or wampum, which the Indians misinterpreted as unjust punishment imposed by the Dutch government for misdeeds of which they were innocent.

When the Raritan refused to make reparations for some pigs they were blamed for killing, Kieft sent soldiers to force them to pay, and a fracas ensued in which several Indians were killed. This was followed by retaliations and more serious incidents, and at midnight on February 25, 1643, a force of Dutch soldiers hacked to death from 80 to 120 Indians while they slept—men, women, and children. The Indians then sought revenge and later lay waste the Dutch boweries and murdered a number of settlers, taking women and children as captives. An uneasy peace was concluded, but in 1655 there occurred a second Indian outbreak that was followed by more burnings, atrocities, and the taking of prisoners.[7]

The arrival of the Swedes brought a new European nation to the land of the Delawares, and this new threat to the Dutch position in the New World had repercussions that also directly affected the Indians. The first Swedish expedition was under the leadership of Peter Minuit, the former director-general of the New Netherland who had fallen out of favor with the directors of the West India Company and had left their service to obtain employment with the New Sweden Company.

The fact that the Swedes could lay no claim to the Delaware Valley, either by right of prior exploration or by discovery (as did both the Dutch and English), did not deter Minuit from building a stronghold he named Fort Christina at the mouth of the Christina River (present Wilmington, Delaware) in honor of the young Swedish queen. There he left a number of colonists who were later reinforced as additional Swedish expeditions came to America. Although the motives of the merchant sponsors of the New Sweden Company were also commercial, unlike the Dutch they immediately sought to acquire extensive territorial rights from the Indians on both sides of the Delaware River. If they could establish their ownership through title deeds negotiated with the Indians, the Swedes believed they could exclude Dutch and English trespassers from the lands and monopolize the beaver trade.

The first land purchase that Minuit negotiated, on March 29, 1638, was with "five sachems or princes, by the name of Mattahorn, Mitot Schemingh [Mitatsemint], Eru Packen [Elupacken], Mahamen, and Chiton, some being present of the Ermewormahi [Armewamex], the others on behalf of the Mante *and Minqua* nations." [8] (Italics added)

The documents covering the purchase are missing, but an affidavit made later in Holland by four members of Minuit's crew indicates the Delaware Indians "transported, ceded, and transferred all the land, as many days' journeys on all places and parts of the river as they requested; upwards and on both sides." For this land the Indians were "paid and fully compensated for it by good and proper merchandise, which was delivered and given to them in the personal presence of the above-mentioned witnesses . . . ." [9]

Minuit could well afford to be liberal in this first land purchase since his cargo included several thousand yards of duffels and other cloth; several hundred axes, hatchets, adzes, and knives; dozens of tobacco pipes; mirrors, looking glasses, gilded chains, finger rings, combs, and earrings. Having served the West India Company in the New Netherland, Minuit knew exactly what commodities the Indians were most desirous of having, and he convinced the Swedish merchants to outfit his vessel accordingly. He not only used his cargo to purchase land but also to trade for furs, and he bartered with the Indians for 1,769 beaver pelts, 314 otter, and 132 bearskins—a very profitable exchange for the European merchandise.

Historians have since had differences of opinions about the extent of the land purchase made by Minuit. From his study of contemporary Swedish documents preserved in Stockholm, Dr. Amandus Johnson believed that there were two deeds, one covering the land from the Christina River south to Duck Creek (where the territory of the Sickoneysincks began), and the second from the Christina River north to the Schuylkill River.[10] Peter Hollender Ridder, who came to New Sweden in 1639 as the head of the colony, bought additional land from Delaware chief Kekesikkun as far north as eight miles above present Burlington, New Jersey, and he renegotiated the purchase of lands from the Christina to Duck Creek with the chieftain named Shakapemeck.[11]

It is of interest that some of the sachems present on March 29, 1638, when Minuit negotiated his first land purchase, were there on behalf of the "Minqua." Some ethno-historians have interpreted this to mean that, having dominated the Delawares in warfare, the Minquas were exercising a sort of benign overlordship in their land transactions with the Swedes. Thomas Campanius Holm, using the journal notes of his grandfather, who was in America from 1643 to 1648, stated that the Minquas "forced the other Indians, whom we have before mentioned [the Delawares] and who are not so warlike as the Minquas, to be afraid of them, and made them subject and tributary to them . . ."[12]

A deposition made in 1697 by Captain John Hance Steelman (quoted in the next chapter) confirms Campanius's statement that the Delawares became tributary to the Susquehanna Minquas. My study of contemporary documents leads me to believe that, having dominated the Delawares, the Minquas exercised a protectoral role, which is the real explanation why Minquas witnesses were present during Minuit's first meeting with the Delawares—and later when Stuyvesant was also negotiating for lands on the Delaware.

As time went on, Swedish influence spread from Fort Christina, which remained the seat of authority; and scattered hamlets of Swedish and Finnish settlers appeared along the Christina, at present Marcus Hook and Chester, and along the Schuylkill in present Philadelphia. When Johan Printz arrived as governor of New Sweden in 1643, he built a two-story gubernatorial mansion of logs and established a small Swedish settlement on Tinicum Island in the Delaware River immediately south of Philadelphia.

By the time of Printz's arrival, his predecessors had negotiated additional land purchases from the Indians, and the Swedes could show Indian deeds giving them ownership of lands from Fort Christina as far south as Cape Henlopen, and from Fort Christina as far north as the Sankikans near present Trenton. These deeds, according to instructions issued to Printz and as interpreted in Sweden, gave the Swedes legal right at any time to "occupy as much land as they like." The Swedish and Finnish population then amounted to not more than a hundred persons scattered along the western side of the Delaware River between present Wilmington and Philadelphia, and amicable relations had been maintained with the natives. The Delaware Indian communities on the Brandywine, on White Clay Creek, along the Schuylkill, and elsewhere remained unmolested, although the Indians did not realize that the deeds they had signed had, in fact, conveyed to the Swedes not only their hunting territories south of Trenton but the lands on which their villages stood. According to their concepts of land, they had, with genuine native hospitality, allowed the Swedes to share their territory with them. They were under the impression that the Swedes had given them presents as a token of appreciation for allowing them to use the land—not as the consideration for ceding full ownership rights.

From the viewpoint of Swedish authorities, as long as the Delawares were a source of valuable furs to be exported to Sweden for the benefit of the merchant sponsors of the New Sweden Company, it was highly desirable not to disrupt Delaware village life. Moreover, until the Swedish and Finnish farmers could produce sufficient crops to feed the colonists, the Indians were a source of corn and other foodstuffs, which they willingly supplied in exchange for European merchandise.

Printz was instructed, not only to treat the Indians with respect and do them no violence or wrong, but also "at every opportunity exert himself that the same wild people may gradually be instructed in the true Christian religion and worship . . ." [13] Accompanying him was the Lutheran pastor John Campanius, who was supposed to attend to the spiritual needs of the colonists and was also dedicated to the task of converting the heathens to Christianity. Campanius traveled among the Delaware Indians, compiled a vocabulary of many of their words, and by 1646 had made a manuscript translation of Luther's *Little Catechism* into the Delaware dialect. In 1656, eight years before John Eliot's Indian Bible was published, Campanius presented a complete translation of his catechism to the King of Sweden, although it was not published until 1696. The first edition of this catechism, which contained an addendum with Delaware Indian vocabulary and idioms, is a very rare volume; only a few copies are still in existence.

Prior to Printz's arrival, the Swedes had given little attention to the eastern side of the Delaware, and their negligence opened the way for a group of English settlers from the New Haven colony to move down to the Delaware from Connecticut and establish a small and short-lived English colony along Salem Creek in Salem County, New Jersey. They had no royal patent for the land on which they settled, but this did not deter them from negotiating land purchases from the Indian owners. [14] It also introduced another European contender not only for the Indians' lands but also for the beaver trade. The Delaware Indians were now in the preferred position of having Swedes, Dutch, and English all competing for their furs, and they had their choice of trading with the one who bid highest and gave them the most merchandise. Aware of this competitive situation, the Swedish merchants instructed Printz to ". . . allow the wild people to obtain the necessary things they need at a somewhat more moderate price than they are getting them of the Hollanders from Fort Nassau or the adjacent English . . ." [15] This price cutting by the Swedes upset the rates of exchange established by the Dutch, forcing both English and Dutch traders to meet Swedish terms, which, of course, reduced their profits and caused resentment.

By the end of the first year of his administration, during which time he had ample opportunity to familiarize himself with all facets of the commercial situation on the Delaware, Printz came to two important conclusions. First, the ruthless slaying of beavers along the

Delaware and its tributaries during the twenty-five years the Indians had been accommodating European traders had almost destroyed the beaver population in this immediate area. As Professor Francis P. Jennings has pointed out, where subsistence was the first consideration, primitive hunters like the American Indians were careful not to kill the breeding stock, thus acting as conservators as they sought wild animals for their livelihood.[16] Once the Indians became dependent upon the white man's goods, they had to hunt with such unnatural and destructive intensity that they indiscriminately exterminated the game on which their survival formerly depended. In aboriginal times the native hunter killed only what was needed to support his family— after white contact, hunting became an orgy of destruction. The Swedish and Dutch traders, with the willing cooperation of the Delawares, emptied the Delaware Valley of the beaver as well as other fur bearers, before the white settlements were well established.

Printz's second conclusion was that there still remained an excellent source of beaver and otter pelts in the deep waters and hills of Minquas country, especially along the tributaries of the Susquehanna. Some of these tributaries, like the Juniata and the smaller streams that emptied into the west branch of the Susquehanna, took the Minquas hunters farther westward through the mountain valleys toward the Allegheny River and its tributaries, where beaver also abounded. Printz realized that to monopolize the Minquas fur trade he must not only solicit the friendship and close cooperation of the Susquehanna Indians but must also do his utmost to block Dutch access to Minquas country.

Whereas Printz spoke highly of the Minquas in his reports to Sweden, he had a very low regard for the Delaware Indians and referred disparagingly to them. He said in one of his reports that the Delawares "are a lot of poor rogues . . . we have no beaver trade whatsoever with them but only the maize trade. Nothing would be better than to send over here a couple of hundred soldiers . . . until we broke the necks of all of them in this River . . . Then each one could be secure here at his work, and feed and nourish himself unmolested without their maize, and also we could take possession of the places (which are the most fruitful) that the savages now possess; and when we have thus not only bought this river, but also won it with the sword, then no one, whether he be Hollander or Englishman, could pretend in any manner to this place either now or in coming times, but we should then have the beaver trade with the Black and White Minquas alone, four times as good as we have had it, now or at any past time." [17]

To exclude the Dutch from the Minquas trade, Printz built a series of forts and fortified trading posts, which guarded the entrance of the Delaware and blocked the mouths of the tributaries, the trade routes to the Minquas country. In so doing he put the Swedish traders in a favorable position, not only in traveling to the Minquas country, but in meeting the Minquas trading parties when they came to the Delaware with their pelts. Intensification of trade with the Minquas imposed a heavy drain on the merchandise used for barter, and Printz knew that, unless Swedish vessels continued to replenish the supply, the Minquas would seek out the Dutch or English to take their furs.

No longer the recipients of large quantities of Swedish trade goods, their ancient lands used as the base for trade with their former Minquas enemies, the Delawares became resentful of the Swedes. One of the belligerent factions of Delaware braves killed a Swede and his wife in their bed, and a few days later murdered two soldiers and a workman. The same group of braves started a fire on Tinicum Island and burned the wood that Swedish carpenters had cut and sawed to build a keelboat. Several of the more conservative Delaware chiefs came to Printz, asking his forgiveness for these crimes, which they said had occurred without their knowledge or consent. During the peace treaty that ensued, they gave him 30 pelts and some wampum beads as evidence of their good faith. Printz agreed to maintain the peace, but he told the chiefs in strong language "that in case they hereafter practice the smallest hostilities against our people then we would not let a soul of them live . . ." [18]

In view of Printz's militant attitude toward the Delawares, it is difficult to predict what might have happened if he had continued in office and Sweden had adequately reinforced and supplied her New World colony. Actually—despite the thousands of beavers and other pelts shipped to Sweden—the cost of supporting the American colony was so excessive that Swedish merchants lost interest in the project, and political changes in Sweden diverted the attention of the government to other matters. During a two-year period Printz was without any merchandise to trade, because no Swedish vessels had arrived, and he claimed that the Minquas had taken eight or nine thousand pelts to the Dutch. "God knows," he wrote, "what difficult eleven years, and now soon twelve years, I have experienced among the heathens and a turbulent people, with so little assistance from the Kingdom . . . in six years [I] have not had the slightest letter or message from my fatherland . . ." [19]

Sweden's vulnerability encouraged the Dutch West India Company to move into action to regain control along the Delaware River, which they had temporarily lost, and Governor Peter Stuyvesant started a political and military offensive that ultimately resulted in Dutch dominion over New Sweden. Part of Stuyvesant's political strategy was to win over the Indians with presents and secure from them title deeds to the lands claimed by the Swedes, in order to nullify Swedish ownership. The Delawares were pawns in his game of maneuvering the Swedes into an indefensible position, with the objective of giving the Dutch the upper hand in the Minquas trade and undisputed control of the Delaware River. The Delawares were unaware that the generous and friendly Dutchmen were using them for selfish purposes.

For suitable merchandise, Mattahorn (the same chief who had participated in the transfer of land to Peter Minuit) and two other Indians—Sinques and Alibakinne—were persuaded to declare that a plot of land on the Schuylkill where the Dutch erected a trading post called Fort Beversreede, had been purchased previously from them by a Dutchman many years before. This enabled Stuyvesant to maintain that a nearby Swedish trading post erected by Printz was actually on Dutch-owned land.

Following this transaction, Stuyvesant had a second meeting with Mattahorn, Sinques, and a third Delaware Indian proprietor named Pemenetta. He asked them through his interpreters if they were indeed owners of lands on the western side of the Delaware River. Mattahorn answered "that they were great Chiefs and Proprietors of the lands, both by ownership and by descent and appointment of Minquaas and River Indians; wherefore they had power to sell and make over the lands; and what they did, that should be done and remain." [20]

Stuyvesant's next question, as recorded, was "What and how much land the Swedes had bought from the Sachems or Chiefs on this river?" Mattahorn replied that all nations coming to the river had been welcomed by the Indians, who "sold" their land indiscriminately to the first who asked for it.[21] Furthermore, he said, the Dutch were the earliest comers and discoverers of the river. Queried about the

land that Minuit had purchased on behalf of the Swedes, Mattahorn
gave the following reply:

That when Minuyt came to the country with a ship, he lay before the
Minquaas kill, where he the Sachem then had a house and lived; that
Minuyt then presented him with and gave him a kettle and other trifles,
requesting of him, as much land as Minuyt could set a house on, and a
plantation included between 6 trees, which he, the Sachem, sold him, and
Minuyt promised him half the tobacco that would grow on the plantation,
although it was never given to him. He declared further that neither the
Swedes nor any other nation had bought lands of them as right owners
except the patch on which Fort Christina stood and that all the other
houses of the Swedes built at Tinnecongh [Tinicum Island], Hingeesingh
in the Schuylkil [Kinsessing, a tract between Cobbs Creek and the Schuyl-
kill], and at other places were set up there against the will and consent
of the Indians, and that neither they, nor any other natives, had received
anything therefore.

Mattahorn went on to say that Printz had also obtained land rights
on the western side of the river from two Mantes Indians named
Siscohoka and Mechekyralames but that the true proprietor of this
land was Kyckesycken ("in our tongue, Live Turkey"), who had never
consented to the transaction.

Stuyvesant asked about the land south of Fort Christina to Cape
Henlopen at the mouth of the Delaware. Had that land been sold
to the Swedes? "Why do you ask that question so often?" replied
Mattahorn. "We told you the lands are not sold to any person."
This was the opening Stuyvesant wanted; if this land had not been
sold to the Swedes, would the Indians now sell it to him?

"Will the houses of the Swedes remain?" asked Mattahorn. "Will
the Sachem of the Swedes, then, not do us harm, on that account,
or put us in prison or beat us? . . . We will rather present than
sell the Great Sachem the land." Further discussion disclosed that
in offering to give the lands to Stuyvesant, the Indians reserved the
right to hunt and fish on it.

Stuyvesant promptly accepted as a gift the territory from Fort
Christina to Duck Creek, and to reciprocate the gift he gave the
chiefs twelve coats of duffels, twelve kettles, twelve axes, twelve adzes,
twenty-four knives, twelve bars of lead, four guns, and some powder.
Pemenetta was referred to in the Dutch document as "the present

and ceding proprietor," and he was apparently a member of the band of which Mattahorn was the chief. Pemenetta stipulated that if anything happened to his gun the Dutch should repair it gratis, and, if he ever came hungry to the Dutch settlements, they would remember to give him some maize as a token of friendship. To this Stuyvesant agreed.

Among those present at this transaction were four Minquas sachems: Jonnay, Tonnahoorn, Pimadaase, and Cannowa Rocquaes. These chieftains were evidently present as witnesses and perhaps as advisers to give approval to the transaction. They probably received their own share of the gifts.

Even at this late date, one can read between the lines and realize that the differences between whites and Indians with respect to concepts of land tenure had not yet been reconciled. In these accounts of discussions with the Indians the word *sell* was a European word inserted in the records in its legal sense, but it had a different meaning to the Indians. It is quite clear from Mattahorn's statements that the Indians intended only to give the Swedes use rights to the lands, just as they were intimidated into giving the same rights to Stuyvesant, but this did not mean that the Indians were excluding themselves or the Swedes from the lands they had given the Dutch. In fact, they specifically stipulated that they were not giving up their hunting and fishing rights. Stuyvesant, on the other hand, believed he had received an outright gift and that the land now belonged to the Dutch, and the Dutch alone.

Except for the handful of English settlers on Salem River, which Printz had brought under Swedish jurisdiction, there had yet been no European colonization in New Jersey. Aware of Stuyvesant's activity, Printz sent for a New Jersey sachem named Wappanghzewan and attempted to buy lands from him, but the Indian refused to sell to the Swedes. Wappanghzewan claimed to be the proprietor, not only of lands in New Jersey running from "Nariticon Kill [Raccoon Creek] and extending westerly down the river unto Maetzingsingh," but on the west shore from "a certain little Kill named Neckatoensingh [possibly Namaan's Creek] extending westerly from the river unto Sittoensaene otherwise called the Minquaas Kill, where Fort Christina stands; all of which lands with their kills and superficies both on the west and on the east shores have always been the property of, and still belong to him."

Under strong Dutch influence, Wappanghzewan, as had Matta-horn, Sinques, and Pemenetta, *gave* his hunting territories on both sides of the river to Governor Stuyvesant. This further strengthened Dutch claims and gave Stuyvesant reason to claim ownership of the property where Fort Christina stood.

On a tract of land along the Delaware River south of Fort Christina, known to the Delaware Indians as Tamecongh, Stuyvesant began to erect Fort Casimir. When Governor Printz realized that this was the reason Stuyvesant had been so eager to purchase the land from Pemenetta, he immediately set about to marshal evidence that Pemenetta was not the real proprietor and had no right to give the land to Stuyvesant. Printz, too, was trying to use the Indians to serve his own selfish interests.

This land, Printz maintained, was the territory of Mitatsimint, who had sold it to Minuit on behalf of the Swedes in 1638. Since Mitatsimint was then dead, Printz located his widow Kiapes, his son Notike, and a relative and "heir" Quenieck. The Indian widow testified that her husband had granted Pemenetta rights to hunt on the land called Quinamkot for certain gifts which were never given to Mitatsimint. Pemenetta, she declared, was not the owner, and, according to Printz, the gift to Stuyvesant should be "revoked."

Printz negotiated two legal documents with Mitatsimint's wife, son, and heir, which reconfirmed Swedish ownership of the tract where the Dutch were then building Fort Casimir, but Stuyvesant ignored the Swedish protests and finished erecting the stronghold. The Swedes later seized the fort, but after a series of confrontations, the Swedes were defeated and the Dutch took over complete control of New Sweden. A little Dutch town called New Amstel sprang up around the fort, and new families came from Holland to increase the population.

From 1655 to 1665, the political authority on the Delaware was vested in the Dutch officials at New Amstel, although Peter Stuyvesant continued as the ranking official over all the New Netherland. The Swedish and Finnish settlers living along the Delaware fell under the jurisdiction of the new government, but they were permitted to retain their lands, their church, and their Lutheran clergyman. If any of the Indian chiefs were sufficiently interested to ask questions about what was going on, they must have been thoroughly confused at the turn of events. Governor Printz, and Johan Rising, who succeeded him, had both returned to Sweden, and whatever territorial rights Sweden formerly claimed now belonged to the Dutch. With their apprehension of the Dutch, because of the difficulties and harassment experienced by their Algonkian brethren in the environs of Manhattan Island, the Delawares could not have been overjoyed with their new masters. After the change in administration, the population increased, and Dutch families, as well as Swedes and Finns, were soon clearing additional lands on the former Indian hunting territories to expand their farm holdings. The Dutch authorities at New Amstel now considered themselves indisputable owners of all the territory on both sides of the river from Cape Henlopen as far north as the river flowed, and the Delawares were not sufficiently unified, nor aware of the inevitable consequences, to challenge the Dutch claims to their lands.

Having learned to wear cloth garments and to use European utensils and tools, the Delawares were becoming dependent upon the Dutch to supply them with these commodities. Many of the men had now been taught the use of guns, and the younger hunters were no longer satisfied to use bows and arrows. A decade earlier Governor Printz had blamed the Dutch "who strengthen the Savages with guns, shot and powder," but the Dutch accused the English and Swedes of introducing firearms to the Indians, and the English traders in Virginia placed the blame on the Swedes and Dutch. The truth is that, in outbidding each other for the fur trade, all shared the responsibility of making the Indians aware that firearms had more practical utility than Jews' harps, mirrors, glass beads, and other similar wares. Unknowingly they were arming the natives with weapons that in a few short years would be turned against the white settlers. Initially the whites were able to exercise a certain control over the weapons, because they could withhold powder and lead or refuse to mend the guns when the Indians broke them, which happened very frequently.

When a party of Delaware chieftains came to New Amstel on December 28, 1655, representing several of the river bands, it was not to complain about the settlers moving on their lands but to try to persuade the authorities to establish a fixed rate of exchange so the traders would not take advantage of them. Unprincipled traders had begun to use many deceptive practices; they stretched the cloth when measuring it for barter, and what should have been a full yard was much less; in measuring out handfuls of powder, they cupped their hands tightly to reduce the amount, and the Indian received less than he had bargained for; they also watered the brandy or rum to cheat the natives.

After listening to the chiefs' protests, the Dutch officials told them they could do nothing about it, that everyone was free to trade with whomever he pleased.[22] Two years later the Dutch had a change of heart when they saw that it was to their own advantage to fix prices because some traders were giving more than others, and the price of some skins had already been run up by more than a third. Since the fur trade was still the mainstay of the economy, it influenced the price of other goods and was causing a hardship for the poor farmers and artisans.

It was agreed on January 10, 1657, that the following rate of exchange should be established and anyone violating it should be deprived of trading rights for one year, severely punished for a second offense, and expelled from the colony if he offended for a third time:

> For a merchantable beaver two strings of wampum,
> for a good bearskin, worth a beaver, two strings of wampum
> for an elkskin, worth a beaver, two strings of wampum
> otters accordingly
> for a deerskin one hundred and twenty wampum
> foxes, catamounts, racoons and other to be valued accordingly.[23]

Changes in regulations governing the fur trade during the various administrations were difficult for the Indians to grasp, since they did not understand the reasons for such laws in the first place. Prior to white contact they had traded among themselves and with other Indians, free from such restrictions, which were completely alien to their society. The early Dutch traders carried on unrestricted barter, which the Indians could understand; but after the Swedes established a colony, they found it necessary to enact ordinances governing the Indian trade along the Delaware, and the Dutch also passed similar regulations. One of the ordinances passed at New Amstel provided that "no persons shall go to the Indians, by land or water, to trade with them, or offer them gifts by sailing up and down the [Delaware] river." This regulation was intended to eliminate abuses that occurred when individual Dutch traders sought out the Indians in their towns and traded with them beyond the eyes of the authorities and the hand of the law. The effect of the ordinance was to force the Indians to bring their furs to New Amstel, where fair treatment could be guaranteed them since the transactions were completed in public. Although this eliminated the evil of illicit traders taking advantage of the Indians, it brought on another problem when large numbers of Indians were thrown into close association with the residents within the town limits.

The Delaware Indians had never seen anything to equal the little Dutch settlement at New Amstel, which must have been a source of wonderment to them. There were more than one hundred houses, mostly of planks or clapboards, some with tiled roofs, many surrounded by paled fences, built in rows on the narrow streets. One of the houses was outfitted with a bell and used for church services, and nearby there was a horsemill, later replaced by a windmill, to grind corn and other grains to flour. The fort itself was a rambling palisaded structure containing barracks for the soldiers, a separate dwelling for the vice-director, a building whose second floor was used as a courtroom, and a number of other structures serving various uses.

There were usually sailing vessels at anchor before the fort, bringing supplies from Holland or Manhattan Island, and as the town grew there was an increase in the foot and horse traffic back and forth across the dykes from the outlying Swedish and Finnish farms and hamlets. The town's population consisted largely of clerks, tradesmen, soldiers, servants, women, and children who had constant need for corn and venison, which the Delawares could supply; and furs, of course, continued to be in demand with from thirty to forty thousand beaver pelts exported each season. New Amstel was the center of commercial activity on the Delaware; and Minquas from the Susquehanna, and Delawares from both sides of the river, were frequent visitors, all anxious to obtain duffels, guns, powder, lead, clothing, and other commodities kept in the storehouse in the fort where the Commissary resided. The chiefs were usually entertained within the fort; bark wigwams built outside the palisades accommodated the others. Friendly relations now existed between the Minquas and Delawares, the former holding a sort of protective position and on several occasions serving as intermediaries when friction developed between Dutch and Delawares.

The Delawares were brought into intimate contact with Dutch

officials and townsfolk, and it was inevitable that interpersonal problems would develop, which is well illustrated in the traffic in intoxicants. An ordinance had been enacted and posted forbidding anyone to sell brandy or strong drinks to the Indians, because it was well known that the natives were crazed by alcohol, but the prohibition came to be generally disregarded. In 1656, Dirck Michielsen, a Finn, and Cornelis Martensen, a Swede, were jailed for selling beer to the Indians, but they were released shortly. Martin Roseman received as wages three ankers of wine, which he sold to a party of Delawares; and Jan Juriaensen Becker openly bartered with liquor, which made the Indians noisy and unruly. Night after night they staggered through the town shouting and shooting off their guns.

A townsman encountered a Delaware Indian in the woods with a two-quart can full of liquor which he had obtained from Becker. The next morning the Indian was found dead in the woods, apparently from consuming the alcohol. Some of his friends blamed Becker for poisoning him; they erected a scaffolding of tree limbs opposite Becker's house and placed the corpse on it. "Some say, that, whereas he has drunk himself to death, he is not yet worthy of a grave, other savages say, that he must curse the house where he got the liquor." [24] (The Delawares believed the spirit hovered around the body for a number of days following death.) On another occasion a group of Indians obtained "an anker of anise-liquor," and they sat around it drinking boisterously in the middle of the street near the church.

After Becker was arrested for violating the ordinance, he introduced witnesses who said that liquor was widely and openly sold to the Indians, and "that if the poor inhabitants of the Colony of New Amstel and others did not sell or barter liquor to the savages for Indian corn, meat or other things, they would perish from hunger and distress." Moreover, Becker produced another set of witnesses who testified that one of New Amstel's top officials had sent them "with several ankers of brandy and Spanish wine in a sloop to the savages to trade them for Indian corn or wampum, whatever they, deponents, could best obtain for them."

The older Delaware chieftains were concerned over this debauchery of their people, and in 1662 a number of chiefs held a powwow at Tinicum Island to discuss corrective measures. They sent a message, following their discussions, to the Dutch authorities at New Amstel, asking that the traffic in liquor with the Indians be prohibited. The demand for liquor was so persistent, and the Dutch traders so intent upon making profits, that the illicit traffic continued. The traders knew that if they did not satisfy the Indian demand for liquor others would. Alcohol was the great compeller that induced the Indians to work harder hunting and trapping in order to bring in more furs.

Wampum beads played an increasingly important role in the fur trade and, as the Indians became more sophisticated in the ways of the white man they learned that, by using beads as a medium of exchange, cheating was minimized. There were two kinds of wampum beads in use during this period, both cylindrical in shape and drilled longitudinally so they could be strung. The white was the more common, but the blue-black bead, similarly made from shells, was more valuable on an approximate ratio of two to one. The term *sewan* or *sewant* (from an Algonkian word meaning "scattered") was used by both Dutch and Swedes in referring to wampum, and the New England traders generally called the bead money *wampum* or *peake* (from the Algonkian word *wampumpeake*, meaning a "string of white beads"). In Virginia the white beads were called *roanoke*, the dark ones were known as *peake*.

Among the Delawares, the beads were strung in standard lengths of one fathom, although they were also exchanged in loose, unstrung quantities. A string measuring a fathom in length consisted of three ells, a unit of measure used by both Dutch and Swedes. An ell was originally equal to the approximate length of a man's forearm. In bartering with the natives, the white trader had to have a supply of bead money, as well as European goods, and the beads were principally obtained from the seaside Indians in New England, New York, and Virginia. The trader exchanged European merchandise for beads, and then used the beads, augmented by trade goods, to buy furs. There was also a traffic in beads between white traders, wherein one trader used European money to purchase beads from another. On one occasion an English trader from Virginia brought 862½ yards of beads to New Sweden to be sold to the Indian traders at an approximate price of four florins (approximately four dollars per yard). Governor Johan Printz complained bitterly that the Delaware Indians were poor and that he could obtain very little wampum from them, which forced him to purchase beads on Manhattan Island and in New England at a high price. Several efforts by the Dutch and others to counterfeit the Indian beads proved a failure. Native-made wampum beads were perforated with a stone drill, their exteriors polished with an abrading stone. The Indians could readily recognize native handicraft and would not accept beads made by white men with metal tools. The Dutch failed to understand why the Indians were unwilling to accept manufactured beads, which to them appeared to be of higher quality than the native products, and this was another situation that caused misunderstanding.

Various other incidents perpetrated by individual Indians or whites for personal reasons, or to avenge misdeeds, tended to strain further the relations between the Dutch and the Delawares. Most of these incidents occurred in the woods some distance from New Amstel, and the authorities had difficulty getting the facts or apprehending the culprits. Three Indians were murdered—a man, woman, and child —allegedly by a Dutchman and a Swede who stole their wampum; a Dutch boy was kidnaped by the Indians and later ransomed with clothing and duffels; the grave of the Delaware Indian chief Hoppe-mink (Ahopemack) was robbed by unknown white persons who stole the wampum and duffels that had been buried with him. Then there was general ferment up and down the river when the Dutch at Manhattan attacked the Esopus Indians to avenge murders committed by the Esopus, and there were eleven Minisinks among the Esopus who were killed. It was reported in 1663, incidentally, that the Esopus, driven from their villages on the Hudson, had joined the Minisinks and were living in their village.

The Dutch documents state that the "Seneca" (by which they meant the Five Nations) attacked the Minquas on the Susquehanna, and a number of warriors of the Armewamex band of Delawares left New Jersey to assist the Minquas in their defense. Meanwhile, the same records provide the information that a "Seneca" war party came down the Delaware River and killed twelve Delaware Indians "living here on the river a little above the Swedish settlement"; they also murdered and scalped an old Swedish farmer.[25] This leaves no reason to doubt that open conflict existed between the Five Nations and the Delawares, which is further corroborated by archeological evidence uncovered at the well-known Minisink site in Sussex County, New Jersey. Dr. Charles A. Philhower conducted extensive excavations at this site (where in 1893–94 Dr. Edward S. Dalrymple excavated twelve Delaware Indian skeletons associated with glass beads, copper kettle, silver spoon, thimbles, bells, combs, and other trade goods), uncovering 180 burials. Dr. Philhower's excavations revealed that the inhabitants had stockaded their village for protection, but this did not save the seventy-five villagers whose skulls had been crushed by their attackers—possibly one of the Five Nations war parties who were raiding the Delaware Indian settlements.[26]

With the Five Nations roaming in the Delaware Valley spreading terror, the settlers lived in fear of having their crops destroyed and their cattle stolen by enemy Indians. The problem was how to distinguish peaceful Indians from those who were hostile, and there was apprehension when *any* Indian appeared. Friendly Delawares found themselves being challenged to prove that they were not enemies, which they felt was an insult. Furthermore, the dread smallpox, which broke out among the Minquas in 1661, spread to the Delawares, and in the spring of 1663 many of the latter were dying of a disease they accused the whites of spreading deliberately.

On June 17, 1660, the Dutch records state that some of the Delawares were beginning to leave their ancestral lands. Seven canoes filled with men, women, and children came down the Delaware, intending to settle in the Minquas country. "It was said that they had lived near the Menissing [Minisink] Indians and had fled for fear of a certain Manitto." [27] Perhaps they believed that one of the manitowuk was displeased with them and had sent the white man's disease as a form of punishment.

To aggravate a situation that was almost ready to explode, there occurred in the fall of 1664 an unexpected event, which disrupted the political situation, resulted in the downfall of Dutch power in America and the loss of their colony, and put another European nation in control of the Delaware River Valley. Charles II of England on March 12, 1664, granted to his brother James, Duke of York (who would later become James II), a patent conveying proprietary rights to land in America from the St. Croix River in Maine to and including the east side of Delaware Bay and River. The Duke sent strong naval forces to America to reduce the Dutch "to submission and obedience" and to claim his lands. In successfully doing so, his forces, heavily armed, sailed up the Delaware in two warships and seized New Amstel. The Dutch officials were ousted, their properties confiscated, and the Duke of York imposed a new government on the Dutch, Swedish, and Finnish settlers. The Duke had never seen a Delaware Indian, never participated in a treaty with them, knew nothing about their traditions or culture, and, of course, never offered to purchase from them one square inch of their lands. By right of conquest over another European power, he had become the new owner of all the territory which the Delaware Indians once considered theirs. Now they were subjects of the English government.

Notes—Chapter 6

1. A. J. Van Laer, trans. and ed., *Documents Relating to New Netherland, 1624-26*, San Marino, Cal., 1924, p. 17.

2. Ibid., p. 244.

3. Ibid., pp. 258–59, 266–67.

4. Weslager, *Dutch Explorers*, p. 272.

5. Myers, *Narratives*, pp. 16–17.

6. Ibid., p. 20.

7. See chapter 3 of Allen W. Trelease, *Indian Affairs in Colonial New York*, Ithaca, 1960; cf. Adrian C. Leiby, *The Early Dutch and Swedish Settlers of New Jersey*, Princeton, 1964, especially chapters 3, 4.

8. Myers, *Narratives*, p. 87.

9. Ibid., pp. 87–88.

10. Amandus Johnson, *Swedish Settlements on the Delaware*, Philadelphia, 1911, vol. 1, p. 184.

11. Cf. C. A. Weslager and A. R. Dunlap, "More Missing Evidence: Two Depositions by Early Swedish Settlers," *Pennsylvania Magazine of History and Biography*, vol. XCL, no. 1, January 1967, p. 38.

12. Thomas Campanius Holm, "A Short Description of the Province of New Sweden . . . ," trans. du Ponceau, in *Memoirs of the Historical Society of Pennsylvania*, vol. 3, Philadelphia, 1834, p. 158.

13. Amandus Johnson, trans., *Instruction for Johan Printz*, Philadelphia, 1930, p. 80.

14. This is fully discussed in my *English on the Delaware*, New Brunswick, N.J., 1967.

15. Johnson, *Instruction for Printz*, p. 80.

16. Francis P. Jennings, "The Indian Trade of the Susquehanna Valley," *Proceedings of the American Philosophical Society*, vol. 110, no. 6, December 1966, p. 407.

17. Johnson, *Instruction for Printz*, p. 117. The Susquehannock were known as the White Minquas. The Black Minquas, who lived farther west, were so called because they wore black stone pendants round their necks.

18. Ibid. Campanius claimed that the Delawares seriously considered wiping out the entire Swedish colony and even had a big powwow where the subject was debated; Holm, A *Short Description* . . . , p. 74.

19. Johnson, *Instruction for Printz*, pp. 194–95.

20. The information relative to Stuyvesant's transactions with the Indians is found in *Pennsylvania Archives*, 2d series, 19 vols., ed. John B. Linn and William H. Egle, Harrisburg, Pa., 1874–90, vol. 5, 1890, passim. The excerpts I have quoted are taken directly from pp. 262–68. William Christie MacLeod cited Stuyvesant's transactions in support of the existence of the family hunting territory among the Delawares in his "The Family Hunting Territory and Lenape Political Organization," *American Anthropologist*, vol. 24, no. 4, 1922, pp. 448–63. I went into the subject further in my "A Discussion of the Family Hunting Territory Question in Delaware," addendum to *Indian Land Sales in Delaware* . . . by Leon de Valinger, Jr., Wilmington, 1941.

21. Stuyvesant was apparently not aware that on September 25, 1646, Andries Hudde purchased from the Delaware Indians for the Dutch a tract of land within the bounds of Philadelphia; see transcript of the document in Weslager, *Dutch Explorers* . . . , Philadelphia, 1961, pp. 307–8. On April 7, 1649, Simon Root bought land from the New Jersey Delawares extending from Rancocas Creek to Burlington Island; *NYCD*, vol. 12, pp. 48–49.

22. Ibid., p. 136.

23. Ibid., p. 157.

24 Ibid., p. 291. All the references I have quoted pertaining to the Indian problems at New Amstel may be found in the section of this volume entitled "Fifth Period," passim.

25. Ibid., pp. 357, 409.

26. Charles A. Philhower, "The Munsee-Lenape Site, Sussex County, N.J.," abstract of paper, *Bulletin of the Eastern States Archeological Federation*, no. 12, September 1953, p. 9.

27. NYCD, vol. 12, p. 315.

7

The Duke of York Takes Over

The Duke of York's seizure of the New Netherland had commercial implications that went far beyond the Indian fur trade, since the underlying reason Charles II granted the territory to his brother was to dispossess the Dutch. Economic and political unification of the English colonies was an impossibility as long as the Dutch held the expanse of territory wedged between New England on the north and Maryland and Virginia on the south—especially since the Dutch were in control of the two major rivers, the Hudson and the Delaware. By terms of his royal grant, the Duke of York was given broad administrative powers, which he delegated to a governor assisted by a provincial secretary and four councilors, all appointive, who constituted the highest authority in the colony.

The Delaware Indians were perplexed by this incomprehensible interplay of European politics that brought to their lands along the Delaware River first the Dutch, then the Swedes, then the Dutch again and, finally, the implanting of an English government and the uprooting of both Swedish and Dutch authority. To add to the confusion, these three nationalities all spoke different languages (which they tried to teach the Indians to understand) and attended different churches (to which their pastors tried to convert the Indians); and each owed allegiance to different European heads of state who were friends at one time and enemies at another. Filed in the archives at Stockholm and Amsterdam, no longer worth the parchment they were inscribed on, were the deeds negotiated with the Passayunk, the Mantes, the Armewamex, the Sickoneysincks, and other Delaware Indian bands. There were no longer any Swedes or Dutch in authority in America to keep the solemn promises each nation had made to the Indians when the chiefs and great men affixed their marks to the documents and took back to their villages the merchandise given them.

One can imagine what might have happened if old Pemenetta had decided to bring his broken flintlock musket to New Castle (as the English then called New Amstel), asking that it be repaired, as Governor Stuyvesant promised when he warmly clasped the chief's hand to pledge his sacred word. Stuyvesant was broken in spirit and politically defrocked after the fall of the New Netherland, and Pemenetta would have learned at New Castle that the Duke of York had enacted a new set of laws governing relations with the Indians living in his province. No person could barter guns, powder, shot, bullets, lead—nor mend an Indian's broken gun—without a license from the English governor who resided in New York, as New Amsterdam was then called. There were some exceptions. The constable at New Castle, who imperiously patrolled the town carrying a long stave with the King's arms on it, could sell an Indian such quantities of powder as he thought necessary to kill wolves (which were a nuisance to the colonists), mend a gun, or provide food for the Indian's family. If the constable made any exceptions, he was supposed to keep a detailed record of the reasons for each transaction.[1]

And how about Indian sachems like Mattahorn, who had been wined and dined, first by Swedes, then by Dutch, in return for lands and furs? The Duke's laws forbade anyone to purchase land from the Indians without the Governor's permission, although any colonist was at liberty to barter for furs if he applied for a license. But all licensed traders were prohibited from trading rum, brandy, or other strong liquors, either with chiefs like Mattahorn or their followers, and violation of this law would subject the offender to a fine of forty shillings per pint. However, in an emergency, an Indian could be given two drams of liquor "in case of sudden extremity sickness faintness or weariness." [2]

There were other loopholes in the Duke of York's liquor laws: The Governor could make an exception and license persons to sell strong liquors to the Indians, provided the licensee would stand security for the Indians' good behavior after indulging in the beverage. The officials at New Castle in the Delaware colony were given permission to exercise their own discretion in selling liquor to the Indians, provided the quantity sold was "not *under* a quarter of an ancker, half, or a whole ancker." An ancker (or anker) varied at different times from seven to ten gallons, and this meant that an Indian could not tipple in a New Castle tavern, where drinks were sold by the cup or bottle, but he could purchase and carry away into the woods a cask containing enough rum or brandy to debauch all the men and women of his village! The intent of this law seems to have been to try to keep Indians from getting drunk in taverns within the town limits and making a nuisance of themselves. During several emergencies that later developed, the authorities attempted to clamp down on the sale of liquor in any quantity to Indians, but none of these regulations was ever strictly enforced or uniformly obeyed.

With the best of intentions, the Duke of York, who remained in London, permitted other laws to be enacted by his governor and councilors to regulate commerce with Indians he had never seen and whose culture he didn't understand. The enforcement of these laws rested with the local officials, and good treatment and friendly relations were naturally what the Duke sought to obtain. "On the other hand," wrote Trelease, "there is no doubt that the Indian was relegated to a position of second-class citizenship. He was subject to racial discriminations, as well as to racial exemptions. Possessing no political rights, he was at the same time free of direct taxation. Throughout the province, and particularly where he found himself in the midst of colonial settlements, a system of legal safeguards developed to assure the Indian of at least minimal human rights. In many ways his status resembled that of free Negroes in the ante-bellum south." [3]

There was a sharp decline in the Indian population of the Atlantic seaboard during this period, as the Algonkian bands found themselves directly in the path of European colonization. Regrettably, no systematic effort was ever made, by Dutch, Swedes or English, to take an accurate census of the Delaware Indian population at different points in time. In 1671 Peter Alricks, an official in both Dutch and English administrations, estimated that the population of the Mantes band in New Jersey had declined to a total of 50 or 60 men, women, and children. This was a substantial decrease from Robert Evelyn's estimate thirty-seven years earlier that the band could muster 100 warriors, which meant the total population of this group was about

400 or 500. Alricks estimated that the *total* Delaware Indian *warrior strength* on both sides of the Delaware River in 1671 had declined to 1,000.[4]

In 1697 Captain John Hance Tillman (Steelman) reported as follows to the Maryland Council regarding the Delaware Indian population:

That the Delaware Indians live at Minguannan about nine miles from the head of Elke river & fifteen miles from Christeen & thirty miles from Susquahanah river & *are about three hundred red men* & are tributary to the Senecars and Susquehannahs fifty of them living at Minguhanan & the rest upon Brandywine and Upland Creeks.[5] (Italics added)

Steelman's estimate of three hundred Delaware warriors obviously did not include a warrior count of the bands still living on the upper Delaware River in the environs of Easton, Pennsylvania, those remaining in northern New Jersey, and elsewhere beyond the territory with which he was familiar. At the time he made this estimate, Steelman said the Delawares from the Minguannan village (located on White Clay Creek) were at the head of the Chesapeake on a hunting trip and were temporarily camped with the Minquas. This is further evidence that the ancient enmity between Delawares and Minquas had given way to friendly relations.

The Delawares seem to have had much greater difficulty getting along with the English settlers than with Dutch or Swedes, even though there was considerable friction with the Swedes during Printz's administration. The extant records, which are incomplete, altogether too sparse, and reflect the English viewpoint, suggest that there was always trouble when English and Delawares were brought into contact. "When the English come," the Delaware sachems were reported as saying, "they drive them from their lands." [6] The Delawares were familiar with the harassment in Maryland of their Algonkian brethren, the Nanticoke, Choptank, and Conoy, and the persecution of the Powhatan tribes of Virginia under English administrations. The result was that anti-English sentiment took root at a very early date, and the Delawares became suspicious of the motives of all English colonists.

The Maryland colonists, especially those living along Bush and Gunpowder rivers, were in an area where "foreign," i.e., non-Maryland, Indians such as the Seneca, Minquas, Shawnee, and Delaware, frequently were seen in their canoes or log dugouts. The Marylanders knew the Delawares as the Mattawas (also spelled Mathes and Mathwas), a designation they picked up from the Nanticoke, which in Nanticoke dialect had the unfavorable connotation of someone who was bad. Some of the Delawares went to Maryland to hunt and also to satisfy their curiosity about what was going on in the Indian villages and white settlements. Young Delawares, like most adolescent Indian males, were notorious wanderers, usually traveling in small parties, and they were no less inclined to mischief than carefree youth of other races or nationalities. If they had been white lads the settlers would have had a different attitude toward them, but to the Marylanders all "foreign" Indians, particularly those carrying guns, were potential enemies. There was adequate justification for their fears, because of the property damage and personal injury many of the settlers had sustained from attacks by Maryland Indians, some of whom had been officially declared "enemies of the Province." The problem was that a Maryland settler couldn't distinguish hostile Indians from peaceful ones, unless he allowed them to come close enough to identify themselves, and there was grave danger in being exposed to that risk.

In the spring of 1661 a party of Delaware hunters had a confrontation with several Maryland planters along Gunpowder River. A Minquas party had previously robbed one of the farms, killing the settler's wife and livestock, and the Delawares were evidently mistaken as Minquas. Seeking revenge, the planters shot at them, overturned their dugout, and killed one of the Indians as they swam ashore and fled into the woods. On their homeward route, the Delawares encountered four white travelers at a place known to them as Saquasehum on present Iron Hill near the Delaware-Maryland border. To avenge the death of their companion, they murdered the four whites who had done them no injury and stole their clothing and belongings.[7]

Shortly thereafter a second party of nine Delaware braves, who lived at Passayunk, made their way into Maryland and paddled down Bush River in two canoes. One of the canoes pulled up to the land, and as an Indian lad stepped ashore he was viciously attacked by a settler's dog. The Indian, in self-defense, shot the dog. At the sound of the gun the animal's owner appeared with several other white farmers. Indians and whites then began firing at each other, and in the exchange of shots one white man and five Indians were killed. One of the victims was the younger brother of Pinna, a chief of the Passayunk Delawares.[8] (*Pinna* can be translated as "Look," probably a nickname.)

In view of these incidents, the Maryland authorities were fearful of further violence, and Governor Philip Calvert invited Chief Pinna to attend a peace conference, which was held at Appoquinimink (near present Odessa, Delaware) on September 19, 1661. Prior to the meeting, Calvert had made a thorough investigation and found that the white planters had provoked the first incident, which resulted in the vengeance-murder of the four men on Iron Hill. Calvert felt that in order to achieve peace he must convince Pinna that the acts of the planters were illegal and did not have the sanction of the Maryland government. Through his interpreter, Pinna replied that "as he did believe all those outrages were committed by the English without order from the Governor and Councell soe he did assure the Governor and Councell that those revenges were taken by his Indians without his or any of his greate mens knowledge . . ."

Pinna went on to say that, notwithstanding the cruel deaths of his Indians, including his own brother, he was willing and desirous to enter into peace with the Maryland government. Treaties later negotiated with William Penn are often incorrectly referred to as the first between Delawares and Englishmen, but they were preceded by the treaty between Philip Calvert and Pinna made September 19, 1661, and quoted in full herewith:

Articles of peace and amity concluded betwixt the honorable Philip Calvert Esq. Governor Henry Coursey Secretary and Mr. John Bateman Councellor on the behalfe of the Lord Proprietary of this Province of Maryland and Pinna King of Pickhattomitta on the behalfe of the Passayonke Indians on the other parte (viz.)

Imprimis that there shall be a perpetuall peace betwixt the people of Maryland and the Passayoncke Indians

2[ly] It is agreed betwixt the abovesaid partyes that in case any English man for the future shall happen to finde any Passayoncke Indian killing either Cattle or Hoggs that then it shall be lawfull for the English to kill the said Indian.

3[ly] It is agreed betwixt the abovesaid partyes that in case any Indian or Indians shall happen to kill any English man for the future (which God forbid) that they the said Indian with all the company of Indians with him which consented to the said murder shall be delivered up to the

English there to be pceeded against according to the lawe of this Province.

4^{ly} It is further agreed betwixt the abovesaid partyes that in case any English man shall happen to run amongst the Passayoncke Indians that the said Indians bring them to Peter Meyors and there for every English man that they shall deliver they shall Receive one Matchcoate[9]

The disharmony between Delawares and English was not confined to Maryland during the Duke of York era; the Delawares living in New York, New Jersey, Pennsylvania, and Delaware were also involved. One source of friction was the way the white farmers allowed their cattle to run loose and unattended in the woods and fields. The Delawares had never fenced their villages or cornfields, and there were numerous incidents when a white farmer's cattle wandered into an Indian village and foraged in the native crops. The Duke's government enacted laws that cautioned farmers to keep their cattle from destroying the Indian cornfields "where they have a right to plant," and the colonists were told to encourage the natives to fence their fields, assisting them if necessary. This was wishful thinking because, if there was need for any fences to be erected, the Indians believed that the pales should be built around the animals, since a fence around a cornfield didn't exclude cattle and swine from nosing around their wigwams.

Other inflammatory incidents along the Delaware River during the Duke of York's government included a number of murders of both whites and Indians, numerous thefts, several cases of arson, and even the rape of a white woman by a Delaware Indian.[10] Perhaps the most provocative was the murder of two servants of Peter Alricks on Burlington Island, then known as Matinicum Island, which almost caused an open war with the Indians. The culprits were two Mantes Indians, Tashiowycam and Wywannattamo, and their crime was the result of Tashiowycam's sister suddenly falling ill and dying. A contagion befell the white settlements in 1658–59, spreading fever and sickness that affected both adults and children, and many children died. This epidemic, which spread from whites to Indians, may have been the cause of the girl's death. Tashiowycam told other Indians, who reported it to Alricks, that a Manito had killed his sister and that he would avenge her death by slaying the Christians. He and his companion then assaulted Alricks's two servants, evidently while they were working in the fields, murdering them in cold blood. Retribution, the reader will note, consisted of *two* males for the life of a female. The cruelty of the crime caused the English authorities to demand of the Mantes chief that the two Indians be apprehended and brought to New Castle to stand trial. The chief agreed and sent two of his followers to track down the assassins. One of the Indians found the criminals in hiding, and he shot one twice in the breast and killed him, but the other one escaped and fled into the woods. The body of the dead Indian was turned over to English authorities, who carried it to New Castle and hung it up in chains for public view.

The Mantes chief came to town with a number of his young men to show them by the example of the dead Indian what would happen if they killed any Englishmen. The chief promised the authorities that "if any other murder were committed by the Indians upon the Christians that they would bring the murderer to us," and for his cooperation the chief was given five matchcoats.[11]

There was much talk of reprisals during the time the Indian murderers were being sought, and the fear of a general Indian uprising spread terror among all the colonists on both sides of the river. A blockhouse was hastily erected in New Castle, since the old Dutch fort was then in decay, to help protect the town against a possible Indian attack. Governor Francis Lovelace called an executive conference in New York because he was concerned "how a Warr may be prosecuted on those Villaines." [12] Cooler heads prevailed, and it was decided that, not only were the available military forces inadequate to withstand an Indian assault, but there would be irreparable loss of crops and cattle if the Indians were provoked to attack. The execution of one of the Indian murderers was a sort of retribution that appeased the authorities, at least temporarily, but this incident, among others, caused strained relations between the settlers and the Delawares to continue.

In 1674 the Duke of York sent a new governor to his colony—Major Edmund Andros, who proved to be the most energetic of the English governors and one of the most perceptive in his grasp of Indian affairs. Andros fully realized that peaceful relations with the natives were necessary to secure the interests of the British empire in the New World. He not only inherited the trouble with the Delawares, but there were other problems based on native rivalries that his predecessors, Colonel Richard Nicolls and Governor Lovelace, had not fully understood: the ancient feud between the Mahican and the Mohawk in the Hudson Valley; discontent among the Algonkian bands in the vicinity of Manhattan and Long Island, as a result of earlier mistreatment by the Dutch; the fact that King Philip's War was just about to break out among the New England tribes; and that the Five Nations war parties were harassing the Minquas on the Susquehanna and the Delawares in the upper Delaware Valley. Andros may have been the first Englishman in a high government position to appreciate the important role the Five Nations could play in aboriginal society. He recognized that, not only were the Five Nations a source of the lucrative fur trade, but that Iroquois warriors could constitute a protective barrier against any attacks on the English in New York by the French of Canada and the French-allied western Indians.

In their intercourse with the Indians, the Dutch had developed the concept that an imaginary chain held them and the native tribes together in a bond of friendship that could never be broken. This imagery caught the fancy of the Indians, who must have been awed when they saw the first unbreakable iron chain carried on a Dutch vessel and impressed with its strength in contrast to their own rope made of vines or plaited grass. Andros carried the metaphor further than the Dutch by associating it with a covenant by which the Five Nations and the English were so welded together that "if the very thunder should breake upon the Covenant Chain, it would not break asunder." [13]

Andros and his successor, Thomas Dongan (who was governor of New York from 1682 to 1688), both continued to brighten the Covenant Chain, and each did his utmost to persuade the Five Nations chiefs to declare themselves subjects of the King of England, offering to give them the same loving care and military protection that the King accorded his other loyal subjects.

The attempt to bring the Five Nations into the British empire as subjects of the King was unrealistic and was not supported by the Iroquois themselves, who did not believe it was to their best economic interests to do so. The Five Nations consistently acted in their own interests, declared their independence of both England and France, and even entered into formal peace treaties with both nations. Although they tried to hold to a neutral position, the Five Nations developed a personal affection for Andros, calling him *Corlaer* (a term they used when addressing a succession of later New York governors), their rendition of the surname of Dutchman Arent Van Curler, who had been "esteemed deare" among them. From the Five Nations sachems and councilors Andros learned how forest statecraft was conducted—the use of metaphoric language; the slow progress of diplomacy, because each area of discussion had to be translated into the Indian tongue; and the need to allow time for the Indians to withdraw from meetings to deliberate before giving their answers. Above all he learned the importance of using strings and belts of wampum beads without which no negotiations could be conducted with any of the eastern tribes.

On May 13, 1675, Andros arranged a treaty conference at New Castle, attended by government officials and four Delaware chiefs from the New Jersey side of the river representing the bands who were most hostile to the English. These chiefs were identified in the records as Renowewan of Sawkin, Manickty and Ipan Kickan of Rancokeskill, and Ket-marius of Soupnapka. Andros declared his desire to be friendly with them and his willingness to protect them. He told them that the Indians must not kick beasts or swine belonging to English farmers when they trespassed in their fields, and that he would see that justice was done in the event the Indians suffered any damage to their crops. The Indians were impressed, and Renowewan then rose and unfolded a long belt of fifteen rows of wampum beads, which he placed at Andros's feet as a token of friendship. Another chief presented a second belt of twelve rows of wampum as evidence of the amity that should exist between Indians and the English. Andros replied that he would retain the belts, properly tagged, as messages of a continuance of peace, and he presented the chiefs with four coats and four "lapp-cloathes." [14]

Wampum belts became widely used by the Delawares to commemorate important events, such as the signing of peace treaties or the sale of lands. Stylized human figures and simple geometric designs were often worked into a pattern with white and purple beads, and the mnemonic designs had a special meaning for those Indians trained to read and interpret them. The white authorities usually tagged the belts with written descriptions of their significance for future reference, and the Indians often retained a duplicate of the belts as their record of the transaction. Years later, Heckewelder wrote that, for the purpose of refreshing their own memories and of instructing their most capable and promising young men, the chiefs assembled their people once or twice a year to review the wampum records.

The belts were taken in order one by one, and the chief would "read" their meanings aloud, sentence by sentence, as he scanned the belts, faithfully repeating the discourse that had taken place at the time the belts had been exchanged. The so-called keeper of the wampum, usually a chieftain, had the stewardship of all of the wampum belts covering transactions with which his people were concerned. Individual wampum beads were also used as a medium of exchange among whites and Indians. On June 24, 1673, the Duke of York proclaimed six white beads equal in value to three black beads, the value being set at one stiver, or a penny.[15]

The white population continued to grow as additional English settlers took up lands on the New Jersey side of the Delaware River, the territory there having been granted by the Duke of York to two of his favorites, Sir John Berkeley and Sir George Carteret, who were eager to colonize. On July 20, 1672, Carteret granted seven hundred acres to Edmund Cantwell and Johannes de Haes, with the provision that they should first extinguish the Indian title. On February 8, 1673, the two purchasers paid the Indian proprietors, Sospanninck and Wicknaminck, two matchcoats, two axes, two bars of lead, four handfuls of powder, two knives, some paint and one-half "Anker of Drinke" to obtain clear title.[16] Thereafter, other Delaware Indians living in New Jersey also sold lands to white buyers. When John Fenwick seated a Quaker colony along Salem Creek, there was a further increase in the New Jersey white population. On the opposite side of the Delaware at New Castle, and along Cedar Creek, Duck Creek, St. Jones River, and the Whorekill, other English families started to take up land. The Dutch, Swedes, and Finns, who had declared their allegiance to the Duke of York, were also growing in numbers as their families increased, which meant that more and more whites were thrown into contact with the Indians. Despite the increased number of settlers, Andros was able to maintain good relations with the Delawares, and on September 22, 1675, he welcomed a delegation of Delaware chiefs at New York, promising to visit them at their campfires on his next trip to the Delaware River.[17]

On May 11, 1676, an English official at New Castle reported that the Delaware Indians were as civil as he had ever known them to be, and that they were peacefully planting and hunting, causing no trouble.[18] It seemed that Andros's policy of fair treatment of the natives was beginning to show results, and the English authorities were following a different policy with regard to Indian land ownership than had been the case in Maryland and Virginia. According to English law, the Duke of York, as the royal proprietor, had the right to issue patents for the disposition of lands covered by his charter without giving any consideration to the Indians living and hunting on the lands. Nevertheless, Andros and his successors required the patentee to make a settlement on the Indian owners in order to extinguish native title. This was done out of prudence, to avoid later trouble and misunderstanding, and to soothe the consciences of the purchasers and the government, who did not want to be confronted later by Indians claiming their lands had been stolen from them. This resulted in a curious situation, because individual English patentees thus paid Indian owners for tracts that were part of the lands the Indians had sold to Swedish and Dutch buyers three or four decades earlier. Of course, many of the original Indian vendors were deceased and a new generation of Indians lived and hunted on the lands.

By this time, the native mind must have been able to grasp the white man's concept of outright land sale, since there had been considerable friction over land matters for a number of years. Typical of the negotiations to extinguish Indian title by English patentees are the records that have been preserved covering the dealings with four different Indians for lands in the present state of Delaware. Starting February 20, 1674, Delaware Indian chief Mehocksett, from Cohansinck in New Jersey (present Cohansey River), participated in six different transactions covering the confirmation of title for lands between Appoquinimink and Duck creeks. The deeds refer to Mehocksett as the "Indian lord" and "natural owner" of lands that were obviously his own hunting territory as well as that of his family or perhaps his band. Although he resided in New Jersey, his hunting territories also lay in Delaware. For a tract containing several thousand acres, one white buyer paid the chief "one gun, four handfuls of powder, three matchcoats, one ancker of liquor, and one kettle." The gun, like most of those traded with the Indians, was probably a cheap weapon, which is why so many of them were soon in need of repair.

A matchcoat was not a coat with sleeves; it was the way the Algonkian word *matchcore* was etymologized by the English. The Indian word was originally applied to a winter robe or cloak made of skins with the fur on the interior side; whereas the European matchcoat was simply a piece of coarse woolen cloth, dyed in a color to suit the

Indians' tastes. The cloth was draped around the shoulders and upper parts of the body during cold weather as one might wrap in a blanket, and it was also used as a coverlet at night.

From another purchaser Mehocksett received "two half anckers of drink, one blanket, one matchcoat, two axes, two knives, two double handfuls of powder, two bars of lead and one kettle" for a tract consisting of several thousand acres.[19]

Mehocksett's brother Petequoque, who was called Christian, probably because of his conversion to Christianity, was referred to as the "lord and owner" of a hunting territory called Missawakett lying between Duck Creek and the Murderkill, south of and coterminous with his brother's lands. He, too, signed a number of deeds extinguishing titles from his territory to various individuals, and received varying quantities of English merchandise in return. On September 20, 1676, Petequoque sold two thousand acres on the south side of Duck Creek to an Englishman for eight bottles of rum, three matchcoats, four and a half yards of cheap cloth, and some buttons and thread. He also agreed to assist the Englishman to protect the property in the event other Indians trespassed and, if the new owner's cattle or hogs strayed into the woods, Petequoque agreed to drive them back to the plantation. There can be little question that Petequoque understood that, as specifically expressed in the deed of sale, he was not only relinquishing the right of occupancy but was also ceding the use rights of "hawking, hunting, fishing and fowling," as stipulated in the deed. In fact, the document clearly stated that "myselfe or no other Indian shall hunt or kill either deare, fish, foule or any other game either wild or tame upon the said land forever." There is no reason to doubt that Petequoque and the other native owners knew they were permanently conveying their lands to the English buyers.

Adjoining Petequoque's lands to the south was the hunting territory of the Delaware Indian Socoroccet, also bounded by named streams, and he, too, deeded portions of this territory to a number of English buyers. Socoroccet also received matchcoats, powder, and shot for his land, and in one transaction a cotton waistcoat was included. But he did not receive any liquor—possibly he may have been an abstainer.

South of Socoroccet's lands were those belonging to the Indian sachem named Parritt, one of the last of the Sickoneysinck chiefs to cling to his native land. Parritt complained on January 10, 1681, to the magistrates of the English court at Lewes (as the Whorekill came to be called) that settlers had moved on his lands without giving him satisfaction. The court ordered that anyone who took up any of Parritt's lands should extinguish title by paying him one matchcoat for each parcel of six hundred acres or less, and two matchcoats for quantities in excess of six hundred acres. If anyone refused to pay, the court instructed the sheriff to force the collection.

Here at the mouth of Delaware Bay on the site of the destroyed Swanendael, the little town of Lewes became permanently rooted, and the influx of new settlers brought strong pressures on the handful of Sickoneysincks that remained. The band had been much reduced, starting with the earlier Minquas attacks and the white man's diseases, which must have decimated their villages. Some of the Indian families may have moved upriver to join the northern Delaware bands; or more likely they went over to New Jersey, because the records state that in 1671 the majority of the Indians were then living on the New Jersey side of the river.[20] The Sickoneysincks ceased to exist as a separate native community during the Duke of York period, although a few conservatives like old Parritt were still living, but for all practical purposes the Indians of lower Delaware Bay had vanished. The western shore of the Delaware River was now populated by white colonists from Lewes on the south to the Schuylkill on the north. The population was not heavy, to be sure. It consisted of only a few thousand families of Swedes, Finns, Dutch, and English, but their occupation reduced the native hunting territories, and the Indians had difficulty finding wild game. Some of the natives moved north to join their brethren at Shackamaxon, at present Kensington, where the Delawares had also given temporary haven to a number of Minquas warriors who had fled from the Susquehanna to escape their enemies.[21]

Although the records are vague about how the end came, the Minquas were broken up and dispersed, and their former ally, the English of Maryland, turned against them. In the end, the Five Nations Iroquois, with English support, were victorious, and the military power of the Minquas ceased to exist. Some Minquas survivors were absorbed by the Five Nations, others went west, and a few families remained on the lower Susquehanna at a town known as Conestoga near present Lancaster. The Five Nations maintained that they defeated the Minquas, and as a result of this defeat they claimed ownership of the entire Susquehanna Valley.[22]

The same method of extinguishing Indian title that was followed

in the state of Delaware also characterized relations with the Delawares in New Jersey. The records relating to the settlement by John
Fenwick clearly show how the Indians slowly dispossessed themselves.
Fenwick himself on November 17, 1675, purchased a tract from
"Mahawksey [Mehocksett, the same chief who owned land on the
opposite side of the river] Allowayes, Myopponey, Saccutorey, Ne-
conis, and his mother Necosshesseo, and Monutt" bounded by the
Delaware River, Game Creek (a tributary to Salem River), and Can-
nahockinck Creek. On February 12 and March 14, 1767, Fenwick
negotiated additional deeds with the Indians to extinguish their title
in the same area.[23]

The published *New Jersey Archives* contain numerous references to
the purchases made by white buyers (as well as land purchases made
at an earlier date) who obtained title to the Indian lands.[24] It seemed
to the Indians that the settlers were impelled by an urge to ruin the
woods, the habitat of the birds and animals. It probably never occurred
to the colonists, as they cut down the trees to obtain logs for building
cabins, barns, and fences—and to make cleared land for fields and pastures, so necessary for their survival—that they were destroying the
means by which the Indians obtained a livelihood. In so doing, they
were contributing, perhaps unknowingly, to a breakdown of native
society.

Despite Governor Andros's efforts to maintain harmony with the
Indians, and to prevent whites from debauching them with liquor,
the laws continued to be broken. An English settlement called Crewcorne was established near the "falls of the Delaware" not far from
present Trenton. The inhabitants were soon complaining that they
were aggrieved by drunken Delaware Indians who "break our fences
and steales our Corn & breaks our windows & dores and Carryes away
our goods, and worryed 3 of our chatle in one day with their dogs,
which oppression if it Continues will forc som of us from our plantations, we being very weake at ye prsent for rsistance & ignorant in their
Lingo whereby we Can not appease them when they are mad with
drink . . ."[25]

The residents pleaded that strong liquor be "wholly suppressed
amongst us," because the laws against vending liquor at retail were
flagrantly violated by one Gilbert Wheeler, who operated a tavern at
Crewcorne. The Upland Court later fined Wheeler four pounds for
selling liquor at retail in small quantities in disregard of the law, but

as long as the Indians could pay for the intoxicants there was always a white vendor ready to accommodate them.

It is uncertain whether overindulgence in alcohol or smallpox was the principal cause of the rapid decline in the Indian population along the Delaware River. At a conference held at Burlington, one of New Jersey's early settlers, Thomas Budd, was told by a Delaware Indian that three separate smallpox epidemics had ravaged the native villages. The Indian said the first epidemic occurred in his grandfather's time, a second in his father's time, and a third, which he himself well remembered, spread through the Indian settlements. With each recurrence of the disease bringing disastrous results, the Indians believed the whites wanted to get rid of them and deliberately infected them by selling them matchcoats that had been exposed to smallpox germs.[26] The Indians were helpless to treat the disease; the incantations of the medicine men, the sweat baths, and herb cures brought no relief to the victims. There were other factors which caused deaths and contributed to the decrease in Indian population, such as tuberculosis, venereal disease, malnutrition due to removals and being subjected to unaccustomed conditions, as well as low vitality resulting from mental depression caused by white abuses.

NOTES—CHAPTER 7

1. *Charter to William Penn and the Laws of the Province of Pennsylvania* (containing the Duke of York's "Book of Laws") Harrisburg, 1879, pp. 32, 58.

2. Ibid., p. 32.

3. Allen W. Trelease, *Indian Affairs in Colonial New York*, Ithaca, 1960, p. 185.

4. *NYCD*, vol. 12, p. 484.

5. *Maryland Archives*, vol. 19, p. 520.

6. *NYCD*, vol. 12, p. 493.

7. *Maryland Archives*, vol. 3, pp. 412–16.

8. Ibid., p. 414.

9. Ibid., pp. 431–33. On August 30, 1663, Governor Charles Calvert entered into a second treaty at New Amstel with "Hocpeckquomeck, Lennoswewigh, & Colaccameck, Kings of the Delaware Bay Indians by their Embassadors, Monickta, Chehoock, & Tichacoon"; ibid., p. 486.

10. These incidents are all described in *NYCD*, vol. 12, section entitled "Sixth Period," p. 457 and passim. There is reference to a woman and her children being murdered by Indians at Parde Hooke; p. 488. It is a

myth that relations between Delawares and Swedes were also always amicable, whereas blood was shed on both sides.

11. Ibid., pp. 484–85; cf. Samuel Hazard, *Annals of Pennsylvania*, Philadelphia, 1850, p. 393.

12. NYCD, vol. 12, p. 485

13. *Maryland Archives*, vol. 5, pp. 256–58. On September 24, 1659, a Mohawk chief told a group of Dutchmen, "Brothers, sixteen years have now passed [i.e., 1643] since we made the first treaty of friendship between you and all the Dutch, whom we joined together with an iron chain"; NYCD, vol. 13, p. 112. For reference to the Dutch forging a chain with the Scaticook as early as 1618, I am indebted to Francis P. Jenning's paper, unpublished at this writing, titled, "The Constitutional Evolution of the Covenant Chain." Dr. Jennings is the author of a second unpublished paper, "How the Covenant Chain Changed Direction, 1677–1732." These papers cover the subject so completely that there is little to add.

14. NYCD, vol. 12, p. 523. Renowewan is referred to elsewhere in 1677 as the sachem of the "most quiet" Indians on the Delaware; *Upland Court Records*, Historical Society of Pennsylvania, Philadelphia, 1860, p. 49. Mrs. Dean translates his name as "A manly Man."

15. *Pennsylvania Archives*, 2d series, vol. 5, 1890, p. 659; see also Francis P. Jennings, "Glory, Death, and Transfiguration: The Susquehannock Indians in the Seventeenth Century," *Proceedings of the American Philosophical Society*, vol. 112, no. 1, 1968, pp. 15–53.

16. *New Jersey Archives*, ed. Wm A. Whitehead, vol. 1, Newark, 1880, p. 111.

17. NYCD, vol. 12, p. 541.

18. Ibid., p. 545.

19. The deed conveyances by Mehocksett and the other three chiefs are enumerated and discussed by Leon de Valinger, Jr., *Indian Land Sales in Delaware*, Wilmington, 1941, pp. 5–9.

20. NYCD, vol. 12, p. 493; "most of the Indians living upon his [Carteret's] side [of the river]."

21. *Upland Court Records*, p. 49. There were a number of other deeds obtained from Indians along the western shore of the Delaware River which space does not permit discussing but which follow the same pattern.

22. Although I agree with most historians that the Five Nations defeated the Susquehannock, this idea has been challenged by Jennings in "Glory, Death, and Transfiguration," *Proceedings of the American Philosophical Society*, vol. 112, no. 1, Feb. 15, 1968, p. 21.

23. Wm. Nelson, ed., *New Jersey Archives*, Paterson, 1899, vol. 21, p. 559.

24. Ibid., passim, for other Indian purchases in New Jersey; see also vol. 2, ibid., for listing of early deeds in East and West Jersey. On Sept. 23,

1675, Andros bought land from four Delaware chiefs in the vicinity of the falls of the Delaware; *Pennsylvania Archives*, 2d series, 1890, vol. 5, pp. 703–4. A number of the New Jersey deeds are transcribed in Frank H. Stewart, *Indians of Southern New Jersey*, Woodbury, N.J., 1932, pp. 60–87.

25. *NYCD*, vol. 12, pp. 658–59. The liquor laws had been changed, and it was then illegal to retail to the Indians in quantities less than two gallons; ibid., p. 526. For the court entry regarding Wheeler's fine, see *Upland Court Records*, p. 194.

26. Samuel Smith, *The History of the Colony of Nova-Caesaria, or New Jersey*, Burlington, N.J., 1877, note on p. 100.

8

The Delawares and William Penn

The government along the Delaware River changed again in 1682 with the arrival of William Penn to claim lands granted him by Charles II and to take possession of the three lower counties, which he leased from the Duke of York for ten thousand years. The entire western shore of the Delaware and the land lying between the river and Lord Baltimore's Maryland province again felt another political upheaval, which was to affect colonists and Indians alike. Penn's grant embraced territory as far north as the 43d parallel—considerably beyond the present New York-Pennsylvania line—and, because of the movement of Indians from New Jersey to Pennsylvania, the large majority of Delawares soon fell under the jurisdiction of Penn's government.

Actually, Penn's influence was felt to some extent in New Jersey, for Edward Byllynge, a Quaker who acquired a large part of that state, appointed three trustees to administer his territory, one of whom was William Penn, who served *in absentia*. "The Concessions and Agreements" issued as a constitution for the New Jersey colony anticipated the later "Frame of Government" with which Penn launched the province of Pennsylvania, and both documents included recognition of the rights of native Indians.

Penn's "holy experiment," as he termed his colony, was essentially a trial democracy, because he promised unconditional religious and civil freedom to colonists who were to be governed by laws of their own making. The details of the rights guaranteed the colonists have been fully discussed in numerous works; suffice it to say that the foremost reason Penn became interested in American colonization was to provide asylum for his own Quaker fellow sufferers and other victims of religious intolerance. Unlike the earlier Dutch and Swedes, the followers of Penn did not come to America primarily in search of wealth. Settlers came to the colony principally to find peace and justice, relief from religious persecution; and secondarily for better economic conditions. Not only Quakers but people of other religious denominations, such as the German sectists, were welcomed to Pennsylvania, and they arrived in great numbers during the eighteenth century.

The principle of goodwill and friendship toward all men lay at the very root of Quaker belief, and in this context it is not difficult to understand why Penn's treatment of the Indians differed from that of his predecessors. He was determined, even before he left England or had seen his first Indian, to treat them as brothers and win their confidence and friendship. This sprang from his deep sense of humanity and a conviction that the Indians, no less than the whites, were children of God, entitled to love and respect. Before coming to Pennsylvania, Penn sent a letter, to his commissioners who preceded him, to be translated into the Algonkian dialect and read to the Indians. The following excerpt epitomizes his whole philosophy of Indian relations: ". . . the king of the Countrey where I live, hath given unto me a great Province therein, but I desire to enjoy it with your *Love and Consent* that we may always live together as *Neighbours and friends* . . ." [1] (Italics added)

So much has been written about Penn's exemplary treatment of the Indians that it would appear little more remains to be said; still, I do not believe the significance of the word *Consent*, as he used it, has been fully explained or appreciated. The use of this one word signified a radical change in Indian colonial policy; and used in connection with the word *Love*, which was also applied in a new connotation in relation to the "savages," it had a deep meaning in Indian affairs.

The British Crown, long fortified with its traditional divine power, completely ignored and, in fact, denied the Indian tribes any ownership rights to lands in the New World "discovered" by English navigators or explorers, or navigators in English employ. Basic in the territorial concepts of the Stuarts, who occupied the throne during the critical period of American settlement, was that land not yet discovered nor yet in the possession "of any Christian Prince, County

or State" belonged to its discoverer, irrespective of its native population. If the savages living on land discovered by Englishmen made any
effort to oppose the exploitation of their country, they were to be
treated as enemies of England. To Charles II the idea that he should
demean the throne to obtain the consent of heathen savages so that
Englishmen might occupy land belonging to the Crown by right of
discovery was preposterous. To deny the right of the King to newly
discovered land, as Attorney General John T. Kempe later informed
Sir William Johnson, "is in Effect denying his Right to Rule there." [2]

Under this legal interpretation, the lands granted to Penn previously belonged to the Crown, and authority for their disposition,
under the law as it was then accepted, was vested exclusively in the
King. Under this legalistic concept, the Delaware Indians had no
more right to the lands on which they had lived for many years than
did birds flitting in the trees or wild animals roaming the forests.
When Penn insisted that the Indians give their "Consent" to his
occupation of lands in Pennsylvania, he recognized their prior right
as legal owners. During the Duke of York period, it became the usual
practice for landowners to extinguish Indian title to lands patented to
them by the Duke, which, in effect, implied a recognition of Indian
ownership. In the Duke's government, this was an individual matter
between the Indian owners and the patentee who had received his
patent from the Duke. In no way could it be interpreted to weaken
the position of the King or the Duke of York as absolute owners, with
or without Indian consent. It wasn't the King or the Duke who found
it necessary to extinguish Indian title, but one of their subjects. In
Penn's case it became an official policy of his government, under the
"Love and Consent" clause, to extinguish native title before any lands
were patented to colonists.

The charter for Pennsylvania that Charles II issued under the Great
Seal, and the two leases and deeds of feoffment for the three lower
counties which Penn received from James, Duke of York, in no way
obligated Penn to acknowledge that the Indians had any land tenure
rights, and he had no legal responsibility to pay them anything for
their lands. Under the terms of his charter for Pennsylvania, Penn was
named "the true and absolute proprietary," committed only to the
extent of rendering the Crown a token payment of two beaver skins
on the first of January each year, and one-fifth of any gold or silver

ore found in his province. All the laws enacted in the province were to be transmitted to the King, who reserved the right to repeal those he did not favor. Penn possessed almost unlimited power over the Indians living in his province, but it was a power he never invoked.

One section of the charter specifically stated that, because the country was so remote "and situate near many barbarous nations, the incursions as well of the savages themselves, as of other enemies, pirates and robbers," Penn was authorized, if it became necessary, to arm soldiers, make war against the Indians, and put captives to death under the laws of war. To a man of peace whose religion did not countenance wars or violence, Penn's conciliatory approach to the Indian problem was not through the use of armed force, for as he wrote, "Don't abuse them, but let them have Justice and you win them."

In addition to the "Love and Consent" clause in Penn's letter to the Indians, he told them he was sensible to the unkindness and injustice to which they had long been exposed and which had caused animosities and bloodshed. He promised them fair treatment, an opportunity for a redress of grievances, and, above all, peace. Penn knew that many of his predecessors had made idle promises to the Indians and that he must demonstrate his sincerity through his actions. He laid down a number of "conditions or concessions" for the guidance of both the colonists and his Quaker officials in their conduct in dealing with the Indians. If an Indian wronged a settler, the settler should not be his own judge but should carry his complaint to an official level to be adjusted. All Indians were to be entitled to the same liberty as the white settlers to improve the ground and to provide sustenance for their families. Goods traded to the Indians must be of the same quality as that sold in the marketplace, with no attempt to deceive the natives. If anyone by word or deed affronted or wronged an Indian, he should be subject to the same penalty under the law as if he had offended a white settler. In case of serious differences, a jury of six planters and six Indians would pass final judgment. This latter provision was more idealistic than practical, because trial by a jury of their peers was something the Indians did not understand; nevertheless, it is illustrative of Penn's desire to be fair with Indians and whites alike.

On the subject of liquor, Penn wrote as follows:

. . . they are an Extreordinary people; had not the Dutch, Sweeds, and English learn'd them drunkenness (in wch condition, they kill or burn one another) they had been very tractable, but Rum is so dear to them, yt for 6 penny worth of Rum, one may buy yt Furr from them, yt five Shillings, in any other Commodity shall not purchass. yet many of the old men, & some of ye young people will not touch with such Spirits; & Because in thos fitts they mischeif both themselves & our folks too, *I have forbid to sell them any*.[3] (Italics added)

Among the sections in William Penn's "Great Law" passed by the first legislative assembly of Pennsylvania on the 5th of the 10th month 1682, was a provision stating in part "that no person within this Province doe from hence forth presume to Sell or exchange any Rhum or brandy or any Strong Liquors at any time to any Indian within this Province & if any one shall offend therein ye person convicted Shall for every Such offence pay five pounds." [4]

Although the Pennsylvania Assembly could no more legislate sobriety among the Indians than it could prevent certain whites from engaging in illicit traffic in liquor, the reported violations were apparently less flagrant than in former years—at least for a little while. Enforcement was possible in Philadelphia, where merchants and traders were under the watchful eyes of the authorities, and in other well-policed towns, but unscrupulous traders continued to smuggle liquor into Indian villages without the knowledge of the Penn government, risking conviction and fine. A few years later, after Penn's return to England, members of the government had private financial interests in the Indian trade, and the authorities closed their eyes to violations of the law as traders hauled thousands of gallons of liquor to their eager Indian customers.

If Penn had remained in America, he would never have tolerated this debauchery, because his main concern was in uplifting the Indians. This is well illustrated in his land dealings wherein he attempted to reconcile his legal rights under British law with the principles of equity. Penn interpreted his charter as giving him preemptive rights to *buy* from the Indians the lands conveyed to him by the Crown. Although his charter from the King gave him clear title, he felt that this was intended to be invoked against rival white claimants, such as the Marylanders, New Englanders, Dutch, or Frenchmen. He believed that there could be no true ownership in clear conscience if he violated the natural rights of the original inhabitants, who were, in his opinion, the true owners of Pennsylvania. Thus the process of first extinguishing Indian title before the proprietor would transfer any lands to white settlers became a policy in Pennsylvania. This concept was embraced by the United States two hundred years later, when the government went to great pains to extinguish Indian title to lands west of the Ohio before it officially transferred those lands to American citizens.

Penn's acute and practical mind seems to have understood the underlying causes of earlier land controversies between Indians and whites, and he was well aware that a series of Indian "owners" often conveyed the same tracts, with ill-defined boundaries, to a succession of different white buyers. He not only recognized the Indian concept of land tenure but knew how it clashed with English common law. He also understood the frequent complaint made by the Delaware chiefs that certain white buyers purchased lands from Indian vendors who did not have the authority to sell those tracts.

The policy Penn decided to follow, under advice given him by Henry Compton, Bishop of London, was to extinguish title to the lands in his province through fair and honest negotiation, either with individual Indian owners or chieftains and great men representing the individual bands. He was careful not only to have the bounds of each tract clearly understood and recorded so far as it was possible to do so but also to make certain that all possible native claimants were paid to their satisfaction.

One of the problems in extinguishing Indian title was the paucity of knowledge about the geography of the country west of the Susquehanna River. Not until Indian traders pressed westward to the Alleghenies—and later to the Ohio River—was much known about how far the American continent extended. That there was a western sea, the Pacific, had been reported by the Powhatan Indians to the first English settlers in Virginia, but even experienced explorers like Captain John Smith thought that the Pacific was not far distant from Virginia. The Delaware Indians themselves were vague not only about the country to the west but also about the geographical limits of their own territory. They were aware that the lands of the Minquas lay west of them and those of the Five Nations north of them. But with no formal maps, there were no established geographical bounds to delineate the different areas of tribal sovereignty. Penn's Dutch and Swedish predecessors had made no effort to resolve this question, and some of the lands they purchased from the Delawares along the western side of the river either had unspecified western boundaries, or else the documents covering the transaction were vague—stating only that the western limit of the purchase was "as far as the land extended."

Penn himself had little information about the western boundary of his province, which, according to his charter, lay five degrees longitude west of the Delaware River, the eastern boundary. The location of the western bound, the nature of the terrain there, and whether or not it was occupied by Indians was unknown to Penn when the charter was granted. He knew only that this boundary was well beyond the Susquehanna River, and that the Delawares whose lands lay along the Delaware River and its tributaries had no claim to the western interior.

Prior to Penn's first voyage to America, he sent his cousin William Markham as his deputy and advance representative to handle various items of business pertaining to the colony and to prepare for his arrival. Through Markham's acts, the Delaware Indians were to gain their first impression of the new proprietor. Markham's first step was to seek the counsel of a Swede, Captain Lasse Cock, long experienced in Indian affairs, fluent in the Delaware dialect, and well regarded by the Delawares. At the time Cock lived at Shackamaxon (now the Kensington section of Philadelphia), where he had earlier purchased property. He summoned the Indians together and wined and dined them preparatory to the meeting with Markham.

At the conference held with the Delawares on July 15, 1682, Cock advised Markham on the nuances of native diplomacy, and he translated for both parties. At this meeting Markham, on behalf of William Penn, purchased from the Delaware Indians Idquayhon, Janottowe, Idquoqueywon, Sahoppe, Merkekowen, Oreckton, Nannacussey, Shaurwaughon, Swanpisse, Nahoosey, Tomackhickon, Westkekitt, and Tohawsiz—lands from the falls of the Delaware opposite Trenton extending to Neshaminy Creek in Bucks County, including three small islands in the river.[5] One of the reasons Markham wanted to extinguish Indian title to this particular tract was to obtain land for Penn's estate on the Delaware north of Philadelphia, where Pennsbury was later laid out. Penn's generosity was shown in the variety and quantity of merchandise Markham gave to the Indians:

350	fathoms of wampum half white, half black	24	pounds of red lead
20	white blankets	200	small mirrors
20	fathoms of stroudwater cloth	2	handsfull of fishhooks
60	fathoms of duffels	2	handsfull of needles
		40	pounds of shot
20	kettles, including four large ones	10	bundles of beads
20	guns	10	small saws
20	coats	12	drawing knives
40	shirts	4	anckers of tobacco
40	pair of stockings	2	anckers of rum
40	hoes	2	anckers of cider
40	axes	2	anckers of beer
2	barrels of powder	40	copper boxes
200	bars of lead	40	tobacco tongs
200	knives	2	small barrels of pipes
12	pair of shoes	40	pair of scissors
		40	combs
		100	awls
		300	guilders

Never before had the Delawares received such a wealth of goods in a land transaction, a quantity large enough to divide among all the members of the band. In fact, on the first day of the following August, Pytechay, Essepamachatte, and Kekerappamand—three chiefs who were owners of the island in the Delaware called Soepassincks but who were not present at the signing of the deed—appeared at Captain Lasse Cock's house to add their names. They, too, received their share of merchandise.

Some years later Delaware sachem Nutimus explained why a number of Indians were usually represented when a land purchase was made, and outlined the chieftain's role when owners of a family hunting territory disposed of their lands to the whites:

. . . when they sold, the Chief always with the Leave of the others undertook to sell & when he had agreed he called together the heads of the families who had any Right in the Land sold & divided among them Goods he got for the Land telling them for what they recd those Goods; then the Heads of the families again divide their portion among the Young people of the Family & inform them of the Sale & thus every individual, who have any right must be fully acquainted with the matter. Besides whenever a Sale is made, the Chief who sells calls the Chiefs of the Neighbouring Tribes who are his friends but have no right, in order to be Witnesses of the Sale & to make them remember it he gives them a Share of the Goods. So that no Land can be sold without all the Indians round being made acquainted with the Matter.[6]

With Indians from a number of locations represented in the initial purchases made by Markham, the news quickly spread to other Indian towns that the new proprietor was different from other Englishmen because he spoke from his lips and also from his heart. When Penn arrived at New Castle on the *Welcome* in the fall of 1682, his reputation had already preceded him, not only with the Indians, but also with the Swedish and Dutch population, whose land holdings he confirmed as he welcomed them as citizens of his province. (Penn remained in Pennsylvania until 1684, when business necessitated his return to England. In 1699 he returned for his second and last visit, and he again remained in Pennsylvania for two years.)

On his first visit, Penn initiated and personally participated in a number of land purchases from the Delaware Indians. The first of these took place on June 23, 1683, when he purchased land between Neshaminy and Pennypack creeks, contiguous to the lands Markham had purchased for him the previous year, from Metamequan and Tamany (whose name appears in the deed records and other accounts as Tamanen, Tamanans, Taminen, Taminent, and Tamanend). Penn consummated the purchase with the two sachems in the newly built Friends Meeting House in Philadelphia, and the Indians remained overnight after dining with him. The next day, which was a Sunday, he persuaded them to attend Quaker Meeting with him. In exchange for their lands, the two chiefs were given an assortment of shoes, stockings, lead, blankets, hoes, combs, knives, fishhooks, awls, scissors, needles, two guns, six coats, and five English hats.[7]

On the same day Penn extinguished title from four other Indians—Essepenaikes, Swanpees, Okettarickon, and Wessapoat—for lands running along Neshaminy Creek. Swanpees was the same chieftain (in a slightly different spelling, Swanpisse) who participated in the

previous sale to Markham. He and his native associates were satisfactorily compensated in trade goods; they also dined with the proprietor and attended Quaker Meeting with him as his guests. It is
of interest that, as stated in the deed, one of the bounds of the tract
they sold Penn was "to Run Two days Journey with an Horse up
into ye Country as ye sd River doeth go," a further example of the
inexact knowledge of the natural landmarks of the interior of Pennsylvania.[8]

On October 2, 1685, land lying between Chester Creek and a
stream known to the Indians as Quing Quingus (present Duck Creek
in Delaware) was purchased from several chiefs and great men (councilors). The western boundary of this purchase was given as a point
inland as far "as a man can ride in two days with a horse." [9] This
deed has often been interpreted by historians to mean that Duck
Creek was the southernmost boundary of Delaware Indian territory,
but this is incorrect. Penn and his agents did not feel it necessary to
extinguish Indian title to the lands south of Duck Creek because
Englishmen had already paid the Delawares for those lands during
the Duke of York period.

In addition to delineating the length of boundary lines in terms of
the time required to ride its length on horseback, another deed extinguishing Indian title to land that lay between Chester and Pennypack creeks refers to the northwesterly boundary point in the woods—
as far as a man could go in two days, presumably on foot.[10] This
deed was one of the forerunners of the more famous "Walking Purchase" discussed in the next chapter.

Obviously, not all the Indians named in the instruments herein
cited were chiefs, although there was a tendency on the part of white
scribes to identify all Indian sellers as "sakimas," perhaps because it
made the records appear more official. Actually, some of the native
vendors were "owners" of hunting territories, and others were councilors, who were present along with the chiefs when land sales were
consummated, in order to share the European merchandise which
was generously distributed by the recipients.

The other land purchases made by William Penn or his emissaries
from Delaware Indians (with names often written in different spellings each time they were recorded) have been enumerated in other
sources.[11] The important thing is that Penn systematically extinguished title to Indian lands along the western shore of the Dela-

ware River. These purchases included the heart of his colony—Philadelphia, Chester, Marcus Hook, Wilmington, New Castle—and in many cases he paid the Indians a second time for lands for which earlier Swedes or Dutch had compensated them. There was one important difference: When Penn paid the Indians for title to their lands, they clearly understood that *they were permanently conveying all ownership rights to him.* There was no longer any question of "use" rights, and it was understood that, thereafter, Penn was the absolute proprietor of any lands covered by an Indian deed.

It was never Penn's intention to dispossess the Indians, or to force them away from their homes on the lands he had purchased from them. As the owner of a vast expanse of territory, he delegated to his Commissioners of Property authority over the locations and the sizes of tracts that were sold to white settlers. The commissioners recognized that lands on which the Indian villages were situated were reserved for their use by the proprietor and should not be sold while the Indians still resided there.

As long as Penn lived, he held to the belief that Indians and whites could live together in harmony in his province if they were treated as equals, and during his lifetime the Indians had no complaints over land matters that were not resolved to their satisfaction. In one instance, Penn arranged for the resettlement of a number of Delaware Indian families by moving them from Ridley and Crum creeks to a tract of five hundred acres between Newtown Square and West Chester known as the Okehocking Reservation, which he set aside for their use in 1701. The title deed given chiefs Pokhais, Sepopawny, and Muttagoopa transferred perpetual ownership to them and their descendants, but if they moved from the tract it was to revert to Penn.[12]

When Delaware chiefs Seketarius, Kalehickop, Nochcotamen, Toonis (Town), Leleghanan, and Wippais sold their territory between the Christina River and Chester Creek to Penn in 1683, they reserved for their own use, with Penn's agreement, lands along the Brandywine one mile on each side of the creek. This reserved land included their village—Queonemysing in the Big Bend—and also gave them access to the stream for fishing, and the privilege of hunting in the woods that bordered it.[13]

Apart from Indian approval of these two reservations, Penn earned the respect of the Delawares in many other ways. For example, unlike the earlier colonial administrators, he developed a studious interest in their language. "I have made it my business to understand it, that I might not want an Interpreter on any occasion," he wrote. "And I must say, that I know not a Language spoken in Europe that hath words of more sweetness in Accent and Emphasis, than theirs." [14]

The Delawares devised their own name for Penn; they called him Miquon, which to them meant quill (a pen), for which the Iroquois equivalent was Onas. The latter became the preferred form, and eventually it was used by all Indians in referring to the proprietor. In fact, in their metaphorical language the Delawares used "Brother Onas" when addressing Penn and, after his death, as a generic referring to the Pennsylvania government and its successive administrations.

In Mattahorn's dealings with Stuyvesant and Pinna's negotiations with Philip Calvert, both proved to be capable diplomats—not ignorant savages, as the Indians were usually characterized by early writers. After numerous dealings with the Delaware chiefs Penn said: "I have never seen more natural Sagacity . . . and he will deserve the Name of Wise, that Outwits them in any Treaty about a thing they understand . . . In treaties about land, or traffic [trade], I find them deliberate in council, and as designing as I have ever observed among the politest of our Europeans." [15] This was a sage observation, because time and again the Delawares proved to be excellent diplomats and negotiators.

In describing his conferences with the Indians, Penn wrote that the chief sat in the middle, the members of his council—the old and wise men—on either side. When a man rose to speak, the other Indians sat silently, gravely, and attentively until he was finished, and the discourses were usually lengthy. When a proposition was made, the Indians deliberated, and no answer was given by the chief until the subject was carefully weighed by the council. "Nothing of Moment is undertaken," Penn wrote, "be it War, Peace, Selling of Land or Traffick, without advising with them; and which is more, with the Young Men too. 'Tis admirable to consider how Powerful the Kings are, and yet how they move by the Breath of their People."

Penn traveled extensively in the eastern portion of his province, visiting the Indians in their towns. In one of his letters he describes a visit to the headwaters of the Schuylkill to call on "Tenoughan, the Captain General of the Clan of [Delaware] Indians of those Parts." Penn found the Indian chieftain ill with a fever and in much pain, and during his visit his native host underwent a sweat bath treatment, assisted by his wife. Penn made note of such details as how the squaw cut a hole through the ice in the river into which her sweating husband plunged after crawling out of the stone bagnio. After drying and warming himself by the fire in his wigwam, Tenoughan arose and "fell to getting us our Dinner, seeming to be as easie and well in Health, as at any other time." [16]

In the lore that has been handed down about Penn are stories of his riding from one Indian town to another on a white horse; sitting on the ground with the Indians in their villages, sharing their venison, roasted acorns, and hominy; joining some of the young braves in leaping and other athletic contests; entertaining groups of Delawares in the downstairs hall at his Pennsbury mansion; and allowing them to perform their ceremonies in his garden.[17] But the event that has persisted longest in Pennsylvania tradition is his negotiating a treaty with the Delawares under a giant elm at Shackamaxon, memorialized in the well-known painting by Benjamin West.

Since there is no documentary record of this treaty, West, who was born twenty years after Penn's death, apparently based the scene on imagination and hearsay, portraying Penn as a portly old gentleman instead of the active, thirty-eight-year-old man he was in 1682 when the meeting is supposed to have taken place. Despite the lack of documentation, tradition persisted among both Indians and Quakers that Penn negotiated a treaty of peace with the Delawares at Shackamaxon under an elm tree following his arrival in Philadelphia in the fall of 1682. The Shackamaxon elm was uprooted in a storm in 1810, and the trunk, which measured 24 feet in circumference, was ascertained by its rings to be 283 years old, which meant it was standing when the proprietor arrived.[18]

After reviewing the evidence pro and con, I see no reason to doubt that Penn held such a treaty, either in 1682 or early in 1683, to establish a league of peace with the Delawares not necessarily connected with any land purchases. Since the Indian village at Shackamaxon had long been a gathering place for the Delawares, it was a convenient and suitable treaty site for both Penn and the Indians. If, as tradition also has it, the chief Tamany was one of the spokesmen on this occasion, it can be assumed that among those attending were members of the Delaware band with whom Tamany was affiliated. According to the land sale negotiated with Penn, Tamany's lands lay between

Neshaminy and Pennypack creeks, and he was one of several Delaware chiefs having limited authority over a relatively small number of Indians.

Contrary to popular belief, Tamany was not a king over *all* the Delawares, for in William Penn's time the Delawares did not have a single leader. A release of land to Penn in 1692 was signed by "King Taminent [Tamany], King Tangorus, King Swanpes [Swanpisse], and King Hickoqueon." [19] In addition to these sachems, there were other chieftains, also having limited authority, whom the English categorized as kings. In other words, Tamany was one of a number of Delaware chieftains, and there is reason to believe that he lived in the village of Perkasie in present Hilltown Township, Bucks County, some distance from Shackamaxon, for Penn went there to see him in May of 1683. The Delaware chief Sassoonan said that he was a small lad when William Penn came to Pennsylvania, and that he remembered when Penn met three Delaware chiefs at Perkasie: "Menanget, Hetkoquean, and Taminy." [20]

Tamany had a brother named Weheeland, and two of Tamany's sons are referred to in a 1697 deed as "Yaqueekhon alias Nicholas, and Quenameckquid alias Charles." [21] Yaqueekhon was probably the "King Hickoqueon" and the "Hetkoquean" cited above.

For reasons that have never been satisfactorily explained, the whites exaggerated Tamany's fame and fabricated many legends about him for which documentary proof is lacking. In 1798 a society was organized in New York to counteract the combined influences of the Federalists and the Society of Cincinnati, the latter then looked upon as aristocratic and hostile to democratic institutions. The new organization, which sprang from the people, was called the "St. Tammany Society, or Independent Order of Liberty." The addition of "St." is believed to have been used to ridicule the propensity for calling social clubs St. George, St. Andrew, St. David, and so forth. Thus Tamany became "canonized" as the patron saint of America, and it was curious that an unchristian Indian would be so designated. The festival in the chief's honor was celebrated the first day of May each year, and the patriot members were "solemnly consecrated to the independence, the popular liberty, and the federal union of the country." As time went on, the "St." was dropped, and in 1805 the organization was incorporated under New York state laws as "The Tammany Society or Columbian Order." [22] The chief's name was later transferred to a New York political machine wielding vast power, whose history was darkened with many scandals.

Unpublished documents indicate that Tamany was not the benevolent chief portrayed in some of the popular writing that dealt with the Indians. On the 8th of the 12th month, 1684, after Penn had returned to England, Thomas Holme wrote a letter in which he stated:

I formerly writ to you about Tameney who played the rogue in hindring our peopl to plant and setl upon their lands by warrt; he threatens to fire their houses. I have lookt in the Governors papers and do finde that he hath sold the Governor all his land between Pemapecca & Neshemineh Creek . . . he hath so discouraged our peopl that we cannot get them to go into Bucks County to settle . . .[23]

Tamany made such dire threats to the English, who attempted to settle on the lands he had previously sold to Penn and who had warrants from the government, that they were frightened and moved across the river to New Jersey.[24] When the news reached Penn in England, he wrote a strong letter to Thomas Holme dated at Kensington the 6th month, 8th day, 1685, stating:

I gave them many matchcoats, stockings & some Guns in earnest; if therefore they are rude and unruly, you must make them keep their word by Just course. The vast number of Matchcoats & other things that I have given Sciotick & his family over & above should compell them to a better & easier compliance, *for Tamine, he sould all & if the Indians will not punish him, we will & must,* for they must never see you afraid of executing the Justice they ought to do.[25]

This reveals a side of Penn's character that was rarely seen in his relations with the Indians. As far as Penn was concerned, Tamany was bound by an honest sale of his lands, and Penn expected him to stand by his word.

Tamany and several other Delawares took their complaints to the Commissioners of Property, and at a meeting held on May 28, 1692, demanded that they be paid nine guns, ten matchcoats, and ten blankets, which they said had been promised them for the land they sold to Penn, and which they said they had never received. The commissioners said they would look further into the matter, and in the meantime gave the Indians two dozen rolls to eat and two gallons of rum to wash down the rolls.[26] Penn was in England, and too long a delay would be necessary to communicate with him, so the commissioners decided that they should make some gesture of appeasement to preserve good relations with the natives. At a later meeting they gave Tamany and his associates six guns of a grade better than ordinary, ten Dutch blankets, ten kettles, and a quantity of bread and beer.[27]

While Penn was in America, he conferred at different times with various Delaware Indian bands to make a firm peace with the several kings from whom he had purchased land. These treaty conferences to confirm peaceful relations were separate from those held for the specific purpose of acquiring land, and either Penn did not feel it necessary to keep a detailed record of them or the records have been lost or deliberately destroyed.[28] Some of these official conferences took place at Pennsbury; others were held either in the native villages or in Philadelphia. Following established custom, Penn doubtless gave the Indians suitable presents to brighten the Covenant Chain of peace and friendship, and wampum belts were exchanged to make a record of the meetings for the Indians.

Between 1682 and his death in 1718, Penn was in Pennsylvania for a total of only four years. During the thirty-two years he was absent in Europe, the Indians lost the personal influence of his guiding hand, even though the Quakers tried to follow his policies. Penn was beset by many problems in England; he had unhappy experiences with several of his deputy governors in whose choice he had shown poor judgment; a number of lawsuits were brought against him; there was conflict with Lord Baltimore over the bounds between Maryland and Pennsylvania; he suffered substantial financial losses from his Pennsylvania venture; the reprehensible conduct of his oldest son, William Penn, Jr., brought him shame and expense; the Crown seized the government of Pennsylvania in 1692–94; he spent time in debtor's prison in 1708; and finally he was the victim of a stroke that paralyzed him and led to his death.

Despite all this adversity, Penn held the confidence, respect, and friendship of the Delawares because his government gave the Indians a "new deal." Unfortunately, this was only a brief interlude in the long and tragic history of the Delawares, because an eventual military clash with the Anglo-Americans was inevitable, and "Brother Onas's" kindness merely served to postpone it.

NOTES—CHAPTER 8

1. Myers, *William Penn*, pp. 66–67. See Penn's second letter to the Indians, ibid., p. 72, and a third to an unnamed Indian chief, ibid., p. 74.

2. Alexander C. Flick, ed., *The Papers of Sir William Johnson*, Albany, 1925, vol. 4, p. 818.

3. Myers, *William Penn*, p. 47.

4. Ibid., p. 85.

5. Ibid., pp. 76–79. I have taken liberties in spelling the names of the Indians, as did Myers; cf. *Pennsylvania Archives*, 1st series, vol. 1, p. 47.

6. Papers Relating to the Friendly Association, . . . Department of Records, Philadelphia Yearly Meeting of Friends, vol. 1, pp. 406–7.

7. Myers, *William Penn*, p. 91; cf. *Pennsylvania Archives*, 1st series, vol. 1, pp. 62, 64, 117.

8. Charles S. Keyser, *Penn's Treaty with the Indians*, Philadelphia, 1852, p. 22; cf. *Pennsylvania Archives*, 1st series, vol. 1, p. 63.

9. Penn-Physick Manuscript, vol. 4, p. 160, Manuscript Room, Historical Society of Pennsylvania, Philadelphia. cf. *Pennsylvania Archives*, p. 95; see p. 124 for a third deed where one bound was "so farr as a horse can travel in two summer dayes."

10. Keyser, *Penn's Treaty with the Indians*, p. 24. It is next to impossible for a modern Delaware to translate these names, because as recorded the original sounds of the words are completely garbled.

11. Ibid., pp. 22–34; cf. Paul A. W. Wallace, *Indians of Pennsylvania*, Harrisburg, 1961, pp. 133–38; *Indian Treaties Printed by Benjamin Franklin, 1736–1762*, with notes by Julian P. Boyd; Philadelphia, 1938; Leon de Valinger, Jr., *Indian Land Sales in Delaware*, Wilmington, 1941.

12. Quoted by C. A. Weslager, *Red Men on the Brandywine*, Wilmington, 1953, pp. 139–40. "The delicate and difficult task of removing the tribe of Indians called the Okehockings from their lodges on the banks of Ridley and Crumb creeks in the vicinity of Chester to a new reservation provided for them" was accomplished by Caleb Pusey, Nicholas Pyle, Nathan Newlin, and Joseph Baker; see "Caleb Pusey, Historical Memoranda," Manuscript Room, Historical Society of Pennsylvania, Philadelphia.

13. Weslager, *Red Men on the Brandywine*, Chap. 6.

14. "Letter from William Penn to the Committee of the Free Society of Traders, 1683," Myers, *Narratives*, p. 230.

15. Ibid., pp. 235–36.

16. Myers, *Narratives*, p. 55.

17. Avis Mary Custis Cauley, ed., *Remember William Penn*, William Penn Tercentenary Committee, Harrisburg, Pennsylvania, 1944, Chap. 5; Samuel M. Janney, *The Life of William Penn*, Philadelphia, 1852.

18. For an investigation of the treaty elm, see Robert Vaux, "Memoir on the Location of Penn's Treatry," *Memoirs of the Historical Society of Pennsylvania*, Philadelphia, vol. 1, 1864, p. 105; cf. John F. Watson, "The Indian Treaty, . . . ," ibid., vol. 3, pt. 2, 1836, pp. 131–99; cf. John W. Graham, *William Penn*, London, 1916, pp. 157–58; Frederick D. Stone, "Penn's Treaty with the Indians. Did It Take Place in 1682 or 1683," *Pennsylvania Magazine of History and Biography*, vol. 6, no. 2, 1882, pp. 217–38.

19. An original copy of this release can be found in the Gratz Papers, Case 4, Box 5, Manuscript Room, Historical Society of Pennsylvania, Philadelphia.

20. Penn Manuscripts, Indian Affairs, vol. 1, 1687–1753, p. 35, Manuscript Room, Historical Society of Pennsylvania, Philadelphia.

21. *Pennsylvania Archives*, 1st series, vol. 1, pp. 124–25. Among the many legends about Tamany is one that he was buried along the right bank of the Neshaminy Creek in New Britain Township, Bucks County; see Henry C. Mercer, "The Grave of Tamenend," *Bucks County Historical Society Papers*, vol. 2, Doylestown, Pa., 1909, pp. 58–66.

22. The spread of the Tammany Society is discussed in an article by Samuel W. Williams, "The Tammany Society in Ohio," *Ohio Archeological and Historical Publications*, vol. 22, 1913, pp. 349–70.

23. This document may be found in the Pemberton-Etting Papers, vol. 1, p. 7, Manuscript Room, Historical Society of Pennsylvania, Philadelphia.

24. Ibid., p. 8.

25. This excerpt occurs in the Albert Cook Myers Papers, Box CXXXVll, Chester County Historical Society, West Chester, Pa. A volume by Joseph White Norwood, *The Tammany Legend* . . . , Boston, 1938, adds nothing factual to what has been recorded about Tamany, and is historically inaccurate in parts.

26. *Pennsylvania Archives*, 2d series, 1890, vol. 19, p. 86.

27. William Penn Account Book, 1691–93, Division of Public Records, State Library, Harrisburg, Pa.

28. In his doctoral dissertation, "Miquon's Passing—Indian-European Relations in Colonial Pennsylvania, 1674 to 1675" (submitted to the faculty of the University of Pennsylvania), Francis P. Jennings suggests on p. 68 that Penn's heirs may have destroyed the documentation when they found its language "inconveniently explicit about their obligations to the Lenape."

9

Pennsylvania's New Indian Policy

After William Penn's death in 1718, which marked the end of an era in Pennsylvania's colonial history, the responsibility for his affairs was taken over by his second wife, the former Hannah Callowhill. Penn's wastrel son by his first wife, William Penn, Jr., was disinherited, and Hannah's three sons, John, Thomas, and Richard, fell heir to their father's American lands. Although the three brothers were joint proprietors—and all spent time in Pennsylvania—they delegated many of their administrative powers to a succession of deputy-governors.

In the decade following Penn's death, there was considerable unrest among the Delaware Indians. Hunters had to travel longer distances than in the past to find game and were thus compelled to remain away from their villages for longer periods of time. Styles changed in Europe, and the demand for beaver pelts decreased to such a point that in 1721 Governor William Keith told the Indians, "We deal but very little in *that* Commodity But Deer Skins sell very well amongst us . . . ." The Indians were bewildered by this phenomenon of supply and demand, which resulted in fluctuating prices, and they could not understand the decline in the price of beaver pelts just because there was a new vogue in men's hats in Europe.

Men and boys in England, especially those in rural areas, were now wearing deerskin breeches and jackets, a type of male garb also used widely in the American colonies, which was the principal stimulus for the demand for deerskins. Bearskins also continued to be in demand for making robes and coats, and there was a ready market among the

hatters who fabricated the type of military headdress made popular
by the Grenadier Guards. A market continued to exist for fox, otter,
muskrat, squirrel, and rabbit pelts (although there was periodic price
fluctuation), but suddenly deerskins were most in demand. In lieu
of beaver pelts, the deerskin became the medium of exchange by which
the Indian could obtain European goods, but the problem was that
deer had become scarce in the Delaware Valley. To satisfy the demand, Indian hunters had to travel to the Elk River and to Susquehanna country to find the herds, and this kept them away from their
villages for extended periods of time.

Most of the old village sites in Delaware and southern New Jersey
had been abandoned as the white settlements expanded, and in some
towns it was not healthy for an Indian to make an appearance after
dark for fear that a slave trader might seize him and sell him illicitly
into slavery as he would an itinerant Negro. Some Negro slaves had
escaped their masters and found refuge in Indian villages, and there
had been black intermarriage with Indian women. The children of
such marriages were always in danger of being sold into slavery, and
that created new fears of mixing in white society.

A much-reduced Delaware Indian population found haven in three
different enclaves along the western shore of the Delaware River. The
first of these was in the upper Schuylkill drainage in Pennsylvania
between the South Mountains and the Blue or Kittatinny Mountains
in a rich, beautiful valley called Tulpehocken ("place of the turtle"),
a name derived from one of the largest Delaware villages situated in
the environs of the present town of Stouchsburg. Other smaller Indian
towns and camps were scattered in this intermontane area along Tulpehocken Creek, which in the old days had primarily been hunting
grounds for the Delawares. In a book published in 1897 entitled *The
Indians of Berks County*, the author, D. B. Brunner, illustrates some of
the typical stone artifacts found abundantly at Tulpehocken and in
the vicinity of Reading, Kutztown, and Maxatawny. He quotes a letter
from an amateur archeologist who in 1848 excavated Indian graves a
half mile northwest of Kutztown. Grave accompaniments included
European glass beads and a copper kettle, which suggests the remains
were those of Delaware Indians who died and were buried during the
period of contact with white traders.

The Delawares who formerly resided at the downstream villages
(Shackamaxon and Passayunk among them) could not withstand the

influx of the thousands of Germans, Swiss, and Scotch-Irish pouring into Philadelphia. English and Welsh Quakers had already converted the wooded area between the Delaware and Schuylkill rivers into a busy commercial town with wharves, banks, inns, churches, and several hundred brick and frame residences. With the influx of new immigrants, there was no end in sight to the population growth, which by 1717 already exceeded 10,000. Philadelphia was destined to become the largest city in the thirteen colonies.

The earlier white settlements at Wilmington, New Castle, and Chester caused the Delawares to move north, and the Indian population became consolidated at villages near the mouth of the Schuylkill. The development of a town at Philadelphia again pressed the Delawares northwesterly toward the headwaters of the river where, in an area not yet settled by Europeans, they felt they could live unmolested, at least for a while. Their squaws could plant corn without fear of its being trampled and eaten by horses, cows, and swine. And Delaware hunters could pursue deer, and hunt and trap smaller game in the woods without encountering surveyors or axemen preparing the land for farms and dwellings. Delaware Indians from a number of scattered locations were attracted to the Tulpehocken settlement; among these were some of the restless Okehocking, who deserted the Chester County reservation laid aside for them by William Penn. A few Indian families still living on Chester Creek and along neighboring streams also decided to move to Tulpehocken to escape the incursions of English, Irish, and Welsh families spreading through the countryside. The paradox was that, although the Delawares wanted to live apart from the white man, they were rapidly becoming dependent upon him for clothing, household utensils, farm implements, and especially for guns and ammunition.

Among the chieftains named in records of the early settlements beginning to take shape on the upper Schuylkill were Manangy ("left handed"), Skalitchy, and Sassoonan (who was also known as Alumapees or Olumapies in various spellings). Some writers have speculated that Skalitchy was Tamanend's successor, but there is no documentary evidence to support this assumption. It has also been said that Skalitchy and Tamanend were the same person who, like many other Delawares, had two or more names. According to Rafinesque's "Fragment on the History of the Linapis" a chief named "Skalichi" was also called the "Last Tamenend." The inference to be drawn is that there were earlier leaders named Tamanend. One author has gone so far as to speculate that the Tamanend (Tamany) of William Penn's time was the third chief to bear this name; the writer has even given dates when the two earlier Tamanends supposedly "reigned" over the Delawares, "facts" that are without historical foundation.[1]

Manangy, whose name appears a number of times in Pennsylvania provincial records, was formerly chief of one of the Delaware bands settled near the falls of the Delaware in the Trenton vicinity, but when the Indians converged at Tulpehocken these former geopolitical bands had lost their separate identities and autonomy. Some had been wiped out by disease; other bands had been reduced to one or two families; and in some instances probably only an elderly chieftain and his immediate household were left from their original village. Although the natives who came together at Tulpehocken continued to be called Delaware Indians, the term *Unami* began to appear now and then in the records to distinguish them from the Munsies. There was also intermarriage between Unami and Munsie, and children grew up knowing there was a Munsie ancestor in their background; but outside of differences in dialect there was no practical difference between a Unami-Delaware and a Munsie-Delaware.

The Pennsylvania authorities did their utmost to enhance Sassoonan's stature by elevating him to the position of titular head of these Unami-Delawares. In fact, "Brother Onas" (the name used by the Delawares for Pennsylvania officials after Penn's death) was more than willing to crown Sassoonan the king of *all* the Delawares, including those called Unami and Munsie—or by any other name. Brother Onas continued to try to create *one* Delaware Indian potentate "with whom Public Business shall be transacted." This was the only kind of political leadership the English understood, having been conditioned to the prerogatives of the throne in their native land. From a practical viewpoint, if they could single out one Indian leader to deal with, they would reduce the cost of buying presents and liquor for the numerous chieftains who paraded to Philadelphia with their entourages to renew the Covenant Chain and be entertained. Also the whole diplomatic process would be simplified.

Evidently the men in authority at Philadelphia were not as well acquainted with Delaware Indian custom as William Allen, a contemporary Pennsylvania landowner, who wrote that "there never was any Time to his Knowledge and Belief One Head, Sachem, King or

Chief who presided or pretended to preside or excercise a Power over the whole Delaware Nation . . ." [2]

As we have seen, Tamanend was only one of a number of band chieftains, and although he may have possessed personal qualities that made him more admired and respected than the others, the assumption that he outranked them in political authority is in direct contradiction to what is known of the autonomy of Delaware communities. Sassoonan was also a band chieftain before the Delawares converged at Tulpehocken, but he was made the Delaware "King" by the Pennsylvania government, which repeatedly addressed him by this title, and so referred to him in dialogue with other Indians. Through the simple expedient of singling him out to deal with, instead of negotiating with other chiefs, and by bestowing on him gifts of merchandise which he could redistribute at his discretion, Pennsylvania authorities set him up as a puppet monarch. They manipulated him with gifts which contributed to his popularity with his followers and which if withheld would lower Sassoonan's status.

Since public records continually refer to Sassoonan as the Delaware king, someone writing about the period got the notion that he was Tamanend's successor, and another suggested that the two men may have been father and son. Neither assumption is founded in fact. Before he became the beneficiary of Pennsylvania's generosity, Sassoonan himself referred to Skalitchy, who predeceased him, as "the Delaware King." Obviously the term was inappropriate, and Sassoonan did not understand the meaning of the English word, which had no equivalent in the Delaware language. Nevertheless, Sassoonan did become King, if in name only, with Brother Onas's blessing. A stronger personality than Sassoonan might have taken Pennsylvania at its word and seized the opportunity to become the protagonist for the Delawares in their moment of greatest need. But Sassoonan was a weak-willed man, lacking both the moral strength and leadership qualities possessed, for example, by the legendary Deganawidah, founder of the Iroquois League, or by the aggressive Pontiac, which might have unified the Delawares and made the white authorities more conciliatory. What happened, in fact, was that a succession of Pennsylvania's deputy-governors continued to try to make him appear to his own people as a great man and king, fully aware that they controlled him body and soul.

Members of the second group of Delawares lived in the valley of the Brandywine, and their largest village called Queonemysing stood in the Big Bend, with smaller Indian towns situated elsewhere along the east and west branches of the stream. Among the town chieftains whose names have been preserved were Oholykon, Peyeashickon, and Wililikyona, and the leader of the band, Checochinican ("person of few words"). In his role as spokesman for the Brandywine Indians during negotiations with the Pennsylvania government, Checochinican acted as a king in his own right, for he and only he spoke for his people, according to ancient custom. As long as this band of Delawares remained on the Brandywine, they behaved as an independent political group, having their own sachems, as in the early days. They had no political affiliation with Sassoonan and the Unami-Delawares at Tulpehocken, nor the Munsie-Delawares on the upper Delaware River. The authorities knew them as "the Brandywine Indians" or "Indians of the Brandywine."

The third Delaware Indian community was situated in the area where the Lehigh River, also called the West Branch, joined the Delaware River. The land at the point of junction, and the territory within the two streams extending all the way to the Blue Mountains, was known as "the Forks." The term was also loosely applied to the territory north from Tohickon Creek (also spelled Tohiccon) to the Kittatinny Mountains, which had long been the hunting grounds of the Unalimi-Delawares, or "upstream people." This territory was associated with the lineages of Menakihikon, Tishecunk (sometimes given as Tishcohan), Lappawinzo, and Nutimus, and the Indians claimed that their title to the land had never been extinguished by the Penns. The native villages in the area, such as Wechquetank, Welagameka, Hociundoquen, Nockamixon, Meniolagomeka, and others, became havens for numerous dispossessed Indian families who came chiefly from New Jersey. The Tatamy family of Delawares and a few others from the Minisink lands moved down to settle in the Forks, and Captain Harris, a noted Delaware, brought his family across the river from Trenton to settle at Pocopoco. One of Captain Harris's sons, "Honest John," also moved from Trenton to the Forks—his Indian name was Teedyuskung.

These Delawares in the Forks community considered themselves a different political entity from their red brethren at Tulpehocken or on the Brandywine. The chief Nutimus ("striker of fish with a spear") was regarded by Pennsylvania authorities, at least for a while, as the titular head of the Indians at the Forks, but since he was not as tractable as Sassoonan, he was unable to hold Brother Onas's love and esteem. Nutimus was born in New Jersey, but his mother came from the Pennsylvania side of the Delaware River, and he said the Indians did not consider the river a boundary "for those of the same Nation lived on both Sides of it." The chief Mehocksett said it more poetically, "Tho' wee live on the other side of the river, yet we reckon orselves all one, becaus wee drink one water." [3]

These Delawares at Tulpehocken along the Schuylkill, on the Brandywine, and at the Forks, it should be noted, were still occupying parts of the homeland that had belonged to their people as long as anyone could remember. William Penn had assured them he would never allow lands to be taken away from them, but the proprietor was now dead, and his sons thought only of their own best interests. Unwritten promises made to the Indians by their father were ancient history. Furthermore, the deputy-governors had to mesh the treatment accorded the Delawares with the province's official Indian policy in which the Five Nations were given a favored position. To understand how the Pennsylvania government acted in its own selfish interests at the expense of the Delawares, one must recognize that the Delawares for a number of years were held in a sort of voluntary bondage by the Five Nations.

In 1661 war parties of Senecas—early writers used the term *Seneca* in a generic sense to describe any of the Five Nations—had come to the Delaware River and attacked and killed some of the Delawares. This occurred during the same period when the Iroquois were also warring against the Minquas and is historical evidence of open warfare between the Five Nations and certain of the Delaware bands. When the Five Nations conquered other Indian tribes, it was their custom to exact tribute in the form of strings and belts of wampum beads, which was paid to them at regular intervals at Onondaga or to special Iroquois messengers who visited the towns of the tributary people. For example, of the Susquehanna Minquas, it was officially noted in 1722, "That they actually pay tribute to the Five Nations, and either from natural affection or Fear are ever under their Influence and Power." [4] The Nanticoke and Conoy, who fell under Five Nations dominion, also paid bead tribute, and Captain Arent Schuyler's note to the effect that the Minisink Indians failed to pay their "Dutty," in 1694, *as usual*, also indicates that the Munsie-Delaware community had also been reduced to a tributary people, and were under Five Nations dominion. (Hereafter I shall designate the Five Nations as the *Six* Nations, as they were called after the Tuscarora joined the confederacy.)

Chieftains representing the Six Nations on numerous meetings with Pennsylvania authorities mentioned, sometimes boastfully, that they had defeated the Delawares in warfare. The Delawares never publicly contradicted this charge; in fact, they admitted it. In relationships between the Delawares and the Six Nations, the former were assigned the position of women, and the symbolic attributes of the female were applied to them.

In the Appendix to Jefferson's *Notes on the State of Virginia*, Charles Thomson, whose sympathies were pro-Delaware, referred to the Six Nations as having made women of the Delawares. Thomson stated that the Delawares (to whom he referred as the Lenopi) were so hard pressed by the Iroquois that they were compelled to sue for peace, which was granted them "on the condition that they should put themselves under the protection of the Mingoes [Six Nations] confine themselves to raising corn, hunting for the subsistence of their families, and no longer have the power of making war. *This is what the Indians call making them women.* And in this condition the Lenopis were when William Penn first arrived and began the settlement of Pennsylvania in 1682."

There is no doubt that the Six Nations had relegated the Delawares to the position of women, and in this role the Delawares were prohibited from going to war or negotiating treaties. The questions that have been raised are concerned with when this occurred and whether the deprivation of masculine prerogatives was a result of conquest, as related by Thomson, or whether the Delawares were somehow duped into accepting a role that they believed was an honored one but that brought them shame instead. According to this latter version, as told by the Moravian pastors Loskiel and Heckewelder, the Delawares agreed to accept what they believed was an honorable position among the Indian tribes as "peacemakers," a role played by some women of royal lineage among the Iroquois. Under this interpretation, as "matrons" in the society of Indian nations, the Delawares were delegated, by the Six Nations, the responsibility of negotiating peace between warring tribes. In this context, it is claimed, there was no shame attached to their being placed in the role of women and figuratively wearing petticoats. The weakness of this position is that there is absolutely no existing documentation wherein the Delawares were recognized as honored peacemakers, whereas there are numerous references to their being degraded to a shameful position as noncombatants.

I still hold to the view I first expressed in a paper in 1944, which has been reinforced by subsequent study, that the Delawares had been subjugated, and the Iroquois reduced them to a subservient position.[5] In the circumstances the Delawares were placed in, there was no honor attached to being looked upon as women, rather they were humiliated because they were reminded constantly that they lacked political or military power. Canyase, a Mohawk, expressed it thus, "We, the Mohocks are Men; we are made so from above, but the Delawares are Women, and under our Protection, and of too low a kind to be Men . . ."[6]

Beaver, a Delaware chief, once addressed the Six Nations as follows, "Uncles: I still remember the time when you first conquered us and made Women of us . . ."[7] Beaver may not have meant that he personally remembered the conquest, which probably took place before he was born, but that he *knew* it to be a fact. A conquest does not imply that *all* of the autonomous Delaware bands living in the Delaware River Valley suddenly fell in battle before the Iroquois, but as Dr. Paul A. W. Wallace wrote, they were "conquered by the Iroquois in a cold war—with a little heat turned on in judicious spots."[8]

On July 26, 1709, the Delaware sachems Owechela, Passakassy, Sassoonan, and Skalitchy met with Governor Charles Gookin and his council at Philadelphia. They wanted to inform the governor that they intended making a journey to visit the Six Nations "and had provided for their Journey Twenty four Belts of Wampum, to be presented to them as their Tribute . . ." Their trip was in question when they received a message from the Six Nations stating that some of their chiefs were coming down to Conestoga to receive the tribute from the Delawares and from the Maryland Indians "who are all Tributaries to the said five nations."[9]

An even more significant entry occurs on May 19, 1712, when Sassoonan, Skalitchy, and eleven other Delaware chieftains or great men again appeared before Governor Gookin and his council. Skalitchy, as spokesman for the delegation, informed the governor that "many years ago being made Tributaries to the Mingoes or 5 nations & being now about to visit them," they thought fit to show him the tribute they were carrying. They placed on the floor in front of the governor thirty-two belts of wampum with various figures worked into the beads and a long calumet smoking pipe with a stone bowl and feathers affixed to it like wings, which had been given them by the Six Nations "who had subdued them and obliged them to be their tributaries." [10] By showing the calumet on their passage through the country of the Six Nations when, as instructed by their conquerors, they went to make their payment, they were able to identify themselves as a peaceful tributary people. Their destination was Onondaga (present Syracuse), where the council fire of the Six Nations League was lighted and where each member had a designated position in the council.

The Six Nations, whose total population numbered fifteen or sixteen thousand, not only exercised dominion over the Delawares, but brought other Indian refugee groups under their authority and settled them in Pennsylvania on lands the Six Nations claimed. The Shawnee, for example, moved north from their southern homes to escape white pressures, and they came under Iroquois protection along the Susquehanna. The Nanticoke and Conoy from Maryland (the latter were sometimes called the Ganawese) also left their homes and were seated on the Susquehanna by the Six Nations. "The People of Maryland," said the Iroquois speaker Canasatego to Brother Onas, "do not treat the Indians as you & others do, for they make slaves of them & sell their Children for Money . . ." [11] The fear of enslavement and other white persecution also caused the "naked Indians" or Twightwee (later to be known as the Miami) to move up the Chesapeake from Virginia and North Carolina to settle along the Susquehanna under the watchful eyes of the Six Nations. The Tutelo, who lived in the piedmont of Virginia and North Carolina, also moved north into Pennsylvania to ally themselves with the Six Nations and live under their protection.

It might appear that the government of Pennsylvania unnecessarily exposed itself to Indian problems by allowing this influx of alien Indians into the province. With hot-headed Scotch-Irish settlers on the western frontier willing to spill Indian blood at the least provocation, young braves from the dispossessed tribes wandering around frontier settlements seeking rum and excitement, and a strong pacifist Quaker element in the Pennsylvania Assembly opposed to the use of force, the situation called for diplomatic genius. That genius was supplied by James Logan, an Irish-born, English-educated Quaker who served successively as the provincial secretary, commissioner of property, president of the council, receiver of the proprietary rents, chief justice of the supreme court, and *de facto* superintendent of Indian affairs. Logan was aided and advised by Conrad Weiser, Indian ambassador and interpreter to the Six Nations, and Shickellamy ("he causes it to be daylight for himself"), a highly intelligent Oneida Indian who was sent by the Onondaga Council as a sort of resident agent to keep an eye on the Indians living in Pennsylvania under Iroquois sufferance. Fully aware of the activities of the French, who were doing their utmost to win the Indians over to their side and gain control of the Ohio Valley, these three men were the architects of new Indian policy. The keystone of this policy was to win the Six Nations over to Pennsylvania's cause, strengthening them in every possible way with supplies and financial aid, and giving full recognition to their dominion over the Delawares and other subjugated tribes. The importance of the Six Nations to Pennsylvania was not in the number of their warriors (Conrad Weiser conservatively estimated the warrior population as less than two thousand) but in the strength of the allied or dependent nations under their supervision. As Governors Andros and Dongan both recognized some years before, the Iroquois League was the main link if the English expected to forge a lasting Covenant Chain of peace and cooperation with the Indians and to block French expansion.

Having both the physical and moral support of the Pennsylvania government, the Six Nations were free to use their authority to restrain and direct the Delawares, Conestoga, Shawnee, Nanticoke, Twightwee, Conoy, Tutelo, and any other Indians who settled in the province. It was to Pennsylvania's best interest to encourage refugee Indians to come to the province to live, because the more Indians who fell under Six Nations dominion, the more useful the Six Nations would be to Pennsylvania. The new policy delegated to the Six Nations full suzerainty over all the migrant Pennsylvania Indians, and, in any confrontation with the French, Pennsylvania would have a mighty force of Indian allies ready to do the bidding of the Six Nations, who would act in Pennsylvania's interests. Also peace with the Indians would be automatically maintained, because in return for the Six Nations police action over the tributaries, Pennsylvania recognized the superiority of the league and was prepared to do its utmost to strengthen the league even further.

It was an ingenious, well-conceived policy, but it had an inherent weakness that neither Logan, Weiser, nor Shikellamy then recognized. Smoldering in the breasts of the Delawares was bitterness and resentment toward the English that dated back to earlier trickery and mistreatment. Moreover, their pride would not allow them to accept much longer the humiliation caused them by the Six Nations, who continually reminded them of their inferior position as women every time they attempted a political move to serve their own interests.

In the spring of 1723, fifteen families from Schoharie, a German settlement about forty miles west of Albany, moved their families and household goods to Pennsylvania. At Tulpehocken they "took lands without permission of the authorities . . . and against the will of the Indians for the land had not yet been bought from Them." [12] Governor William Keith, traveling to Albany the previous year in an attempt to build up a personal constituency, had invited the Palatines to settle on Pennsylvania's fertile lands. In what is now the Lebanon Valley, with Reading and Harrisburg at either gateway, these sturdy, industrious Schoharie Germans settled. They felled and squared tree trunks for log houses (later replaced with stone dwellings), laid out their farms and pastures, and began to cultivate the soil.

This was done to the distress of the Indians, because the valley was the heart of Sassoonan's refugee settlement, which by now also included a number of Shawnee families that had joined the Delawares. The Delawares had refused to sell this land to the whites, because they knew what was destined to happen when white settlers took possession. The authorities in Philadelphia faced a serious problem, because if they turned away the Germans they would do an injustice to people who came into the valley in good faith on Governor Keith's invitation. The easiest thing to do was exert strong pressure on the Indians to sell the lands, thus extinguishing their claim to the territory, and then convey residential tracts to dependable German farmers who would be an asset to the province. Aging Sassoonan, any diplomatic skill he had possessed befogged by rum, might have negotiated to the advantage of his people in his younger years, but now he was ever willing to exchange lands for goods and drink. When the agents of the three Penn brothers persuaded him to sell the lands at Tulpehocken he did so, indifferent to the fact that he was divesting the Delawares living there of the last property they could call their own.

On September 7, 1732, "We Sassoonan alias Allumapis, Sachem of the Schuylkill Indians . . . Elalapis, Ohopamen, Pesqueetomen, Mayeemoe, Partridge, Tepakoaset alias Joe" released to Thomas, John, and Richard Penn the lands at Tulpehocken including "all those Lands situate lying and being on the said River Schuylkill and the branches thereof, Between the Mountains called Lechaig to the South, and the Hills or Mountains called Keekachtanemin on the North, and between the branches of Delaware River on the East, and the Waters falling into Susquehanna River on the West, etc."

The deed went on to say that the Delawares hereafter forfeited any right, title, or interest in the land from which they "shall be Excluded and forever debarred." In payment, the Indians received a large quantity of trade goods—shirts, hats, blankets, ribbons, looking glasses, coats, shoes, stockings, hats, brass kettles, guns, hoes, and other items, including twenty gallons of rum and fifty pounds in money.[13] As some of the Shawnee chiefs later said of the Delawares, "they was Dry and wanted to Drink ye land away." [14] So many thousands of acres of land in the Delaware Valley had been drunk away that, from the date of this deed on, the Schuylkill Delawares were trespassers on their former hunting territories. After the rum was consumed and the merchandise distributed to the Indian residents at Tulpehocken, the land, as another Shawnee once said of the Delawares, had gone through their guts.

The Brandywine Delawares were also troubled and harassed after William Penn's death by Englishmen settling on territory that belonged to them. They complained bitterly to Pennsylvania authorities that their fishing in the Brandywine was hindered by the building of mill dams which blocked the shad and herring from coming upstream to spawn. They protested that the whites were also building houses and mills on lands one mile to either side of the stream, which they claimed William Penn had reserved for their exclusive use. The white man's cattle foraged on this land, leaving nothing for the wild animals to eat. The Delawares were becoming destitute because they could no longer obtain deer pelts to barter with white traders.

James Logan replied that he could find no record in the provincial files at Philadelphia to indicate that William Penn reserved lands one mile on each side of the stream for the exclusive use of the Indians, as they maintained. He asked the chiefs to produce documentary proof of their claims. They replied that Penn had given them a document many years before, which had long been in their possession but was destroyed when a fire consumed one of their cabins.

On June 24, 1729, Checochinican, probably aided by a friendly and literate Quaker, wrote a letter to Governor Patrick Gordon in Philadelphia, which read as follows:

. . . in time past we Sold our interests to Wm. Penn (our Brother) he was pleased to grant us a Wrighting for the Creek of Brandywine up to the Head thereof which said Wrighting by some Accident was Lost with all ye Land a mile wide of ye Creek on each Side which afterward we Disposed of so far up as to a Certain known Rock in ye said Creek, it being in the Line of the Land, belonging to one Abraham Marshall, and of Late to ye great prejudice and Disquiett of us a people that has done and Still Desiers to do, *to continue in peace and Love, and be as one Heart and Soule* with Wm. Penn and his People, the Land has been unjustly Sold whereby we are redused to great wants & hardships notwithstanding . . . nay we have been so much interrupted that we have been forbid So much as to make use of timber growing thereon, for ye Convenience of building some Cabins & further, that the [Indian] Town at the Head of Brandiwine is Survey'd to one James Gibbins and many more . . .[15]

A phrase in the letter has been italicized to illustrate how certain metaphoric expressions Penn used in his negotiations were long remembered by the Indians. When he held council with them, he promised them so much love and friendship that he said he would not call them brothers, because brothers sometimes differed. He added that he would not call them children, because children might offend and require correction, "but he would reckon them as one Body, one Blood, One Heart and One Head." This concept of whites and Indians joined together both spiritually and physically as one person was memorable verbal imagery, which was more meaningful to the Indians in some ways than the metaphor of the Covenant Chain. The idea of oneness in heart and body with William Penn was repeated years after, not only by the Delawares, but also by the Six Nations, the Conestoga, and Shawnee.

But the Brandywine Indians received no relief for their problems, and the illicit occupation of their lands by white settlers, with the full knowledge of the Pennsylvania government, imposed unbearable pressures. They had no recourse except to retaliate, which would have been useless, or to move away. Checochinican and his people were peaceful folk, and they elected to take the latter course, seeking haven on Minquas lands along the Susquehanna River, where no white families were yet settled.

At the Forks of the Delaware, white settlers were also encroaching on the Indians' lands, and the chiefs Nutimus and Tishecunk lodged protests with John and Thomas Penn, claiming their ancestors had never sold these particular lands to William Penn. The Indians did not know that the Penns were badly in need of funds to pay their creditors, and Thomas decided that money could be obtained most readily by selling lands in the Forks to white settlers. Because Indian title had not been extinguished, this was a violation of his father's policy, which had long governed Pennsylvania's relations with the Indians in land matters. Having prematurely disposed of numerous tracts, Thomas Penn could not issue any patents to white buyers until he had paid the Indians for the lands—and he knew they didn't want to sell. The problem was to devise means that appeared to be legal to extinguish Indian title, thus concealing acts that were illegal and also permitting additional sales to be made.

In May of 1735, Nutimus and Tishecunk, along with other Delawares, were invited to Pennsbury, where they were entertained and softened for the blow that was to be dealt them by James Logan, acting in behalf of the proprietor's sons. Logan produced what he purported to be a *copy* of an old deed executed in 1686 and recently brought to America by Thomas Penn. The original was allegedly missing—and there was no record of the transaction in the archives at Philadelphia, nor has the original yet been found. Logan told Nutimus and Tishecunk that the document proved their forebears had transferred land to William Penn on the west bank of the Delaware, *north* of Tohickon Creek including lands in the Forks which the Indians were then occupying. When the names of the deceased Indians, supposedly the signatories, were read, Nutimus recognized them and protested that they were not proprietors of the lands in question but the former owners of lands *south* of Tohickon Creek. They would not have sold lands north of Tohickon Creek, to which they had no own-

ership rights, Nutimus maintained, and this territory, including the
Forks, belonged to the "up River Indians," of whom he was the chief.

Logan, with sarcasm, then asked Nutimus how he came to own
land in the Forks on the west side of the Delaware River when it was
common knowledge that he had been born on the east side in New
Jersey.

Nutimus said his Mother came from this side the River & by her he had
a Right here as he likewise had to some Lands in the Jerseys which his
Father left him & besides the Indians did not consider the River as any
boundary for those of the same Nation lived on both sides of it. As
Nutimus thought this a trifling Question he in banter asked how he [Logan]
came to have a Right here as he was not born in this Country.[16]

This was a biting question because, while he was transacting business for the proprietors, Logan had a special personal interest in the
lands in the Forks. He was a partner in the Durham Ironworks situated north of Tohickon Creek on land that he had purchased independently from Nutimus. In his private business Logan was also
deeply involved in the Indian trade, not as a trader but as an entre-
preneur who made a double profit on his transactions. A London
merchant, John Askew, with whom he had a joint account, purchased
goods in England which were shipped to Logan, who resold the merchandise on credit to the Indian traders at a profit. They paid their
debts to him in pelts, which he shipped to England, also to be sold
at a profit. Logan, and a younger partner he took into the business,
Edward Shippen, operated well-stocked stores in Philadelphia and
Lancaster, where the traders loaded their wagons with powder, lead,
axes, kettles, and the blue and red woolen cloth brought from England known as "strowdwaters," which had grown in popularity with
the Indians.[17]

After considerable argument, innumerable threats, and strong pressures from Logan and the Penns, Nutimus, Tishecunk, Lappawinzo,
and Menahihikon ("a King of the Minissincks") finally agreed to confirm the 1686 deed. On August 25, 1737, they signed what later became known as the Walking Purchase Deed. It was a confirmation of
the bounds given in the first document, wherein one of the bounds
extended from a fixed point (present Wrightstown in Bucks County)
as far into the woods as a man could walk in a day and a half. Having
convinced the Indians that their father had purchased the land in

1686, the Penns, aided and abetted by Logan, then insisted that the bounds had never been laid out in the manner prescribed by the conveyance. The unwilling and resentful Indians, aware that control of lands in the Lehigh Valley was at issue, were forced to agree that the line should be paced off as specified in the document. So much has been written about the walk that was made on September 19–20, 1737, that the incident needs only a brief summation here to show how the Delawares were cheated of their lands in the Forks.

With the assistance of surveyors and draughtsmen, Logan, Thomas Penn, and James Steel, the Receiver-General, put their heads together and found a way that a day-and-a-half walk could be made to take in practically all the land claimed by Nutimus and his followers. By cutting a path through the woods in advance, and using three fast walkers who had been specially trained and rehearsed for their mission—followed by horses carrying provisions—the whites began the walk, accompanied by two Indian observers. Two of the white walkers became so exhausted that they were forced to give up after the first day, but the third walker endured the complete walk which took in about sixty miles. The Indian signatories intended the bound to be an ordinary walk, which would have taken a man about twenty-five or thirty miles in a day and a half, not a pace that caused the Indian observers to quit, one saying in disgust, "You Run, thats not fair, you was to Walk." [18]

Later, Lappawinzo (whose portrait, and also that of his colleague Tishcohan, painted by Gustavus Hesselius, now hangs in the Historical Society of Pennsylvania in Philadelphia) described the walk this way: "no sit down to smoke, no shoot a squirrel, but *lun, lun, lun* all day long!" [19]

By the terms of the old deed, a line was to be run from the point where the walk ended back to the Delaware River. Although the deed did not describe the course the line should take, one would assume that this should have been the shortest distance. Quite the contrary. By a manipulation of angles, a line was squared off at a right angle from the point at the end of the walk and projected to the banks of the Delaware, sixty-five miles away by this longer measurement. By deception, the tract took the shape of a triangle whose base was the Delaware River and whose apex was the end of the walk—and the triangle included all the lands occupied by the Delawares and some Shawnee families who had settled among them.

Having acquired everything he wanted, Logan benevolently set aside ten square miles at the Forks as a reservation for the Indians, but this miserable token did little to lessen Indian resentment toward the English caused by the walk. Feeling frustrated and tricked, the Delawares refused to move and threatened to meet any intruders on their lands with force. Meanwhile, Thomas Penn released a flood of patents to new buyers, and by 1740 more than a hundred white families were settled in the territory included in the walk. Several incidents provoked by the Indians convinced Pennsylvania officials that they must rid themselves of this thorn in their sides and guarantee clear title to the English residents. It was precisely to solve such bothersome problems that Logan's new Indian policy had been formulated, and the proprietors turned to their Six Nations allies: "We now expect from You that you will cause these Indians to remove from the Lands in the fforks of the Delaware," Governor George Thomas charged the Six Nations chiefs, "and not give any further Disturbance to the Persons who are now in Possession." [20]

A large contingent of Six Nations chiefs and great men were summoned to an important meeting in Philadelphia, and on July 10, 1742, Governor Thomas presented them with a varied assortment of goods including 24 guns, 10 dozen knives, 25 pairs of shoes, 25 pairs of stockings, 25 hats, 50 hatchets, 50 hoes, 30 blankets, and other items adding up to a value of £300. In fact, these gifts, added to merchandise given the Six Nations several days earlier in return for certain lands west of the Susquehanna River, necessitated loaning the chiefs horses, wagons, and drivers to carry it back to their homes in upper New York state.

The goods presented to the Six Nations on July 10 were given as a gesture of friendship, but the Indians knew what they were supposed to do in return. Canasatego was their speaker on July 12, when in open council he addressed himself to Nutimus and the Indians from the Forks.

The speaker at Delaware and Iroquois councils and treaties was not the chief sachem and did not have to be a sachem at all. He was a special orator, qualified for the job by a knowledge of council procedures and an ability to express eloquently the thoughts and decisions of the chieftains and policymakers. It was a highly formalized procedure, with introductory remarks, words of welcome, and strings of wampum with which the speaker ceremoniously wiped dust from the eyes of his listeners so they could see the truth, cleansed their throats so they could speak, and bored open their ears so they could hear.

Canasatego spoke as follows to the Delawares, according to Conrad Weiser's English translation of the much-quoted speech:

We have seen with our Eyes a Deed signed by nine of your Ancestors above fifty years ago for this very Land, and a Release Sign'd not many Years since by some of yourselves and Chiefs now living to the Number of 15 or Upwards. But how came you to take upon you to Sell Land at all? We conquer'd You, we made Women of you, you know you are Women, and can no more sell Land than Women. Nor is it fitt you should have the Power of Selling Lands since you would abuse it. This land that you Claim is gone through Your Guts. You have been furnished with Cloaths and Meat and Drink by the Goods paid you for it, and now You want it again like Children as you are . . . And for all these reasons we charge You to remove instantly. We don't give you the liberty to think about it. You are Women; take the Advice of a Wise Man and re-move immediately. You may return to the other side of Delaware where you came from, but we don't know whether, Considering how you have demean'd yourselves, you will be permitted to live there, or whether you have not swallowed that Land down your Throats, as well as the Land on this side. We, therefore, Assign you two Places to go—either to Wyomin or Shamokin. You may go to either of these Places, and then we shall have you more under our Eye, and shall see how You Behave. Don't deliberate, but remove away . . .

This String of Wampum serves to forbid You, Your Children and Grand Children, to the latest Posterity, for ever medling in Land Affairs, neither you nor any who shall descend from You, are ever hereafter to presume to sell any Land, for which Purpose you are to Preserve this string in Memory of what your Uncles have this Day given you in Charge.[21]

Canasatego probably exceeded the authority delegated to him by the Six Nations chiefs in denying *all* Delawares the right to sell land, if that was his intention. The issue in question involved only those settled in the Forks. Nevertheless, it was an undeserved and unex-pected insult that he hurled at Nutimus and Sassoonan, who was also present, and what made it worse was that Nutimus knew that Canasa-tego's order to remove his people from the Forks had the complete backing of Brother Onas. The Delawares stood alone with no one on their side.

Canasatego's performance was even better than Governor Thomas expected, and later when Canasatego suggested that the Six Nations had been stinted of rum while in town and that Brother Onas should "open the Rum Bottle" on the road, the council responded with a sum of money sufficient to buy twenty gallons. This comfort for the road was put aboard the wagons with the other gifts when the Six Nation emissaries, having completed their assigned task, headed homeward.

The two places where Canasatego ordered the Delawares to go were on the Susquehanna River, where tributary Indians were placed by the Six Nations under the watchful eye of their viceroy Shickellamy until his death in 1748, and after his death by his son John. From 1727 to 1756, Shamokin (present Sunbury), probably first settled by Shawnee migrants, became the largest and one of the most important Indian settlements in Pennsylvania. It was not one Indian town but a series of settlements on an island and on both sides of the river. In 1745 Presbyterian missionary David Brainard described it as partly on the east side of the river, partly on the west, and partly on an island, all in all housing three hundred Indians, half of which were Delawares and the others Seneca and Tutelo.[22]

Wyoming, situated above Shamokin on the north branch of the river, was on the site of present Wilkes-Barre, and its large flats and hunting grounds beyond the hills were of critical importance to the Six Nations. Whoever owned Wyoming blocked white expansion northward from Pennsylvania into Six Nations country and controlled the war and diplomatic trails to Onondaga from Pennsylvania. Although the Susquehanna River system originally belonged to the Minquas, from whom William Penn had purchased the land many years before, the Six Nations claimed ownership by right of conquest of the Minquas. The river system was strategically important not only as a place to assign the subjugated tribes but as a barrier to white expansion because, while protesting friendship with Brother Onas, the Six Nations were also thinking of their own protection.

Sassoonan and his people also moved over to the Susquehanna from Tulpehocken, and Sassoonan first set up his cabin at the old Indian settlement called Paxtang, at the mouth of a creek by the same name within the limits of present Harrisburg. He, Owechela, Passakassy, and Skalitchy were settled there in 1709.[23] Later he and a brother chieftain, Lingehanoa, moved to Shamokin with some of their followers.

After leaving the Brandywine, Checochinican's band of Delawares also settled at Paxtang, where some Shawnee and Conoy were living. In time, the Brandywine Delawares merged with Sassoonan's people, with whom there had been Shawnee intermarriage, and Brother Onas thereafter considered the combined group Sassoonan's subjects.

Following the July 12, 1742, conference, Nutimus, Lappawinzo, Tishecunk, and the majority of Indians living in the Forks picked up their belongings and moved to the Susquehanna, as ordered by Canasatego. Some settled at Shamokin; a few went to Wyoming; another faction established a little hamlet at the mouth of Nescopeck Creek that became known as Nutimy's Town. They, too, were joined by some Shawnee and Mahican.

The Munsies living north of the lands included in the Walking Purchase were settled on territory claimed by the Six Nations, and for a time were left unmolested. Eventually a number of them and other Delawares joined the pious Moravians, including Teedyuskung ("he who makes the earth tremble"), and his wife and family, who moved from Meniolagomeka to make their home with the Moravians at Gnadenhütten.

The fraudulent Walking Purchase has often been regarded as the turning point in English relations with the Delaware Indians, but this is something of an exaggeration. Many of the Delawares who became hostile to the English were not directly affected by the Walking Purchase. It should be clear that the loss of the Tulpehocken lands and the illicit white occupation of territory along the Brandywine were as disastrous to those two bands of Delawares as was the loss of the property at the Forks to Nutimus and his associates. The real turning point occurred when William Penn's humanitarian policy toward the Delawares gave way to Logan's new policy of strengthening their uncles, the Six Nations. Not only did Nutimus and his followers feel that they were helpless and frustrated victims of an injustice from which they had no recourse, but the entire Delaware Indian society resented the favoritism shown thir former enemy and overlords. As a result of Logan's policy, Nutimus knew, as did Sassoonan and Checochinican, even if the full realization had not yet dawned on their followers, that there was no longer any land in the Delaware Valley they could call their own. They were innocent victims of an Indian policy that served the best interests of the English in their resistance to the French—a policy that strengthened the Six Nations but left the Delawares in the sorry status of a people without a country of their own.

NOTES—CHAPTER 9

1. Joseph White Norwood, *The Tammany Legend*, Boston, 1938, p. 11.

2. See Allen's deposition of June 24, 1762, Board of Trade Properties, vol. 21, pt. 1, Historical Society of Pennsylvania, Philadelphia.

3. *Pennsylvania Colonial Records* (also called *Minutes of the Provincial Council*), 16 vols., vol. 1., p. 447. Joseph Severns & Co., Philadelphia, printed the first three vols.; Theo Fenn of Harrisburg printed the balance, 1852–53. Hereinafter cited as *Colonial Records*.

4. Ibid., vol. 3, pp. 204–5. The Shawnee joined themselves to the Susquehannock Indians "who were dependent on the five Nations, they thereby fell also under their Protection"; ibid., p. 442.

5. C. A. Weslager, "The Delaware Indians as Women," *Journal of the Washington Academy of Sciences*, vol. 34, no. 12, December 1944, pp. 381–88; also "Further Light on the Delaware Indians as Women," ibid., vol. 37, no. 9, September 1947, pp. 298–304.

6. *Colonial Records*, vol. 7, p. 297.

7. Ibid., vol. 6, pp. 155–56.

8. Paul A. W. Wallace, "John Heckewelder's Indians and the Fenimore Cooper Tradition," *Proceedings of the American Philosophical Society*, vol. 96, no. 4, August 1952, p. 499. The heat was still turned on in certain places in 1692–93 because Delaware representatives asked Governor Benjamin Fletcher to persuade the Seneca from doing them any harm "as was done some of them last summer"; *Colonial Records*, vol. 2, p. 372. In this same paper Wallace wrote that Heckewelder's story that the Delawares were duped by the Six Nations into becoming female peacemakers was "at best a piece of folk-rationalization, at worst a piece of political propaganda"; *Proceedings of the American Philosophical Society*, vol. 96, no. 4, August 1952, p. 497. In 1732, incidentally, a Shawnee chief said that the Five Nations had also put petticoats on the Shawnee; *Pennsylvania Archives*, 1st series, vol. 1, p. 329.

9. *Colonial Records*, vol. 2, p. 471.

10. Ibid., p. 546. One of the wampum belts was sent by a Delaware man who was an infant "at the time of their agreemt. or submission."

11. *Colonial Records*, vol. 5, p. 402.

12. Paul A. W. Wallace, *Conrad Weiser*, Philadelphia, 1945, p. 31. James Logan was party to the shameful treatment of the Delaware Indians at Tulpehocken, and it is possible that he was guilty of outright embezzlement, as discussed by Francis P. Jennings, "Incident at Tulpehocken," *Pennsylvania History*, vol. 35, no. 4, October 1968, pp. 335–55.

13. *Pennsylvania Archives*, 1st series, vol. 1, pp. 344–45. There was also a later deed with the Delawares, signed August 22, 1749, whereby they conveyed lands between the Delaware and Susquehanna for £500; ibid., vol. 2, p. 33.

14. Ibid., 1st series, vol. 1, p. 330.

15. Ibid., pp. 239–40; see also C. A. Weslager, *Red Men on the Brandywine*, Wilmington, 1953, pp. 89–90. Note that Nemacolin, a son of Checochinican, complained to both Christopher Gist and James Kenny that his father had been cheated out of lands along the Brandywine; ibid., pp. 93–94.

16. Papers Relating to the Friendly Association, Department of Records, Philadelphia Yearly Meeting of Friends, Philadelphia, vol. 1, pp. 406–7. The most complete and authoritative account of the Walking Purchase, from which I have liberally borrowed, is Francis P. Jennings, "The Scandalous Indian Policy of William Penn's Sons: Deeds and Documents of the Walking Purchase," *Pennsylvania History*, vol. 37, no. 1, January 1970, pp. 19–39.

17. This is fully discussed by Albright Zimmerman in his dissertation, "The Indian Trade of Colonial Pennsylvania," University of Delaware, 1965.

18. Lewis R. Harley, *Life of Charles Thomson*, Philadelphia, 1900, p. 54.

19. Wm J. Buck, "Lappawinzo and Tishcohan," *Pennsylvania Magazine of History and Biography*, vol. 7, no. 2, 1883, p. 216.

20. *Colonial Records*, vol. 4, pp. 575–76.

21. Ibid., pp. 579–80.

22. Rev. Jonathan Edwards, ed., *Memoirs of the Rev. David Brainerd*, New Haven, 1822, p. 233.

23. *Colonial Records*, vol. 2, p. 469.

10

Trouble on the Susquehanna

Originally the autonomous bands of Delaware Indians were dispersed along tributary streams in the Delaware River system from Cape Henlopen at the mouth of the bay to the territory of the Minisinks, well beyond the head of tidewater. The exodus to the Susquehanna River brought survivors of these scattered bands together at a common location for the first time. This convergence of Delaware Indians from New Jersey, Delaware, southern New York, and southeastern Pennsylvania, on the lower Susquehanna, where Minquas blood flowed in the veins of the handful of Conestoga still living there, was a remarkable movement of native peoples who had been reduced numerically and demoralized culturally. What made it noteworthy in Indian history was that the Delaware migration was either preceded, accompanied, or followed by similar migrations to the Susquehanna of expatriated Shawnee, Conoy, Nanticoke, Mahican, Tutelo, and Twightwee families who had also been driven from their native hearths by Anglo-American pressures on their societies.

Ownership of the Susquehanna and of contiguous lands continued to be claimed by the Six Nations; and the Cayuga and Oneida, fully supported by the other members of the Iroquois League, exercised a specific responsibility for the Susquehanna Valley. This territory, the Onondaga Council decided, must be withheld from intrusions of the white man. "No body," they agreed, "shall have this Land." Old Shickellamy and his son John (Tachnechdorus), who succeeded him, were appointed by the Six Nations, not only to watch over the Delawares and other tributary Indians living on the Susquehanna, but also to make certain no white men settled on the river, particularly at Shamokin or Wyoming.

The Susquehanna, with its north and west branches, is really two rivers, and a few miles above Harris's ferry (present Harrisburg) a third branch, the Juniata, whose valley leads into the heart of the Alleghenies, swells the main stream with its waters. The terraces and coves of the main river give way to extensive flatlands and bluffs south of Harrisburg, as one proceeds downstream toward the Chesapeake. To the displaced Delawares almost any location along the Susquehanna was a wilderness paradise, because its virgin forests had not yet felt the slash of the white man's axe nor the earth the bite of his plow. The Indian expatriates seated themselves at the native towns of Paxtang, Shamokin, Nescopeck, Wyoming, and at villages farther north on the river—such as Lackawacka, Adjouquay, Tunkannock, Wyalusing, Tioga, Oswego, Otseningo, Assinisink, and Wilawane in the Seneca country on the Chemung. (Additional information about these sites can be found in Appendix 1.) Many of the Indians now owned horses; a few had cows; their gardens along the river banks were green with corn; they fished in the river and hunted in the woods for deer and other animals whose pelts continued to be in demand by the white traders. It was like old times to stalk the herds of deer again and not be forced to complain, as Canasatego once did in a conference with the whites, that "your Horses and Cows have eat the Grass our Deer used to feed on." [1]

Half-naked children sprawled in the dirt around their huts, and the squaws cooked and sewed as their mothers and grandmothers had done before them. Now they used iron and brass pots, European needles and thread, and their dresses were made of strouding decorated with bands of colorful ribbons as well as of other cheap, woven woolens that continued to be imported from England. The Indian men wore breechclouts, leggings made of cloth, mantles of matchcoats, stockings, shirts, shoes, coats, hats, and other articles of European manufacture obtained either from the fur traders or as gifts presented by Brother Onas to their chiefs and great men. Sassoonan was treated liberally by Pennsylvania's governors (and he conferred with a succession of governors appointed by the Penns during his lifetime) when he went to Philadelphia on official business. Sometimes he was summoned to the conference table, along with other chiefs, because the authorities had matters to discuss with the Indians; at other times he and some of his native associates went without invitation to reconfirm the peace, which was always a good excuse to collect gifts. Whatever the occasion, Brother Onas, having made Sassoonan the king, rarely failed to give him quantities of matchcoats, powder, lead, hats, stockings, shoes, red pigment for use as face paint, and the perennial strings of wampum used to clear dust from the eyes and remove obstructions from the road. Once as evidence of affection, Sassoonan was given a horse, saddle, and bridle, because who could expect a king to walk to Philadelphia? [2] On another occasion, after presenting the governor with pelts valued at eight pounds, the chief, in turn, was given merchandise worth thirty pounds. Another time he received a matchcoat laced with silver and a silver-laced hat, because a king must give the appearance of being a royal personage.[3] Usually on the last day of the meeting, the jug was uncorked to drink to everyone's health and a safe journey home.

A chief returning from Philadelphia dressed in European finery, with a quantity of merchandise to share with friends and relatives, made a favorable impression among the Indians, who naturally assumed he must be regarded highly by the white leaders. Thus, they were inclined to observe his wishes, and he did his best to oblige his benefactors by doing their bidding, realizing that an uncooperative attitude would result in shutting off the supply of presents. Sassoonan enjoyed playing the role of king of the Delawares, and at a session with Governor Gordon in Philadelphia on September 11, 1728, the secretary recorded the following passage from one of Sassoonan's discourses:

That the Governour now sees but a very small Number of their People: there are only present some of the Delaware & Brandywine Indians, & none of the Shawanese, but the Governour must not think strange of it, because at this time of the year they cannot conveniently come; *that nevertheless, he now speaks in the Name & Behalf of them all.*[4]

The words I have italicized indicate how Sassoonan exaggerated his authority, since he was well aware that he was not appointed to speak for the Delawares at Shamokin, the Munsies living upstream on the Susquehanna, nor the Delaware survivors still living in northern New Jersey. He also knew that the Shawnee were fully capable of speaking for themselves and usually addressed the Pennsylvania authorities through their own sachems or speakers. Sassoonan went on to say that he hoped the Delaware Indians and Brother Onas would continue to be good friends forevermore, and he gave the following tenuous reason as one justification for the peaceful and friendly attitude of the Delawares toward the English:

He says the five Nations have often told them that they were as Women only, & desired them to plant Corn & mind their own private Business, for that they would take Care of what related to Peace & War, & that therefore they have ever had good and peaceable Thoughts toward us.[5]

Governor Gordon was so impressed with the Delawares' peaceful intentions that he presented Sassoonan with the following merchandise, as recorded in the minutes of the meeting:

6 Strowds	12 Duffells
6 Shirts	1½ Barrel Powder
12 Blanketts	1 Cwt Lead
with Bread, Rum, Pipes, & Tobacco.	

After receiving these gifts and loading them on a pack horse to carry to Wyoming, Sassoonan said that he appreciated this kindness and "will not only remember it carefully, but likewise publish it among all his Friends & Brethren . . . and they [the Indians] all express'd their Satisfaction by a harmonious Sound peculiar to them, in which they all joyned." [6]

This "harmonious Sound," which flattered Governor Gordon, was the well-known "Yo Hah," a chant of approbation given by the Delawares (as well as the Shawnee, Six Nations, and others) when they were especially pleased. The Indian speaker enunciated the first syllable, and the others repeated it in unison; then came the second syllable, which was also repeated in unison. This was done a number of times, resulting in a striking vocal effect, particularly when a large number of Indians participated.

For a while things seemed to go fairly well with the Indians on the Susquehanna, although the threat that their uncles and hosts, the Six Nations, might find it necessary to chastise them for some indiscretion seemed to annoy the Shawnee more than it did the Delawares. There was, however, freedom to roam, which gave the Indian occupation a sort of fluidity reminiscent of the good old days before the white man came, when the Delawares and their Algonkian brethren were not obligated to affix themselves permanently to a particular piece of property. For instance, after moving into Pennsylvania from Maryland, the Nanticokes first lived at the mouth of the Juniata; then they moved upstream to Wyoming; and later they went up farther to the Six Nations town of Otseningo (present Binghamton, New York). The tameless and restless Shawnee moved back and forth from Paxtang to Shamokin to Wyoming. Some went to Tulpehocken and the Forks of the Delaware; others were seen hunting as far south as Cecil County, Maryland. The Delawares, like the Mahican, lived at one village site or on a series of sites on year and then moved elsewhere the next. Some of the Indian families pushed into the Alleghenies through the valley of the Juniata and its tributaries, returning to the Susquehanna when they felt so inclined. Sometimes in the fall it seemed that the woods and mountains had swallowed up the Indians entirely, except for a few of the old men and women who remained behind when the younger families deserted their wigwams for the chase.

It was a small party of young Shawnee braves who first decided to go west of the mountains with their families and settle on the Ohio River, where game was more plentiful than along the Susquehanna. They didn't ask permission of Brother Onas or Shickellamy, who were both concerned for their welfare—they just took off. Shortly thereafter, some of the young Delaware men, uneasy in their Susquehanna villages, expressed their wanderlust by paddling their families in dugouts up the west branch of the Susquehanna to the headwaters of the stream, and portaging over to the Allegheny River to join the Shawnee. They founded a village at "Allegheny on the Main Road," known as Kittanning ("place on the big river"), destined within a few years to become the largest Indian town west of Shamokin.

These Delawares who departed from the Susquehanna probably did not consult with old Sassoonan before they left, because they owed no fealty to him. Most of them were indifferent to his views, feeling no responsibility to either him or Brother Onas. Some had been members of Checochinican's Brandywine band; others formerly owed their loyalty to Oholykon, Tishecunk, Lappawinzo, or Nutimus;

still others had been followers of Menakihikon, Echgohund, Owechela, or Kindassowa—the latter being one of the chieftains of the
Minisinks (Munsies) settled on the upper Susquehanna. None of
them felt affection for a has-been Delaware king who seldom left his
smoky cabin at Shamokin because he was too old and feeble to participate in the chase and too proud to work in the cornfields with
the women.

Incidentally, the affection Sassoonan showed Brother Onas, whether
real or pretended, was not shared by most of the other Delaware
sachems. Some, like Menakihikon, had a special grudge against the
English because one of his relatives, Wequeald (also spelled Weeque-
helah), was hanged in New Jersey for killing a white man, Captain
John Leonard, in the spring of 1728.[7] Wequeald, who lived in a well-
furnished house, spoke English, and owned a farm with cattle and
horses, shot Leonard when he seized property Wequeald claimed to
own. After a legal trial Wequeald was executed, which aroused the
anger of those who were related to him.

Eventually the members of Sassoonan's band paid little attention
to him, except when he returned from Philadelphia with presents to
distribute. He was not in good health, having never fully recovered
from a contagious fever that swept the Susquehanna in 1744, killing
a number of his "subjects." He had also become a chronic alcoholic.
He developed such a compulsion for rum that in the depths of his
degradation he sold, one by one, the precious belts and strings of
wampum entrusted to his care, thus depriving the Delawares of official records of the transactions in which he represented them during his more sober moments. Conrad Weiser tells how the old chief
had deteriorated in a letter to Richard Peters dated July 20, 1747:

Olumapies would have Resigned his Crown before now, but as he had
the keeping of the public treasure Consisting of Belts of Wampum, for
which he buys Liquor and has been Drunk for this two or three years,
allmost Constantly, and it is thought he won't Die so long as there is a
single wampum left in the bag.[8]

Brother Onas knew all about Sassoonan's weakness for the hard
liquor that was originally imported from Europe but was now being
distilled in various parts of the province as well as in nearby Maryland. Once on a visit to Philadelphia in June, 1715, dressed in a

braided coat and breeches Brother Onas had given him, his face striped with paint and his shoulder-length hair glistening with its dressing of bear fat—Sassoonan went on a bender as soon as the session with Governor Gookin ended. He and several other chiefs became drunk, making a nuisance of themselves in the streets and taverns of Philadelphia. Several days later, after the Delaware chief and his companions had sobered up, the governor cautioned them that he "wished they had more effectively taken the advice that was given them to forbear Excessive Drinking, & especially to avoid Rum, wch since it disorders them so very much & ruins their health they ought to shun it as poison; for tho' valuable and Good men when sober yet when overcome with that unhappy Liquor, they are quite lost & become beasts." [9] Gookin was well aware that only feeble efforts were made to enforce the liquor laws, because the livelihood of too many whites depended upon this commerce. In both Virginia and Pennsylvania, government executives were personally involved in liquor profiteering at the expense of the Indians.

The liquor problem among the Delawares continued to be as acute as it had been years before when the Dutch and Swedes were in control, and it was paradoxical that chiefs like Sassoonan, who knew that intoxicants debauched their people, were the worst offenders. Time and again Sassoonan complained to the authorities that English traders were bringing quantities of rum to Indian villages on the Susquehanna, and requested that the practice be stopped. On August 12, 1731, he protested to Governor Gordon "that many Horseloads of it [rum] pass by his Door & it all comes from Philadelphia and that he cannot understand why such Quantities should be sent up." [10] On the other hand, he said he didn't want it entirely prohibited, but his main concern was that he didn't want the traders to bring it to Shamokin. He urged that inventories of intoxicants be kept at certain convenient locations where the Indians could go and buy it when they wanted it, or send their women after it, since "they would not wholly be deprived of it, but they would not have it brought by the Christians."

The Delawares who had gone over the mountains from the Susquehanna to Kittanning also petitioned Governor Gordon regarding certain white traders who followed them and violated the provincial liquor laws. They asked him to "Suppress Such numbers of them from Comeing Into the woods and Esspecially from bringing such Large quantityes of Rum . . ." [11] Some of the unlicensed traders came to Indian towns with nothing else to trade but rum. To satisfy their craving for alcohol, the braves brought out the furs they had been saving to pay for clothing for their families, or to buy powder, lead, gun flints, and other essentials. They exchanged the pelts for liquor, which they consumed until they were senseless. After their furs were all gone, the Indians in their drunken frenzy often tore off their own clothing and exchanged it for a final drink of rum. When the bacchanal was over, the trader departed, his horses loaded with valuable skins representing a full season's hunting, and the Indians had nothing useful to show for their long days of work, nor could they discharge their debts to the legitimate traders who had extended credit to them.

Governor Gordon reminded the Indians that there were adequate laws on the books forbidding traffic in liquor, but the natives not only refused to obey these laws but encouraged unscrupulous traders to bring liquor to their towns. The governor said he realized that a principal cause of dissension between Indians and whites was rum "of which you are so fond that you will not be denied it." He enjoined them to "behave themselves, Soberly like Men of Thought and understanding." [12] At the same time he issued instructions to the licensed traders, reminding them that liquor traffic with the Indians was prohibited by law, and should the Indians get it from sources outside the province the traders were to avoid drinking it with them.[13]

In 1738 the Delawares, Shawnee, and other Indians living on the Ohio held a council and decided to permit no rum in any of their towns for four years. Responsible Indian leaders were appointed in each town to see that no traders brought liquor but, if they did, to stave the casks and spill the contents on the ground "in the presence of the Whole Town." [14] Permission to stave casks of liquor illegally transported to their villages had been given the Indians many years before in William Penn's time, but this was not a realistic approach to the problem, nor did the four-year moratorium declared by the Indians prove to be an enforceable solution.

"You go yourselves & fetch Horse loads of strong Liquor," Conrad Weiser told these same Delawares and Shawnee at one of their Ohio towns. "But the other Day an Indian came to this Town out of Maryland with 3 Horse loads of Liquor, so that it appears you love it so well that you cannot be without it." [15] Weiser put his finger precisely on the problem, for which there was no easy solution. The whites must accept the blame for introducing alcohol to Indian society without trying to teach moderation, but the Indians, in their craze to drink more and more, even after experience had taught them the consequences, must also assume a responsibility for their foolish conduct. Sassoonan and other Delaware chiefs failed to set an example of sobriety for their people and deserve censure for their actions.

As time went on, more Delawares moved from the Susquehanna to settle on the Ohio, which the French called *La Belle Rivière* and which also included the Allegheny River system. Where Pittsburgh is situated, the Allegheny merges with the Monongahela to form the Ohio proper, and about eighteen miles south of the junction of the three rivers was an Indian settlement called Chiningué or Logstown (present Ambridge), a cosmopolitan community of Delawares, Shawnee, and other Indian migrants. There were other smaller towns in the immediate area also occupied by Delawares, some named for a leading Indian resident. Shingas lived for a while at Shingas's Town, for example, in the vicinity of present McKees Rocks; and Shannopin's Town, named for another prominent Delaware, was on the Allegheny above the junction of the three rivers and within the city limits of present Pittsburgh. At present Franklin, where French Creek joins the Allegheny, there was an old Indian town named Venango, and a group of Delawares under the chief Custaloga settled there. A town called Loyalhanning at the mouth of Loyalhanna Creek (near present Ligonier) was the residence of another prominent Delaware named Kichinipallin, and along the Indian path that ran from Loyalhanning to Kittanning there were at least two smaller Delaware hamlets, one containing eleven and the other seven cabins.[16]

Although the Delawares knew these various settlements as their homes, they realized that they actually had no ownership rights to the lands on which they lived, planted, and hunted. The Six Nations claimed this territory, and two Iroquois representatives, a Seneca called the Half King whose native name was Tanacharison, and an Oneida named Scarouady, supervised and kept a close protective scrutiny over the Delaware and Shawnee living on the Ohio lands. The Six Nations maintained that they were proprietors of the Ohio territory by right of conquest, insisting that it was their prerogative to determine who, whites or Indians, or either, should occupy the territory.

With the exception of the warlike Eriechronons ("Cat Nation"), who formerly occupied the area south of Lake Erie and were defeated by the Six Nations, the question of what other Indian tribes living in the Ohio Valley were conquered by the Iroquois was never fully answered. It is true that by 1657, following their defeat, the Eriechronons were forced to move, but the Six Nations did not settle in the depopulated territory, nor did they apparently use it as hunting grounds. When the rivalry between France and England for colonial power in northeastern North America became heated, the English upheld the right of the Six Nations to the Ohio Valley. They did so for a very selfish reason—the same reason that had caused Governors Andros and Dongan to bend their efforts to make the Six Nations subjects of the King of England. They wanted to dispossess their French rivals from the Ohio, and they claimed the territory that their subjects, the Iroquois, had allegedly conquered. In short, they magnified Iroquois conquests for their own aggrandizement.

Of course, England's claim to the Ohio Valley was part of her broader claim to possession of North American lands entirely apart from the Six Nations. The situation was further complicated because the King of France had annexed all the land discovered by La Salle, and this included the full extent of the Ohio Valley. Neither French nor English monarch had privy counselors wise enough to lay down accurate bounds on a map for this vast domain each claimed. The land was then being policed by Six Nations overseers and occupied by sundry bands of Indian hunters. The Penns and their appointed governors, supporting the Six Nations, maintained that the charter of Pennsylvania included lands at the forks of the Ohio, but they were in a weak position to enforce ownership because the Quaker-dominated assembly refused to become involved in hostilities. To confound matters further, Virginia insisted that part of the Ohio Territory, of indeterminate size, belonged to her by right of a royal charter, and the Ohio Company, supported with Virginia money, was starting to sell lands and promote settlement along the Allegheny and Monongahela.

At this critical period neither France nor England knew the size and extent of the mobile Indian population along the Ohio River and its tributaries, although an English trader in 1731 reported there were then 300 Delawares and 260 Shawnee at Kittanning, including men, women, and children.[17] It continued to be the largest Indian settlement on the Ohio River at the time of the report, although there were Wyandot villages along the Sandusky, the Muskingum, and elsewhere in the area that had been vacated by the Eriechronons. By 1748, according to information given to Conrad Weiser by the Indians—using small sticks as counters to record the population—there were 789 *fighting men* on the Ohio, exclusive of their women and children. This warrior population consisted of 165 Delawares, 162 Shawnee, 15 Mahican, 163 Seneca, 100 Wyandot, 40 Tisagechroanu (a Chippewa subtribe also called the Mississauga), 74 Mohawk, 35 Onondaga, 20 Cayuga, and 15 Oneida.[18] Evidently the Seneca, Mohawk, Onondaga, Cayuga, and Oneida warriors were mostly opportunists who had left New York and struck out on their own, but some had left their homes because of a famine. A number of these Iroquois initially settled on the Cuyahoga River, but they also lived at other locations in Ohio, independent of the Onondaga Council.

The Six Nations were not able to control the movements or action of their Ohio brethren, and still less, as time went on, the Delawares and Shawnee, although the English authorities did their utmost to try to keep the Indians living in Ohio under the authority of the Six Nations. Within a few years the Ohio faction of Iroquois warriors and hunters were to become known as Mingoes and to win a reputation as fierce and ruthless warriors.

Pennsylvania, Virginia, and the Onondaga Council—each for reasons of its own—became seriously concerned about French activity along the Ohio when reports were received that the tribes living and hunting there, including the Delawares and Shawnee, were turning an attentive ear to the French. The Six Nations, encouraged by the English, believed that a quick and certain solution was to bring the Delawares and Shawnee back to the Susquehanna, removing them from the French sphere of influence. They first tried to persuade the Shawnee to return, but the Shawnee said they would starve on the Susquehanna because of the scarcity of game. Then the Six Nations instructed Sassoonan to bring back the Delawares, "upon which he had sent Messengers to his People at Ohio, requiring them to return." [19] The Delawares at Logstown and Kittanning turned a deaf ear to the request of a king who was now growing senile. He "has lost his Senses," Weiser wrote, "and is uncapable of doing anything."[20]

Pennsylvania authorities believed that, if Sassoonan couldn't bring the Delawares back to the Susquehanna, it was more important than ever that his successor be an Indian respected among his people—influential, yet amenable to the English political interests. Pennsylvania's deputy-governors, preconditioned by English politics, stubbornly continued to think in terms of nominating a new king who could exercise authority over *all* the Delawares—those on the Susquehanna as well as those who had moved west to the Ohio. This was alien to a basic Delaware concept of hereditary chiefs whose lineage was the nucleus of the matrilinear band structures, each independent of the other. Pennsylvania's first choices, from whom they hoped Sassoonan's successor could be selected, were two of his blood relatives: Opekasset, the elder heir apparent, and Shackatawlin, described by James Logan as "the truest, honestest young fellow I ever knew among Indians."

Opekasset, who had attended numerous conferences and peace renewals between Sassoonan and Brother Onas, and Shackatawlin, who had rendered valuable services as a Delaware-English interpreter, were both pro-English in their sympathies. Logan knew that either could be influenced as readily as Sassoonan, and kept under the authority of the Six Nations consistent with Pennsylvania's Indian policy. But neither was destined to succeed Sassoonan. Opekasset died of smallpox, which continued to break out at intervals and take its toll of the Indians, and Shackatawlin was stabbed to death by his uncle Sassoonan in a fit of temper when the old chief was so drunk he didn't know what he was doing. Later Sassoonan was so remorseful that he refused to eat, and sorrowed almost to death, until Brother Onas summoned him to Philadelphia and forgave him.[21]

With the two best-qualified candidates dead, Conrad Weiser suggested that Lappapitton (also spelled Lappachpitton, "does it over again"), a sober and honest Delaware Indian between forty and fifty years of age, would make an acceptable alternate. Weiser was sure that Brother Onas could handle him. When Lappapitton, who lived at Catawissa, called Lappapitton's Town, on the north branch of the Susquehanna, was approached by Weiser who tendered him the "crown," the Indian politely declined the honor. "He is afraid he will be Envyd and consequently bewitched by some of the Indians,"

Weiser wrote Logan.[22] Lappapitton was fully aware that a "stump chief," who was not a birthright "king" in the line of succession, would have difficulty imposing himself on the Delawares, and that the traditionalists would lose no time in "bewitching," i.e., "removing," him permanently from office.

Sassoonan favored as his successor another one of his nephews, named Pisquetomen ("he that keeps on though it is getting dark"), an intelligent, courageous, strong-willed member of the "royal family." He had also attended many conferences with Brother Onas, often serving as a Delaware-English interpreter. In fact, Pisquetomen had interpreted for Nutimus when the latter's lands were fraudulently taken, and he was strongly pro-Delaware in his views. Perhaps Sassoonan saw in him the man he had always wanted to be before he became a slave to liquor, but James Logan was also perceptive—he knew he would never be able to force his will on Pisquetomen. He instructed Weiser to do his utmost to prevent Pisquetomen's accession to the chieftaincy, and he also enlisted Shickellamy's assistance to thwart any action by the Indians that would be considered inimical to English interests. When Sassoonan died in 1747, there was no one satisfactory to succeed him, since the ominous shadow of Brother Onas hung over the Delaware "throne." Aware that either he or one of his two younger brothers, Shingas ("wet, marshy ground") or Tamaqua ("Beaver") were by heredity eligible to the chieftaincy, Pisquetomen left Shamokin to settle on the Ohio, more resentful than ever of Brother Onas's interference with ancient Delaware custom.[23]

It should not be inferred that the Delawares lacked leaders after Sassoonan's death. In the various Delaware and Munsie towns on the Susquehanna and Ohio, there were band and village chiefs who acted as spokesmen for their followers. The Pennsylvania provincial records refer to such sachems as Nenathcheeon, Custaloga, Nowchikano, Nutimus, Kachhawatichiky, Shawanasson, Schamanatainu, Quetekund, Tishecunk (who formerly lived at Hociundoquen in the Forks of the Delaware, but who had moved to Ohio), and many others. Most Delaware villages on both the Ohio and Susquehanna waterways were now composed of families of mixed affinity, with Shawnee, Mahican, and persons of other tribal blood intermingled with the Delawares. Culture changes were beginning to take place as the Delawares borrowed traits from other Indian groups with which they were thrown into contact.

The government of Pennsylvania continued to seek a suitable candidate who could be elevated to king of the Delawares, because this would greatly facilitate dealings with the Indians. At the signing of a treaty with the Six Nations, Delawares, Shawnee, Wyandot, and Twightwee, held at Logstown on May 28, 1751, George Croghan—Irish-born trader, land speculator, Indian emissary for Pennsylvania, and later deputy-agent to Sir William Johnson—addressed the Indians as the personal representative of Governor James Hamilton. Speaking to the Delawares in particular he said:

. . . I desire you may choose amongst Yourselves one of your wisest Counsellor and present to your Brethren of the Six Nations and me [i.e., Governor Hamilton] for a Chief, and he so chosen by you shall be looked upon by us as your King, with whom Publick Business shall be transacted.[24]

During this conference the speaker for the Delawares was Beaver, whom James Kenny described as "a steady, quiet, middle-aged man of cheerful disposition, but low stature." The following day, Beaver spoke, declaring that since their wise men were not all gathered together "it would take some time to consider on a Man that was fit to undertake to rule a Nation of People, but as soon as possible they would make a full answer, which they hoped would give Satisfaction to their Brothers the English and the Six Nations." Governor Hamilton had been careful to emphasize to the Delawares that their nominee must meet the approval of the Six Nations. Beaver, in his desire to please Hamilton, acknowledged the necessity of obtaining this approval, although many of the Delawares resented the Six Nations intervention in the selection of their chief. It was, of course, one of the many gestures by the Pennsylvania government intended to strengthen Six Nations control over the other Indians, the essence of its Indian policy.

By 1752 the Delawares on the Ohio had a new chief who came of "royal lineage," a man the Six Nations found satisfactory, because they made the selection themselves after consultation with Brother Onas. At a treaty-signing at Logstown in 1752, Tanacharison addressed Beaver as follows: "We let you know that it is our Right to give you a King, and we think it proper to give you Shingas for your King, whom you must look upon as your Chief & with whom all publick

Business must be transacted between you & your Brethren the English." [25]

Shingas, who then lived near the "Fork of Mohongalio" (present Pittsburgh), was not present at his coronation, so Tanacharison put a laced hat on the head of Beaver, who stood proxy for his brother, and presented him with a rich jacket and a suit of clothes supplied by the Virginia commissioners. Within a few years, the governments of Virginia and Pennsylvania would both regret having endorsed the crowning of Shingas, when frontier families were frightened almost to death by the sound of his name, and tales of his atrocities made him known as "Shingas, the Terrible."

Many of the Ohio Delawares did not favor the choice of Shingas, but, whether they liked it or not, the Six Nations had named him the principal chief and official agent with whom business with the English had to be conducted. Actually, Shingas was never the spokesman for *all* the Delawares, because those living on the Susquehanna and others still in New Jersey felt no fealty toward him, having their own chiefs.

In the meantime, a new leader was coming up from the rank and file of the Delawares living on the Susquehanna, an aggressive and eloquent man conversant in the English language, but one who lacked hereditary claim to chieftaincy—Teedyuskung, alias "Honest John." Following the Walking Purchase, Teedyuskung did not move to the Susquehanna with Nutimus and his people, but went to Bethlehem and became associated with the Moravians. This carefully planned industrial community, regulated by severe religious disciplines, was the American headquarters of the German-speaking United Brethren, who came predominantly from Saxony and Bohemia (Moravia).

Not far from Bethlehem, at present Lehightown on Mahoning Creek, a tributary of the Lehigh, the Moravians, motivated by intense zeal to Christianize the Indians, founded an Indian mission. This tiny sylvan utopia called Gnadenhütten ("tents of Grace") was the first of several Moravian Indian missions to bear this name. At Gnadenhütten in the solemn Moravian ritual of adult baptism, conducted by Bishop Cammerhoff, the fifty-five-year-old Teedyuskung, robed in white, was reborn a Moravian convert under the name Gideon, and his Munsie wife was baptized Elisabeth. His twenty-two-year-old son Tachgokanhelle and his wife, Pingtis, were baptized Amos and Justina. At Gnadenhütten, homeless Mahican families from the Hudson Valley and Wampanoag Indians from New England joined the Delawares and, under the tutelage of industrious Moravian pastors, tended their gardens, assisted in the orchard and in the grist- and sawmills, and attended daily religious services in the chapel, where they participated in communion, love feasts, and other church rites.

On July 18, 1753, a company having both commercial and religious objectives was organized in Windham, Connecticut. The Susquehanna Company was to play an important part in the life of Teedyuskung and other Moravian Indians. The stockholders intended to take up lands along the Susquehanna River in Pennsylvania that they claimed had been included in an early grant Charles I made to the Plymouth Company and later conveyed and confirmed to Connecticut in another royal patent. Although Connecticut was far from overcrowded, many of its residents, like those in the other growing American colonies, were intent upon acquiring land at low prices per acre. The company's published aims, "To Spread Christianity and also promote our Own Temporal Interest," were a gross understatement of the mania for land speculation that developed along the Susquehanna. As time went on, a second organization, the Delaware Company, was formed in Norwich, Connecticut, and its members also turned covetous eyes in the direction of Pennsylvania.

This complicated and confusing chapter in American colonial history, wherein the citizens of Connecticut tried to take lands claimed by the citizens of Pennsylvania—which were extremely critical to Pennsylvania's Indian relations—is the subject of a twelve-volume study called *The Susquehanna Company Papers*.[26] For the present purpose, suffice it to say that the people from Connecticut began to survey and make maps of the lands, rivers, and tributaries in the vicinity of Indian settlements at Wyoming. This was disturbing to the Six Nations, who claimed the land, and to the Delawares who had been placed there by the Six Nations with the assurance of Brother Onas that they would not be annoyed by white people. A Delaware Indian started a rumor by saying that he had overheard one of the Connecticut leaders saying that he intended to return the following spring with 1,000 white settlers. When the Six Nations learned what was happening, they protested loudly to Pennsylvania, and at the same time attempted to block Connecticut expansion by placing more Indians on the Susquehanna.

There is no reason to think that Teedyuskung had any interest in assisting the Six Nations to preserve their lands when he and a Mahican comrade, Mamalatasecung (baptized Abraham, the first Moravian convert in America), decided to leave Gnadenhütten and settle at Wyoming. On April 24, 1754, along with sixty-five other Indians, they left the mission town, and, as Nutimus and the Forks Delawares had done twelve years before, found a new home in the flat green plain of Wyoming, where the Susquehanna flows southward to the Chesapeake. Although they left without a white missionary, the majority of the group promised they would cleave unto the Lord Jesus and remain faithful to Christian teachings.[27]

While Teedyuskung was leading his polyglot Indian followers to the Susquehanna, the French were moving southward from the Great Lakes into the forests of the Ohio. Their intention was to link Louisiana with French Canada, and in 1753 they built forts at Presque Isle (modern Erie) and Le Boeuf (Watertown) without obtaining permission from the Six Nations to occupy the territory. The French maintained they had discovered the Ohio River long before the Six Nations knew of its existence. As they pressed into the Ohio country, the French were assisted by Indian allies from Canada and the Great Lakes, and Peter Chartier, son of a French father and Shawnee mother, had already consolidated a pro-French faction among the Shawnee to prepare for their coming.

In October of 1753, twenty-one-year-old George Washington left Williamsburg, Virginia, with a message from Governor Robert Dinwiddie warning the commandant of French forces to leave the Ohio country, which, the message said, was the property of Virginia and the King of England. On this journey Washington visited Shingas, whom he referred to in his journal as "King of the Delawares," at the chief's home about two miles below present Pittsburgh. Washington accompanied Shingas to a meeting attended by Tanacharison (the Iroquois Half King) at Logstown, where he learned that the Indians were equally concerned about French intrusion in the Ohio Valley. In fact, it was the Delawares living at Venango who had sent a formal notice to the French commander warning him not to advance beyond Niagara, but this had no effect. As the French continued their march, the Indians held a council at Logstown, and a second notice was sent to the French to leave the country and return home. The French officer replied that he was ordered to build four forts along the Ohio, and this he intended to do since all the land and the water west of the Alleghenies belonged to the French.[28]

Washington exchanged wampum belts with the Indians at Logstown, where he learned that Tanacharison had sent a third warning the previous month to the French that said in uncompromising terms, "I tell you in plain Words you must go off this land." [29] It is of interest, in view of what ensued, that the Ohio Delawares at this stage of their diplomacy fully supported Tanacharison in his opposition to the French advance. Washington exchanged wampum belts with the Indians, and Tanacharison and Shingas pledged him their full support as allies of Virginia. Tanacharison, a man of unusual intelligence and foresight, had repeatedly urged Virginia to build a "strong house" at the forks of the Ohio, recognizing the military importance of this site long before his English contemporaries. When Washington viewed the triangular point at the junction of the rivers, he quickly came to the same conclusion and noted in his journal that the land was "extremely well situated for a Fort, as it has the absolute Command of both Rivers." [30]

Neither the English warning delivered by Washington nor the three Indian protests deterred the French. At Fort Le Boeuf, Washington was greeted with Old World military courtesy by the ailing fifty-two-year-old commander Legardeur de Saint-Pierre, whose troops were then busy building pirogues and bateaux for a campaign down the Allegheny to construct a fort at the forks of the Ohio. Saint-Pierre sent a written reply to Dinwiddie's letter in which he blandly said that he thought himself "not obliged to obey it" but would forward it to his superior, the Marquis Duquesne, French governor at Quebec. Saint-Pierre knew that the lordly and arrogant Duquesne had deliberately adopted a strong and aggressive policy so far as the Ohio country was concerned, and Dinwiddie's letter could not change his plans.

It is unnecessary to recount the well-known details that led to the outbreak of hostilities between the French and English, except to emphasize that it was Virginia, not Pennsylvania, that took the offensive. At a treaty held in Lancaster, Pennsylvania, Virginia bought from the Six Nations "all the lands within the said colony as it is now or hereafter may be peopled and bounded by his said Majesty." At the time, the Iroquois were not aware that, according to her charter, Virginia's official bounds extended well beyond the Alleghenies. From Virginia's viewpoint, extinguishing the Indian title was to pave the way for expansion. Yet a few years later when another treaty was signed at Logstown, the Virginia commissioners assured the Six

Nations chiefs ". . . that the King, our Father, by purchasing your lands, had never any Intention of takeing them from you, but that we might live together as one People & keep them from the French, who wou'd be bad Neighbours." [31]

In 1747 the Crown approved a petition submitted by the organizers of the Ohio Company of Virginia for two hundred thousand acres on the consideration that it seat one hundred families within seven years and maintain a garrison to protect them. When these conditions were satisfied the company would then be entitled to take up an additional three hundred thousand acres. Subsequently the Ohio Company sent a group of men to the forks of the Ohio, not to erect the kind of stronghold Tanacharison had recommended as a fortress to protect the mouth of the Ohio River, but to build a small fort where trade goods could be secured.

In 1754 Washington led a small detachment of Virginia soldiers across the Alleghenies, and before reaching the Ohio River learned that a strong French force had seized the junction of the three rivers, torn down the English post, and erected a formidable fortress called Fort Duquesne. At Great Meadows, after making a surprise attack on a small party of French soldiers, Washington hastily threw up Fort Necessity, which he was forced to surrender to a French force that outnumbered him. Politically the defeat was a severe blow to English prestige, and it marked the opening of the French and Indian War in which the Delawares were to become deeply involved. Washington's defeat also tended to weaken James Logan's well-laid Indian policy, because it showed the Shawnee and the Loups ("Wolves"), as the French called the Delawares, that the French had adequate supplies and sufficient men under arms to oppose the English effectively. Thus it brought the Ohio Indians closer to the French orbit, even though the Delawares had initially resented French intrusion on their hunting grounds.

The defeat at Fort Necessity also tended to dilute the authority of Tanacharison and Scarouady in their dealings with the Delawares and Shawnee. It also removed from the Indians their primary source of trade goods, because English traders were afraid of what the French would do to them, and they fled from the Ohio. One English trader was apprehended by French soldiers from Fort Duquesne who seized his thirteen horses laden with goods and took him to Quebec as a prisoner.[32] Soon French traders, or those acting in French interests working out of Fort Duquesne, were monopolizing the Indian trade, and the French assumed both military and economic control of the Ohio Valley. Sentiment grew among the Indians that "Onontio" (their name for the governor of Canada, as well as the King of France) had sufficient strength to emerge victorious if open war broke out with the English.

At this time the English themselves had serious doubts of their ability to withstand French attack, and, despite repeated brightening of the Covenant Chain with the Six Nations, some English leaders were apprehensive that their Iroquois friends would betray them by joining the French. In 1754 the English colonies called a joint meeting in Albany to discuss the best way to unify their forces. The words italicized below in a representation written at the meeting reflect their grave concerns:

That it is the evident Design of the French to surround the British Colonies, to fortify themselves on the Back therof, to take and keep Possession of the Heads of all the important Rivers, to draw over the Indians to their Interest, and with the help of such Indians, added to such Forces as are already arrived and may be hereafter sent from Europe, to be in a Capacity of making a general Attack upon the several Governments. *And if at the same Time a strong Naval Force be sent from France, there is the utmost Danger that the whole Continent will be subjected to that Crown.*[33]

At the Albany conference, Pennsylvania's representatives insisted that the Six Nations convey to them the unexplored, vaguely bounded territory west of the Susquehanna, which, after much persuasion, the Indians reluctantly agreed to do. They reserved from the sale the lands at Wyoming and Shamokin "to settle such of our Nations as shall come to us from the Ohio or any others who shall deserve to be in our Alliance." [34] Pennsylvania officials were anxious to extinguish title to this land in order to be able to show the world an Indian deed that would brand the French as intruders—and would also strengthen Pennsylvania's claim against Virginia's, since the two colonies overlapped on the lower Ohio. The Pennsylvania authorities had no opposition to the Six Nations reserving Wyoming and Shamokin from the sale, since friendly Delawares, including Teedyuskung and his people living in those settlements—and any other Indians who might be placed there—constituted a buffer against Connecticut.

In view of the adamant position the Six Nations held regarding ownership of Wyoming and Shamokin, what occurred at Albany five days later, on July 11, becomes inexplicable. The Susquehanna Company designated Gideon Hawley of Bridgeport to establish an Indian mission on the Susquehanna, and, in order to acquire land for the mission, Timothy Woodbridge was given the task of negotiating with the Six Nations. Not feeling qualified in Indian statecraft, Woodbridge delegated his authority to an Albany trader of ill repute named John Henry Lydius. Working under cover, Lydius, who knew the ways of the Indians and their love for liquor, bribed several Iroquois sachems with rum and Spanish dollars, obtaining their signatures on a deed which conveyed to the Susquehanna Company a tract of land between the Delaware and Susquehanna, including the Wyoming valley.[35] The signatories were not representatives of the Onondaga Council, which later disavowed the conveyance. Nevertheless a document existed, signatures were on it, a consideration had been paid, and the Susquehanna Company could point to it as proof of having extinguished Indian title.

Not until the end of October, four months after the Albany conference, did Nutimus and his Delawares at Nescopeck, Teedyuskung and the Christian Indians at Wyoming, Kindassowa and the Munsies upstream, and other Delawares living on the Susquehanna learn that the Connecticut people claimed to have bought their Wyoming lands. This was a flagrant breach of all the promises made to them, and it meant that they would soon be facing the same influx of white settlers that had driven them from their original homes. In December, when some of the Connecticut people came to Wyoming to look over the territory that they believed now belonged to them, John Shickellamy lodged a complaint with the authorities at Philadelphia, stating that New Englanders were "coming like Flocks of Birds to disturb me and settle those Lands," and he told the Delawares, Shawnee, and Mahican to prepare a strong remonstrance to be sent to the Onondaga Council.

A hundred miles to the west on the Ohio frontier, King Shingas and his brothers Beaver and aging Pisquetomen were brooding over the old scores the Delawares had to settle with the English. The survival of their people was now dependent upon white traders providing the needed guns, powder, lead, cloth, kettles, hoes, knives, blankets, and other essential tools and clothing. The Delawares had learned no new manufacturing techniques to produce the goods they needed, and through disuse had practically lost their own skills. When the English traders fled in fear of losing their scalps, after Washington's capitulation at Fort Necessity, the Delawares had no alternative except to turn to French traders to keep them supplied. Now in return for being suppliers of needed merchandise, the French were demanding that the Delawares become their allies against the English.

There was another consideration that frustrated the Delawares in Ohio: the Six Nations continued to look down upon them as women and had repeated the instructions that they "must not meddle with Wars, but stay in the House and mind Council Affairs." Under these restrictions, the Delawares could not invoke the prerogatives of warriors, although as Beaver told the Iroquois chiefs: "We have hitherto followed your directions and lived very easy under your Protection, and no high Wind did blow to make us Uneasy; but now Things seem to take another turn, and a high Wind is rising. We desire you, therefore, Uncle, to have your Eyes open and be watchful over Us, your Cousins, as you have always been heretofore." [36]

The Delawares on the Susquehanna, both frightened and angered by the Connecticut menace and made uneasy by French pressures on their brethren west of them, turned to John Shickellamy and warned him that although they were in the noncombative position of women they were reaching the end of their patience. "Uncles the United Nations," they addressed the Iroquois, "We expect to be killed by the French your Father; We desire, therefore, that You will take off our Petticoat that we may fight for ourselves, our Wives and Children, in the Condition We are in You know we can do nothing." [37]

In March of 1755 John Shickellamy bluntly informed Pennsylvania authorities that if any white men presumed to settle at or near Wyoming, the Indians there would kill first their cattle, then the people. Shickellamy was well aware that a faction of young Delaware warriors were eager to demonstrate their manhood in battle, and if provoked further would divest themselves of their figurative petticoats without the acquiesence of their Iroquois uncles. The thoughtful, peace-loving faction among the Delawares looked hopefully to Brother Onas at Philadelphia to do something in their behalf, and waited patiently for the nonviolent Assembly to take action to assist them. In the confusion, some of the Delawares living on the north branch of the Susquehanna moved to the Ohio; this time it was the Delawares who tried to persuade some Shawnee stragglers to move west with them.[38]

In retrospect it now seems clear that Pennsylvania and Virginia acting promptly and in concert, fully utilizing their Indian allies, might have prevented the French from entrenching themselves at the forks of the Ohio. By blocking the French advance down the Allegheny, they could have maintained the prestige that was needlessly lost at Fort Necessity. On April 18, 1754—more than a month before the Fort Necessity engagement—Tanacharison sent an urgent message to the governors of Pennsylvania and Virginia. He indicated that he believed the French could be repulsed by immediate military resistance and said that the Indians on the Ohio—the Delawares, Shawnee, Mingoes, and their allies—were prepared to strike the French and would move into action as soon as Pennsylvania and Virginia pledged themselves to fight.[39]

Governor Dinwiddie evidently understood the seriousness of the situation, and he wrote several letters to Governor Hamilton of Pennsylvania, urging him to raise troops to join those that Virginia was raising "for defeating the Design of the French." [40] Hamilton had to contend with an Assembly that refused to appropriate money for military uses, and while Dinwiddie was offering land bounties on the east side of the Ohio River, in addition to soldiers' pay to all volunteers for military service, Pennsylvania was doing nothing. If Pennsylvania, which then had no militia, had provided supplies, weapons, and ammunition to its Indian allies and volunteers to join the Virginians, the French could have been turned back before they had an opportunity to seize the forks of the Ohio and consolidate their forces. But wars between European nations, whether fought in Europe or in foreign fields, have a way of taking slow, costly, bloody courses. It would take a worse defeat than Washington's to show the Pennsylvania Assembly that Tanacharison was right—although they could not have been expected to admit that a "savage" had given sound military advice.

NOTES—CHAPTER 10

1. *Colonial Records*, vol. 4, p. 571.
2. Ibid., p. 446.
3. Ibid., pp. 308, 311.
4. Ibid., vol. 3, p. 334.
5. Ibid.
6. Ibid., p. 337.

7. Samuel Smith, *The History of the Colony of Nova-Caesaria, or New Jersey*, Burlington, N.J., 1877; see note, p. 440. Cf. *Colonial Records*, vol. 3, p. 330.

8. *Pennsylvania Archives*, 1st series, vol. 1, pp. 761–62.

9. *Colonial Records*, vol. 2, p. 603.

10. Ibid., vol. 3, p. 405.

11. *Pennsylvania Archives*, 1st series, vol. 1, p. 255.

12. Ibid., p. 262.

13. Ibid., pp. 243–44.

14. Ibid., vol. 2, 549.

15. *Colonial Records*, vol. 5, p. 357.

16. See "The Captivity of Charles Stuart, 1755–57," ed. Beverley W. Bond, Jr., *Mississippi Valley Historical Review*, vol. 13, no. 1, June 1926, p. 65.

17. *Pennsylvania Archives*, 1st series, vol. 1, p. 299.

18. *Colonial Records*, vol. 5, p. 351. Writing in 1750, Christopher Gist said the Delawares in Ohio had five hundred fighting men; Charles A Hanna, *The Wilderness Trail*, 2 vols., New York, 1911, vol. 2, p. 150.

19. *Colonial Records*, vol. 3, p. 442. As late as 1754 the Onondaga Council was still trying unsuccessfully to persuade the Delawares to return to the Susquehanna, as George Washington learned in a conference with Shingas; William A. Hunter, *Forts on the Pennsylvania Frontier, 1753–58*, Harrisburg, 1960, p. 56. Sir William Johnson in July of 1758 was urging the Delawares to return; *Colonial Records*, vol. 8, pp. 153–54.

20. *Colonial Records*, vol. 5, p. 88.

21. Ibid., vol. 3, p. 403.

22. Ibid., vol. 5, p. 139.

23. Cf. Francis P. Jennings, "The Delaware Interregnum," *Pennsylvania Magazine of History and Biography*, April 1965, pp. 174–98.

24. *Colonial Records*, vol. 5, p. 533.

25. "The Treaty of Loggs Town," *Virginia Magazine of History and Biography*, vol. 13, 1905–6, p. 167, The Onondaga Council, concerned about Sassoonan's successor, sent representatives to Philadelphia in 1748 to discuss the matter; *Colonial Records*, vol. 5, p. 222.

26. *The Susquehanna Company Papers*, ed. Julian Boyd and Robert Taylor, Wyoming Historical and Geological Society, 1930– . Twelve volumes are planned in this series. As of 1970, vol. 8, edited by Robert Taylor, had become available to supplement seven earlier volumes. For a brief account of the company's further activities, see Julian Boyd, *The Susquehanna Company: Connecticut's Experiment in Expansion*, published for the Tercentenary Commission by Yale University Press, New Haven, 1935.

27. This is fully discussed in Anthony F. C. Wallace, *Teedyuskung, King of the Delawares*, Philadelphia, 1949, chap. 4.

28. *Colonial Records*, vol. 5, pp. 666–67.

29. Ibid., p. 668; cf. Donald H. Kent, *The French Invasion of Western Pennsylvania*, Harrisburg, 1954, p. 49.

30. This quotation is found on p. 4 of *The Journal of Major George Washington*, a Newberry Library reprint, Chicago, 1958, of the 1754 journal originally printed by William Hunter, Williamsburg, 1754. A second journal from March 31 to June 27, 1754, edited by Donald H. Kent, entitled "Contrecoeur's Copy of George Washington's Journal for 1754," was published in *Pennsylvania History*, vol. 19, no. 1, January, 1952, pp. 3–36.

31. "The Treaty of Loggs Town," *Virginia Magazine of History and Biography*, vol. 13, 1905–6, p. 161. At this treaty Shingas and Beaver were "dressed after the English fashion [but] had silver breast plates and a great deal of Wampum about them"; ibid., p. 155.

32. *Pennsylvania Archives*, 1st series, vol. 2, p. 240.

33. *Colonial Records*, vol. 6, p. 103.

34. Ibid., p. 116.

35. Wallace, *Teedyuskung*, pp. 61–62.

36. *Colonial Records*, vol. 6, p. 156.

37. Ibid., pp. 36–37.

38. *Pennsylvania Archives*, 1st series, vol. 1, p. 615.

39. Penn Manuscripts—Indian Affairs, vol. 2, 1754–56, p. 2, Manuscript Room, Historical Society of Pennsylvania, Philadelphia; cf. "Croghan's Journal," R. G. Thwaites, ed., *Early Western Travels*, 1784–1846, Cleveland, 1904, vol. 1, p. 78.

40. *Colonial Records*, vol. 5, pp. 714–15. It was ironical that Hamilton persistently reminded Dinwiddie that the forks of the Ohio belonged to Pennsylvania, not Virginia, and yet Pennsylvania did nothing to defend it; ibid., vol. 6, pp. 4–7.

11

The Warriors Shed Their Petticoats

The unexpected defeat of Major-General Edward Braddock's well-equipped military forces on July 9, 1755, by a party of numerically inferior French and Indians brought a disastrous climax to the English campaign designed to seize the forks of the Ohio and expel the French. Coming so soon after Washington's capitulation at Fort Necessity, it had a catastrophic effect on Indian relations with the English colonies, which is the major significance of the defeat, because the Indians held the balance of power between France and England in North America.

Six months previously the governors of Maryland, Virginia, and Pennsylvania had proclaimed to the Six Nations and their allies that the great General Braddock, an invincible military leader sent by the King, had arrived in America. They instructed traders to spread the news among all the tribes that the general's formidable army of some 2,200 men, including English foot soldiers and troops from South Carolina, Maryland, and Virginia, would drive the French trespassers from territory that belonged to the King of England. Braddock's military objective—to capture Fort Duquesne—was intended to force the French to retreat and thus display the might of the British lion to the Indians.

Pennsylvania's Governor Robert Hunter Morris sent messages to keep the Delawares and Shawnee posted on Braddock's progress from the time the general joined his forces at Fort Cumberland in May and then laboriously crossed the Allegheny Mountains—range after range, with snorting horses and sweating men dragging siege guns, howitzers, six pounders, twelve pounders, and tremendous quantities of ammunition and supplies. Braddock followed an Indian trail called Nemacolin's Path (named after a son of the Brandywine chief Chicochinican), which had been widened here and there but was not designed for military traffic and required improvement (see Fig. 14). A detachment of several hundred men preceded the main army felling trees, bridging creeks, laying causeways in swamplands, and opening a twelve-foot-wide road across a formidable array of mountains. A group of sailors, proficient in the use of block and tackle, had been brought along to pull wagons and guns out of mud holes and up slippery banks as the foot soldiers forded the rivers and creeks.

The Indians did not need the colonial governments to enlighten them about Braddock's progress because they knew from firsthand

Figure 14. The author tracing the route of the old road, built by Major General Edward Braddock through the Alleghenies, as it crosses the ridge of the Summit near Farmington, Pa., on the old Nemacolin Trail (Courtesy Hugh Johns, Uniontown, Pa.)

observation the obstacles the troops were surmounting as the army moved slowly but surely toward the West. Fifty natives, mostly Delawares, brought by George Croghan from his trading post, Aughwick (near present-day Shirleysburg, Pennsylvania), with their women and children, joined the English army. These natives, friendly to the English, had assembled at Aughwick after Washington's defeat at Fort Necessity, and they were fed at the expense of the Province in the expectation that the warriors would fight on the side of the English. The squaws consorted with Braddock's officers and then gave their husbands "money in Plenty which they got from the Officers, who were scandalously fond of them." [1] When General Braddock learned of this liberality, he issued orders that the Indian women should be sent to their homes and none admitted to his camp thereafter. Later Braddock, who had contempt for Indians, also sent the male Indians back to their homes—except for eight or ten whom he used as scouts—but as Scarouady said, the obstinant, sixty-year-old general "looked upon us as dogs, and would never hear anything what was said to him." [2]

Considering that the theater of operations was in an unknown wilderness, that good roads were nonexistent and the lines of communication inadequate, Braddock's strategy was sound and his troop movement well conceived and boldly executed. Only one thing went amiss: his careful preparations and long march ended in a resounding defeat instead of the victory that Braddock had confidently predicted.

The defeat was a more severe blow to British prestige than the fall of Fort Necessity, and, when the smoke of battle cleared, the general was mortally wounded, 63 of his 83 commissioned officers were either killed or wounded, and the looted bodies of more than 450 of his enlisted men lay dead on the battlefield, their blond, brown, and black scalps torn from their heads. All told, 977 of his men were either killed or wounded. When John Heckewelder and Christian Frederick Post were on their way to the Muskingum in the spring of 1762, the bones and skulls of the fallen men and officers were still strewn on the battleground. Heckewelder wrote that "the sound of our horses' hoofs continually striking against them made dismal music, as, with the Monongahela full in view, we rode over this memorable battleground." [3]

Following the battle, the British troops fell back in a panic, leaving their supplies and artillery, Braddock's personal chest with his military papers, and a substantial amount of cash in the hands of the enemy. Braddock was dying, and his second in command, Colonel Thomas Dunbar, ordered the senseless retreat to Fort Cumberland without either man knowing that the forces who cut their regiments to shreds consisted of fewer than 300 French regulars, no artillery support, and about 630 undisciplined Indians whose war whoops and painted faces, according to French accounts of the battle, "struck terror into the hearts of the entire enemy." The majority of these so-called French Indians who accompanied the French troops down the Allegheny River from Fort Le Beouf represented Ottawa, Huron, Chippewa from beyond Lake Michigan, natives from other parts of the Great Lakes region, and a few Mingoes.

Although historians writing of the battle refer to Delawares and Shawnee fighting with the French, evidence to support this assumption is contradictory. During his trip to western Pennsylvania in 1761–63, James Kenny overheard one Delaware Indian telling another "that at Braddock's Defeat there was not One of ye Delawares & only four Mingoes & three Shawnas, all ye rest North[n] Indians." [4] Delaware chief Shingas said that a small party of Delawares joined the French, "But the Greater Part remained neuter till they saw How Things wou'd go Between Braddock and the French in their Engagement." [5] This latter version is in keeping with the character of the opportunistic Delawares, who wanted to be on the side of the victors.

Although much has been written to explain Braddock's defeat, his tactless handling of the Delaware chiefs was a factor in depriving him of their overt assistance. Instead of fighting at Braddock's side, the Delawares held to a neutral position, as Shingas pointed out, to await the outcome of the clash. Behind these circumstances lies an interesting and little-known story.

George Croghan wrote that a month prior to the battle, General Braddock told him that Governor Dinwiddie had led him to expect four hundred Catawba and Cherokee warriors to join his forces. Instead, Braddock complained that he was provided with only fifty poorly equipped Indians brought by Croghan from Aughwick on the instructions of Governor Morris of Pennsylvania. Recognizing the inadequacy of these limited Indian forces, Braddock asked Croghan to summon some of the Delaware chiefs on the Ohio to confer with him in the hope of enlisting their assistance. Croghan said he promptly sent to the Ohio a messenger who returned to Braddock's camp at Fort Cumberland in eight days with three Delaware chiefs. Croghan's interpretation of what then happened was that the three Delaware chiefs met in Braddock's tent to accept presents he had prepared for them and to ask how they might assist him. Braddock allegedly replied that he could use all the warriors they could supply when he assaulted Fort Duquesne, and, "The Indians told him they would return home and collect the warriors together and meet him on the march." [6] Croghan added that the Delawares did not keep their promise, but he did not know the reason why.

Fortunately, Shingas's account of what happened in Braddock's tent has been recorded, and it differs from Croghan's version. Shingas said that he was one of *six* Ohio chiefs, representing Delaware, Shawnee, and Mingoes, who met with Braddock while he was preparing to march on Fort Duquesne, and they asked Braddock what he intended to do with the Ohio lands *after* he drove the French away. The general replied that the English should "Inhabit & Inherit" the land, and Shingas then asked him if the Indians who had been friendly to the English might not be permitted to live and trade on the Ohio, and have access to hunting grounds sufficiently large to support themselves and their families. Braddock haughtily replied "that no Savage Shoud Inherit the Land," and when the chiefs put the same question to him the following morning they received an identical and uncompromising answer. Shingas and the other chiefs then replied, "That if they might not have Liberty to Live on the Land they woud not Fight for it To wch Genl Braddock answered that he did not need their Help and had no Doubt of driveing the French and their Indians away." [7] Braddock's exalted view had been expressed several months earlier when Benjamin Franklin warned him about an Indian ambush and Braddock smiled at Franklin's ignorance.

Following his conference with the Ohio chiefs, Braddock, confident of victory with no need to obligate himself, sent away the Indians who had been on the march with his troops, and who appeared to him to be of little use and a possible source of trouble. Shingas and his fellow chiefs went back to the Ohio, according to his account, and communicated to their people what had passed between them and the English general. As a result they remained neutral, awaiting the outcome of Braddock's march against the French. Shingas added,

"And they made it their Business to draw nigh the place where the Engagement Happened that they might see what passd at it and were still in hopes that the English woud Be Victorious." [8]

The Delawares not only saw the defeat and the rout that followed; they witnessed the French victory celebration at Fort Duquesne, where naked British soldiers were tortured and burned at the stake. They also watched Braddock's demoralized troops withdraw after destroying their own wagons, ammunition, and stores to keep them from falling into the hands of the enemy. If Braddock had utilized the Indians from Aughwick who were familiar with the terrain and the native way of fighting in the woods, the outcome of the battle might have been different. Having contemptuously sent these Indian allies away, he retained only a few Iroquois to assist him in the battle at the Monongahela, among whom were Silver Heels; Johnny, the Half King's son; Tohashwuchtonionty, or the Belt; and a son of Queen Allaquippa named Kanuksusy, whose English name was New Castle. Croghan himself stated, "But I am yet of the Opinion that if we had fifty Indians instead of Eight, that we might in a great measure have prevented the Surprise that Day of our unhappy Defeat." [9]

Whereas Washington's defeat at Fort Necessity brought the Delawares closer to the French, Braddock's imperious and insulting attitude toward the Delaware warriors sent to assist him, followed by his defeat, resulted in complete alienation of Delawares and Shawnee on the Ohio; and even some of the Seneca and Cayuga, the westernmost members of the Iroquois Confederacy, defected to the French, much to the abashment of those members of the League who continued to hold fast in the English cause.

On September 11, 1755, the Oneida sent a belt of black wampum a fathom long to the Delawares who remained at Shamokin on the Susquehanna, urging them to come to their assistance because they momentarily expected to be attacked by the French. Scarouady, who had fled from the Ohio after Braddock's defeat and was then serving as a Six Nations messenger on the Susquehanna, reported to Brother Onas that the "Six Nations have ordered their Cousins the Delawares to lay aside their petticoats and clap on nothing but the Breech Clout." [10] The Six Nations intended the Susquehanna Delawares to attack the French—not the English.

The Delawares at Shamokin and Wyoming were in no condition to desert their families, assume the posture of warriors, take up the tomahawk and scalping knife, and travel north to aid their distressed uncles. An unseasonal frost the night of May 29, 1755, the second that year since the corn came up, completely destroyed the Indians' crops. There had been no rain in eastern Pennsylvania for the two months that followed, which prompted Governor Morris to proclaim June 19 throughout the Province as a day of "Public Humiliation, Fasting and Prayer." [11] Their corn ruined, their garden vegetables destroyed by drought, and the waters so low in the tributary streams that the fish could not live, the Susquehanna Delawares refused to leave their women and children to starve to death. Their survival depended upon hunting game in the woods, or by obtaining aid either from Brother Onas—or Father Onontio.

Weeks before, Teedyuskung had asked the provincial government to assist the Delawares on the Susquehanna by supplying them with guns and ammunition, but the pacifistic Pennsylvania Assembly was reluctant to appropriate funds to accommodate the Indians, nor would the members then consent to build a fort on the Susquehanna to protect their Delaware allies from the French attack that the Indians feared. From 1681, when William Penn received his charter, until 1755, Pennsylvania was under a government that erected no forts, maintained no militia, and was notorious for evading royal appeals for money to be used in intercolonial defense. While Teedyuskung patiently waited for a change in policy that would result in the assistance he requested, Shingas, apprenhensive that a French attack would find the Susquehanna Delawares defenseless, made a fateful decision. Still smarting from Braddock's rebuff, and now certain that the English would be defeated, he allied the Delawares on the Ohio with the French. The Shawnee also joined the French, and events began to move swiftly.

On October 16, 1755, a party of Shingas's warriors attacked a white settlement along Penn's Creek south of Shamokin near what is now Selinsgrove, Pennsylvania, murdering and scalping thirteen men and women and an infant, and capturing eleven young men and children.[12] While this was happening, another group of Delaware warriors, their faces painted black, appeared at Shamokin to advise the Delawares that their brethren on the Ohio had joined the French and had taken up arms against the English. They brought a message from Shingas urging the Susquehanna Delawares to join him in ridding the land of the English.

The Susquehanna Delawares remained neutral, ignoring this invitation, and the following November two messengers from Shingas brought a string of beads in confirmation of their action, saying, "We, the Delawares of Ohio do proclaim War against the English. We have been their Friends many years, but now we have taken up the Hatchet against them, & we will never make it up with them whilst there is an English man alive." [13]

Shingas, Pisquetomen, Killbuck, Delaware George (Nenatcheehunt), and war captains named Captain Jacobs, Captain John Peter, and Captain Will were the most notorious leaders of the Delaware war parties who obtained ammunition and supplies from the French at Fort Duquesne and terrorized the settlers in Pennsylvania, Virginia, and Maryland. French officers commanded some of the war parties, such as those that raided the Potomac settlements, cut off communications between Winchester and Fort Cumberland, and ascended the Kanawha to burn, loot, massacre, and take captives. Ensign Dagneau Douville, with a party of fifty Indians, attacked a settlers' fort on Cacapon River, about twenty-five miles east of Fort Cumberland, where he was surprised and then killed by a Virginia detachment. Following this incident, another party of French and Indians attacked a group of Virginians, killing two officers and fifteen men. During this engagement nine Indians were killed, and Shingas was wounded, although not seriously. On another foray, a war party commanded by Captain Coulon de Villiers consisting of twenty-three Frenchmen and thirty-two Shawnee, Delaware, and Illinois Indians, including Captain Jacobs, returned to Fort Duquesne with twenty-seven prisoners and four scalps. [14]

There was no organized military defense against the Indian raids, except for the troops Maryland and Virginia had raised to protect their own borders. Unlike the Pennsylvania Quakers, neither Virginians nor Marylanders had any scruples about shedding Indian blood, and their militia laws provided men to defend their settlements from Indian war parties. Before the end of November, 1755, the Pennsylvania frontier from the Maryland border to the Delaware Water Gap was aflame—houses were set afire by howling warriors, barns destroyed, farms raided, livestock seized, and men, women, and children scalped or carried away into captivity. Those whose homes had not been attacked fled to nearby towns to seek safety.

Until late November most of the atrocities were committed by the

Delawares and Shawnee who had gone to the Ohio. The Delawares living on the Susquehanna continued to hold a neutral position. Their mood changed on November 24, 1755, when a group of Susquehanna Delawares led by Captain Jachebus, a Munsie warrior from Assinisink, attacked Gnadenhütten, burning many of the buildings, including the little log chapel where Teedyuskung, Nutimus's son (Isaac of Nescopeck), and a number of other converted Delawares had been baptized. They murdered and scalped eleven of the unarmed white Moravian brethren, including men, women, and children. The Delaware and Mahican converts living at the mission hid in the woods while the attack was in progress.[15]

Following this massacre, some Delawares living at Wyoming and elsewhere on the Susquehanna went on the warpath. War parties swept into the settlements in the region north of the Forks of the Delaware; they burned and scalped in the Tulpehocken Valley; some crossed the Delaware and raided homes in New Jersey. Not all of the Delawares took up the war hatchet at this time. Some, including Teedyuskung and his former Moravian Indians, continued to remain neutral. But with victorious warriors tasting blood and bringing back scalps, prisoners, and the spoils of war to Wyoming, Teedyuskung, who had already waited too long for the Pennsylvania authorities and his own Six Nations uncles to act in his behalf, could no longer contain himself. He seceded from the neutralists and joined the growing faction on the Susquehanna that was working in concert with the French and Shingas's warriors to exterminate the English.

Teedyuskung did not think that Shingas possessed any authority over the Delawares and Munsies living on the Susquehanna, nor did he feel bound to old Nutimus, now regarded as a head chief of the Susquehanna faction. Having no recognized superior, he gathered together his own followers and called himself a war captain. In the winter of 1755 he organized a party of about thirty warriors and set out in quest of scalps, prisoners, and plunder. His war party was a sort of family affair because it included three of his sons, three half brothers, and a nephew; and they raided and sacked the white settlements north of the Kittatinnies. Teedyuskung himself apparently participated only in this one foray, which involved scalpings, burnings, and thefts; and when his party returned to Wyoming on January 3 with their white prisoners, they found the place deserted. Fearing a reprisal from the English, the Delawares had moved upstream to the village of Tunkhannock. Teedyuskung and his warriors followed, taking their prisoners with them. From there he led one hundred Delawares and an unknown number of white prisoners to Tioga at the forks of the north branch of the Susquehanna and the Chemung. Later he settled at Pasigachkunk, a village on the Cowanesque River, a tributary of the Chemung.

Teedyuskung won sufficient honor and prestige from one successful foray to assure his status as a war captain. His family, followers, and friends continued to attack the English settlements, bringing back prisoners and scalps, and Teedyuskung cinched his reputation as a warrior-leader by assuming the role of coordinator and planner.[16] The weakness in the Delaware military system was a lack of disciplined organization to maintain a sustained offensive; the war parties, who acted independently of each other, often dispersed at the close of a raid. Tactically the war captains showed skill, bravery, and the ability to lay waste the enemy, but an overall strategy was lacking.

When Shingas and his war captains from the Ohio launched their attacks—and when Captain Jachebus, Teedyuskung, and other Susquehanna Delaware captains took their braves on the warpath—it was with malice in their hearts and an obsession to destroy white people. This hatred caused them to inflict terrible atrocities on settlers of all nationalities and of all ages. No white family was safe, as warriors seemed to swoop down from nowhere with bloodcurdling war whoops, their faces and bodies covered with paint. They set fire to houses and barns, killed some of the residents, and took others into captivity. There was no single cause to which these attacks can be attributed; they were not designed to avenge a single incident like the Walking Purchase. It was a matter of retaliation against successive broken promises made over a period of years by Dutch, Swedes, and English—and against unscrupulous traders who cheated Delawares, debauched their people with rum, and took liberties with their squaws when their husbands were hunting in the woods. They were expressing a deep-seated hatred of white people who spread smallpox, contagious fevers, venereal diseases, and other ailments that decimated the Indian population. They were also flaunting in the faces of the Six Nations the folly of the myth that, since they had been figuratively emasculated, they must permanently play the undignified role of pacifistic women. The determination to express their manhood was a motivation, especially of the young warriors, that has not been fully recognized.

Despite the lack of an overall military strategy, some two hundred Delaware warriors living on the Susquehanna and seven hundred from the Ohio waged a commando war which was an orgy of blood-letting that marked the Delawares as brutal and ruthless warriors who showed no mercy. As one looks back at the sequence of events in Anglo-American relations with the Delawares, there can be little question that the English brought this disaster on themselves, although they would have been the first to deny it. Governor Morris in a letter to Sir William Johnson, appointed by the King of Superintendent of Indian Affairs for the Northern Colonies, blamed the Delaware uprisings entirely on the "Artifices and Intimidations of the French." He took the position that the English were "innocent Brethren and allies who have never hurt them [the Delawares] in Thought or Action." [17]

Pennsylvania's Indian policy, based on the supremacy of the friendly Six Nations, began to fall apart in the wake of the kind of warfare conducted by the Shawnee and Delaware warriors who turned a deaf ear to their Iroquois uncles who were supposed to control their behavior. At a meeting of the Onondaga Council, two Delaware representatives summoned by the Six Nations chiefs were censured and told that "they were drunk and out of their Senses, and did not consider the consequences of their ill Behaviour . . ." [18] The Delawares said they would tell their warriors that their uncles were displeased, but the Delaware warriors paid no attention. They continued to treat the Six Nations insolently and told them that if they did not assist in the war against the English the Delawares would make women of them! [19] The Delawares knew, of course, than an anti-English faction of Seneca and Cayuga had defected to the French, thus dividing the Iroquois in their loyalties.

Governor Morris officially declared war on the Delaware Nation on April 14, 1756, and at the same time offered cash bounties for Indian prisoners, and 130 Spanish dollars (also called pieces of eight) for the scalp of any enemy male Indian over twelve years of age, and fifty Spanish dollars for the scalps of enemy Indian females.[20] Morris was not setting a precedent by paying scalp bounties. As early as 1641 Governor Willem Kieft had offered friendly Indians ten fathoms of wampum for each scalp of an enemy Raritan brought to him. In 1693 Governor Benjamin Fletcher, the ranking English official at Albany, had offered a bounty of fifty shillings for the scalps of enemy Indians, and other instances could be cited where colonial governments had encouraged this practice.

Morris was later forced to withdraw the scalp bounties in deference to strong protests raised by Quakers in and out of the government, but pressures from angry frontiersmen finally compelled the frugal, Quaker-dominated Assembly to vote funds for the defense of the Province. Out of the crisis, at long last, a chain of forts and block-houses was built in the spring of 1756 and garrisoned against Indian attack. The largest, Fort Augusta, erected at Shamokin, commanded the junction of the two branches of the Susquehanna. Funds were also provided to equip and maintain soldiers to defend the Province, and Pennsylvania was able to strike directly at the main body of Delawares and Shawnee on the Allegheny with a force of three hundred troops led by Colonel John Armstrong.

On the morning of September 8, 1756, having the advantage of surprise and superiority in numbers, Armstrong fell on the village of Kittanning, which the French called Attigué, its Iroquois name. He set fire to thirty Indian cabins, destroyed food, supplies, and a large quantity of French ammunition, and during the battle Captain Jacobs and his squaw and a son were killed.[21] The victory bolstered English morale, although of one hundred white prisoners reportedly held at the village only eleven were found and set free. The others were carried away by the Indians to less exposed Delaware villages at Shenango (near present Sharon, Pennsylvania); Saukunk (at present Beaver), also known as Shingas's Old Town or King Beaver's Town; and Kuskusky (at present New Castle) on the Beaver River, a tributary of the Ohio. Of these settlements, Kuskusky, or "the Kukuskies," as the community was better known, became the largest Delaware settlement after Kittanning was vacated. It consisted of four separate villages with ninety huts, which housed two hundred warriors and their families.

The defeat at Kittanning did not bring Shingas and his war captains to the peace table; but back on the Susquehanna, Teedyuskung, now claiming to be a king, was being drawn closer to the English. Of his own volition and completely independent of the Six Nations, Teedyuskung entered into peace discussions with Robert Hunter

Morris, and with William Denny who succeeded Morris as governor of Pennsylvania in August of 1756. Peace was made at Easton, where, following a series of meetings in July and August of 1757, Teedyuskung and a group of three hundred Indian men, women, and children were entertained at a sumptuous dinner at which an armistice was proclaimed with the Susquehanna Delawares. Teedyuskung left the conference promising to announce the peace to Indians everywhere.[22]

Although arrogant and bombastic, and, like many of his native contemporaries, having a psychopathic craving for liquor, Teedyuskung brought a leadership to the Susquehanna Delawares that had been lacking. He went to conferences accompanied by councilors and his own interpreter, even though he could speak English. He was the first Indian to demand the right to have his own clerk to record the minutes of conferences, a position to which sagacious twenty-seven-year-old Charles Thomson, master of the Quaker school in Philadelphia, was reluctantly appointed by Brother Onas.[23] Teedyuskung boldly assumed authority that he did not have, and at the signing of the Easton treaty he said he was "impowered by the ten following Nations, vizt: Lenopi, Wename [Unami], Munsey, Mawhickon [Mahican], Tiawco, or Nanticokes, and the Senecas, Onondagoes, Cayugas, Oneidoes, and Mohawks, to settle all Differences subsisting between them and their Brethren the English . . ."[24] He gave Brother Onas the kind of Delaware king that a succession of English governors had long sought. He maintained that the Delawares were now independent of the Six Nations, that ". . . formerly we were Accounted women, and Employed only in women's business, but now they have made men of us . . ."[25]

The truth was that the Six Nations chiefs had upbraided Teedyuskung for allowing "the string that tied your petticoat to be cut loose by the French, and you lay with them and so became a common Bawd, in which you did very wrong and deserve Chastisement."[26] The Mohawk chief Canyase had figuratively cut off Teedyuskung's petticoats and made a "partial" man of him in the fall of 1756 but refused to consider him a warrior. "I know what is good for you," Canyase said, "and therefore I will not allow you to carry a Tomhawk."[27] This was utter nonsense, because Canyase knew full well that the war parties directed by Teedyuskung paid no attention to the Six Nations, and that the Delaware king would not be restrained if he felt it necessary to go to war again.

There was, of course, considerable bravado in Teedyuskung's pretense at being a great sachem, because he had no birthright claim
to chieftaincy, having years before eked out a gypsy livelihood on the
fringes of the New Jersey white settlements as a basket- and broom-
maker. Now high-level conferences were frequently delayed, sometimes for three or four days, because the "Delaware King was in Liquor," and the gallon of rum he could consume in a single day gave
him further cause to declare, "I *am* a Man!"

In July of 1756, old "King" Nutimus and three others went to represent the Delawares in peace negotiations with Sir William Johnson,
and it was at that meeting that Sir William took it upon himself to
make men of the Delawares. He put the war hatchet in their hands
as he emancipated them, so they could use it against the French. He
removed their petticoats with the following speech:

I do in the name of the Great King of England your father declare
that henceforward you are to be considered as Men by all your Brethren
the English and no longer as Women, and I hope that your Brethren of
the 6 Nations will take it into consideration, follow my example, and
remove this invidious distinction which I shall recommend to them.[28]

In the meantime, Teedyuskung, resplendent in a gold-laced coat,
riding boots with silver shoe buckles, checkered cloth breeches, and
stockings with scarlet gartering, was boasting to Governor Denny that
eight more tribes had taken hold of the Covenant Chain, and he now
represented eighteen Indian nations, the additional eight being, as the
words were spelled by the colonial scribe, the "Ottawaws, Twightwees,
Chippewaws, Toawaws, Caughnawagos, Mahoowa, Pietoatomaws,
Nalashawawna." [29] Teedyuskung claimed that in the interest of peace
he had persuaded these tribes to join hands with himself and the
English, and that they had delegated him as their spokesman. Governor Denny and his council may have had their doubts about the
truth of Teedyskung's claims, but they did not want to jeopardize
the peace by antagonizing him. There was also the possibility that
he might exert a favorable influence on the Ohio Delawares.

There was still another reason why Pennsylvania authorities deferred to the Delaware king: he had gained the moral support and
financial assistance of influential Philadelphia Quakers who formed
an organization called The Friendly Association for the Gaining

and Preserving Peace with the Indians by Pacific Measures. The Quaker intervention in Indian politics was a departure from precedent, since the proprietors, their appointed governors, and the council had wielded authority over Indian affairs. Now prominent members of the Quaker organization, such as Israel Pemberton, were working behind the scene at Indian conferences as secret advisers to the natives. The Quaker faction was seemingly doing its utmost to reduce the prerogatives of William Penn's non-Quaker sons and wrest political advantage from them. Teedyuskung was unaware that he was being used as a pawn by the Friendly Association when they encouraged him to resurrect the issue of the Walking Purchase and claim that the Indian uprisings and massacres were a result of the fraudulent seizure of lands at the Forks through the use of forged deeds.

The intent was to maneuver Teedyuskung into making such loud protests that the dispute would eventually reach the ears of the King of England to the embarrassment and detriment of the Penn government, and this is exactly what happened. In 1759 Benjamin Franklin brought the Walking Purchase issue before the Privy Council in London, and Sir William Johnson was instructed to investigate and report whether Teedyuskung's complaints were justified. This led to letters, reports, and hearings, and finally Teedyuskung backed away from the position in which the Quakers had placed him, declaring that he was misinformed when he charged the proprietors with forging any deeds.

Teedyuskung received a handsome present from Governor Denny for withdrawing his charges, which cleared the proprietary government of wrongdoing and enabled Sir William Johnson in his report to the Lords of Trade to accuse the Quakers of inciting the Delawares to magnify the Walking Purchase far beyond its real proportions. At another meeting held at Lancaster in August of 1762, Teedyuskung was given additional gifts of goods and cash, with a big surplus for distribution to his people. Before a large assembly of Indians, he turned to the representatives from Pennsylvania and said, "Now, Brother Governor, our Children and Grandchildren shall never be able to say hereafter that they have any right or claim to the Lands that have been in dispute upon that [the Delaware] River." [30]

Earlier, in October of 1758, when another important treaty conference was being held at Easton, the Six Nations chiefs had done

their utmost to discredit Teedyuskung. The peace he had independently concluded with Pennsylvania detracted from their dignity
and authority. They hoped that if they repudiated him Pennsylvania
would be compelled to desert him too, and if that happened he
would lose prestige among his followers. In a private session with
Governor Denny, the chiefs, one after the other, denied that Teedyuskung was the great man he claimed to be and that he had
authority over other Indian nations.[31] The irony was that the Six
Nations had failed to make the Delawares and Shawnee lay down
their arms, even though Sir William Johnson assured Richard Penn
that these Indians were the subjects of the Six Nations and were
obliged to do their bidding.[32] The Delawares were defiant. "We are
men," they told a delegation of Six Nations chiefs sent by Sir William
to force them into peace, "and are determined not to be ruled any
longer by you as women." [33] They insulted Scarouady and John
Shickellamy, the Iroquois agents, and threatened to kill them.

Since the essence of Pennsylvania's Indian policy was to uphold
the authority of the Six Nations, Governor Denny had no alternative,
and the treaty marked the reascendancy of the Six Nations and the
decline of Teedyuskung as an arbiter. Denny listened patiently as the
Seneca chief Tagashata went through the motions of making peace
on behalf of the Susquehanna Delawares and Munsies by removing
the French hatchet they had struck into the heads of the English.
Then, speaking as though the Six Nations hadn't tried it unsuccessfully before, he said that messengers were also being sent to the Ohio
to instruct the Delaware and Shawnee to lay down their tomahawks.[34]

The facts, well known to Denny, were that through the intermediary of Teedyuskung the majority of Susquehanna Delawares
were already at peace with the English, and Teedyuskung had given
the big "halloo" to the Ohio Delawares to cease fighting. The peace
he had concluded with Denny was having an influence on Shingas,
who had sent two of his sons to the Ohio the previous spring to try
to promote peace on behalf of the English. Even while the discussions
were in progress at Easton, these efforts were starting to bear fruit,
for Shingas's elder brother, Pisquetomen, delivered a written message
signed by fifteen Delaware chiefs, captains, and councilors on the
Ohio, including Beaver, Shingas, Delaware George, and Killbuck.
The message stated frankly, "We long for that Peace and Friendship
we had Formerly." [35]

The willingness of the Delawares on the Ohio to listen to a peace message was not due to their love for Brother Onas, nor to the fear of the Six Nations, but to a very practical consideration having to do with their trade relations with the French. The French had done their best, not hesitating to use lies or insinuations, to keep the Indians prejudiced against the English, but with their supply lines stretched and their ports blockaded, they were unable to supply the quantities of merchandise the Indians needed. At best, French trade goods were never equal in quality to those supplied by the English, but since French goods were all that was available, the Ohio Delawares had no other recourse than to barter their furs with French traders. The war resulted in a reduction in the receipt of merchandise from France, and French traders were unable to fill the needs of the Indians, which weakened the Delawares' sense of loyalty. Having a constant supply of goods was vital to their survival, and their own best interests necessarily determined who their political allies would be.

There had also been a sudden change in leadership among the Ohio Delawares, the less belligerent Beaver having replaced his brother Shingas. Pennsylvania had offered a reward of seven hundred pieces of eight for any person who brought the scalp of Shingas the Terrible to Philadelphia, and Virginia also offered a reward of "an Hundred Pistoles" for Shingas's death. With these rewards on his head, Shingas lived in fear of being captured and hanged, even though sanctuary had been promised him if he entered into peace negotiations. This may have been one of the reasons he passed on the "scepter" to his brother Beaver, but the diplomatic skills of the Delaware councilors should not be underestimated. They may have come to the conclusion that it would be easier to arrive at peace with Brother Onas by having a new pacifist king to conduct the negotiations.

Governor Denny was amenable to almost any terms that would put an end to murder and pillage, and which would result in the release of several hundred women and children from Indian captivity. The position of the Ohio Delawares could be summed up simply as, "Supply us with traders who will give us goods for our furs, but keep white settlers off our lands." Denny in turn was more than willing to give the Indians his word that no white families would be permitted to settle on Indian lands west of the Alleghenies.

Apart from the peace missions, and the intercession of Christian Frederick Post (a Moravian who spoke the Delaware tongue fluently and made two trips to the Ohio in 1758),³⁶ the cessation of hostilities came about when the forks of the Ohio were occupied by Brigadier-General John Forbes. Forbes succeeded where Braddock had failed. On November 25, 1758, he seized the smoking ruins of Fort Duquesne, which the French had destroyed prior to their withdrawal. When the Delawares and Shawnee saw the most formidable fortress in colonial America—Fort Pitt—arising from the ruins of the French fort, there was no doubt who was in command of the situation, and they had no alternative except to look to the English for trade goods.

On July 9, 1759, King Beaver, with his Delaware and Shawnee associates, entered into a treaty of peace at Fort Pitt with George Croghan, deputy agent for Sir William Johnson; and in the fall of 1762, at the invitation of Denny's successor, Governor James Hamilton, a delegation of Ohio Delawares headed by Beaver, Wendocalla (also spelled Windaughala or Wandohela), and Tissacoma, came to confer with him at Lancaster, Pennsylvania. The purpose of the meeting was to remove the rust from the ancient Covenant Chain and to discuss the release of white captives still being held by the Indians.³⁷ A friendly dialogue ensued, mutual promises to maintain peace were made, the Delawares were given presents of merchandise and cash— and they left agreeing to free all their captives. For some time an uneasy peace—perhaps an armed truce would be a better description— existed between the English and the Ohio Delawares, largely because the older men in the tribe were tired of war. But Colonel Hugh Mercer wrote from Fort Pitt that "the young Villains who have swilled so much of our Blood, and grown rich by the plunder of the Frontiers, have still some French poison lurking in their Veines that might perhaps break out at a Convenient Opportunity." ³⁸

Back on the Susquehanna, Teedyuskung continued to press the Pennsylvania authorities to give him a title deed to lands at Wyoming on which the Delawares could live and which could never be expropriated. But the proprietary government continued to dodge the issue. Officials knew that to deal directly with Teedyuskung on land matters would be interpreted by the Six Nations as furthering the independence of the Delawares and would negate their own Indian policy. Moreover, Brother Onas could not deed land at Wyoming because it still belonged to the Six Nations. The Delawares were once more caught in a bind. Teedyuskung suddenly grew humble and turned to his Six Nations uncles with a pathetic and eloquent plea to give his people a deed to lands at Wyoming.[39] The Onondaga Council refused to deed any lands to the Delawares, but told Teedyuskung that he and his followers were free to live and plant at Wyoming, though not to the exclusion of other Indians they might place on the Susquehanna.

Although Pennsylvania could not assure the Delawares land tenure at Wyoming, carpenters and laborers were sent to build houses and assist them in clearing the fields for cultivation. The Indians had not inhabited their new town long when woodcutters hired by the Susquehanna Company broke through the forests, and Connecticut settlers appeared with their tools and farming implements.[40] Beaver, who knew about the controversy between Pennsylvania and Connecticut, sent a special messenger to Teedyuskung at Wyoming and Nutimus at Tioga inviting them to come west with their people and join him. Teedyuskung seriously considered doing so, but Governor Hamilton did not favor the move—not only because of the investment he had made in the houses, but because he hoped that the presence of Delawares might help to deter the Connecticut settlers.

The situation was rapidly reaching a climax as more Connecticut people trespassed on Indian lands; then on April 19, 1763, tragedy befell the Indians. Teedyuskung was killed as he lay asleep in his house, some said in a stupor from liquor given him by his assailants. His house of hewn logs was set afire from the outside, and the Delaware "king" was burned to death within the flaming walls.[41] Almost simultaneously the twenty surrounding dwellings, some of frame and others of log, were also set afire, and within a few hours the Indian town of Wyoming lay in ashes. The Delawares fled—some to Moravian missions, others to the Big Island in the west branch of the Susquehanna (present Lock Haven) where other Delawares and Munsies had gathered.

Two weeks after Teedyuskung's death, a dozen families from Connecticut were busily engaged in erecting houses and tilling the soil at Wyoming. Before the end of April, more New Englanders returned, their cattle trailing behind wagons loaded with farming implements, supplies, and seed corn. It is not known whether it was the Iroquois he had offended—or white men from Connecticut or the hired Indians working in their behalf—who were responsible for Teedyuskung's murder, but the Susquehanna Company gained most by Teedyuskung's death and the dispersal of his followers. With the Delaware chief and his people out of the way, one of the obstacles that had thwarted their expansion plans was removed.

Pontiac's War, coming as a natural aftermath of the French and Indian War, was another futile, although better organized, native effort to resist the westward expansion of English civilization. After the English drove the French from the forks of the Ohio, and then prepared to make their own occupation permanent, the Indians became alarmed. On his peace missions, Christian Frederick Post solemnly assured the Delawares and their Indian allies that the sole object of the English was to drive the French away. Complying with the instructions he had been given, he told the Indians that following the French retreat the English would depart, leaving the Ohio, with its forests and wild animals, as an exclusive game preserve for the Indians. George Croghan gave the Indians similar assurances, but, while these guarantees were being made, the Ohio Company, as required by its charter, was making plans for settlers to cross the mountains.

To aggravate the situation further, the directives of General Jeffery Amherst, appointed Governor-General of British North America in the fall of 1758, ignored Indian needs by severely limiting the sale of powder and lead and prohibiting all trade in rum. The frontier Indians by now were completely dependent upon a trading economy, and Amherst's curtailment of ammunition meant privation for their families. Lacking an understanding of Indian economic life, General Amherst was not aware that guns, powder, and lead were not luxuries (or that they were used only as military weapons) but, like animal traps, were absolute necessities to the Indians. They had to have them to obtain pelts to trade for the manufactured goods that replaced the artifacts produced by their former arts and crafts. In a desire to economize, Amherst also reduced the merchandise gifts normally distributed to the Indians and this, too, aroused resentment among natives taught to share possessions with their friends.

In 1758 the Pennsylvania Assembly passed a law to concentrate the Indian trade at Fort Augusta and Fort Pitt under the supervision of commissioners appointed by the Assembly. By so doing the government was trying to consider the Indians' best interests and put an end to the dishonest practices of unlicensed traders. Actually the restriction proved to be a hardship because the Indians were forced to make long journeys to the two forts with their furs and often found upon their arrival that the supply of trade goods was insufficient to meet their needs.

"There is a great Demand for Indian Goods," wrote Captain Hugh Mercer from Fort Pitt on January 8, 1759. "I have refused great Quantities of Skins and Furs." What he meant was that his supply of merchandise was exhausted, and he had nothing to give the Indians in exchange for furs. The Indians were also becoming more particular in their choice of merchandise. "Course Goods will not do," he wrote in a later letter, "such things as the Indians have formerly dealt in must now be more Showey and of the finest Sort." [42] The goods in biggest demand at this time included blankets, blue, black, and scarlet in color; flowered serges; calicoes and wash cottons in lively colors; red, yellow, blue, and green ribbons, with which the Delaware women decorated their dresses; linens and ready-made shirts; needles, awl blades, clasp knives, scissors, razors, hatchets, beaver and fox traps, vermilion pigment for use in making face paint, looking glasses, horn combs, finger rings.

Guyasuta, a Seneca chief on the Ohio, also complained about the shortage of trade goods, and he was especially angered at Amherst's prohibition of liquor. "You make Rum and have taught us to drink it," he said, "you are fond of it yourselves; therefore don't deprive us of it, or of the liberty of purchasing Goods . . ." [43]

The disruption in normal trade relations contributed to the disharmony between whites and Indians, and caused each side to try to take advantage of the other. The converted Munsie chieftain Papunhank told Governor Hamilton that under the circumstances it was next to impossible to maintain amicable relations. He said:

You make it publick that you will give a Certain price for our Skins, and that they are to weighed and paid for at that set price, according to their Weight. Brother, there are two bad things done in this way of dealing; You alter the price that you say you will give for our skins, which can never be right; God can not be pleased to see the prices of one and the same thing so often altered and changed; our Young Men, finding that they are to receive for their skins according to the weight, play tricks with them and leave on them several parts which are of no use, only to make them weigh more, such as some of the flesh, the Ears and the paws . . . Brother, you see there is no Love nor honesty on either side.[44]

Indian-white relations could not be more aptly characterized than in the words italicized above, and it was in this atmosphere of misunderstanding and suspicion that seeds were sown for the Indian uprising, which Francis Parkman popularized as a "conspiracy" in the title of his book *The Conspiracy of Pontiac* (1870). The title reveals the bias of an author who was a spokesman for New England Indian prejudices, and it discredits the Indian movement to drive the English—but not the French—out of the country. It was not a conspiracy, nor was there a preconceived military plan; it was a series of uprisings that had their origin when the Seneca in 1761, and again in 1763, sent war belts to the western tribes. They urged these tribes to arise with them against the English, whom they accused of purposely withholding powder from the Indians to weaken them prior to annihilating them. This accusation—added to the decreasing number of presents given to the Indians (which Amherst considered unwarranted bribes); the prohibition of the sale of liquor; English deceit in not leaving Indian territory after the defeat of the French, as they had promised; a general dislike for English arrogance; and friendship for the French—incited Pontiac to action. An intelligent Ottawa war captain, Pontiac was also influenced by a Delaware shaman who preached that the Indians should change their way of living, purify themselves of sin, and drive the white man from their lands. Evidently, it was not Pontiac who aroused the Delawares, but the reverse, as the following quotation from Pontiac himself seems to indicate: "The Delawares told us this spring that the English sought to become masters of all and would put us to death. They told us also, 'Our brethren, let us die together, since the design of the English is to destroy us. We are dead one way or another.' " [45]

Pontiac's main role in the uprising was in uniting his immediate Indian neighbors the Huron and Potawatomi, aided by the Chippewa of Saginaw and his own Ottawa warriors, for an attack on the English at Fort Detroit. While the fort was being besieged, some of Pontiac's Indian followers also made sporadic attacks along the Detroit River on English military parties, traders, and small river vessels. News of Pontiac's siege of Detroit was carried to other Indian tribes, including the Delawares, and the war he started gained momentum as others were encouraged to strike the English. There was no master strategy in these attacks, nor was Pontiac responsible for planning simultaneous thrusts against English installations and frontier settlements by various tribal war parties.

Prior to Pontiac's attack on Detroit, there had been a pronounced shift in the Delaware population along the Allegheny and Ohio. As early as 1739, the Delaware sachem Wendocalla ("one who is brought this way") had taken his band to found a town on the south bank of the Ohio near the mouth of the Scioto River, and later moved to a less exposed site on the banks of the Scioto.[46] Other displaced Indians also settled in what is now the state of Ohio in the early eighteenth century. A famine in 1741–42 drove a number of Seneca families to the Cayuga River. There were also Wyandot families moving about in the area of the Cayuga and Scioto rivers, although the majority of the Wyandot had settled on the Sandusky River.[47]

In late 1758 or early 1759, a Delaware chief named Netawatwees ("skilled adviser," also known as Newcomer although his Indian name was also given as Netahutquemaled or Netodwehement), founded a village on the Cuyahoga River near present Cuyahoga Falls. In July of 1758, Netawatwees, called "ye great man of the Unamie nation," lived at the mouth of Beaver Creek on the Ohio below Fort Duquesne.[48] After a sojourn at Cuyahoga Falls, Netawatwees and his people moved to the Tuscarawas River where they founded another village which was popularly known as Newcomer's Town. Other Delawares, upon invitation of the Shawnee, moved from western Pennsylvania to Lower Shawnee Town on the Scioto, so designated to distinguish it from the town of Waketameki on the Muskingum River near what is now Dresden, Ohio.[49]

During this unsettled period, Beaver and Shingas also left Pennsylvania and went to Ohio, although a number of Munsies continued to occupy "the Kuskuskies," as well as Goschgosching on the Allegheny. Captain White Eyes (sometimes called Grey Eyes, whose Indian name was Coquetakeghton, also spelled Koquethagecthon, "that which is put near the head") and a few other conservative Delawares lingered for a while at the mouth of Beaver Creek where the Moravian missionaries Heckewelder and Post, in the spring of 1762, obtained venison and fowl from them.[50]

The destination of the two Moravians on this journey was a new Delaware town on the west bank of Tuscarawas Creek, situated in the vicinity of present Bolivar, Ohio. It was founded by Beaver and

Shingas and known as The Tuscarawas, Beaver's Town, or Shingas's Town. When the two Moravians arrived, they found the Delawares living in forty huts.[51] It was here that Heckewelder attended the funeral of Shingas's wife, and in his journal he describes the warrior who had terrorized hundreds of white settlers, his cheeks now wet with tears, his head bowed in grief, as his wife's body was laid in the earth.[52] The occupants of Shingas's Town later moved to the head of Hocking River, at or near Standing Stone, at present Lancaster, Ohio, where they built a new village called Hockhocking, sometimes known as Beaver's New Town. With characteristic mobility, other Delawares, prior to 1764, lived or camped in small settlements at or near what is now Zanesville, Cambridge, Duncan Falls, Chillicothe, Circleville, Warren, Youngstown, and elsewhere in eastern Ohio.

On October 6, 1763, Sir William Johnson reported to General Amherst intelligence he had received from the Indians indicating that Ottawa and Huron emissaries had gone to the Tuscarawas River, the principal tributary of the Muskingum, where the Delawares and Shawnee had assembled to listen to their message. Sir William said that the war hatchet and the bow and arrows of the warrior were delivered to the Delawares, and the messengers said they hoped the Delawares would lose no time in taking Fort Pitt and Fort Augusta.[53] The messengers also said that while the Delawares and their allies were taking these two strongholds, the Ottawa, Twightwee, Huron, and their allies would demolish the two French forts seized by the English—Detroit and Niagara. With these strongholds in their hands, the Indian warriors could march on to Philadelphia and burn it to the ground. The forts at Venango (where the Seneca butchered the garrison), at Le Boeuf, Presque Isle, and Sandusky, were all taken by Indian war parties, but the major strongholds were able to hold out against the Indians. In addition, Pontiac failed to capture the two most important forts, Detroit and Niagara, which remained in English hands.

The Delawares, Shawnee, Mingoes, and other Ohio Indians besieged Fort Pitt, where Captain Simeon Ecuyer had brought in several hundred men, women, and children from the adjacent settlement for protection. According to William Trent's Journal, an eyewitness account, Shingas, Beaver (Trent said they were commonly called "King B. and King S."), White Eyes, and Wingenum tried to persuade Ecuyer to vacate Fort Pitt to prevent bloodshed. He replied that the English had taken it from the French and would defend it to the last against Indian attack. Two other Delawares, Turtle's Heart and Mamaltee, visited Ecuyer to tell him that the forts on the Allegheny had fallen and to advise him to give up Fort Pitt before the Indians overran it and put all the occupants to death. According to Trent's Journal, Ecuyer thanked them for their warning, and as a token of appreciation he gave them a present of two blankets and a handkerchief which he had taken from the beds of smallpox patients at the fort.[54] General Amherst, who approved of using whatever stratagem was necessary to defeat the Indians, including germ warfare, wrote Colonel Henry Bouquet, "You will do well to try to inoculate the Indians by means of blankets, as well as to try every other method that can serve to extirpate this execrable race."

When Ecuyer failed to vacate the fort, the Delawares took part in a number of forays against settlements in Juniata, Tuscarora, and Cumberland valleys, again spreading terror wherever they attacked. Near Bushy Run, Westmoreland County, Pennsylvania, about twenty-six miles east of Pittsburgh, on August 5, 1763, a large party of Delaware, Mingoe, Shawnee, and Wyandot warriors from Sandusky attacked Bouquet's force of four hundred men marching to the relief of Fort Pitt. Bouquet, a Swiss soldier who had entered British service, was an outstanding officer and military tactician, and the engagement stands as an example of his skill and resourcefulness. His troops, for the most part, were as little accustomed to backwoods fighting as those who fought under Braddock, but Bouquet had served in America for a number of years and had a healthy respect for Indian warriors. To rest his tired men and horses Bouquet camped for three days at Bedford, where he had the good fortune to engage a group of backwoodsmen to accompany him. He then proceeded cautiously along the military road made by General John Forbes five years before. His forces continued on to Fort Ligonier, where he left oxen and wagons, which helped to lighten his columns and permitted faster maneuvering should he encounter enemy Indians on the march toward Fort Pitt. His men were within a half mile of Bushy Run when the Indians attacked, killing fifty soldiers and wounding sixty others.

On the second day Bouquet ordered two companies of infantry, who were exposed to the hottest fire, to fall back. The Indians mistook the movement for a retreat and rushed headlong after the infantrymen. At the crucial moment, Bouquet ordered troops he had hidden on either side to close in. They inflicted decisive losses on the enemy, and the warriors were driven into the woods, having no time to rally or to pick up their dead and wounded.[55] Bouquet's forces then continued on to Fort Pitt, arriving four days later in time to save the civilian families from death or captivity. The siege was broken, and the Delawares and Shawnee, having failed to capture the stronghold, retreated to their Ohio villages.

Back east on the Susquehanna, Captain Bull, one of Teedyuskung's sons, organized a war party that swept through the Wyoming Valley in the fall of 1763. Many settlers, including women and children, were tortured and killed, and about twenty prisoners were taken in what has been recorded as the *first* Wyoming massacre. (The second took place on July 3, 1778, when four hundred British and seven hundred Indians raided the valley, the Indians collecting more than two hundred white scalps which they sold to the British for ten dollars each.)

The atrocities of 1755 and 1756 were repeated in the summer of 1764, with raids, murders, scalpings, mangled bodies, prisoners taken into captivity, livestock stolen, and houses and barns set aflame. In September, Colonel John Armstrong, hero of the attack on the Delawares at Kittanning, led an expedition to Big Island, to which Tapescawen (one of Teedyuskung's former councilors), Nutimus and his son Joseph, Captain Bull and his family and followers, and sundry other Delawares had retreated. Armstrong's soldiers set fire to the Indian cabins and destroyed the corn which the natives had harvested and stored for winter use, and on which the livelihood of their families largely depended.

Captain Bull, whose vendetta against the whites was carried on because of his father's murder, now had an additional reason to seek vengeance, because the attackers had destroyed the Indians' food. In October he took a war party into Northampton County, Pennsylvania. Bull later boasted that on this foray he killed twenty-six whites with his own hands. Returning to Wyoming with his victorious warriors, Bull seized and tortured nine men and one woman. The woman was roasted alive over an open fire, and the men had awls thrust into their eyes, and spears, arrows, and pitchforks stuck into their bodies. About twenty others, who were not harmed, were led off into captivity.[56]

The taking of prisoners by the Indians has been much misunderstood, and it is not generally realized that captives were usually treated as well as members of the tribe. Prisoners were recognized as an important population increment, and most of them were adopted by bereaved families to take the place of deceased husbands, wives, or children. Shingas, for instance, adopted two white boy captives as his own sons, and accorded them equal treatment with the children he fathered. His brother Beaver once liberated two white female prisoners with the remark, "One is my Mother, the other my Sister . . . I love them as well as I do my own Mother and Sister." [57]

Although some prisoners taken by the Delawares were tortured and killed, this was the exception rather than the rule. Only if adoption was refused a prisoner was he killed because no Delaware families wanted him. Not infrequently white prisoners found the Indian way of life more to their liking than the society from which they had been taken. When the authorities demanded release of captives as terms of peace, the Indian chiefs in good faith tried to comply, but many captives refused to be liberated. When some were forcibly set free and given to the whites, they ran away and returned to their adopted Indian relatives. With this intimate association between Indians and white prisoners, white blood continued to infiltrate the veins of the Delawares in a process of assimilation that had its beginning a century before.

Many friends or relatives of persons who had been massacred or taken into captivity by Indian war parties—particularly those who had seen mutilated bodies of loved ones lying in the smoldering ashes of a destroyed home—became "Indian haters" and sought reprisal. They called the Indians "dogs" and "thieves," and cursed them to their faces. The so-called Paxton Boys, in December of 1763, perpetrated two massacres on peaceful, unarmed Conestoga Indians living in Lancaster, Pennsylvania, killing, scalping, and then hacking the limbs from the bodies of defenseless men, women, and children. Following these murders, the Paxton men threatened to kill a group of about 140 peaceful Moravian Delawares, averse to war, whom Governor John Penn housed in the military barracks in Philadelphia for safety. Public opinion in Philadelphia and in the frontier settlements was divided. Some supported Penn, but a strong segment opposed his pacifism, claiming that he was appeasing potential murderers. The sentiment began to grow that the only good Indian was a dead one, and, when a gang of settlers threatened to attack the barracks, Penn decided to send the Indians under military escort to Sir William Johnson at Johnson Hall on the Mohawk and let him take further action to protect them.

To do so the Indians had to travel the full length of New York state to Albany, but Lieutenant-Governor Cadwallader Colden and his council refused to let the Indians pass, sending a message to Penn that "this Government are rather disposed to attack & punish, then to support and protect them, whom they still consider as their enemy." [58]

As a result, the Moravian Indians were forced to remain for a year and four months in the army barracks in Philadelphia under heavy guard. There they suffered an epidemic of smallpox and undiagnosed fevers which killed fifty-six Indians, who were then interred in a potter's field. The Presbyterians living in Philadelphia, who sympathized with their long suffering Scotch-Irish brethren on the frontier, were accused by the Quakers of aiding lawbreakers who wanted to murder the Indians. The Presbyterians charged the Quakers with supporting a weak government that had failed to protect its citizens, and of coddling red devils who would butcher and scalp white people the next spring, when they were released. After a notice of peace was brought to Philadelphia on December 4, 1764, and a proclamation issued, the Indians were permitted to leave the barracks in March. They withdrew to Nain and then to the banks of the Susquehanna at Wyalusing, where they settled under the protection of Moravian missionaries.

In 1764 public opinion forced John Penn to reinstate the bounties for scalps of enemy Indians, a plan which Sir William Johnson endorsed. Pennsylvania now offered 130 pieces of eight for the scalps of Indian boys and girls under ten years of age; 134 pieces of eight for the scalps of Indian males over ten; and 50 pieces of eight for the scalps of Indian females above the age of ten.[59] The bounties applied to all enemy Delawares—but what government official had the wisdom to determine whether a bloody scalp turned in for cash had been torn from the head of a friendly or unfriendly Indian?

Having failed in their objective of taking Fort Pitt, the Ohio Delawares fell back to the Tuscarawas and Scioto rivers, and their war parties, in a sort of guerilla warfare, continued to harass the settlers and to inflict whatever damage they could on English troops. This was a thorn in Bouquet's side, and the contempt the Delawares and Shawnee showed him was a factor that prompted him to organize an expedition to march into the Muskingum Valley for the purpose of subduing the Delawares and their allies.

Bouquet went overland into the Ohio wilderness, where no army had yet penetrated, driving cattle and sheep and a train of pack horses laden with provisions for his fifteen hundred troops. Virginia woodsmen, skilled as Indian fighters, moved in front and on either flank to prevent a surprise attack. The strategy called for Bouquet to attack the Delawares, Shawnee, Mingoes, and Mahican occupying the area between the Ohio River and Lake Erie, and simultaneously for Colonel John Bradstreet to move against the Wyandot, Ottawa, Chippewa, and their allies in the vicinity of the Great Lakes.

Neither the social organization nor the economy of the Delawares could sustain lengthy warfare as practiced in more complex European societies. The Indians had no specialized class of soldiers; their warriors were also the laborers who cleared the fields for their women to cultivate, pursued the game, and engaged in other activities necessary to feed, clothe, and house their families. Outnumbered by the superior and well-armed British troops, lacking powder and lead for their guns, their wives and children in jeopardy, their homes and fields in danger of destruction, the Delawares had no alternative except to admit defeat and lay down their arms. The Shawnee were soon compelled to follow their example.

Bouquet summoned the Delaware chiefs and captains to meet him to discuss peace terms, and all except Netawatwees complied with instructions. Bouquet promptly deposed this leader and ordered the Indians to name an alternate chief to join in discussing armistice terms. On November 15, 1764, Bouquet wrote as follows to John Penn at Philadelphia from his camp "at the forks of the Muskingum" where the town of Coshocton now stands:

I have the Pleasure to inform you that the Mingoes, the Delawares & the Shawonese, after a long Struggle, have at last submitted to the Terms prescribed to them, vizt:
    1st. To Deliver all the Prisoners without Exception
    2d. To give fourteen Hostages to remain in our Hands as a Security for the strict performance of the 1st Article, and that they shall commit no Hostilities against his Majesty's Subjects.
    Upon these Conditions they are permitted to send Deputies from each Nation to Sr. William Johnson to make their Peace.[60]

Bouquet added that he had already liberated two hundred white captives, although this caused a severe problem because he had to station armed guards over many of them to prevent their running away and returning to their Indian homes. Some of the younger prisoners turned over to him were children of white women prisoners and Delaware Indian fathers.

In discussing the surrender and temporary peace terms, which had to be confirmed and made final by Sir William Johnson, Bouquet held a series of conferences with Indian leaders, among whom was the now elderly Beaver. Neither Shingas nor Pisquetomen are named in the minutes of these conferences; younger leaders had apparently taken their places. In a meeting held in May of 1765, the following Delaware chiefs are named: "Neattawatways [Newcomer], Custaloga, The Beaver, Latort, Tepiscochan, Kelopum, Spoagusa, Nesseuletham, Cuscalethon, Kehewenum, Captain N. Jacobs [possibly a son of the Captain Jacobs killed at Kittanning.]" In addition to these chiefs, 215 Delaware braves attended, along with their "Chief Warriors" whose names are also given in the minutes as follows: "Wingenuna, Cutfinger Peter, Captn. Pipe, Captn. Johnny, Captn. Grey Eyes, Turtle Heart, Sun Fish, White Wolf, John Peters, Thomas Hickman, Kecholan, Opeloawethin, Wessoaux, Simon Girty [Katepacomen]." [61]

Consistent with the traditional Delaware institution of decentralized authority, no single individual could speak with finality, because the lines of responsibility ran to a number of sachems and war captains. Although the war captains, who were responsible for declaring war, had to care for the people while war was in progress, they could not conclude peace. This was the function of the civil chiefs, and, if peace terms were offered to a war captain, it was necessary that he place the matter in the hands of the civil chief.[62] The Delawares were now divided into three camps. The minutes of Bouquet's conferences with Delaware leaders contain significant references to the three groups, which hearkens back to the controversial animal associations discussed briefly in chapter 3 and which now occur for the first time in official military documents.

Beaver is referred to as the chief of the "Turkey Tribe," Kelipama (also given as Kalatama) as the "acting chief" of the "Turtle Tribe" (serving as an alternate for the deposed Netawatwees), and Custaloga as the chief of the "Wolf Tribe." The terms Unalachtigo, Munsie, and Unami were not associated with the animal terminology used in these negotiations.[63]

George Croghan spoke of having a meeting on April 29, 1765, at Fort Pitt with the principal warriors "of the *three Tribes of the Dela-*

wares," although he did not use the animal names.[64] The three tribes referred to both by Bouquet and Croghan were Delawares then living in Ohio. Those still living on the Susquehanna, the conservatives on the Brotherton Reservation in New Jersey (see chapter 12), and the Munsies still living along the Allegheny River were not included in this tri-tribal classification. Although it is not certain how these animal terms may have been used in the distant past—either for clans or phratries (groups of clans)—the concept of animal eponyms clung to the Delawares after this as descriptive terms for three political divisions. The three groups were called "tribes" by Bouquet, but the words *bands* and *subtribes* were later used to refer to them. The three groups were subdivisions of what had formerly been called the Unami or the Delaware proper. Although there was considerable fluidity in the Indian settlements in Ohio, the members of the Turkey, Turtle, and Wolf divisions of the Delawares lived separately, and each had its own chiefs, captains, and councilors. The Munsies were treated separately from the Delaware proper, and it is likely that they, too, had similar subdivisions with animal names, although the evidence is not positive.

While Colonel Bouquet was preparing for his march against the Delaware and Shawnee on the Muskingum, Sir William Johnson dispatched a force to punish the Delawares on the upper Susquehanna for raiding the settlements during Pontiac's uprising. Pontiac fought a losing war and made peace without attaining his objectives; then he was assassinated by a nephew of Black Dog, a Peoria chief. When things had settled down, Sir William invited the Delawares to join him in a treaty, and the Indians conferred with him on May 8, 1765, at Johnson Hall, where a treaty of peace was signed by representatives of both the Ohio and Susquehanna Delawares.[65] The Delawares were now in the position of a vanquished enemy, for the document contained twelve articles which, among other requirements, obligated them not to molest the King's subjects either on land or water, and to keep all routes open; to bring in any white prisoners they still held captive, as well as any deserters, Frenchmen, or Negroes living in their towns; never to take revenge on any British subject who might harm them, but to take their complaint to the authorities, who would bring the culprit to trial; to protect any traders sent to the principal posts to deal with them, and not to impede or injure them in any way. Perhaps the most punitive clause in the document related to lands. It stated that whenever the English and Six Nations ultimately agreed on land limits, the Delawares were required to abide by the decision and not offer any retaliation against white settlers.[66] In effect, as punishment for their part in Pontiac's War, the Delawares forfeited all land rights until the English and Six Nations decided where they might live and hunt.

This was another instance wherein Sir William Johnson did his utmost to restore the hegemony of the Six Nations over the Delawares, but the question of which lands still belonged to the six Nations—and thus where they could place the Delawares—was now a clouded issue. At Albany the Six Nations sold to Pennsylvania their lands west of the Allegheny Mountains—and lands on the Susquehanna to Connecticut—although in 1758 Governor Denny returned to them the lands west of the Alleghenies because their warriors and hunters voiced such strong disapproval to the chiefs who had consented to the sale. At the Treaty of Fort Stanwix (now Rome, New York) in 1768, the Six Nations reconveyed to Pennsylvania all their land in the province extending from the New York line on the Susquehanna over the west branch to Kittanning, and down the south side of the Allegheny and Ohio rivers as far as the mouth of the Tennessee River.[67] This meant, of course, that the Delawares and Shawnee were deprived of some of their best hunting lands, and that the Ohio River became the western limit of white territory, leaving to the Indians the lands west of the Ohio. There was doubt about Six Nations ownership of these western lands.

Not only did white settlers come over the Alleghenies and seat themselves on Red Stone Creek and on the Monongahela as soon as the Fort Stanwix treaty was signed, but Pennsylvania became further embroiled with her English-speaking neighbors, which tended to put added pressures on the Indians. For instance, the dispute with Connecticut had not yet been resolved and, with the Delawares on the Susquehanna committed to peace by their treaty obligations, nothing could be done when Connecticut settlers began to take up lands on the Susquehanna again. Newalike ("the four steps"), a chief of the Munsies on the Big Island in the west branch, complained because white men were surveying lands and marking trees under the pretense of hunting.[68] Brother Onas was no less displeased than the chief, and later when Pennsylvania tried to offer resistance the Connecticut people took possession by "riotous Conduct." The

Pennsylvanians resisted the Connecticut people with force of arms in what was a disgraceful chapter in American history, and in this strife the Delaware and Munsie families were caught in the middle. They had no alternative except to leave before becoming enmeshed in the controversy.

Pennsylvania was also in the midst of compromising an old boundary dispute with neighboring Maryland, which the heirs of William Penn and Lord Baltimore were striving to settle; and Virginia still insisted that her territory included the forks of the Ohio and that segment of Pennsylvania south of the Ohio claimed by the Penns. In his determination to extend Virginia's dominion, her governor, John Murray, Earl of Dunmore, sent agents to explore and survey the territory on the lower Ohio and Kentucky rivers, which was part of the land Pennsylvania bought from the Six Nations at Fort Stanwix, and settlers from Virginia soon came over the mountains to take up ownership of western lands.

Fully aware that they had no claim to lands along the Susquehanna, Allegheny, or Ohio, the Delaware leaders wanted to believe the assurances given them when they agreed to cease hostilities "that the King of Great Britain will take under his protection all nations of Indians in this Country to the Sun Setting & restore tranquility amongst all nations, that your Children unborn may enjoy the blessings of a lasting peace." [69]

As the Virginians encroached on the Shawnee and Cherokee hunting grounds in the area with the general name of "the Kentucky Country" (south of the Ohio River and west of the Great Kanawha), infuriated Shawnee braves resisted in a series of raids, counterraids, and bloody incidents that became known as Lord Dunmore's War. One might think that the direct challenge to the land rights they had assigned the Shawnee would have aroused the Six Nations either to come to their assistance or to act as intermediaries between the Shawnee and Virginia. Nothing like that happened, and the Shawnee stood alone in their resistance, unsupported by the Six Nations.

The younger, more daring Delaware warriors were ready to join the Shawnee, but they were deterred from doing so by Delaware chief Captain White Eyes. Lord Dunmore himself wrote that he received "great Service from the faithfulness, the firmness, and remarkable understanding of White Eyes," who was able to hold the Delawares steady in their attachments to the English in accordance with the treaty they had made.[70] Small in stature, his eyes a lighter color than the eyes of most Indians, White Eyes, a resolute yet thoughtful man who acted with sound judgment, was a good friend of the English. He later became even more attached to the Americans.

The essential vulnerability of the Shawnee during Lord Dunmore's War caused them to retreat west of the Ohio, where there were already some Shawnee villages. After the war, the Shawnee gathered along the Muskingum, the Tuscarawas, and the Scioto rivers in what is now the state of Ohio. White families promptly took possession of the vacated hunting grounds, leaving a hatred burning in the breasts of the Shawnee that encouraged them to massacre American families during the Revolution. Although the Delawares remained peaceful during Lord Dunmore's War, they were fully aware of the treatment the land-hungry Virginians had accorded the Shawnee in an unjustified war.

On May 3, 1768, the garrison at Fort Pitt counted fourteen canoes containing Indian men, women and children, moving slowly down the Allegheny. The officer of the day learned that the party comprised Munsies, who had recently resided at the head of the west branch of the Susquehanna. A few old-timers among these Munsies remembered when they had lived happily along the upper Delaware before they were forced to move to the Susquehanna. During the trials and tribulations of the years that followed, they were shunted back and forth, finally reaching the shallow headwaters of the west branch. Now with the troubles between Yankees and Pennsylvanians, and new white families entering the upstream lands, they belatedly decided to join the Delawares and Munsies living on the Muskingum.[71]

Another Delaware faction living at Tioga (which became Athens, Pennsylvania) moved upstream with other Indian migrants to Oswego and Otseningo, and then settled at Albany. Historical records provide little information about these conservatives who chose not to go west with their brethren but realized they had to leave the Susquehanna. In 1932 eighty-eight-year-old Chief Joseph Montour, one of Teedyuskung's descendants, who lived on the Six Nations Reservation in Ontario, Canada, gave Dr. Frank G. Speck the account handed down orally among his people of the route their ancestors followed after they left the Susquehanna. He said they first settled at a place near

Albany called Alaping ("hemp place"), and from there moved to Lackawanna Flats adjacent to Lake Ontario some five or six miles south of modern Buffalo. Then they moved to a place beyond Irving, New York, on the east side of Cattaraugus Creek opposite a Seneca village on the same stream.[72] During their migrations, these Delawares cemented their associations with the Cayuga, who became their sponsors for their reception into the Six Nations as a "prop" in the confederacy, which is believed to have occurred in the year 1763.

With the exodus of the main body of the Delawares—and some Munsies—to Ohio, and the movement of others across the boundary line into Canada, Pennsylvania appeared to be divesting herself of her bothersome Indians. But the problem was far from settled—it was merely moved to new locations and given to others to solve. Actually the problem was all out of proportion to the number of Indians involved. In 1765 Croghan estimated there were 150 Munsie warriors and 150 Delaware warriors on the Susquehanna, and 600 Delaware warriors living in the area between the Ohio and Lake Erie.[73] That meant the total Delaware Indian population had declined, at most, to about 3,000. As long as France and England were competing for supremacy, both sides courted the Indians and made their political policies accordingly. With the defeat of the French, the western Indians were left to the mercy of the English, who now considered them a costly nuisance.

NOTES—CHAPTER 11

1. *Colonial Records*, vol. 6, p. 397.

2. Ibid., p. 589.

3. Paul A. W. Wallace, *Thirty Thousand Miles with John Heckewelder*, Pittsburgh, 1958, p. 40. As late as the spring of 1775, Cresswell saw "great numbers of bones, both men and horses" on the site of the battle; *The Journal of Nicholas Cresswell, 1774–1777*, New York, 1924, p. 65.

4. "Journal of James Kenny, 1761–1763," *Pennsylvania Magazine of History and Biography*, vol. 37, no. 1, 1913, p. 183.

5. "The Captivity of Charles Stuart," ed. Beverley W. Bond, Jr., *Mississippi Valley Historical Review*, vol. 13, no. 1, June 1926, p. 63.

6. "Croghan's Transactions with the Indians Previous to Hostilities on the Ohio," *Early Western Travels, 1748–1846*, ed. R. G. Thwaites, Cleveland, 1904, vol. 1, pp. 97–98; cf. "The History of an Expedition against

Fort Duquesne," *Memoirs of the Historical Society of Pennsylvania*, Philadelphia, vol. 5, 1856, p. 380. Braddock wrote Governor Morris asking him to have the Indians from Aughwick join him at Wills Creek, *Pennsylvania Archives*, 1st series, vol. 2, p. 290.

7. "The Captivity of Charles Stuart." The records are clear that Braddock held conferences in his tent with the Indians prior to his march over the mountains; see Peter Halklett's Orderly Book, *Braddock's Defeat*, ed. Charles Hamilton, Norman, Okla., 1959, pp. 88–90. Out of fairness to Braddock it should be noted that prior to the march, on April 15, 1755, he wrote Governor Morris that he intended to restore the Ohio country to the Indians (*Pennsylvania Archives*, 1st series, vol. 2, p. 290), but evidently something happened to make him change his mind prior to the conference reported by Shingas.

8. "The Captivity of Charles Stuart."

9. Penn Manuscripts, Indian Affairs, vol. 1, 1687–1753, p. 52, Manuscript Room, Historical Society of Pennsylvania, Philadelphia.

10. *Colonial Records*, vol. 6, p. 615.

11. Ibid., pp. 423, 443.

12. Ibid., pp. 647–48.

13. Ibid., p. 683.

14. For an account of the raids herein mentioned, see William A. Hunter, *Forts on the Pennsylvania Frontier, 1753–58*, Harrisburg, 1960, pp. 123, 125. Scarouady had warned the Pennsylvanians that if they did not provide assistance against the French, "it would occasion the absolute Defection of the Delawares"; *Colonial Records*, vol. 6, p. 692.

15. George H. Loskiel, *History of the Mission of the United Brethren*, trans. Christian Ignatius La Trobe, London, 1794, pt. 2, pp. 166–67.

16. Anthony F. C. Wallace, *King of the Delawares: Teedyuskung*, Philadelphia, 1949, pp. 83–86.

17. *Colonial Records*, vol. 7, p. 99.

18. Ibid., p. 71.

19. Ibid., p. 75. Their actual words were, "Say no more to us on that Head lest we cut off your private Parts and make Women of you, as you have done of us"; ibid., p. 522.

20. Ibid., pp. 88–89.

21. For a detailed account of the attack see William A. Hunter, "Victory at Kittanning," *Pennsylvania History*, vol. 23, no. 3, July 1956, pp. 3–34.

22. *Colonial Records*, vol. 7, pp. 705, 713.

23. Charles Thomson, *Alienation of the Delaware and Shawanese Indians*, Philadelphia, 1847 (reprint of 1759 edition). See also Lewis R. Harley, *Life of Charles Thomson*, Philadelphia, 1900, wherein Harley says Thomson was adopted by the Delawares and given the name Wegh-wu-

law-mu-end, which he says meant, "the man who tells the truth"; p. 49.

24. *Colonial Records*, vol. 7, p. 665. Teedyuskung's definition of the Unami was that they "were a distinct Tribe of Delaware Indians and that Alomipus was formerly King of that Tribe"; ibid., p. 726. The implication of his statement is that he did not consider himself a Unami, yet the records make it very clear that he was not a Munsie; ibid., p. 284. At the conference in Easton that opened on Oct. 8, 1758, the Indians in attendance were "Chehohockes, alias Delawares and Unamies, Teedyuskung with Sundry Men, Women and Children . . . Munsies or Mini-sinks . . . Egohowen . . . with Sundry Men, Women, and Children"; ibid., vol. 8, p. 176. In the Appendix to Jefferson's *Notes on the State of Virginia*, Thomson wrote that the Chihohocki was one of the five Lenape tribes, and its members dwelt on the west side of the Delaware River. An earlier variant of the name, Chickahokin, is found on Captain John Smith's map of Virginia; cf. A. R. Dunlap and C. A. Weslager, *Indian Place-Names in Delaware*, Wilmington, 1950, pp. 14, 49. A complete and colorful account of the Easton fall conference of 1758 is given by Paul A. W. Wallace in *Conrad Weiser*, Philadelphia, 1945, chaps. 59, 60, and 61.

25. *Colonial Records*, vol. 7, p. 213.

26. Ibid., p. 218. At a meeting with Sir William Johnson on July 11, 1756, the Delaware spokesman said, "We are looked upon as Women, and therefore when the French came amongst us, is it to be wondered that they were able to seduce us?" *NYCD*, vol. 7, p. 157.

27. *Colonial Records*, vol. 7, p. 297.

28. *NYCD*, vol. 7, p. 119. After concluding peace with the Delawares and Shawnee, Sir William Johnson gave the Delawares a war belt signify-ing that they were now English allies against the French, and they danced a war dance all night; ibid., p. 159.

29. *Colonial Records*, vol. 8, p. 35.

30. Ibid., p. 751; see p. 708 for the presents promised Teedyuskung to withdraw his charges, cf., pp. 739–40. See also Wallace, *Teeduskung*, chap. 8, for discussion of Teedyuskung's relations with the Friendly Association.

31. *Colonial Records*, vol. 8, pp. 190–92.

32. Milton W. Hamilton, ed., *The Papers of Sir William Johnson*, Albany, 1957, vol. 12, p. 937.

33. *Colonial Records*, vol. 7, p. 522.

34. *Colonial Records*, vol. 8, p. 181.

35. Ibid., p. 188.

36. The details of the mission may be found in Francis P. Jennings, "A Vanishing Indian," *Pennsylvania Magazine of History and Biography*,

vol. 87, no. 3, July, 1963, pp. 322–23; see also "The Journal of Christian Frederick Post," *Early Western Travels*, ed. R. G. Thwaites, vol. 1, Cleveland, 1904, p. 273.

37. *Colonial Records*, vol. 8, pp. 386, 723.

38. Ibid., p. 268.

39. Ibid., p. 203.

40. *Colonial Records*, vol. 9, pp. 6–7.

41. George Henry Loskiel, *History of the Mission, of the United Brethren* . . . , trans. Christian Ignatius La Trobe, London, 1794, pt. 2, p. 203.

42. *Colonial Records*, vol. 8, pp. 292, 311.

43. Ibid., vol. 9, p. 261.

44. Ibid., vol. 8, p. 489.

45. Howard H. Peckham, *Pontiac and the Indian Uprising*, Princeton, N.J., 1947, p. 147.

46. Defendant (Government's) Exhibit No. 538 in Docket 13-6 *et al.* before the Indian Claims Commission, prepared by Dr. Erminie Wheeler-Voegelin; see also Defendant's Exhibit No. A-322 in Dockets 13-E *et al.* I am deeply indebted to Senator J. Caleb Boggs of Delaware for his cooperation in obtaining these exhibits from the Department of Justice for my examination.

47. Ibid.

48. Ibid. Dr. Wheeler-Voegelin says in the report she prepared for the government that Newcomer founded the town on the Cuyahoga between 1756 and 1758, but this is unlikely since he was still living on Beaver Creek in July of 1758; see card no. 1954, *Papers of the Provincial Council* (microfilm), Bureau of Archives and History, Pennsylvania Historical and Museum Commission, Harrisburg. Under date of July 9, 1758, card no. 1960, Newcomer "at ye mouth of Beaver Creek" is called "a very considerable man." I am indebted to William A. Hunter for providing me with these citations. In 1754, when Newcomer attended a meeting with George Croghan at Logstown, he apparently had not attained the position of eminence that he later held, for Shingas was referred to as the Delaware king; "Croghan's Journal, 1754," in R. G. Thwaites, ed., *Early Western Travels*, vol. 1, pp. 79, 80; cf. *Colonial Records*, vol. 5, p. 735. By 1761 Newcomer was recognized as one of the Delaware leaders, for when White Eyes came to Philadelphia on May 22 of that year he stated he was "sent by his chief men at Allegheny—Tomaqui, or King Beaver and Netalwalemut [Netawatwees]"; *Colonial Records*, vol. 8, p. 618. In 1771 he was the head chief on the Ohio; ibid., vol. 9, p. 735.

49. *Colonial Records*, vol. 7, pp. 172, 381, 466.

50. Wallace, *Thirty Thousand Miles with John Heckewelder*, Pittsburgh, 1958, p. 41. White Eyes lived on Beaver Creek in a "Good Shingled

House & several Stables & Cow houses"; see "Journal of James Kenny," *Pennsylvania Magazine of History and Biography*, vol. 37, no. 1, 1926, p. 22. After the Battle of Bushy Run, the majority of the Delawares and Shawnee forsook their settlements on Beaver Creek, and Thomas Hutchins states that they destroyed their houses before moving to Ohio; Charles A. Hanna, *The Wilderness Trail*, 2 vols., New York, 1911, vol. 2, p. 203.

51. Wallace, *Thirty Thousand Miles*, p. 41.

52. John Heckewelder, *History*, p. 272.

53. *Colonial Records*, vol. 9, p. 63.

54. "William Trent's Journal at Fort Pitt, 1763," ed. A. T. Volwiler, *Mississippi Valley Historical Review*, vol. 11, 1924, p. 400.

55. Niles Anderson, *The Battle of Bushy Run*, Harrisburg, 1966.

56. *Pennsylvania Archives*, 1st series, vol. 4, pp. 125–27. The Delaware atrocities are fully described by C. Hale Sipe, *The Indian Wars of Pennsylvania*, Harrisburgh, 1931.

57. *Colonial Records*, vol. 8, p. 839.

58. Ibid., vol. 9, p. 122.

59. Ibid., p. 189.

60. Ibid., p. 207.

61. Ibid., p. 256.

62. *David Zeisberger's History*, p. 98.

63. *Colonial Records*, vol. 9, pp. 214–33. Note, pp. 226–27, that Kalatama (Kelipama) was a brother of the deposed Netawatwees; cf. ibid., p. 229. For additional details, see *Historical Account of Bouquet's Expedition against the Ohio Indians in 1764*, Ohio Valley Series, Cincinnati, 1868.

64. *Colonial Records*, vol. 9, p. 254. In 1758 Delaware George told Christian Frederick Post, "Look brother, we are here of three different nations. I am of the Unami nation"; "The Journal of Christian Frederick Post," *Early Western Travels, 1748–1846*, ed. R. G. Thwaites, Cleveland, 1904, vol. 1, p. 220. Beaver also said, "We are three tribes . . ."; ibid., p. 271.

65. *Colonial Records*, vol. 9, p. 280.

66. Ibid., pp. 277–80.

67. Ibid., pp. 554–55.

68. Ibid., p. 426.

69. Ibid., p. 258; see also Randolph C. Downes, "Dunmore's War: An Interpretation," *Mississippi Valley Historical Review*, vol. 21, no. 3, December 1934, pp. 311–30.

70. *Documentary History of Dunmore's War, 1774*, ed. R. G. Thwaites and Louise P. Kellogg, Madison, Wis., 1905, p. 384. White Eyes complained that he had spent so much time assisting Dunmore than he

neglected his fields, and that his wife and children were in need of bread; *The Revolution on the Upper Ohio*, ed. R. G. Thwaites and Louise P. Kellogg, Madison, Wis., 1908, p. 40.

71. *Colonial Records*, vol. 9, p. 529.

72. Frank G. Speck, *The Celestial Bear Comes Down to Earth*, *Scientific Publications Series*, no. 7, Lancaster, Pa., 1945, p. 10.

73. "Croghan's Journal, 1765," in R. G. Thwaites, ed. *Early Western Travels*, vol. 1, pp. 167–68.

12

Keeping Peace in New Jersey

Although there had been a series of movements of New Jersey Indians across the Delaware River—to settle in the Forks at Easton, Pennsylvania, to affiliate with the Moravians at (the first) Gnadenhütten, and later to join other migrants at Shamokin and Wyoming— a small group of Delawares clung tenaciously to their New Jersey homes. They no longer resided in villages but were scattered in rural areas, a few families here, others there, usually housed in wretched cabins. These families had their own cornfields and vegetable patches. Perhaps they owned a horse and cow, or a few pigs, and some raised chickens. They fished and crabbed in season; some made splint baskets, brooms, cornhusk mats, and wooden bowls, and peddled them from door to door.

This conservative faction, numbering a few hundred at most, was separate from and independent of those who had moved to Pennsylvania, although some were blood relatives. These natives fell under the jurisdiction of the New Jersey government, which became a royal establishment in 1702 and soon had a governor, council, assembly, and other distinct organs of government. For a while, very little attention was given to these Indian remnants who kept to themselves, because there were other more important matters to keep officials busy. As the economic situation of the Indian families worsened, Presbyterian ministers in New York and New Jersey began to take an interest in them as forgotten children of God. They reported to the Society for Propagating Christian Knowledge, which had been formed

in Scotland, that the plight of unconverted Indians in the Colonies
was deplorable, and the society appropriated money to send two
missionaries to live there and preach the gospel. One of these, an
ordained minister named David Brainerd, not yet thirty, spent a year
administering to the Indians at the Forks, during which time he also
made two discouraging journeys to the Susquehanna to preach to the
Delawares and other Indians living at Shamokin. There he had long
discussions with old Sassoonan, who understood English and "was
willing to be instructed," but Brainerd found most of the Delawares
on the Susquehanna too bibulous to listen to the Christian message.[1]

In 1745 Brainerd turned his attention to the conversion of the
Delawares remaining in New Jersey, and in June he went to a place
called Crosswicks (also known to the Indians as Crossweeksung),
near present-day Bordentown, about ten miles southeast of Trenton,
where several Indian families were living. The Indians built a crude
hut for Brainerd to live in, and he traveled around the countryside
preaching to any Indians he could find. The women and children
were willing to be taught, but most of the men refused to listen.
Nevertheless, he persisted, and by August had found and persuaded
about sixty-five Delawares to attend Christian services regularly, including a few of the old men "who had been drunken wretches for
many years." [2] Soon thereafter he noted in his journal that he had
baptized thirty-five of the Delawares, a notable achievement, since
he had not yet mastered their language and was forced to depend
upon an interpreter to translate his words into the native dialect. He
was further handicapped by a pulmonary affliction that sent him
into fits of coughing during his sermons and caused him to spit
blood. He soon learned why the majority of Indian men were averse
to Christianity, for one Delaware told him that "the white people
lie, defraud, steal, and drink worse than the Indians . . . that the
English have by these means, made them quarrel and kill one another,
and in a word, brought them to the practice of all those vices which
now prevail among them. So that they are now vastly more vicious,
as well as much more miserable, than they were before the coming
of the white people into the country." [3]

Brainerd's devotion to his mission dispelled some of these prejudices, and, before six months had passed, twenty Indian families built
huts at Crosswicks to be near the magnetic young pastor. He also
started a school where children and young persons attended by day

and married couples came at night to be taught. By March of 1746, the Delaware population at Crosswicks had increased to 130 persons, but the land would not yield sufficient crops to feed so many mouths, and the Indians, with their pastor's agreement, decided to move elsewhere. They selected a site about fifteen miles distant— two miles northeast of Cranbury in Middlesex County, where the soil was more fertile and there was better grazing land for their cows. They intended to build a new school and a church at this place, which Brainerd called Bethel, and "settle an Indian town, which might be a mountain of holiness," as he noted in his journal. By May most of the Delaware community had moved to their new home, although about twenty remained at a place in Burlington County called Weekpink, now Vincentown, on a tract secured by an English right granted the family of the Indian Mahamickwon, who was known to the whites as "King" Charles.[4] Brainerd's labors brought most of the dispossessed Delawares together in a self-contained Indian community where the New Jersey government could not escape paying attention to them.

After David Brainerd's death in 1747, his brother John, also a minister, carried on with the mission at Cranbury, and he attempted to obtain a larger tract of land to which the natives would have undisputed title. He was given financial assistance by a group of Quakers called the New Jersey Association for Helping the Indians, but his plan to acquire land where the Indians could live in peace and security was interrupted by the outbreak of the French and Indian War.[5] Although New Jersey was some distance from the fighting in Pennsylvania, Governor Jonathan Belcher of New Jersey reported to his council on December 2, 1755, that the war resulted in murders and depredations by the French and Indians "near our borders." [6] Later some Indian war parties crossed the Delaware in their canoes, and among the warriors who terrorized the settlers were former residents of northern New Jersey, who sought to avenge wrongs done them before they left their homeland. During this critical period, Governor Belcher received a petition from the peaceful Delawares settled at Cranbury, stating that they were not only in danger of being killed by the New Jersey settlers (who then considered all Indians enemies), but their lives were being threatened by hostile war parties fighting for the French interests.[7]

In an effort to protect the friendly Delawares, New Jersey enacted a law stipulating that any of the Cranbury Indians could go to a magistrate and obtain a certificate testifying to his status as a non-hostile. The statute further provided that the magistrate "should at the same time give him a Red Ribbon and desire him to wear it upon his head when he happens to be in any place where such Accident may be Likely to happen that he may not be taken by any of the People of this Province for an Enemy but known as a friend." [8]

On June 2, 1756, Governor Belcher, thrown into a panic when a war party of enemy Indians staged a raid in Sussex County, issued a proclamation in which he stated that the Delaware Indians were "Enemies, Rebels & Traytors to his most Sacred Majesty & I do hereby require all his Majestys Subjects within this Province to be Assiduous Within the Government in taking or Destroying the said Delaware Indians . . ." [9] He was, of course, referring to the hostile marauders, not to the residents at Cranbury authorized to wear identifying red ribbons.

Following the example set by Pennsylvania's Governor Morris two months before, Governor Belcher also offered a bounty of 150 Spanish dollars for every male enemy Indian above the age of fifteen delivered to one of the New Jersey jails or to forts that had been hastily thrown up for defense; 50 Spanish dollars to any inhabitant of the colony who killed a male enemy Indian above the age of fifteen and produced the Indian's scalp; 130 Spanish dollars for any male or female enemy Indian under the age of fifteen delivered to the authorities. The friendly Indians at Cranbury and Weekpink were told to confine themselves within certain bounds prescribed for their protection, and all ferrymen were forbidden to carry any Indians across the Raritan or Delaware rivers without special orders granted either by the governor or two justices of the peace.[10] This was to prevent any of the New Jersey Indians from moving to Pennsylvania to join those warring against the colony, and it led to a later misapprehension that New Jersey was holding the friendly Indians captive against their wishes.

Because of the slowness of communication, Governor Belcher was unaware that Sir William Johnson was then negotiating a peace treaty with Delaware chief Nutimus and the Shawnee, hoping to persuade them to turn against the French. When Governor Belcher received the news that Sir William Johnson had successfully concluded a treaty on July 11, he hastily rescinded his proclamation and issued a new one on July 23, 1756. In the second proclamation he instructed both military and civilian personnel "to forbear carrying on an Offencive War against th said Indians, and all others to the Eastward of the said River [the Susquehanna] until my further Order therein." [11]

Recognizing that settlers on the Pennsylvania frontier were still apprehensive of Indian brutalities, that influential Quakers and Presbyterians living in New Jersey believed the natives had been abused (which had brought on the hostilities in the first place), and that the Indians themselves were discontented, New Jersey authorities decided to attempt to right the wrongs and prevent further bloodshed in the province. Commissioners were appointed to examine the treatment the Indians had received; they met with a group of Indians in the winter of 1756 and heard their grievances. Upon the advice of the commissioners, the legislature in 1757 passed laws intended to protect the Indians—for example, by making it illegal to sell strong drink to them and by prohibiting the imprisonment of an Indian for indebtedness.[12]

The commissioners also learned that New Jersey really had two serious problems relating to the Indians' lands. First, the Munsies then living in Pennsylvania claimed that they were still owed for lands in New Jersey illegally confiscated by white settlers. Second, the Delawares settled at Cranbury and the few remaining at Crosswicks, having no title to the lands they were occupying, were fearful that the whites would soon drive them away.

The commissioners again met with the Indians at Crosswicks on February 20, 1758, and among those attending were resident natives from New Jersey as well as Delawares from the Susquehanna, including Teedyuskung, who was described in the minutes of the conference as "the king of the Delawares." The Indians gave the commissioners a list of specific parcels of land which they claimed had not been paid for but which were in the possession of settlers. Even Teedyuskung claimed that he was the owner of a certain plot that white men now occupied. Since the matter required further investigation, the Indians appointed five Delawares to transact with the commissioners all future business relating to land matters: Tom Store, Moses Tatamy, Stephen Calvin, Isaac Stille, and John Pompshire.[13]

It was apparent to the commissioners not only that it would be necessary to compensate the Indians who had left New Jersey for the lands they still claimed, but also that some place would have to be found where the resident Indians could live without interference. An act passed by the General Assembly in 1758 authorized five commissioners—Andrew Johnston, Richard Salter, Charles Read, John Stevens, William Foster, and Jacob Spicer—to make a just settlement on the Indians, and also to purchase "some convenient tract of land for their settlement, and shall take a deed or deeds in the name of his said excellency or commander in chief of this colony for the time being, and of the commissioners and their heirs, in trust, for the use of the said Indian natives who have or do reside in this colony, south of Raritan, and their successors forever . . ." The sum of sixteen hundred pounds was appropriated for use by the commissioners, half of which was to be used to pay the Indians for the lands they still claimed and the other half to buy new lands for their occupancy.[14]

In the meantime, new governor Francis Bernard in the summer of 1758 sent a message to Governor William Denny of Pennsylvania, advising him that he was mortified upon his arrival "to have advice of an incursion made upon our Province, attended as usual by great Barbarities, by Indians who are suspected to be of those who made peace with your Honour's Province." [15] He suggested that the two provinces act in concert, to which Governor Denny consented, and, in a meeting arranged between the two governors in Philadelphia, it was agreed that Governor Bernard would send a message to the Munsies and invite them to meet him in Burlington, New Jersey, to discuss their grievances.[16]

When the Indians arrived on August 7, 1758, Governor Bernard was introduced to the nuances of Indian statecraft when he was told that a Six Nations representative accompanied the Delaware delegation. The messenger from the Munsies, Otawopass, whose English name was Benjamin, opened the discussion by offering a belt of wampum, but native protocol prevented his standing until the Six Nations representative had first spoken; therefore he spoke from a sitting position. He explained that when the Munsies received Governor Bernard's invitation to confer with him, they immediately informed their Iroquois uncles, who sent an agent to accompany them and witness the negotiations. This agent, Apewyett, whose English name was John Hudson, then rose, and, presenting a wampum belt, informed the governor "that the Munseys are women and cannot hold Treaties for themselves . . ." [17] Continuing, he said that the Indians would be glad to have a formal session with the governor, at which time all the principal chiefs and councilors of the Munsies and Six Nations would be present, but this could not take place in New Jersey, where no council fire had ever been lit. He said they would be glad to meet with him at the Forks of the Delaware, where the ancient council fire had been kindled and (figuratively) was kept burning for such discussions.

Benjamin then stood and told Governor Bernard that at the next full moon the Indian nations would be present at the Forks of the Delaware for an important meeting with Brother Onas and would notify him in advance of the exact day. Bernard replied that he would be glad to join them at the great council fire, at which time he was certain that any differences they had about the land could be resolved. Sincere expressions of peace and amity were made by both the governor and the Indians, and the conference ended harmoniously.

Prior to the scheduled meeting at the Forks, the New Jersey commissioners on August 29, 1758, purchased as a reservation for the Indians a tract of 3,044 acres in Evesham Township, Burlington County, for seven hundred forty pounds.[18] Benjamin Springer was the owner of this property, which contained two houses, one occupied by Springer and the other by a settler named James Denight.[19] The property also included an orchard, fences, an old sawmill on a stream called Edgepillock Branch, and a new mill on another branch. The indenture provided that Denight's house and a hundred acres of land would continue to be reserved for his use, but that the Indians would possess the rest of the property. The accompanying surveyor's drawing, which appears in the deed of conveyance, shows the bounds and shape of the property (see Fig. 15).

Although this tract was the first Indian reservation (and the last) in the state of New Jersey, it was by no means the first Indian reservation in the country, as some New Jersey writers have suggested.[20] Reference has already been made to the reservation laid out in 1701 in Chester County, Pennsylvania, for the Okehocking Indians, and another on the Brandywine during the same period. The Province of Maryland laid out a reservation of five thousand acres for the Nanticoke Indians as early as 1698, and a second reservation of three thousand acres in 1711.[21]

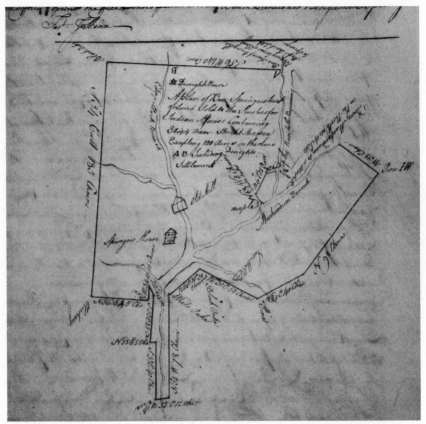

Figure 15. Contemporary surveyor's drawing, 1758, of 3,044-acre Brotherton Indian Reservation, Evesham Township, Burlington County, N.J., purchased by funds raised through a lottery (Courtesy New Jersey Historical Society)

The conference at the Forks at Easton, Pennsylvania, convened on October 8, 1758, with political dignitaries present from both Pennsylvania and New Jersey, and a total of 507 Indian men, women, and children representing the Six Nations—Nanticoke, Tutelo, Unami, Munsies, Mahickon, and Pomptons. The Pomptons, also designated as Wapings, were New England Algonkians who established a central village at the junction of the Pompton and Pequannock rivers near modern Paterson and later left New Jersey, claiming their lands had been taken away from them without payment. Much of the conference was devoted to discussing the causes of the Indian war and the release of white prisoners, which was of particular concern to

Governor Denny and his associates. When the question of New Jersey lands was finally broached, the Oneida speaker, whose English name was Thomas King, took the floor in behalf of his nephews, the Munsies, claiming they had been wronged out of a great deal of their territory and that the Pomptons had been similarly injured.

> . . . you claim all the Wild Creatures [he said on behalf of the Munsies and Pomptons] and will not let us come on your land to hunt for them. You will not so much as let us peel a Single Tree. This is hard and has given us great offence. The Cattle you raise are your own; but those which are Wild are still ours, and should be common to both; for our Nephews, when they sold the Land, did not propose to deprive themselves of hunting the Wild Deer or of using a Stick of Wood when they should have Occasions.[22]

Through Stephen Calvin, his Delaware Indian interpreter, Governor Bernard replied that he would be glad to make diligent inquiry as to which specific lands in New Jersey were still claimed by the Munsies and Pomptons. He said this would take considerable time, and he hoped that some means of settlement could be agreed on that would eliminate all delays and also give the Indians fair treatment. The Munsies and Pomptons withdrew to confer about the matter, and, when they returned, the Munsie sachem Egohohowen said that it was the consensus that Governor Bernard should make them a cash settlement in a lump sum which would then be distributed to the Indians. After consulting with his commissioners, Bernard told the Indians he believed eight hundred Spanish dollars would be "an extraordinary price" for their unpaid lands in New Jersey. The Munsies then asked the advice of their uncles. Thomas King said it appeared to be a fair and honorable offer, but, since there were so many Indians to share in it, he believed that an additional two hundred dollars was in order.

After consulting again with the commissioners, who were themselves doing some rapid calculations—having already spent seven hundred forty of the sixteen hundred pounds appropriated for their use—Governor Bernard said it was more than he intended to pay, but that he was willing to do so as evidence of his desire to be just. However, he said he wanted the Indians to understand clearly which lands were being purchased so that there would be no trouble in the future, and he laid a map before them showing the exact location and bounds. The Indians said they were in agreement, the cash exchanged hands, and two deeds were executed.[23] The Indians further agreed that from this time on the Province of New Jersey would be considered free of any claims by Munsies and Pomptons. The money was distributed by the chiefs to their followers, and the Indians returned to their Susquehanna homes content—at least for a time. In reality the Delawares never rid themselves of the belief that the English defrauded them of their lands in the Delaware Valley, even though on this occasion the conference ended with a friendly feeling on both sides.

A majority of the Indians remaining in New Jersey moved to the lands purchased for their occupancy at the place on the road from Medford to Hammonton called Edgepillock (apparently named for the creek of that name on the tract; see Fig. 15), which became Indian Mills. There, with financial assistance provided by the government, they built new cabins, a log meeting house, and a gristmill.[24] Governor Bernard was responsible for naming the reservation, as indicated in this excerpt from a letter he wrote on June 15, 1759, to the Commissioners for Trade and Plantations, "To this place I went with 3 of the Commissioners for Indian Affairs, where we laid out the plan of a town, to which I gave the name of Brotherton . . ."[25] In the same letter he pointed out that there were then about three hundred Indians living in New Jersey and that approximately two hundred were settled on the reservation. The place-name Brotherton, also found in England, apparently was selected by Governor Bernard to connote brotherliness, although he gave no reason for his choice. It was explained to the Indians that the land would be held in trust for them, tax free, by the commissioners, and that it was not within the power of any of them, or their descendants, to lease or sell any part of it. It is clear from a study of the documents that Governor Bernard and the commissioners intended that the Indians and their descendants would have the privilege of occupying the reserved lands exclusively, forever.

To repay the government the money it had advanced from the treasury for the cash settlement made at the Forks at Easton, and to purchase the lands at Brotherton without burdening the taxpayers, the General Assembly empowered the commissioners to conduct a lottery to raise sixteen hundred pounds covered by the appropriation act of 1758. Some 3,200 tickets were printed and offered for sale to the people of New York and Pennsylvania, as well as to residents of New Jersey. This was a precedent in Indian affairs, and the commissioners hoped that many persons would buy tickets when they realized how much Christian blood had been saved by New Jersey's fair and humane treatment of the Indians.[26]

The Reverend John Brainerd was engaged on March 22, 1762, as "Superintendent and Guardian" of the Brotherton Reservation, subject to such orders or regulations as the governor or commissioners should make.[27] He served on the reservation for a number of years, during which time he preached to the Indians, visited the sick and elderly, gave advice to parents about their children, and performed other services. The families, who soon became known as the Brotherton Indians, were engaged primarily in farming, although the land and waterways of the reservations and the adjoining marshland yielded a variety of fish, birds, and small game. At its population peak there were between two hundred and three hundred Indian residents, but as time went on the population decreased due to deaths and departures, and in 1774 it is said there were only fifty or sixty persons remaining on the reserve.[28]

The main body of Delawares, who had now moved from the Susquehanna to the Ohio Valley, were not content that a group of their people continued to live separately in New Jersey. When Joseph Peepy, a converted Delaware, went as an interpreter in 1766 with Charles Beatty, the Presbyterian pastor, to the Delaware towns on the Muskingum, the Indians pressed him for information about their New Jersey brethren. Peepy explained that they were living at Brotherton, under the supervision of the government, and the council gave him a belt of wampum to carry back to New Jersey with an invitation to the occupants of the reservation to move to Ohio.[29]

Peepy delivered the message, and in the spring of 1767 he returned to the Muskingum with a reply written by John Brainerd on behalf of the Indians in his charge. The message said that the Brotherton Delawares were ready and willing to accept the invitation to come to Ohio, provided three obstacles could be removed: First, they needed money to defray their moving expenses; second they couldn't leave without the "consent, assistance, and protection" of the New Jersey authorities; third, they had a church, schoolhouse, residences, and other accommodations on the reservation that would be lost if they vacated.[30] There was no immediate reply to the message, but the

Ohio Delawares did not forget their New Jersey brethren. In May of 1771 New Jersey Governor William Franklin, on business in Philadelphia, received a request for an audience from Captain Killbuck, a prominent Delaware from the Muskingum who was in the city on official business with Pennsylvania authorities.[31] Killbuck told Governor Franklin that he was a messenger from "Na-taut-whale-mund [another name for Netawatwees or Newcomer] the great Chief of the Delawares, and at the request of all the other Indians of that Nation on the Ohio to desire that the Governor would let the New Jersey Indians loose that they might go and live with the rest of their Nation. And lastly that he expected that the Governor would furnish them with Money to Enable them to remove either the Ensuing Fall or next Spring." [32]

Governor Franklin asked Killbuck whether he was certain the Brotherton Indians were willing to leave their reservation, and Killbuck replied affirmatively. He said he had learned that the only thing holding them back was money to make the trip, and he told Franklin that it would be necessary for them to sell the reserved lands to pay their debts and defray the expenses of the journey. The governor replied that the reservation was secured to the Indians forever by statute, and it would have to be repealed before they could offer the land for sale. He said if the Brotherton people would lay a request before his council and the General Assembly, the honorable gentlemen might consider enacting legislation to permit them to dispose of the land held in trust for them. Killbuck said that he must return to Ohio but would leave matters to be handled by Stephen Calvin, who was fully empowered to act in Killbuck's absence. Stephen Calvin promptly composed a petition to which he affixed the names of several of the Indians and submitted it to the council and General Assembly.

On June 1, 1777, representatives of the Brothertons met with the governor and members of his council at Burlington, New Jersey. The manuscript minutes of this meeting have been preserved:

. . . The Board being informed that a number of the Brotherton Indians were now in Town ready to attend the Council agreeable to the Notice they had received for that purpose, they with Stephen Calvin were called in and his Excellency acquainted them that Stephen Calvin having presented a Petition to him in the name of himself and sundry other of the Brotherton Indians praying that a Law might be passed to enable the said Indians to sell the Lands allotted and secured to them by the Government in this Province and have leave to retire to the Ohio, he had sent for them that he might be informed from their own Mouths of their inclinations respecting this matter.

Thomas Store an antient Indian, and the person whom Stephen Calvin assured his Excellency was the principal person confided in by the Brotherton Indians when they had any Business to transact then declared that he did not sign the said Petition [although his name was on it] nor had he ever seen it, or heard of it: and that he did not chuse the Land should be sold, nor did he want to go away.

Merrien Claus an Indian Woman of good Repute and Mother of one of the Persons whose names were affixed to the Petition being ask'd by the Governor whether she had a Son named Ben Claus [whose name was also on it], and what the Age of her Son was. She answered she had such a Son who was now in the 15th year of his Age. That she had not signed the said Petition, nor seen it, and she was sure her Son had not, nor did she or her Son choose to have the Land sold, or to leave the Province.

Stephen Calvin then Acknowledged that Thomas Store and Ben Claus had not signed the Petition, but said he thought himself Authorized to put their names to it, and that he was determined the Land should be sold, whether they would nor not. He was somewhat in Liquor & talked very absurdly and impertinently. On the whole it appeared to the Board after a good deal of Conversation with the Indians present on the Subject, and a Strict Examination into the Matter, that there was not above two of the Indians whose names were signed to the Petition who were anyways privy to it, or had any Inclination to remove. Whereupon his Excellency acquainted them that as some of the principal of the Brotherton Indians did not choose the said Lands should be sold and some others of them were not here to answer for themselves, it was not proper to pass such a Law at present as had been requested. That nevertheless the Indians were at full Liberty to go to the Ohio whenever they pleased, but that such of them as chose to remain here on the Lands secured to them by the Government should be kindly treated, as they had always hitherto been.[33]

Although the records are not clear, evidently a few of the Indians left the reservation to go west, but the majority preferred not to move. Nevertheless, as time went on, the population at Brotherton continued to decline.

In 1801, the Indians remaining on the reservation petitioned the state government to sell their lands and give them the proceeds to enable them to move to New Stockbridge in Oneida County, New York. They had received an invitation to reside among the so-called Stockbridge Indians, then living near Oneida Lake.[34] In a speech made before members of the New Jersey Historical Society, January 21, 1875, Samuel Allinson said that in 1832 he had seen a copy of this invitation, which could no longer be found, and that the Stockbridges urged the Brotherton people to "pack up their mat" and "come and eat out of their dish," adding that "their necks were stretched in looking toward the fireside of their grandfather till they were as long as cranes."

The Stockbridge Indians were mostly displaced Mahican families, many of whom had formerly lived along the Housatonic River in Massachusetts who left their homes there after the French and Indian War to join one of the bands of Oneida Indians. In November of 1792 David Zeisberger referred to these Mahican when he wrote that he had ". . . learned that the Indians have all left Stockbridge (in Massachusetts), and now live with the Oneidas, who have given them land . . . and it was reported that the Indians from the Jerseys will also move thither." [35] This suggests the Indians had been discussing the removal of the New Jersey people from the Brotherton Reservation several years before the written invitation was received.

The contemporary documents do not explain why the New Jersey Brothertons did not move to Ohio and accept the long-standing invitation to join the main body of the Delawares. There had been ferment on the Ohio during the Revolution, with a schism in the tribe, and this may have deterred the Brothertons from going west. It is also possible that the population of the Brotherton Reservation included some Mahican who preferred to rejoin their own people and who influenced the others. The New Jersey government acted favorably on the Indians' petition, and commissioners were appointed to divide the tract into lots of not more than one hundred acres each, and to sell them at public sale, provided that three-fourths of the Indians consented. At that time there were sixty-three adult Indians who had rights in the tract. The commissioners announced that the sale would begin on May 10, 1802, and the tract was disposed of to twenty-two different purchasers at prices ranging from two to

five dollars per acre.[36] By the end of the year, the Indians had departed, some of the proceeds of the sale having been given to them
outright for use in defraying the expenses of their removal. The
balance of the money was invested in United States securities and
held for the benefit of the Indians.

In 1822 the Brothertons, then settled in Oneida County, New
York, petitioned the New Jersey legislature to ask that the balance
in their account be transferred to their credit in a Utica bank. The
balance, which amounted to $3,551.23, was delivered to them by a
special agent.[37] In 1824 the former New Jersey Brothertons, the Stockbridges, and a second group of New England Indians also called
Brothertons moved to a tract near Green Bay (then in Michigan Territory, now in Wisconsin) on lands which the group purchased jointly
from the Menominee Indians.

The last reference to the New Jersey Brothertons in the New Jersey records is found in 1832, when the survivors, reduced to about
forty individuals, were living near Green Bay. They delegated one of
their patriarchs, Bartholomew S. Calvin, whose Indian name was
Shawuskukhkung ("place of the wilted grass"), son of their former
schoolmaster, to represent them before the New Jersey authorities in
a final settlement of land rights. Although they had been paid fully
for the Brotherton Reservation, the Indians insisted that they still
possessed the rights to hunt and fish on all the lands in New Jersey
south of the Raritan River, regardless of ownership, as guaranteed
them by an earlier deed. The object of sending Calvin to New
Jersey was to negotiate a cash settlement with the legislature in return for the relinquishment of these rights. Calvin, who had been
educated at Princeton at the expense of the Scotch Missionary Society, addressed members of the legislature in an unusual personal
appearance. The following passages have been extracted from his
speech:

My Brethren,—I am old, and weak, and poor, and therefore a fit representative of my people. You are young, and strong, and rich, and therefore fit representatives of your people. But let me beg you for a moment
to lay aside the recollections of your strength and of our weakness, that
your minds may be prepared to examine with candor the subject of our
claims.

Our tradition informs us, and I believe it corresponds with your records, that the right of fishing in all the rivers and bays south of the Raritan, and of hunting in all unenclosed lands, was never relinquished, but on the contrary was expressly reserved in our last treaty held at Crosswicks in 1758.

Having myself been one of the parties to the sale, I believe in 1801 [he is here referring to the sale of the Brotherton Reservation] I know that these rights were not sold or parted with.

We now offer to sell these privileges to the state of New Jersey. They were once of great value to us, and we apprehend that neither time or distance, nor the non-use of our rights, has at all affected them, but that the courts here would consider our claims valid were we to exercise them ourselves, or delegate them to others. It is not, however, our wish thus to excite litigation. We consider the state legislature the proper purchaser, and throw ourselves upon its benevolence and magnanimity, trusting that feelings of justice and liberality will induce you to give us what you deem a compensation.

And as we have ever looked up to the leading characters of the United States, (and to the leading characters of this state in particular) as our fathers, protectors, and friends, we now look up to you as such, and humbly beg that you will look upon us with that eye of pity, as we have reason to think our poor untutored forefathers looked upon yours, when they first arrived upon our then extensive but uncultivated dominions, and sold them their lands, in many instances, for trifles in comparison as "light as air." [38]

These were words to melt a heart of granite, and the matter was referred to a special committee for study and recommendation. The members of the committee concluded that the state had no legal obligation of any kind to the Indians who had voluntarily abandoned whatever rights they might have had by leaving the state. Nevertheless, the legislators believed that something should be done "as a memorial of kindness and compassion," and by an act of March 12, 1832, they appropriated two thousand dollars to be given to the Indians. Calvin felt that this was a just payment, and he wrote a thank-you letter in which he stated the following:

The final act of intercourse between the state of New Jersey and the Delaware Indians, who once owned nearly the whole of its territory, has now been consummated, and in a manner which must redound to the honor of this growing state, and in all probability to the prolongation of the existence of a wasted, yet grateful people . . .[39]

Before actually paying the two thousand dollars, the legislators drew up a deed of conveyance wherein the Indians acknowledged they had "granted, bargained, sold, and transferred" all their land rights to the state. The Indians living in Wisconsin who signed the instrument were Jeremiah Johnston, Charles Stephens, Austin Quinney, Sampson Marquis, Andrew Miller, and their eloquent spokesman, Bartholomew S. Calvin.[40] Quinney and Miller are family names found among the Mahican, and these signers may have been New Jersey Brothertons of Mahican ancestry. How the Indians disposed of the cash Calvin's oratory had won for them is not explained, but most of the composite Stockbridge-Munsie families in Wisconsin were poor and no doubt made good use of the windfall.

Although it might be assumed that the departure of the Brothertons meant that the last of the Delaware Indians had left New Jersey, this was not the case. Rarely did all Indians desert a particular area en masse; invariably there were individuals unwilling to change their place of residence who remained behind, sometimes unnoticed. Some married white spouses and their children became members of white society; others were absorbed into the black population; and still others contributed Indian blood to the tri-racial groups that may still be found in the East, like the so-called Moors of Delaware and New Jersey, and the Gouldtowners of New Jersey.[41]

Among the best-remembered Indian descendants in New Jersey was "Indian Ann," who lived near Indian Mills and whose surname is said to have been Roberts, taken from her second husband, himself a mixed-blood, by whom she had several children. She was a basketmaker and, when her trade was slack, she picked cranberries and blackberries and sold them door to door. She was said to have been well known to southern New Jersey farmers, who provided her with food and firewood in her declining years. She died in 1894 at an advanced age.[42] Ann's life is reminiscent of that of "Indian Hannah," often referred to as the last of the Delaware Indians, who lived along the Brandywine in eastern Pennsylvania and who died a pauper in the Chester County Poor Home in 1802, aged seventy-two or seventy-three. In her final years, she, too, traveled from town to town and home to home, selling herb medicines, brooms, and baskets woven from oak and ash splints, and sometimes reading fortunes.[43]

A consciousness of Indian identity was kept alive until 1953, when the last formal meeting was held by a group of Indians having Delaware, white, and Cherokee increments, who lived in Monmouth County, New Jersey, only a short distance from New York City. Sometimes called the Sand Hill Indians from a place they occupied in 1875, they continued to perpetuate certain Indian customs, ceremonials, arts, and crafts, and had their own chief and council.[44] Ordinarily dressed like their white neighbors and pursuing similar occupations—they put on their costumes on certain occasions and tried to preserve their Indianism. Although this band no longer exists as an organization, the scattered descendants are still proud of their Indian ancestry. Among these is James Revey (Lone Bear), whose father was a prominent Sand Hill Indian and whose mother's people were New Jersey Delawares. In personal discussions and correspondence with me, Mr. Revey has shown his keen awareness of the traditions and affairs of the Delaware Indian groups. At present he maintains a shop in New York City, where he makes authentic Delaware Indian costumes and such artifacts as flutes, water drums, horn rattles, war clubs, pump and bow drills, feather fans, and moccasins.

NOTES—CHAPTER 12

1. Jonathan Edwards, ed., *Memoirs of the Reverend David Brainerd*, New Haven, 1822, p. 233.

2. Ibid., p. 218.

3. Ibid., pp. 342–43.

4. Smith, *History*, fn. pp. 95–96; p. 484. I have not tried to search the deeds of King Charles's property, since it is not of any particular significance to the present history. However, this would be a good project for a local scholar to undertake. I am aware of a deed on record in Burlington County for land belonging to King Charles and his son Osolowhenia that was sold on Sept. 19, 1745, to John Burr by another son named Teanish; William Nelson, *Personal Names of Indians of New Jersey*, Paterson, N.J., 1904, p. 63. Evidently the name of the Delaware Indian town at Weekpink was O-ko-kath-see-mee; *John Brainerd's Journal* (1761–1762), Historical Records Survey, WPA, Newark, N.J., 1941, p. 34.

5. For details about John Brainerd's efforts, see *New Jersey Archives*, 1st series, vol. 9, Newark, N.J., 1885, note p. 355.

6. Ibid., vol. 16, p. 565.

7. Ibid.

8. Ibid., p. 567. See letter written by Rev. William Tennent describing Indian affairs at Cranbury, March, 1756; William Nelson, *The Indians of New Jersey*, 1894, pp. 141–42.

9. *New Jersey Archives*, vol. 17, pp. 30–31.

10. Ibid.

11. Ibid., vol. 20, pp. 53–54.

12. Smith, *History*, p. 441.

13. West Jersey Deeds, Liber O, pp. 401–3. A transcript is given by Frank H. Stewart, *Indians of Southern New Jersey*, Woodbury, N.J., 1932, pp. 82–83; see Smith's *History*, pp. 443–45, for a list of the specific lands for which the Indians claimed no payments had been made.

14. A transcript of the law is in *Indian Land Cessions in the United States*, Bureau of American Ethnology, 18th Annual Report, Washington, D.C., 1899, pt. 2, 590.

15. *Colonial Records*, vol. 8, p. 139.

16. Ibid., p. 140.

17. Ibid., pp. 156–61; cf. Smith's *History*, pp. 450–53, where the note appears about Benjamin talking while seated.

18. I am indebted to Kenneth W. Richards, head of the Archives and History Bureau of the State of New Jersey, for a transcript of this deed, which may be found in West Jersey Deeds, Liber O, pp. 394–400.

19. The note on p. 356, *New Jersey Archives*, 1st series, vol. 9, to the effect that one tract was bought from Springer and two from Richard Smith is incorrect. It is true that Smith was a previous owner of part of the land, but his property was subsequently bought by Springer as cited in the Springer deed to the commissioners.

20. This statement is made in Alfred M. Heston, ed., *South Jersey, a History, 1664–1924*, New York and Chicago, 1924, vol. 1, p. 12; also Frank H. Stewart, *Indians of Southern N.J.*, p. 9; and in other sources.

21. C. A. Weslager, *The Nanticoke Indians*, Harrisburg, 1948, p. 49.

22. *Colonial Records*, vol. 8, p. 199; cf. minutes given in Smith, *History*, pp. 455–83. According to Richard Peter's *Diary* (Historical Society of Pennsylvania), Oct. 10, 1758, Seneca chief Tagashata said the Minisinks had asked the Six Nations to handle their affairs "as they are women and and not in a Condition to travel and don't understand State Affairs."

23. *Colonial Records*, vol. 8, p. 216. These deeds or releases were recorded in West Jersey Deeds, Liber O, p. 401 ff. and p. 464 ff. A transcript of one of them is given by Charles A. Philhower, "The Indians of the Morris County Area," *Proceedings of the New Jersey Historical Society*, vol. 54, no. 4, October 1936, pp. 251–55.

24. *New Jersey Archives*, vol. 9, p. 140.

25. Ibid., p. 175.

26. In the collection of original manuscripts owned by Herbert Bernstein of Vineland, N.J., there is a document that is not on record—a bill empowering the commissioners to conduct a lottery to pay for the reserved lands, which passed the House on Nov. 25, 1760, and the Council on

Nov. 27 but was never signed by the governor. It was followed by a second bill, which passed the House on Dec. 3, 1760, the Council on Dec. 4, and signed by Governor Thomas Broome on Dec. 5. This act authorized the commissioners to offer the lottery tickets in three series: Nov. 1, 1761, in the amount of £600; Nov. 2, 1762, in the amount of £500; and Nov. 1, 1763, in the amount of £500. I am deeply grateful to Mr. Bernstein for making both documents available to me for study. The tickets sold for $4 each—the two top prizes were $800 each, and there were numerous lesser cash prizes.

27. *New Jersey Archives*, vol. 9, pp. 355–56.

28. Edgar Jacob Fisher, *New Jersey as a Royal Province, 1738–1776*, New York, 1967, p. 383. Brainerd also conducted worship in an Indian hut at Weekpink as late as 1775; William Nelson, *Indians of New Jersey*, pp. 143–44.

29. .Charles Beatty, *The Journal of a Two Month Tour in America*, London, 1768, p. 52.

30. Milton W. Hamilton, ed., *The Papers of Sir William Johnson*, Albany, 1957, vol. 12, p. 305.

31. By the Treaty of Fort Stanwix the Delawares received a pass from Sir William Johnson permitting them to go to New Jersey to arrange for any Brothertons who wanted to do so to go west; *Colonial Records*, vol. 9, p. 738.

32. This information is contained in an unpublished seven-page manuscript recording a council meeting at Burlington on May 30, 1771, which is in the possession of the New Jersey Historical Society. I want to gratefully acknowledge the society's permission to quote from the manuscript, and to express particular thanks to Dr. Robert M. Lunny and Thaddeus J. Krom.

33. This second manuscript (four pages), recording the council meeting on June 1, 1771, is also in the collections of the New Jersey Historical Society, whose permission to quote it is gratefully acknowledged.

34. Major E. M. Woodward and John F. Hageman, *History of Burlington and Mercer Counties*, Philadelphia, 1883, p. 5.

35. Eugene F. Bliss, trans. and ed., *Diary of David Zeisberger*, Cincinnati, 1885, vol. 2, p. 289. Twelve wagons carried their baggage, and those too feeble to go on foot; Thomas Brainerd, *The Life of John Brainerd*, Philadelphia, 1865, p. 419. Among the Delaware Indian victims of the Gnadenhütten massacre was a former Brainerd convert from New Jersey named Samuel Moore, who had become a Moravian elder; also a New Jersey Indian named Tobias was killed in the massacre; William H. Rice, *David Zeisberger and His Brown Brethren*, Bethlehem, Pa., 1897, p. 58.

36. Woodward and Hageman, *History of Burlington and Mercer Counties*, p. 5. A surveyor's drawing showing the subdivisions sold to various

white owners appears on p. 415, ibid. Since the Indians paid no taxes, the white owners insisted that they, too, were exempt from taxation, which led to litigation; *New Jersey Archives*, vol. 9, fn. p. 355.

37. Woodward and Hageman, *History of Burlington and Mercer Counties*, p. 6.

38. John W. Barber, *Historical Collections of the State of New Jersey*, New York, 1844, pp. 510–11. Probably E. M. Ruttenber, *History of the Indian Tribes of Hudson's River*, Albany, 1872, p. 293, borrowed this quotation from Barber, although he does not say.

39. Barber, *Historical Collections . . .* , 1844, pp. 510–11.

40. A transcript of the deed may be found in Frank H. Stewart, *Indians of Southern New Jersey*, pp. 83–85.

41. C. A. Weslager, *Delaware's Forgotten Folk*, Philadelphia, 1943; the Murray family of Gouldtown is one of the tri-racial families known to have Indian increments, and there are others; William Steward and Theophilus G. Steward, *Gouldtown: A Very Remarkable Settlement of Ancient Date*, Philadelphia, 1913, p. 63. Brewton Berry in *Almost White*, New York, 1963, refers to two hundred or more mixed-blood groups having Indian increments in the eastern United States, p. 11.

42. See pt. 11 of twelve articles by Charles A. Philhower entitled "Indian Lore of New Jersey" reprinted from the *Newark Sunday Times*, undated; also clippings in scrapbook in collections of Camden County Historical Society.

43. The story of "Indian Hannah" is told in my *Red Men on the Brandywine*, Wilmington, 1953, chap. 1.

44. The Sand Hill Indians are referred to briefly by A. Hyatt Verrill, *The Real Americans*, New York, 1954, p. 100.

13

Turmoil in Ohio

Despite obstacles and wilderness hardships, dedicated Moravian missionaries, working without compensation, followed their Delaware converts and potential converts as the Indians moved westward. In the summer of 1747 the Moravians erected a small chapel at Shamokin on the Susquehanna; they also rendered a much-needed service by providing the Indians with a blacksmith, Anton Schmid, whom they brought from Bethlehem.[1] Not only were the natives unable to do a blacksmith's work, but rarely did the white settlers possess either the skills or the tools to shape a horseshoe and nail it to a horse's hoof, to make a grubbing hoe and other farm tools, or to forge an iron rod into a gun barrel. The blacksmith was one of the most essential craftsmen in the colonial community, but to ply his trade he needed a bellows, a vise, sledges, small hammers, tongs, files, rasps, chisels, wedges, cooling tubs, and a kiln in which wood could be burned to yield charcoal. Most of the Moravian pastors were craftsmen in their own right, and knew how to equip a blacksmith shop so that their smithy could work efficiently. No Protestant body was more consecrated to the task of establishing missions than the Moravians, but in administering to the spiritual needs of the Indians they never lost sight of practical matters. Schmid repaired the Indians' broken guns, straightened out their bent implements, and made new tools and utensils in exchange for payment in animal skins.

Within a few years the Moravians built another mission town on the Susquehanna, near Wyalusing, where the Cayuga gave them permission to settle. This new mission, which they called Friedenshütten ("tents of peace"), was a larger and more important town than the first Gnadenhütten, and its population increased rapidly. In 1765 the Christian Indians, numbering eighty adults and ninety children, whom John Penn protected from mob attack at Philadelphia, found haven at Friedenshütten, and it was there that David Zeisberger baptized the Munsie chief Papunhank, naming him John. Under Papunhank's influence other Munsies and Unami living in the environs of Wyalusing became Christians, and the chief later went to Ohio with the Moravians as a "helper" to assist in the mission work.

Friedenshütten contained a main street, twenty-nine log houses, thirteen bark huts, and a chapel of hewn pine logs, with a shingled roof, cupola, and bell—a permanent fixture on Moravian chapels—whose ringing always delighted the Indians. Behind the houses were gardens, orchards, and pastures enclosed by post and rail fences. John Jacob Schmick, sent by the parent church at Bethlehem, succeeded Zeisberger as the pastor and teacher at this mission when the latter went west to locate new mission sites.[2]

Not only were Moravian teachings directed at the religious life of the Indians, but the native social and economic patterns were also directly affected. The pastors taught the Indians the sanctity of monogamous marriages, and that husband and wife should provide for their children and be "cleanly in all things," that strong drink should be detested, that the converts must obey their teachers and helpers, that they must not contract debts with traders, that Sunday was a day of rest.

Moravian disciplines also required, among other things, abstention from idolatry, witchcraft, "deceits of Satan," murder, lying, scolding, and idleness, also from going on journeys or hunting trips without informing the minister or one of the stewards. Young people were taught not to marry without the consent of their parents and the minister, and everyone was expected to attend meetings for divine service, to honor father and mother and assist them in the distress of old age, to assist in the erection of fences and buildings, and in doing other work for the good of the community. In the event of hostilities, the Indian converts were forbidden from going to war and shedding blood, and also from purchasing plunder from warriors. Since Bible study and hymnody were important, the brethren were intent upon establishing schools where Indian children could be taught to read

and write. Also, in giving up their native ways, the natives discontinued
painting their faces, became modest in their dress, and allowed their
hair to grow long instead of shaving their heads and leaving a scalp
lock.

After the Six Nations sold their Susquehanna lands to the English
by the Treaty of Fort Stanwix (Wyalusing and Shamokin were included in this territory), the brethren knew that the Indians would not
be able to occupy Susquehanna lands much longer. Things worsened
as Connecticut and Pennsylvania settlers clashed over possession of
the upper Susquehanna valley. Even before the situation became critical, it was farsighted David Zeisberger who convinced the church
fathers at Bethlehem that the future of the missionary effort lay in
the Ohio wilderness west of the Alleghenies, where the main body of
the "heathen" Delawares had been pressed following Pontiac's War.

In 1767 Zeisberger went over the mountains and founded a new
mission near the Munsie settlement called Goschgosching ("place of
hogs") on the Allegheny River near present Tionesta, Pennsylvania.
Goschgosching consisted of three separate Indian towns, and Zeisberger built his mission, which the Indians called Lawunakhannek
("middle stream place"), two or three miles above the Indian settlements. These Munsies had gone to the Allegheny from their former
towns on the Susquehanna, Tioga, and Chemung rivers, and were
seated on lands set aside for them by the Seneca, whose principal
villages were then on the headwaters of the Allegheny. The Munsie
sachem at Goschgosching was a blind chief named Allemewi on
whom Zeisberger concentrated his attention and whom he soon
baptized and renamed Solomon.[3]

Because the land at Goschgosching was poor, the Indians had difficulty raising sufficient corn to feed their families; they depended
largely upon hunting and fishing for a livelihood. (Zeisberger wrote
that in the fall of 1759 Munsie hunters from the three towns killed
three thousand deer.) Since the Moravian mission towns were founded
on an agricultural economy, Zeisberger became disenchanted with the
location when he learned that the land was not fertile. To make
matters worse, he was harassed by a Delaware shaman, Wingenund
("well beloved"), who tried to turn the Indians against him; and the
Seneca chiefs also objected to his presence on their lands. At the
invitation of another Delaware chief named Pakanke and his captain
Glickhican ("sight on a gun barrel"), who lived at the Kuskuskies

Indian community, Zeisberger abandoned Lawunakhannek and moved south to Beaver Creek. There he founded a new mission town which he called Friedensstadt ("peace village"), located near what is now Moravia, about six miles south of "the Kuskuskies." There he converted both Pakanke and Glickhican, the latter proving to be of invaluable assistance in helping to spread the gospel among the Delawares. The story has been preserved that one day after listening to a sermon on sin and grace, Glickhican, now named Isaac, was seen walking through the village sobbing. "This is wonderful," Zeisberger wrote in his journal, "a proud war-captain sheds tears in the presence of his former associates. Thus the Saviour by His word breaks the hard hearts and humbles the pride of the Indians." [4]

Soon after Friedensstadt was established, the Moravian Indians who still remained on the Susquehanna decided to move west to the new mission town. In September of 1771 the church sent John Heckewelder to assist Zeisberger at Friedensstadt. He was living there when about two hundred Indians from Friedenshütten and Sheshequin (another small mission on the Susquehanna) arrived, having been conducted westward by the Reverends John Rothe and John Ettwein. Unknown to the newcomers, a decision had already been made to vacate Friedensstadt, because of trespassing and other annoyances caused by the rum-soaked element among the Munsies at the nearby Kuskuskies. In the summer of 1772 Heckewelder, who traveled more than twenty-six thousand miles during his active years as a missionary and crossed the Alleghenies thirty times, assisted Zeisberger in leading the first group overland from Friedensstadt to a new destination—the Tuscarawas branch of the Muskingum where the Delawares under Beaver's leadership had found refuge years before.

The new site selected by Zeisberger, which he named Schönbrunn ("beautiful spring"), was on the east bank of the Tuscarawas about two miles southeast of present New Philadelphia, Ohio. The Moravians and their Indian converts had received repeated invitations from the Delawares living on the Tuscarawas to come and settle among them. Netawatwees, the principal Delaware chief, who had been reinstated by his people after Bouquet's departure, sent a personal invitation to Zeisberger to bring his charges to the Tuscarawas, evidently believing that the Delawares would be strengthened as a political force if all of them—Christians and non-Christians—could be brought together at one location. There was also another reason:

An epidemic had broken out among the Indians, and the Delawares blamed the deaths of some of their people on sorcery or witchcraft. Some of their leaders believed that if more of the Indians embraced Christianity the witchcraft would be overpowered and the contagion would end.

The Wyandot, an Iroquoian-speaking tribe also known as the Huron, assured Zeisberger that suitable land would be set aside for his mission if he accepted the Delawares' invitation. Although the Six Nations claimed title to some of the lands on the Ohio, the Wyandot considered themselves proprietors of the territory between the west bank of the Ohio and Lake Erie. The Wyandot gave the Shawnee, Delawares, Munsies, and Ottawa permission to reside and hunt in what is now eastern Ohio and part of western Pennsylvania. By accepting this invitation, the Delawares had no need to depend on the Six Nations to allot lands to them. They had a clear understanding with the Wyandot as to the bounds of the territory, which were cited by White Eyes at a meeting with commissioners of the Continental Congress held in Pittsburgh in the fall of 1775, as follows:

> Beginning at the Mouth of Big Beaver Creek and running up the same where it interlocks with the Branches of Guyahoga Creek and down the said Creek to the Mouth thereof where it empties into the Lake along the Side of the Lake to the Mouth of Sandusky Creek and up the same to the head untill it interlocks with Muskingum down the same to the Mouth where it Empties into the Ohio and up the said River to the Place of Beginning.[5]

White Eyes added for the benefit of the commissioners, and as a veiled threat to the Six Nations, "I now also Acquaint you that my Uncles the Wiandots have bound themselves, the Shawanese, Tawaas [Ottawa] and Delawares together and have made us as one People . . ." Perhaps the crafty Wyandot gave lands to the Delawares, Shawnee, and Ottawa in order to place them in a buffer zone to repel the surge of white expansion, and then persuaded them to unite their forces in a military alliance to help protect Wyandot territorial interests.

The Muskingum, from its point of juncture with the Ohio at present Marietta, was navigable into the Tuscarawas, and the latter stream was a connecting link with Lake Erie either via the Sandusky or the Cuyahoga River routes. Situated along this important avenue, the Delaware towns not only benefitted from its commercial and military usefulness, but the bottom lands along the Tuscarawas were fertile and yielded abundant crops. To the Delawares a navigable stream teeming with edible fish and bordered with rich soil where the women could plant their crops was reminiscent of their original homes along the tributaries of the Delaware River. They rapidly adjusted to the new environment and lived without interference until the outbreak of the American Revolution (see Fig. 16).

The Christian Delawares on the Tuscarawas, under Moravian leadership, and the non-Christian Delawares, under their own native chiefs, were near neighbors, although they occupied separate towns. The relationship was generally harmonious, even though the Christian Indians pursued an entirely different religious, social, and economic life from the nativists. The converts prospered in the mission towns, learning such new and useful crafts as carpentry, milling, masonry, weaving, and woodworking. Pastors and converts labored together in the fields and pastures, the brethren teaching the Indians how to

Figure 16. View along the Tuscarawas (tributary to Muskingum River) in Ohio where Delawares lived following the French and Indian War until they moved to Indiana Territory after the Greenville Treaty of 1795 with the United States

obtain maximum productivity from the soil and how to breed and care for livestock. The pastors set a high moral example by their almost apostolic conduct, and Netawatwees, who respected and admired the Moravians, had a special regard for Zeisberger. Netawatwees was torn between becoming a Christian and his responsibilities to the main body of Delawares, who continued to adhere to nativistic beliefs, and he never consented to conversion.

As time went on, other Delaware chiefs and captains followed the example of Allemewi, Papunhank, Pakanke, and Glickhican, by becoming Christians. This caused an unusual situation to develop, which came to a head when Echpalawehund ("he that missed the object he shot at"), Netawatwees's right-hand man in the Delaware Great Council, became a Moravian convert and was baptized Petrus. The Council, or Lupwaaeenoawuk ("wise men"), composed of chiefs and captains—as well as warriors and patriarchs—representing the three divisions, faced a new political issue. Should Echpalawehund and others who became Christians be permitted to maintain their seats in the Council, or should they be expelled? Lengthy deliberations took place, and although this dialogue has not been preserved, Zeisberger describes the Council meetings. They were, he wrote, quiet and orderly, like devotional ceremonies. There was no levity, no talking in the audience, and no laughter, because undivided attention was given each speaker, as the chiefs and captains spoke in a prescribed order. No one interrupted the person who was talking, and everyone sat silently and attentively until the speaker finished and sat down. Members of the Council brought their pipes and tobacco, and smoked thoughtfully throughout the sessions. Food, when called for, was distributed by the women, who remained outside the Council House and were admitted only for the purpose of handing the victuals to the attendants and keeping up the fires.[6]

After much discussion, the Great Council ruled that Echpalawehund would be permitted to retain his seat, and any other converts should be similarly treated. The Council also solemnly adopted the following statement of policy:

Liberty is given the Christian religion, which the Council advises the entire nation to adopt. The Christian Indians are on an entire equality with the Delawares, all constituting together one nation. Christian Indians have like property rights in the nation's lands with the rest of the nation. Only converts may settle near the towns of the Christian Indians.[7]

Even Zeisberger, an adopted Munsie, was accepted as a member of the Great Council, where he was able to exercise considerable influence in the decision making. He also acted as a scribe when the chiefs or captains needed to send written messages to military authorities at Fort Pitt or to interpret written messages the Delaware leaders received from the government. Heckewelder also prepared written messages for the Indians when requested to do so, and he interpreted incoming messages into the Delaware dialect and read them to the Council. These messages became more frequent during the early days of the Revolution. Newspapers published in Philadelphia, which reported colonial victories, were sent to the Moravian missionaries by the Continental Congress to be translated and read aloud in the Great Council. The government felt that this was tangible evidence to convince the Indians that the British would ultimately be defeated.

Both Zeisberger and Heckewelder were responsible for insisting that Christian Indians continue to live separately from non-Christians. They knew they could handle the Indians in the mission towns, particularly since these Indians were not exposed to alcohol and other temptations present in the native villages. There was also a matter of conformity, because the converts not only observed church disciplines but were obligated to work in one of the crafts or in the fields as their contribution to the Christian community.

The pastors were prolific in their writings, and the Moravian records include a manuscript diary in the German language written by Zeisberger during the period 1772–77, translated into the English language by Professor August C. Mahr for the Ohio State Historical Society but not yet published.[8] Therein Zeisberger reveals the surprising information that Gelelemend ("leader," also called Captain John Killbuck, Jr.) Netawatwees's grandson, grew weary of the burden of Delaware political affairs and was on the verge of accepting Christianity and becoming a worker in one of the Moravian mission towns. His grandfather persuaded him not to leave the Great Council or to change his residence, because the old chief, then nearing ninety, felt he needed the assistanec of his grandson, in whom he had the utmost confidence. Gelelemend observed the old man's wishes, but after his grandfather's death he was baptized and became a member of the Moravian church.

In the same diary Zeisberger notes that Gelelemend's father, John Killbuck, Sr., Netawatwees's eldest son, was strongly opposed to the

Moravians and what he felt was their unwelcome intrusion in Delaware society. He was one of those who argued in the Great Council, where he was opposed by White Eyes, against permitting Christian Delawares to retain their membership. He also insisted, with considerable logic, that since the Moravians were pacifists who shunned war, they would be useless as allies in the event of an attack on the Delawares, either by whites or enemy Indians. The elder Killbuck, who became blind in his later years, stirred up other traditionalists against the Moravians, and the Delawares became divided between the political views of the son and grandson of their aging chief.

Zeisberger's mission town of Schönbrunn, known to the Delawares as Welhik-Tupeek, surpassed any of the previous Pennsylvania missions, containing sixty dwellings mostly built of round or hewn logs. There was a main street running east and west, and from the place where the log chapel stood a second street ran off to the north. This property is now owned by the Ohio Historical Society which, as a memorial and educational exhibit, has reconstructed a number of the log buildings to simulate the original appearance of the mission (see Fig. 17). The Indians living at Schönbrunn planted vegetables in well-

Figure 17. Reconstruction of the Moravian mission town called Schönbrunn, which stood near present New Philadelphia, Ohio. Here the Delaware Indian converts lived and worked under the supervision and care of Zeisberger, Heckewelder, and other Moravian pastors.

paled gardens, cultivated extensive corn fields, grew fruit in orchards, and raised cattle, horses, and hogs. The community prospered from the industry of the residents, who attended daily worship in the chapel and sent their children to the log school, the first school west of the Ohio, where they were taught in the Indian language. Zeisberger compiled a spelling book in the Delaware dialect, and he also translated a dictionary, sermons, hymn books, and religious tracts into the Delaware language.

A sister town, Gnadenhütten, named in honor of the destroyed mission in Pennsylvania, was built about ten miles downstream, and its native population included a number of Mahican who in time merged with the Delawares and lost their separate identities.

A third mission town founded in 1776 on the east side of the Muskingum below present Coshocton was called Lichtenau ("meadow of light"). The Christian Delawares were largely confined to these three towns during the early years of the Revolution, although there were movements of families from one town to another, including visitations by non-Christian Delawares, who came to see their converted relatives and listen to the preachers. The pastors welcomed these visitors, because they were all potential converts, as long as they were well behaved and did not try to smuggle intoxicants into the mission towns. In 1775, when Captain James Wood, a Virginia officer, visited Gnadenhütten, he wrote that the pastor prayed in the Delaware language, preached in English, and sang the Psalms in German—and that the Indians joined in.[9]

The largest settlement of non-Christians prior to the Revolution was the village south of Gnadenhütten founded by Netawatwees at what is now Newcomerstown in Tuscarawas County, Ohio. It was then variously known as Gekelmukpechink ("still water"), Negh-ka-un-que ("red bank"), or Newcomer's Town. The old chief lived in a two-story dwelling with a shingled roof, wood floors, staircase, and stone chimney. On Zeisberger's first visit to this town, the seat of the Great Council in the spring of 1771, he wrote that the Indians lived in a hundred houses, mostly of logs.[10] The Council continued to meet here until Coshocton, formerly a Wyandot town known to the French as Conchaké, became the Delaware "capital."

The wars the Delawares had fought against the whites, as well as other adversity, tended to bring the Indian leaders together despite divisive influences. The chiefs and captains of the Wolf and Turkey divisions willingly ceded a superior position to Netawatwees, the Turtle chief. Members of the Turtle group now claimed preeminence over the other two, because, as all Delawares knew, the turtle, symbolical of Mother Earth, was the first of living things. Unlike the wolf, who moves from place to place in search of prey, and the turkey, who is limited to the earth, the turtle can live either on land or in water. The preeminence of the chief of the Turtle division may have become institutionalized with Netawatwees, because his predecessors, Shingas and Beaver, were members of the Turkey division.[11]

The Delaware war captains, who were the military leaders during the French and Indian War and also Pontiac's uprising, began to assume wider authority during the Revolutionary period as the war came closer. They outranked the civil chiefs in military matters and were very jealous of this prerogative, but they also participated actively in all Great Council discussions. The office of the captain was not hereditary but was attained through the prowess of the individual, demonstrated feats of valor, or personal aggressiveness resulting from dreams or visions wherein he was endowed by the Spirit Forces with fighting skills. As time went on, captains and chiefs had overlapping authority, and the terms came to be used interchangeably as the strongest, most intelligent, and persuasive individuals influenced the policy decisions made in the Council.

It was the duty of the civil chief to maintain peace as long as possible, since he did not have the power to begin a war if his captains opposed it. If the captains decided to declare war, the chief was obliged to turn the people over to them while the war was in progress because they were the warrior leaders. The captains also exercised authority in the selection and inauguration of new chiefs from among the eligible candidates. In addition, they had a lot to say about forsaking a chief who ignored custom, or who refused to accept their advice. Although the succession and deposal of chiefs is mentioned in accounts written by Moravian pastors, the subject is confusing and the writings are so contradictory that it is next to impossible to reconstruct the actual procedures that were followed.[12]

Brief descriptions exist of the Council House where the chiefs, captains, and other leaders met, and one wonders if the Big House, where Delaware survivors in Oklahoma and Canada later held their annual ceremony, may not have been a vestige. In the period 1772–73, a Baptist minister, the Reverend David Jones, strongly motivated by a desire to convert the Indians to Christianity, spent nearly a year among the Delawares and Shawnee in Ohio. In his account Jones describes the locations of a number of Shawnee and Delaware towns along the Scioto and Muskingum, which he visited, including Newcomer's Town. He was invited to attend a meeting of the Great Council when he sought permission to preach Christianity in Delawares' towns. He wrote that there were about twenty males present when he appeared before the Council to present his request, which, after due deliberation, was granted. He said that the Council House measured fifty feet by twenty-four, having one post in the middle and two fires.[13]

Another contemporary minister, a Presbyterian named Charles Beatty, visited Newcomer's Town in the fall of 1776. He said the town stretched about a mile and a half along the south side of the river, and the population of from six to seven hundred persons then occupied sixty or seventy houses, some built of logs, others of bark.[14] Beatty not only visited the Council House but was permitted to preach a sermon there based on the text of the Prodigal Son, which was translated into the Delaware tongue by an Indian accompanying Beatty. Beatty's description of the Council House, which follows, is more detailed than that given by Jones:

This house is a long building, with two fires in it, at a proper distance from each other, without any chimney or partition. The entry into it is by two doors, one at each end. Over the door a turtle was drawn, which is the ensign of this particular tribe. On each door-post was cut out the face of a grave old man, an emblem I suppose of that gravity and wisdom that every senator there ought to be possessed of. On each side, the whole length of the house within, is a platform, a bed, five feet wide, raised above the floor one foot and a half, made of broad split pieces of wood, which serves equally for a bed, on which to sleep, and a place on which to sit down. It is covered with an handsome matt, made of rushes, near the end of which the king sat.[15]

Beatty said that Netawatwees greeted him warmly by rising from his seat and extending his hand. Some of his councilors sat on the platform with him; others occupied the platform on the opposite side of the room. The minister was invited to sit near Netawatwees and, although he was treated politely, neither the chief nor the Council reacted favorably to his request that Presbyterian ministers be allowed to come and live among the Delawares. At first the Indians, to spare his feelings, pretended that they did not understand fully the meaning of his request. When he persisted with further argument through his interpreter, the members of the Council told him that if they gave their permission they feared this might break an agreement they had made with Sir William Johnson!

The Reverend David Jones had learned the truth about the Delawares' attitude toward the Presbyterians on his earlier visit—since he was a Baptist, they didn't hesitate to talk about the other denominations. He found that though the Delawares held the Moravian missionaries in high regard, they were not kindly disposed toward the Presbyterians. Captain John Killbuck, Sr., who spoke fairly good English, according to Jones, told the minister that the Delawares had forbidden any Presbyterian ministers or teachers to live in their towns because ministers of this denomination had gone to war against them. Evidently the Delawares carried with them to Ohio deep-seated prejudices against the Scotch-Irish, who were mostly Presbyterians, after the raid by the Paxton Boys, the confrontation in Philadelphia, and other reprisals taken against the Pennsylvania Indians.

On May 3, 1773, Heckewelder took a group of Christian Delawares from Friedenshütten up the Muskingum in twenty-two canoes en route to Schönbrunn, where they intended to settle with their brethren. He wrote that there were 106 Indians gathered on the river bank at Newcomer's Town who hailed the passing canoes with shouts of joy.[16] Two years later Loskiel wrote that there were "414 believing Indians" in the Moravian towns on the Tuscarawas, although he made no estimate of the number of non-Christian Delawares and Munsies, whose numbers greatly exceeded those of the converts. When the first shots of the Revolution were fired at Lexington, the total Delaware Indian population west of the Alleghenies, including Christians and non-Christians, probably did not exceed 2,500 to 3,000 men, women, and children, of whom 300 to 400 had been converted to Christianity. In the context of modern population figures, this may seem insignificant; but the Continental Congress felt the Delawares had far-reaching influence on other tribes, who looked upon them as their uncles or grandfathers, and heeded their advice.

During the early days of the Revolution, the non-Christian Delaware population continued to be centered at Newcomer's Town, with other towns of lesser size scattered along the Tuscarawas and neighboring streams. Among the towns at this particular period—whose populations ranged from three and four families to those housing fifty or more people—were Kokosing ("place of owls") on the Kokosing River; Kinshanschican, on the eastern headwaters of the Scioto, residence of Wingenund; Assinink ("the standing rock") near modern Lancaster, Ohio; White Eyes's Town, a small village that stood on the south bank of the Tuscarawas about four miles above Lichtenau; Old Hundy, a Munsie town on the north side of the Walhonding between the mouths of Killbuck and Mohican creeks; New Hundy, built two or three miles west of Old Hundy, where in 1775 the chief Windaughala ("council door"), father of Buckongahelas, had his residence.

There were other Delaware towns on the Cayuga, Mahoning, and Hocking rivers, although neither Christian nor non-Christian Delawares lost their wanderlust, continuing to move from one place to another. (Appendix 1 gives sources where the interested reader can obtain detailed information about these locations.) None of the native villages in Ohio were permanent in the European sense of fixed settlements, and for various reasons thriving towns were deserted and new ones founded as the population shifted from time to time. Even the Moravians moved around: In 1778 the occupants of Gnadenhütten and Schönbrunn moved to Lichtenau, and some time later they left Lichtenau for a newly built mission town near present Port Washington, Ohio, which was called Salem.

The transfer of the "capital" from Newcomer's Town to Coshocton, where the Tuscarawas and Walhonding meet to form the Muskingum proper, was agreed upon after discussion in the Great Council. According to Zeisberger, the Christian Indians needed more territory for expansion, and the underlying reason for moving the capital was to make available to the Christians additional lands in the immediate vicinity of Newcomer's Town. The Council, under David Zeisberger's influence, continued to insist that the communities of converted Delawares and non-Christians should remain separated.[17]

The government strongly favored concentrating the Delaware warrior population at one location to facilitate keeping an eye on them during the war. The government not only endorsed the shift of the capital to Coshocton but encouraged the Council to seat the entire non-Christian Delaware and Munsie population there. This is clarified in the manuscript letter books of Colonel George Morgan in posses-

sion of the Pennsylvania Division of the Carnegie Library in Pittsburgh. Morgan, a capable executive, fur trader, and colonizer, was
appointed agent for Indian affairs at Fort Pitt. The Delawares thought
so well of him that they adopted him, bestowing on him the honored
name Taimenend, after their ancient chieftain. Morgan had a very
high regard for White Eyes, and White Eyes admired the officer. A
letter in one of Morgan's books sent to him by White Eyes on July 19,
1778, contains this sentence: "I shall hold fast to our friendship as
long as the Sun shall shine and the Rivers run."

Morgan urged White Eyes to use his influence on the Great Council to bring all the scattered Delawares together at Coshocton. That
meant gathering together the Delaware families from along the
Kokosing,Walhonding, Cuyahoga, Scioto, and other streams, and
persuading the village chiefs and captains to abandon their homes and
settle at a new location. The creation of what the government conceived as a sort of city-state was a radical departure from Delaware
economic and social patterns, and many Indian families did not want
to move to Coshocton, nor was the Great Council inclined to take
positive action on the recommendation. After caustic argument in the
Council, and strong opposition to the proposal, White Eyes made an
eloquent speech and then resigned. Colonel Morgan recorded the substance of this unusual speech in one of his letter books as follows:

Don't you see, says he to the Council, the Mingoes and Wiandots insult us in our own Town & take those People Prisoners whom we ought
to protect. they kill our Cattle daily & frighten our Women & Children—
but this is not the worst, for our young Men when scatter'd abroad in
little Towns are liable to be deluded by their Warriors & may utterly break
our Friendship with the United States. I am determined not to be acces-
sory to such a breach of Faith and therefore resign all the Authority you
have vested me with until you all consent to collect yourself into one small
Circle, that your Chiefs & old Men may have an Eye to & be answerable
for the conduct of the young men—untill this is done, I will not speak to
the United States because I will not impose upon them.—Collect yourselves together; *resolve one & all to be govern'd by the Chiefs of your
choice* & I will join as heartily as ever in promoting your interest with the
United States—until then I will withdraw myself from your Councils.[18]
(Italics added)

In White Eyes's reference to the Delawares' accepting the government of the chiefs of their choice, he was referring to himself, for he

had been chosen by the Council as the head chief of the nation. This is brought out in a report that George Croghan made to Sir William Johnson in 1774, wherein Croghan stated that the Delawares at Newcomer's Town had chosen White Eyes as their chief in place of Netawatwees, "who they thought unfit for the charge & desire that all the neighbouring Indians will take notice, etc." [19]

White Eyes's sagacity, recognized by Indians and whites alike, and his diplomatic skill in negotiations with the government, were assets well known to Killbuck, Welepachtschiechen ("erect posture", also known as Captain Johnny), Echpalawehund, and the other members of the Great Council. His resignation and withdrawal from the Council was a loss they could not afford and were unwilling to accept. In the end, White Eyes had his way, and his associates deferred to him, as they had done previously when he insisted that the Christian Delawares be accepted in the Council on an equal basis with non-Christians.

Netawatwees seems to have continued to hold a position of prestige after White Eyes was appointed chief, for he was one of the participants on October 31, 1776, at a conference at Fort Pitt where he was taken ill. His dying message was a plea to his people to heed the teachings of the Moravians, and White Eyes delivered this message to the Great Council.[20] Had the old chief's advice been followed, a pro-American Christian Delaware commonwealth might have been born, but the tensions increased after his death, and an articulate anti-American faction was formed in the Council.

When the conflict broke out between England and the American colonies, the Delawares held a neutral position, although the sympathies of the Moravian pastors and their converts were with the Americans. Both Zeisberger and Heckewelder supplied intelligence to the American commanders at Fort Pitt and used their influence with members of the Council to persuade the Delawares to refuse to have any dealings with the English. White Eyes continued to assure Colonel Morgan that he was determined to adhere to a friendship with the United States, and he reported that the Delawares were complying with the government's request to gather their people together at Coshocton. In the spring of 1778, he wrote Morgan to tell him that three hundred men capable of bearing arms had assembled at Coshocton, and more were coming there to live, including seventeen Shawnee families.

The Delawares who gathered at Coshocton became divided in their loyalties, due largely to the influences of a captain of the Wolf division, Konieschquanoheel ("maker of daylight"), nicknamed Hopocan ("tobacco pipe"), also known as Captain Pipe. A bold and ambitious schemer and a man of courage, he succeeded his uncle Custaloga as the Wolf chieftain. While White Eyes, representing the Turtle group, and Captain John Killbuck, Jr., representing the Turkey division, both exhibited firm attachments to the Americans, Pipe and his Wolf warriors turned pro-British, and Delaware neutralism gave way to a quarrelsome partisanship.

Knowledge of the succession of Delaware chiefs and captains during this chaotic period is incomplete, and unfortunately no information is available to help understand the circumstances leading to White Eyes's elevation to head chief. Perhaps Colonel Morgan may have had something to do with it, although at that time there does not seem to have been much governmental tampering with native custom. It seems, however, that there was a birthright heir who had a better right than White Eyes to succeed Netawatwees—a youth to whom Heckewelder refers all too briefly as "the person on whom by lineal descent, the station of head chief of the nation devolved, being yet young in years." [21]

It would appear that White Eyes's seniority may have been the reason the Delawares chose him to succeed Netawatwees. The young chief fell victim to an attack by armed civilians and was killed before he was able to take office. The details of what happened seem to have been covered up, although, when Brigadier General William Irvine took office at Fort Pitt, he learned something of what had happened, which he reported to George Washington in a letter dated April 20, 1782. He said that on March 24, 1782, a group of settlers attacked a party of friendly Delaware Indians then living on a small island in the river below Fort Pitt, killing several, including two who had received captain's commissions and had assisted the Americans in expeditions and on scouting parties. During the assault, according to Heckewelder, a chief fled and escaped the attackers by swimming to shore, but he left behind "the bag containing all the wampum speeches and written documents of William Penn and his successors for a number of years together, which had for so long a time been so carefully preserved by them, but now had fallen into the hands of a murdering band of white people, who also at the same time killed the promising young chief above-mentioned." [22]

With the support of Captain Pipe, English sympathizers spread propaganda that the Americans were pretending to be friends of the Delawares in order to seize all their lands at the crucial moment and destroy them. Pipe believed this to be the secret policy of the Continental Congress and felt it was his duty to organize a strong force to prevent the destruction of his people. As he reflected on White Eyes's friendship with Morgan, he became certain in his own mind that the head chief had entered into a clandestine dialogue with the deceitful Americans, and was being well paid to betray his people. As a result, Captain Pipe succeeded in strengthening the pro-English faction.

The Delawares did not understand the nuances in the political conflict between England and the colonies resulting from mercantilism, which was foreign to Indian economic life. The divided attachments among the colonists themselves, which caused some to remain Loyalists and others to side with the rebel patriots, puzzled the Indians. For many years the Delawares had been told repeatedly by colonial officials that the King of England, whose word was law, was the Great Father of whites and Indians alike. This propaganda made such an impression that Netawatwees unsuccessfully sought Richard Penn's permission to prepare a vessel for him to "go over the Great Waters to see *that* Great King." [23] Netawatwees was so confused by the conflicting teachings of the Moravians, Quakers, Baptists, Presbyterians, Roman Catholics, and others that one of the questions he intended to ask the King was what denomination he wanted the Delawares to embrace! [24] White Eyes also wanted to go to England and lay before the King the whole problem of the conflict between whites and Indians. He envisioned a country where the converted Delawares, as Christian people, were in possession of an expanse of territory separate from that occupied by whites, but his dream was never fulfilled. [25]

At first, the Congress assured the Indians that the dispute with the Great Father across the sea was a family spat, and the Indians should sit still and take as little notice of it as possible. At the same time the Congress recognized the importance of the Indian tribes as potential allies and as early as July 12, 1775 went on record, "That the security and preserving the friendship of the Indian Nations appears to be a subject of utmost moment to the colonies." [26]

In time both English and Americans attempted to win over the Indians, and the Americans encouraged the bewildered natives to destroy the King's soldiers whom they previously had been enjoined to aid. The English took full advantage of the investments made by earlier colonial officials to strengthen the Six Nations, but the League was again divided, and a majority of the Tuscarora, Oneida, and Onondaga elected to remain neutral. In December of 1777 the Continental Congress sent a message to the Oneida and Onondaga commending them for maintaining friendly relations with the Americans.²⁷ Other members of the League held fast to English interests, little suspecting that the Americans would ultimately be victorious and that General John Sullivan, under direct orders from George Washington, would lay waste the heart of Iroquois country, destroying the main Cayuga and Seneca towns, to punish the Iroquois who took the side of the English. The Indians were confused as to the issues between the colonies and England, and the Americans were mystified as to where some of the Indians stood. Many of the tribes, like the Delawares, had both pro-British and pro-American factions, and even a well-informed Indian agent like Colonel Morgan was uncertain where all the Indians stood. His letter books record a conference with White Eyes on April 26, 1778, wherein he asked the chief to tell him frankly who the Indian enemies of the Americans were. White Eyes made the following reply:

At present your Enemies are the Banditti of Mingoes & the Wiandots of Sandusky & Detroit & a few of the Ottawas & Chippewas & some Shawnese & a few Delawares have been deluded by them—the whole number of all these Nations now engaged or that have been engaged against you do not exceed 400 warriors . . . . The Munsies except about thirty have gone to live in the Seneca country—They are so distant from us & times have been so troublesome that we have had no intercourse with those People latterly—those who remain wish to live in Peace if they know how to do it.

When he referred to thirty Munsies, White Eyes must have meant only those then living at or near Coshocton, because there were Munsies living on the Sandusky with their chief Newalike who sided with the English. Newalike, who was converted by the Moravians, renounced the church to become an anti-American belligerent, encouraged by the English. White Eyes's estimate of four hundred warriors having joined the British cause was a conservative figure, although at that early date some of the tribes had not yet decided to support the redcoats openly. White Eyes was probably unaware that his associate Captain Pipe was scheming to go over to the British and within a few months would be giving the death yell at Detroit, with dried American scalps tied to the staff he flourished and presented to the English commandant.

During this indecisive period, parties of Wyandot warriors came to Coshocton at three different times, each time offering the war belt to the Council, urging the Delawares to join them against the English. White Eyes reminded the Wyandot messengers that they and the Delawares had both signed peace treaties with the Americans. He said, "That they, the Delawares, had engaged to hold the chain of friendship with *both* their hands, and therefore had no spare hand to take hold of the war belt." [28] The Ottawa and Shawnee had already agreed to fight alongside the Wyandot, and after the Wyandot messengers returned to their homes they persisted in sending messages to Coshocton to the effect "that the Delawares should keep their shoes in readiness to join the warriors." Meanwhile the deceitful Wyandot were pretending to be friendly to the Americans.

Those of the Six Nations who held firm in English interests were also applying pressure on the Delawares to ally with them, and, at a meeting of the Seneca and Delawares, White Eyes stated frankly that he was in sympathy with the Americans and had no intention of joining the English. A Seneca speaker then reminded the Delawares of their ancient femininization, telling them they should take instructions from their superiors, the Six Nations. White Eyes then rose, and replied that he was well aware that the Six Nations still considered his nation as an inferior, conquered people. Then he spoke as follows:

You say you had conquered me that you had cut off my legs—had put a petticoat on me, giving me a hoe and cornpounder in my hands, saying, "now woman! your business henceforward shall be, to plant and hoe corn, and pound the same for bread, for us men and warriors!" Look at my legs! if, as you say, you had cut them off, they have grown again to their proper size!—the petticoat I have thrown away, and have put on my proper dress!—the corn hoe and pounder I have exchanged for these fire arms, and I declare that I am a man.[29]

This declaration of manhood, followed White Eyes's statement favoring the American cause, caused some of the Delawares to fear that the Six Nations would take up arms against them and that further animosities would develop. In commenting on this situation, Heckewelder stated that the Munsies "made this a pretence of withdrawing themselves from the councils of the Turtle tribe and joining themselves to the Wolf tribe." Perhaps this may have contributed to the notion that the Munsies were called the Wolf tribe. The warriors of the Wolf group, under Captain Pipe, had congregated in Ohio, having moved from Venango, where the Six Nations had assigned them, to Beaver Creek, on Wyandot lands, and from there to the Tuscarawas.[30]

There were other influences working to bring the Delawares to the support of the English. Three frontier diplomats, Alexander McKee (whom Sir William Johnson had sent to Fort Pitt as his representative to the Ohio Indians), Simon Girty, and Matthew Elliot, all strong in British interests, kept repeating the old story that the Americans were deceiving the Indians and intended to send soldiers to murder them and burn their villages to the ground. Sir Henry Hamilton, in command of British forces at Detroit, where supplies for the Indians were received, stored, and distributed, encouraged the Ohio Indians to turn against the Americans and offered cash rewards for American scalps. This was a repetition of the disgraceful bounty system Pennsylvania had adopted twenty years before to encourage the frontiersman to bring in scalps of enemy Delawares. Although Hamilton was criticized for his barbarism, the Pennsylvania government on April 7, 1780, again offered liberal cash bounties for the scalps of enemy Indians.

To win the friendship and support of the Indians, the Continental Congress on July 12, 1775, created three departments, or geographical divisions, to handle Indian affairs, Northern, Middle, and Southern. Each had a board of commissioners, elected by the Congress, whose members changed from time to time, supplied with moderate amounts of money to buy presents, make treaties, and otherwise negotiate with the Indians. The Delawares fell under the jurisdiction of the commissioners of the Middle Division, who usually met with the Delaware leaders at Fort Pitt, where a (figurative) council fire had been lighted. On August 14, 1776, the commissioners received a message from "King Newcommer, Capt. White Eyes, Captain Killbuck and

John Killbuck, Chiefs of the Delaware Nation" which was directed "to the thirteen States of Amaraca." The Delawares requested that someone be appointed to live with them as their liaison officer with the Congress, one who could read written messages to them, and translate their messages into English. The commissioners appointed John Anderson on August 17, 1776. Shortly thereafter, Colonel Morgan presented White Eyes to the Congress in Philadelphia, where the sachem was officially thanked for promoting good relations between the Delawares and the Americans which had preserved the peace.[31]

Largely as a result of a high regard the Congress had for White Eyes, the members, in compliance with a request made by the chief, authorized Morgan to employ a Christian minister to reside among the Delawares, to engage a schoolmaster to teach the Indian children and a blacksmith to attend to their needs. It is difficult to understand why White Eyes asked the Congress to provide a preacher and a teacher in view of the activities of the Moravian pastors, and one can only conclude that he must have been trying to achieve a closer Congressional involvement in affairs of the Delawares.

While he was in Philadelphia, White Eyes made a brief speech to the members of Congress, and before he left to return to Coshocton the president of the Congress addressed him as follows:

We desire you will inform your nation, your uncles the Six Nations and Wyandots, and your grandchildren the Shawnees, and all the other nations what you have seen and heard among us, and we exhort them to keep fast hold of the covenant chain of friendship, which we have so lately repaired and strengthened. As you are now about to depart we present you with some money to buy clothes and necessaries and pay your expenses, and we wish you a good journey and bid you farewell.[32]

With that, White Eyes was given three hundred dollars in cash, and two fine horses equipped with saddles and bridles.

When he returned to Coshocton and explained the request he had made of the Congress, White Eyes received no support from the Council. The Moravian pastors would not endorse a plan to have a minister and teacher of another denomination compete with them for the souls of the Indians. Thus his program was effectively blocked.[33]

Two years later, White Eyes, Captain Pipe, and Captain John Killbuck, Jr., representing the three divisions, were invited to another important meeting at Fort Pitt with commissioners of the Middle Department. The Americans were planning to move against Detroit, and the troops under command of General Lachlan McIntosh could not undertake the three hundred-mile march from Fort Pitt through Delaware Indian country without guarantees that the Delawares would not oppose this trespass on their territory. In their neutral position the Delawares lived precariously between the English, the Wyandot, their Indian allies on the north and west, and the Americans to the east. The Americans feared the Delawares would resist any violation of their neutrality, and Congress authorized the commissioners to buy off the Delawares by distributing goods valued at ten thousand dollars, and to negotiate a treaty that would allow McIntosh's troops to march through their territory. The commissioners realized that the hostile tribes would interpret this act of aggression as having the full support of the Delawares, and that the news would spread that the Delawares were allied with the Americans.

The treaty signed by White Eyes, Pipe, and Killbuck on September 17, 1778, provided for an offensive and defensive alliance between the United States and the Delawares. It is usually referred to as the first formal treaty between the United States and an Indian nation, but the Delawares were party to three previous treaties at Fort Pitt—in 1775, 1776, and 1777—although I have not found any formal written instruments prior to the pact of 1778. The 1778 treaty provided that United States troops would have free and safe passage through Delaware territory, that the Delawares would supply the soldiers with meat and corn, as well as guides to show them the way, an assignment for which White Eyes promptly volunteered. The United States also agreed to erect a fort in Delaware territory "for the better security of the old men, women, and children . . . whilst their warriors are engaged against the common enemy." [34] The erection and maintenance of a fort was an important consideration, because it was intended to protect the Delaware community against probable retaliation by the Wyandot and their allies.

Of this treaty Colonel Morgan later wrote, "There never was a Conference with the Indians so improperly or villainously conducted." [35] Excess quantities of liquor were distributed so that the Indians did not always have their full senses, and the articles written into the treaty were misrepresented by deliberate deceptive interpretation when translations were made into native dialect. Some of the Delawares, perhaps the majority of those attending, were not aware that they were obligating themselves to take up the war hatchet against the English. When Killbuck was later questioned about it he said, "I have now looked over the Articles of the Treaty again & find they are wrote down false." [36]

On the other hand, it is difficult to believe that White Eyes, a perceptive man even though he could not read or write, could have been fooled. Intelligent enough to be commissioned a lieutenant-colonel by General McIntosh, he came to the conference to obtain support for a unique proposition—namely that the Delaware Indians should be permitted *to form the fourteenth state in the American union.* White Eyes may have felt that, if he could persuade the commissioners to accept this new and unprecedented proposal, he could agree to almost anything, including going on the warpath against the English. In the absence of detailed information, one can only speculate about his motives. Perhaps the commissioners never had any thought of aggressively supporting the idea, and were willing to agree to it in order to win White Eyes's signature on the treaty, although this, too, is speculative. The fact remains that before the conference was over the Indians had signed a treaty which made them American allies in the war, and the commissioners had included the following proposal as Article 6 of the treaty:

Whereas the enemies of the United States have endeavored, by every artifice in their power, to possess the Indians in general with an opinion, that it is the design of the States aforesaid, to extirpate the Indians and take possession of their country: to obviate such false suggestion, the United States do engage to guarantee to the aforesaid nation of Delawares, and their heirs, all their territorial rights in the fullest and most ample manner, as it hath been bounded by former treaties, as long as they the said Delaware nation shall abide by, and hold fast the chain of friendship now entered into. *And it is further agreed on between the contracting parties should it for the future be found conducive for the mutual interest of both parties to invite any other tribes who have been friends to the interest of the United States, to join the present confederation, and to form a state whereof the Delaware nation shall be the head, and have a representation in Congress: Provided nothing contained in this article to be considered as conclusive until it meets with the approbation of Congress.* And it is also the intent and meaning of this article, that no protection or countenance shall be afforded to any who are at present our enemies, by which they might escape the punishment they deserve.[37] (Italics added)

White Eyes was overjoyed when this article became part of the treaty, of that we may be sure, and no doubt Killbuck also heartily approved. It is difficult to attempt to explain Captain Pipe's feelings or the motivations that brought him to the council table with the despised Americans. Perhaps he may have had a change in attitude when his two associates left the conference convinced that an Indian state with the Delawares at the head of it would soon be a reality. It is more likely, and in keeping with his character, that in making pretenses of friendship he deliberately deceived the Americans to put them off guard.

Because of his familiarity with the terrain in Western Pennsylvania and Ohio, White Eyes offered his services as a guide and scout for the American forces. General McIntosh was delighted to take advantage of the opportunity of having the principal Delaware chief lead his troops across Delaware territory. On November 10, 1778, the Delawares at Coshocton received a messenger bringing the almost unbelievable news that White Eyes had succumbed to smallpox during McIntosh's march from Fort Pitt. That is how his death was officially accounted for and so reported in contemporary records, including the journals of the Moravian pastors who believed the lie. The truth is that White Eyes was murdered. What happened is only briefly hinted at by Colonel Morgan in an unpublished letter written to Congress on May 12, 1784, six years after the chief's death:

[White Eyes] was treacherously put to death, at the moment of his greatest Exertions to serve the United States in whose Service he held the Commission of a Colonel . . . I have carefully concealed and shall continue to conceal from young [George] White Eyes the manner of his Father's death, which I have never mentioned to any one but Mr. [Charles] Thomson, the Secretary, and 2 or 3 members of Congress.[38]

Who killed White Eyes and the circumstances surrounding his death were never revealed. The lie about the smallpox covered up facts which if disclosed could have resulted in the Delawares' deserting the American cause and turning on McIntosh's forces with vengeance. By White Eyes's murder the Americans lost their most loyal and trusting Indian friend. His untimely death left Killbuck still pro-

American, but with Captain Pipe now on the verge of joining the enemy.

Other Delaware guides took White Eyes's place, and when McIntosh reached the Tuscarawas he built Fort Laurens (named for Henry Laurens, who was elected president of the Continental Congress in 1777) at present Bolivar, Ohio, near the site of King Beaver's old village. But as a result of the mismanagement of his supplies, lack of food for his horses, and other bungling, McIntosh was forced to give up the campaign against Fort Detroit. His militiamen, hungry and bedraggled, disbanded and fell back on Fort Pitt, thence to their homes, leaving only a small garrison at Fort Laurens that was insufficient to protect the Delawares in the event of attack. McIntosh's failure to move on to Fort Detroit was not the first time the Americans had broken their word to the Delawares. His predecessor Brigadier-General Edward Hand had also promised that he would capture the English fort. The inadequacy of Hand's troops and supplies had never permitted him to launch a campaign, and McIntosh repeated the failure, with one important exception. This time the Delawares were deeply involved because they had signed a treaty making them American allies, and now their ally had retreated, leaving them unprotected in the event of an enemy attack.

It appeared to the Delawares that the Americans continually boasted of their military victories in the East but did nothing to punish the enemy on their western border. On October 1, 1777, after he had received news of the Battle of the Brandywine, General Hand had sent a dispatch to the Delaware Great Council claiming a military victory and promising the Indians that "You may depend the English will soon be ashamed of their foolish conduct." [39] The Battle of the Brandywine was actually an American defeat, but there was no way at the time for the Indians living on the far-off Tuscarawas to find that out.

Less than two weeks after Hand's message was received, Colonel Morgan had sent another dispatch to the Delawares to advise them the Americans had surrounded part of the British Army at Germantown, killing, wounding, and capturing fifteen hundred enemy troops. Morgan went on to say that as soon as the Americans captured General Howe and his army, "which I hope to inform you of before many moons," they would then strike at the Wyandots and Mingoes supplied from Detroit.[40] Morgan's letter was written from York, Pennsylvania, but the Delawares had no way of knowing that Germantown was also an American defeat and that the enemy had gone on to capture Philadelphia, forcing the Continental Congress to flee to York.

A full year later, the Delawares were still waiting for the long-promised attack on Detroit. Instead of covering himself with glory when he marched into Indian country, McIntosh lost face because he had to turn back. The three years Morgan had spent cultivating the friendship and support of the Delawares were in danger of being undone, due to McIntosh's blundering. Morgan later denounced McIntosh openly to Congress, and when Morgan resigned on May 28, 1779, he left no doubt that he had opposed McIntosh's policies, which he felt would alienate the Delawares and lead to a general Indian war—and that's exactly what happened.

Following White Eyes's death, Killbuck and Captain Pipe continued to retain authority, but other Delawares also assumed active leadership roles. Among the most prominent were Machingwe Pushis ("large cat"), Buckongahelas ("one whose movements are certain," also spelled Pachgantschihilas), Tetepachksit ("one who has been split"), Wingenund, and Welepachtschiechen, also called Captain Johnny. Around this time Captain Pipe decided to leave his home on Walhonding Creek. He gathered his warriors at Pluggy's Town, a place near present Delaware, Ohio, which was occupied by Mingoes openly hostile to the Americans.

To placate the Delawares, Colonel Morgan in April of 1779 arranged for an Indian delegation from Coshocton to meet with representatives of the Continental Congress. This was an opportunity the Indians had sought to tell Congress that the Treaty of 1778 had been falsely interpreted to them, and that they did not want to become belligerents. They wanted to inform Congress that, since they were not allied with the English, they were deprived of the supplies the Wyandot, Shawnee, Ottawa, Mingoes, and other tribes fighting on the side of the English could obtain for their pelts in Detroit. They also wanted Congress to know that they were sorely in need of merchandise in exchange for their furs, since these goods were "absolutely necessary for the Subsistance of their Women and Children." [41] In addition, they wanted to ask Congress if the members thought they ought to take their pelts to Detroit, where the English were eager to trade with them. Finally, they wanted to remind the honorable gentlemen that Congress had sent commissioners to meet with them in Pittsburgh in 1775, 1776, and 1777,[42] and each time they had been promised clothing and goods in exchange for their peltries, but none of these agreements had been "complied with in any degree, whereby the said Delaware Nation have become poor and naked."

Killbuck, a member of the Turtle division, described in the Congressional records as "the first chief," was the ranking member of the mission, and evidently the Americans now looked to him as White Eyes's successor. Two other members of the delegation were Welepachtschiechen, spokesman for the Turkey division, referred to as the "second chief," and Peykeling, a councilor who represented the Wolf division. Captain Pipe did not attend, although there were eleven other Delawares in the party, including Tetepachksit, a councilor.

The Delawares brought with them three young males: George White Eyes, eight-year-old son of Captain White Eyes; John Killbuck, age sixteen, son of Killbuck; and Thomas, age eighteen, half brother of Killbuck. As arranged by Colonel Morgan and approved by Congress, the three lads came east to enroll as students at Princeton University.[43]

After being entertained by Colonel Morgan at his Princeton home, the Delaware delegation was granted an interview with General Washington at his Middlebrook headquarters. Washington was not pleased that the Delawares had come to see him before first visiting the Continental Congress, because he was not certain what position the Congress wanted to take, and he didn't want to give answers that might deviate from the government's policy. An old hand in Indian negotiations who had visited the Delawares in their camps years before, Washington spoke to the Indians in the familiar terms of native diplomacy. He assured them that the English would soon be defeated and punished for their wickedness, and he told them that the King of France had promised aid to the Americans.[44] Perhaps the irony of the situation was not lost on the chiefs, who remembered that during the French and Indian War they were on the side of the French and Washington was their enemy. The Indians asked if they could have a written copy of Washington's remarks, for, as Morgan informed the General, the Delawares had discontinued the use of wampum in favor of the same kind of written records the government used. This was only partially correct—the Delawares continued to use wampum beads in certain transactions—but it was a good way for the Indians to acquire a transcript of his remarks.

The Delawares were also formally received by M. Gerard, the newly arrived French ambassador, who reminded them that the French and Delawares were old friends, that the French would now stand by their side against the murderous Englishmen, and that the scarcity of trade goods had been due to the English blocking of American ports, which the French Navy would soon unblock.[45]

Later, when they met with the Congressional Committee for Indian Affairs, the Delawares reiterated that they wanted to remain neutral. A committee member replied that Congress had been told that some Delaware warriors had joined the Seneca (Mingoes) and taken up the English war hatchet against the Americans. To this accusation, the Delaware spokesman made the following reply:

We are told that there are in several of your states People you call Tories—but as that does not make those particular States your Enemies, so we hope you will make a proper Distinction between our Nation and Individuals—who, on Account of their Conduct have become Outcasts from it and whom we will never receive again as Friends until you agree to receive them as your Friends or you obtain full satisfaction for the Injuries they have done you.[46]

The Delaware delegation also pressed Congress for clothing to dress their families, as well as powder and lead with which to hunt in order to provide food for their women and children. They didn't ask that this merchandise be given them gratis—they wanted to buy it with their animal skins. They received no encouragement. The committee answered that Congress had sent to Europe for a large supply of clothing and other merchandise for their Indian brethren, but the English, having more ships than the colonies, had attacked the vessels and plundered the goods earmarked for the Indians.[47] The committee said the Indians should be patient and that as soon as the English were defeated everything would work out to their advantage.

Congress seemed to feel that the conference cleared the air and contributed to a better understanding with the Delawares. The Indians felt that leaving three of their boys in the custody of the Americans to be educated was evidence of their "firm Resolution to continue an inviolate Friendship with the United States of America to the end of time." (The two older lads were soon having trouble in the white man's world. Thomas Killbuck became addicted to "Liquor & to Lying"; and, just as he was beginning to show an aptitude for geography, mathematics, and Latin, John Killbuck had an affair with one of Colonel Morgan's maids and became the father of her child. In 1785 Thomas and John returned to their people in Ohio, John bringing his wife and child with him. Meanwhile, George White Eyes progressed to Virgil and Greek and even won a prize at his grammar school commencement. But when he reached the college level he neglected his studies and sold his clothes, books, maps, and instruments to obtain money to return to Ohio. Some time after passing his eighteenth birthday his academic career came to an end, and he, too, went home to his people.[48])

The Delaware chiefs did not suspect that the boys would not respond to the white man's educational processes. They headed west after the conferences, convinced that forward steps had been taken toward creating a better understanding with the Americans. En route to Coshocton the delegation stopped at Fort Pitt, where they were assured by McIntosh's successor, Colonel Daniel Brodhead, that they could depend upon getting goods very soon in exchange for their furs.[49] Brodhead also discouraged them from trading with the British at Detroit, although he knew he was unable to satisfy their needs. He didn't have enough supplies to clothe and feed his own troops properly, and he continually complained in his dispatches to General Washington that his men were ill fed and poorly clad. The best Washington could do was to offer his sympathies and forward Brodhead's requests to Congress, because other continental officers, confronted by the British in the East, were registering similar complaints. Congress had the responsibility of establishing priorities for the pitifully small resources at its disposal, and the members felt the battles being fought along the Atlantic seaboard were the most critical.

Brodhead, who was named Maghingua Keeshoch ("the great moon") by the Delawares, managed to gather sufficient livestock and supplies to launch a small expedition up the Allegheny River against enemy Indians in the fall of 1779. His purpose was to punish the Seneca, and also to chastise the Munsies, because their war parties fighting in the British cause had terrorized settlers in western Pennsylvania. At the same time Brodhead was making his way up the Allegheny, General John Sullivan was invading the heart of Six Nations territory via the Susquehanna River. Both campaigns were successful; Sullivan laid waste forty Iroquois towns, forcing those who had supported the British to retreat into Canada; Brodhead destroyed the Munsie and Seneca villages on the Allegheny, as the Indians fled in advance of his troops. To give evidence that the Delawares in Ohio were holding fast to American interests, the Council at Coshocton in 1780 declared war against the Mingoes.[50] Welapachtachiechen, who had been a member of the delegation insisting on neutrality in the visit to Congress, sent a message to Brodhead stating he was now ready to march with the Americans against their Indian enemies.[51]

Brodhead next intended to march on Detroit, finally fulfilling the promises made by Hand and McIntosh, but he was unable to gather enough men and supplies, nor could General Washington assist him. Brodhead's failure to move against Detroit was the last straw, worsened by the fact that he also failed to rebuild Fort Laurens, which was in ruins, as he had also promised. He also had declined a request made by the Delawares that he build a fort at Coshocton and place men there to assist the Indians against a threatened attack.[52] During the severe winter of 1779–80, when the Delawares were in dire need and their families almost perished due to lack of food and clothing, Brodhead was not able to comply with their pleas for aid.

Because of the Americans' failure to render assistance, Killbuck, still a staunch American supporter, lost prestige, and the members of the Council turned against him. This was the moment Captain Pipe was waiting for, and he argued that the only course left to the Delawares was to join forces with the English. The logic of his position could not be refuted, since the English could supply the clothing, powder, lead, firearms, and other supplies which the Americans failed to provide, and which the Indians needed to survive. It also seemed apparent that the Americans did not intend to move against Detroit. In the meanwhile, the Wyandot Half King was threatening to drive the Delawares off Wyandot lands if they did not come into the war on the side of the English. At a session of the Council held when Killbuck was absent, the members, after lengthy discussion and under Pipe's influence, decided to ally the Delaware Nation with the English.[53] The dream of an Indian state envisioned by White Eyes, with the Delawares in a dominant position, lost any chance it might have had of being realized when the Council decided to take up the war hatchet against the Americans. It was no longer safe for Killbuck and others in the pro-American faction to remain on the Tuscarawas, and they left to join Brodhead at Fort Pitt.

As one reviews the events leading up to the action of the Council, it is difficult to know where to place the blame for the Delawares' turning against the Americans. The Continental Congress fully understood the importance of having friendly Indians on the west, and, following the 1778 treaty with the Delawares, special commissioners had been appointed specifically to preserve peace and amity with the Delawares and Shawnee.[54] Congress was also desirous of carrying the war to the English at Detroit, which would have relieved the Delawares of the pressure exerted by enemy Indians. Yet when the Delawares made their special trip to seek relief from the Congress, they received no satisfaction. The Congress, in effect, failed to implement its own policy.

The immerging American state was beset with countless problems during the critical war period. In addition to the lack of supplies, there were faulty communication in the military establishment, poor discipline, weak lines of authority, and differences of opinion, all of which contributed to the failure of the government to gratify the needs of the Delawares. Bloodshed and widespread frontier atrocities resulted when the Delaware warriors again ran amuck, and this might have been avoided by diverting a small quantity of goods to Fort Pitt as a token of support and understanding. "I have never been furnished with any article of goods for the Indians," Brodhead wrote from Fort Pitt on January 23, 1781, "nor a shilling of money to enable me to transact business with them, neither has any person been employed to take the trouble of them off my hands." [55] The Delawares joined the English largely because of the default of the Americans, whose crowning failure was in not capitalizing on the alliance with the French for whom, as the English General Frederick Haldiman wrote, the Ohio Indians "had an old and very firm attachment." [56] Brodhead wrote Washington that if supplies were not made available to the Delawares, "I conceive they will be compelled to make terms with the British *or perish*." [57]

When the day of reckoning finally arrived, and Brodhead received intelligence that Pipe and Wingenund had taken their warriors on the warpath, he knew that attacks on the settlements would follow, and the intertribal influence of the Delawares would result in a general Indian uprising against the Americans. After receiving secret intelligence from Heckewelder that three separate war parties of Delaware braves were being organized on the Tuscarawas for an attack on Pittsburgh, he decided that his best defense was an offense. In the emergency he was able to arouse some members of the Pennsylvania militia, who considered killing Indians the same as hunting wild animals. He gathered enough supplies and horses to outfit a striking force of three hundred soldiers, half militiamen, half Continentals. In the spring of 1781 he marched on to Coshocton, where he found only fifteen warriors, who were captured, tried by a council of war, and sentenced to death. Their limbs bound, the warriors were taken beyond the town limits, killed with tomahawks and spears, and then scalped.[58] A number of old men, women, and children were also taken captive, and Brodhead's troops burned all the cabins, destroyed poultry and forty head of cattle, and confiscated large quantities of animal skins and other plunder, which they later sold at a good price.

Although the majority of Delaware warriors were elsewhere at the time of Brodhead's arrival, a group of some forty drunken braves were dancing on the banks of the Muskingum opposite Coshocton. They were apparently celebrating their return from a raid with prisoners and scalps, but due to heavy rains the river was swollen and Brodhead's men could not get across. During the night, Killbuck (who had been commissioned as Colonel William Henry) and a party of Delawares who marched with Brodhead were able to cross the stream. They struck their brethren, killing and scalping—a ruthless encounter of Delawares fighting Delawares.[59] Brodhead suffered no casualties during the campaign, although many shots were fired at his men by Indians hidden in the woods. In a letter written prior to the march, Heckewelder cautioned Brodhead to do everything in his power "to prevent *mistlisting* anybody belonging to our Towns," by which he meant the Moravian Delawares, who were still living at the mission towns on the Tuscarawas.[60] Brodhead complied with the request by ordering his men not to harm the friendly Delawares they found at Newcomer's Town, nor the Christian Indians in the mission towns, who, incidentally, supplied his troops with meat and corn.

Heckewelder was at Brodhead's side at Coshocton when a message was received that one of the militia units—doubtless a group of fanatic Indian haters—was getting ready to destroy the settlements of the Christian Indians. Brodhead immediately took measures to prevent this disobedience of his orders, but it illustrates the hatred some Americans felt for *all* Indians because close friends or members of their immediate families had been the victims of massacres.

After Brodhead's troops left the Tuscarawas and were well on their way back to Fort Pitt with their plunder, a party of Delaware warriors under Buckongahelas returned to the Tuscarawas from a foray. Buckongahelas assembled the Moravian Indians at Gnadenhütten, and he told them he had learned that Brodhead's militiamen had intended to murder them, just as the Paxton Boys murdered the peaceful Conestogas. He said that, although Brodhead had been able to prevent such an assault, they were not safe at Gnadenhütten, because other Americans would return and destroy them. He continued as follows:

Have you not discovered the footsteps of the long knives [i.e., the Mechanshican, or Americans] almost within sight of your towns, and seen the smoke arising from their camps! Should not this be sufficient warning to you; and lead you to consult your own safety! . . . Friends and relatives! —Now listen to me and hear what I have to say to you.—I am myself come to bid you rise and go with me to a secure place! Do not my friends, covet the land you now hold under cultivation. I will conduct you to a country equally good, where your fields shall yield you abundant crops; and where your cattle shall find sufficient pasture; where there is plenty of game; where your women and children, together with yourselves, will live in peace and safety; where no long knife shall ever molest you!—Nay I will live between you and them, and not even suffer them to frighten you!— There, you can worship your God without fear.[61]

His listeners replied that they trusted the Americans and were sorry that Buckongahelas, Captain Pipe, and other militant Delaware war captains had violated the Christian commandments by going on the warpath. They said they were living very happily in their present homes and did not want to go elsewhere. Buckongohelas, described by Heckewelder as "mild and affable in his manners; friendly and humane," answered that the right of choice was theirs, although he believed they were making a serious mistake they would live to regret. He then departed with his warriors to join Pipe along the Sandusky where they allied themselves with Pomoacan, the Wyandot Half King. Along with the Wyandot, they turned to the British at Detroit to keep them supplied with powder, lead, and provisions to maintain their families, and also to enable their war parties to harass the Americans.

Had the villagers at Gnadenhütten heeded Buckongahelas's advice, a terrible tragedy might have been averted. What happened was that the residents who had been subject to brutal Indian attack in Washington County, western Pennsylvania, organized a militia commanded by Lieutenant-Colonel David Williamson. Under orders issued by Colonel James Marshall, the highest military authority in Washington County and the man who was partly responsible for the tragedy, Williamson led a raiding party with some 160 volunteers against the Delawares on the Tuscarawas. His militiamen, burning with hatred, blamed the Christian Indians they found there for having taken part in the raids, which was untrue. They also accused the Christian Indians of harboring enemy Delaware, Munsie, Shawnee, Mingo, and Wyandot warriors. There was some truth to this accusation, as Gnadenhütten was a convenient stopping-off place for war parties to camp and refresh themselves. The Moravian Indians knew that if they did not give food to the warriors, the Wyandot would kill their cattle and burn their fields and houses. From the viewpoint of the Moravian Delawares, they were feeding needy brethren, just as they fed Brodhead's soldiers—not giving aid and comfort to enemy Indians in order to facilitate attack on the Americans.

The militiamen held a council, and by majority vote decided to put all the Indians to death. On the pretext of leading the Indians to safety, they gathered together the residents of Salem and Gnadenhütten in the latter village. When the Indians were assembled, they were formally accused of being accessories to murder, and all were sentenced to death. March 8 was set as the day of execution, and while the Indians sang hymns taught them by their pastors, prayed, pleaded for their lives, and protested their innocence, they were beaten to death with mallets and hatchets, and scalped. According to Moravian records, 56 adult Indians were killed (29 men, 27 women) and 34 children of various ages—a total of 90 victims. The militiamen returned with 96 scalps—they must have killed six unconverted Indians somewhere along their route.

Williamson's men burned the buildings at Gnadenhütten to the ground, including the structures in which they heaped up the corpses of the victims. They also burned to ashes the neighboring villages of Schönbrunn and Salem and then loaded their horses with the spoils of the raid, which they divided and took home with them.⁶² When the news of the tragedy reached the main body of the Delawares, it convinced them that the Americans were evildoers, and they lost all respect for the white man's religion and his God. White men of sound judgment knew that Williamson's troops had not found and punished the guilty but, their emotions at a high pitch, they had vented blind hatred on noncombatants. "That affair is a subject of great speculation here, some condemning, others applauding the measure," wrote a contemporary observer from Pittsburgh, ". . . they killed rather deliberately the Inocent with the guilty and it is likely the majority was the former." ⁶³

The victims of the massacre included such respected converts as Glickhican, Echpalawehund, and Welepachtschiechen, whose friends and relatives in the non-Christian group sought revenge. An opportunity came the following June when Colonel William Crawford, a Virginia landowner and one of Washington's friends, under Williamson's command marched a company of militiamen against the tribes on the Sandusky. Crawford was taken prisoner by Captain Pipe, and, to avenge the massacre at Gnadenhütten, he was cruelly tortured and burned at the stake.⁶⁴ Colonel Williamson, however, was never taken by the Indians, nor was he tried in a white man's court for the crime that occurred that bleak March day of 1782.

After the defeat of the English at Yorktown, it took more than a year and a half to end the war, one of the last Indian land battles occurring in November of 1782 when George Rogers Clark routed the Shawnee on the Scioto, burning their villages and destroying their corn stores. A preliminary treaty was signed with England on November 30, but not until the next year were definitive peace terms agreed upon at Paris. The thirteen colonies not only achieved their independence and became masters of their own destiny, but Britain ceded territory extending to the Great Lakes on the north, Spanish Florida on the south, and the Mississippi on the west. Congress set up this new land as the Northwest Territory, appointing General Arthur St. Clair governor of an area that would eventually include the states of Ohio, Indiana, Illinois, Michigan, and Wisconsin.

Through ownership of these lands the new government had territory into which colonists could expand, and the vast acreage could be sold as public lands to pay off the nation's debts. The problem was that the territory was occupied by Delawares, Munsies, Shawnee, Ottawa, Wyandot, Mingoes, Kickapoo, Potawatomi, Chippewa, Miami, Peoria, Kaskaskia, Wea, Piankashaw, Sauk, Fox, and other tribes all hostile, in whole or in part, toward the Americans. Deprived of their British allies, the Indians sought to unify their forces during the postwar period, and in 1783 thirty-five different tribes or nations, including the Delawares, met on the Sandusky River to form an Indian confederacy "to defend their country against all invaders."

The Indian problem was only one of myriad complexities confronting the Continental Congress, which was attempting to fuse the thirteen colonies into a new nation, but it was apparent that a confederacy of Indian tribes was not in the national interest. How the Six Nations—treated as a subdued people, the majority of their villages reduced to ashes—were compelled to relinquish their claims to lands has been related elsewhere.[65] The government also proceeded to negotiate individually with the western tribes, as a means of breaking up the confederacy. An internal pact made by the confederacy bound its members not to cede any lands in the Northwest Territory without the consent of all the tribes. At the Treaty of Fort McIntosh (present Beaver, Pennsylvania) the United States, on January 21, 1785, met with the Delawares, Wyandot, and a few wandering Chippewa and Ottawa. All were members of the confederacy, and, despite having agreed not to deal separately with the Americans, they entered into the treaty negotiations. By the terms of the treaty, the Indians placed themselves under the protection of the new government and promised to "deliver up" all white prisoners in their possession. Boundaries were laid down for a small area of land within the Northwest Territory which would be reserved for the Wyandot and Delawares to live and hunt on, and for any members of the Ottawa nation then occupying any part of the area. The Indians agreed that lands not lying within the stated bounds belonged to the government and they would not presume to settle thereon.[66]

The treaty also provided that "Kelelamand or lieut. col. Henry [i.e., Captain John Killbuck, Jr.], Hengue Pushees or the Big Cat, Wicocalind or Capt. White Eyes, who took up the hatchet for the U.S., and their families shall be received in the Delaware nation with the same rank as before the war." (The Captain White Eyes referred to was Joseph White Eyes, a son of the great Delaware diplomat.) Through the inclusion of this clause the government was trying to heal the internal wounds by encouraging a reconciliation of the pro-English and the pro-American factions. Despite this effort, there continued to be a strong, militant anti-American party to challenge those who favored the government's policies. After the cessation of hostilities, Captain Pipe was accused by the chiefs of the Turtle and Turkey divisions of having displayed incompetence by joining the English cause since "nothing but disaster had been brought upon them from the time he usurped this power" and tried to govern the nation.[67] Buckongahelas confronted Pipe and blamed him for all the ills that had befallen the Delawares after White Eyes's death.[68] Apparently Machingwe Pushis, the "Big Cat," succeeded Pipe as the chief of the Wolf group following the war.

At the time the Fort McIntosh treaty was signed, the Delawares were living at various places in Ohio to which they had retreated from the Tuscarawas—on the Sandusky, the Mad River, the Maumee, the Auglaize, and elsewhere. A splinter group left the main body in 1789 to follow a band of Shawnee across the Mississippi and by permission of the Spanish governor, Baron de Carondelet, settled near present Cape Girardeau, Missouri, in Spanish territory. The sites of the former villages on the Muskingum and Tuscarawas were not included in the lands reserved for the Delawares and Wyandot at Fort McIntosh, and white farmers would soon be cultivating the bottom lands in the valley of the Muskingum. Already the Ohio Company of Associates had contracted with the government to purchase acreage at the confluence of the Ohio and Muskingum where the town of Marietta would be laid out. With the Delawares and Shawnee out of the way, there was nothing to deter white expansion on the lands where the Wyandot had seated the Delawares.

The Moravian Delawares continued to remain separate from the main body of the Delawares. They moved from a settlement on the Upper Sandusky called Captives Town to establish New Gnadenhütten above Detroit. From there they went to a site on the Huron River near what is now Milan, where they built New Salem at a place known to the Indians as Pettquotting. No matter where they went they seemed to encounter problems, and they didn't want to be drawn into disputes over land matters that caused continuous unrest among non-Christian Indians. "How could we live in the midst of warriors," the seventy-two-year-old Zeisberger wrote about his Indian wards, "who are every day going out and in with shouts and songs. We would be swallowed and devoured." [69] Finally, to escape trouble and to be alone, he led his converts to a refuge in what was then Canadian wilderness, establishing in May of 1792 the mission town of Schönfeldt (Fairfield) on the heights overlooking the north bank of the Retrenche River, now the Thames, in Kent County, Ontario. Thirty miles up the Thames from Fairfield, there was a prior settlement of migrant Munsies from Pennsylvania who had founded Muncy Town. Their chieftain, Lohachkes, permitted his people to sell the Moravian Indians corn, which provided food for their families until their own crops were sown and harvested. Thus remnants of the Christian Delawares—who moved from Philadelphia to the Susquehanna to escape harassment from rioters; and from there to western Pennsylvania, as trouble broke out on the Susquehanna; thence to the Tuscarawas, where they experienced a terrible massacre —now hoped to find peace at a location many miles removed from the conflict taking place in the Northwest Territory.

The heart of the controversy was the Indians' insistence that the Ohio River had been established by the second Fort Stanwix treaty of 1768 as the boundary between whites and Indians. This was consistent with the promises, repeatedly given the Indians *before* the Revolution, that the English had no design on Indian lands north and west of the Ohio. But the situation had substantially changed with the victory of the colonies. As the Congress saw the situation, England and her Indian allies had been defeated, and the western lands won from England and the Indians belonged to the new United States government by right of conquest. England may have had prior treaty commitments to the Indians regarding this land, but this did not obligate the United States, and the new government took the position that it alone had the right to decide what should be done with the territory acquired by the Treaty of Paris. The Americans felt they had been magnanimous at the Treaty of Fort McIntosh, permitting, as a generous conqueror, the vanquished Delawares, Wyandot, Ottawa, and Chippewa to continue to live on assigned lands in the Northwest Territory, instead of forcing them to leave.

On the other hand, the Indian confederacy renounced the Fort McIntosh treaty because it had been negotiated without the approval of all the tribes who jointly claimed they still owned the Northwest Territory. The Mohawk captain Thayendanega ("two sticks bound together"), whose English name was Joseph Brant, one of the prime movers of the confederacy, was outspoken in his criticism of American policy. Like the other Indian leaders, he sought to restore the boundary antedating the Fort McIntosh treaty—namely, the Ohio River. It was a hopeless cause, because the American government could not suppress the pioneer spirit or the commercial aggressiveness that motivated its growing population to expand westward. The enterprising young nation could not be held back, and it was the tragic lot of the Delawares and their Indian associates to be occupying the territory into which the whites expanded. As the differences mounted and the controversy became more heated, blood was spilled again on the Ohio frontier. The Indians took up their war hatchets and scalping knives to attack wagon trains coming west from Fort Pitt, as well as supply boats moving down the Ohio, once more committing atrocities against white families. The United States was forced to take retaliatory action, and an expedition was sent under General Josiah Harmer in 1789, and a second under General St. Clair in 1791. Both suffered crushing defeats as they faced the allied forces of Little Turtle and his Miami braves; Blue Jacket and his Shawnee fighters, and Buckongahelas and his Delaware warriors.[70]

To agitate the Delawares, Captain Joseph Brant revived the whole question of the Delawares' wearing petticoats, and he conducted a gratuitous ceremony of making men of them again. During the ceremony, an Indian was dressed like a warrior of old, his head shaved, face painted, wearing only a breechclout and carrying a war club. Turning to the Delawares, Brant then said:

Cousin, beforetimes we put on thee a woman's garment; hung at thy side a calabash, with oil to anoint they head; put into they hand a grubbing axe and a pestle, to plant corn and to grind it, together with other housegear, and told thee to support thyself by agriculture, together with thy children, and to trouble thyself about nothing else. Now we cut in two the band wherewith the garment is bound, and throw it among these thick, dark bushes, whence no man shall bring it again or he must die. Thou art thus no longer in thy former form, but thy form is like this Indian's, whom we now present to thee, that thou mayest see who thou now art, and instead of grubbing axe and corn-pestle we put into thy hand a war-beetle and feathers upon thy head. Thou goes about now like a man.[71]

The absurdity of this speech should be readily apparent, because the Delawares had proved repeatedly to be ruthless warriors in battle, and had shed their petticoats years before. The Six Nations, routed by the Americans, had lost the vast territory they once controlled and no longer had effective military strength as a confederacy. The Delawares' reaction to his speech was not what Captain Brant expected. "What shall we do with this murderous club," a Delaware leader was quoted as saying, "except to use it against you our uncles who have so often and so richly deserved such treatment at our hands." [72]

Congress sent a third expedition, under General "Mad" Anthony Wayne, to avenge the defeats of Harmer and St. Clair and to eliminate for all time the Indian menace to white settlement in eastern Ohio. Wayne dealt the confederacy a crushing defeat at the Battle of Falling Timbers where the Indians, expecting English supplies and reinforcements that never came, had to stand alone against a stronger and better equipped American force. The battle broke the back of the confederacy and proved to the Indians that it was not only futile to look to the English for assistance but that the Americans were undisputed masters of the Northwest Territory.

Following this victory, Wayne concluded an important treaty on August 3, 1795, at Greenville, Ohio, with the following vanquished tribes: Delawares, Wyandot, Shawnee, Ottawa, Chippewa, Potawatomi, Miami, Eel River, Wea, Kickapoo, Piankashaw, and Kaskaskia. The United States gave the Indians rights to occupy the land lying between the Cuyahoga River and the Mississippi, which permitted them to hunt in northern Ohio as well as in the territory now comprising Indiana and Illinois. The government reserved for itself nearly seventeen million acres in eastern and southern Ohio, embracing about two-thirds of the state, from which the Indians had to move.[73] The Greenville treaty opened up the Northwest Territory, and, as the Indians departed, the Americans seized control of the Ohio River Valley.

Notes—Chapter 13

1. John W. Jordan, "Bishop J. F. C. Cammerhoff's Narrative of a Journey to Shamokin, Pennsylvania in the Winter of 1748," *Pennsylvania Magazine of History and Biography*, vol. 29, no. 2, 1905, pp. 160–79.

2. Kenneth G. Hamilton, "Cultural Contributions of Moravian Missions Among the Indians," *Pennsylvania History*, vol. 18, no. 1, January 1951, pp. 1–15.

3. A. B. Hulbert and W. N. Schwarze, eds., "Diary of David Zeisberger's Journey to the Ohio from Sept. 20 to Nov. 16, 1767," *Ohio Archeological and Historical Society Publications*, vol. 12, 1910, pp. 96–97. The likelihood is that Lawunakhannek was on the east bank of the river and the three Munsie towns were on the west side; see M. H. Deardorff, "Zeisberger's Allegheny River Indian Towns, 1767–1770," *Pennsylvania Archeologist*, vol. 16, no. 1, January 1946, pp. 2–19.

4. Wm. H. Rice, *David Zeisberger and his Brown Brethren*, Bethlehem, Pa., 1897, p. 34.

5. R. G. Thwaites and Louise P. Kellogg, eds., *The Revolution on the Upper Ohio*, 1775–1777, Madison, Wis., 1908, p. 86. On April 11, 1776, Congress told White Eyes that, since the Six Nations also claimed the same lands the Wyandot gave to the Delawares, he should obtain their consent in a public council, *Journals of the Continental Congress*, Library of Congress, Washington, 1904, vol. 4, pp. 269–70. I have as yet found no evidence that he did so.

6. A. B. Hulbert and W. N. Schwarze, eds., *David Zeisberger's History of the Northern American Indians*, Ohio Archeological and Historical Society Publications, vol. 19, 1910, pp. 96–97.

7. Rice, *Zeisberger and His Brown Brethren*, pp. 35–36.

8. I am indebted to Donald Hutslar, Assistant Curator of History, Ohio State Historical Society, and his wife Jean for bringing this diary to my attention and making it available for study. For a discussion of other Zeisberger diaries, see Archer B. Hulbert, "The Moravian Records," *Ohio Archaeological and Historical Publications*, vol. 18, 1909, pp. 199–226.

9. Thwaites and Kellogg, eds., *Revolution on the Upper Ohio*, p. 64.

10. Edmund de Schweinitz, *The Life and Times of David Zeisberger*, Philadelphia, 1870, p. 366.

11. *Colonial Records*, vol. 9, p. 226.

12. Hulbert and Swarze, eds., *Zeisberger's History*, pp. 98–100; cf. George H. Loskiel, *History of the Mission of the United Brethren . . . ,* trans. Christian I. La Trobe, London, 1794, pt. 1, pp. 130–31.

13. David Jones, *A Journal of Two Visits Made to Some Nations of Indians, . . . ,* Sabina Reprints, New York, 1865, p. 104.

14. Charles Beatty, *The Journal of a Two Months Tour . . . ,* London, 1768, fn. p. 71.

15. Ibid. See entry which begins on September 18, 1776, the day he arrived at the Indian town.

16. Paul A. W. Wallace, ed., *Thirty Thousand Miles with John Heckewelder*, Pittsburgh, 1958, p. 111. See also Wallace's paper, "They Knew the Indian: The Men Who Wrote the Moravian Records," *Proceedings of the American Philosophical Society*, vol. 95, no. 3, June 1951, pp. 290–95.

17. De Schweinitz, *Life and Times of David Zeisberger*, p. 422.

18. There are three letter books containing documents written from March 2, 1775, to May 28, 1779. Since the documents are arranged chronologically, they may readily be located by date.

19. Milton W. Hamilton, ed., *The Papers of Sir William Johnson*, Albany, 1957, vol. 12, p. 1047. When Custaloga became aged and unfit, he voluntarily turned the chieftaincy over to Captain Pipe; ibid.

20. Loskiel's *History of the Mission of the United Brethren* . . . , pt. 3, pp. 116–17. The Cherokee came to the Muskingum and conducted condolence rites following Netawatwees's death; ibid., pp. 122–23; cf. Hulbert and Schwarze, eds., *Zeisberger's History of the Northern American Indians*, pp. 150–51. It was not unusual for other tribes to console the Delawares on the death of a noted civil chief. The Shawnee had conducted condolence rites for Sassoonan in 1748; *Colonial Records*, vol. 5, p. 354. The purpose of the ceremony was to comfort the bereaved tribe with speeches, presentation of wampum strings, prayers, and singing.

21. John Heckewelder, *A Narrative of the Mission of the United Brethren* . . . (hereafter cited as Heckewelder, *Narrative*), Philadelphia, 1820, p. 193. There is a legend that two Pennsylvania militiamen, William Boggs and Lewis Wetzel, tomahawked a young friendly Delaware chief to death at Wheeling, and that the Indian's name was Killbuck. This younger member of the Killbuck family could have been the young chief-elect; see Louise P. Kellogg, ed., *Frontier Retreat on the Upper Ohio, 1779–1781*, State Historical Society of Wisconsin, *Collections*, vol. 24, Madison, Wis., 1917, pp. 419–20; fn. 3, p. 376. Heckewelder, however, wrote that Killbuck, Jr. (Gelelemend) was "not in a direct line entitled to the Chiefdom," Maurice C. Jones, "Memorandum," *Proceedings of the Historical Society of Pennsylvania*, vol. 1, no. 9, February 1847, p. 150.

22. Heckewelder, *Narrative*. Cf. Consul Wilshire Butterfield, ed., *Washington-Irvine Correspondence*, Madison, Wis., 1882, pp. 99–100. Butterfield insists that the murders were not committed by soldiers returning from the Gnadenhütten massacre, as Heckewelder stated, but by a separate group of armed civilian Indian haters. One of the Delawares killed on this island (known as Killbuck's Island) was named Captain Wilson; Archibald Loudon, *A Selection of the Most Interesting Narratives of Outrages Committed by the Indians in Their Wars with White People*, Carlisle, White Hall, 1808–11, vol. 1, pp. 54–55.

23. *Colonial Records*, vol. 9, p. 738; ibid, vol. 10, p. 62.

24. De Schweinitz, *Life and Times of David Zeisberger*, p. 387.

25. Ibid., p. 418.

26. *Journals of the Continental Congress*, vol. 1, p. 175.

27. Ibid., vol. 9, under entry of December 3, 1777.

28. Heckewelder, *Narrative*, p. 159.

29. Ibid.

30. Milton Hamilton, ed., *Papers of Sir William Johnson*, vol. 12, 1957, p. 1047.

31. The message from the Delaware chiefs and the details of John Anderson's appointment may be found in the Jasper Yeates Papers, Correspondence 1762–80, Box 129-E, Manuscript Room, Historical Society of Pennsylvania, Philadelphia. For an account of White Eyes's appearance before the Congress, see Richard C. Adams, *A Brief History of the Delaware Indians*, Senate Document no. 501, 59th Congress, 1st session, 1906, p. 22.

32. *Journals of the Continental Congress*, vol. 4, pp. 266–68. A copy of White Eyes's speech to the Congress in Philadelphia December 9, 1776, may be found in the Jasper Yeates Papers, Correspondence 1762–80, Box 129-E, Manuscript Room, Historical Society of Pennsylvania, Philadelphia.

33. The unpublished Zeisberger Diary translated by Professor August C. Mahr describes White Eyes's return from his visit to the Continental Congress and the cool reception he received from Council members who felt he had exceeded his authority. Despite his keen intelligence, White Eyes could not read; see "Journal of James Kenny," *Pennsylvania Magazine of History and Biography*, vol. 37, no. 1, 1913, p. 178.

34. Charles J. Kappler, ed., *Indian Affairs, Laws And Treaties*, Washington, 1904, 3 vols., vol. 2, pp. 3–5. Hereinafter as Kappler, *Indian Affairs,*

35. Randolph C. Downes, *Council Fires on the Upper Ohio*, Pittsburgh, 1940, p. 216. The complete text of Morgan's letter to Colonel Daniel Brodhead is given in Louise P. Kellogg, ed., *Frontier Advance on the Upper Ohio, 1778–1779*, State Historical Society of Wisconsin, *Collections*, vol. 23, Madison, 1916, pp. 216–17. For a transcription of the Treaty of 1778, see ibid., pp. 138–45.

36. Downes, *Council Fires*, p. 17. Killbuck later told Colonel Morgan that at the Treaty of 1778 at Pittsburgh he did not intend to commit himself to lift the tomahawk in a warlike manner against the English; Kellogg, ed., *Frontier Advance*, p. 204. On the other hand, a review of the minutes of the conference with White Eyes and his associates held prior to the signing of the treaty leaves no doubt that White Eyes was aware of the commitment; David Bushnell, "The Virginia Frontier in History, 1778," *Virginia Magazine of History and Biography*, vol. 24, p. 175.

37. Kappler, ed., *Indian Affairs*, vol. 2, pp. 3–5. The proposal was never acted upon by Congress. Later there were a number of serious proposals both by Indians and Americans relative to creating an Indian state, see Annie H. Abel, "Proposals for an Indian State, 1778–1878," *American Historical Association, Annual Report*, 1907, vol. 1, pp. 89 ff.

38. A page from the letter containing the excerpt quoted may be found

in the Morgan Letters, 1775–87, Library of Congress. I want to express my thanks to Senator J. Caleb Boggs of Delaware for his assistance in obtaining a copy of this page for me.

39. R. G. Thwaites and Louise P. Kellogg, eds., *Frontier Defense on the Upper Ohio, 1777–1778*, Madison, Wis., 1912, pp. 112–14.

40. Ibid., pp. 136–37.

41. Kellogg, ed., *Frontier Advance*, p. 318. The quotations I have cited from this splendid compilation of primary source material are all transcripts of documents largely taken from the Draper Collection.

42. For reference to the treaties of 1775 and 1776, see Thwaites and Kellogg, eds., *Revolution on the Upper Ohio*, p. 80 ff.; pp. 216–17. At the treaty of 1775 White Eyes referred to the three Delaware subtribes in these words ". . . we now inform you that there are three tribes of us Kalamint [Gelelemend] Walapachakin [Welepachtschiechen] and Ohokon [Opokan] are the Chiefs appointed for the Delaware nation"; ibid., p. 88.

43. Kellogg, ed., *Frontier Advance*, fn. 1, p. 319. Killbuck (Gelelemend) had at least two other sons, Charles Henry Killbuck and Christian Gootlieb Henry Killbuck; see Gratz Papers, Case 4, Box 5, Manuscript Room, Historical Society of Pennsylvania, Philadelphia, wherein they acknowledge receipt of rifles from the Pennsylvania government in August of 1811.

44. Kellogg, *Frontier Advance*, p. 322. Washington must have known that Governor Patrick Henry sent instructions to the County Lieutenant of Ohio to use every means to protect the Delaware Indians who had befriended Virginia during Dunmore's War. "In one word, support, protect, defend and cherish them in every Respect to the utmost," he wrote; see Thwaites and Kellogg, eds., *Revolution on the Upper Ohio*, pp. 244–45. Washington's account of his conference with the Delaware delegation is recorded in his letter of May 14, 1779, to John Jay; Colonial Society of Massachusetts, *Transactions*, vol. 13, 1910–11, pp. 261–62.

45. Kellogg, *Frontier Advance*, pp. 354–56.

46. Ibid., p. 352.

47. Ibid., p. 341.

48. Varnum Lansing Collins, "Indian Wards at Princeton," *Princeton University Bulletin*, vol. 13, pp. 101–6. As I state in Chap. 14, George White Eyes was killed by the Osage in Missouri.

49. Kellogg, *Frontier Advance*, p. 370.

50. Kellogg, *Frontier Retreat*, p. 301.

51. Ibid., p. 172.

52. Ibid., pp. 315–16.

53. Ibid., p. 339; cf. pp. 337–38.

54. *Journals of the Continental Congress*, vol. 9, pp. 942–44.

55. Kellogg, *Frontier Retreat*, p. 326.

56. Ibid., p. 122.

57. Downes, *Council Fires*, p. 265.

58. Kellogg, *Frontier Retreat*, pp. 378–79.

59. *Pennsylvania Archives*, 1st series, vol. 1, p. 770.

60. Ibid., p. 771. Brodhead's letter of May 22, 1781, giving his account of the engagement is found on pp. 161–62. For other accounts, cf. Kellogg, *Frontier Retreat*, p. 376 and passim.

61. Heckewelder, *Narrative*, p. 216. Evidently Buckongahelas was the leader of the war party of 80 Delawares who came to the Tuscarawas for the main purpose of finding and killing Killbuck and his followers; Kellogg, *Frontier Retreat*, p. 380.

62. A list of the names of some of the militiamen and their officers is given in *Pennsylvania Archives*, 2d series, vol. 14, pp. 753–54; cf. Kellogg, *Frontier Retreat*, pp. 461–69; Thomas H. Johnson, "The Indian Village of Cush-og-wenk," *Ohio Archeological and Historical Quarterly*, vol. 21, 1912, pp. 432–35.

63. *Pennsylvania Archives*, 1st series, vol. 9, p. 540; see pp. 524–25 for account of the massacre.

64. John Heckewelder, *History*, pp. 285–89, which describes how Crawford asked Wingenund to save him, but was refused.

65. Downes, *Council Fires*; also by the same author, *Frontier Ohio, 1788–1893*, Ohio Archeological and Historical Society, Columbus, 1935; cf. Anthony F. C. Wallace, *The Death and Rebirth of the Seneca*, New York, 1970.

66. Kappler, *Indian Affairs*, vol. 2, pp. 6–8. In 1875 Congress granted 12,000 acres on the Muskingum to the Moravian Indians and the descendants of Gelelemend and White Eyes, as a reward for services rendered during the Revolution. Since the Indians could not return because of unsettled conditions, the land was vested in trust in the Society of the United Brethren for Propagating the Gospel among the Heathen. It was later ceded to the government by the Moravians in 1823; Elma E. Gray and Leslie Robb Gray, *Wilderness Christians*, Toronto, 1956, pp. 85–86, 206, 269–70. In the summer of 1797 Heckewelder and others were sent by the Moravian Church to survey the 12,000 acres; they found a number of Captain White Eyes's children and grandchildren still living in the vicinity of Newcomers Town aware that they were entitled to a share of the lands covered by an act of Congress of June 1, 1796; see "Notes of Travel of William Henry, John Heckewelder, John Rothrock, and Christian Clewell," *Pennsylvania Magazine of History and Biography*, vol. 10, no. 2, 1886, pp. 125–27. Some of the relatives of White Eyes later moved to Moraviantown in Ontario, where his descendants may still be found.

67. Heckewelder, *Narrative*, p. 350.

68. Ibid., p. 351. In Captain Pipe's favor, it should be said that he was responsible for the release of Zeisberger, Heckewelder, and others when

they were captured by the English and charged with treason at Detroit; Paul Wallace, ed., *Thirty Thousand Miles with John Heckewelder*, Chapter 21.

69. Eugene F. Bliss, trans. and ed., *Diary of David Zeisberger*, Cincinnati, 1885, vol. 1, p. 242. This published diary should not be confused with the unpublished diary cited in the text, nor with the one listed above in n. 3.

70. See *American State Papers, Documents Legislative and Executive of the Congress of the U.S.*, vol. 1, Indian Affairs, 1789–1814, Washington, D.C., 1832, p. 489, where two Shawnee warriors testify regarding the number of Delawares.

71. Bliss, *Diary of Zeisberger*, vol. 2, p. 410; cf. p. 381.

72. De Schweinitz, *Life and Times of David Zeisberger*, p. 642.

73. Kappler, *Indian Affairs*, vol. 2, pp. 39–45; cf. *American State Papers*, pp. 562–63. One of the white prisoners freed in 1795 was a lad named John Brickell, who had been taken captive near Uniontown, Pa., in 1781, and was adopted by Machingwe Pushis; "Narrative of John Brickell's Captivity among the Delaware Indians," *American Pioneer*, vol. 1, Cincinnati, 1842, pp. 43–56.

14

Haven in Indiana Territory

Under the terms of the Greenville treaty, General Anthony Wayne distributed goods valued at $20,000 to the defeated Indians—gifts that were intended to buy their friendship and soften the blow of forcing them to vacate a large part of what is now the state of Ohio but was then part of the old Northwest Territory.[1] In addition, every year *"forever after"* the government agreed to deliver to the Indians at some convenient place north of the Ohio River useful goods worth $9,500. Each tribe or nation—the government continued to prefer the latter word, considering each tribe a foreign nation under the treaty-making powers of the Constitution—who signed the treaty was to receive a pro-rata share of trade goods annually. The quantity allotted the Delawares under the Greenville treaty was supposed to amount to $1,000 a year—not a lavish sum to be spent on merchandise intended to be divided among some two thousand men, women, and children. This was the first of the so-called annuities the government paid the Delawares, and it would later be followed by others in cash instead of trade goods, as covered by treaty arrangements.

Fourteen chiefs and great men represented the Delawares at the signing of the Greenville treaty, including the warrior Buckongahelas, Kikthawenund ("creaking boughs"), who was better known as Chief William Anderson, and Tetabokshke (Tetepachksit), referred to in the document as the "Grand Glaize King" but who had now become the nominal head of the Delaware Nation.[2] Although the Delawares had only a vague claim to ownership of the Muskingum lands where they were formerly seated (part of the territory the Wyandot were forced to cede to the United States), they carried away their share of trade goods the army wagons brought to Greenville for distribution to the Indians. Like other natives, they continued to expect either merchandise or cash presents following a conference with the authorities, and the Americans continued to oblige them even when, as at Greenville, the Indians were a conquered enemy.

The twelve Indian nations participating in the Greenville treaty were represented by 1,130 individuals, among whom the Delaware contingent of 381 persons was the largest. The treaty contained specific clauses to the effect that the Indian signatories acknowledged that henceforth they would be under the protection of the United States and no other power, and, if any white men settled on the lands being allotted the Indians, the natives were within their rights to drive them off or punish them in any manner they thought fit. After the treaty was signed, Buckongahelas in his role as a hero war captain was quoted as saying, "All who know me, know me to be a man and a warrior, and I now declare that I will for the future be a true and steady friend of the United States as I have heretofore been an active enemy." [3] These words did not mean that Buckongahelas now loved the white man—only that he would not again take up arms against the Americans, a promise he never broke.

After agreeing to cease hostilities and to release their white prisoners, the Indian signatories were given the right to dwell, plant, and hunt "as long as they pleased" on the lands set aside in common for them. These lands lay north of a boundary across Ohio and south and west of the Great Lakes as far as the Mississippi—then the western bound of United States territory. The Indians wanted the lands allocated tribally instead of being held in common, but General Wayne elected to treat them on equal terms, knowing if he did otherwise it might cause intertribal problems he could not cope with. His answer was, "You Indians know best your respective boundaries," a naïve reply when one considers that most of the signatories had been dispossessed and were living in unfamiliar territory. Wayne was probably unaware that the Delawares were present in Ohio as invited guests of the Wyandot, and that the Wyandot were living and hunting on lands that formerly belonged to the Erie and were later claimed by the Six Nations. When the second Fort Stanwix treaty of 1784 with the Iroquois was signed, the United States commissioners told the Seneca, Mohawk, Onondaga, and Cayuga that, having sided with the British during the Revolution, they were now a subdued people, and the United States as conqueror had the right to seize all their land, but, instead of exercising this right, would take only a portion of their territory. By terms of the treaty, the Six Nations gave up all their rights to the lands west of the Ohio River, and consequently were not even represented at the Greenville treaty.

Apart from the fact that General Wayne gave equal territorial rights to Indian hosts and guests alike, neither he nor the Indians anticipated what soon would happen. With southeastern Ohio open for settlement, successive waves of land-hungry settlers inundated the Ohio Territory, spilling over into lands reserved for the Indians. The population increased so rapidly that less than ten years later Ohio became a state.

Prior to the admission of Ohio, President Jefferson had the idea that the territories could be divided into farms cultivated by white settlers and Indians, both living and working together in peace. He later realized that this hope could never be fulfilled—it proved impossible time after time for whites and Indians to live together in harmony. When the Louisiana Territory was purchased from France, Jefferson's main objective was to acquire the port of New Orleans, but he later concluded that the wild, unsettled, and largely unexplored country west of the Mississippi would be an ideal place to move those Indians who persisted in refusing to become part of the white man's world. Jefferson may have reasoned that no white American would ever have need to live on the remote western lands when there seemed to be plenty of living space east of the Mississippi River. He believed that if the Indians were placed in the West they could hunt, fish, plant their cornfields, and live contentedly without white interference. This does not mean that he was not sympathetic with the problems faced by Indians who were being overwhelmed by the white man's civilization and relentlessly driven before it. Knowing that wild game was being greatly reduced east of the Mississippi, in his second inaugural Jefferson called upon all Americans to cooperate in teaching the natives agriculture and the domestic arts to help them change their status from huntsmen to farmers and artisans, which is what the Moravians had been trying to do for many years. But the Delawares were tired of the continual pressure exerted on them by Christian missionaries—and by American officials urging them to settle down to steady labor, practice agriculture at a fixed location, cease going on extended hunting trips, and send their children to schools where they would be taught to accept the white man's ways. Far-seeing though he may have been, Jefferson and his successors Madison and Monroe, during the formative years of the Republic, underestimated the tenacity of the Indians to adhere to their own social and political systems. Even today there are still Indian groups in the far west that have never been "Americanized" despite many efforts to bring "civilization" to them.

When the Wyandot ceded the lands on which they were living to the United States at the Greenville treaty, the Delawares moved to new territory that had formerly been claimed by the Piankashaw and the Miami proper. Like the Wea and Eel River Indians, the Piankashaw was a subtribe of the Miami, whose earlier name Twightwee had now generally fallen into disuse. The United States considered the Miami to have a legitimate claim to lands in the Wabash drainage system in Indiana Territory, as well as to parts of western Ohio adjoining Wyandot lands. The government offered no objection when the Miami extended their hospitality to the Delawares and other Indian tribes, inviting them to live on specified parts of their territory, for, as General Wayne had indicated to the Indians, this was something they could decide for themselves. This whole subject of lands allocated by the Miami is not well understood because no written leases changed hands, and no surveyors' drawings were made to show the bounds of tracts the Miami assigned to the newcomers. The guest tribes understood where their Miami hosts expected them to live and hunt, since there were natural boundaries that both recognized, but lacking documentation the white authorities were often nonplussed by these unwritten tribal agreements.

In 1804 the *Piankashaw* chiefs stated that thirty-seven years before they had invited the Delawares to live on specified lands along the White River, one of the major tributaries of the Wabash, and this would seem to indicate that, as early as 1767, land in Indiana Territory became available for Delaware occupancy.[4] Whether any Delawares settled in Indiana at this early date is not certain, but by 1794 there were Delaware families residing on the White River. A difference of opinion later developed among the Indians as to which tribe or band was responsible for issuing the invitation to the Delawares to settle in Indiana, for on December 12, 1808, it was recorded that,

"The land which we now inhabit [on the White River] was granted by the Miamies and *Pottawatomies*, which they renewed last September in their general council held at Fort Wayne, in the presence of the agent of Indian affairs, Captain [William] Wells, and the commanding officer of that place." This statement was negated by a deposition made by President Jefferson on December 21, 1808, to the effect that the Miami "have granted to the Dellawares Mohiccaners and Muncies and their descendants forever a certain portion of their Lands on the White River . . ." [5]

In traditional Indian fashion there had been an oral agreement, punctuated with appropriate strings of wampum, whereby the Delawares were permitted to move to the White River country, but no written records exchanged hands. Irrespective of the identity of the original owners—Piankashaw, Potawatomi, or Miami proper—the important point is that the Delawares had no land of their own and resided in Indiana Territory by the sanction of a host tribe and the blessing of the United States government.

The other tribes that had settled in Indiana Territory by Miami invitation included the Eel River Indians residing on Eel River, a branch of the Wabash, and the Wea, who lived downstream near present Lafayette. The Shawnee were on the Auglaize, a branch of the Maumee River in Miami County, Ohio, and also on Stoney Creek, one of the tributaries of the Miami River. The Potawatomi were on the lower end of Lake Michigan and on the Saint Joseph, which flows into the same lake. The Piankashaw and Kickapoo were settled in the neighborhood of Vincennes on the Wabash and Vermilion rivers. The principal villages of the Miami themselves, who were the most numerous, were along the Wabash River south of Fort Wayne and on the Mississinewa River.

By 1801 the main body of Delawares was well established in a series of villages, variously estimated at from nine to eleven, on the West Fork of the White River between the present cities of Muncie and Indianapolis. The most easterly town, situated about three miles south of present Muncie on the left bank of the river, was called Buckongahelas's Town, but it was also referred to as Wapicomemoke or Wapekommekoke, a variant of the Delaware name *Wapeksippu*, which means White River. The gallant war captain Buckongahelas lived here, as did the well-known white trader and interpreter John Conner, who had an Indian wife.

The most westerly town was on the east side of the river, near present Noblesville and about twelve miles north of Indianapolis. It was called the Lower Delaware Town. Between these two towns lay the other Delaware settlements strung out along both sides of the river. One of the largest was Wapeminskink ("chestnut tree place") at the site of modern Anderson. It was also known as Anderson's Town because it was the home of Chief William Anderson and his family. John Conner's brother William Conner, also a trader and interpreter, lived at Anderson's Town after his marriage to Mekinges, also spelled Ma-cun-chis ("last born"), a daughter of Chief Anderson. He and Mekinges later moved and established a trading post four miles south of present Noblesville, where he built a log cabin large enough to house his family and stock the beads, lead, flint, steel, knives, hatchets, and other merchandise used in the Indian trade. The couple raised their six half-white, half-Indian children in what, in effect, was an Indian household, and the entire family conversed in the Delaware language.

John and William Conner were sons of Richard Conner and his wife Margaret Boyer, a white captive who had been raised among the Shawnee. The Reverend David Jones visited Richard Conner and his wife in 1773 in an Indian village on Ohio's Scioto River occupied by Shawnee and Delawares. He wrote that Mrs. Conner spoke broken English and behaved like an Indian. Not surprisingly, the Conner boys were raised on the Ohio frontier like Indians. Before coming to Indiana they not only spoke fluently the Shawnee, Delaware, and Munsie dialects, but the language of the Chippewa and Wyandot as well. Married to Indian women, and having a familiarity with the dress, customs, and language of the Delawares, William and John Conner became very useful emissaries for General William H. Harrison, Governor of Indiana Territory and Superintendent of Indian Affairs as well as for the Indian agents employed by the War Department in their dealings with the Delawares.

Among the other Indian settlements on the White River was Killbuck's Village, settled at a later date than some of the neighboring towns. Located about a mile northeast of present Chesterfield, it was the home of one of Gelelemend's sons, Charles Henry Killbuck, who was converted by the Moravians in 1789. Nancy Town, about four miles overland from Anderson's Town in a northwesterly direction, was the home of James Nanticoke and a handful of Nanticoke Indians originally from southeastern Delaware and the eastern shore of Maryland. After leaving their homeland, the Nanticokes established a village on the Susquehanna as early as 1747, and from there the main body gradually moved up the river, finally settling in Canada under the protection of the Six Nations. James Nanticoke and his family on the White River were members of a small splinter group, and through intermarriage with the Delawares they eventually lost their tribal identity. Some of the Delaware families in Canada and Oklahoma are aware of Nanticoke increments, and some remember being told about witchcraft, which the Nanticoke practiced.

There was also a Delaware village on the White River called Tetepachksit's Town, and another called Hockingpomska's Town, named for two Delaware chiefs who, like Buckongahelas, were former residents of the Muskingum.[6] Tetepachksit, the traditionalist and former councilor of the Turtle group, had become the principal chief; and Hockingpomska ("hard walker"), Captain Pipe's and Big Cat's successor—who was called "a great witch doctor"—was a member of the Wolf group. In 1801, during their residence in Indiana, both chiefs were described as having grown old and venerable, wearing broad blue belts and silver collars and carrying turkey-wing brushes to switch at flies. Buckongahelas, observing Indian style, had a heavy piece of lead decorating each ear lobe which caused the skin tissue to stretch so far he could put it in his mouth.[7]

Buckongahelas died in 1805, after having urged the Delawares not to forsake their ancient customs but to live as their fathers did before them, and never, as he had warned the converts at Gnadenhütten, to trust the white man. Captain Amochk (in German, "Beaver") succeeded him, but he was a weak man addicted to alcohol. "If I see it," he once said, "I have to drink it."[8] He lacked the character and the judgment to become a leader of the tribe, and Chief Anderson's stature grew following Buckongahelas's death, although he did not actually become the principal chief until after the death of Tetepachksit. Anderson, like his predecessors Beaver and Shingas, was a member of the Turkey group. A Moravian pastor living on the White River wrote of Anderson, "He was a half-breed who belonged to a certain family by that name at the ferry at Harrisburg. He was not inclined, however, to Christianity, but sought to make his people averse to it."[9] The chief was later described as "the son of Mr. Anderson by a Delaware woman, who resided prior to the Revolutionary

War, below Harrisburg on the Susquehanna, and gave name to the ferry long within my remembrance called 'Anderson's Ferry.' " [10]

The Moravians eagerly sought the opportunity to regain the respect and affection of the Delawares, and they took advantage of an invitation their Indian converts had received from the Delaware Great Council on the White River. Apparently the members of the Council wanted to draw together any Christian Delawares remaining on the Tuscarawas, with the objective of bringing together all scattered members of the tribe. Although the Moravian pastors were not included in the invitation, they nevertheless accompanied thirteen Delawares, five of whom were children, to Indiana Territory. There they established a mission town on the east bank of the West Fork of the White River about three miles east of what is now Anderson. The mission, called Woapimintschi ("chestnut tree"), was in existence from May, 1801, until September of 1806, and the diary notes of one of the missionaries, John Peter Kluge, provide important information about the status of the Delawares in Indiana during this five-year period when they were seized with strong desires to revert to old Indian customs.

Kluge wrote that the Delawares continued to be divided into three groups—Turtle, Turkey, and Wolf—each with its own chief and its own captain or captains. He added that, "These deliberate together as circumstances demand it on the welfare of their nation." [11] No longer were the Moravian pastors permitted to share in these deliberations in the Great Council where Zeisberger and his associates had been able to influence the decisions at Coshocton. In the aftermath of the Revolution there had been a complete change in Indian attitude, and the Delawares had become openly hostile to the Moravian Church; and, by the time they settled on the White River, a strong non-Christian faction had ascended to power and there was opposition to all Christian missionaries.

The soil along the White River was well suited to agriculture. Along with the indigenous Indian crops planted in the fields at Woapimintschi, the Moravian pastors tried to teach the handful of Delawares that could be lured to their mission how to raise turnips, cucumbers, beets, and kohlrabi. The pastors built log cabins as residences for their own families and the Indian converts; but, as part of their return to nativism, most Delawares were living in bark huts. A few built homes of notched logs, as they had done in Ohio, in imitation of the Moravian cabins, but they did not construct chimneys, merely leaving a hole in the roof to vent the smoke as in their traditional bark wigwams. Living in an environment where the Indians were making a deliberate effort to break away from white influences on their culture, the Moravians were subject to annoyance and harassment, which became intolerable, forcing them to abandon the mission as a failure.

In the meantime, General Harrison as the chief executive of the territory was doing his utmost to encourage the Delawares and other tribes to raise cattle and cultivate large tracts of land like white farmers. Harrison was assisted by the United States Indian Agency established at Fort Wayne, where the personnel were supposed to help him carry out national policies. Among the agents appointed by the War Department to handle the affairs of the Delawares (also the Miami, Wea, Eel River, and some Potawatomi), the best known was John Johnston, a twenty-seven-year-old Scotch-Irishman named as agent or factor in 1802 at a salary of $1,000 per year and three rations per day. In addition to implementing Governor Harrison's instructions, the agent received orders from the War Department, relating to the functions of the agency, to grant licenses to traders, pay annuities, hold councils with the Indians as the intermediary between them and the government, and furnish the natives with useful domestic animals, farm implements, goods, and money, when deemed proper by the President.

Through the combined efforts of Harrison's office and the Indian Agency, the Indians were offered farm implements, plows, and oxen at reasonable prices, and men were sent to teach them how to fence their cultivated fields, the expenses to be deducted from the Indian annuities. The Delawares continued to resist building fences, and the Indian women shunned the use of the plow, continuing to use hand hoes and digging sticks to prepare the earth for seeds. When governmental pressures increased for the adoption of more efficient agricultural methods, the Delaware chiefs talked over the situation, and one of them told the others, "This time we have to agree to the proposition, for they continue to bring up the matter and give us no rest. If we agree they will say no more about it." [12]

The Delaware men were not ready to give up their activity in the woods and along the streams to allow the white men to turn them into dirt farmers to do the work of their women. They had neither the inclination nor the ambition to develop large farms—nor to work to accumulate wealth—and they quietly ignored the pressures to cultivate the land and raise herds of cattle. This had been the downfall of the Christian Delawares on the Tuscarawas whose burnt bones were rotting at Gnadenhütten. There was an abundance of fur-bearing animals in the woods bordering the White River, including deer, bear, wild cat, panther, fox, otter, beaver, squirrel, rabbit, and raccoon; and traders were still willing to buy pelts. It is true that prices had declined. In 1802 the traders paid only $1.00 for a deerskin, $1.50 to $2.00 for a bear pelt, $4.00 for an otter skin, and $1.00 for a pound of beaver hair.[13] Even so, the Delawares persisted in following their old-time custom of going into the woods each fall to hunt and trap, although when they returned the traders wrangled with them over the reduced prices offered for peltries.

The well-watered country along the West Fork, with such tributaries as Duck Creek, Pipe Creek, and Buck Creek, was more like their homeland along the coastal plain of southern New Jersey and Delaware than any place the Delawares had lived since leaving the Delaware River Valley a hundred years before. Nevertheless, they were not happy in their Indiana homes, and there were reasons for their discontent other than the government's determined effort to make farmers of them. Uncertainty over the ownership of the lands they were living on gave them a feeling of insecurity, particularly as the increasing white population got uncomfortably close. Squatters, expecting that government lands would be offered for sale at low prices as soon as Indian title was extinguished, settled in Indiana Territory and later claimed preemptive rights, which the United States recognized. There was land speculation by both individuals and syndicates, and large quantities of land were sold for as little as $2.00 per acre and even less. Revolutionary soldiers were also given western lands as a bonus for their services, bringing added pressures on the Indians.

General Harrison's instructions were to treat the Indians patiently in the hope of civilizing them, but if that failed to remove them beyond the Mississippi. As a result of a conference he held at Vincennes on September 17, 1802, with chiefs of the Potawatomi, Kickapoo, Eel River, Kaskaskia, Wea, and Piankashaw, a wave of resentment against the United States government spread through the tribes. The Delawares and Miami decided to take their complaints directly to President Jefferson; and in December, Tetepachsit, Buckongahelas, and other Delaware chiefs appeared before the President in Washington. Their principal grievance was that white settlers were encroaching on land that belonged to the Indians. The Indians said they had not signed any treaties permitting white families to settle on their territories.

On June 7, 1803, at a conference at Fort Wayne, General Harrison put such strong pressure on the Indians in attendance that the Miami, Kickapoo, Potawatomi, Eel River, Wea, Piankashaw, and Shawnee chiefs formally agreed to cede the lands discussed at the Vincennes conference. Notwithstanding their earlier protests to the President, the Delaware chiefs also put their marks on the treaty the other chiefs had signed in 1802, and a large tract of Indiana land, including a valuable salt-lick springs, came into United States possession.

Following the Fort Wayne treaty, which, in effect, ratified the Vincennes agreement, Harrison negotiated four separate treaties with the Indians for the cession of more of their land in Indiana. Congress passed the act of March 26, 1804, for the government of the Louisiana Territory, Section 15 of which authorized the President to give the Indians land west of the Mississippi in exchange for land they were then occupying east of the river. It was some years before this was put into effect, but Harrison was making a good start. One negotiation of immediate concern was consummated with the Delawares on August 18, 1804, at Harrison's home near Vincennes called "Grouseland." According to the terms of this treaty, the Delawares ceded to the United States certain lands between the Ohio and Wabash rivers. Harrison was aware that the Piankashaw obstinately refused to recognize the Delawares as proprietors of any lands in Indiana; and, to eliminate their objections, on August 27 he obtained the Piankashaw's release for the identical property.[14] By buying off both Indian groups, Harrison was reasonably certain the government would have legal title that the Indians could not later challenge. His mission in life at this time seems to have been to win the Midwest from the natives, and by the close of the year 1805 he had persuaded the Indians to cede more than 56 million acres to the United States.

When news of the 1804 transaction with the Delawares reached the ears of the Miami chiefs, they were angered. They said the Delawares had been given permission to live along the White River but had no authority to sell land there—or anywhere else in Indiana Territory. The Delawares, "for the sake of peace and good neighborhood," agreed to cancel the sale and released the government from the payment stipulated in the instrument. Pastor Kluge noted in his diary on September 17, 1805, that the Delaware chiefs were hurt for the following reason:

. . . the Delaware nation has no land of its own any more. The fact was announced to them at a recent gathering of chiefs from the Twitwees [Miami], Pottawottamis and other nations in Post Vincennes. The lands along the White River where we and they live, were therefore, taken away from them.[15]

Kluge was probably unaware that the Delawares never owned any land on the White River, and were living there only by sufferance of the Miami. He went on to say that some of the younger Delawares were threatening to leave the main body and go west beyond the Mississippi, because they were proud and didn't want to be dependent upon the charity of neighboring Indians for land to live and hunt on. A new demand was developing for buffalo skins. The young hunters knew that vast herds of buffalo roamed the western plains, some even coming as far east as Indiana Territory; but older and wiser men persuaded them not to leave.

Later the Miami did an about-face, and in an important treaty with General Harrison on September 20, 1809, they acknowledged the equal rights of the Delawares as co-owners of the country watered by the White River. During this negotiation the Indians transferred additional lands in Indiana to the United States (the bounds are not relevant to the story of the Delawares), for which they were given goods amounting to $5,200. The Delawares received a proportionate share of these goods, and Chief Anderson was one of the signatories; after making his mark on the document he also made a mark for Hockingpomska who, like Tetepachksit, was absent. By the terms of the treaty the Delawares, Miami, and Potawatomi were each guaranteed *"forever more"* an annuity of $500 each, and the Eel River Indians $250.[16] This was in addition to other annuities the Indians were then receiving.

The intemperate use of alcohol continued to debase the Delawares, even though an Act of Congress on March 30, 1802, empowered the President to take whatever measures appeared expedient to prevent or restrain the sale of intoxicants to Indians. Harrison did his best to prohibit the liquor traffic in Indiana Territory by issuing a strongly worded proclamation on October 24, 1802, and the traders were so apprehensive of losing their licenses that they stopped transporting whiskey to Indian towns. But the Delawares themselves were so intent on obtaining hard liquor that they went long distances, bought it surreptitiously, and transported it in quantity by pack horses back to their towns.

When the annuities were paid in Fort Wayne, the traders knew that hundreds of Indians with parched throats would converge there from the native towns. A contemporary observer explains how the traders sold liquor but escaped the arm of the law: Prior to paying the annuities, the traders hid kegs of whiskey in the woods beyond the town limits. When the Indians received their annuities—blankets, clothing, and so forth—they sold this much-needed merchandise for cash, paid the traders at the exorbitant rate of two dollars per pint, and then went into the woods, as directed, to find the liquor cached there for them.[17]

Hockingpomska became a drunkard, and, instead of setting an example for the young men of the tribe, he became an illicit dealer and sold whiskey to them. Some of the Delaware women also engaged in the liquor traffic, and there are accounts of quantities up to one hundred gallons being transported to a Delaware town on the White River and consumed by the occupants in one night of noisy revelry. Like many other Indians, the Delawares drank and drank until the supply was exhausted or they fell down, paralyzed. On one occasion some Delawares carried eighty gallons of whiskey to one of their towns, and, since there were only a few men present when the liquor arrived, intemperate squaws consumed it all.[18]

The Moravian missionaries not only had great difficulty winning converts; the few whom they converted to Christianity, after promising to abstain, often ran away from the mission to join their non-Christian brethren in revelry when a shipment of whiskey arrived.

The Baptist minister Isaac McCoy, who, like the Moravian missionaries, settled on the White River in the hope of Christianizing the Delawares, paints a sordid picture of the effect of alcohol on his potential converts.[19] On a trip to Vincennes he found Billy Killbuck and two other Delawares in jail for having killed a white man while they were drunk.[20] McCoy and others living in the vicinity of Fort Wayne formed a society whose aim was to prevent the Indians from obtaining liquor. The success of the society, McCoy later wrote, was "not equal to the kindness of its resolutions," because one individual who refused to join continued to supply liquor illegally to the Indians, and it was not long until others followed his example.[21] While censuring the Indians for drunkenness, the whites continued to make whiskey available to them and, in fact, encouraged them to consume it in large quantities.

The Delawares never forgot the Gnadenhütten massacre, and some families on the White River were still grieving over close relatives murdered by Williamson's militiamen. The belief was widely held that the Moravian missionaries at Gnadenhütten made the Indians "tame" in order to soften them for destruction and, after taming them, summoned the American soldiers to kill them. When the Moravian mission was established on the White River, news went from one Delaware village to another that these missionaries were also under orders from the United States government to tame the Delawares and that those foolish enough to accept Christianity would soon be "knocked in the head." Chief Tetepachksit came forward to lend the weight of his office to this accusation. He said he had known more than one Indian who had been dead for a day or longer and had come back to life to tell about the world after death. These persons told him, he assured his listeners, that they saw no Indians in hell—only white people! [22] Hockingpomska and Chief Anderson, who also opposed the Moravians, were responsible for encouraging strong nativistic feelings and noninvolvement in the white man's world.

The White River flooded its banks a number of times during Delaware occupancy of Indiana, which further convinced the chiefs that the Spirit Forces were not happy that the Indians were imitating the way of life of the whites. In 1806 high waters washed out the cornfields and scattered the oak rails from fences built by General Harrison's workmen to protect the Indians' crops. Delaware medicine men interpreted this disaster as a warning from Kee-shay-lum-moo-kawng that Indians should not live like white farmers. With crops scarce that year, hunger was felt in all Delaware towns, and the Delawares saw this famine as another evil omen to punish them for deserting native institutions. Their shaman told them that if they returned to their old ways their corn would thrive and not be injured by worms and frost, and the deer and other game would return.

The most disturbing influence that caused unrest among the Delawares was the appearance in Indiana Territory of the notorious shaman, the one-eyed Tenskwatawa ("the open door"), brother of the Shawnee chief Tecumseh. The "Prophet," as he was known to Indians and whites alike, claimed that while in a trance he had been conducted to the land beyond the grave where he was introduced to the mysteries of the Spirit World. He insisted he could read the thoughts of other men, see what was in a person's heart as well as his face, lift the veil from past and future—and perform supernatural feats. The Prophet was a magnetic personality. When he preached about his visions in the Delaware White River towns, he drew large crowds of listeners eager to hear his condemnation of the ways of the white man.

The Prophet taught that Indians should shave their heads and live as warriors did in the olden days; that they should stop caring for cattle and raise only horses; that Indian women should cease intermarrying with white men; that white man's clothing should be discarded, and the Indians return to their native garb and face paint; that there were plenty of deer underground to feed and clothe the Indians, and they would be made to come forth by the Creator as soon as the Prophet's teachings were observed. He preached against the use of whiskey, and warned that those who drank it would be tormented after death with pains of fire, and consumers of this evil "firewater" would give forth flames from their mouths. He convinced the Delawares that many of their people who had died in recent years had been bewitched by members of the tribe who had either poisoned them or destroyed them by applying supernatural power. The guilty ones must be found, he maintained, and put to death by fire, or the tribe would be slowly destroyed by their malevolence. In the Delaware Indian world of anxiety, insecurity, and frustration, at a time of a strong nativistic trend, the Prophet was a religious revivalist who gave the Indians something to cling to. His preachings were more in keeping with native cosmology than the theology of the Moravians and Baptists, and the Indians followed him blindly.

The Prophet's incredible power over his listeners is illustrated by the cruel way in which he excoriated some of the old Delaware chiefs, alienating them from their followers. He accused both Tetepachksit and Hockingpomska of practicing black arts on their people, and he turned the Delawares against their two aged leaders. Tetepachksit was struck on the head with a tomahawk by the son of his first wife, who was under the spell of the Prophet and who had long resented his father's taking two wives. The old chief was then thrown half alive into an open fire, where he burned to death in front of his people. Hockingpomska would have suffered death in the same manner, but at the last minute some of his close friends rescued him.[23] The Prophet also inflamed the other migrant Indiana tribes by his teachings, and Governor Harrison, learning that "black clouds were rising," sent messages to the Indians denouncing the Prophet and scolding them for listening to him. This had little effect on the Delawares, some of whom sent the Prophet strings of wampum and bribes of silver and cows in the expectation that their lives would be spared by offering these tributes.[24]

In the meantime, Tecumseh was traveling from the Great Lakes to Florida, and west to the Missouri, speaking in Indian councils in an attempt to win support for his cause. One of the most extraordinary Indians who ever lived, Tecumseh was a man of brains and ingenuity whose ambition was to unite the Indians against the usurpation of their lands by the whites. Like White Eyes and Joseph Brant, both of whom envisioned an almost identical concept, Tecumseh's aim was to weld the Indian tribes into a great confederacy occupying a separate Indian state located somewhere between Canada and the United States. Tecumseh underestimated the power and drive of American nationalism, which would not have tolerated an enclave of red men in the center of a white society, and he overestimated the feasibility of unifying the Indian tribes under one banner. Although he was treated with dignity and respect by General Harrison and others, Tecumseh's ideas were rejected by the United States government and indifferently received by many of the Indian tribes, who were in fear of losing their own independence. The Indians he was able to rally to his cause were so outnumbered by the more than a million white Americans of arms-bearing age that he never could have attained his objective by force when diplomacy failed, although his brother the Prophet evidently felt otherwise.

In the spring of 1808, the Prophet started to bring together at his village on the upper Wabash near the junction of the Tippecanoe River a force of warriors who formed raiding parties and harassed the white settlers during the following months. They stole horses and other private property, and, furnished with guns and ammunition by the British, displayed such insolence and belligerency that, as time went on, General Harrison, in the interests of orderly government, could not permit the Prophet to continue unchallenged. He organized a force of eight or nine hundred men to march along the Wabash from Vincennes to the Prophet's town, hopeful that a display of military strength would dissuade the Prophet from further hostility. At the time Tecumseh, who might have recognized the futility of resisting Harrison, was on a journey to enlist the support of southern tribes to his cause. The Prophet scorned any effort at conciliation and insulted a delegation of Delaware chiefs sent by Harrison in a final effort to persuade the Prophet to lay down his arms. When Harrison's forces arrived in view of the Prophet's town, where his warriors had also gathered their women and children, an Indian appeared with a flag of truce. A parley followed between Harrison and the Indian delegates, who assured him they desired peace, solemnly promising to meet him in a council the following day to settle on terms.

Harrison's forces encamped overnight, but he wisely issued orders for his troops to sleep with their firearms at hand. Before daybreak the Indians attacked, led by White Loon. The Prophet had spent the night and spent the following morning on a hill behind the battle lines praying to the Great Spirit to assist his Shawnee braves and their allies. In the Battle of Tippecanoe on November 7, 1811, the Indians, numbering five to eight hundred, met a resounding defeat; Harrison's forces drove them from the Prophet's town and burned their huts to the ground.

The Delaware Council had voted not to support Tecumseh, and there were no Delawares sanctioned by the Council with the Prophet's forces at Tippecanoe, although there may have been a few impulsive young warriors looking for excitement who may have disregarded their elders. The military records indicate that one of Harrison's units marching up the Wabash was joined by several Delaware chiefs who told the officer in command that thirty young Delaware braves were on their way to assist the American forces.[25] The records are not clear as to whether they arrived in time for the engagement, which lasted only a few hours.

Having demonstrated their friendship by supporting the American cause, the Delawares continued to receive their annuities from the government, which would have been discontinued if they had become enemies. The goods distributed to them each year at Fort Wayne, valued anywhere from $1,600 to $1,800, consisted of powder, lead, gun flints, calico and linen, brass kettles, strouds and blankets dyed blue, knives, thread, vermilion face paint, scissors, rifles, and cotton shawls a yard square.

With the defeat of the Indian forces at Tippecanoe, Tecumseh's cause collapsed, and the uncommitted tribes, who were beginning to turn attentive ears to his idea of reviving the Indian confederacy, lost interest in his cause. The chiefs and war captains were realistic. They knew that the United States would offer strong military opposition to a continuation of Tecumseh's movement and that unless they were overtly aided by the British their cause would be hopeless. Nevertheless, the defeat at Tippecanoe tended to increase Indian resentment against the Americans, and the warriors waited for an opportunity to strike back again. Tecumseh and the Prophet withdrew into Canada, and when war between the United States and England was declared on June 18, 1812, Tecumseh was commissioned a brigadier-general in the English army and placed in command of Indian volunteers. Many of the braves from Indiana Territory joined his forces, their smoldering hatred now inflamed as they sought the opportunity to take American scalps. The British high command did not wholly approve of the Indian method of warfare and the atrocities committed by the warriors, but they closed their eyes to the savagery of their red allies.

The Delawares, Wyandot, Seneca, and Shawnee tried to hold a position of neutrality; wheras the Miami, Piankashaw, Chippewa, Ottawa, Wea, Eel River, Osage, Sauk, Fox, Kickapoo, Pawnee, and others took the side of the English. The Delawares did their utmost to induce their Miami hosts to remain neutral, but the latter took part in an attack on Fort Harrison and participated in the siege of Fort Wayne. Harrison, in retaliation, found it necessary to destroy Miami villages on the Mississinewa River to prevent the Miami from assembling hostile tribes and giving them assistance. This destruction of their homes drove the Miami into the arms of the British and further kindled their hatred of the Americans. They sent repeated messages to the Delawares urging them to join them in warring against the United States, as the Wyandot had done during the American Revolution, but the Delawares held to their neutrality. The influence of John Conner and his brother William, who were interpreters and witnesses in many treaty negotiations in which the Delawares were involved, is believed to have been an important factor in keeping the Delawares neutral.[26] Although Harrison deplored Indian brutality and actually had a low opinion of the Indians as soldiers, in the spring of 1813, apprehending a British invasion, he enlisted a number of Delawares, Wyandot, and Seneca in his forces. He was quoted as saying that the Delawares "ever performed with punctuality and good faith their engagements with the United States . . ."[27]

The Moravian Delawares whom Zeisberger had taken to Fairfield in Ontario in May, 1792, were the innocent victims of Harrison's forces when the British were retreating before the American advances. During their twenty-year sojourn on the Thames River, the Indians, under their Moravian teachers, built an oasis of peace and prosperity, erecting a shingle-roofed church of hewn logs, two hewn-log schoolhouses, two homes for the families of the missionaries, twenty-eight dwellings of hewn logs for Indian families, nineteen smaller log cabins, barns, smokehouse, stables, and other farm buildings.[28] They cleared hundreds of acres for farm fields, pastures, and orchards, and manufactured baskets, brooms, bowls, mats, benches, chairs, barrel staves, rifle stocks, and maple sugar boiled down from sap for sale in Detroit and elsewhere. Fairfield was an unusual community, having an Indian population that never exceeded two hundred, and its residents lived beyond the jurisdiction of British law, governed by the moral code of the Moravians, the precepts of the Gospel, and Indian custom. English towns grew up nearby, and, by the time the war broke out, the main road linking Niagara to Sandwich and Fort Malden on the Detroit River ran through Fairfield. Post riders from Niagara clattered into Fairfield to change to fresh mounts, and the town became a stopping place for visitors to and from Detroit. The Moravian pastors were always glad to receive travelers who brought news, and both white and Indian members of the community extended hospitality to visitors who stopped overnight on their journeys.

This hospitality proved to be the downfall of Fairfield, for British soldiers, including Brigadier-General Henry Procter, were garrisoned there as the English prepared to repulse the Americans, and the church and the larger of the schoolhouses were used temporarily as a hospital for English soldiers. Harrison's forces caught up with the retreating British east of Fairfield and defeated them in the Battle of the Thames, sometimes called the Battle of Moraviantown. Procter, in a hasty withdrawal from Fairfield, left behind in one of the missionary's houses, which he was using as his headquarters, several boxes of official army documents and military letters.[29] When the American forces entered the town, found these documents, and learned that the Indians had fled into the woods, allowing their houses to be occupied by British soldiers, Harrison decreed that Fairfield was an English garrison town and should be destroyed. The town was plundered of everything worth carrying away, and then the American soldiers set all the buildings afire, putting the first torch to the Moravian church. The missionaries and their families had been given prior notice that the town would be burned and were permitted to leave and join their Indian converts camped in the woods some miles away.

Tecumseh, who commanded a force of Indians, was killed in the Battle of the Thames, although it was never determined who fired the fatal shot. Colonel Richard M. Johnson, whose regiment of mounted Kentucky rangers made a spectacular and decisive frontal charge, was later given credit for the act. When he became Martin Van Buren's vice-presidential running mate in 1836, one of the campaign slogans went like this:

Rumpsey, dumpsey, rumpsey, dumpsey
Colonel Johnson killed Tecumseh [30]

The Prophet, incidentally, escaped the guns of the Americans, and after the war was given a pension by the English government for his services. He resided in Canada until 1826, when he returned to the United States. By that time most Americans had forgotten his exploits. He was living in Wyandotte County, Kansas, in 1832 when George Catlin painted his portrait, and he died there in 1837, still convinced that he was a shaman with a divine mission.

A separate volume could and should be written about the Delawares during their residence in Indiana Territory, since there are still untapped documentary sources pertaining to this approximately fifty-year period of Delaware Indian history. In the present volume space permits discussing only the highlights of each period as we trace the migratory route of the Delawares.

The defeat of the British and their Indian allies in the War of 1812 brought settlers from Pennsylvania, New York, Virginia, Kentucky, and North Carolina seeking western lands, and on December 11, 1816, the state of Indiana was admitted to the union. General Harrison had long before given up any hope of a part-Indian, part-white Indiana, and he knew that the Indians occupied the best-cleared land, which was the property the settlers wanted most. He also knew that, if the whites encroached on those lands, the Indians would be up in arms again to burn the homes and kill the intruders, and, as he saw the situation, the only practical solution to the problem was to get rid of the Indians.

Subsequent negotiations between the United States and the dozen or more Indian tribes or nations living in Indiana are too numerous and complicated to discuss here. Basically, the United States took the position that absolute right to the soil was vested in the government, and that American soldiers had shed their blood for the land acquired from Great Britain in the Treaty of Paris, which included Indiana Territory. The government also held that it alone owned the land between the Mississippi and the Rocky Mountains by right of the purchase from France at a cost of fifteen million dollars in public funds. As owner of these lands, the United States had the right to grant Indian tribes the privilege of occupancy through the instrument of formal treaties made by the President, with the "advice and consent" of the Senate. It made no difference to the government that the Indians claimed title to the same lands—even though, as in the case of Indiana Territory, the native occupants (like the Delawares) were newcomers to the territory, having disposed of their ancestral lands long before the United States of America had come into being.

When a tribe ceded its territory to the United States by formal treaty, the government inferred that the Indians sold only what they possessed, which was the *right of occupancy*. Title to the lands they sold, or the lands to which they removed, rested with the United States. As fiduciary wards of the government, therefore, the Indians owned no land themselves and thus could not transfer title to anyone else, since title rested with the power that held the jurisdiction. The only party to which the Indians could cede their land occupancy—and this legal philosophy continued to follow the Delawares as they went farther west—was to the United States. There was, of course, an inconsistency in the government's position when it paid the Indians to extinguish their occupancy right, because such payment tacitly admitted the validity of Indian ownership, which the government denied.

It would be untrue to say that the United States deliberately attempted to cheat the Delawares out of any of their lands. In retrospect, what happened in both Ohio and Indiana Territory was that the government, in good faith, assigned large tracts to the dispossessed tribes, fully expecting the Indians to be able to live there in peace. But as settlers pressed west of the Ohio River in increasing numbers, the government found itself under strong public pressure to remove the Indians and make way for white settlements. This meant simply that another place had to be found for the Indians to live and hunt. Harrison followed the repossession and relocation policy very successfully, and the Delawares were one of the many tribes caught in the movement.

This does not mean that the United States seized the land and then brutally drove the Indians away homeless—an American myth that has little foundation in fact. In return for lands ceded to the government, Harrison pledged the protection of the United States to the tribe or tribes involved, and typically agreed to pay cash or annuities, or both, supposed to be equal to the current value of the land. There were also agreements with some of the tribes whereby, in addition to paying for vacated lands and providing new territory for the Indians to settle on, the United States agreed to erect schools, hospitals, churches, gristmills, sawmills, and the like; to provide teachers, physicians, millers, blacksmiths; to furnish food, blankets, tobacco, farm implements, weapons, horses, and other domestic animals.

Following the War of 1812, commissioners appointed by President Madison called the Indian tribes together to establish peace and amity and settle claims of land ownership. The government generously pardoned the chiefs who had fought on the side of the British, and agreed to restore to them their stations and the property they enjoyed before the war. During the administration of President Monroe (1817–25), the policy of moving the Indians west of the Mississippi in accordance with the Act of March 26, 1804, began to take shape, but the government had a big job on its hands before this could be accomplished effectively. First, it was necessary to persuade the Indians to cede the lands they were occupying east of the Mississippi, and this required threats, cajolery, bribes, and all manner of intimidation, even though the Indians were paid for the territory they vacated.

The Delawares, along with other tribes, were signatories to a series of postwar treaties with the government covering the cession of lands.[31] Perhaps the most significant treaty involving the Delawares was held at Saint Marys, Ohio, on October 3, 1818, whereby the Delawares gave up their occupancy rights to Indiana. The Miami, by terms of the same treaty, ceded more than seven million acres in Indiana and Ohio to the United States, and other tribes claiming lands in Indiana also ceded their properties to the government. The Miami permitted the Delawares to participate in negotiations and share the purchase money. In addition to making payments for the lands the Indians were vacating, the government agreed to provide lands of at least equal worth west of the Mississippi.

Each of the numerous treaties contains provisions applying specifically to the individual tribes who were parties to the agreements. For instance, the government not only promised to provide the Delawares with suitable lands beyond the Mississippi, in exchange for the lands they were vacating, but to reimburse them in full for whatever improvements they had made on the lands they had been occupying along the White River. The government also agreed to give them a *perpetual annuity* of $4,000 in silver coin, in addition to the other annuities then being paid. In today's market this seems a small amount, but one must realize that, under the Land Act of 1820, the government was selling western lands to pioneer families and speculators for $1.25 per acre.

The United States allowed the Delawares three years in which to prepare for their removal from Indiana and from Piqua, Ohio, where agent John Johnston had gathered a large number of friendly tribes during the war. The government further agreed to supply the Delawares with 120 horses, suitable provisions, a sufficient number of pirogues to transport their families across the Mississippi, and also to provide and maintain a blacksmith for them at their new homes. As far back as the time they lived on the Susquehanna, the Delawares had demanded blacksmiths, because this was one of the European crafts for which Indians could not be easily trained, or perhaps they did not take to the work. The Treaty of 1818 also contained less important clauses dealing with payments made to individual Delaware claimants covering the costs of improvements made on the lands they were leaving.

The Delaware chiefs, captains, and great men who made their marks as signers of the 1818 treaty were "Kithteeleland or Anderson, Lapahnihe or Big Bear, James Nanticoke, Apacahund or White Eyes, Captain Killbuck, The Beaver, Netahopuna, Captain Tunis, Captain Ketchum, The Cat, Ben Beaver, The War Mallet, Captain Caghkoo, The Buck, Petchenanalas, John Quake, Quenaghtoothmait, and Little Jack." [32] (White Eyes and Killbuck were descendants of revolutionary leaders bearing these same names.)

Accounts of the meeting indicate that most of the chiefs, including Anderson, signed the treaty with much reluctance. Three years later agent Johnston explained in a letter to J. C. Calhoun, Secretary of War, how he and the commissioners appointed by Congress were able to get the signatures on the document of the two chiefs, Anderson and Lapinihile. (Although the latter's nickname was Big Bear, his Indian name is translatable as "one who must be killed twice.") They secretly agreed to pay Anderson and Lapinihile life annuities of $360 and $140, respectively. No record of this transaction was kept in official records because Johnston said "the personal safety of the Chiefs required the utmost secrecy." Apparently it would not have been healthy for the chiefs if other Delawares knew they were collecting money from the government.[33] With the business acumen that characterized most Delaware leaders, both chiefs forced Johnston to give them signed agreements guaranteeing the annuities, which they held in confidence. Neither was willing to trust the promises of white negotiators—and who can blame them?

At this time, before the removal across the Mississippi, there were probably about two thousand persons in the main body of Delawares living at Piqua and along the White River, but this figure by no means constituted the total Delaware Indian population in the United States and Canada. There were a number of separatist communities, such as the Moravian Delawares on the Thames in Ontario, who returned after General Harrison's forces withdrew; the Munsies, living at Muncy Town on the Thames above the Moravian group; and a third Canadian group of mixed Delawares, Mahican, and Munsies seated at the mouth of the Grand River under the protective wing of the Cayuga. There had also been about 150 Delawares who moved from Pennsylvania to Cattaraugus, New York, under the care of the Seneca, and they, too, in due course, made their way into Canada. The three Canadian groups may have represented a total Delaware population of one thousand or twelve hundred men, women, and children. In Wisconsin, a small group of the original New Jersey Brotherton Delawares, numbering less than one hundred, were living with the Stockbridge Indians. Along the Sandusky River in Ohio there still remained another small enclave of less than one hundred Delawares clinging to lands alloted them by the Wyandot, which the United States permitted them to occupy after the main body moved from Ohio. In 1829 the government signed a treaty paying them to abandon these lands and move west to join the main body. Among these Sandusky Delawares was a chief named Solomon Joneycake, whose descendants under the name Journeycake were later to become prominent leaders of the tribe in Kansas and Oklahoma.[34]

Finally, there was the faction of Delawares who moved to southeastern Missouri, with permission from the Spanish government, and were living on lands (in what is now Cape Girardeau County) assigned them by the Baron de Carondelet, the Spanish governor at Saint Louis, on January 4, 1793. As recorded in the office of the Recorder of Land Titles in Saint Louis, this land was, "East by the Mississippi river, west by White River, north by St. Come River and south by Cape Girardeau, equal to twenty five miles square." With the influx of white settlers, the Delawares left here in different parties between 1807 and 1815. Some settled temporarily in what is now Pope County, Arkansas, and others went to Texas.

Chief William Anderson proved an outstanding leader among the Delawares, and one who was much respected and admired by his people. Thomas Dean, a Quaker visitor who lodged overnight at Anderson's house on the White River in Indiana during the summer of 1817, described the chief, who was about six feet tall, as a "plain, majestic-looking man, sixty or sixty-five years old." [35] Dean was acting as an agent for the Stockbridge Indians then living in Madison and Oneida counties in New York state, who requested his assistance in finding a new home for them among their Delaware and Munsie kinfolk in Indiana. This was before the New Jersey Brothertons joined them. Although Chief Anderson and his councilors were willing to share their White River lands with the Stockbridge people and had, in fact, issued an invitation for them to come to Indiana, the Treaty of 1818 removed the Indiana lands from Indian control. The migration of the whole body of Stockbridges, as planned, had to be deferred, although some Stockbridge families came to the White River after the land had been sold to the United States.

Baptist minister Isaac McCoy also visited Chief Anderson's residence in Indiana on several occasions in 1818 and 1819. The chief apparently lived in a large log house, and McCoy on one of his visits found the Delaware Council meeting in the chief's residence. On another of McCoy's visits, the chief did his best to make the preacher comfortable and personally prepared food for him. The minister conversed with Anderson through a Negro who served as the chief's interpreter since Anderson was not fluent in the English language. The following is McCoy's direct quotation of Anderson's remarks relative to the lands in Indiana:

A little more than a year ago the United States agent advised us to adopt the habits of civilized life. At that time his word was very good; accordingly many of us procured cattle and hogs &c. Scarcely had we commenced this course, when we were asked to cede our lands to the white people. Some thing of this has been done; the white people now claim our country, and desire that we should leave it—and now we know not what to do. I think that the men who made the bargain with us have done wrong, and that they had not been authorized to purchase our country; and I hope the transaction will not be approved by Congress.[36]

Anderson was unaware not only that was Congress eager to approve any transaction that would result in moving the Indians farther west—but also that, to please their constituents, congressmen were putting pressure on the Commissioner of Indian Affairs to make haste in placing the Indians beyond the Mississippi. Anderson told the minister that he had dispatched a letter asking Congress "to send me a paper that will give us a sure title to the land to which we are going, so that the white people may no more disturb us." [37] The chief's concern about having a deed in fee simple for lands west of the Mississippi was premature, for at this time the government didn't know exactly where to seat the Delawares. Knowledge of the territory beyond the Mississippi was still incomplete, despite the report of Lewis and Clark, and the United States was apprehensive about possibly fomenting more Indian troubles by placing eastern Indians on land claimed by western tribes. This is exactly what was destined to happen, for, as the Delawares were pushed westward, they ran into conflict with their Indian brethren, the Pawnee and Osage, which added to their sorrows.

NOTES—CHAPTER 14

1. Kappler, *Indian Affairs*, vol. 2, pp. 39–45.

2. When Heckewelder revisited the Muskingum area in 1797, he wrote that "Tetepachkschi" was then Delaware chief; Paul A. W. Wallace, *Thirty Thousand Miles with John Heckewelder*, p. 336. During this unsettled period there appear to have been a number of changes in leadership. For example, in 1791 the Mahican chief Hendrick Aupaumut, sent by the United States to negotiate peace with the western tribes, refers in his journal to "Puckonchehluh" (Pachgantschihilas) as the "Head Heroe" of the Delawares. He also makes reference to the sachems "Tautpuhqtheet [Tetepachksit], Pohqueonnoppeet, and Big Cat," stating that he comforted Big Cat on the death of his brother, the previous spring, who had been the chief sachem of the Delawares; "A Narrative of an Embassy to the Western Indians," *Memoirs of the Historical Society of Pennsylvania*, Philadelphia, vol. 2, 1827, pt. 1; pp. 96, 98, 99, 105, 106.

3. American State Papers, vol. 1, p. 582; cf. Charles Elihy Slocum, *The Ohio Country Between the Years 1783 and 1815*, New York, 1910, p. 142.

4. Kappler, *Indian Affairs*, vol. 2, pp. 70–72; cf. p. 81.

5. This quotation appears in a letter written by Hendrick Aupaumut and Beaver to President Jefferson on December 12, 1808, partially quoted in chap. 12, p. 393, of a report prepared by Erminie Wheeler-Voegelin, Emily J. Blasingham, and Dorothy R. Libby, entitled *An Anthropological Report on the History of the Miamis, Weas, and Eel River Indians*, one of the documentary exhibits put before the Indian Claims Commission in the Delaware litigation over lands in Indiana, consolidated Dockets Nos. 15-H, 29-F, 307, 314, 137, 253, 131 (Defendant's exhibit no. 163). The complete deposition may be found in Gayle Thornbrough, ed., *Letter Book of the Indian Agency at Fort Wayne, 1809–1815*, Indiana Historical Society, 1961, pp. 53–54.

6. Information regarding the locations of Delaware towns has been taken largely from Charles N. Thompson, *Sons of the Wilderness, John and William Conner*, Indiana Historical Publications, vol. 12, Indianapolis, 1937; see notes to chap. 4.

7. Lawrence Henry Gipson, ed., *The Moravian Indian Mission on White River*, Indianapolis, 1938; pp. 107–8.

8. Ibid., p. 322.

9. Ibid., p. 608. In *Colonial Records*, vol. 6, p. 160, there is a 1754 reference to "William Anderson the Delaware." For evidenec of Chief Anderson's Turkey affiliation, see Rev. Jedidiah Morse, A *Report to the Secretary of War* . . . , New Haven, 1822, p. 110.

10. John Johnston, *Recollections of Sixty Years*, Dayton, Ohio, 1915; p. 45; cf. Grant Foreman, *The Last Trek of the Indians*, Chicago, 1946, p. 47, note 46. I am indebted to Mrs. Henry A. Secondine of Delaware, Oklahoma, for information that Marietta, Pa., is on the site of what was was known as Anderson's Ferry.

11. Lawrence Henry Gipson, ed., *The Moravian Indian Mission*, pp. 166–67. The Moravian pastors indicated there were eleven Delaware towns on the White River in 1801 and nine in 1802; ibid., pp. 104, 476. This contradicts a notion expressed in some historical sources that the Delawares had only six villages on the White River.

12. Ibid., p. 297.

13. Ibid., p. 484.

14. Kappler, *Indian Affairs*, vol. 2, pp. 101–2. General Harrison had also negotiated a treaty the previous year, on June 7, 1803, at which time the Delawares were present and the lands allotted the Indians were redefined. All treaties in which the Delawares participated can be found in this source.

15. Gipson, *Moravian Indian Mission*, p. 544.

16. Kappler, *Indian Affairs*, vol. 2, pp. 101–2.

17. Harlow Lindley, ed., *Indiana as Seen by Early Travellers*, Indiana Historical Commission, Indianapolis, 1916, p. 249.

18. Gipson, *Moravian Indian Mission*, p. 158.

19. Isaac McCoy, *History of the Baptist Indian Missions*, Washington, D.C. (printed by P. Force), 1840, p. 59; cf. pp. 57–58.

20. Ibid., p. 55

21. Ibid., p. 144.

22. Gipson, *Moravian Indian Mission*, p. 406.

23. Ibid., pp. 415, 420.

24. Ibid., pp. 420, 421. Cf. Harrison's speeches to Delawares in Logan Esarey, ed., *Governors Messages and Letters: Messages and Letters of William Henry Harrison*, 2 vols., *Indiana Historical Society Collections*, vols. 7 and 9, 1922.

25. *John Tipton Papers*, Indiana Historical Society Collections, 1942, vol. 24, p. 70. For an eyewitness account of the parley before the battle, see "The Battle of Tippecanoe—as described by Judge Isaac Naylor, a Participant," *Indiana Magazine of History*, vol. 2, no. 4, December, 1906, pp. 163–69; cf. Alec R. Gilpin, *The War of 1812 in the Old Northwest*,

East Lansing, 1958, p. 13, wherein the Delawares try to dissuade Prophet from attacking.

26. Thompson, *Sons of the Wilderness*, p. 83. Harrison temporarily moved some of the Delawares from the White River to Shawnee towns on the Auglaize River in Ohio to protect them from whites who had turned against all Indians; ibid., p. 64. Other Delawares, including Chief Anderson, moved temporarily to Piqua, Ohio; ibid., p. 66. In the spring of 1813, John Johnston had 10,000 Indians under his care at Piqua, where the government had placed them to keep them from joining hostile tribes; Charlotte Reeve Conover, *Concerning the Forefathers (Col. Robert Patterson and Col. John Johnston)*, Dayton, Ohio, 1902, p. 50. Cf. Thornbrough, ed., Letter Book of the Indian Agency, p. 202, fn. 96, in which agent Johnston reported on August 3, 1813, that 200 Delaware and Shawnee joined Harrison's forces.

27. Ibid., pp. 75, 64. For details on Miami participation in the war, see Bert Anson, *The Miami Indians*, Norman, Okla., 1970.

28. Elma E. Gray and Leslie Robb Gray, *Wilderness Christians*, Toronto, 1956; see p. 337 for a complete list of buildings destroyed by the Americans.

29. Ibid., p. 239.

30. Samuel Eliot Morison, *The Oxford History of the American People*, New York, 1965, p. 454. See Gray, *Wilderness Chronicle*, p. 236, for information that the Indians secretly buried Tecumseh in the hollow of an upturned tree and visited the grave annually thereafter to conduct secret rites.

31. See R. C. Adams, *A Brief History of the Delaware Indians*, Senate Document no. 501, 59th Congress, 1st session, 1906, pp. 65–66, for list of Delaware treaties, although Adams omitted the important Greenville Treaty of 1795. For an excellent summary of the government's Indian policies, see Francis Paul Prucha, *American Indian Policy in the Formative Years*, Cambridge, Mass., 1962.

32. Kappler, *Indian Affairs*, vol. 2, pp. 170–71.

33. The complete letter dated October 22, 1821, is quoted verbatim by Richard C. Adams, *A Delaware Indian Legend and the Story of Their Troubles*, Washington, D.C., 1899, pp. 43–45.

34. On August 3, 1829, the United States entered into a treaty with the Delawares still residing on a three-mile-square tract on the Sandusky River, reserved to them by a treaty of Sept. 29, 1819. Under terms of the new treaty, the Delawares agreed to move west to join the main body and were given $3,000 in cash, and horses, clothing, and provisions for the journey. Signatories were "Capt. Pipe, William Matacur, Capt. Wolf, Eli Pipe, Solomon Joneycake, Joseph Armstrong, George Williams";

Kappler, *Indian Affairs*, vol. 2, pp. 303–4. Cf. *American State Papers*, vol. 1, *Indian Affairs*, *1789–1814*, Washington, D.C., 1832, p. 744 for reference to the Delawares living in two towns on the Sandusky, ten miles apart, with the population as of 1806 reduced to 47–50 men.

35. Paul Weer, "Thomas Deans and the Delaware Towns," *Proceedings of the Indiana Academy of Science*, 1946, vol. 56, p. 29. In 1821, John Johnston wrote that Anderson was aged sixty and Lapanihile fifty; see his letter to Calhoun in Adams, A *Delaware Indian Legend*, pp. 43–45.

36. McCoy, *Baptist Indian Missions*, pp. 52–53; cf. p. 58. John Johnston wrote in 1819 that the Delawares were more opposed to the Gospel and to the white people than any other Indians with whom he was acquainted; "Account of the Present State of the Indian Tribes Inhabiting Ohio," letter from Johnston to Caleb Atwater, in *Transactions and Collections of the American Antiquarian Society*, Worcester, Mass., 1820, p. 271. Note also, on p. 270, that Johnston stated that in October 1819 there were 29 Delaware men, 21 women, and 30 children on the Upper Sandusky.

37. McCoy, *Baptist Indian Missions*, p. 59. Inventories of merchandise on hand and quantities of pelts obtained from the Delawares in Indiana are given in the "Col. John Johnston Indian Agency Account Book, 1802–1811," pp. 405–663 of *Fort Wayne: Gateway of the West*, Historical Bureau of the Indiana Library and Historical Department, Indianapolis, 1927. As the factor, Johnston bartered with the Indians on behalf of the government, not for profit, but to serve their needs and to keep them from contact with British traders.

15

From Missouri to Kansas

The Delawares were one of twenty or twenty-five Indian nations or tribes (both terms were used interchangeably in government documents) who were swept west of the Mississippi in an uncoordinated series of migration waves. During their movements the Indians were supervised by representatives of a young government who had no experience in transplanting groups of people. At this time the military were in charge of Indian affairs, a continuation of the colonial policy wherein the suppression of hostilities and the regulation of trade were the chief concerns of the Continental Congress. Army officers, such as Hand, McIntosh, Brodhead, Wayne, Harrison, Clark, and Cass, negotiated with the Indians until a separate Indian agency was set up in the War Department in 1824. In 1832 the office of Commissioner of Indian Affairs was created within the War Department; but not until 1849, when the Department of the Interior was established, was the administration of Indian affairs transferred from military to civilian control.

While the Delawares were living in Indiana, the Secretary of War bore the full responsibility for Indian matters, and although some civilian agents and subagents were employed in Washington and in the field offices, the philosophy of the military continued to be reflected in the administration of the department. Before Ohio and Indiana were rid of "the Indian menace" the representatives of the War Department held numerous separate conferences with the tribal leaders. Between 1778 and 1830, for instance, the Delawares were party to sixteen separate treaties, and after 1830 they signed a number of others. This was no exception—eighteen separate treaties were negotiated with the Potawatomi prior to 1830, and about seventeen more after 1830. Wyandot, Miami, Piankashaw, Kickapoo, Shawnee, and others participated in countless treaty negotiations with the War Department. Most of these treaties had to do with giving up lands east of the Mississippi in exchange for lands farther west. The negotiations were often argumentative, because, in general, the Indians resisted the government's insistence that they uproot themselves and find new homes. When negotiators from the War Department were confronted with stubborn chiefs, slow in yielding to the blandishments of the government, the threat of a discontinuance of tribal annuities—or the application of military force—usually elicited their reluctant cooperation.

The fact that the Indians were compensated for lands they ceded to the government, and given new lands gratis on which to settle (for which the government had to pay the western tribes residing on those lands in order to extinguish title) did not lessen the hardship and inconvenience. With their family life disrupted, the Indians had to travel over unfamiliar trails, suffering many privations, as they sought new homes in strange territory. Some owned horse-drawn vehicles in which they transported their families; others crowded their wives and children into farm wagons hired by the government for their use; many went on horseback, and some walked. Blankets, clothing, furs, and bedding were packed in haphazard fashion, usually piled in wagons already overloaded with broadaxes, adzes, augurs, chisels, saws, and other tools, bags and barrels of sweet corn and beans, sacks of peachstones, and other vegetable and fruit seeds. When they reached the new location their livelihood would depend upon the crops they could raise and the wild animals they could kill. The aged and infirm, who were least inclined to leave their homes, usually constituted a special problem, and sometimes they almost had to be carried off bodily.

Some of the Indians, like the contingent of fifty-eight Delawares who had been living on reserved land along the Sandusky River (and a large party of Seneca who accompanied them), were afraid of boarding a steamboat. This group, which included a Delaware named Solomon *Joneycake*, as his name was spelled in the government records, rode overland all the way to Saint Louis on horseback.[1] No matter what means of transportation was used, the pace was slow and painful, and weeks, sometimes months, were required for the Indian families to reach their destinations due to rains, windstorms, and heavy snows. Many of the children died en route from epidemics of measles and undiagnosed diseases, while others suffered from frozen fingers and toes, as well as malnutrition, during the winter. Sickness often delayed a party. They were forced to set up temporary camps, and during the delay they used up all the food, and families went hungry.

In the summer of 1820, 1,346 Delawares from Indiana and their 1,499 horses were taken across the Mississippi River via the boat ferry at Kaskaskia, Illinois, by Pierre Menard, an Indian subagent who was responsible for moving groups of Indians across the river. Because the ferry could carry only a limited number of people and horses at one time, many trips back and forth were required to transport the large contingent across the river. In the confusion, white thieves stole thirteen of the Indians' horses.[2] This was not a rare incident—stealing horses from migrating Indians was a common occurrence. The thieves were seldom apprehended, because the animals were not branded, and the Indians had difficulty proving legal ownership. In fact, they did not even have rights as American citizens.

Crossing the Mississippi was an ordeal for the women and children, as well as for the old men and women, many of whom had never seen a boat, and they were frightened by the swift-flowing current. Depending upon the number of persons and animals to be carried, some had to camp on the east bank for several days while waiting their turn. After finally getting across the river, one of the groups of Delawares decided to camp along the Current River, which flows through Carter and Shannon counties in Missouri. The women dug up the earth along the river banks and planted their seed corn, hopeful of raising food to carry with them, but the young plants were killed by an early frost. Hunger and sickness followed, and during this trying period even Chief Anderson was taken ill. A large number of Delawares were still camped on the Current River in July and August of 1822, when the government paid the annuities. Another group from the White River in Indiana were delayed by illness before reaching the Mississippi, and were forced to spend the winter of 1820–21 near Vincennes, badly in need of food.

One of the family groups which had left Indiana in the fall of

1821 with Chief Anderson included his daughter Mekinges, wife of William Conner, and their six children, John, Nancy, Harry (or Hamilton), James, William, and Eliza. William Conner knew that his squaw belonged with her tribe and must go where her people went, and that, according to custom, Delaware children went with their mother. It was a sad parting when the white father bid good-bye to his dusky wife and children, and gave a parting handshake to his nephew, the half-Indian son of John Conner, who accompanied them.[3] William Conner was generous with his wife and children at the time of their departure, giving her money and a herd of ponies which they drove ahead of them. Conner later married again—this time his wife was a white woman who wed him in a Christian ceremony, and who gave him seven sons and three daughters. At the time of his death in 1855, aged eighty-two, William Conner was a well-to-do Indiana businessman who had served several terms in the state legislature.

The records are silent as to whether Conner ever saw Mekinges and his half-Indian children again, but he probably would have been proud that his progeny became prominent members of the Delaware Nation. His son John was made the principal Delaware chief about 1858. His daughter Eliza married into the Bullitt (Bullet, Bulette) family, and Nancy Conner's grandson, Richard C. Adams, became noted for his speeches and articles relating to the Delawares. Mekinges, who lived to an old age, is believed to have married into the Ketchum family, although there is some doubt about this. She died a much-respected matron among her people in Oklahoma.

The separate migratory groups, constituting the main body of the Delawares, converged by prearrangement on the James River, then called James Fork, a tributary of the White River in Missouri. This stream, not to be confused by the river of the same name in Indiana, was selected for their occupancy by the territorial governor, General William Clark, former cocaptain of the Lewis and Clark expedition. The tract General Clark assigned to the Delawares, which they had not seen in advance, was described as extending seventy miles from east to west, forty-four miles to the south, and this area now includes the present counties of Barry and Stone, and parts of Christian, Greene, and Lawrence.[4] The main Delaware settlement, known as Anderson's Village or simply Delaware Village, was located on James Fork near Wilson's Creek in the northwest part of Christian County.

Typical of Indian communities, it extended haphazardly up and down the river bank, with the cornfields planted by the Indians lying between their cabins and the river. There were also scattered areas of occupation elsewhere on both the James Fork and Wilson's Creek, each housing Indian families having kinship ties.

The infusion of white blood continued during the period of Delaware occupancy of Missouri. William Gillis, a white trader, who is said to have had three Delaware wives—not at one time but successively—and his business partner, Joseph Philabert, kept a trading post at the main Delaware village. Another trader, William Marshall, had a Delaware wife; and James Wilson, who also did business with the Indians, is said to have had three Delaware wives at different times.[5] In the white man's society these were known as common-law marriages, since no formal civil ceremony took place, and no license was issued, which makes it next to impossible to ascertain the names of the Indian spouses and their children. Some of the white traders believed it was good for their business to have as a wife a member of the tribe with whom they traded, whereas a true affection existed between others and their Indian mates.

The James Fork, chief tributary of the White River, rises in the Ozarks, and when the Delawares settled along its banks, the surrounding country was rough, hilly, and densely forested. The alluvial bottom land on the margins of both the James Fork and the White River was fertile but subject to severe flooding in the spring and summer when the snows in the mountains melted. The White River was named because of the transparency of its waters, and the French called it *la rivière au Blanc*, a translation of its Indian name. In 1818, explorer and ethnologist Henry R. Schoolcraft visited the White River where he found large numbers of bear, elk, deer, beaver, raccoon, duck, geese, brant, and wild turkey,[6] but white and Indian hunters in search of pelts soon devastated the game. By the time the Delawares arrived along the James, there were scarcely enough animals on the lands set aside for them to provide meat for their families. They needed to take pelts in order to purchase clothing and other supplies for their families, and were soon in such distress that Chief Anderson, Black Beaver, and Natcoming (one of the former band captains of the Cape Girardeau Delawares who joined Chief Anderson) addressed a pathetic letter to General Clark in February, 1824, reading in part as follows:

Last summer a number of our people died just for want of something to live on . . . We have got in a country where we do not find all as stated to us when we was asked to swap lands with you and we do not get as much as was promised us at the treaty of St. Marys neither . . . Father— We did not think That big man would tell us things that was nor true [Jonathan Jennings, Lewis Cass, and Benjamin Parke were the commissioners at the Saint Mary's Treaty]. We have found a poor hilly stony country and the worst of all no game to be found on it to live on. Last summer our corn looked very well until a heavy rain come on for 3 or 4 days and raised the waters so high that we could just see the tops of our corn in some of the fields, and it destroyed the greatest part of our corn, punkins and beans and a great many more of my people coming on and we had to divide our little stock with them. Last summer there was a few deere here and we had a few hogs but *we was obliged to kill all of them and some that was not our own* but this summer there are no game nor no hogs and my old people and children must suffer. Father—You know its hard to be hungry, if you do not know it we poor Indians know it . . .[7]

The italicized words indicate a new area of conflict between the Delawares and the white farmers. A few white families had already crossed the Mississippi to become squatters in Missouri, where they were grubbing a bare living from the soil and raising a few cows and hogs. The Indians who were facing starvation stole some of the hogs, which caused bad relations with the whites; and after the farmers complained, the government agent had to reprimand the Indians. In fact, he insisted that the Delawares pay for the stolen hogs from their next annuity payments.[8] When annuities were paid in 1826, a deduction of $300 was also made to compensate a white miller for damage done his mill by the Indians (see voucher in Appendix 4).

Apart from floods and lack of wild game, there was another serious drawback to living in Missouri. The land where General Clark placed the Delawares had long been the home of the Siouan-speaking Osage tribe. Although by a treaty dated November 10, 1808, the Osage had ceded to the United States lands where the displaced eastern tribes could be seated, the Osage continued to hunt on these lands and regarded with animosity any trespass of alien Indians on their hunting grounds. The Osage position was that they had sold their lands to the United States, but not the beaver, bear, deer, buffalo, and other animals living on the lands, because the animals were needed for their survival. To make matters worse, the government also moved the Shawnee, Piankashaw, Kickapoo, Arkansas, Cherokee, Creek, Peoria, Wea, and other tribes into this same territory. This was not done purposely to antagonize the Osage, but it made a confrontation inevitable between them and the newcomers.

The scarcity of game on the reserved lands along the James Fork sent Delaware hunters west to the plains and prairies, the habitat of thousands of buffalo which wintered along the Red River, the Brazos, and the Rio Grande, traveling north in the spring when new grass appeared on the plains. The herds made their way through what was to become Oklahoma, Kansas, and Nebraska, and were followed by bands of Osage hunters who found their food, clothing, and fuel in the herds, and who challenged white men and other Indians who ventured on the plains to compete with them.

Swift horses were as vital to the buffalo chase as bows and arrows or rifles and bullets, and the Osage obtained needed animals by stealing them from other tribes. An Osage hunter's skill as a horse thief increased his esteem among his tribesmen.

In the autumn of 1824, Chief Anderson's young son left Delaware Village with a party of hunters for an extended hunting trip on the plains, and while they were camping, a party of Osage hunters stole some of their horses during the night. During the fracas which took place when the Delawares tried to recover their animals, Anderson's son was killed. The old chief was deeply grieved when the returning hunters reported the tragedy to him, and his young men, under the leadership of a war captain whose name is given in the records only as Killbuck, launched a bloody campaign against the Osage to avenge the death of Anderson's son.

In February of 1826, the Osage killed another Delaware lad and ran off with twenty-six horses he was driving, after which an Osage war party killed George Bullet, George White Eyes, and some other young Delaware hunters. Brash, hot-blooded Delaware braves, eager to test their skill as warriors and ambitious to be known as heroes, could not be restrained from avenging these deaths. A month later, within three miles of the place where Anderson's son was killed, a hunting party of ten Delawares and ten Kickapoos killed five Osage warriors. This called for retaliation by the Osage, and a party of fifty or sixty Osage braves invaded the Piankashaw and Delaware towns. So it went, one hostile act leading to another. The Cherokee, who had been warring against the Osage for several years, also became involved in the attacks. These incidents, which are described in full detail in another source,[9] have been cited to illustrate that disharmony in Missouri existed, not only between whites and Indians, but also among the Indian tribes themselves. To restore law and order, the government was forced to intervene, since the Indians were supposed to be under United States protection, according to past treaties. General Clark and others contrived a treaty of peace between the Osage and Delawares at Saint Louis in October 1826, but this by no means healed the wounds nor settled the animosity. Trouble continued off and on for a number of years thereafter.

The Delawares not only hunted on the plains, but their hunting parties backtracked to the Mississippi, pursuing game in the newly admitted state of Illinois. The residents found this objectionable, because they didn't want wild Indians roaming over their lands. In January of 1825, government representatives visited the Indian hunting camps scattered in Illinois to urge the natives to return to their home villages early the following spring. A party of Delawares hunting along the Kaskaskia River agreed that they would return to the James Fork as soon as the grass was high enough to feed their horses during their journey homeward. The agent reported: "These Indians conduct themselves well & are generally esteemed among the settlers, but like the Kickapoos, drink to access when they can get whiskey & dislike to leave a country which afford them such facilities in obtaining that article." [10]

The following May 19, the Indian agent wrote from Delaware Village on the James Fork that Chief Anderson was distressed because a white man who stole a horse owned by his son was also selling whiskey to the Indians. Anderson also accused white men of stealing a number of horses belonging to his people.[11] There was nothing new about corrupting Indians by selling whiskey to them, but stealing their horses was a crime associated with the West. Life west of the Mississippi was entirely different from the life the Indians had known in the East, and the horse brought a new influence on Delaware Indian culture, completely changing their mode of living. Horses were indispensable to whites and Indians alike in Missouri, and in the vast western prairie lands where the Plains tribes had long pursued wild herds sired by Spanish stallions. When the Delawares settled in Missouri, they found that the horses they brought from Indiana were useful, not only for transporting heavy packs of furs and dragging overloaded wagons across what seemed to be boundless stretches of land, but also for hunting down the buffalo and other prairie animals. Horses became such a vital necessity that when an Indian's horses were stolen he was immobilized and severely handicapped. His recourse was to steal horses from white men or other Indians, and this could lead to serious consequences.

While they were living in Missouri, the Delawares also had trouble with their former hosts from Indiana, the Miami, and if the government had not taken a hand, their differences would have flared in open warfare. When the Delawares left Indiana for Missouri, there were unsettled differences between them and the Miami, having to do with the murders of six Delawares, which Chief Anderson claimed had been committed by irresponsible Miami braves. These killings occurred over a period of years, the first in 1809 or 1810, when a Delaware named Washum was shot near Anderson's cabin and later when a Delaware named Lanaquis was slain near Fort Wayne by Indian assailants who were trying to steal his gun. Four other Delawares were killed at a later date and under different circumstances, including a daughter of the chief Lapinihile (Big Bear). The killer also stole two of her horses and other goods.[12]

Anderson sent a message to the chiefs of the Miami in the fall of 1825, demanding an indemnity of $500 for each of the victims, $3,000 in total, reverting to the ancient practice of expiating a crime by compensatory gifts. When the Miami refused to pay, Anderson sent a second message to which he added a note from Captain Killbuck, reading in part, "I am the war man and the war counciler . . . you have heard a great deal from my head chief and you have not listened to him. I now speak as the war chief of my peoples to you." [13] The Miami chiefs understood the significance of this threat, yet they took no action, and on February 28, 1827, Anderson sent what he said was his third and final message. He offered to make a compromise, stating he would accept $2,000 as the wergild, and would give the Miami four months to pay. "If you doe not settle in that time," he warned, "I shall then let my people goe and they must doe as they please." [14]

The son of the principal Miami chief, acting on behalf of his father who was ill, consulted with the other chiefs and councilors, and with their consent, made the following reply:

My Grand Father: Your Miami children have listened to what you have said. Their ears are never stopped when you speak to them.

Grandfather: You must recollect that when you passed over the great mountains [Alleghenies], and come to our country, that you were poor and destitute; you placed yourselves under our protection: we gave you lands, and *at the treaty of St. Mary's you sat in council with us. There we consented to let you sell the land and keep the money for it.—This we considered enough to satisfy you for all the injury our bad young men had done to you;* but it appears otherwise, for you to continue to beg for more notwithstanding all that has been told you by our old Chief who now lies sick in his wigwam. His words I now speak to you . . . The Miamis have already done much for your people; but they will extend their bounty. They have instructed their agent . . . to send . . . five hundred dollars, which sum is to be taken out of our present year's annuity . . . This is all we will give to you . . . If you accept this, it will be well, and we will then take you by the hand and live with you in harmony, as we have done ever since you crossed the mountains . . .[15]

The italicized words explain why nine years earlier the Miami permitted the Delawares to share in the purchase money for Miami lands, whereas prior to that time they had refused to allow the Delawares any right to sell the territory where they were seated.

When the Delawares flatly refused to accept a total of $500 to resolve their differences, the government saw that it must step in and halt the dispute to prevent the bloodshed that seemed inevitable. Pierre Menard was sent to Delaware Village where he arrived on February 13, 1828. Chief Anderson and Captain Beaver dispatched runners to call in their chiefs and captains, who assembled seven days later in a council meeting. Menard minced no words in describing the consequences to be faced by the Delawares if they shed "the Blood of their Grand Children with whom they had been for a long time friendley, and allied by intermarriage, and beside they would incur the displeasure of the Government." This veiled threat meant that the annuities might be withheld, and perhaps other punitive action would have to be taken. The Delawares had no alternative except to accept the $500 as blood money, and with that the matter was closed.[16] But from that time on, relations between the Delawares and Miami were not as harmonious as they formerly had been.

On September 24, 1829, the government negotiated a new treaty with the Delawares which canceled their rights to the lands they were occupying on the James Fork in Missouri, and allocated them land lying at the junction of the Kansas and Missouri rivers in Kansas. The tract extended up the Kansas River (also known as the Kaw) to the Kansas line, and up the Missouri River to Camp Leavenworth, the first military post in the territory. A strip ten miles wide coextensive with the reservation, extending westward approximately 210 miles from the Missouri boundary line, was also reserved for the Delawares as an outlet or passageway to the buffalo hunting territory. According to terms of the treaty, the United States pledged "the faith of the government to guarantee to the said Delaware Nation forever, the quiet and peaceable possession and undisturbed enjoyment of the same against the claims and assaults of all and every other people whatsoever." [17]

The government agreed to furnish forty horses and six wagons and an ox team to assist the poor and desolate members of the Delaware Nation to move from the James Fork to the new location. Apparently most of the Delawares, with the exception of some of the poor old people, now owned horses and wagons. The government further agreed to supply farm implements and tools for building houses, provisions for the journey, and one full year's provisions after the Indians arrived in Kansas. In addition, the government agreed to erect a gristmill and sawmill within two years. Another annuity of $1,000 was to be added to annuities then being paid, and thirty-six sections of the best land relinquished by the Delawares in Missouri were to be sold by the government, the proceeds to be applied to the support of new schools to be built in Kansas to educate Delaware children. This land was ultimately sold for $46,080, which the government invested at 5 percent interest. The twelve Indians who signed the instrument were "Wm. Anderson, principal chief, Capt. Paterson, 2nd chief, Pooshies, or the Cat, Capt. Beaver, Capt. Suwaunock, or white man, Johnny Quick, John Gray, George Guirty, Naunote-tauxien, Little Jack, Capt. Pipe and Big Island." [18] Paterson was a former chief of the Cape Girardeau Delawares who had joined Anderson; and Captain Pipe, namesake of the Delaware leader during the Revolution, was a member of the group who had moved to Missouri from the Sandusky. Although these signers were not identified by animal eponyms, there is no reason to doubt that three different groups, or subtribes, continued to be represented.

To make certain the new lands assigned his people were satisfactory Chief Anderson sent a committee of six prominent Delawares to examine the proposed reserve (located in what is now the state of Kansas, but was then unorganized territory) before agreeing to accept it. The delegation was favorably impressed with what they saw, and on October 19, 1829, the members signed a treaty of acceptance with United States commissioners at a camp in the fork of the Kansas and Missouri rivers.

When this treaty was sent to the Senate for ratification, a special resolution was passed authorizing the President to employ a surveyor to lay out the lands and establish markers and boundary points on both the reserve and the outlet—in the presence of an agent designated by the Delaware Nation. In the fall of 1830, Isaac McCoy, the same Baptist minister who had labored among the Delawares in Indiana, was employed by the government to survey the lands which the Indians had approved. He was accompanied by a Delaware patriarch who identified himself as the "second chief," Captain John Quick, one of the signers of the 1829 treaty.[19]

On a drawing he made during the course of his survey, McCoy noted that the reserved lands contained 1,759,361.77 acres. In a letter to the Secretary of the Interior dated May 20, 1854, Indian Commissioner George W. Manypenny stated that, according to an updated estimate made by McCoy, the reserve contained 924,160 acres, and the outlet 1,318,000 acres, a total of 2,242,160 acres.[20] A figure of 2,808,000 acres was also given in other correspondence as the approximate content of the Delaware reserve and outlet. The wording of the original treaty was not clear regarding the bounds of the outlet, and the exact acreage was never actually ascertained, except that the total Delaware reserve was well in excess of 2,000,000 acres.

McCoy kept a journal describing his trip, and the hardships he endured in the course of making the survey, such as sleeping ninety-six successive nights without being sheltered by the roof of a house.[21] He referred to his companion, John Quick, as "an old Delaware" appointed by his nation as "a commissioner to attend the surveying of their lands." Quick was pleased with the new territory, and even before McCoy completed the survey, the old Indian returned to Missouri to assure the other chiefs that the land was good, and that

Delaware families should move west promptly and take possession before the onset of winter. Doubtless Quick had talked to some of the Shawnee who had settled first in Kansas—another instance of the Delawares following their Shawnee friends into new territory.

Although the 1829 treaty obligated the government to supply provisions to sustain the Indians on the move to Kansas, Chief Anderson with about a hundred of his people set out of their own volition in the fall of 1830, carrying their provisions and driving their herds of horses ahead of them. The old chief, now in his early seventies, was anxious to leave Missouri, because neither he nor his people had been happy there. His fond hope was that before his death he could lead the Delawares to a promised land they could call their own where they could live in peace without interference from whites or enemy Indians. He and his party arrived in Kansas prior to November 1, 1830, and the next spring the remainder of the nation followed their chief to their new homes.

The movement to Kansas was not confined to the Delawares, because other displaced Indian tribes were also moved to westerly locations. Following his election, President Andrew Jackson was authorized by an act of Congress passed on May 26, 1830 to cause certain lands west of the Mississippi to be divided into a suitable number of districts for the habitation of the Indian tribes. The idea was that Indians living east of the Mississippi, or immediately west of it, were to swap the lands on which they were living for equivalent tracts farther west. The sum of $500,000 was appropriated to carry the provisions of the act into effect. To prepare lands to seat the tribes, like the Delawares then living in Missouri, the government paid the Osage for extensive tracts in Kansas. President Jackson was empowered to assure every tribe that exchanged its land holdings for property in the then unorganized territory that the government would "forever secure and guarantee to them, and their heirs and successors, the country so exchanged with them."

Although the main body of the Delawares living in Missouri were party to a treaty which allocated lands to them in Kansas, the splinter group formerly settled at Cape Girardeau had not been given satisfaction for their lands. On October 26, 1832, the government entered into a treaty at Castor Hill, Saint Louis County, Missouri, with some Delawares, accompanied by Shawnee, who had formerly lived in the Cape Girardeau environs. These Delawares maintained that when they left Cape Girardeau they did not receive any compensation for the lands they had vacated or the cattle they lost. Furthermore, they complained that they had never had any share of the annuities or other gifts that the main body received from the United States. This was a curious position for them to take in view of their having left United States territory at the invitation of a foreign power (Spain) in a transaction which the United States was not asked to approve or sponsor. Now that the United States had acquired the land on which they were living, as a result of the Louisiana Purchase, these Delawares insisted that the new owner should indemnify them for losses sustained when they were living under the jurisdiction of the former government. Since Congress was then bending over backward to appease the Indian tribes, in the expectation of inducing them to go west, three commissioners were appointed and authorized to make a settlement on these Delawares.

In the negotiations that followed, the Indians drove a hard bargain, forcing the government to agree to pay them $2,000 for injury to their livestock at Cape Girardeau; $1,000 for assistance in breaking ground at the new location, which was not specified in the treaty; $2,500 to pay a person to operate a gristmill for them for five years and keep it in good repair; $1,500 to support an Indian school. In addition, merchandise worth $5,000 was to be paid them when they reached their new homes, and a cash settlement of $12,000 was made to enable them to discharge their debts.[22]

Three of the Delaware leaders of the Cape Girardeau band also fared very well individually. The government agreed that an annuity for life of $100 should be paid each of them. One of the recipients was Meshe Kowhay (Chief Paterson), who had been the principal chief of the Cape Girardeau Delawares and who joined the main body on James Fork as second in command to Chief Anderson. The two other recipients of annuities were two band captains who also joined Anderson—Natcoming and Tah-whee-lalen. The latter Indian name was the scribe's rendition of a Delaware expression translatable as "catch him," which was later corrupted into English as "ketchum," and was used as a family name. According to Delaware folk etymology, a young brave, fleet of foot, once outran and caught a deer, and was given a nickname in the Delaware language which meant "catch him." The Indian named Tah-whee-lalen may have been the same person called "Captain Ketchum" who enlisted in the service of the American government at Fort Wayne during the War of 1812 and, along with several other Delawares, served in a detail that accompanied General Lewis Cass to Canada.[23]

Whether or not the government fulfilled all the terms of the treaty of 1832 is difficult to ascertain because of divisions within the splinter group from Cape Girardeau. Some settled with Chief Anderson and went to Kansas as part of the main body. Others continued to absent themselves from the main body, and finally ended in Texas. Regrettably the Delawares kept no written records of their movements, nor when they collected money owed them by the government.

The main body of the tribe seemed to have adjusted quickly to their new location in Kansas, which was conducive to agriculture and cattle raising. This tended to make them less dependent upon hunting than they had been in Missouri. Of course, some of the men continued to hunt and trap each fall and winter, but instead of becoming an equestrian tribe, wholly dependent upon the buffalo, antelope, and other game for a livelihood, they began to make strides toward adopting the ways of the whites. The venturous young Delawares still considered themselves hunters, not farmers or cattlemen, but some of the mature married men now began to realize that the only certain way of making a livelihood for their families was to cultivate the land and raise herds of cattle like the prosperous white men.

The reserved land was owned in common, each Delaware family selecting a place of its own choosing, where no one else lived; and there was plenty of land for everyone. At first, nearly all the Indian families erected small cabins of round or hewn logs, but it wasn't long before a few of the more ambitious men built modest frame houses for their families, patterned after the white man's dwellings they had seen in Indiana and Missouri. A few of the energetic Delaware farmers, definitely in the minority, erected barns and outbuildings, and some acquired from twenty-five to a hundred head of cattle, as well as swine, sheep, horses, wagons, and farm implements. Those whose farms were most productive adopted the farming methods of the white man, and, at long last, erected rail fences around some of their fields, built smokehouses and stables, and turned up the soil with horse-drawn plows. Their crops included corn, beans, pumpkins, Irish potatoes, melons, and small amounts of oats and wheat. Not only was the soil watered by the rivers rich and black, but there were hundreds of acres of virgin trees, the reservation containing some of the best timbered land in Kansas.[24]

On July 3, 1834, a white visitor wrote as follows:

The Delawares number about 1000 souls, have also a Government teacher & blacksmith . . . they have saw & grist mills—furnished by [the] Government, raise some wheat, considerable corn & vegetables, there [sic] land is good, they also raise some cattle, horses, sheep—& hogs. live on the north banks of the Kansas River about 5 m from its mouth, there land extends up the South side of the Mo [Missouri] River within 4 m of the Garrison [Fort Leavenworth].[25]

Another visitor, Lewis Henry Morgan, famous for his Indian studies, visited the Delawares twenty-five years later, and his journal, written in the summer of 1859, provides valuable information about the Indian communities in Kansas. He wrote that at the mouth of the Kansas River, on the north bank, was a Wyandot settlement on land they had purchased from the Delawares. Next on the west were the Delawares, and west of them were the Potawatomie. The Shawnee lived on the south side of the Kansas River, their reserved lands extending from present Kansas City to Lawrence. Seated on reserved lands south of the Shawnee were the Sac and Fox, Pianka-shaw, Miami, Peoria, Chippewa, and Ottawa. Morgan noted that there were short gaps between settlements of the various tribes, where a few white settlers, contrary to the treaties made with the Indians, had taken up lands by the simple expedient of marrying Indian women.[26]

At the time of Morgan's visit, thirty years had elapsed since the Delawares had come from Missouri, poor and demoralized, and many changes for the better had taken place in their economic life, due to federal aid. Chief Anderson died in 1831, after having had the satisfaction of living long enough to see his people settled in their new homes. One of his last messages was a letter written at his di-rection (probably by the Indian Agent) to Secretary of War Lewis Cass on September 22, 1831, which began as follows:

Father Cass: I inform you that nearly all our nation are on the land that the Government has laid off for us; and I hope that if the Government fulfill all its promises, that before many years the balance of my nation who are now scattered, some on Red River and some in Spanish country [Texas] will all come here on this land. We are well pleased with our present situation. The land is good, and also the wood and water, but the game is very scarce.[27]

Chief Anderson went on to say that his young men had to go great distances to hunt in order to get pelts to pay their debts. Cass probably knew that distance had never been a deterrent to Delaware hunters, who for years had wandered far from their villages to track down game.

The old chief was survived by four sons, Captain Suwaunock, Secondyan, Pooshies, and Sarcoxie (their names were variously spelled), who are believed by some to have been adopted. This is possible, inasmuch as Anderson referred to the son killed by the Osage in Missouri as "my only one boy." [28] The records are not clear in this connection, since the use of the term *son* by the Delawares did not necessarily mean a blood offspring. The four men named as his sons, who certainly loved Anderson as a father, became well-known scouts and guides on the western frontier, and descendants of Sarcoxie and Secondyan (modified to Secondine) may be found today among Delaware survivors in Oklahoma.

When the movement to California began in the 1840s—followed in 1859 by the "Pikes Peak gold rush" to Colorado—Kansas lay on the route to the Far West. Trains of canvas-covered prairie schooners were made up at Independence, Missouri, and all of the wagon trains heading in the direction of the Pacific hired Delaware Indian guides to lead them across the plains and through the mountain passes. Astride his swift, shaggy pony, knife in belt, bullet pouch and powder horn at his side, rifle resting on the high pommel of his saddle, the taciturn Delaware "guide and hunter" was a picturesque figure. The safety of the families in the wagon train depended to a large extent on his knowledge of the terrain, when and where to travel, and where to camp at night.

The pioneer families left civilization behind when they reached the mouth of the Kansas River, and immediately ahead lay the bleak prairie inhabited only by herds of buffalo and antelope, small prairie animals, snakes, and Indian hunting parties. The pioneer going southwest took the Santa Fe trail, which entered Kansas on the south side of the Kansas River. If he was headed for California he traveled an-

other route that ran along the south bank of the river. If his destination was Oregon, or the gold fields of Colorado, he followed another
route through northern Kansas, or took the Butterfield Trail along
the Kansas and Smoky Hill rivers. An almost endless procession of
men, animals, and wagons wore the trails deeper and wider until
wagon roads developed. Over a period of time debris gathered where
the families passed—broken and rusted mining tools, wagon wheels
with missing spokes, bleached bones of cattle, and here and there a
forlorn grave on which was heaped stones and a wooden cross.

In *The Oregon Trail*, Francis Parkman has written a vivid description of his trip to Kansas in the spring of 1846, preparatory to completing a journey across the continent to the Pacific on horseback.
He went to Saint Louis by train and left by steamboat, mingling in
the growing town with gamblers, land speculators, adventurers, and
emigrants going to the Far West. It was a week's trip from Saint
Louis to Kansas, as the boat fought the current of the muddy Missouri River. After debarking, he visited Independence, a town of
transient families whose canvas-covered wagons, pulled by oxen or
strong draught horses, followed by droves of cattle, were being organized on the prairie eight or ten miles beyond the town for the
slow procession westward. The rutted, unpaved streets thronged with
people, horses, oxen, mules, and shaggy Indian ponies all throwing
up clouds of dust. Some of the men carried long whips and wore
loaded pistols in their belts and spurs on their boots. Blacksmiths
and wagonmakers were constantly hammering and banging, as the
heavy wagons were being repaired, iron rims secured to the wheels,
and the horses and oxen shod for the journey ahead.

Parkman and his companions camped on Delaware reserved lands
at the Lower Delaware Crossing on the Kansas River, where, after
some difficulty, they rafted their horses and equipment across the
stream. They ascended the steep bank on the opposite side of the
river, and followed the military road to Fort Leavenworth, and from
there they headed across the plains to the mountains. Parkman com-
mented in his book about the small log houses occupied by Delaware
Indian families scattered at intervals along the route crossing their
reservation. At one of these cabins he paused to talk to an old Delaware woman, weighing about three hundred pounds, who was seated
on the porch of a cabin, while a pretty child, part white, was feed-

ing a flock of turkeys. He also encountered a Delaware hunting party returning from the plains, their pack mules laden with bundles of furs they had taken, together with their kettles, buffalo robes, and other camping gear. Parkman described the leader of the party as a sullen fellow wearing a buckskin jacket and fringed leggings blackened with grease, with an old handkerchief tied around his head, his rifle resting on the saddle before him. This unsociable Delaware probably resented white men from the East trespassing on the Indians' reserved lands.

When the Delawares resided in Missouri, their hunters had become acquainted with the plains country, but when they settled in Kansas they went even farther west to pursue the buffalo herds. As soon as they began to hunt in that part of their reserve called the outlet, they ran into trouble with the Pawnee, a resident tribe angered by the appearance of strange Indians whose language and customs differed from their own. In an effort to repulse the strangers, the Pawnee organized war parties and ambushed the Delaware hunters. According to their custom, the Delawares were forced to retaliate to save their honor, and injury and death resulted on both sides, a repetition of the same kind of trouble the Delawares had experienced with the Osage in Missouri. As an act of vengeance, Chief Anderson's son, the war chief Captain Suwaunock ("white," named no doubt because of his white increments), led a party of Delaware warriors to the main Pawnee town on the Platte River in what is now Nebraska, and destroyed all the dwellings.

The United States sent commissioners to assuage the jealousies and bring the warring tribes together to halt hostilities. John Treat Irving, Jr., the twenty-year-old nephew of Washington Irving was present with Indian Commissioner Henry L. Ellsworth and others on November 12, 1833, when peace was concluded between the Pawnee on one side, and the Delawares and other tribes on the other. In describing this conference, Irving wrote that the Delaware warriors were "glittering with trinkets; their silver ornaments glistening in the sunshine, and their gay ribbands fluttering in the wind. They were a gaudy, effeminate-looking race, yet beneath all their frippery of dress lurked that indomitable courage, and thirst for glory, which not even intemperance, and their intercourse with the whites could destroy." Behind the warriors came Captain Suwaunock, and the

Delaware delegation took their seats opposite the Pawnee chiefs and councilors, the members of both groups wearing grim expressions, all fearful of compromising their dignity as proud warriors. When it came his turn to speak, Suwaunock made no apology for his attack on the villages of the enemy. "The Pawnee met my young men upon the hunt and slew them," he said through the translator. "I have had my revenge. Let them look at their town. I found it filled with lodges: I left it a heap of ashes." [29]

When one considers that the Pawnee population was probably ten times larger than that of the Delawares, Suwaunock's admission in an open meeting might have provoked a disastrous attack on the Delaware villages by a superior force of Pawnee warriors. Fortunately, Commissioner Ellsworth was present to pour oil on troubled waters, and arbitrate the differences, having been instructed to purchase the contested lands from the Pawnee, induce them to move north of the Platte River, and effect peace between them and their Indian neighbors.

Although the meeting resulted in a peace agreement between Delawares and Pawnee, sporadic killings and horse thievery continued. In 1848, and again in 1857, the government paid the Pawnee off to extinguish title to their lands. In due course the Pawnee moved to what is now Oklahoma, where their descendants may still be found, and the Delawares were rid of this problem.

Congress was aware of the intertribal jealousies and the constant friction that resulted from transplanting eastern tribes to western lands. There was much discussion and debate in the halls of Congress, but no one could offer a solution to which the legislators could agree. In March of 1836 Senator John Tipton had introduced a bill that was intended to solve the problem by establishing an Indian territory of more than 70 million acres, where *all* the Indians could be placed under the jurisdiction of a congress made up of Indians elected by their people. He estimated there were then 74,241 Indians living west of the Mississippi and east of the Rockies, among whom he said there were 921 Delawares living in Kansas.[30] Senator Tipton's proposal ran into stiff political opposition and was tabled.

In the fall of 1838, the United States decided to employ Indian soldiers as mercenaries in the war against the Seminole in the Florida

Everglades, which began in 1835. The government urged the south-eastern tribes to cede their land and move to Indian Territory west of the Mississippi and, although some of the Seminole moved after a treaty was signed, most of the tribesmen refused to recognize the treaty. About eighty Delawares from Kansas, and an equal number of Shawnee, "prompted by fidelity to the United States, and the promise of high wages, enlisted and performed a six months tour in Florida." [31] Because of an ill-advised government policy, the Indians had to wait more than ten years before they were able to collect the back pay due them.[32]

Another interesting episode which occurred during the time the Delawares were living in Kansas, was the participation of a number of Indian hunters, including several chiefs, in the Frémont expeditions. John C. Frémont, the first distinctively scientific explorer produced by the United States, conducted several expeditions to the West Coast to obtain data for the government about unexplored areas of the country. On his first trip in 1842, he engaged an unnamed Delaware father and son as hunters to help provide food for the more than thirty men in the party.[33]

In 1844, President Tyler appointed Frémont a captain by brevet, and, on his third trip to the Far West, in 1845, Frémont engaged twelve Delaware Indians as scouts and hunters for his party. Among these Delawares, as given in Frémont's spellings, were James Swanuck (Suwaunock, sometimes given as Shounack), James Saghundai (same family name as Secondyan or Secondine), James Conner, Delaware Charley, Wetowka, Solomon Everett, Crane, and Bob Skirkett.[34] One of Frémont's objectives was to examine the ranges of the Cascade Mountains and the Sierra Nevadas, and other parts of California which then belonged to Mexico but which President Polk had a fixed determination to acquire. In the middle of May 1846, while he was still exploring California, Frémont received orders from Washington which changed the nature of his mission. He learned that the United States was going to war against Mexico and intended to seize California. His exploring party was suddenly converted into an offensive force, and Frémont promised his Delaware scouts that he would endeavor to obtain *additional compensation* for them if they would enlist as soldiers in the service of the United States, which they did.

Thus, beginning in May, the Delawares and other members of

the party were all belligerents in the Mexican War, and Frémont later commended the Indians highly for "performing their duties with remarkable courage and fidelity." [35] Upon his return to Washington, Frémont recommended, not only that the War Department give the Delawares the soldiers' pay he had promised them, in addition to their pay as scouts, but also that they receive land warrants being awarded to American soldiers who fought in the war. The Delawares were never given any land for their services, and there is serious doubt that they ever received the military pay which had been promised them and to which they were fully entitled. [36]

After resigning his commission, Frémont made a fifth trip to California in 1853–54 as a private citizen. He arranged with James Secondine to engage ten Delaware hunters to accompany him, each to furnish his own horses, Frémont to supply ammunition, saddles, and wages of $2 per day. In the event of one of the Indian's horses dying while they were in Frémont's service, he agreed to compensate the owner for the loss. In 1886—more than thirty years later— one of the Delaware hunters named George Washington was still trying to collect the pay owed him and other members of the party. The Secretary of War refused to assume the debt, stating that the government was not responsible for the expenses of an expedition conducted by a private citizen. [37] At that late date the Indians had no way of locating Frémont, and the whole issue got bogged down in government red tape, and it is unlikely that they ever received this pay either.

During his western trips, Frémont had many hazardous experiences, which were shared by his Indian companions, and are related in his memoirs. During his third trip, when attacked by a party of hostile Klamath Indians, the explorer lost several men, including the Delaware named Crane. The other Delawares mourned the death of their companion by blackening their faces, and they were not satisfied until they avenged Crane's death by taking the scalps of two Klamaths. In his narrative Frémont also described how James Secondine, for whom he had a particular admiration, saved the life of Kit Carson when a Klamath Indian tried to kill Carson with a poisoned arrow. [38]

The Delawares in Kansas received government annuities based on six different treaties as follows:

$1,000 annually in accordance with the Greenville Treaty negotiated on August 3, 1795

$100 annually for salt money, to compensate for land sold the government in Ohio on which a salt spring was located, per treaty of June 7, 1803

$500 annually, per treaty of September 30, 1809

$940 blacksmith annuity, to compensate a blacksmith to serve them, per treaty of October 3, 1818

$4,000 annually also per treaty of October 3, 1818

$1,000 annually per treaty of September 24, 1829

The grand total of these annuities, which were supposed to be paid in perpetuity, amounted to $7,540. In addition, the government was secretly paying individual personal annuities to certain chiefs. The government was also holding in trust for the Delawares the capital it had paid the nation for lands vacated, on which the interest was usually disbursed annually in the form of separate annuities. Where a written document existed in which the government agreed to do certain things, or pay certain amounts of money, it usually fulfilled its commitments. For example, the Treaty of September 24, 1829, obligated the United States to furnish tools and farm utensils, and to erect a sawmill and gristmill when the Delawares arrived in Kansas. At first, two mills were built at government expense, but on August 10, 1857, the Indian agent made an agreement with a miller, a white man paid by the government, to consolidate the milling operations in one building. At that time the gristmill was located four miles above Delaware Crossing on the Kansas River, and the stones and equipment were moved to the point where Strangers Creek empties into the river. The sawmill and gristmill were combined in the new building, and at this time both were operated by steam. The operator was permitted to retain half the lumber he sawed for his own use. Corn was ground for the Indians free of charge, and the operator was permitted to have any needed repairs to the mill made free of charge at the Delaware National Blacksmith Shop.[39] The blacksmith was also paid by the government, and his services were available gratis to the Delawares.

In June of 1859 Lewis Henry Morgan witnessed the Indian agent paying annuities to the Delawares while some one hundred white spectators and traders shared in the excitement. The payment was made on a site situated on the side of a hill near the Baptist Mission. The amount distributed in gold and silver amounted to $78,000—approximately $83 for each of the 941 men, women, and children officially listed as bona fide Delawares on the agent's rolls. Actually two annuity payments were combined at this time, making the individual payments larger than usual. The Delawares, according to Morgan, had more than $1 million in their name in the United States treasury accumulating 5 percent interest. On this occasion there were about eight hundred Delawares present to receive their payments; some had remained at home to watch over their properties, and others were unable to come because of sickness or old age among other reasons.

Merchants and traders set up stands with canvas canopies under which they offered for sale grains of all kinds, tinware, washtubs, washboards, coffee mills, calico and muslin, costume jewelry, salt, pork, flour, bacon, and other commodities. The stellar attraction was the display of bridles and saddles, the latter of the Mexican type having a high pommel, quilted seat with a high rear plate, and wooden stirrups. These sold from $15 to $50—an amount that few Delawares could afford, except on annuity day. The pay wagon, marked U.S., was guarded by a file of soldiers, and the cash was disbursed in an army tent which the Indians entered single file to have their names checked off on the official enrollment list. When all the Delawares were paid, the paymaster left with his military escort to pay annuities due to the other tribes.

Morgan described the Delaware women as no longer wearing Indian skirts but dressed in the long frocks worn by white females, although the cloth was much more colorful. Some wore richly brocaded silk gowns, crimson, black, and fiery red in color. A few were dressed in print muslins, but, regardless of the cloth used in their dresses, all wore expensive silk shawls of many colors and shades, most of them fringed. The dresses were worn without hoops or petticoats, and all of the Indian women wore silk handkerchiefs on their heads. The light complexion of many Delaware women was unmistakable evidence of the frequency of white increments in past years, and Morgan said the females appeared strong, clean, and healthy.

He wrote that the men were "more fantastically dressed than the women, and did not appear half as well. Their fancy dresses were cheap and absurd, rendering their general appearance ridiculous. There were many good faces among them, and also well dressed Indians who speak our language and have the manners and address of gentlemen. Some of the old men and some of the young men had on colored calico frock coats of the most gaudy colors. Many had vermilion on their faces, thus giving them a low appearance, and I saw a few girls with spots of it on their cheeks. One man I saw with a silver ornament in his nose, which covered part of his mouth. Many of the men wore leggings with a wide side projection, ornamented, and the breech cloth, over which they wore vest or shirt, and perhaps one of the frock coats of calico above named, with head bands of bead work over the shoulder and meeting in a large bead work pocket on the right hand side." [40]

The paying of annuities was a gala event, and by all odds, the biggest single day in the life of a Delaware Indian family. When they were first settled in Indiana, they went to Fort Wayne to collect their annuities, some traveling as far as a hundred miles, and at that time, payment was made in merchandise. This continued until 1804, at which time each Indian man, woman, and child received clothing amounting to about $12 per person. That year the paymaster advised the Indians that thereafter annuities would be paid in cash because General Harrison wanted them to hire laborers to help them build fences and houses.[41] Subsequently, William Conner was deputized to pay the annuities in cash, and prior to making payment he would distribute sticks of three different lengths to the men, women, and children. When the money was apportioned, each Indian turned in his stick, the older ones receiving payment in silver dollars, the next youngest in half dollars, and the youngest in quarter dollars.[42]

Usually, regardless of how much cash they received, the money was all gone by the time the Indians were ready to go home. Some purchased worthwhile goods sold on the grounds, but others wasted their cash in surreptitious drinking and gambling, both of which were prohibited by the paymaster or government agents. After the officials left, almost anything could happen. One of the popular games of chance played by the Indians was Moccasin, a variety of the old shell game, which apparently originated with the Delawares "who were great experts in playing it." Usually four, or sometimes six, moccasins were placed upside down between the betters on a well-dressed deerskin, and as the dealer shuffled the moccasins he hid a lead bullet under one of them. The players bet that they could pick the moccasin under which the bullet was concealed. The white settlers borrowed this game from the Indians, and players in Indiana used men's caps instead of moccasins, and changed the name of the game to Bullet.[43] When the Delawares settled in Oklahoma the game ceased to be played as a pastime and became associated only with the rites performed at funerals.

In addition to the Baptist Mission located near the site of the annuity payments, and owned by the American Baptist Mission, the Methodist Episcopal Church, and the United Brethren (Moravians) were active among the Delawares in Kansas. The Methodists opened their mission in 1832 at what is now the White Church Community about five miles north of the old Delaware Crossing on the Kansas River. A report made the following year indicated that membership consisted of five whites and twenty-seven Indians, and the outlook for growth was said to be very good. The Methodists also established a school for Delaware children, but an agreement was made in 1844 between the Shawnee and the Delaware Council whereby the Delawares diverted funds to the Shawnee Manual Labor School, and the Methodist school was closed.[44] By 1844, the Methodists had 108 Delaware converts, and among the prominent members were Charles Ketchum and James Ketchum, both of whom became ministers preaching in the English and Delaware languages.

The Moravian Mission, established in 1837, was situated on the north bank of the Kansas River near the town of Munsie. The composition of this group, usually termed Christian Indians, was principally Munsie, but a few Stockbridge Indian families were also included.

The American Baptist Missionary Union was the sponsor of an extremely successful mission which owed its origin to the prestige of the Reverend Isaac McCoy, who was held in high regard by the Delaware chiefs. As far back as 1818, when McCoy traveled from one Indian town to another along the White River in Indiana, several Delaware chiefs, despite the prevailing anti-Christian sentiment, promised him that when the tribe was permanently settled west of the Mississippi they would allow him to build a school to teach their youth.[45] Holding the Delawares to their promise, the Baptist pastor, Reverend Ira D. Blanchard, built a mission school of logs at present Edwardsville, Wyandotte County, Kansas, in 1836. It was used for a number of years, but in 1844 the Kansas River overflowed its banks, inundating the school and forcing its abandonment.

In 1848, the Reverend John G. Pratt, a native of Massachusetts, and his wife Olivia took charge of this mission. Pratt hauled the logs from the site of the original school and used them to rebuild a new schoolhouse at a location on higher ground about four miles northeast of Edwardsville. Pratt was an unusual and versatile man who had been apprenticed to a printer prior to his ordination, and he first came to the Shawnee Mission in Kansas as a printer in the employ of the Baptists. Later he was placed in charge of the Stockbridge Baptist Mission near Wadsworth, Kansas, following which he was assigned to the Delawares as a missionary. Like McCoy, Pratt came to be held in very high regard by the Delawares, and after he served at the Baptist missionary for many yeras, the Delaware agent Fielding Johnson engaged him as a practical physician to the Delawares at a salary of $1,000 a year. This was an extraordinary assignment for a man who had no formal medical training, but he was nevertheless very successful in his ministrations.

On April 18, 1864, President Lincoln appointed Pratt to a four-year term as United States Indian agent to the Delawares, succeeding Johnson. At this time the Indian agents were paid an annual salary of $1,500, and were allowed certain expense funds to run the agency. It was a difficult job requiring long, hard work, an incredible amount of paper work, including lengthy correspondence between Washington headquarters and the district offices of the Bureau of Indian Affairs.

When the Delawares first came to Kansas, they, along with the Shawnee, Kickapoo, Stockbridge, Munsie, and Kansas Indians, fell under the jurisdiction of the Fort Leavenworth Indian Agency. In 1851, the Kansas Agency was created, with jurisdiction restricted to the Delawares and Wyandot, but in the spring of 1855 the Delaware Agency was established exclusively for the Delawares. A former army officer, Major B. F. Robinson, was appointed the first Indian agent in this new agency.

In 1859 Miss Clara Gowing, a twenty-seven-year-old Massachusetts schoolteacher, came to Kansas to serve as a missionary-teacher, along with Miss Elizabeth S. Morse. At that time Pratt was still the superintendent of the Baptist Mission, which Miss Gowing described as a cluster of wood structures, including a chapel, stables, smokehouse, and washhouse. The old one-room log schoolhouse, covered with clapboards, formed the middle part of a rambling two-story frame house, built in stages, then occupied by the Pratts and their seven children. Another house was used as a dormitory for the Indian boys and girls who boarded at the school, ranging in ages from six to eighteen, and another building was used as the school proper.[46] The school fund of $46,808, set aside by the government in accordance with the Treaty of 1829, yielded interest which partly paid the school expenses. The tribe was assessed $75 for each pupil, later raised to $100, which covered room, board, clothing, and tuition for two terms of five months each. The Delaware children were taught to read and write English, and to sing hymns in their own language, using hymnals translated into the Indian tongue, which Pratt printed when he was at the Shawnee Mission. The curriculum also included arithmetic, geography, and scripture-reading. The girls cleaned the bedrooms, made the beds, dusted the furniture, and served food at the tables. In addition to the academic subjects they were taught sewing and the domestic arts. When the boys were not busy with their studies, they carried water, split and sawed wood for the stoves, and worked in the fields. Both boys and girls were taught to knit, and they made their own stockings. The number of boys attending the school generally exceeded the girls, because Indian mothers were inclined to keep the girls home to care for the younger children. Health was a problem, because Indian children seemed more susceptible to colds, fevers, and eye irritations than white children, and it was here that Pratt learned which medicaments to prescribe for the most common childhood ailments. Evidently some of the children were quite willing to devote time to their studies—one of the boys was prompted by an unusual motivation. In a progress report, Miss Morse commented on the aptitude of this particular boy, whose English composition contained this revealing sentence: "We must know books for whiteman know much. He cheats us much. Therefore I want to look hard on my book and slate." [47] Appendix 7 lists the names of the Indian children attending the Baptist Mission school in 1858 and in 1867. Both lists are published for the first time.

In an interesting account of life at the school, Miss Gowing wrote that among her pupils were Adeline and Emeline, identical twin daughters of Charles Journeycake, a son of the Solomon Joneycake, or Journeycake, previously mentioned. In the spring of 1860, their older sister Nannie Journeycake married Lucius, the eldest son of the Pratts.[48] Four years later, when Pratt was appointed Indian agent, Lucius succeeded him as superintendent of the school. After Lucius's death on September 7, 1865, his widow Nannie became head of the school, although her father-in-law continued to devote attention to the education of the Indian children despite the demands on his time as Indian agent.

Charles Journeycake, who had apparent white increments, could read and write, and he became a Baptist in 1833. Like the Ketchums, he became a devout Christian and exerted a strong influence in improving the moral behavior of the Delawares and in teaching temperance. He was one of the charter members of the Baptist Mission in Kansas. The Baptists were reinforced by the teachings of Methodists, Moravians, and Presbyterians, all of whom were opposed to intoxicants, which led to a determined effort on the part of the converted Delawares to suppress intemperance. The story is told that Charles Journeycake, whose Indian name was Ne-sha-pa-na-cumin ("he who stands twice at daylight"), was asked by a group of Delaware hunters to lead them on a beaver-trapping expedition because of his skill as a hunter and trapper. He agreed, provided the Indians would attend prayers at camp every night and morning, and spend the Sabbath in rest and religious exercises. The men were absent from their homes for six weeks, during which time they not only kept their promises to be present at prayers, but also participated in singing hymns, and listened while Journeycake read the scriptures to them.[49]

Captain Ketchum, former leader of one of the Cape Girardeau bands of Delawares, who joined Chief Anderson on James Fork, also went to Kansas with the main body.[50] Ketchum's brother, Chief Lapinihile, died on James Fork in 1826, and after his death Captain Ketchum apparently assumed his brother's mantle as a chief. After the deaths of Chief Anderson and Chief Natcoming, Ketchum was made the principal chief of the Delawares in Kansas by appointment of Superintendent Cummings of the Department of Indian Affairs.[51] From this time on, the Indian agents and commissioners had something to do with the selection of the principal and assistant chiefs.

Captain Ketchum, who was born on the Tuscarawas in Ohio, was a heavy drinker in his younger years. After his conversion to Methodism he became a total abstainer, and by example he, too, influenced other Indians to give up alcohol. On October 20, 1856, a dignified and venerable man in his seventies, he drew up his last will and testament, perhaps the first Delaware Indian to have a formal will. Since this document has not previously been published, it is quoted verbatim below:

Delaware Nation
October 20, 1856

I Capt Ketchum   )   X
Chief of the Delawares)

being feeble in body, give this my wish and *will* to my *people* and if in the *Providence* of Almighty God I should not recover I hope you remember and regard, as my last will

1. I want my nephew Ah-lar-a-chech or James Conner to be a Chief and my people look upon him as such, I think he is suitable man to fill the place as Chief

2. And I also wish you all to help one to another in business and try to promode the nation of our people.

3. As to my private anuity I want that to pay my depts first, all that I owe then divited with my children in first payments.

Witness—Henry Tiblow   U.S. Intr

I Certify that the foregoing instrument of writing was this day proved to be the last will of Capt Ketchum by Henry Tiblow before me this 15 day of Feb 1858.

(signed) B. F. Robinson
Indian Agent [52]

Captain Ketchum died on July 12, 1857, and is buried in the graveyard of the White Church about seven miles west of Kansas City, Kansas.[53] At the time the will was made, and at the time of his uncle's death, James Conner was away from home, having been engaged by the government as a hunter and scout. When he learned of the will upon his return, he sought the assistance of his nephew William Adams, an educated Delaware, to write a letter for him to the government. In the letter he said that he felt most of the Delawares would be opposed to his elevation to the chieftaincy, although he did not give any reason for this belief. In his stead he nominated his brother John Conner "for he is an aged man and I'll do all I can for him." [54]

At this time John Conner was in his late fifties, and he had been living on the Texas frontier for more than thirty years. Following the admission of Texas as a state, he served the United States as an Indian interpreter; in fact, he rendered such useful services that he was given a plot of land and made a citizen of Texas.[55] When Colonel Richard Irving Dodge was stationed at Fort Martin Scott, Texas, John Conner and a band of Delawares were living nearby, and Dodge and Conner became good friends. In his book *Our Wild Indians . . .* , Dodge relates that Conner told him that as a lad of eighteen or nineteen he was living within the limits of the then recently admitted state of Illinois. Like other young Delawares he had wanderlust and decided to go west. Traveling on foot and generally alone, he made his way across the continent to the mouth of the Columbia River. From there he went to the Southwest, then occupied by Mexicans, and learned to speak the Spanish language with ease and fluency. After about three years he went to Texas and joined a band of Delawares living there. Thereafter he made frequent journeys to Mexico and the West Coast as a hunter and scout, and Dodge says he "was justly renowned as having a more minute and extensive personal knowledge of the North American Continent than any other man ever had or probably will have."

When John Conner came to Kansas, he brought with him a "to whom it may concern" letter written by the United States Indian agent in Texas, stating that he "has devoted the best of his life trying to make peace with the wild and warlike tribes on our frontier, who has often risked his life and lost his property, is certainly entitled to the kindness and respect of the people he has served so faithfully." John Conner was then the owner of a sizeable tract of land in Haskell County, Texas, consisting of about 4,000 acres.[55]

John Conner made such a good impression on Delaware agent B. F. Robinson that he attached the letter of recommendation from Texas to a letter he wrote his superior on May 8, 1857, in which he strated: "Believing that the interest & well being of the tribe would be greatly advanced by putting John Conner in authority among them I would be pleased the Indian department would authorize me to treat him as a principal chief."

The Department of Indian Affairs gave its approval to the recommendation and authorized Robinson to deal with John Conner as the principal chief of the Delaware Nation. What the Delawares thought of their new chief, who had deserted the main body following their departure from Indiana, who had been absent for more than thirty years, and whose father was a white man, has not been recorded. If there were some who felt lukewarm toward the appointment, none could deny Conner's eligibility on his mother's side, since he was descended from Chief Anderson through Mekinges. Having the full support of the Great White Father living in Washington, no one attempted to block his elevation to the highest office in the tribe. At the first treaty-signing in which he participated at Sarcoxieville on May 30, 1860, the records identify him as "head chief of the whole tribe." The other chiefs who were present, as their names were spelled in the document, were "Sarcoxie ['as tall as he is'], chief of the Turtle band; Ne-con-he-con ['he who is pushed in front'], chief of the Wolf band; Kock-a-to-wha ['he who walks with crooked legs'], chief of the Turkey band, and assistants to the said chief, chosen and appointed by the people, and James Conner, chosen by said chief as a delegate." [56] The scribes who took down the minutes of the proceedings generally referred to the three animal groups as "bands" of the Delaware Nation.

In the first report he submitted dated September 13, 1864, following his appointment as the Delaware agent (printed in the 1864 *Report of the Commissioners of Indian Affairs*), Pratt wrote: "The Delaware tribe is divided into bands known as the Wolf, Turtle and Turkey bands, each band having its representative head (except the former, which is for the present, without a chief), and the tribe by a principal chief. There is also a council consisting of five members, who are selected according to fitness, which constitutes a legislative body or court."

Miss Clara Gowing, who was still employed as a teacher in the Baptist school in 1861, wrote that Charles Journeycake had been chosen chief of the Delawares, and she was very pleased because he was a Christian and a Baptist.[57] However, since she was a relative newcomer, and had little understanding of the Delaware political structure, she made a grievous error when she came to this conclusion. It is obvious that she was unaware that there was a principal chief and three band chiefs; nor did she know that Kockatowha, one of the band chiefs, died in April of 1861. Furthermore, she was unaware that Indian agent Fielding Johnson had recommended to the government that Charles Journeycake be appointed to succeed Kockatowha as a band chief, not as the principal Delaware chief, which her statement has caused many historians to erroneously assume. If there is any doubt about this, Johnson's letter dated July 5, 1861, addressed to his superior in the district office at Saint Joseph, Missouri, makes it very clear that he recommended Journeycake to succeed Kockatowha. He said in his letter that Journeycake was "one of the most intelligent Indians belonging to the tribe, honest and upright in his dealings deservadly popular with all classes and what makes it more desireable to have him appointed I think he is beyond the reach of bribery and would look after and protect the interests of the people and particularly the industrial and moral interests of the tribe . . ." [58]

The Saint Joseph office approved Johnson's recommendation and forwarded it for final approval to Washington, where it was decided that Johnson should first consult with other members of the Delaware Nation. He wrote subsequently on October 14, 1861, that "pursuant to the suggestion of the department, I had the Delawares called together for the purpose of nominating a chief to fill the vacancy of R[K]ocka-to-wha deceased. I nominated Charles Journeycake whose nomination was unanimously confirmed by the tribe." [59] This is another instance of the Department of Indian Affairs prompting the selection of a chief who met their approval. There can be no question that Journeycake, in the eyes of the authorities, was a man of integrity, having a reputation for high moral conduct. He was not, however, a Turkey like his predecessor Kockatowha, but a member of the Wolf division, which shows how government influence altered the native system of having a chief from each of the three groupings.

When Lewis Henry Morgan visited the Delaware reservation in Kansas in 1859, he conversed with Charles Journeycake's elderly mother, who was born Sally Williams, and who died in Oklahoma on February 6, 1873, at the approximate age of seventy-six.[60] She told Morgan that she was a member of the Wolf "tribe," but that her husband was a member of the Turtle tribe. She said that, according to Delaware tradition, children followed their mother's lineage, and all her offspring were considered Wolves. She went on to explain to Morgan that the words *wolf, turtle,* and *turkey* were not the correct literal translations of the three Delaware words used to identify the three groups. She said that in the dialect of her people the word translated into English as *wolf*, i.e., "Took-seat" actually meant "round foot" and could be applied to that class of quadrupeds which included the wolf but was not restricted to it. The word translated as *turkey*, i.e., "Pal-la-ooh," actually meant "fowls" or "scratchers," including the turkey. The word translated as *turtle*, i.e., "Poke-koo-ring," meant a class of reptiles that carried shells on their backs. These three terms were generic descriptions of the hairy, the feathered, and the hairless, nonfeathered creatures that inhabited the earth. She told Morgan that anciently there had been a number of subdivisions of the three tribes, each of which bore special names. The members of each group were prohibited from marrying persons within their group.

Although she may not have been aware of it, it would appear that Journeycake's mother was describing the vestiges of a clan structure which had been disrupted by wars, disease, and shifts in the Indian population after the arrival of Europeans. The three tribes, bands, or subtribes named after the three animals may have survived from phratries, each composed of a number of clans, but the former rules of marriage, kinship, and lineage of chieftains had given way to something else. In the true clan system, members of the same clan claimed descent from an animal, bird, reptile, or from some legendary creature associated with each animal grouping. The members of each clan looked upon this totemic animal for protection, guardianship, and support. The totems also served to define marriage relationships because when blood relationships were forgotten, some method had to be found for a man to determine whether he was related to a woman he selected as his mate. If they both were descended from the same totemic animal, thus owing allegiance to the same totem, it was assumed that they were related and it was taboo for them to marry.

Evidence that vague clan concepts and taboos were embodied in the three Delaware divisions is indicated in a statement made as follows by Zeisberger:

No Indian will marry a person in his own tribe, as he is too closely related to all in it. Herein, the Indians allege is to be found the reason for the existence of the tribes. Were it not for these, they could not be quite sure whether persons to be married are near relatives or not.[61]

In this statement, Zeisberger must have been using tribe in the sense of a small subdivision, such as a band or clan. Speck, who possessed a knowledge of ethnology that Zeisberger lacked, did his utmost to arrive at some rational meaning for the three "zoonymic" divisions, as he called them. He found that the three groupings were perpetuated by the three generic terms—wolf, turtle, and turkey—in the Big House Ceremony, but he wrote that the association between human members of the groups and the animals whose classification they bore was not clear.[62] That statement still stands unchallenged.

NOTES—CHAPTER 15

1. Grant Foreman, *The Last Trek of the Indians*, Chicago, 1946, p. 67.
2. Ibid., p. 41.
3. Charles N. Thompson, *Sons of the Wilderness, John and William Conner*, Indiana Historical Society Publications, vol. 12, 1937, p. 124. According to a deposition made by an elderly Delaware woman, Sarah Kinney of Coffeyville, Kan., on June 16, 1924 (in possession of the Bartlesville, Okla., Public Library) Mekinges, whose English name was Elizabeth, later married a man named Ketchum.
4. Joab Spencer, "Missouri's Aboriginal Inhabitants," *Missouri Historical Review*, vol. 3, no. 4, July, 1909, p. 291; cf. pp. 199–211, Marvin E. Tong, Jr., "The Indian Heritage of Christian County," of *Christian County, Its First 100 Years*, published by Christian County Centennial, Inc., Ozark, Mo., 1959.
5. *History of Greene County, Missouri*, Western Historical Company, St. Louis, 1883, pp. 131–32.
6. Henry R. Schoolcraft, *Scenes and Adventures in the Semi-Alpine Region of the Ozark Mountains of Missouri and Arkansas*, Philadelphia, 1853.
7. Grant Foreman, *Indians and Pioneers*, Norman, Okla., 1936, p. 197.
8. Richard Graham Papers, John Campbell to Richard Graham, September 20, 1825, Manuscript Collections, Missouri Historical Society, St. Louis. In 1826, $300 was deducted from Delaware annuities to pay for a mill owned by John Sample that had been burned by the Indians; ibid., annuity voucher, June 10, 1826.
9. Foreman, *Indians and Pioneers*, chap. 16; cf. R. C. Adams, *A Brief History of the Delaware Indians*, Senate Document no. 501, 59th Congress,

1st session, 1906, p. 29. See also Richard Graham Papers, John Campbell to Richard Graham, September 20, 1825.

10. Richard Graham Papers, Richard Graham to General William Clark, January 15, 1825.

11. Ibid., John Campbell to Richard Graham, May 19, 1825.

12. *The John Tipton Papers*, 3 vols., Indiana Historical Bureau, Indianapolis, 1942, vol. 1, pp. 469, 477, 486.

13. Ibid., pp. 500–1.

14. Ibid., p. 666.

15. Ibid., p. 764.

16. Ibid., vol. 2, pp. 40–41.

17. Kappler, *Indian Affairs, Laws and Treaties*, Washington, 1904, vol. 2, pp. 304–5. This treaty supplemented the St. Mary's Treaty of October 3, 1818; ibid., pp. 170–71.

18. Ibid., p. 305.

19. Foreman, *The Last Trek*, p. 55. The 1829 treaty is found in Kappler, *Indian Affairs, Laws and Treaties*, vol. 2, pp. 304–5.

20. Before the U.S. Court of Claims, Appeal No. 6-69, the United States of America vs. the Delaware Tribe of Indians and the Absentee Tribe of Oklahoma, on appeal from the Indian Claims Commission Docket nos. 27-A and 241.

21. Isaac McCoy, *History of Baptist Indian Missions*, New York, 1840, p. 404.

22. Kappler, *Indian Affairs*, vol. 2, p. 262; pp. 370–72.

23. Mrs. Mary Smith Witcher kindly made available to me a copy of this document in which Captain Ketchum testified as to his military service before Indian agent Robinson, June 20, 1855, National Archives, Record Group 13 A, B L Reg. 183943.

24. Lewis Henry Morgan, *The Indian Journals, 1859–1862*, ed. Leslie A. White, Ann Arbor, Mich., 1959, pp. 28, 55.

25. "Letters concerning the Presbyterian Mission in the Pawnee Country," *Kansas Historical Society Collections*, vol. 14, 1915–16, p. 693.

26. Morgan, *The Indian Journals*, passim.

27. See the transcript in the Secondine-Anderson Folder, Washington County History Room, Bartlesville (Oklahoma) Public Library.

28. Richard Graham Papers, Reply of Anderson and Killbuck to Richard Graham, May 29, 1856.

29. John Treat Irving, Jr., *Indian Sketches Taken during an Expedition to the Pawnee Tribes*, ed. John Francis McDermott, Norman, Okla., 1955, pp. 242–47; fn. 1, p. 6; cf. McCoy, *Baptist Indian Missions*, p. 492, wherein McCoy refers to Delaware war parties returning with eleven Pawnee scalps. On another hunting trip two sons of Captain Ketchum were killed

by a Sioux war party, and their furs, horses, traps, and blankets were confiscated; Foreman, *Last Trek*, p. 183.

30. *John Tipton Papers*, vol. 3, p. 595.

31. McCoy, *Baptist Indian Missions*, p. 545.

32. Foreman, *Last Trek*, p. 183; cf. McCoy, *Baptist Indian Missions*, p. 545.

33. J. C. Frémont, *Report of the Exploring Expedition to the Rocky Mountains in the Year 1842, . . . ,* Washington, D.C., 1845, p. 174.

34. Allan Nevins, ed., *Narratives of Exploration and Adventure by John C. Frémont*, New York, 1956, p. 437; cf. Richard C. Adams, *A Brief History*, p. 34.

35. Adams, *A Brief History*, p. 34.

36. On microfilm roll no. 5, John G. Pratt Papers, Kansas State Historical Society, a letter from Thomas Benton to George Manypenny dated May 10, 1854, relative to the back pay claimed by the Delawares, states: "I have to say that I have heard him often speak in great commendation of those [Delaware] Indians both as hunters and warriors in the conquest of California, and am very well assured that he considered them entitled to all the benefits of the acts for the reward and compensation of soldiers in the service of the United States, . . ." Following this letter are depositions from James Secondine, James Conner, and Delaware Charley stating they were paid $480 each for services to Frémont per agreement as hunters and scouts, but had not yet received any military pay still owed them.

37. Adams, *A Brief History*, pp. 34–35. According to information handed down among the Delawares in Oklahoma, the 10 Indians on this expedition were George Washington, Andrew Miller, John Smith, James Harrison, Wa-hoo-ney, James Wolf, John Moses, Jacob Eneas, Good Traveller, and Solomon Everett. It was a terrible trip, and the party numbering several hundred was snowbound in snows 15 to 30 feet deep, and were forced to eat some of their horses and mules to survive.

38. *Narratives of Exploration by John C. Frémont*, pp. 501, 505.

39. Microfilm, M 234, roll 275, Letters Received by the Office of Indian Affairs, 1824–81 (1858–61 Delaware Agency), National Archives, agreement dated Aug. 10, 1875. See also agreement of June 11, 1860, ibid., for contract made with another individual to take charge of the mill. These contracts were renewed periodically with both blacksmiths and millers, and there were a number of changes in the personnel. I am deeply indebted to Mrs. Mary Smith Witcher for lending me this microfilm.

40. Morgan, *The Indian Journals*, pp. 49–50. During this period Chief Anderson regularly collected his secret and private annuity of $360 per

year from the government; in the Richard Graham Papers there is a receipt bearing Anderson's mark and dated at the Delaware Agency, James Fork of White River, June 14, 1826, acknowledging payment for the year 1826.

41. Lawrence Henry Gipson, ed., *The Moravian Indian Mission on White River*, Indianapolis, 1938, p. 297.

42. Charles N. Thompson, *Sons of the Wilderness*, p. 222, note 7. Zeisberger also wrote that when the Indians went each year to collect their annuities, each chief or captain delivered as many little sticks as there were persons, which provided a check on the Indian population; Bliss, trans., *Diary of David Zeisberger, Cincinnati*, 1885, vol. 2, p. 288.

43. Robert B. Duncan, "The Games of Moccasin and Bullet," *Indiana Magazine of History*, vol. 1, 1905, pp. 17–18; cf. *John Tipton Papers*, vol. 1, p. 204, wherein a "professional" dealer played the Delawares.

44. See J. J. Lutz, "The Methodist Missions among the Indian Tribes in Kansas," *Kansas Historical Society Collections*, vol. 9, 1905–6, p. 204, note 66, for agreement. Evidently a school was later reopened in association with the Methodist Episcopal Church. On July 21, 1860, Indian agent Thomas B. Sykes signed a contract with Nancy Boles for three months "to teach them such studies as in her opinion are best calculated to enlighten their minds." She was paid one dollar per month per child, the Indians to supply the books and stationery; Pratt Papers, roll no. 5. Three years later, agent Field Johnson contracted with Miss Helen E. Tuttle to "teach school at the Methodist Church near James Ketchem's" for six months at a salary of twenty-four dollars per month; ibid., roll no. 6, agreement dated Nov. 24, 1863.

45. McCoy, *History of Baptist Indian Missions*, pp. 59–60.

46. Clara Gowing, "Life among the Delaware Indians," *Kansas Historical Society Collections*, vol. 12, 1911–12, pp. 183–93. See notes 3 and 4, p. 183, for information about location of the first mission and biographical data about Rev. John G. Pratt. Roll no. 9 of Pratt Papers also contains biographical data about Pratt; cf. Esther Clark Hill, "The Pratt Collection," *Kansas Historical Quarterly*, vol. 1, no. 2, February 1932, pp. 83–88.

47. Pratt Papers roll no. 5, report dated Sept. 17, 1866.

48. Gowing, "Life among the Delaware Indians," p. 187. Additional data about the Baptist mission may be found in Esther Clark Hill, "Some Background of Early Baptist Missions in Kansas," *Kansas Historical Quarterly*, vol. 1, no. 2, February 1932, pp. 89–103.

49. McCoy, *History of Baptist Indian Missions*, fn. p. 580.

50. Among the chiefs on the James Fork who acknowledged receipt of the government annuity in 1826 was "Captain Catchum"; Richard

Graham Papers, Vouchers for Annuities, June 10, 1826; see copy of voucher in Appendix 4 of this book.

51. In a letter written July 5, 1861, agent Fielding Johnson explains that Cummings appointed Ketchum the principal chief in the year 1829 and that Commissioner Mix in effect appointed John Conner to the same post in 1858; Microfilm, M 234, roll no. 275, National Archives.

52. I am further indebted to Mrs. Witcher for a transcript of this will found in the National Archives, Record Group no. 75, 1858, Delaware R 600.

53. Mrs. Witcher, who is descended from Captain Ketchum, sent me photos of the inscriptions on his grave and the grave of his son Charles Ketchum, a deacon in the Methodist Episcopal Church, who died July 20, 1860. Both are buried in the graveyard of the White Church.

54. James Conner's letter and B. F. Robinson's letter endorsing the nomination of his brother John are on record in the National Archives Record Group no. 75, 1858, Delaware R 600.

55. Microfilm M 234, roll 275, letter dated Jan. 1, 1857; cf. Adams, A Brief History, p. 33. John Conner later claimed compensation for losses suffered by him and his family in moving from Texas to Kansas, but he did not have adequate proof to satisfy the government, Pratt Papers, roll no. 5, letter dated Dec. 8, 1857, from the Acting Commissioner to the St. Louis office. The manuscript collections of the Oklahoma Historical Society include a letter dated Sept. 11, 1896, written by Andrew J. Baker, Commissioner of the General Land Office, Austin, Texas, indicating that a certificate for one league of land (4,428 acres) located in Young and Haskell counties was issued to John Conner on Feb. 7, 1853. The certificate stated that the land shall not be sold or transferred by Conner; it would be interesting to know what eventually happened to it. I am indebted to Mrs. Rella Looney, Indian archivist, for providing me with a copy.

56. Kappler, Indian Affairs, Laws and Treaties, vol. 2, p. 803.

57. Gowing, "Life Among the Delaware Indians," p. 190. Her exact words were "In October Charles Journeycake was chosen chief, thus making two Christian chiefs, as his brother Isaac had been chief for some years." This is a palpable error—Isaac Journeycake was never considered a Delaware chief.

58. Microfilm M 234, roll 275.

59. Ibid.

60. Morgan, The Indian Journals, p. 52. For information about Sally Journeycake see Rev. S. H. Mitchell, The Indian Chief Journeycake, American Baptist Publication Society, Philadelphia, 1895. Although Morgan apparently considered her a reliable Delaware informant, one wonders

if he was fully aware that she was only part Indian, her father being a white man.

61. Hulbert and Schwarze, eds., *David Zeisberger's History of the Northern American Indians*, p. 98. In *The Indian Journals*, Morgan indicates that the Munsies were also divided into the same three groupings, having the identical eponyms, p. 59.

62. Frank G. Speck, *Big House Ceremony*, p. 75. Note that Brinton, *Lenâpé Legends*, p. 39, also uses the identical generic terms which Sally Journeycake explained to Morgan.

16

On to Oklahoma—
The End of the Road

During the thirty-eight years the Delawares lived in Kansas—from 1830 to 1868—they were party to four separate treaties with the United States which were ratified by the Senate. The first was ne-gotiated in Washington, D.C., on May 6, 1854; the second at Sar-coxieville on the Kansas reservation, May 30, 1860; the third at Leavenworth City, July 2, 1861; and the final one at the Delaware Agency in Kansas on July 4, 1866.[1] After the Indians' signatures were affixed to the Treaty of 1866—the last one between the United States and the Delawares—the 2 million acres that had constituted the re-served lands in Kansas were no longer owned by the Indians.

The attrition of these lands occurred in a series of steps involving not only the government but four railroad companies, individual white citizens, squatters, townsite companies, and other Indians as well. For example, on December 14, 1843, the Wyandot, having ceded to the government all their lands east of the Mississippi, pur-chased 23,000 acres from the Delawares for $46,080, of which $6,680 was to be paid in 1844 and $4,000 annually thereafter for ten years. This land ran west of the Kansas River, thence north to the Missouri River and back to the place of beginning "in as near a square form as the rivers and territory ceded will admit of." [2] In deeding lands to their former hosts, the Delawares reciprocated for the hospitality extended to them by the Wyandot in Ohio. The agreement between them stated they had been ardent friends for many years, and the Delawares went on record as saying they were glad to have their uncles settle down near them.

The converts known as Christian Indians, who lived near Munsie, Kansas, also purchased lands from the Delawares. The nucleus of this group was a band of about 200 Moravian Indians formerly from New Fairfield along the Thames River in Ontario who came to Kansas in 1837, accompanied by the Reverend Jesse Vogler and John Killbuck.[3] In May of 1854 the leaders of the group formally purchased four sections of land from the Delawares for $2.50 per acre.[4] In the Moravian records the mission town in Kansas where these Indians settled, and where a succession of pastors ministered to them, was known as Westfield.

In 1858 Joseph Killbuck and Frederick Samuel, members of this group, complained in a letter to President Buchanan on behalf of the congregation that they had been happy and had prospered in their new homes on the land purchased from their Delaware hosts "until the avaricious white man came to Kansas. From that time until now we suffered great wrongs until now which we can no longer endure. There are now about fifteen [white] families and individuals living on our land." [5] White incursions forced the Christian Indians to sell their property, and in 1859 some of them settled with the Chippewa in Franklin County, Kansas, where their descendants may still be found. Another group returned to their previous homes in Canada.

In December of 1838 a group of Stockbridge Indians from Wisconsin came to what is now Delaware County, Kansas, where they applied to the Delaware Council and were granted permission to live on the reserved lands. Among these migrants were a few families of Brotherton Indians, direct descendants of Delawares who occupied the New Jersey reservation until 1802, when they joined the Stockbridges in New York, and from there went to Wisconsin. All of the Stockbridges who remained in Kansas (some returned to Wisconsin) were eventually absorbed into the Delaware Nation, although as late as 1860 there were still a few individuals on the reservation maintaining their Stockbridge identity. Seven of them were members of a family named Dick, and the wife of A. D. Dick was described as being a white woman.[6] Others bore the names Clark, Abrams, and Toucy.

It is also of interest that in 1856 a Brotherton Indian named Jacob Scioket living on the Kansas reservation complained to the Delaware agent that he believed he was entitled to money still owed the Brothertons for the reservation they vacated in New Jersey when they went to New York. The agent referred the question to his superiors, letters were written to Washington, and an investigation was made. After a lapse of time, a reply was received from Thomas S. Allison, New Jersey's secretary of state, in which he stated that in 1801 the Brotherton Indians reconveyed their reserved lands to the state for an agreed upon price, and that Jacob Scioket's name was the first on the list of thirty-eight Brothertons who signed the deed of conveyance.[7]

The age-old conflict with white settlers over possession of land occupied by the Indians was repeated after the Kansas-Nebraska Act created the Territory of Kansas in 1854. Congress was well aware that confrontations with the Indians could not be avoided, and an act had been passed on March 3, 1853, authorizing the President to negotiate with Indian tribes in Kansas and Nebraska to extinguish their title to the lands they then occupied, in whole or part, which would permit United States citizens to settle on their lands legally. Indian Commissioner George W. Manypenny conducted preliminary discussions with the tribes living in Kansas during the summer and fall of 1853, in the hope of persuading them to move. He explained to them that the acquisition by the United States of California, Oregon, and New Mexico would bring hundreds of new families to the West, and it would not be healthy for the Indians to be living in the paths of the migration. In view of previous promises made to the Indians by the government that Kansas would be their homes forever and ever, most of them, including the Delawares, were unwilling to give up the land and move again.[8]

One could scarcely conceive of a worse place for Indians to be living during the chaotic period after 1854 when Kansas became a territory. After bitter debate in the Congress, Senator Stephen A. Douglas, a heavy investor in real estate and railway stock, threw his weight behind a plan whereby the citizens of the new Kansas Territory would decide whether they wanted to have slavery or not.[9] If Kansas, lying immediately west of slaveholding Missouri, decided to become a slave territory, there was no question that this would be bitterly opposed by the North. If it decided to be a free state, then southern supporters would be angered. Indian Agent B. F. Robinson warned the Delawares that white men in Kansas might go to war with each other over the slavery question, but that the Indians should not be drawn into the dispute "taking sides with neither the Missourians or Yankees." [10] This was easier said than done, because it was difficult to remain neutral when opponents and proponents of slavery flocked into the territory from the North and South, each side hopeful of gaining enough political strength to swing the issue in its favor. There then followed numerous outbreaks in "bleeding Kansas" over the slavery question, including John Brown's raid at Pottawatomie Creek, as seeds of the Civil War were being sown.

With the influx of settlers, especially the proslavers from adjacent Missouri, it was inevitable that a town would be built on the Missouri River, even though the land there legally belonged to the Delawares. The general belief of the newcomers was that the Delaware Indians owned more land than they could possibly utilize, and even the Office of Indian Affairs thought the Indians had much more land than they needed. As a consequence, the whittling away of Delaware territory began when a townsite company was formed on June 13, 1854, and building lots were laid out near Fort Leavenworth. Two high-ranking officers in the garrison were among thirty organizers of a land syndicate, which not only laid out the lots but advertised them for sale *before* the company had obtained title to the property. Since the Delawares were prohibited by treaty from selling their lands to anyone except the government, which actually retained title, potential buyers had difficulty acquiring lands. To do so, a buyer was first obligated to enter into negotiations with the government, and if the government approved, then representatives were obliged to discuss the matter with the Indians and obtain their consent. Finally, the government was not supposed to favor one buyer over another, but was required by law to offer the land for public sale, and dispose of it the highest bidder. In the case of the Leavenworth townsite company, the Indians had little choice in the matter, although the government interceded in their behalf, forcing the company to pay $24,000 for 320 acres. The towns of Lawrence and Topeka were founded soon after, and the whole situation, which involved not only the Delawares but their Indian neighbors, was a repetition of what had happened to the Indian lands in Ohio, Indiana, and Missouri as the settlers overran the territory.

The Delawares had been bothered intermittently by emigrants stealing their horses and causing other annoyances as they passed across the reservation en route to California, Colorado, and Oregon; but now with towns springing up, the trouble became chronic. Almost all the Indian families now owned horses, and some had large herds which grazed unattended in open fields, where they became easy prey to horse thieves. In October of 1858 the Delaware chiefs complained as follows in a letter to President Buchanan: "Since the opening of the Territory, thieves (white men) have come in and are constantly stealing our horses, and in many instances have stripped some of our people of almost everything they owned." [11]

The four Kansas treaties were intended to settle differences between the Delawares and their white neighbors, or to adjust problems relating to lands, and one might devote many pages to a discussion of these treaties. For example, the second treaty dated May 30, 1860, obliged the United States to indemnify the Delawares in the amount of $30,000 for timber illicitly taken from their lands, and $9,500 for ponies and cattle stolen from them. What had happened was that white squatters drove away bulls, cows, and oxen owned by the Delawares; and, as though to add insult to injury, they cut down trees growing on the Indians' property to obtain logs to build their cabins. (On January 19, 1869, the Delawares claimed that, since signing the 1860 treaty, they had lost to white thieves an additional 428 horses, 10 mules, 112 cattle, 10 sheep, and six hogs having a total valuation of $26,284. Detailed lists were submitted in evidence along with names of the Indian victims and specifically what animals they had lost.[12])

Settlers continued to stream into Kansas by covered wagon, by steamboat up the Missouri, on horseback, and on foot, some alone, others with their families or in the company of other families. It seemed that nothing could hold them back, and, since the Delawares were not American citizens, they did not have recourse to the courts to protect their persons or properties. They knew that, if they attempted to offer resistance to the trespassers, there was always the possibility of the whites forming vigilantes, who would burn their houses to the ground, and steal all their livestock. The only practical course open to them was to demand of the United States that the squatters be compelled to pay for any lands they occupied illegally. Actually, the Delawares did not want to divest themselves of any of their lands, but as this was the only alternative, it became one of the main provisions of the first Kansas treaty of May 6, 1854. By the terms of this instrument, the Delawares were compelled to authorize the President to offer acreage from their reservation for sale at public auction, except for a strip forty miles long and ten miles wide. This tract was called a "diminished reserve," and the Delawares were given the impression that they could retain this smaller property as their own and never be crowded out by trespassers. The President was empowered to invest the money for the lands sold to incoming settlers and speculators, in safe and profitable stocks, the principal to remain unimpaired and held in the account of the Delaware Indians as their "national fund." The interest on the principal was disbursed to the Delawares at intervals, and divided among the men, women, and children on the official enrollment lists on a per capita basis. Eventually, some 558,555.46 acres of the choicest lands were sold, bringing a total of $1,054,943.37 to the "national fund." [13]

Those Delaware families who were living, ranching, or farming on the lands offered for sale were forced to vacate and move to their "diminished reserve" to live. In doing so they needed cash to erect dwellings and farm buildings, and to replace livestock lost or stolen while they were vacating their old homes and moving to new ones. To provide financial aid to these needy families, the Delaware Council requested that instead of continuing to pay annuities of $7,540, which amounted to an insignificant amount per capita, the government should make a cash settlement by giving the tribe a lump sum. The United States agreed to this request, and consented to give the Delawares $148,000 outright in two payments as covered in the Treaty of 1854. Thereafter, the government would no longer be obligated to pay $7,540 annually.

The United States paid the Indians $10,000 for the "outlet" (also by terms of the Treaty of 1854), which was not included in the "diminished reserve." This was a paltry sum for a tract containing more than a million acres, which in litigation between the Delawares and the government a hundred years later, was found by the Indian Claims Commission to be worth at least $617,980 at 1854 land prices.

The $10,000 paid by the government in 1854 was distributed among the five chiefs who signed the treaty: "Captain Ketchem, Sarkoxey, Segondyne, Neconhecond, and Kockkatowha, in equal shares of two thousand dollars each, to be paid as follows: to each of the said chiefs annually, the sum of two hundred and fifty dollars, until the whole sum is paid." The treaty specified that this money was being given to the old chiefs because the Delawares felt grateful for their long and faithful services, and since the chiefs were poor, their people believed it was their duty to keep them from want in their old age! The truth is that the rank and file of the tribe were unaware of what was going on. Richard C. Adams, an educated Delaware, wrote later that the Council never formally approved this treaty, which he said was concocted in defiance of the law and in violation of former treaties for the express purpose of taking the Indians' lands away from them. He said that when they learned what had happened, the Delawares "exasperated and outraged by this proceeding, were cajoled into acquiescence by the specious argument that although the proceeding was irregular and unjust, yet as it would doubtless result in their perpetual peace and undisturbed possession of their remaining lands, it was worth the sacrifice." [14]

Indian agent B. F. Robinson seems to have been sincerely concerned for the welfare of the Indians and was indignant about the indiscriminate trespassing on Delaware lands which continued despite the 1854 treaty. On September 29, 1857, he wrote his superiors as follows:

Hundreds of whites have simultaneously invaded the Delaware reservation and are engaged in surveying the country, marking lines, making claims &c preparatory, I presume, to permanent settlement. I am informed the movement has been set on foot by an illegal combination of several hundred persons at Leavenworth City and vicinity.[15]

Under the regulations then in effect covering intrusions on Indian property, the Indian agent was helpless to do anything until he posted a public notice for twenty days, warning trespassers that the land they occupied was on an Indian reserve. After this he had to serve a written notice individually on each intruder in person. If the intruder then disregarded the warning, the agent was authorized to request the assistance of military forces from the nearest fort. Robinson estimated the number of intruders at about one thousand, in such numbers he said that he alone was incapable of halting "such iniquitous and flagrant violations of the laws of the country." To his credit it must be said that he did his utmost to deliver warning notices, and some squatters were frightened away when threatened that they would be ejected by soldiers from Fort Leavenworth—but then they returned later.

While Robinson was issuing warnings to settlers at one location on Indian lands, other settlers were cutting timber and erecting log cabins on more distant parts of the reservation, and it was beyond the capacity of one man to police the Indians' lands. Trespassers began to erect a ferry on the Kansas River opposite Lawrence, which Robinson, fortunately, was able to stop, thus halting this encroachment on Indian property.[16] In the winter of 1857 he dispatched a letter to the United States District Attorney's office in Kansas Territory complaining about the intruders. "It is important," he wrote, "that prompt and sufficient action be taken or the whites will soon overrun the whole reserve."[17] The local government officials, who were hearing similar complaints from agents stationed with neighboring tribes, had no inclination to commit political suicide by siding with Indians. Even if they had wanted to, they lacked sufficient personnel or large enough budgets to patrol the millions of acres constituting lands reserved to the Indian tribes. Many officials held to the view that Indians should not be allowed to wander around aimlessly in search of game, but should settle down to family homesteads, and they deliberately closed their eyes to white encroachment.

From the viewpoint of the Department of the Interior, where the major policy decisions were made, the most practical solution was to hasten the sale of the Indians' lands and get them out of the way by moving them elsewhere. According to the Indian Appropriation Act of March 3, 1855 (as stipulated in the 1854 treaty), the President had appointed a special commissioner to supervise the disposition of lands belonging to the Delawares which he was empowered to put up for sale. Although it was intended that the money go into the Delaware national fund, the chiefs requested that some of the receipts be turned over to them immediately to meet the needs of their people. Accordingly, in the spring of 1857, Robinson was authorized to distribute $60,000 on a per capita basis, and in November of the same year he distributed an additional $100,000.[18] If these and other monies had been allowed to collect in the national fund and accumulate interest, the Delawares would have become a wealthy tribe, but by such disbursements, which amounted to about $160 or

$170 for each man, woman, and child, the national fund was continually reduced. Much of the money was wasted by the recipients, and in the long run did little good.

In 1858 members of the Delaware Council sent a message "To Our Great Father, the President of the United States," in which they said they would like to have the lands in their "diminished reserve" surveyed and apportioned to them in severalty, because "many of us have adopted the manners and customs of our White Brothers, we have in many instances large farms fenced and under cultivation, we have good houses, have our children educated, and notwithstanding this, we have nothing we can call our own." [19]

In a second letter written the same year, the chiefs admitted that some members of the tribe did not pay as much attention to agriculture as they should, and even those who were learning to become farmers were at the mercy of bad weather. "We have all ceased to hunt for a living," the letter went on to say, "and some of us are necessarily compelled to look to the government of the United States for support and assistance while we are endeavoring to throw off the habits of our fathers and assume those of the White Man." Although these thoughts were doubtless those of the Indians, the words were probably those of agent Robinson because none of the signatories could write. The chiefs who put their marks on the letter were John Conner, Neconhecond, James Secondine, and Kockatowha. The three councilors, who also made their marks, were James Conner, James Ketchum, and Big Raccoon. The communication stated that one of the chiefs, Captain Sarcoxie, and several of the head men were absent on a visit to the Cherokee. [20]

By 1860 the situation had grown much worse on the Delaware reservation, and to add to the Indians' troubles, a new agent, whom they did not trust, Thomas B. Sykes, had been appointed to succeed Robinson. By custom established some years before, the Indian agent always attended the meetings of the Delaware Council, and he not only knew what was going on, but could influence the decisions. In the spring of 1860 the Council convened a number of times without Sykes's knowledge. He later learned what had transpired, and he wrote his superior as follows:

Many things tended to bring about their discontentedness. This Winter they have had a great many Ponies stolen from them, not a neighborhood or settlement has escaped the thieves. They are out of money, and have gone to the extent of their credit with their merchants.[21] The white people around them are continually annoying them with threats, telling them they cannot nor shall not long own so much land here among them. People are cutting timber continually, and hauling it off, and according to Judge Pettit's (the Judge for this District) decision they cannot be punished for it. And to bring a civil action against them would be only running the United States to great expense, and not even the cost of the suit could be made out of such men as are doing this. The law should be amended.[22]

At the time of Sykes's appointment, John Conner continued to hold office as head chief, with his brother James as a councilor. Sarcoxie was chief of the "Turtle Band," as Sykes's records identified the subgroup, and he was also an assistant to the head chief. His councilors, in the spelling given in Sykes's reports and letters, were Chal-lo-ese, Buffalo Wilson, and John Wilson. Neconhecond was still the chief of the "Wolf Band" and an assistant to the head chief. His councilors were Big Nigger, John Sarcoxie, Jim Simond, Big Raccoon, and George Washington. Kockatowha, who was then still alive, was chief of the "Turkey Band" and assistant to the head chief, and his councilors were White Turkey, Tongie-noxie, Captain Beaver, and Pe-ne-a-tut.[23] (The last name is a variant of the Delaware word meaning "little boy," and was the Indian name for the Turkey chieftain and ma-ta-en-noo, "medicine man," known as Colonel Jackson. He is included in the Indian group in Fig. 18.) These men were the mainstays of the Council, and Sykes learned from an Indian informer that the discussion at the Council meeting in May 1860 was whether the Delawares should move to the Rockies, the Far West, the Southwest, or elsewhere to escape being harassed by white people. This was obviously the reason they did not want Sykes present at the meeting while their plans were being discussed and formulated. Sykes also learned that the Council had taken a ballot among Delawares living on the reservation, and, with the exception of ten or fifteen negative votes, the consensus was to leave Kansas Territory.[24]

Subsequently, the Delaware spent $874.50 from their national fund to cover the expenses of a delegation sent to visit the country of the Cherokee and Choctaw. The records are clear that this delegation headed by Sarcoxie and the aging Neconhecond left the reservation on November 6, 1860, on a mission to inspect the lands in

Figure 18. Group of Delaware Indians who came from Kansas to Indian Territory (now Oklahoma) in 1867–68. Front row: Richard C. Adams, Herbert Ketchem, Willie Nicholas. Second row: William Adams, Abe Ketchem, Colonel Jackson (a chief and ceremonial leader), "Old Man" Curlyhead, Andrew Miller. Top row: John Sarcoxie, Charles H. Armstrong, Julius Fouts, Albert Curlyhead, Arthur Armstrong. (From Richard C. Adams, A Delaware Indian Legend and the Story of Their Troubles)

what was then called Indian Territory—now Oklahoma. The initiative was taken by the Delaware Council, not the government, and the following passage is quoted from a letter written by the delegation from the Cherokee Station on the Neosho River on November 28, 1860:

Our object in holding a conference with the chiefs & people of the Cherokee Nation is that we wish to buy about two hundred sections [a section was 640 acres] of Land from the Cherokee Nation and at the same time to become citizens of said Nation to abide and come under your Laws and Government, for which we will pay a fair price for the Land if the arrangement can be made.[25]

In addition to Sarcoxie and Neconhecond, the letter was signed by Delaware Charlie, Big Nigger, and Joseph Thompson (grandfather of Mrs. Nora Thompson Dean), who were members of the mission. In the light of subsequent events, it is important to note that the Delawares independently made a proposal to the Cherokee to settle on their land as early as 1860.

Prior to the departure of the delegation, the Treaty of May 30, 1860, was signed, in which the government agreed to comply with the Delawares' request that their "diminished reserve" be allotted in severalty to members of their nation. This meant that every man, woman, and child would be allocated a certain plot of land—finally agreed on as eighty acres—and each family was expected to live thereafter on its particular allotment. The land thereafter could not be sold to anyone except the United States or another Delaware Indian, after permission was obtained from the Indian agent. Each individual would receive a certificate from the Commissioner of Indian Affairs which contained a description of the eighty acres set apart for the exclusive use and benefit of himself and his heirs.

The treaty also stated that there were about two hundred Delawares "among the Southern Indians," which referred to the splinter group who had gone to Cape Girardeau, and were later called Absentee Delawares. Since the Council had reason to believe these absent people, some of whom were in Texas, might rejoin the main body, eighty acres were also reserved for each of them when and if they came to Kansas. A delegation was later sent to invite the absentees to come to Kansas and claim their lands, but the Indian agent wrote that "these efforts were unavailing." [26] There were other provisions in the 1860 treaty, such as reserving 320 acres where the mill, the schoolhouse, and Ketchum's store stood; 320 acres where the Council House stood; 160 acres where the Baptist Mission stood; 160 acres for the Agency House; 40 acres for the Methodist Episcopal Church South, and 40 acres for the Methodist Church North.

After all these allocations were made from the "diminished reserve," there still remained a large surplus of unallocated lands. The treaties of 1860 and 1861 provided for the Delawares to be relieved of this excess acreage, which was being eyed hungrily by railroad promoters. Therein lies another story.

The white man's determination to improve the means of transportation in the West caused friction with the Indians even before any railroads existed. So far as the Delawares were concerned, their trouble began with the Kansas Stage Company, which was operating stagecoaches between Lawrence and Leavenworth in 1858. In addition to transporting passengers, the company contracted with the United States to carry mail in an efficient manner, and the fastest and most direct route between the two cities ran across the Delaware reserve. The owners of the stage company obtained permission from "two leading Indians . . . Sarcoxie and Packague" to build a stable where they could exchange relays of horses, which seemed a reasonable arrangement since the stage was also a convenience for the Indians. On September 25, 1858, Isaac E. Eaton, Secretary of the Kansas Stage Company, notified the Commissioner of Indian Affairs that a white man, John Kinney, whose wife was a Delaware, and a half-breed Delaware named Zeigler were erecting a saloon to retail "ardent spirits" in the vicinity of the stable.[27] The owners of the stage company could not be blamed that persons not in their employ, and over whom they had no control, decided that this was a good location to vend liquor to drivers and passengers—and illegally to the Indians. Nevertheless, it illustrates how the advances made by the white man seemed always to clash with the interests of the Indians.

The dynamic American Midwest could not limit its growth to the stagecoach, and strong pressures soon developed to extend railroad transportation into Kansas Territory, and from there to the Far West. Railroads represented year-round transportation in spite of fall rains, winter blizzards, and spring thaws that interrupted the stage schedules. The Kansas legislature, which assembled in July, 1855, chartered five railroads, and it was inevitable that the coming of rail lines would deal the final blow to all of the Indian reservations in Kansas. Looking back from the perspective of modern business when antitrust laws and state and federal regulations, to say nothing of the tax structure, restrict the conduct of business corporations, what happened during the infancy of American railroads is almost beyond comprehension. States granted the right of eminent domain to rail operators, permitting them to take over land without the owner's consent through condemnation proceedings. In many instances the states bought railroad bonds with public monies to help the railroads pay their construction costs. From 1850 on, huge grants of state and federal lands were made as construction subsidies to railroad companies for the declared purpose of bringing the general blessings of railroad service to the people, and to contribute to the economic growth that accompanied the expansion.

Not only were railroad promoters extended privileges unheard of today, by state, territory, and federal officials who were catering to voters clamoring for rail service to the West, but there were also many shady dealings. Negotiations that would be illegal today were carried on with the knowledge of Congress and the President. It was not unusual for responsible government officials to buy stock privately in budding railroad companies in the expectation of making large profits on their investments. Others, who were participants in decision-making before public announcement was released, speculated in western lands whose values increased dramatically when news of the coming of a new railroad appeared in the newspaper headlines.

A railroad company had to acquire a right-of-way on which to lay its tracks, but it is not generally recognized that it also needed land for other purposes. The company had to acquire timberland as close as possible to the right-of-way so that trees could be obtained for conversion into the countless number of ties on which the tracks were laid. The earliest locomotives used wood for fuel, and wood was also needed to build depots, freight stations, trestles, platforms, water towers, houses for employes, and other structures. Once the tracks were in place, the company's income depended upon the volume of freight it was able to haul, because, if freight did not materialize, the receipts from passenger service would be inadequate to keep the line in operation.

The most practical freight route in Kansas Territory was directly across the reserved lands—but the railroad companies had to get rid of the Indians who stood in their way. The companies wanted enterprising white farmers and cattlemen to be in possession of the lands, not unprogressive Indians who had little need for either freight or passenger transportation. Railroad officials had to find a way to acquire ownership of the Indian reservations so they, in turn, could transfer the land in smaller parcels to white farmers and ranchers. By buying the lands cheaply from the Indians, the railroad companies made a profit by selling the acreage to settlers at higher prices, and that meant extra income for their stockholders. Since the Indians were wards of the United States, government officials necessarily had to involve themselves in the transactions. They convinced the Delawares to sell their excess lands by assuring them that the railroads were being laid to accommodate the Indians as well as whites and would increase the value of the lands the Indians retained for themselves. By terms of the old treaties, the Delawares were permitted to sell their lands only to the government, but the treaties of 1860 and 1861 permitted sale to the railroads as well.

These two treaties provided for the newly organized Leavenworth, Pawnee and Western Railroad Company to purchase all surplus Delaware lands after the allotments had been made to the Delaware families. After the lands were allocated and surveyed, the surplus amounted to 223,000 acres. It was agreed that the railroad company would pay the Indians on the basis of an appraisal made by three commissioners appointed by the Secretary of the Interior, but in no event less than $1.25 per acre. When their study was concluded, the commissioners appraised the surplus territory, which included some of the choice corn and ranch lands in Kansas, at $1.28 per acre.

The surplus land was strictly a real estate investment for the railroad company, because they laid their right-of-way across the "diminished reserve" wherein the Delawares had their eighty-acre plots. The proposed line was to extend from Leavenworth to a point on the Kansas River opposite Lawrence, and the treaty gave the company a perpetual right-of-way across the territory. The Indian owners were again given assurance that the railroad tracks crossing their property would greatly enhance the value of their individual eighty-acre plots. They were given the impression that everything was being done for their benefit.

When the time came for the railroad company to pay $286,742.15 "in gold or silver coin," the appraised evaluation of the 223,000 acres, the company claimed it was short of cash because "of the general derangement of business conditions." In lieu of paying cash, its officers conceived of the idea of printing its own bonds to pay the Indians for the lands. Since it had no cash or other collateral, the company used 100,000 acres of the land it could not pay for as security for the bonds. The company then offered for sale the remaining 123,000 acres at prices ranging from $20 to $50 per acre, thus making a huge profit without investing a cent of its own money. A letter (quoted in Appendix 5) written on April 30, 1861, by the Secretary of the Interior to President Lincoln, and the letter of June 4, 1861 (Appendix 6), written by a law firm representing the Delawares, reveal how this irregular financing, which might be considered extortion, was arranged and approved in Washington.

In October of 1860, the President received a message from Kansas signed by fifty Delaware Indians stating that "we will not and shall not consider the Treaty [1860] recently made between Mr. T. B. Sykes Agent on the part of the United States and *three of our Drunken Chiefs as Legal.*" The letter went on to accuse Sykes of giving intoxicating liquor to the four chiefs who signed the treaty, and to state that three of them were drunk when they affixed their marks. The letter concluded with this plea: "Now with the mind and heart of a kind and compassionate man, can you consider this as legal—Never! Never!" [28] The treaty had already been signed by the President with the "advice and consent of the Senate" and, having been ratified on July 11, 1860, it was a binding legal instrument.

Apparently there was more hanky-panky involved in getting the chiefs' signatures than merely serving them arduous spirits. Article 7 stated that each of the Indian signatories, "in consideration of long and faithful services," would be allotted an extra large tract of his own choice, and for his own personal use, for which he would receive a patent in fee simple from the President. Accordingly, John Conner received 640 acres; Sarcoxie, 320 acres; Kockatowha, 320 acres; Neconhecond, 320 acres; and Henry Tiblow, the Delaware Indian interpreter, 320 acres. The treaty stated further that $1,500 would be appropriated each year from the national fund "as the annual salary of the councilmen of the said tribe of Indians." [29] The chiefs at this time were each receiving $250 per year as a private annuity, according to the Treaty of 1854, and the final installment was paid in 1861.

One wonders if those Delawares eking out a bare livelihood from tending their small herds, raising corn, and splitting logs to keep their cabins warm during the cold winters were aware that their chiefs and councilors were being handsomely rewarded by the government. During their later days in Kansas, each chief was receiving a salary of $800 a year, and the councilors $750. Isaac Journeycake, who succeeded Henry Tiblow as interpreter in 1861, was paid $400 annually. At today's price levels, these may seem insignificant sums, but a century ago, when a full-time Indian agent was paid only $1,500 per year, these salaries were not inconsiderable.

Although the Leavenworth, Pawnee and Western Railroad (later consolidated with the Union Pacific) was the first to acquire lands from the Delawares by the treaties of 1860 and 1861, there were three other railroad companies whose tracks were eventually laid across the reserved lands. These were the Eastern Division of the Union Pacific, which ran up the Kansas River through the "diminished reserve"; the Missouri River Railroad, which ran from Leavenworth to Wyandotte, Kansas, passing through the eastern boundary of the reserve; and the Rocky Mountain Railroad, which ran from Fort Riley to the Missouri River. It was well known among the white population in Kansas that certain of these railroad interests encouraged squatters to harass the Delawares in the expectation that they would vacate their eighty-acre allotments if their lives were made miserable enough.

If, as the documentary evidence suggests, agent Sykes was influenced by a desire for personal gain at the expense of the Indians, then one can understand the frustration of the Delawares. If their intermediary with the Great White Father in Washington was not sympathetic toward their problems, and if he failed to protect their interests, they became fearful and anxiety-ridden. On July 2, 1861, they registered a complaint which indicates they had completely lost faith in Sykes, "representing that he is connected with unprincipled & unscrupulous speculators who are endeavoring to defraud the Indians. They complain of want of integrity in him & his associates & of the utter unreliability of their statements." [30] Apparently the disdain shown by the Delawares became more than Sykes could stand, or perhaps his superiors may have caught up with his malfeasance. In any event, he resigned his position, and later became an officer in the Confederate army. He was succeeded in 1861 by Fielding Johnson, who served the Delawares honorably until 1864, when Reverend John G. Pratt, whose record was unblemished, was appointed to the post by President Lincoln.

On a number of occasions, certain members of the Delaware Council were invited to Washington for high-level conferences, and this was always an experience the Indians enjoyed. It gave them a rare opportunity to ride in a passenger train, to see new places and people, to put up in a hotel, and eat good food, with all expenses paid from the national fund. In the spring of 1864, Pratt received orders through official channels to bring a delegation of Delawares to Washington for further discussions of land matters. The group consisted of ten individuals, including chiefs, councilors, and an interpreter, each of whom, in addition to having his expenses fully paid, received $100 for his services. The delegation, dressed in new suits, white shirts, and cravats, stayed for twenty-nine days at the Kirkwood House, where the total bill for board, room, and laundry amounted to $907.75.[31]

More than a century has elapsed since this delegation, and many others, went to the capital to meet representatives of the Department of the Interior and railroad executives to discuss land matters. With the passage of time some of the facts have been obscured—the documents were so phrased that any unwholesome influences in the form of threats or bribes never found their way into the records. There is no question that the railroad interests constituted a strong lobby, influencing decisions made by both the legislative and executive branches of the government. Now and then a militant newspaper editor spoke out about what was going on, such as the editorial in the *Leavenworth Daily Bulletin* commenting on the trip the Delawares made to Washington in 1864. According to the editorial, the Department of the Interior was the most corrupt department of the government, and was guilty of perpetrating a "consummate swindle upon the Indians." [32]

In view of the duplicity of some of the government officials, and the abuses the Delawares suffered at the hands of white settlers, it is ironical that they volunteered to fight for the Union during the Civil War. On December 31, 1862, agent Fielding wrote that the Delaware Council was willing for Indian males to engage in military service on the side of the United States government against the rebel states.[33] The North was glad to have the Delawares and any other Indians as allies, and the Commissioner of Indian Affairs reported in 1862 that, of a total of 201 Delaware males between the ages of eighteen and forty-five, 170 had volunteered and were then in the service of the Union. He added, "It is doubtful if any community can show a larger proportion of volunteers than this." [34] There is no question that the percentage of the Delaware male population in the military service was high, because in 1866 the total Delaware population on the Kansas reservation was 1,072, comprising 235 men, 327 women, and 510 children.[35]

I have not yet been able to find a list of all the Delawares who took up arms during the Civil War, but the names of twenty-six Delaware Indian members of M Company, 6th Kansas Volunteer Cavalry, are listed in Appendix 9. Six additional names of members of Company E of the 15th Kansas Volunteer Cavalry are also on record: Doctor Black, Thomas Lewis, Wilson Sarcoxie, Charles W. Ketchum, Big Moccasin, and George Pempsey.[36] Since many of the Delawares were then using the same kind of names as white men, it is next to impossible to identify all of the Indians on a military list. Captain Falleaf and Black Beaver both distinguished themselves during the Civil War. Prior to the outbreak of hostilities, Black Beaver was a guide for the naturalist John J. Audubon in his travels through the West looking for new birds to paint (see Fig. 19). Cap-

Figure 19. Black Beaver (Suck-tum-máh-kway), famous scout, guide, interpreter, and captain of a company of Delaware soldiers who fought for the United States during the Mexican War. He died in 1880 in Anadarko, Okla., aged seventy-four; note his name heading the list in Appendix 11. Taken by an unidentified photographer before 1869, this is one of the earliest photographs of a Delaware Indian. (Courtesy Smithsonian Institution National Anthropological Archives)

Figure 20. A Delaware traditionalist, the late John Falleaf of Oklahoma, taken in the early 1920s with his five daughters, Irene, Myrtle, Mona, Alona, and Nancy (Courtesy Elmer J. Sark)

tain Falleaf's descendants are still living today in Oklahoma (see Fig. 20).

When the Delaware men returned to their homes at the close of the war, they were restless, and it was difficult for them to settle down and adjust to civilian life again. In his annual report for 1865–66, Pratt in a classic understatement referred to the "rude behavior" of these discharged veterans, who drank whiskey to excess, and then fought among themselves with revolver and knife. The situation became so critical that, he wrote, "The Council has passed a code of laws—the hope is a more cautious manner of life." [37]

This code constituted the first written laws the Delawares ever had. Phrased in legal language (probably written for the Indians by a Leavenworth lawyer), the ten articles adopted by the Council on July 21, 1886, set up punishments for such crimes as murder, bodily injury, theft, arson, rape, adultery, and slander. Thenceforth it was unlawful for any Indian to bring to the reservation more than one pint of spirituous liquor at any one time. A jail was to be built where the Council House was situated, and the laws provided for the head chief and the Council to appoint three sheriffs, a clerk, a jailer, and a treasurer, all to be paid salaries from the national fund. [38] The adoption of such laws may have been a commendable undertaking from the government's view, but the traditionalists said their forefathers had lived happily without such laws, and it was just another step toward making Indians like white men. The new laws were not obeyed, nor apparently was there a serious effort to enforce them.

Over the years, two schools of thought had been developing: first, there were the traditionalists, who would not accept many of the white institutions, and who fought to preserve certain elements of the Indian way of life. These adherents refused to send their children to school or to the Christian missions, and they continued to observe their ancient religion. They gathered together each fall in the Big House—which stood in a cluster of walnut trees, later known as Bismarck Grove, about six miles east of Lawrence—dancing around the sacred centerpost with the carved faces of the M'sing (see Fig. 21). They also conducted family feasts and ceremonies, spoke the

Figure 21. Model of the Big House built by the late Reuben Wilson (Week-peh-kee-Xeeng) now in the collections of the museum at Seton Hall University, South Orange, N.J. Roof has been removed to show carved faces on two posts at the west doorway and on the centerpost. Posts on the interior of the eastern doorway were similarly carved, as were inside posts on the north and south sides of the structure. (Courtesy W. R. Blakemore, The Frank Phillips Foundation, Inc.)

Delaware language, and tried to preserve tribal folklore. Meanwhile they did not object to using the tools and weapons of the white man, and in following many of his economic practices which they recognized as improvements over their own.

In contrast were those who might well be called modernists who sent their children to mission schools and attended Christian churches with their families. Many of them were bilingual, speaking both English and Delaware, and some had succeeded in learning to read and write. They looked on the Big House Ceremony and other feasts and dances as unchristian, and some Delaware converts overtly opposed these ceremonies as pagan expressions from a past that was best forgotten. The extreme modernists believed that the future welfare of themselves and their families depended upon their adopting the culture of the white man. At the same time, they wanted to preserve their identities as Delaware Indians, just as any other national group might want to perpetuate itself, perhaps for the purpose of using its influence for social progress or political gain.

The most outspoken family among the modernists was the Journeycakes, whose most influential members were Charles Journeycake, his daughters, his brother Isaac, and Robert J. E. Journeycake, who was elected clerk of the Council. Of course, there were others, such as the Adamses, Youngs, and Ketchums, who veered away from the traditionalists, but did not fully accept the views of the modernists. Then there were some who vacillated back and forth between the two factions, and John Conner, the principal chief, was one of those having divided loyalties. Although he was an intelligent man, spoke English as fluently as he spoke Delaware, and had a wider knowledge of geography than any of his associates, he never learned to read and write. Under the strong influence of Charles Journeycake, Conner and his wife Charlotte were baptized and taken in as members of the Baptist Church, which the Journeycakes and others had formed.[39] But strong forces pulled him in the direction of the traditionalists, for when the Baptist Church was reorganized on August 12, 1848, following his conversion, John Conner's name was conspicuously missing from the list of members then in good standing. In contrast, Charles Journeycake, his mother Sally, and his wife Jane (Sosha), remained firm in their church attachments.[40]

It may have been Conner's leanings toward the traditionalists that prompted the modernists to prepare a written protest on October

15, 1861, which they sent to the government. They said that anciently the Delaware Council had been the tribe's decision-making body, which acted on all important policy matters, but that their former agent Sykes took it upon himself to change this custom. Instead of referring business matters to the Council, he obtained the signatures of the chiefs only on important papers, "the meaning of which they did not comprehend, but binding the nation to arrangements highly injurious to its interests and prosperity." The authors were obviously referring to the treaties of 1854 and 1860. The letter continued: "Our desire is that you, if consistent with official proceedings, appoint one of our enlightened sober men, as Chief, to take effect before proceeding to other business with the Council. We have no one from this class in authority at the present time."

This was an indictment of John Conner, and the criticism was made more pointed by this statement: "Any fancy of the present Chieftaincy can be gratified from the general treasury." The letter then concluded: "If our business be left either to the Chiefs, or Council, as it is now organized, then there is nothing for us to expect but submition and the future is only sure to reveal fearful ruin to all we hold most dear." [41]

Having acted as a kingmaker by elevating John Conner to the status of principal chief, and having bought the support of other chiefs and councilors with gifts of money and land, the United States was not now disposed to depose those it could manipulate. Moreover, there was nothing innovative about the government's position—it was merely following a precedent established by the Province of Pennsylvania almost 150 years before in its dealings with old Sassoonan.

In the winter of 1866, the Department of Indian Affairs brought to Washington the chiefs and councilors representing the Indian tribes living in Kansas for the purpose of persuading them to sell their reservations and move to new homes in what was then called Indian Territory, or even farther west. Treaties were made with the Kansas, Sauk, Fox, Quapaw, Kaskaskia, Shawnee, Peoria, Miami, Ottawa, Wyandot, Kickapoo, Potawatomi, Wea, Piankashaw, and the Delawares. The treaty with the Delawares was finalized at the Indian Agency in Kansas on July 4, 1866, with Thomas Murphy, the Superintendent of Indian Affairs, John G. Pratt, the Delaware agent,

and William H. Watson, special commissioner, acting on behalf of
the United States. Representing the Delawares were John Conner,
principal chief, Sarcoxie and Charles Journeycake, now referred to
as assistant chiefs, and four councilors—James Ketchum, James Conner, Andrew Miller, and John Sarcoxie.[42] Although the animal
eponyms are not mentioned in this instrument, it is known from
previous citations that John Conner was a member of the Turtle
group—Sarcoxie was also a Turtle—and Journeycake a Wolf. There
was no chief of the Turkey group present at the signing of this treaty,
which would seem to indicate that the subdivisions were beginning
to lose their previous political importance.

This treaty stated that since the Delawares had expressed a wish
to move from Kansas, which was now a state, the United States
would agree to sell them a suitable tract of land of their choosing,
lying between Kansas and Texas. This land would be taken from
territory already ceded to the government by the Choctaw, Chickasaw, Creek, or Seminole—or to be ceded by the Cherokee. The
United States had concluded treaties with those four tribes, obtaining from them lands on which to seat the Indians who were leaving
Kansas, and was then conducting negotiations with the Cherokee
to buy some of their lands for the same purpose. The Delawares
would be allowed to select a tract that met with their approval,
equal in size to 160 acres for every man, woman, and child who
moved from Kansas. The treaty provided that the Delawares would
pay the government the same price for the new land that the government paid the former Indian owners. This money would be
raised through the sale of the "diminished reserve" the Delawares
were vacating in Kansas, and the government would also reimburse
them in cash for the lands sold to the Leavenworth, Pawnee and
Western Railroad, which the railroad company had not yet paid for.

The treaty also stated that the Missouri River Railroad Company
had expressed a willingness to purchase the lands owned in severalty
by the Delawares (the eighty-acre allotments), and any other unsold
land on the Kansas reservation. The Delawares agreed to accept this
offer at $2.50 per acre, each Delaware man, woman, and child to
receive that amount per acre for his eighty acres, plus a fair increment for whatever improvements he had made on the property. All
other unallocated lands would be sold to the railroad company at
the same price, the receipts deposited in the national fund. It would

gather interest there, along with other monies being held by United States, on which the interest was periodically disbursed as annuities. (It is of interest that $187,000 of the Delaware national fund were then invested in the bonds of five southern states—Florida, Georgia, Louisiana, North Carolina, and South Carolina.) The annuity payments at this time were usually made twice a year, and the amount per person varied with the interest accumulation. In November, 1864, the payment amounted to $12 per person; in May of 1865, $30; in October of 1865, $40; in May 1866, $24, etc.[43]

The 1866 treaty also stated that it was the duty of the Secretary of the Interior to give all adult Delawares the opportunity to dissolve relations with the tribe and become citizens of the United States, if they wanted to do so. The eighty acres which had been certified to a Delaware who decided to become a citizen, and the acreage belonging to his minor children, would not be sold to the Missouri River Railroad. When the Indian filed a certificate of citizenship, after furnishing proof that he was self-supporting, and meeting other legal requirements, he would be entitled to receive a patent in fee simple, with power of alienation, for the land allotted him and his minor children. He and his children were also entitled to receive their share of the national fund held by the United States, either as annuities or as any other disbursements were made. They were also eligible to participate in distribution of the proceeds of the sale of any unallocated lands.

The treaty was ratified by the Senate on August 10, 1866, and the Delaware leaders lost no time saddling their horses for another visit to Indian Territory to explore the lands available to them. After looking over the territory occupied by the so-called Five Civilized Tribes—the Cherokee, Creek, Choctaw, Chickasaw, and Seminole—the Delawares concluded that they wanted to live in what is now northeastern Oklahoma. The land there belonged to the Cherokee, who had not ceded this particular territory to the United States, which meant that the government could not convey to the Delawares the land they wanted as provided in the treaty. Therefore, on August 11, 1866, the United States entered into an agreement with the Cherokee whereby the latter consented to permit the government to settle any civilized Indians friendly with the Cherokee on unoccupied lands east of 96°, on such terms as were agreed to by any such tribe and the Cherokee, subject to the approval of the

President. Should any such tribe decide to give up its own tribal organization and affiliate with the Cherokee, it was their privilege to do so, with the following provision:

. . . there being first paid into the Cherokee national fund a sum of money which shall sustain the same proportion to the then existing fund [of the Cherokee] that the number of Indians sustain to the whole number of Cherokees then residing in the Cherokee country, they shall be incorporated into, and ever remain, a part of the Cherokee Nation on equal terms in every respect with native citizens.

Since the Delawares wanted to leave Kansas as soon as possible, the leaders were desirous of conducting negotiations with the Cherokee without delay. Through a letter dated October 13, 1866, agent Pratt authorized the Delaware Council to select a delegation to meet with the Cherokee.[44] At a meeting in Pratt's office the same day, the Council authorized the following individuals to act in behalf of the tribe: John Conner, principal chief; Charles Journeycake and John Sarcoxie, assistant chiefs; Joseph Armstrong and Andrew Miller, councilors; and Isaac Journeycake, interpreter. On November 7, 1866, the Cherokee Council passed a resolution providing that their principal chief, assistant principal chief, and three others to be appointed by their principal chief as commissioners, were authorized to enter into discussions with the Delaware delegation.[45]

An agreement was finally consummated at Washington, D.C., on April 8, 1867, and it is important to note that the agreement was between the two Indian nations. The United States government was not a party to the contract. The Cherokee signers, William P. Ross (the principal chief), Riley Keys, and Jesse Bushyhead, were intelligent, sophisticated men, literate and experienced in business negotiations. The Delaware signatories—John Conner, Charles Journeycake, Isaac Journeycake, and John Sarcoxie—were no less capable of handling the business interests of their people, and they examined the agreement with the utmost care before signing it.[46] These men might have been mistaken for white men by their dress and deportment (see Fig. 22).

The members of the Delaware delegation were not fully satisfied with the terms of the agreement, and there was considerable discussion, and some argument, between the Delawares and Cherokee. Rep-

Figure 22. Delaware Indian leaders who participated in negotiations in Washington, D.C., in 1867. Seated, left to right: James Ketchum, James Conner, John Conner (Principal Chief), Charles Journeycake, Isaac Journeycake, John Sarcoxie, Sr. Standing left to right: James McDaniel, a Cherokee present at discussions, Black Beaver, Henry Tiblow, interpreter, John G. Pratt, the U.S. Indian Agent, Charles Armstrong, and John Young. (Courtesy Bartlesville Public Library)

resentatives of the Department of the Interior, who had arranged for the meeting, kept pressing the Delawares to sign. They assured the Delawares that everything was in their best interests, and that the government would make certain that the Cherokee lived up to the terms of the agreement. With this assurance, although still reluctantly, the Delawares affixed their signatures to the instrument, and three days later President Andrew Johnson approved it.

According to the agreement, the Cherokee agreed to sell the Delawares a quantity of land east of the line of 96° west longitude, equal in the aggregate to 160 acres for each individual Delaware man, woman, and child "who has been enrolled upon a certain register made February 18, 1867, by the Delaware agent, and on file in the office of Indian Affairs, being the list of the Delawares who elected to remove to the 'Indian country.' " There were 985 names on this enrollment list, a highly important document because it recorded the constituents of the main body and it established the birthright for future generations of Delawares. (A manuscript copy of this list, as well as later enrollment lists, is on file in the Washington County History Room of the Public Library in Bartlesville, Oklahoma.)

A number of Delawares who represented the most extreme modernists elected to remain in Kansas and become American citizens. Appendix 10 lists the names of heads of families who decided to separate from the tribe.

To compensate the Cherokee for the 160 acres each individual was entitled to receive, the Delawares agreed to pay $1 per acre for 157,600 acres to be allocated to those on the official enrollment list.

There was another extremely important provision in the agreement: upon further payment of $123 to the Cherokee national treasury for each registered Delaware (in accordance with the formula quoted above from the agreement of August 11, 1866, between the United States and the Cherokee), a total of $121,824.28— the Delawares who went to Oklahoma became members of the Cherokee Nation. As such they were entitled to the same rights and immunities, *and the same participation in the Cherokee national funds and annuities as the native Cherokee,* "and the children hereafter born of such Delawares so incorporated into the Cherokee Nation, shall in all respects be regarded as native Cherokees." Under the laws of the Cherokee Nation, the Delawares were to be governed by the Cherokee and would no longer have a political identity of their own. Legally, the terms of the agreement eliminated the authority of the Delaware chiefs and councilors who became *personnae non gratae* to the government.

At the outbreak of the Civil War, the population of the Cherokee Nation was about 21,000, but due to casualties during the war, the population dropped to about 14,000 when the Delawares applied for and were granted Cherokee citizenship. The Cherokee Nation, owner of more than 14,000,000 acres of land, was organized along the lines of white society, having a written constitution, and legislative, executive, and judicial departments, with the government centered at the town of Tahlequah. There were elected officials, law enforcement officers, schools, two seminaries for higher education, and a newspaper printed in both English and Cherokee, using a syllabary developed by Sequoyah. As citizens of this Cherokee Nation, the agreement gave the Delawares the right to vote, and to hold elective or appointive offices in the Cherokee national government.

At one of the final meetings of the Delaware Council held at the residence of John Conner on the Kansas reservation on May 2, 1867, Pratt was directed to inform Washington that, as soon as they received the money due them, the Delawares were ready to vacate their lands and move to their new homes.[47] The area agreed on for their occupancy during lengthy discussions with the Cherokee was in the valley of the Little Verdigris, or Caney River, "beginning at the Kansas line where the 96th Meridian crosses the same, and running thence 10 miles, thence south 30 miles, thence west 10 miles, thence north to the place of beginning." Much of this area is included in present-day Washington County, Oklahoma, a long rectangle running north and south, with Nowata County on the east and Osage County on the west. The Cherokee did not intend this area to be set off for the Delawares to the exclusion of Cherokee families, but that registered Delawares be permitted to select their 160 acres from lands not then occupied by Cherokee families. Actually there were not many Cherokee families living on tracts chosen by the Delawares, which were preferably along running streams where the soil was fertile, and where there were also good stands of timber.

The movement to Oklahoma began in December of 1867, continuing during the spring and summer of 1868, each family making its own preparation for the journey, and traveling at its own expense. Some families went alone, but often several families joined together. Sometimes the men returned to Kansas, making two or more trips, to complete hauling all their belongings and livestock. The route was almost directly south, veering a little to the west, and although the distance was only from 180 to 200 miles, progress was slow, especially during the winter. Such livestock as remained in their possession was driven ahead of them (many had to buy horses from the Cherokee because of thefts of their own herds), and the aged and sick had to be transported with care, which made the pace even slower. There were a number of deaths en route, but by 1869 the main body of the Delawares had been transplanted to Oklahoma. To some of the most elderly it was the fourth time they had moved since childhood, when they went from Ohio to Indiana; thence, as they were growing up, from Indiana to Missouri; then from Missouri to Kansas, and now the final move, which would bring them to the end of the road.

Agent Pratt, whose work with the Delawares was almost ended, remained in Kansas as their attorney to represent their interests in concluding unfinished business with the government. (He died near Piper, Kansas, on April 23, 1900.) On January 16, 1869, he wrote that the two Delaware chiefs, John Conner and Charles Journeycake, where then living in Indian Territory.[48] The inference was that other members of the tribe were also settled in their new homes, but the next fall Pratt received bad news from Oklahoma. The Caney River overflowed during the summer and destroyed the crops of the Delawares living on or near its banks, prompting him to recommend that the government give some relief to the Indian families by paying their annuity earlier than scheduled.[49]

Adjusting to the new environment was a slow process, because many families were poor, and there was a long delay before they received compensation due them for the lands they vacated in Kansas. After clearing the land, some of the families found that, through errors made in the surveys, they had settled on tracts claimed by others in the Cherokee Nation, and they had to pick up and move again. Even though they were seated in Oklahoma by permission of the Cherokee government, some Delaware families were harassed by half-breed Cherokee and wandering bands of Osage who resented the intrusion. The Osage had not forgotten their earlier trouble with the Delawares in Missouri, or that, even before this, Delaware warriors allied with the Cherokee had gone as far west as Oklahoma to attack the Osage.[50] Harassment by hostile Indians became so serious that some of the Delawares were forced to flee their new homes, and Richard C. Adams said that "all moved in a body to Quapaw country on the Neosho River." He exaggerated the numbers involved, but his statement illustrates the gravity of the situation.[51] The Neosho cuts across the northeast corner of Oklahoma where the Quapaw had a reservation in what is now Ottawa County. After a year or two, the Delaware families were persuaded by government agents to return. They finally found suitable, unoccupied lands in Washington, Nowata, and Osage counties, where they erected log cabin homes, the typical Indian dwelling of the time (see Fig. 23).

A story about relations between the Osage and the Delawares has been preserved among the Delawares in Oklahoma. It is related below

Figure 23. Old one-room log cabin, Washington County, Oklahoma, similar to those built by the Delawares when they came from Kansas to settle in Indian Territory. The tin roof is a later addition.

in the version told me by Mrs. Nora Thompson Dean, as she heard it from her parents:

Not long after the Delawares joined the Cherokee Nation, a Delaware lad of eighteen or twenty, the only son of "Old Lady Wahooney," was hunting at the foot of the Osage Hills. He encountered a party of young Osage hunters who claimed the area as their rightful hunting grounds through conquest, use, and occupancy, but not through legal title. They recognized him as an intruder and killed him. They left his body lying on the ground and placed two crossed arrows on his breast as a warning to other Delawares not to trespass on their lands.

When the body was found, there was considerable discussion among sober-minded Delaware men as to the appropriate action to take. At that time the aged Pe-ne-a-tut, or Colonel Jackson, was still living—he is buried in the Falleaf Cemetery near Coon Creek northeast of Copan. Subsequently there were discussions between Osage and Delaware leaders, including Colonel Jackson, because both tribes wanted to avoid war and bloodshed, which would occur in avenging the misdeed. Some of them had been told about the war between the two tribes when Chief Anderson's son was killed by the Osage many years before.

It was decided that instead of fighting and shedding blood, the Osage and Delawares would meet every year to have a good time. The Delawares agreed to supply the food for these festivities, and the Osage agreed to bring presents to atone for the misdeed of their young men. These assemblies, which were held outdoors, continued for many years, alternating in Osage country one year and in Delaware country the next. In addition to feasting, and the giving of presents by the Osage, tobacco was smoked by the participants, which resulted in applying the word *smokes* to these outings. The site of the smokes when held in Delaware territory was usually on Post Oak Creek north of present Dewey, on the east side of Highway 75. Mrs. Dean's parents attended these smokes, and on one occasion her father, James H. Thompson (Oh-huh-lum-mee-tahk-see, "the one who can be heard from afar"), received a horse as a present from the Osage visitors. The last smoke was held around 1900, although the exact year is not certain.

A number of families from the Delaware splinter group which left Cape Girardeau in 1815 made their way to eastern Texas, where other uprooted Indians were living with remnants of the Caddo Confederacy. The Caddo were an ancient people who were in their ascendance at the time of De Soto's expedition, and their villages were along the Red River and its tributaries in what is now Louisiana and Arkansas, and along the banks of the Sabine, Neches, Trinity, Brazos, and Colorado rivers in east Texas. The influx first of Spanish, next the French, and finally American settlers during the years that followed, resulted in disintegration of the Caddo Confederacy, a tragic story that has already been told.[52] In 1828 General Teran estimated the total Delaware Indian population (Stephen Austin called them "Deluas") at 225 families, with 75 of the families living "on the Red River of Natchitoches." [53] In 1830 a French biologist in the employ of a Mexican commission visited Texas, and he wrote that the "Delaas" tribe, as he termed the Delawares, numbered 150 families.[54]

Although no separate account of the Delawares in Texas has yet been written, it appears that they and the Shawnee entered into a treaty with the Republic of Texas in 1836, and allied themselves with the Texans in fighting the Comanche.[55]

In 1854 the United States set aside a reservation on the Brazos River as the temporary home for the remnants of the friendly Delawares, Shawnee, Wichita, Caddo, and Tonkawas. The reservation

Figure 24. Mrs. Nora Thompson Dean (Touching Leaves), fluent Delaware Indian speaker of Dewey, Oklahoma, member of the Wolf group, wearing traditional clothing of deerskin which she made according to early patterns. A close friend of the author's, Mrs. Dean was of invaluable assistance during his visits to Oklahoma gathering data about her people.

system in Texas was doomed from the start, because white Texans long exposed to vicious attacks by the Comanche, were resentful of all Indians, including peaceful families living on the Brazos reservation. Much trouble ensued, and the United States was compelled to remove the Indians from their reservation in Texas, and the Delawares were among those transplanted to the Washita River in Indian Territory near present Anadarko, Oklahoma.

The Caddo and their native associates were placed under the jurisdiction of the United States Wichita Indian Agency, established in 1859 to deal with the Indians being moved out of Texas. In the next few years there were a number of changes both in the agency setup and in the movements of the affiliated tribes. In 1874 the Delawares at Anadarko decided to merge with the Caddo and put themselves under the leadership of a Caddo chief, which meant they were sacrificing their own political identity, as the main body did when it joined the Cherokee Nation. In his report for 1875, the United States Indian agent noted that the Caddoes under the jurisdiction of the Wichita agency included sixty-one Delawares who had joined him, and that these Delawares were industrious farmers. He also said that at this time there were thirty Delawares on Kiowa and Comanche reservations where life was still primitive and the standard of living very low.[56]

Fortunately there has been preserved a list of the names of the heads of Delaware families living on the reservation at Anadarko in 1876. At that time the total Delaware population, including men, women, and children, numbered 83 (see list of their names in Appendix 11). Apparently the Delaware population was not fixed, for the annual report of the Indian Agency for 1886 listed only 41 Delawares, although a new list made in 1892 indicated there were 87 Delawares, 530 Caddo, and a number of other tribesmen on the reservation, then under the jurisdiction of what was called the Kiowa, Comanche, and Wichita Agency.[57] A photo of one of the Delawares living there at the time, whose name was also listed among the heads of families in 1876, has been preserved (see Fig. 25). In 1895, Congress ratified an agreement with the Cherokee Commission whereby a reservation was laid out at Anadarko for a total of 965 Indians consisting of Wichita, Kichai, Waco, and the Caddo with their Delaware affiliates.

Figure 25. Jack Harry (Wy-a-wa-qua-cum-an, "Walking everywhere"), a Delaware from Anadarko, Okla., born in 1853, probably a full-blood. His name is on list in Appendix 11. (Courtesy Smithsonian Institution National Anthropological Archives)

One of the Delaware traditionalists at Anadarko who died shortly after Oklahoma was given statehood was Chief Bill Thomas. Upon his death, Chief Jim Bob was considered the titular leader (see Fig. 26). After the latter's death, Jack Thomas was unofficially referred to as the Delaware chief. It is ironical that these Absentee Delawares, after years of wandering, finally arrived at a destination in Oklahoma less than two hundred miles from the last home of the main body. A number of other migrant Indian groups settled in Oklahoma, and those who retain formal organizations are under the general jurisdiction of United States Indian agencies.[58]

Figure 26. Chief Jim Bob, who probably succeeded Black Beaver as the titular leader of the Delawares at Anadarko, photographed in 1898. See his name on list in Appendix 11. (Courtesy Smithsonian Institution National Anthropological Archives)

NOTES—CHAPTER 16

1. Kappler, *Indian Affairs, Laws and Treaties*, vol. 2, contains transcripts of these four treaties. Other than a sixteen-page pamphlet by Alan W. Farley, *The Delaware Indians in Kansas, 1829–1867*, Kansas City, 1955, which is not documented, very little has been written about the Delawares during their residence in Kansas. An article by Rev. J. J. Lutz in *Kansas Historical Society Collections*, vol. 9, 1905–6, p. 206, gives a direct quotation from "the History of the Delawares by Charles R. Green of Lyndon, Kansas," but I have been unable to locate this work. The Kansas Historical Society does not have either a printed or manuscript

history of the Delawares by Mr. Green, although Mr. Nyle Miller, Secretary of the Society, located in their archives a 35-page manuscript by Mr. Green entitled "The Original Settlers and History of the Delaware Reserve," and he kindly made a transcript available to me.

Mr. Green's library of 750 books and 1,000 pamphlets was presented to Fort Hays Kansas State College in 1915 after his death; but Marc T. Campbell, Director of the Forsyth Library at the college, advised me that the collection does not contain a history of the Delawares written by Mr. Green.

A note I found in Mr. Green's hand on the roll list of the Delawares dated November 1863 (Pratt Papers, roll no. 6) states that he copied the names for use in the book he was then writing. The following note in his hand also appears on the list: "There are 404 heads of families and a total of about 1,100 souls returned for pay Nov. 1863 at the Sarcoxie Agency. I taught the first district school in southern Leavenworth County in the Delaware storeroom of Johnnycake sta. (Stranger then and Linwood now) winter 1868–69. In '70 and '71 I taught the first district school in the new school house at Sarcoxieville—Some of the Delawares up from the Indian Ty. where they had been moved visited my school room at Stranger Jany 1869. [signed] C. R. Green."

Green came to Leavenworth County, Kansas, from Milan, Ohio, in 1867, and on p. 33 of the manuscript cited above he states that when he alighted from the Union Pacific train at Lenape Station in Kansas, the first thing that met his gaze was "a lot of Delaware bucks standing around watching the passengers and loafing. They lived in their cabins out on the higher slopes up and down the Kaw Valley and dressed some in blankets, some in suits like a white man, few of them wearing hats, but many wearing feathers, numerous silver ornaments both on their face and breast, red paint being very prominent."

If the history that Mr. Green is supposed to have written ever turns up, it no doubt will contain much of interest.

2. Kappler, *Indian Affairs*, vol. 2, p. 1048.

3. Fred C. Hamil, "The Moravians of the River Thames," *Michigan History*, vol. 33, June 1949, pp. 97–116. An annuity settled on the Delawares by the Canadian government in exchange for some of their lands, and money they collected from the government as a result of damages to their properties during the War of 1812, provided money for them to make the long trip to Kansas.

4. Microfilm M234, roll 275, letter from the Secretary of the Interior, April 12, 1858. The following names of the heads of families among the Christian (Moravian) Indians are given in a letter of Feb. 12, 1858, ibid.: Job Samuel, Anderson Wilson, Christian Snake, Cornelius Charles, John

Young Ignatius Caleb, Frederica Caleb, Jane Caleb, Sibella Nathan, Rachel Henry, Henry Donohoe and his wife Polly Donohoe (formerly Polly Killbuck), John Williams and his wife Abigail Williams (formerly Abigail Killbuck), Lewis Veix and his wife Lydia (formerly Lydia Wilson), Wesley Snake, Claudia Meacham (formerly Claudia Hendrick), and Julia Davis (formerly Julia Caleb).

For information that there were only 38 of these Christian Indians remaining on the Kansas reservation in 1858, see B. F. Robinson's letter of Dec. 20, 1858, ibid.

5. Ibid., letter of Feb. 12, 1858; see Joseph Romig, "The Chippewa and Munsee (or Christian) Indians of Franklin County, Kansas," *Kansas Historical Society Collections*, vol. 11, 1909–10, pp. 314–23. I am indebted to Hilda M. Carpenter of the Carnegie Free Library, Ottawa, Kan., for a photocopy of this article and for a photocopy of an Annuity Roll dated May 31, 1900, listing the names of the Munsies and Chippewa in Franklin County, then under the jurisdiction of the Potawatomie and Great Nemaha Agency of the United States Indian Service. Among the Munsies are families whose names were recorded on the Kansas reservation— Caleb, Donohoe, Killbuck, Veix, and so forth—which corroborates that they came from Canada, settled with the Delawares near Leavenworth, and then moved to Franklin County, where their descendants may still be found.

6. Microfilm M234, roll 275, list dated Mar. 13, 1860, which also includes the names of several Oneida Indians who formerly lived in New York state but had settled in Kansas among the Delawares. Their surnames were Denny, Thomas, Smith, and Woodman, and they were no doubt members of the particular band of Oneida with whom the Stockbridge and Brotherton Indians had affiliated. Following their arrival in Kansas, the Stockbridge people organized a Stockbridge Mission Church in 1845, which in 1848 merged with the Delaware Baptist Mission; see "Two Minute Books of Kansas Missions in the Forties," *Kansas Historical Quarterly*, vol. 2, no. 3, August 1933, p. 243.

7. Pratt Papers, roll no. 5, letter of July 28, 1856.

8. Manypenny's discussions with the several tribes are fully covered in the "Proposed Findings of Fact and Brief dated September 1968" before the Indian Claims Commission, Docket no. 72, Absentee Delaware Tribe of Oklahoma vs. United States of America; also in Docket 298, Delaware Tribe of Indians vs. United States of America.

9. This is fully discussed in many standard American histories; see, for example, chap. 37 in Samuel Eliot Morison, *The Oxford History of the American People*, New York, 1965, chapter 37.

10. Pratt Papers, roll no. 5, Dec. 1, 1855.

11. Microfilms M234, roll 275, Oct. 26, 1858.

12. Pratt Papers, roll no. 8.

13. Richard C. Adams, A *Brief History of the Delaware Indians*, Senate Document no. 501, 59th Congress, 1st session, Washington, D.C., 1906, p. 41. In the proceedings before the Indian Claims Commission, Dockets nos. 72 and 298, the Delawares stated that the trust lands in Kansas after the Treaty of 1854 comprised 557,955 acres, and that the government had realized $1,057,898.19 from the sale, which amount was placed in the national fund.

14. Adams, A *Brief History*, p. 41.

15. Pratt Papers, roll no. 5.

16. Pratt Papers, roll no. 5, letters of Aug. 9, 1856, September 29, 1857, and Nov. 10, 1857. The ferry site where the whites were trespassing was no doubt the location of the earliest ferry across that Kansas River, founded by Moses Grinter, a white soldier who married Ann Marshall, a Delaware woman, and raised a family of ten children. This "rope ferry" was variously called Grinter's Ferry, Military Ferry, Lower Delaware Crossing, and Secondine Crossing; cf. George A. Root, "Ferries In Kansas," Pt. 2, *Kansas Historical Quarterly*, vol. 2, no. 3, August 1933, p. 264. The two-story Grinter mansion built in 1857 is still standing at 1420 South 78th Street, Muncie, overlooking the Kaw.

17. Microfilm M234, roll 275, letter of Dec. 4, 1858.

18. Pratt Papers, roll no. 5, letters of Mar. 25, 1857 and November 10, 1857.

19. Ibid.

20. Microfilm M234, roll 275, Oct. 26, 1858.

21. The records contain lengthy lists of the names of Delaware Indians indebted to the traders; ibid. As of December 1860, one trader was owed $3,048.38; another $7,989.25; and a third $14,134.14. Each trader had to post a bond of $5,000 when he applied for a license to the Indian agent to trade for one year. He had to be a citizen of the United States, and his application had to be approved by the office of the Indian Commissioner. The principal commodities traders sold the Delawares were flour, bacon, sugar, coffee, cotton cloth, dry goods, boots and shoes, hardware, crockery, and groceries. Payment at this time was almost entirely by cash, or on promise to pay cash.

22. Microfilm M234, roll 275, Feb. 10, 1860. Sykes said in a later letter that he had talked to two federal judges who both said there was no law for punishing settlers who stole the Indians' timber, and he added that at least $20,000 worth of timber had been stolen; ibid., Mar. 9, 1860. A firm called the Delaware Lumber Company caused the Indians much loss of timber.

23. Microfilm M234, roll 275, names on list dated Nov. 12, 1860.

24. Ibid., Sykes's letter of Mar. 12, 1860.

25. Ibid., letter of Nov. 20, 1860. On May 29, 1863, three years after the first delegation went to Indian Territory, William P. Dole authorized the expenditure of $800 for another Delaware delegation to go to Indian Territory. They wanted to examine the land in the Rocky Mountain area, but Dole refused to allow the money to be spent unless they looked over lands in Indian Territory; Richard C. Adams, A *Delaware Indian Legend and the Story of Their Troubles*, Washington, D.C., 1899, pp. 47–48. The quoted excerpt is from the letter in the John Ross Collection, Gilcrease Museum Library, Tulsa, File Folder 60-16 (1860), and I am indebted to James A. Rementer for a copy.

26. Pratt Papers, roll no. 8, July 14, 1868.

27. Microfilm M234, roll 275, letter of Sept. 25, 1858; see also letter from the office of Kansas Stage Company, January 10, 1859.

28. Ibid., Oct. 10, 1860.

29. Kappler, *Indian Affairs, Laws and Treaties*, vol. 2, p. 806. Agent Fielding Johnson wrote on May 4, 1861, that John Conner, Neconhecond, and Sarcoxie had all sold the lands given them by terms of the 1860 treaty. Sarcoxie evidently needed cash badly, because Johnson said he sold his land well below its actual value; Microfilm M234, roll 275.

30. Ibid., July 2, 1861.

31. Pratt Papers, roll no. 6. The bill is dated June 18, 1864.

32. The complete editorial, clipped from the paper by Pratt, but with the date missing, is one of the documents on roll no. 6. It names specific individuals and accuses them of misfeasance.

33. Pratt Papers, roll no. 5.

34. *Annual Report to the Commissioner of Indian Affairs*, Washington, D.C., 1862, p. 23; cf. Adams, A *Brief History*, pp. 36–37, for evidence that the Delawares also used their influence to persuade other tribes to join the Union forces. In 1864 two Delaware lads of fifteen ran away from the Indian School, walked seventeen miles to Fort Leavenworth to enlist in the Kansas 16th; *Report of the Commissioner of Indian Affairs*, 1864, p. 358.

35. Pratt Papers, roll no. 6, population figures given in annuity list dated May 4–5, 1866.

36. Pratt Papers, ibid., letter E. N. O. Clough to Pratt, Feb. 13, 1864. For Civil War careers of Black Beaver and Captain Falleaf, see Adams, A *Brief History*, pp. 38–40; Farley, *The Delaware Indians in Kansas*. Cf. Carolyn Thomas Foreman, "Black Beaver," *Chronicles of Oklahoma*, vol. 24, no. 3, 1946, pp. 269–92.

37. Pratt Papers, ibid., report to Thomas Murphy, Atchison, Kansas, Sept. 19, 1866.

38. These laws are given in Adams, A *Brief History*, pp. 66–70.

39. "Two Minute Books of Kansas Missions in the Forties," p. 235.

40. Ibid., p. 250.

41. Microfilm M234, roll 275, Oct. 15, 1861.

42. Kappler, vol. 2, pp. 937–42.

43. Pratt Papers, roll no. 6.

44. Adams, A *Delaware Indian Legend*, p. 22.

45. Ibid., p. 25.

46. The agreement is quoted in Adams, A *Brief History*, pp. 43–44. A faithful reproduction of the original handwritten document was reproduced by Elmer J. Sark in a multigraphed pamphlet, *100 Years in Oklahoma—Treaty Delaware-Cherokee Indians, 1867*, Bartlesville, 1967.

47. Pratt Papers, roll no. 8. The Baptist Indian School was discontinued on Apr. 1, 1869, at which time there were still twenty-six pupils in attendance. Some of these were no doubt children of modernists who decided to become United States citizens and remain in Kansas.

48. Ibid. A story handed down in the Frenchman family, as related to me by Earl Frenchman, a grandson of "Old Man" Frenchman, a registered Delaware, illustrates one of the tragedies on the trek from Kansas to Oklahoma. The elder Frenchman's family consisted of nine girls and two boys; while the family was enroute to Oklahoma seven of the girls died. For an excellent account of the western movement and the nuances in the government's policies, see James C. Malin, "Indian Policy And Westward Expansion," *University of Kansas Humanistic Studies*, vol. 11, no. 3, November 1921, pp. 1–108.

49. Pratt Papers, roll no. 8, letter of Aug. 6, 1869.

50. Adams, A *Brief History*, p. 29.

51. Adams, A *Delaware Indian Legend*, p. 25. Foreman, *The Last Trek*, says about three hundred Delawares moved temporarily to the Neosho River, p. 189.

52. W. W. Newcomb, Jr., *The Indians of Texas*, Austin, Tex., 1961.

53. Jean Louis Berlandier, *The Indians of Texas in 1830*, ed. John C. Ewers, Washington, D.C., 1969, p. 125.

54. Ibid.

55. Adams, A *Brief History*, pp. 30–31.

56. *Annual Report of the Commissioner of Indian Affairs, 1875*, Washington, D.C., pp. 61–62.

57. Ibid., 1886, p. 128. Cf. chap. 16, entitled "Texas Emigrants," in Foreman, *The Last Trek*. See also note 32, p. 295, ibid., and *61st Annual Report of the Commissioner of Indian Affairs, 1892*, p. 792.

58. Muriel H. Wright, *A Guide to the Indian Tribes of Oklahoma*, Norman, Okla., 1965, 3d printing, p. 4.

17

Delawares vs. the Cherokee

As one drives along secondary roads in the rolling country in northeastern Oklahoma drained by the sluggish Caney River, in the environs of the Delaware powwow grounds near Copan, he will see
here and there an isolated cedar, the gnarled limbs of old peach and
apple trees, or the decaying logs that were once part of the walls
of a cabin. These mark the early homesites of the Delaware Indian
families who came from Kansas a century or more ago. Economic
necessity brought about a revival of basketry, woodworking, and other
native crafts that had fallen into disuse on the Kansas reservation
because of the availability of manufactured goods at the traders'
stores. In Indian Territory the women revived some of the domestic
crafts that had almost been forgotten, and they resumed using wild
herbs, folk remedies, and sweat baths as cures for family ailments, as
their forebears had done.[1] Having associated with other Indians during their westward trek over a 150-year period, the Delawares borrowed culturally from the Shawnee, Wyandot, Miami, Nanticoke,
Potawatomi, Kickapoo, and other tribes.

Some of the men again took up hunting as a means of supporting
their families, as though something deep inside them rebelled at
being held to the soil as farmers or homesteaders. Now, more than
fur pelts, the hides of animals were in demand in the marketplace
for making boots, saddles, harnesses, jackets, and trousers. The traditionalists lost no time in building a new Big House, and each fall the
Indian families came by horse and wagon to attend the ceremony,

pitching their tents on the grounds surrounding the "church house."
Every night during a twelve-day period they sang, danced, recited
their visions, and gave thanks to Kee-shay-lum-moo-kawng for bestowing his blessings on them and on all mankind.[2]

At prescribed times during the ceremony they burned the awl-
shaped leaves of the cedar and used the smoke as a purifier, as they
had for generations when they offered prayers to the Creator, or for
other purposes of spiritual purification. They selected land for a
cemetery on a quiet wooded plot not far from the present town of
Dewey, and when a member of the tribe died they buried him there,
placing a kee-keen-he-kun ("identifying thing") on the grave as a
marker during the graveside burial rites in which the family and
friends participated. Made from pine wood by a friend of the deceased (never by one of his blood kin), the marker for a male grave
was a straight piece of wood placed in a vertical position, the top
carved in the shape of a diamond. The marker for a female grave
was similarly carved at the top, but it also had a crosspiece with a
diamond-shaped carving at each end (see Fig. 27). The facing surface of the marker was painted with red crosses by a mourner assigned to this task who dipped his fingers in olumen, a red pigment
mixed with grease, and daubed it on the wood. The dead were placed
in the grave in an extended position, with feet pointing west and
head pointing east. Years before, when the tribe was still living on
the Muskingum in Ohio, Zeisberger wrote that the Delawares placed
their dead in this position, and that a post was erected on the grave,
carved if the deceased was a chief and painted red if he was a war
captain.[3] The old Delaware cemetery in Oklahoma is still in use,
and the same orientation of the corpse is observed. But today one
sees only a few of the kee-keen-he-kun. Most of the graves are marked
with conventional granite and marble monuments inscribed with the
names of the deceased.

Some of the traditionalists never wholly approved of becoming
Cherokee citizens, or of accepting the elected Cherokee chiefs and
councilmen as their leaders. They wanted to continue to be recognized
as Delawares and were reluctant to renounce their right to have
their own chiefs, even though such individuals were not recognized
by the United States government or by the Cherokee council. The
Cherokee Nation at this time was divided into nine districts. Each
district elected two male Indians to what was called the National

Figure 27. Grave markers called Kee-keen-he-kun, male at left, female at right, made of pine two-by-fours 30″ high. The crosses are daubed on the wood with red olumen at time of interment and represent the spirit Len-nay-pay-oakun. The markers remain in place on the grave until they rot away, and are never replaced. (Drawing by Charles Waterhouse)

Committee (the members were also called Senators), and three to the National Council, the two houses constituting the legislative body. The executive branch consisted of a principal chief and an assistant chief elected every four years, lesser officers, and a judicial system consisting of a district court in each of the districts, a circuit court, and a supreme court.

The Delawares had full citizenship rights, which entitled them to vote and to hold office. In 1869 James Conner was elected to the National Committee from the Cooweescoowee District, where most of the Delawares lived. In subsequent years, among the Delawares elected to the National Council were Joseph Thompson, John Bullette, George Swannock, John H. Secondine, John Young, Arthur Armstrong, Samuel Tiblow, and John Sarcoxie.[4]

The traditionalists continued to recognize certain of their own chiefs or captains as unofficial leaders, particularly in the ceremonial life of the tribe. These were the men who perpetuated the Big House Ceremony. They visited the Delaware families to comfort the bereaved at the time of death. They participated in graveside burial rites. Some were name-giving visionaries known as Way-huh-we-huh-lahs ("one who gives names over and over") and were the principals at rites where names were bestowed. Among these early leaders were Weoxalingoat ("light eyes"); Captain Falleaf, whose Indian name was Panipakuxwe ("he who walks when leaves fall"); Delaware Charley, or Chah-la-wees, a mystic who could converse with the spirits of the departed; Joseph Thompson; Colonel Jackson; Ice Wil-

Figure 28. John Brown, a Delaware-Munsie, born in Michigan Territory (present Wisconsin) in 1834, who joined the main body of the Delawares in Kansas and then came to Oklahoma. Delawares named him Weh-wul-i-nund ("He was admired") to replace his Munsie name, which meant "little boy." The picture was taken in 1901 when he was sixty-seven years old. (Courtesy Smithsonian Institution National Anthropological Archives)

son; Suk-kee-loong-gawn ("blackwing"); Bill Swannock, whose Indian name was Espikund ("one pushed upward"); George Swannock,
also called Ulikaman ("he steps on it well"); John Jim John, whose
Indian name was Kapesino ("twin man"); and others.[5]

In contrast to the traditionalists, the extreme modernists deliberately separated themselves and their families from ancient custom.
Their principal spokesman, Charles Journeycake, did not choose
to live along the Caney but selected as his homesite a tract along
Lightning Creek in Nowata County, now covered by the waters of
the Oolagah Reservoir. Journeycake, whose white increments were
pronounced, probably thought, dressed, and acted more like an educated white man than most of his Indian contemporaries. He built
as a family residence a comfortable two-story frame dwelling, with
porches and a bay window overlooking a garden. He was one of the
founders of the first Baptist Church in Oklahoma, a frame structure
with wooden steeple erected on Lightning Creek southwest of Nowata.[6] Journeycake was formally ordained a Baptist minister in 1872.

An impression has been allowed to gather that he was the *first*
Delaware Indian authorized to administer the church ordinances, but
that is incorrect. The Reverend William Adams was ordained a
Baptist minister in Kansas on March 14, 1868, and John Sarcoxie, Sr.,
was ordained May 21, 1888.[7] The Sarcoxies lived on Silver Lake, one
of the natural lakes in the Caney watershed, where they occupied a
serviceable frame house with porticoes on three sides. Another prominent Delaware, Reverend James Ketchum, descendant of Captain
Ketchum, was ordained a Methodist minister about 1860, and when
he came to Indian Territory from Kansas he had considerable means.
He purchased a two-story brick residence near the present town called
Ketchum in the southeast corner of Craig County, which was in the
Delaware District of the Cherokee Nation.[8]

There were many other devout Christians among the modernists,
including Andrew Miller, John Young, Joe Wilson, and Arthur Armstrong, who were all lay preachers. The sermons delivered by these
Indian ministers were usually long ones. Charles Journeycake is
known to have exhorted from the pulpit for as long as an hour and a
half at one time. Reverend John Sarcoxie, Sr., talked slowly and
deliberately when he preached. "If you had been walking," one Delaware told me, "you could have gone a long, long way before he
was through." These ministers all preached in the Delaware tongue,

but, as time went on, whites joined the congregations, and the new Indian generation learned to speak English, with the result that English replaced the Delaware language in church services. Both Baptist and Methodist Delawares repudiated customs they considered pagan, such as the Big House Ceremony, as they observed Christian disciplines in their daily lives, leaving the unchristian ceremonies to be practiced by the traditionalists.

Following the death of her husband, Lucius Pratt, in Kansas, Nannie Journeycake Pratt married Jacob H. Bartles. The couple moved to Indian Territory, bringing with them Nannie's three half-white daughters by her first marriage. The site of their home in the horseshoe bend of the Caney grew into a busy settlement named after Nannie's second husband—Bartlesville. Her daughters by her first marriage and her children by Bartles married white spouses. Other daughters of Charles Journeycake also married white men and separated themselves from the Indian world to become absorbed into Oklahoma's white society.[9]

The payment of annuities and other disbursements were usually made in a frame payhouse built in the yard behind the Journeycake dwelling on Lightning Creek. John Conner predeceased Charles Journeycake; and Journeycake, as the last living assistant chief from the former regime and one who understood the language and ways of the white man, became the point of contact with the United States on business matters. He was not elected to this position; he just fell into it. Both modernists and traditionalists came to the payhouse to collect their annuities, some traveling many miles on horseback, others bringing their families by horse and wagon; a few walked. This was one of the infrequent times when all the Delaware families had occasion to gather together, and it was a sort of homecoming, a forerunner to the Pan-Indian powwows. Many families camped on the property and socialized through feasting, storytelling, and playing games. The amount disbursed to each individual continued to be small. In August of 1876, for example, $27 was paid to each of 786 Delawares. This was semiannual interest on the national fund, which then amounted to approximately $900,000, although the Indians claimed that the government still owed money to the national fund for unpaid lands in Kansas. Storekeepers who had extended credit to the Indian families were always present when the annuities were paid—to collect the money due them before it was spent on new merchandise. Some merchants continued to appear with horses, buggies, saddles, and other miscellaneous merchandise to sell to the Indians, as the traders had done years before in Indiana and Kansas when annuities were paid.

After several years, the Delawares began to feel that the money held in their account by the government should be paid to them outright. When there was a question of taking money from the United States, there was never any disagreement between the traditionalists and modernists, even though it had been proved over and over again that when such funds were distributed the small disbursements per capita were quickly spent and no lasting good ever came of the money. Nevertheless, the principal Cherokee chief, J. B. Mayes, was persuaded to write the Commissioner of Indian Affairs in 1890, requesting that the government distribute to the Delaware citizens of the Cherokee Nation the balance remaining in their national fund.[10] The reason he gave for his request was that this money would enable the poorer Delaware families to build better homes than the squalid log cabins they were living in, and would also give the more fortunate ones who owned frame houses the money to improve their dwellings and their land. The government complied with the request, since the money belonged to the Indians and the argument for its distribution seemed reasonable. In December of 1891, the first installment of $425,000 was paid out to 836 Delawares, amounting to approximately $508 for every man, woman, and child. In August of 1893, the second installment of $459,664, or $527.72 per capita, was disbursed, after which there was no longer any money left in the Delaware account.[11]

At this time controversies developed with the Cherokee over fiscal matters, and these deserve a brief explanation. From time to time the Cherokee received sums of money from the United States for lands in the Cherokee Nation purchased by the government and sold, in turn, to pioneer white families who had gone west to make new homes. The Cherokee also received money from white cattlemen for cattle-ranch leases. All these receipts were distributed to the Cherokee citizens on a per capita basis. In May of 1883, the Cherokee National Council denied the Delawares the right to participate with other Cherokee citizens in the distribution of funds received from the sale of grasslands west of the Arkansas River. Delaware leaders insisted, not only that, according to their 1867 agreement with the Cherokee, they had a right to share in this distribution, but that the government, by terms of the Treaty of 1866, was obligated "to protect, preserve, and defend the Delawares in their just rights." They said that if the United States would not support them in getting what was justly due them, they wanted the $279,424.28 they had paid for land and citizenship rights returned to them, plus their $900,000 national fund, which they claimed had been spent by the recipients to improve the lands and properties in the Cherokee Nation. They went on to say that the government was also responsible for making new lands available to them where they could rebuild their homes and resume their former tribal organization.

On January 21, 1890, six of the modernists—John Sarcoxie, Sr., Arthur Miller, Henry Armstrong, Filmore Secondine, John Young, and Arthur Armstrong—authorized and empowered Charles Journeycake to represent the Delaware tribe in the courts and with boards of commissioners or committees of Congress. How these six men obtained the mandate to speak on behalf of the tribe is not explained in the documentation, although the sincerity of their intentions cannot be doubted—and who would oppose any movement to get money from the government? The contract they entered into with Journeycake specified that he would devote his time to recovering money due the Delawares from the Cherokee Nation; also to recover money for lands they had vacated in Kansas, which were not yet fully paid for; for timber illicitly taken from their lands in Kansas for which they had not been fully paid; and for ponies and cattle stolen from them in Kansas.[12]

Litigation was initiated by Journeycake in the United States Court of Claims, where a decision was handed down in favor of the Delawares, and the Cherokee promptly appealed the decision to the Supreme Court. The case, *The Cherokee Nation and the United States, Appellants vs. Charles Journeycake, Principal Chief of the Dela-Delaware Indians, Appellee,* was tried during the October 1894 term of the Supreme Court. The United States was made a party defendant, not because of any adverse interest, but because it was a trustee holding the funds of its Indian wards. Journeycake was designated as the Principal Chief, probably to add more weight to his role as spokesman for the tribe, even though there had been no formal election of a chief after John Conner's death, so far as can be determined. The paradox is apparent, because the agreement of 1867 marked the complete surrender of Delaware political authority to the Cherokee government, and none of the traditionalists regarded Journeycake as their Principal Chief. They saw him as a well-educated Baptist preacher who lived in the white man's world, occupying a fine house containing a library with books and the latest periodicals. He wore good clothing, owned an elegant carriage with rubber-covered wheels, and a silver-tipped harness for his bays. Preoccupied with his own family, church affairs, and his property and cattle, Journeycake had no interest in preserving such elements in the Delaware culture as the Big House rites, and other old-time ceremonies, which were precious to the traditionalists but heathenish to a Christian minister.

The Baptist schoolteacher in Kansas, Miss Clara Gowing, was indirectly responsible for the myth that Charles Journeycake had been appointed Principal Chief of the Delawares in 1861. Although Miss Gowing did not use the word *principal*, that was the inference drawn by the Reverend S. H. Mitchell, a white minister who succeeded Journeycake in the fall of 1890 as the pastor of the Baptist Church. In a biography of Journeycake which contains other errors of fact, Mitchell perpetuated the myth by stating erroneously that Journeycake became the Principal Chief in 1861.[13] The records leave no reason to doubt that John Conner was occupying the position of Principal Chief in 1861 and continued to hold that office when the Delawares moved to Indian Territory, at which time the agreement of 1867, in effect, abolished the position. Mitchell also referred to Journeycake as "the last chief of his tribe," and other writers have repeated this incorrect and biased statement. The last chief whom the traditionalists considered their nominal leader was Charles Elkhair, Kaw-wul-lup-poo-x-way ("one who walks backward"), whose discourse at one of the ceremonies in the Big House, which took place some years after Charles Journeycake's death, was quoted by M. R. Harrington in his account of Delaware religion.[14] Chief Elkhair, who was born in Kansas, died at the age of eighty-seven on February 6, 1935, at his home in the rural area northwest of Copan, survived by two daughters and a son (see Fig. 29).

In a decision handed down on November 19, 1894, the Supreme Court upheld the Court of Claims, decreeing that the Delawares were, by the agreement of 1867, members and citizens of the Chero-

Figure 29. Charles Elkhair (Kaw-kul-lup-poox-way, "One who walks back-ward"), last ceremonial chief of the Turkey group of Oklahoma Delawares, and his grandson Richard Franklin Falleaf. Chief Elkhair, a master of ceremonies in the Big House, died Feb. 6, 1935, at the age of eighty-seven. (Courtesy Elmer J. Sark)

kee Nation, and, as such, entitled to equal rights with all other Cher-okee citizens in proceeds from the sale of lands or any other income disbursed to Cherokee citizens.[15] This was an important legal victory for which Charles Journeycake must be given full credit, because he had accomplished something that only a man with his sophistication, education, and understanding of the law could have attained. Unfor-tunately he did not live long enough to enjoy the fruits of his labors. He died on January 3, 1894, aged seventy-seven, almost a year before the decision was rendered. The commissions he received for collect-ing money due the Delawares were said to have amounted to more than $100,000 at the time of his death.[16]

One might have thought that following this decision the Delawares and Cherokee would live together in harmony, but soon there was another series of controversies. A new issue had arisen—oil, gas, and coal had been found on land occupied by the Delawares. Some of the enterprising Cherokee businessmen (who were more white than Indian in their viewpoints), as well as whites who married Cherokee women, obtained what were called mineral leases, which they claimed gave them the right to recover what was below the ground. They then subleased these rights to prospectors and business organizations, who spent substantial sums sinking oil wells and then claimed that these expenditures entitled them to preferred rights to the mineral leases—to the exclusion of the Delaware residents. There had also been corruption and bribery among Cherokee officials, and a faction unfriendly to the Delawares had gained control of both branches of the National Council. The Delaware victory in the *Journeycake* case had antagonized many of the Cherokee, who seemed to be looking for pretexts to annoy the Delawares. Personal feuds became common; Delaware social functions were interrupted and broken up; and even some lives were lost. Appeal to the courts, which were under the control of Cherokee judges, was useless. Then, to make matters worse, the Cherokee government took the position that the Delawares did not have any ownership rights to the lands they then occupied and had paid for.

The Cherokee themselves did not own lands individually in their nation. All property was considered public land held in common for the equal benefit of all Cherokee citizens. Although individuals and families could obtain the right to occupy prescribed tracts of land, the occupants were never issued title deeds. The nation remained the owner of the land, whereas the occupants owned only the improvements they made on individual properties. The Cherokee government also took the position that the land set aside for the Delawares according to the 1867 agreement was only for their occupancy and did not belong to them because it was part of the public land held in common for Cherokee citizens. The Delawares protested angrily, insisting that the Cherokee government had guaranteed them full ownership of 157,600 acres of land for which they had paid $157,600. Furthermore, they said that representatives of the Department of the Interior had assured them when they signed the 1867 agreement that they were purchasing outright ownership of this acreage. Having paid an additional $121,824.28 for citizenship rights, the Delawares said they had been assured both by the United States government and the Cherokee government that they would have equal rights, along with native-born Cherokee citizens, to all the remaining lands and funds owned by the Cherokee Nation.

Unable to obtain satisfaction from the Cherokee government, the Delawares had no alternative except to bring another suit against the Cherokee in the United States Court of Claims, which they did on August 4, 1898, for the purpose of defining their rights to title and possession. An educated Delaware modernist, Richard C. Adams, and another Delaware, John Bullette, were entrusted with the responsibility of defending the Indians' rights and protecting their interests as Journeycake had done previously. In the event of their winning a favorable decision, the Delawares agreed that Adams and Bullette were to receive as their compensation 25,640 acres of the land set aside for the tribe. Two prominent New York attorneys, Walter S. Logan, president of the New York State Bar Association, and Marx E. Harby, were also engaged as the tribe's legal representatives.[17] The United States refused to be a party to the suit, claiming it was a dispute between the Delawares and Cherokee, and in doing so it abandoned the guardian role it had long held. By deserting the Delawares, the government left them unaided in an impossible situation in which it had helped to place them.

In addition to the suit to protect their property rights, another complaint filed by the Delawares stated that they had not been paid the full amount of their share of the proceeds received by the Cherokee from the sale of their lands, as directed by the Supreme Court in the *Journeycake* decision. The Cherokee defense was that they didn't have enough money in the treasury to pay the Delawares, to which the Delawares replied that there had been irregularities in the distribution of money, due to misfeasance in high places. The Delawares charged that corrupt Cherokee officials had been bribed to have disbursements made at certain towns where the Indian recipients would immediately squander their payments drinking, carousing, and on lewd women. Some Cherokee recipients got more than they were entitled to, the Delawares insisted, which is why they had been cheated of their fair share.

In a pamphlet printed at his own expense while the litigation was in progress, Adams, frustrated by the failure of the United States to come to the Delawares' assistance, tried to arouse public sympathy for his cause; but the issues were so tangled in complex legalities that they were not fully understood, and even his own people challenged his motives. In 1899 he wrote that he had been working in Washington, D.C., for more than three years in behalf of his people, and "at my own personal expense, I have championed their cause, and the cost of doing this has been many thousands of dollars." [18]

The Court of Claims ruled that the Delawares did *not* have perpetual title to the lands set aside for their occupancy in the Cherokee Nation; that they had only purchased the right of life occupancy, with the additional privilege secured in the event of allotment. The Delawares appealed this decision to the Supreme Court. In the meantime settlers were overrunning Indian Territory; by 1896 the total population of 365,000 included 300,000 whites.[19] Crime was rampant; timber, coal, and oil lands were being monopolized by a few to the detriment of the many, and the Territory had become a place of refuge for murderers, train and bank robbers, horse thieves, and outlaws in general. Even though none of the newcomers could technically own land, they obtained rights of occupancy, and aggressive entrepreneurs, by manipulation, were soon controlling extensive tracts of land—some were even employing Indians as farm laborers. The United States was under pressure from its citizens to do something not only about the Cherokee Nation but about all the lands occupied by the Five Civilized Tribes. As Americans saw the situation, it was an anomaly for their country to be cut in half territorially by lands set aside for Indian occupancy. Although the land actually belonged to the United States, since no title deeds had ever been given the Indians, nevertheless the Cherokee and the other Civilized Tribes had full control through their governments, Congress was without authority, and United States courts had little jurisdiction.

The Dawes Severalty Act (also known as the General Allotment Act) was originally passed by Congress in 1887—it had a number of later amendments—and the intention of this legislation was to eliminate the Indian Territory and create a state, or states, that would embrace the Indians' lands. Senator Henry L. Dawes, chairman of the commission that bore his name, was authorized to enter into negotiations with the Five Civilized Tribes with the objective of purchasing the lands from the Indians on behalf of the government, or making arrangements whereby the lands would be allotted in severalty to the members of the tribes. This meant that the Cherokee Nation would be dissolved, and its lands would be taken over by the Indian citizens as individual property owners possessing title deeds. The commissioners encountered stubborn resistance, and in some instances were treated with disrespect by the Indian leaders, who feared high taxation if their lands became part of a state and complete loss of their Indian identities. Nevertheless, the commissioners persevered, and Congress passed an amendment to the basic act on March 3, 1901, which expressly declared that every Indian living in Indian Territory was a citizen of the United States.

Finally, on August 7, 1902, Cherokee citizens voted in a special election to approve an agreement with the commission. The result was the ultimate erasure of the Cherokee Nation, although several years were required for the complete dissolution of the Cherokee government.

The Curtis Act provided that the Dawes Commission prepare an official roll of the members of each tribe, and that a detailed record be kept of the lands allotted to each Indian. The philosophy behind the land allotment plan was that lands being controlled by whites would be restored to the Indians, and that by becoming individual landowners the Indians would be given an incentive to become ranchers or farmers and support their families without further government intervention or aid.

On February 23, 1904, the Supreme Court handed down its decision in the case of the Delawares vs. the Cherokee, which dealt a severe blow to Adams and his constituents. The Court upheld the decision of the Court of Claims and said that at the time of the 1867 agreement the Cherokee did not have title to the said lands in its nation, and thus were powerless to convey a title in fee simple to the Delawares.[20] This was the old concept under United States laws— that an Indian tribe enjoyed the rights of dwelling, hunting, and planting on lands set aside for its members, but that when the Indians were disposed to sell the lands, they were obliged to convey their occupational rights to the United States, which possessed the title. The Court stated that the registered Delawares acquired only the right of occupancy during their lifetimes to the lands which had cost them $1 an acre. However, the Court said that the registered Delawares had a privilege secured in the event of allotment, which meant that under the General Allotment Act every registered Delaware was entitled to 160 acres, even if there was not enough land in the Cherokee Nation to allot that quantity to every citizen.

This decision applied only to living Delawares whose names were on the February 18, 1867, registration list, of whom there were only 212 when the suit was entered in the Court of Claims—the others having died or being otherwise unaccounted for. The children of living registered Delawares—and the children of registered Delawares then deceased—were to be treated on the same basis as other Cherokee citizens. When the final calculations were made, the allotment was set at an average of 110 acres per individual, based on the *quality* of the land. The land was appraised in terms of its probable fertility— for instance, whether it was hilly or bottom land. Some Indians received more than 110 acres, and some less, the distribution ostensibly based on a fair evaluation of the allotment. Immediately following the Supreme Court decision, the 157,600 acres which the Delawares believed they owned and which had been held intact pending court decision were released for allotment. These lands were treated the same as all other lands in the Cherokee Nation and were released to duly enrolled citizens. Under rules and regulations made by the Dawes Commission, the Secretary of the Interior, and the applicable laws of the United States, these allotments became subject to conveyance by patents which legally transferred to the individual allottee all interest and ownership of the land allotted him.

Since the United States had refused to be a party to the Delaware-Cherokee suit, the rights of the Delawares under their treaty of July 4, 1866, with the United States was not determined. That treaty—and the prior treaty of 1861—had clearly guaranteed the Delawares full and complete ownership of lands to which they moved and which were intended as their permanent homes. By payment of a specified sum to purchase what they thought was perpetual title, the Delawares had been assured that the United States would guarantee this title. In treaty after treaty the Delawares had been assured that the government would protect them "in the quiet enjoyment of their lands against all citizens of the United States, and against all other white persons who intrude upon the same." Time and again the government permitted violation of these promises, and in the Cherokee-Delaware dispute it refused to become involved or to assist its Delaware wards.

In the aftermath of the allotments, a majority of the Indians eventually sold their lands to white buyers, then spent the money, and once again found themselves in need. Others were more prudent, for there are still Indian descendants in Oklahoma who possess acreage allotted to them, or to their parents or grandparents. On the other hand, there are Delawares directly descended from the 985 registered Delawares who no longer have any land they can call their own.

What was expected to be a final cash settlement to satisfy the last of the Delawares' claims against the government for money due them was awarded on April 12, 1904, when Congress authorized the Secretary of the Treasury to pay the Delaware tribe residing in the Cherokee Nation an additional sum of $150,000. This was to settle any and all outstanding claims pending in the courts where the Delawares were plaintiffs and the United States was the defendant. The act stated that "The said sum shall be paid only after the tribal authorities, thereunto duly and specifically authorized by the tribe, shall have a writing stating that such payment *is in full of all claims and demands of every name and nature of said Delaware Indians against the United States . . .*" [21] (Italics added)

The "writing" was given, and the $150,000 was paid, and the government closed its ledger on the Delaware account, hopeful that things would forever after remain quiet. It proved to be a vain hope.

NOTES—CHAPTER 17

1. Many of these old cures are enumerated by George A. Hill, Jr., in "Delaware Ethnobotany," *News Letter,* Oklahoma Anthropological Society, vol. 19, no. 3, March 1971, pp. 3–18.

2. To the Munsies the Creator was known as Ket-tun-it-to-weet ("Great Spirit") or Pa-tu-ma-was ("he who is petitioned").

3. A. B. Hulbert and W. N. Schwarze, eds., *David Zeisberger's "History of the Northern American Indians," Ohio Archeological and Historical Publications,* vol. 19, Columbus, 1910, p. 89; cf. Frank G. Speck, *Oklahoma Delaware Ceremonies, Feasts and Dances,* Philadelphia, 1937, pp. 117–34.

4. Emmet Starr, *History of the Cherokee Indians,* Oklahoma City, 1921, pp. 266–83.

5. Some of these names are found in the unpublished notes Dr. Truman Michelson made during his visit to Oklahoma in 1912; Anthropological Archives, Smithsonian Institution, MSS. 2776. Ives Goddard first brought

these notes to my attention, and Mrs. Margaret Blaker kindly supplied me with transcripts.

6. Photos of both structures appear in Richard C. Adams, *A Delaware Indian Legend and the Story of Their Troubles*, Washington, D.C., 1899, pp. 23, 39.

7. Adams, *A Brief History*, pp. 54–54; see also Elmer J. Sark, *The First Baptist Church*, Bartlesville, Okla., 1964; for data on Sarcoxie residence, see Margaret Withers Teague, *History of Washington County and Surrounding Area*, Bartlesville, Okla., 1967, vol. 1, chap. 1. It is uncertain who was the first Delaware ordained. John Henry Killbuck was ordained a Moravian minister at an early date; Adams, *A Brief History*, p. 52.

8. Claiborne Addison Young, "A Walking Tour in Indian Territory, 1874," *The Chronicles of Oklahoma*, vol. 36, no. 2, 1958, pp. 176–77.

9. A Journeycake genealogical chart is given by Harry M. Roark, *Charles Journeycake, Indian Statesman and Christian Leader*, Dallas, 1970.

10. Adams, *A Delaware Legend*, p. 27. *The Annual Report of the Commissioner of Indian Affairs*, 1877 states that the Delaware national fund then yielded semiannual interest of $28 for every man, woman, and child; p. 109.

11. Muriel H. Wright, *A Guide to the Indian Tribes of Oklahoma*, Norman, Okla., 1965, 3d printing, p. 152.

12. Roark cites the complete contract in *Charles Journeycake*, pp. 61–63.

13. S. H. Mitchell, *The Indian Chief, Journeycake*, Philadelphia, 1895, pp. 43, 45.

14. M. R. Harrington, *Religion and Ceremonies of the Lenape*, New York, 1921, p. 87.

15. 28 Ct. Cl. 281, *aff'd*, 155 U.S. 196.

16. Roark, *Charles Journeycake*. Dr. William Nicholson was a dinner guest at the Journeycake home in November, 1870; his journal contains interesting notes about the family and other prominent Delawares; "A Tour of the Indian Agencies," *Kansas Historical Quarterly*, vol. 3, no. 3, 1934, p. 315. I am indebted to Mrs. Wilma M. Berry for a copy of this article.

17. Adams, *A Delaware Indian Legend*, p. 63. Mrs. Nora Dean has a copy of the contract with Adams and Bullette dated October 11, 1898, and she kindly provided me with a copy.

18. Ibid., p. 33.

19. Charles F. Meserve, *The Dawes Committee and the Five Civilized Tribes of Indian Territory*, Philadelphia, 1896, p. 11.

20. 38 Ct. Cl. 234, *aff'd as modified*, 193 U.S. 127.

21. Kappler, *Indian Affairs*, vol. 3, p. 68.

18

Conclusion

In 1946 Congress established the Indian Claims Commission to act as a court and provide a regular means of adjudicating claims involving injuries to Indian tribal groups. If fraud, duress, or error existed in connection with any treaty or agreement, or if it could be shown that an insufficient consideration had been paid the Indians with respect to lands they formerly occupied, the commission was empowered to settle "all just and equitable Indian tribal claims against the United States," and award suitable monetary recoveries. When President Truman signed this bill into law, he insisted that since the Northwest Ordinance of 1787 the government had set for itself a "standard of fair and honorable dealings" with the Indians, and through the years had "purchased from the tribes that once owned this continent more than 90 percent of our public domain, paying them an approximately 800 million dollars in the process." He added that it would be a miracle if in this course of the largest real estate transaction in history some mistakes had not been made.[1] The Indian Claims Commission was intended as an instrument to try to rectify those mistakes.

In the majority of land cessions, it was not the government's intention to cheat the Delawares, but it can be argued whether all the dealings were fair and honorable. From the several hundred claims that were subsequently filed by Indian tribes and the millions of dollars awarded by the commission, one can only conclude that many mistakes must have been made. Long before the Delawares brought their first action before the Claims Commission, awards to other tribes in excess of $100 million had been granted as compensation for injuries they claimed. The initiative on behalf of the main body of Delawares in Oklahoma was taken by the Tribal Business Committee, which demanded that additional payment be made to the Delawares for lands they ceded to the government in Indiana and Kansas during the last century.

Represented by capable legal counsel before the commission, the Delaware Tribal Business Committee insisted that in all instances the prices paid their forebears by the government for the lands they vacated in Indiana and Kansas were unconscionably low. They further maintained that in some instances the government, in violation of treaty obligations, tolerated squatters on lands set aside for exclusive Indian occupancy; allowed speculators and others to buy reserved lands at fixed prices without competitive bidding, and without regard to the actual market values; and sold potential townsites at the same price obtained for ordinary rural acreage. To compensate for such injustices, the Delawares demanded the difference between the money actually paid them for their land and the amount the same land would have yielded if it had been offered at competitive bidding, or if potential townsites had been offered for sale at higher prices than rural lands. They argued that their lands were not taken away from them through the exercise of the right of eminent domain, with just compensation as determined by a judicial tribune, but were arbitrarily sold; and, although the proceeds from the sale of their lands had been paid them, the amount was far less than the fair market value of those lands.

To support their claims, the attorneys representing the Delawares prepared briefs and exhibits running into hundreds of pages. The Indian Claims Section of the Department of Justice, acting in behalf of the government as the defendant, compiled counterevidence of no less magnitude. These voluminous data were then used in proceedings before the Claims Commission, which passed judgment on the validity of the claims and, where justified, recommended appropriations by the Congress for a cash settlement. Some of the evidence was prepared by professional scholars and experts engaged as witnesses and took the form of anthropological reports, historical studies, and appraisals of lands and timber. Despite a certain bias that is present when evidence is offered to support one side of an issue, many of these documents are worthwhile contributions to Delaware Indian history.[2] For example, since it was generally recognized that the Munsies were originally part of the Delaware tribe, the question of whether the Stockbridge-Munsies living in Wisconsin should share in the settlements had to be resolved. Attorneys for the Delawares produced historical evidence to show that the Stockbridge-Munsie people had become an independent and autonomous tribe (as distinct from the Munsies and Mahican, who came west and were absorbed in the main body of the Delawares) and should not be considered beneficiaries of any claim paid to the main body.[3] The Business Committee also maintained that the fifty or sixty persons of Munsie descent living in Franklin County, Kansas, were not eligible to share in any awards since they had broken away from the main body in 1859 to live with the Chippewa and had a separate trust fund which the government distributed to them in 1900 on a per capita basis of $494.

Although to date Congress has appropriated funds in settlement of some of the claims made by the Delawares, action on other claims is still pending, and it will be months, perhaps years, before the final outcome is known.

One of the problems in disbursing the funds already appropriated has been to validate the pedigrees of those who claim Delaware Indian ancestry. When payment of the awards were authorized by Congress, the statutes specified that the money should be distributed on a per capita basis among bona fide Delaware Indians who could prove their pedigrees. The amount to be awarded each individual depends upon the number of legitimate claimants. So far as the main body was concerned, it was agreed that a claimant should be able to furnish proof that he was a descendant from one of the Delawares whose names were listed on an official roll compiled in 1906, which represented blood kin of those related to one or more of the 985 Delawares whose names were on the official enrollment list in 1867, the time of the movement from Kansas to Oklahoma. Other criteria had to be developed to validate the claims of the Delaware Tribe of Western Oklahoma, because as a splinter group their ancestors were not named in the official 1867 enrollment list; yet they formerly had been members of the main body.

Claimants were required to fill out and submit applications to the Muskogee and Anadarko Area Offices of the Bureau of Indian

Affairs, giving requested data about their ancestry, including the date and place of birth. As a result, the Oklahoma vital statistics office was deluged with requests for birth certificates. The deadline for submitting the applications was December 31, 1969, although this date was later extended by a directive from the Solicitor's Office of the Secretary of the Interior. The applications were then reviewed and approved or rejected by the Delaware Business Committee and the Muskogee Area Office of the Bureau of Indian Affairs. In the event a claimant who had been rejected felt that he had not been treated fairly, he was permitted to appeal to Washington for a special review of his case by the Secretary of the Interior, and several hundred rejected claims were accordingly filed for review. Some 6,446 applications were received from individuals claiming descent from registered Delawares on the 1906 roll list, and 1,480 applications from those who claimed to be descended from the splinter group sometimes called the Absentee Delawares. As of May 1, 1971, the amounts of money involved in awards made or pending were as follows:

Under Claims Docket Number 337, an amount of $1,627,244.64, covering 3,859,000 acres of land ceded to the United States in Indiana under the Treaty of October 3, 1818, was awarded by the Claims Commission on August 5, 1963, and the money appropriated by an act of Congress dated October 7, 1964. From this amount legal fees of 10 percent were deducted, plus $16,306.40 in attorney's expenses, in accordance with the provisions of the contract between the Business Committee and their attorney. In addition, all enrollment costs were deducted. Since no validated list of claimants was yet available in 1964, the money was held by the Treasury Department for a short while, during which time it drew 4 percent simple interest per annum, which was added to the Delawares' account. The money was later transferred to the Delawares in trust, and was used to purchase certificates of deposit and United States Treasury bills at a higher rate of interest. Until the date of its distribution, this money will continue to gather interest, and principal and interest may amount to between $1,800,000 and $1,900,000 to be disbursed.

Another claim awarded the Delawares (Claims Docket Numbers 72 and 298) covers lands in Kansas ceded to the United States before the main body left for Oklahoma, which was sold under the Treaty of May 6, 1854. The actual amount of the claim, representing the difference between the money paid the Delawares for those lands and what the commissioners believed they should have received, amounted to $1,385,617.81. This figure was arrived at by judicial decision—the Delawares contended they were due much more. In this claim, the Delawares also maintained that they were entitled to 5 percent interest on the unpaid amount, and a judgment was awarded them representing $7,808,747.18 interest at 5 percent per annum for the period from April 30, 1857, to January 16, 1970. Thus the Claims Commission decision dated September 10, 1969, provided for a total judgment of $9,194,364.99, including principal and interest. The interest continued to accrue until January 16, 1970, the date the money was transferred in trust to the Indians. From this amount were deducted 10 percent for legal fees and $7,591.80 for expenses. The Delaware Business Committee then invested the net amount in six-month United States Treasury bills at an interest rate of 7.981 percent. As of July 31, 1970, the interest amounted to $332,694.94, bringing the total to $8,513,000. This amount will continue to appreciate through interest accumulation until questions of eligibility are resolved and validation of the claimants permits its distribution.

An amount of $457,980 was awarded the Delawares (Claims Docket Numbers 27-A and 241) covering the so-called outlet in Kansas. In 1854 the government paid certain Delaware chiefs $10,000 for this land, which the Claims Commission agreed was unconscionably low. The original judgment entered in 1959 in favor of the Indians was for $607,980, but during the ensuing years there were further hearings because the government took the position that certain money and things of value, called offsets, that subsequently had been paid the Delawares (after they left Kansas) should be applied to reduce the amount of the judgment. On June 4, 1969, a decision of the Claims Commission held that an offset of only $150,000 should be deducted, leaving a net amount of $457,980 owed the Delawares. This $150,000 represented the sum paid the Delawares under the act of Congress of April 21, 1904. The Delawares were amenable to this reduction, but on August 29, 1969, the government appealed to the Court of Claims requesting that additional offsets also be permitted to apply. The Delawares filed a cross appeal asking that the amount of the offset not be increased, and at the present time this case is still unsettled.

Another claim (Docket Number 289) covers lands in Indiana, in proceedings filed jointly by the Delawares and the Peoria tribe of Oklahoma. The Peoria was originally one of the member tribes of the Illinois Confederacy, who lived above the mouth of the Wisconsin River, but in 1854 they were united with the Wea and Piankashaw in Indiana Territory. Today the Piankashaw and Peoria are part of the Confederated Peoria living in Ottawa County, Oklahoma; like the Delawares, they have a Business Committee to represent their interests in dealings with the government. The joint claim relates to the so-called Vincennes Tract in southeastern Indiana, part of which extends into southwestern Illinois, and which was occupied by the Piankashaw for one hundred years prior to the Treaty of 1803; but from 1770 on the Delawares shared occupancy.[4] On February 24, 1971, an award of $1,497,246.11 was made to the Delaware tribe and another award of $1,501,294.35 to the Peoria tribe on behalf of the Piankashaw tribe. The awards represented additional payments for the equity each tribe had in 2,007,000 acres constituting the Vincennes Tract, as ceded under the Treaties of August 18, 1804, and August 27, 1804.

In summation, the judgments covering principal and interest which have been awarded to the Delawares, and appropriated to date by Congress, amount to more than $12 million, and it is certain that additional amounts will become available in the future from cases now pending before the commission. Needless to say, all the claimants are eager to get their prorated share of the appropriated money. To some of them the process is beginning to take on aspects of a lottery, with a winning ticket consisting of a birth certificate through which the respondent can prove kinship with someone on the official roll. Many of the claimants are middle-class people representing various trades and professions, who, until the present, have been far less interested in Delaware Indian matters than the few traditionalists who have tried to keep Indianism alive.

At the last meeting of persons claiming Delaware Indian descent over which he presided, at Dewey on September 19, 1970, Horace L. McCracken, fully aware of how the numerous government payments and annuities made to the Delawares down through the years had done the individual Indians no lasting good, proposed that a sum of $250,000 be set aside from the awards for such things as scholarships for Delaware children, an arts and crafts center, a museum, or other worthy tribal projects.

"I'm opposed," a female claimant from Tulsa said, according to a news story in the *Bartlesville Enterprise-Examiner*. "The tribe has been owed that money for more than 100 years. All my life I've been waiting for that money, and I think every nickel should be paid to the members of the tribe." The three hundred Delaware descendants seated in the Dewey High School auditorium, many indistinguishable in appearance from white persons, voiced their agreement, each believing he was entitled to his full share of the prize money.

Another lady, whose Indian features were pronounced, agreed that McCracken's idea was a good one, and she suggested a voluntary donation system when the money is distributed, with each recipient making a voluntary contribution to a revolving fund to be used for the benefit of the tribe.

"There ain't nobody going to volunteer," said an old Delaware patriarch from Dewey, "when he gets that money in his hands." *

NOTES—CHAPTER 18

1. William A. Brophy, Sophie D. Aberle, et al., compilers, *The Indian, America's Unfinished Business*, Norman, Okla., 1966, p. 28.

2. In the various chapter notes I have made reference to historical data and exhibits prepared for the government by Erminie Wheeler-Voegelin, and others. Another interesting 53-page printed compilation by Mrs. Gay Ramabhushanam used in the litigation is entitled *A Report on Indian Land Use and Occupation of Ohio South and East of the Greenville Treaty Line, 1795 (Including An Historical Sketch of Relevant Events from 1661 to 1797)*. It carries no date or place of publication. A copy was supplied me by Louis L. Rochmes, Washington attorney for the Delawares. H. L. McCracken loaned me copies of all of the briefs submitted by the Delawares, findings of fact, and so forth, in the various hearings before the Claims Commission. Much of this literature has been printed for the records by the Byron S. Adams Company, Washington, D.C. •

3. This was thoroughly covered in a brief prepared by Bruce Miller Townsend, then vice-chairman of the Delaware Tribal Business Committee,

* The first partial disbursement under Docket Number 337 consisting of $185 per capita was made after this chapter was written, and none of the recipients made voluntary contributions to a tribal fund. What will happen with future disbursements remains to be seen.

on Nov. 28, 1966, and submitted to the Secretary of the Interior under the title *In the Matter of the Proposed Legislative Determination of Identity of the Delaware Nation of Indians as Constituted at the Time of the Treaty of October 3, 1818* (7 Stat. 188).

4. The details in this claim are given in a separate report entitled *Proposed Findings of Fact with respect to the Vincennes Tract (Royce Area 26)*, printed December 1969 by the Byron S. Adams Printing Company, Washington, D.C.

APPENDIXES

Appendix 1

Maps and Drawings Relating to Delaware Indian Villages and Reservations

The serious reader may feel the need for obtaining more detailed information than that given in the text about specific areas of Delaware occupancy at different periods in history. The authors of a number of sectional accounts have included drawings that provide useful information about particular locales. The following list is by no means exhaustive, but it offers selected sources worthy of examination.

For general locations of Delaware Indian villages in the Delaware River Valley in the seventeenth century at the time of white contact:

Peter Lindeström, *Geographia Americae*, trans. Amandus Johnson, Philadelphia, 1925; folding map "A," *Nova Suecia, Eller the Swenskas Revier in India Occidentalis*, drawn by Lindeström, 1654–55, and annotated by Johnson, is an extremely valuable contemporary work for locating Indian villages along the Delaware.

P. L. Phillips, *The Rare Map of Virginia and Maryland*; this is a map made by Augustine Herrman in 1670, and it delineates Indian villages along the Delaware River.

C. A. Weslager, *Red Men on the Brandywine*, Wilmington, 1953; see p. xv for a drawing of the Okehocking reservation; p. xviii for drawing of lands along Brandywine reserved to Delawares; p. xx for contemporary surveyor's drawing showing location of Delaware village in the big bend of the stream.

C. A. Weslager, "Robert Evelyn's Indian Tribes and Place-Names of New Albion," *Bulletin* 9, Archeological Society of New Jersey, November 1954: drawings on pp. 5 and 6 give locations of Delaware villages in New Jersey based on seventeenth-century maps made by Van der Donck, Vingboons, and Lindeström.

A. R. Dunlap and C. A. Weslager, "Toponymy of the Delaware Valley as Revealed by an Early Seventeenth-Century Dutch Map," ibid., *Bulletin* 15–16, November, 1958; see folding map, *Caerte vande Svydt Rivier in Niew Nederland*, c. 1629, annotated by the authors.

C. A. Weslager and A. R. Dunlap, *Dutch Explorers, Traders & Settlers in the Delaware Valley*, Philadelphia, 1961; Dutch map opposite p. 60, *De Zuid Baai in Nieuw-Nederland*, c. 1630–40, shows location of Indian settlement at Swanendael (present Lewes, Delaware).

For locations of Delaware Indian settlements in Pennsylvania and Ohio, 1700–95:

[Charles Thomson] *Alienation of the Delaware and Shawanese Indians*, 1759 (reprint), Philadelphia, 1867; map opposite p. 184 shows purchases made by Pennsylvania proprietors from the Delaware Indians, including the Walking Purchase (a copy of this map is also given on p. 170 of Wallace's *King of the Delawares*, see below).

Charles A. Hanna, *The Wilderness Trail*, New York, 1911; folding map of early Indian villages in Pennsylvania and Ohio by the author.

Paul A. W. Wallace, *Conrad Weiser*, Philadelphia, 1945; drawing on p. 78 shows route of Onondaga Trail and Indian villages on Susquehanna; drawing on p. 138 shows Shamokin Trail; drawing on p. 265 shows Allegheny Trail with such locations as Shanopin's Town, Augwick, and Big Island on the west branch of the Susquehanna.

Grant Foreman, *The Last Trek*, Norman, Okla., 1946; p. 80 folding map of the upper Ohio region showing lands reserved to Delaware Indians by the Greenville Treaty.

Anthony F. C. Wallace, *King of the Delawares: Teedyuskung*, Philadelphia, 1949; see end papers for a drawing of the location of Delaware Indian villages in Pennsylvania 1700–63; map on p. 27 gives approximate location of Minnisink, Esopus, and so forth.

August C. Mahr, "A Canoe Journey—Heckewelder's Travel Diary," *Ohio State Archeological and Historical Quarterly*, vol. 61, no. 3, 1952; drawing opposite p. 290 shows Heckewelder's route from Beaver Creek to Tuscarawas in 1773, with locations of Delaware towns.

Paul A. W. Wallace, *Thirty Thousand Miles with John Heckewelder*, Pittsburgh, 1958; two folding maps in end pocket showing Heckewelder's travels contain important entries relative to Delaware Indian villages.

Nicholas Wainwright, *George Croghan, Wilderness Diplomat*, Chapel Hill, N.C., 1959; drawing on p. 11 shows Braddock's Road, Kittanning, Kuskuskies, Logstown, and other locations.

For locations of Delaware Indian settlements and reservations in Indiana, Missouri, Kansas, and Texas, 1795–1867:

Charles N. Thompson, *Sons of the Wilderness*, Indianapolis, 1937; drawing opposite p. 42 shows Delaware Indian towns along the White River in Indiana.

Grant Foreman, *The Last Trek*, Norman, Okla., 1946; folding map showing lands in Indiana ceded by the Delawares, p. 114; map of Delaware reserved lands in Missouri, p. 34; map of Delaware reserved lands in Kansas, p. 182.

John Treat Irving, Jr., *Indian Sketches* (1833), ed. John Francis McDermott, Norman, Okla., 1955; map on pp. xxxiv and xxxv shows Delaware reserved lands and "the Outlet" in Kansas.

Lewis Henry Morgan, *The Indian Journals*, ed. Leslie A. White, Ann Arbor, 1957; drawing on p. 75 shows Delaware reserved lands in Kansas, as well as adjacent reservations of neighboring tribes.

Jean Louis Berlandier, *The Indians of Texas in 1830*, ed. John C. Ewers, Smithsonian Institution Press, 1969; map opposite p. 22 shows where Delawares were living in Texas in 1830.

Appendix 2

Henry R. Schoolcraft's Letter to E. G. Squier *

Washington Feb. 16th 1849

My dear Sir,

I have, cursorily, examined the "Walum Olum" of the Delawares, as published by you, from the papers of Rafinesque. It is to be regretted, that the elements of such a document should have fallen into the hands of Rafinesque, who spoiled, historically and scientifically, every thing he touched. It is to be lamented the more, because the system of the Walum Olum, or stick writing itself, is a mode of communicating ideas, which, under several names, all the more advanced tribes of the Algonquin groupe, possessed more fully, than the other North American groupes, who are situated north of Mexico.

How far the specimen exhibited by you, is to be regarded as conveying the traditions, ancient and modern, of the Delawares, and to what extent these traditions have been mixed and interpolated, may require more leisure, and minute examination than I have given the paper. I have been impressed with general coincidences and agreements with the Algonquin traditions, and with the pictorial method of notation, as it exists in the North and West at the day. The figures and devices, with the exception of such symbols as Nos. 8. 9. 10. and 16 &c. are well sustained by comparisons with such transcripts as I have obtained from bark rolls, and the tabular pieces of wood called music boards in the North, in which, however these or similar devices are usually applied to spiritual, or monetorian triumphs in necromancy and

* Permission to reprint from the Manuscript Collections of the New York Public Library is gratefully acknowledged.

medicine. I am not generally, impressed as well, with the explanations of the symbols, as the symbols themselves. They fail in fullness and point, and appear to lack that acquaintance with the Olum idiom, and the system of pictorial interpretation, which must be supplied by induction and memory.

I have, however, no where found historical records of such "extent and continuity" as the Walum Olum to which you refer, and cannot point to a single record, of any kind, which aims to perpetuate traditions of more than one or two centuries standing, unless it be in the mooted specimen of the Dighton Rock; while by far the greater number, do not reach back, fifty years.

In the system of the northern tribes, to which I have given attention, the objects of inscriptive art are; to bear testimony to a single exploit—a battle,—a brave man—something like biographical jottings, as numbers of scalps, fierce animals killed, spirit-craft in the priesthood &c. More commonly this art, is applied to record medicine, hunting and war songs. The system is purely ideographic and mnemonic. It is a system of substantives, action being always inferential. Verses of songs are noted by pictures, but it is, so to say, only the key-notes, which are designed to awaken the memory. The words must have been previously committed to memory, in order to be certainly recited. It is a property of the symbols, that they are, like the Chinese, or like words in their own languages, often highly compounded. A dot,—a mark, or some other device, is to be viewed as a pictogrammatical adjunct, giving force or expression to noun-figures. I have never seen the triangle and its combinations, which appear in the symbols 9. 10 &c. above referred to, in the northern bark or block inscriptions, while symbols of the sun and moon are common. It is not improbable that Mr Rafinesque was better acquainted with the doctrines of Zoroaster, and the early oriental nations of a triune power, than the ancient Delawares, to whom these particular figures are ascribed.

In conclusion, allow me to express the satisfaction I feel, that you have contributed this element to our knowledge on this topic, whatever may be its absolute historical value. For one, I am free to confess, that while seeking and appreciating every effort to enlarge the number of facts, on the Indian pictorial system, it appears impossible to me to carry the date of many of the ancient events noted in the Walum Olum, beyond the period of the introduction of christianity among the Lenape by the United Brethren. It is indisputable that the teachers of that early order, were far more celebrated for their devotion and piety, than their learning or research; although they, in our days have had a Schweinitz. Single hearted and unsuspecting themselves, they received the traditions of the Delawares, with undoubting credulity. These Indians were then in their national decline, having fallen before the indomitable courage

and superior diplomacy of the Iroquois. To the tales of their declension;—
of their former power; and of a far off, and past era, which their old
chiefs pictured, as another golden age, these good men listened with unsuspecting belief and characteristic kindness, and were ever more ready
to pity their misfortunes, than to scrutinize the truth of their old narratives, or to compare them with the contemporary traditions of other
stocks. I think the Lenapes had some well founded claims to comparative
antiquity, among the Atlantic border tribes, though none at all, to the
title of original men, which the term's Lenno Lenapi, have been said to
signify. They mean no such thing. Lenapi, is the equivalent for the
northern Algonquin Inabi, meaning Indian, and its prefix, lenno, is the
equivalent for the northern, enno or annish, meaning common, or general. And thus the Delawares, like the Chippewas and their cogenital
tribes, called themselves, as at this day, the common people, or the mass
of men, as contradistinguished from Englishmen, Frenchmen and other
Europeans.

But not to dwell in so minute a point, it is abundantly manifest, that
the Delawares of the olden time, when they had been instructed in
Christianity, saw, or fancied they saw, some things in their mythology
which bore a certain resemblance to scripture history. Their allegories gave
almost every license to the imagination; and it was almost a matter of
course, that they should attempt to adjust these few points, namely, a
tradition of creation, and of a flood, &c. to the highlights supplied by
revelation. It was natural when they heard the miraculous accounts of
Jonah and Noah, that they should discern the exploits of their own
Manabozho in these sacred incidents. Few adult Indians are ever found
to be so thoroughly christians, to turn their backs in toto, upon their
own mythology. In this manner, and upon the banks of the Musking or
White River of Indiana, I think the Walum Olum was drawn. How much
Rafinesque had to do with it, in its transcription from the original sticks
or blocks; and who gave him the interpretations, are questions which
you have not settled, but which have a material bearing upon the historical value of your interestng and ingenious paper. Every element of ethnological knowledge of this kind, is deeply valuable and to none can it be
more so, than to your obliging friend

and obedient Servant.

Henry R. Schoolcraft

P.S.
Mrs S. and the young ladies reciprocate your remembrances. We all expect to see you again soon. Give my respects to Mr Bartlett, and believe
my very truly yours.

H.R.S.

Appendix 3

Account of some of the Traditions, Manners and Customs
of the
Lenēē Lenaūpaa or Delaware Indians [1]

The original and present name of the tribe is Lenēē Lenaūpaa. The
term Lenaūpaa is applied by them to all nations of Indians, and no
doubt means man or people in an extended sense. They call themselves
by this name in ordinary cases, but if it be necessary to distinguish them
from other tribes they prefix the word Lenēē, which signifies common, and
sometimes, as Mr. Heckewelder has said, original; so that Lenēē Lenaūpaa
would mean the common or original people. How far this fact would go
to support the opinion which these people pretend to entertain of their
originality, I will not pretend to say, for all other nations of Indians of
whom I have any knowledge, make the same claim. By the neighbouring
nations they are called Oapunōhkee, or "From the east," from Oāpun,
Light, Daylight.[2] The Moahēēkunee or Stockbridges are known by the
same appellation.

The only nation with whom they acknowledge any relationship by
blood are the Munsee or Mōōnsee; the Oāponoos, the Nanticokes or
Oonaāhteekoa, whom they term their brothers; the Wyandots or Taale-
mūtenoo, their uncles, and the Mohiccans or Mauhēēkunee, their grandchildren. The Shōōpshee or naked, the Oāpingk or Oppossum, and the
Skaāhteekoa (the Schatikoake of the Dutch) nations formerly residing
upon the shores of the Atlantic, are said to have been descendants of the
Delawares. These nations by intermixture with the parent tribe have become extinct as such, with the exception of the Shōōpshee, descendants
of whom are supposed still to exist near Oswego, but under what name I

cannot learn. By an ancient political connection which existed between the Delawares and the other nations residing upon the Atlantic and the great lakes they assumed the office of mediators between those who were so unfortunate as to be engaged in war, and their success in promoting the peace of the surrounding tribes being attributed to their superior wisdom, which with them is always the attendant of age, they were styled Grandfathers by all who had occasion to apply for their mediatory services, and have continued to this day to call the Pottowatamies, Chippeways, Ottawaus and others their grandchildren.

They claim to be descendants of the Wyandots, and relate these circumstances connected with their birth. The Wyandots sprang from a hole in the earth, which is still to be seen on Lake Huron. Not long after their discovery of the world above, a virgin of that nation became pregnant from some unnatural cause and in due time was delivered of twins, a son and daughter, who spoke a language entirely different from their parent, to wit, that of the present Delawares. That it was customary at that time to marry very near relatives; that these twins were so united and from this incestuous intercourse sprang the Lenēē Lenaūpaa, who, by direction of their uncles, the Wyandots, went to the borders of the Ocean and there settled themselves.[3] They deny any connection by blood with the Iroquois, and although they call them Uncles they say it was at first a mere matter of courtesy resulting from their actual relationship in that degree to the Wyandots, who were connected with the Iroquois, and from whom the latter adopted the title of nephew (since the change of the Delawares this is also changed to niece, as is that of the Munsees to Sister) which has been since continued.

The account of their different migrations is very imperfect. They sat out for the Atlantic in pursuance of the advice of the Wyandots, and were about two years in reaching the place of their destination, the precise location of which is lost in the lapse of time. They lived there a long time and became populous; when the frequent and protracted aggressions of the whites thinned their numbers and compelled them to remove from place to place until they reached Hutēēkengk,[4] near Pittsburgh. Thence they went to Kushkūshkingk,[5] on the Big Beaver, where they remained until their removal to the lands of the Tuscarawas. From there they went to Upper Sandusky, whence they scattered through the Ohio country, on the heads of Mad River[,] Sciota and its other tributaries. From these villages the great body of the nation removed to Fort Wayne, where they remained until Harmers' defeat, after which they resided at Delaware Town twelve miles above Defiance, then on the Auglaize and back again to the Town above Defiance whence they migrated to the White River.

They have been at war with the Cataūbas, Cherokees, and Iroquois, but they reccollect no particulars of these wars. Cherokees have been known to go as far as Defiance to commit murder or other depredations upon them, and Pipe reccollects to have seen warriors of his own nation set out to attack them in return. During their residence near Defiance the Cherokees sent Ambassadors there to sue for peace. These Ambassadors were preceded by females carrying presents, and they were admitted to the village through two rows of warriors who fired guns over their heads as they passed. Peace between the two nations was then concluded and has not since been violated by either party.

The tradition of their first acquaintance with the whites has been minutely related by Mr. Heckewelder and agrees in substance with the account now given of that important event. Capt. Pipe says that in those days the Indians were accustomed to worship annually as they now do, in a large building prepared and kept for that purpose. At one of these meetings an old man prophesied the coming of some important and extraordinary events and a few days after a ship hove in sight and a boat with some of the officers came on shore. The Indians, supposing the crew to be inferior deities sent by the great Spirit, spread beaver skins upon the ground for them to walk upon. The whites refused to comply and pointed to their hats endeavouring to make them understand the value and proper use of the skins, but they were compelled to accept the politeness of their new acquaintances who surrounded them and drove them on the skins. When they arrived at the great council house or place of worship one of them took a cup and filling it with liquor drank of it and offered it to the astonished spectators. The cup passed around, refused by all. At length three brave men supposing the Deity would be offended by their stubbornness resolved to undertake the dreadful task, and having drunk the contents of the cup they were taken out of the lodge and seated upon a log. The effect of the liquor soon prostrated them to the ground, and their recovery was despaired of. However they were closely watched and at length one of them lifted up his head and demanded more of the poison. In time they all recovered and their account of its pleasing effects induced others to join, and its use soon became universal.

After becoming familiar with them the whites solicited them to give a small piece of land upon which they might build a fire to prepare their food. They demanded only a piece as large as a Bullocks hide and the request was readily granted, when to their great astonishment the bullocks hide was soaked in water and cut into a small cord with which the land was surrounded. However, they determined to overlook the deception and be more wary in future. They whites presented them with Axes, hoes etc. and departed, promising to revisit them the next year.

Upon their return they were not a little amused to see the Indians walking about with these things suspended from their necks as ornaments. They taught them their use, trafficked a little with them, and at length told them that they wanted more lands, because it was impossible from the smallness of the size of the first grant, to build a fire upon it without being incommoded with the smoke. It was therefore resolved to add to the first piece a quantity large enough to hold the chair of the whites, without the influence of the smoke. Upon this the bottom of the chair, which was composed of small cords, was taken out and like the hide, stretched around the lands. This second deception determined them never to give more lands without fixing some boundary understood by both parties distinctly.

It is difficult to derive from them the history of any of their great men in such manner as to afford interest to the hearer. There is so much of the fabulous in their stories that they become quite insipid and sometimes disgusting. As an instance I could give the substance of a long story about Weekharmookhaas, who lived many ages past and was a mighty hunter. He generally hunted alone and sometimes went a great distance from home. Combinations were often formed for his destruction, but if he heard the approach of any thing or of his enemies he would fly out at the top of his wigwam and alighting upon a neighbouring tree would demand their business. If they had courage enough to declare their intention he attacked them with a huge war club and having destroyed a part despatched the rest with contemptuous expressions to relate their fate. He had unlimited power in the nation and used to go about killing the aged and decrepit, telling them that they lived for nothing.[6]

GOVERNMENT

At the creation of the world the Great spirit himself resided with the Indians and regulated their intercourse with each other. When he left the earth he told them that he would depute a person possessing all his own virtues, at whose death they should choose a successor having as nearly as possible the same qualifications. Since that period the office of chief has been elective, yet the election is not made by the people. Merit alone ensures to a man this distinguished honour. There is among them a body of men called Lupwaaeenoāwuk or Wise Men, (the plural, from Lupwaaoākun wisdom and Lŭnnoa a man). These men from their conduct in early life receive the attention and respect of the aged and as they grow in years they gradually assume the power which is attached to the wise men or counsellors. At length they are received as members of that powerful body and become officially interested in the proper regulation of national affairs. All civil affairs are conducted and ordered by them and when the office of chief becomes vacant they assemble and in presence of the <u>people</u> they consult together upon the qualifications of the aspirants and having decided they appoint another meeting for his inauguration, to which, as to the first, they invite the nation generally. At the appointed time the Lupwaaeenōawuk together with the elected chief and such spectators as choose to attend, assemble at a grand lodge prepared for the purpose, and one of the body in a speech adapted to the occasion declares to the people their choice and then turning to the chief addresses him on the importance of a firm, independent and upright course of conduct, the importance of good examples from the heads of the nation etc. During the speech the speaker holds in his hand a Belt of wampum, which he places around the neck of the chief, telling him, "now you have the speech, see that you keep it, and adhere to the advice contained in it." The ceremonies attending the appointment of chief are practiced also at the reception of one of the wise men, excepting the placing a belt around the neck, which is not used at all. Formerly the authority of the War and Council chiefs was distinctly defined. To use their expression, in a time of peace the war chief sat in the ashes, but upon the declaration of war, the village or council chiefs took his place, and the movements of the war depended solely upon him. At this day however they have equal authority in treaties and the like, that is to say, according to their influence as men.

The Chiefs have no compulsory powers, but instances of disobedience to their commands are very rare. Submission to their will arises from many causes, first because by common consent of the nation expressed through their representatives, the Lupwaaeenōawuk, they are vested with the highest powers which they can confer on a man: secondly, because as a natural consequence of their form of election none arrive at the honors of a chief but such as are distinguished for their bravery and mental capacity, consequently such are feared and respected; and again, because they believe or pretend to believe that no man becomes a chief who has not been intended for that dignified station by the Great Spirit from whom his wisdom and capacity to govern is derived. It is only necessary for a Chief to express his will and it is obeyed, or he who refuses is condemned by the nation.

If a man in drunkenness or in the heat of passion commit any violence or injure another in his person or property, he goes to one of the Council Chiefs, delivers him a string of wampum, describes the circumstances of his transgression, confesses his sorrow for the event and solicits him to heal the breach between him and his friend. With a proper message the chief transmits the wampum to the injured party advising him to overlook the offence, and the matter is thus generally settled. But in case of refusal on the part of the latter it is returned to the aggressor, who prepares himself for any attempt of the other to avenge the wrong in his own way. There are six chiefs, properly so called, in the Delaware nation, three of whom are war and the others council or village chiefs. One of each description is appointed for the Wolf tribe, one of each for the Turkey tribe and the other two for the Turtle tribe.[7]

The Lupwaaeenōawuk are not restricted to any particular number, but accessions are made of such as merit an admission from the general tenor of their lives. The members of this body, or some one of them as occasion may require, are appointed to carry into effect the orders of the chiefs, and any employment, however degrading, is considered by them an honour under such circumstances. In the distribution of annuities and of presents their services are indispensible, and while young they carry the kettles of the war parties while on the march.

As chiefs are elected by the will of the people, in the same manner they are removed from office. Not by direct accusation and trial however, for they are careful not to arraign an individual publicly before the nation whether he be great or low, but by neglecting to invite him to councils or refusal to listen to or execute his orders. This being done by the aged and influential, whose motives are made known at proper times, the neglect becomes general, the people contemn his authority and he is gradually lowered down to the private station, whence he does not attempt to rise but by a long course of good conduct or by some extraordinary effort of genius or political intrigue by which he can overpower his enemies at a single movement.

Notwithstanding the partial amalgamation of the powers of the council and war chiefs of late years, the conducting of war parties is considered the particular duty of that class of chiefs, and in treaties of peace which succeed them the counsellors assume again their authority, subject always however, to the advice of the war chiefs as to the continuance of the war or the necessity of ending it. Unimportant or ordinary occurrences are considered as within the superintendence of the Chiefs without consultation or advice; such as regulating the internal affairs of their villages, settling disputes, etc. but affairs of consequence are never acted upon without the concurrence of the Lupwaaeenōawuk, from whom in fact all important transactions emanate. The consultations of these men precede all treaties declarations of war, etc. and after expressing their opinion as a body each member considers himself individually bound to assist and obey the Chief in the execution of it.

There are no female Chiefs. Some women have been known to assume a kind of superiority in things under the control of their sex, but this was merely the result of superior capacity. The wives or daughters of Chiefs are not particularly respected on that account.

There is no mode of compelling the payment of a debt. Relatives sometimes contribute to pay the debt of another, as well to satisfy the creditor as to secure a reputation for honesty; at others the creditors seizes the property of the debtor, his horse, gun or other article of which he can possess himself, and instances have been known where the property of the debtor's relatives was thus taken, for which they were remunerated by the debtor himself.

There is no law for the redress of civil injuries. The injured party generally obtains satisfaction by application to the Chiefs, but if this fails he resorts to retaliation, a very general mode of procuring satisfaction in such cases.

No offences are considered as such against the body of the nation. To this however there have been some extraordinary exceptions; such were the offences committed by supposed witches and wizzards who were burned on White River in 1810.[8] If a murder is committed the friends and relative of the murderer collect by their own means and the contributions of others a quantity of wampum, which they deposit with the Chief of their own tribe from time to time until the stock amounts to an hundred and twenty fathoms if the murdered person be a man or an hundred and thirty fathoms if a woman. When this is effected the Chiefs call a council at which the nation, or as many as are so inclined, with the friends of the deceased and the murderer assemble. Here, after a few remarks by way of consolation to the afflicted relatives the acceptance of the wampum is proposed to them, and if they refuse eight fathoms are added to it and the presentation is repeated. If they persist in their refusal eight fathoms more are added and should they still reject the offer the connexions of the murderer pronounce themselves ready to meet the opposite party in any way they may propose to avenge themselves. The fear of the anger of the nation always induces them at last to accept the wampum and compromise the matter. Great difficulties sometimes occur in procuring the quantity of wampum required by law. Seven or eight years have been thus employed. In such cases twelve fathoms are presented immediately after the commission of the offence, as an earnest of the desire of the aggressors to settle the difference in an amicable manner. The acceptance of this first offering is a pledge on the part of the injured relatives to receive the balance. No other presents accompany the wampum, as is the case among the northern Indians.

If the murderer or his relatives in his behalf neglect to offer the customary evidences of their desire for peace, some one of the relatives of the deceased avenges his death by killing the murderer. This is sometimes done in the heat of the affray and is considered perfectly justifiable. It does not extend in its consequences as among the Munōāminees, where whole families fall victims to the barbarous custom of retaliation. It is not considered the duty of any particular relative thus to take revenge, but is accomplished by him who has the requisite courage. The guilty person if he be a worthless man, not respected by his own relatives or by the nation will generally effect his escape if possible, for he cannot hope for assistance in obtaining the quantity of wampum necessary. If he be poor but reputable he will probably "deliever his body" as they say, to the relatives of the murdered, and his life being in their hands they have an opportunity to show their generosity which they frequently seize upon.

Offences of this nature are very often settled by a much smaller quantity of wampum than that mentioned, but as the law requires the one hundred and twenty or thirty fathoms, a refusal to accept less does not meet the displeasure of the nation as would be the case if the legal quantity were rejected.

The murder of an individual belonging to a different tribe in the nation of the murderer, is considered as a more heinous crime than if the parties were of the same parent stock, and is treated accordingly.

Rape, adultery and stealing are considered criminal, but no punishment is attached to them save the severe reprimand of the Chiefs, which attracts the notice and disrespect of the community and is often a sure preventive of wrong. Those who commit such and other improper acts habitually, are called men without ears, deaf to the voice of their superiors and worthy of the contempt of the nation.

For the regulation of affairs of internal policy councils of the Lupwaaeenōāwuk are called by the Chiefs who submit such propositions touching the good of the nation as have come to their minds. These being deliberated upon the wise men report their opinion to the chiefs. If they [sic] resolutions are not approved by them, they in their turn submit amendments to the council, or as they say, 'straiten their resolutions.' With these amendments the wise men concur, the Chief approves and if necessary promulgates the proceedings and the resolutions are thenceforward considered as fixed and irrevocable except by the same authority which formed them.

The Delaware nation is divided into three tribes, the Tōōkseet or Wolf (Round foot; from Tookwaa and Oozeet) the Tshēēkunum or Turkey, called by the Munsees and sometimes by the Delawares Pelāāooh, and the Tōōlpaa or Turtle, (in Munsee Skēēhkee). They say that anciently each of these three tribes was divided into four, making twelve tribes, but they do not recollect the names of those subdivisions.[9]

Mr. Heckewelder has strangely mistaken himself when he said that

Unamis (Woonaūmee) meant Turtle, or Turtle tribe, and Unalachtgo (Woonalaūhtekoa) the Turkey tribe. The term Woonaūmee was given by the Munsees to the Turtle tribe of the Delawares because they resided at a place of that name; and Woonalaūhtekoa is the name of one of the twelve divisions just mentioned. Mr. H. made a similar mistake when he distinguished the Munsees as one of the tribes of the Delaware nation. There are descendants of each of the three tribes among them as well as among the Delawares themselves.

The division into tribes is undoubtedly for the purpose of government, for each tribe has a Council and war Chief who do not interfere with the other tribes. In the receipt of annuities and of presents they strongly exemplify this distinction, by dividing the articles received into three equal parcels correspondng to the number of the tribes, notwithstanding one tribe may contain twice as many souls as another.

It should be here observed that children are always considered as belonging to the tribe of the mother, who is the only relative; and the expression "He is my father but not my relative" tho' singular, is said to be very common.

In the relation of their assumption of the character of women, they agree in substance with the account given by Mr. Heckewelder. They say that about the time of the arrival of the whites or soon after, they were a very powerful and warlike nation, superior in number and prowess to all their neighbours. The Iroquois, jealous of their fame told them that as none of the surrounding nations could withstand them it was unnecessary and improper for them to fight, and solicited them to throw aside the weapons of war and become the arbiters between contending tribes. The Delawares deceived by these flattering speeches and the prospect of their enviable situation as mediators to whom all the neighbouring tribes were to bow in abject submission, consented to the change. A grand council was called and a petticoat of wampum together with a hominy block and pounder, emblems of their degradation, were in due form presented to them. They say that this proceeding was ratified by the Congress (by whom they must mean the·Dutch) from whom they received a medal having an inscription together with a female figure in a state of nudity. This they were told to preserve with great care. They consider themselves still in the condition to which they were reduced by the Iroquois, although the latter acknowledge them to be no longer women but men at the treaty of Greenville; but not being able to procure the quantity of wampum necessary for the construction of their warlike weapons the reassumption of their former authority was not completed.[10]

They know nothing of a nation of Taleekāāee, Aleekāāee or Allegewı, of which Mr. Heckewelder speaks as the possessions of the country east of the Mississippi before the arrival of the Delawares: But Pipe says that one of the twelve tribes of the Delawares, before mentioned, was called Aleekāāee, and that they resided on the Allegheny river. When a boy he saw one of them at his fathers, but at that time they were but very few, and are supposed to be now extinct.

WAR AND ITS INCIDENTS

They do not know that they ever commenced a war but in retaliation for some offence. In such cases if one or more of their own nation was murdered they sent to the aggressors to demand the cause. If the act was committed without the authority of the other nation, as was sometimes the case, a present was generally made to the messenger, with assurances of peaceable intentions. But if they confessed the act authorized by the nation the ambassadors returned with their answer to the council chiefs, at whose command the war chiefs and Lupwaaeenōawuk met together and prepared for avenging the wrong. The War Chiefs were formally invested with the power to prosecute the war and thus authorized they dispatched a messenger to the different villages to notify the villagers of such meeting as they had chosen to appoint. This messenger carried with him a string of wampum called the Candle, (because in such cases he was to travel without ceasing until accomplishment of his task) together with a large belt of the same material, having the figure of a hatchet inwrought. When those invited have assembled at the appointed place, one of the war Chiefs holding the great belt in his hands, which is now covered with vermillion, rises and dances the war dance around the circle formed by the warriors. The council thus opened he explains to them the circumstances which occasion the meeting and with all his eloquence enforces the necessity of resorting to war for a redress of their injuries. He then repeats the dance and seats himself, when each one who chooses to declare his intention to join the party takes the belt and dances around the circle as his chief had done. Few resist the desire to emulate their fellows, and thus in most cases all who attend the council pledge themselves to their leader.

There are no important ceremonies attending this meeting. A bear is killed and eaten and the War Chief addresses them again, declaring more explicitly the object of the war, and advising implicit reliance upon Eelauwunūtoo, the God of Warriors, (from Eēlau a warrior and Manūtoo a supernatural being), who will give them victory. When setting out from the village they go a short distance in a confused body, and then having halted, each man fires his gun, when the chief starts ahead singing a war song. The warriors answer with yells and fall into the line in regular succession, and when the leader becomes fatigued by singing one of his associates, or if he be the only chief, a warrior commences the song to relieve him.

They march in single file so long as they suppose themselves out of danger, but when by their spies they learn that caution is necessary, they separate into smaller bodies or form a solid one, as circumstances and the plan of attack render necessary.

Each man carries his own provisions, but there is a special appointment of cooks for the party, with whose business no one pretends to interfere. At noon the party halt to smoke, and then if there be no prospect of danger the chief appoints the place of encampment and gives permission to some of the young men to hunt during the afternoon. When the hunters arrive at night they deposit their game in one pile under direction of the cooks, by whom it is prepared and distributed in equal proportions among the warriors. No one thinks of taking to himself a greater share than is allotted to another, even if he should have been the only successful hunter. These cooks have a permanent appointment during their youth and generally attend all the war parties, as a reward for which they receive an admission into the body of the wise men. When the party encamp they cut two long poles which they fasten to stakes at the distance of three or four feet from the ground, on opposite sides. In the centre between these poles two stakes are fastened in the earth from which their cooking kettle is suspended. On each side of the fire the warriors repose themselves having their weapons at their heads, resting against the poles. The leader places himself at the eastern end of this open encampment, the sides of which are generally made to run east and west; and notwithstanding the ease with which a warrior can creep out at the sides, he is compelled by custom to rise and walk in the line between the feet of his companions and go out at the end. Nor is any person permitted to go under the cooking poles in crossing from one side to the other. In the morning they leave the encampment without eating, following the chief, who goes out at the eastern end of the lodge singing his war song as they march. All are submissive to this leader, who directs the march, determines the question of battle and directs all their movements. He frequently divides his followers into small bands which remain concealed at different posts assigned to them, until a given signal brings them suddenly upon the enemy.

There is no ceremony succeeding a victory. The warriors meet upon the battle ground where they are congratulated by the Chief, who does not fail to ascribe their success to Eelauwunūtoo, the God of the Warriors. Upon returning to their village they are met by the council chiefs and conducted by them to a large council house, where they make a detailed report of all proceedings. After this they are presented with provisions by the women and the warriors are discharged from further service.

When marching to the attack they select a rallying point to which they return in case of a defeat and thence they proceed to the village, where having reported to the chiefs they are dismissed from service until a further plan of operations shall have been agreed upon.

It is not uncommon for a family to ask of the leader of a war party to bring them a prisoner who shall fill the place of some deceased relative. If one be taken answering to the description given, the chief takes from his medicine bag (an important and indispensible part of the accompaniments of a war chief) a large war belt, which he places around the neck or shoulders of the prisoner, who is thereby protected from insult and danger. Other prisoners are under the care of the particular conquerors until their arrival at the village, when they are delivered to the chief to be by him disposed of as he sees proper. They are generally given to those who have lost relatives in the battle, whose place the leader considers himself bound to fill, and therefore spares the lives of the captured. In the adoption of prisoners no particular distinction is made on account of age, save that the person adopted must be youthful to supply the place of a son or daughter, and aged for a father or uncle.

All prisoners are compelled to run the gauntlet. When the party of warriors approach the village a messenger is despatched with the news of their coming, and two rows of men and women, indiscriminately arranged, are extended from the council house towards the place of approach. Each person is supplied with a stick, and between these lines the captured are made to run. If great exertion is made they may reach the house without injury and are then secure from harm, but fear often produces a severe and sometimes a dangerous beating.

The only instance of burning a prisoner in the reccollection of Pipe, is the case of Col Crawford, at which he was present.[11] Pipe agrees with Mr. Heckewelder, that the death of Col Crawford was attributable solely to the previous massacre of the Moravian Indians. The tragical affair took place a mile and a half from Sandusky. Crawford was tied to a sapling, by a rope fastened around his neck. A fire was built near him, and after suffering great pain for some time he was tomahawked and thrown upon the pile. The practice of burning prisoners is said to have been very ancient. It extended particularly to great warriors, whose capture and death was accompanied with loud shouts by the victors.

Formerly no man joined a war party until he was twenty four winters old, as they were thought of to be too imprudent at an earlier age; but of late years this custom has not obtained among them. The aged often continue to bear arms so long as their strength permits, and some have been known to join war parties when from their advanced age they were obliged to ride on horseback; but in these cases they did not approach the field of battle.

There are no feasts or fasts preceding the departure of a war party, nor do they consult the jugglers upon such occasions. The wounded are entrusted to the care of physicians of the juggling class, specially appointed by the chief for that purpose, and are by them removed to the village. The astonishing powers which these men are supposed to possess are too well known to need description here. Besides other medecines they are said to have a piece of the horn of an unknown serpent, which is grated or pulverized and administered from a muscle shell to such as are shot through the body; and they do not doubt that by the appearance of the medecine when sprinkled on the water contained in the shell, the physician can foretell the effect which it is to have upon the patient. Flesh wounds of no great importance are probed with a feather of the bird Iiāāhum, which is previously dipped in a decoction prepared for the purpose.

This Iiāāhum is a very large bird resembling an eagle. They are not seen in summer, during which time they are supposed to live altogether in the air; but in the autumn and winter they are found in the company of Turkeys, which compose their principal food. The tail is black at the extremity and white near the body, and its feathers afford ornaments for the Indian head dresses which you must have seen frequently. They pretend to believe that this bird cannot be killed by a ball, and they relate an instance of a Shawnee who attempted to shoot one of them but was killed by the rebounding of his own ball. The bird flew away but left one of its feathers as a warning to them not to repeat such attempts. There are many stories of this kind in relation to the Iiāāhum which are too ridiculous to be repeated.

Anciently the women were never known to accompany a war party, but since booty has become an inducement they have been much in the habit of joining them.

They do not possess any tradition of battles fought in canoes, nor of any sieges prosecuted by them, but tradition says that the Iroqouis once besieged two forts occupied by the Conestoga Indians on Buffalo Creek, about fifteen miles from its mouth. Four Munsees were of the party of the besiegers from whom the tradition has been handed down. The Indians used no weapons but bows and arrows and after five days exertion they carried both of the works (which were in sight of each other) by assault, and massacred all the occupants but the women and children.

PEACE

It was customary in former times to send Ambassadors from the conquered to the conquerors for the purpose of laying the foundation for a peace. The persons of these ambassadors were held sacred, and although they did not, like the Munōaminees, bear any external marks of their office, such as going naked; painting their bodies etc, yet from their travelling without any weapons and in a free, unreserved manner, they were known and suffered to pass unmolested if met by any of the enemy. The ambassadors carried a belt of white wampum containing the speech with which he was entrusted, and upon his arrival at the place of destination a council was called and the desires of the nation which sent him, there manifested. If his proposition was favorably received he returned to his nation and brought from them to the conquerors an invitation to attend a council to adjust the preliminaries. At this council a grand feast was prepared and was accompanied with dancing. The weaker party made the necessary acknowledgements, the peace belt was delivered to the conquerors as a token of their superiority and the parties returned to their respective homes. They never have used the pipe as is customary among northern nations, nor had they anything like flags or armorial bearings before their knowledge of the whites.

DEATH AND ITS INCIDENTS

As soon as life leaves the body some distant relative of the deceased takes upon himself the charge of paying the last offices. Two men and two women, not related, are employed in washing and dressing the body, (now in a white cloth, anciently in a newly dressed skin,) which is laid upon a kind of a platform where it is kept one day previous to the interment. This time was formerly three days in summer and seven days in winter, because they supposed that the tutelar deity of the deceased might restore them to life; but at this day they seem to have little faith and are apparently anxious to get the corpse out of sight as soon as decency will permit. The two male attendants prepare a coffin in which they place the body, and it is borne by them to the grave, preceded by the relatives and succeeded by the more distant friends. The grave is dug about three feet deep and the coffin is covered with earth as among the whites. Before they knew the use of boards the grave was lined with bark and the body protected by a covering of the same before throwing in the earth. At the grave one of the relatives renders thanks to the bye standers for their assistance and the mourners return home.

For six days after the interment the near relatives visit the grave twice in each day; once at the break of day, and again at the going down of the sun. In the latter case they frequently remain until late at night.

They seat themselves upon the grave, and not a word is spoken, but each is bowed down to the ground in perfect silence. These visits are said to be made to the deceased who may not have set out upon his journey to the land of spirits and would of course like company during his stay. They have no particular ceremony of mourning except that they abstain from games, dances and other amusements for twelve days, which by the husband or wife of a deceased person is continued for nine months, at the end of which time the relatives of this chief mourner make and present to him or her a new suit of clothes and formally pronounce their willingness for another marriage. They never paint themselves during the mourning season, as is the custom among the Chippeway's, but they divest themselves of all unnecessary apparel and of their ornaments, and suffer their hair to flow loosely about their necks.

It is customary among them to offer the first fine products of the hunting season and the first fruits of the earth at the grave of the deceased. The meat or vegetables being cooked are carried thither by the relatives and a guest not connected with the deceased, is invited to eat that portion which would have been his if living. Silence is preserved during the feast and when it is finished the guest addresses the deceased in a kind of prayer, assuring him (or her) of the extreme regret of the friends left behind and imploring him to rest satisfied with the great change and not to return for the purpose of taking away any of the remaining relatives. Mr. Conner once saw the sister of a chief buried upon the banks of white river and this prayer was addressed to her by her brother, before the earth was thrown upon the body. They sometimes omit the ceremony of the feast at the grave, after a short time, but it has been known to continue for years, and is often renewed upon the appearance of any misfortune which can be attributed to the malignant spirit of the deceased.

They never burn the bodies of deceased persons, nor do they take up the bones for reinterment. They say that the Nanticokes were in the habit of placing the body of the deceased upon a scaffold, where it was suffered to remain until the flesh decayed, when the friends and relatives assembled to pay the last duties to the bones. At this time a dance, called the Spirit dance, took place, in which they had the figure of a human being drawn upon a skin which was stretched over a hoop and suspended in the air. Under this figure sat the singers who continued their songs all the night, for if one of them thro' indolence or excessive fatigue stopped his song, it was an indication of his speedy death. The day succeeding the dance the friends assembled again at the same spot and large presents were distributed by one of the near relatives of the deceased. This man held in his hand a small ball, and placing himself in the midst of a circle formed by the spectators he would pretend to make frequent attempts to throw the ball out of the ring. At length he would throw it where it was least expected, and he who was so fortunate as to catch it received a portion of the presents. This was repeated until all the goods were given out, and at each return of the ball the figure on the skin was made to bow to it. After the distribution of the goods the bones were collected, put into a kind of box and buried in the ground. If a death happened at a distance from the village, as in hunting or on a journey, the flesh was separated from the bones by cutting, the bones were burned until they became perfectly dry and then transported to the place of burial, where the same ceremonies took place.

As Mr. Heckewelder has said, many ceremonies take place at the interment of a distinguished personage, which are not common on other occasions; such are distributing presents, feasting &c; but the general customs are such as have been here related.

They sometimes put articles of furniture or clothing in the graves, as a gun for a man, a kettle for a woman; but this is not considered necessary, and arises only from the desire of the relatives to express some marked esteem for the deceased. At the head of a warrior it is common for them to place a white post, upon which is represented in hieroglyphics the tribe to which he belonged, the number of engagements in which he has been engaged, of scalps which he had taken, &c, but no post is placed at the graves of women.

BIRTH AND ITS INCIDENTS

Children are named at one of the grand worshipping councils, and as opportunities do not occur regularly, there is no particular age at which they are formally named. The child when about to be named is taken to the assembly (which will be hereafter described) and there presented to one of the old men of the same tribe with the father, together with a fathom of wampum for his services. This old man taking the child by the hand, rises and proclaims aloud his name, requesting all who hear him to recollect it. He then proffers a short prayer to the Great Spirit in supplication for his blessing on the child during life; after which it is returned to its parents. They sometimes take the name of the father or the mother, and although they never have more than one name at a time it is not uncommon for them when grown up, to change their name, in which case the same ceremonies at the grand council take place. This subsequent naming is sometimes because the original appellation, being descriptive may be more appropriate for children; at others because the subject has performed some remarkable feat of bravery or is otherwise deserving of a favorite name. They are unwilling to tell their names because the interpretation frequently occasions laughter among the whites. During youth they are in the habit of addressing each other by their names, but after the arrival at mature age the terms of relationship are substituted. They always address the father or mother by those titles, which have been already explained. Each man considers it his duty to advise the children of the same tribe with himself, and to instruct them by precept 'the way they should go,' and to this kind of advice the father, though he may be never so great a scoundrel, is very particular, always enforcing the duty of correctness in their moral conduct. There is no system of education among them. Corporeal punishment is said to be very common. In days of yore children were considered as bound to obey their parents, and were not suffered to marry until the age of thirty if males or twenty four if females; but to use their own language, they have so degenerated that in these days, when a boy begins to grow hoarse he assumes the practices of a man, declares himself independent and marries.

In the distribution of property children receive no particular share. Divisions are made by families in which regard is had to their size or number. Orphans and sometmes neglected children are often adopted by good men in the nation, and are in such case considered as the children of the adopting person subject to the same privileges which his own children enjoy.

Parental feelings are very strong and generally continue during life, in consequence of which, aged relatives consider it their duty to advise the young and deter them from the commission of wrong. But no compulsory means are used after their arrival at years of discretion.

During infancy the children are carried in a cradle like that used by the Chippeways and to amuse them they are put into a hammock constructed of a blanket which is fastened by means of bark ropes to two saplings. There is no difference in the treatment of male and female children. In case of the death of the parents, the maternal grandfather or mother is bound by custom to take the children under protection; but if they also be dead the children are adopted by such relatives or friends as may be inclined to take charge of them. There is no difference in the case of the legitimate and illegitimate children, the mother always taking charge of the latter, to whose support the father may or may not contribute by presents or otherwise, as his inclination dictates.

MARRIAGE AND ITS INCIDENTS

There is no ceremony of courtship and marriage in these degenerate days. Anciently, when the father ascertained that his son desired to marry, if he was of proper age, he sought for him a suitable partner in the person of some female of his acquaintance, and carried to her father a bundle of presents, making known to him at the same time the object of his visit. If the father of the female accepted the present it was a signal of his consent to the union and the visitor returned to declare the result of his visit to his son. On the following night the female was conducted by her relatives to the lodge of her intended husband and there delivered to him. The day succeeding was taken up by the relatives of the bride in carrying to those of the groom large presents of corn, squashes &c together with pouches and other ornaments, the products of female labours, and they also gave her a kettle for cooking. This was the conclusion of the ceremony, and the new married couple then set themselves at work to provide for their future subsistence. Instances of refusal to comply with the wishes of the parents have seldom been known. Formerly each man had but one wife, but now they are permitted to marry as many as they can maintain, who generally form the same family, the youngest having the husbands preference.[12] But if they cannot agree to live together they reside in separate cabins and receive the visits of the husband when he deigns to make them. The husband does not consider it a duty to marry any relative of his deceased wife, but it is sometimes done.

Adultery is considered criminal in either sex, but is subject to no punishment, save that either party may separate from the other. On the part of the female this amounts really to a punishment, for it draws upon her the contempt of the nation; but the man suffers little by it, and is sometimes glad to rid himself in this way of a burdensome wife. The husband may for any cause turn away his wife; and she may separate herself from him, but from the dependent situation of women they seldom choose to avail themselves of this privilege.

In the event of a divorce the children are taken by the mother, and retained until they have arrived at years of discretion when they are at liberty to choose for themselves. Many instances have been known where a man having married a widow also marries her daughter, and this has sometimes been at the suggestion of the mother herself. They do not marry relations by blood unless very distant. An instance is reccollected by Pipe, of two cousins having married before a knowledge of their relationship, and although it occasioned great regret, they considered themselves doubly related, and each strove to render the other happy in consequence of the novelty of the case. Young men have been known to join the families of females whom they loved, by hunting for them and performing other services to gain the affections both of the girl and her parents, but there is in such case no previous understanding that his labours will be so requited. It is uncommon for individuals of either sex to live to an advanced age without being married. Necessity and inclination both prompt them to it.

So far as regards the reputation of women who have children without being married it is affected much as that of the whites. They secure to themselves a good deal of contempt and worthless fellows for their husbands.

ASTRONOMY, MATHEMATICS &c.

They suppose the earth (that is, the Am. Continent,) to be a large island which is surrounded by an immense body of water and rests upon the back of a great Turtle. That it is convex, and therefore the rivers have a fall from their sources. That it was at first but a small body of earth placed by the Great Spirit on the back of the Turtle, and has accumulated to its present sise. They ascribe earthquakes to the moving of this supporter and they suppose that he will one day dive so deeply as to sink the earth and destroy its inhabitants. To the question 'What does the turtle rest upon' they shrewdly answer that, being a Deity he requires no resting place.

The sun they suppose to be a human being, and they call him their brother. Tradition says that in early days the sun was in the habit of devouring twelve indian children each day at noon, as a kind of compensation for his labours; but the inhabitants of the earth becoming incensed at his voraciousness remonstrated. He then proposed to reduce the number to six but they still refused and at length agreed upon two, which number they suppose he now receives every day. The light of the sun is occasioned by the brightness of a feathered head dress which he wears. They think that the Indians once possessed the same general character with the sun, that he has retained his original powers and they have degenerated to their present degraded situation. He is supposed to go under the Island at night for rest. The moon is supposed to be the brother of the sun, and they formerly had numerous relatives who warred against each other and were all killed. The moon was made to commence her present employment in consequence of these wars.

Thy can of course have no correct ideas of the planetary system, when they express such ideas as these. They believe the fixed stars to be stationed at their posts, for their particular benefit, instead of which they say the whites have the compass. Eclipses are thus accounted for—Every man as he grows up is visited in his dreams by his tutelar deity in the form of a Bear, Wolf, Dog, Tree, Cornstalk, or anything else which the imagination can conceive, and by this deity he is protected and governed through life. When he dies his protector assumes the mourning garb common to deities, and through his influence the eclipse of the sun or moon takes place in token of the excess of his grief. I think Mr. Hecke-welders account differs materially from this, but I do not recollect it particularly. The meteors called shooting stars are thus described. Like the sun & moon the stars are brothers to the Indians, human beings, and subject to the frailties of man. When one of them begins to practice lying and fraud he is rejected by the others and obliged to fly from his companions to seek a place of refuge.

They have no ceremonies on the appearance of the new moon, nor can they calculate with certainty the time of its reappearance. They believe that there are three separate islands, that on which they live, that of the whites and that of the negroes; and they suppose that there were three distinct creations in the order just mentioned; but they have no idea of the local situation of these islands.

The four cardinal points are

Loowunāāyoongk	To the winter, from Loōwun, winter.	North.
Shauwunāāyoongk	To the south.	South.
Oapunāāyoongk	To the light, from Oāpun, Light.	East.
Woondhunāāyoongk	To the west. (a proper term)	West.

They divide the year into four seasons, viz: Seēkun, Spring, Neēpen, Summer, Tarkōakoo, Autumn, and Loōwun, Winter. And into twelve moons, viz:

Haumoakwheēta keēshooh [March.]	From a species of shell fish found in March at their former residence on the sea Coast.
Kwāātiioahas keēshooh April.	From the shedding of the hair of the deer.
Tiieeneēpen keeshooh May.	Or middle moon. Between spring & summer, when nothing comes to maturity.
Kitshee neēpen keēshooh June.	Commencing summer moon.
Yaukāutamwaa keēshooh July.	The moon of sacrifice and prayer, from Yaupāutamaum. To pray. In this moon the first fruits of the earth are offered as a feast.
Saukiioahaa keēshooh August.	The moon in which the deer get blue hair.
Kītshee Tarkōak keēshooh September.	Commencing cold moon.

Pŏokseet kēeshooh	October.	Broken moon, from the shedding of the leaves.
Wēenee kēeshooh	November.	From Wēenaa. To Snow. The snowy moon.
Haukhŏakwaa keeshooh	December.	The clouded moon.
Arnēekwsee kēeshooh	January.	The squirrel moon.
Tsharkŏalee kēeshooh	February.	Frog moon. Tshārkoal, a frog.

The word keeshooh signifying sun or moon, is seldom used when speaking of the moons, the descriptive terms answering every purpose.

They have no idea of arithmetic in its most simple forms. But they can reckon to one thousand.

RELIGION

They believe in one Supreme being, who is known generally by the appellation Keshaalemŏokungk, "He who created us by his thought;" and sometimes Kaataunutŏowit, The great spirit, from Khit, great; or Waalseet Maunūtoo. He who is the good spirit, from Woolit, good. They suppose that this being created the world and remained sometime upon earth, having the moral superintendency of all affairs therein, and that having perfected the system which he commenced he left it. With the Indians (these indians) all animals, and even animated nature, trees, plants &c, are considered as beings having supernatural powers. This is proved to be a serious belief by the great distinction in the language, which includes trees, plants and some vegetables in the class of animated beings, and by the superstitious notions of these men, who having been prepared by excessive fatigue, long fasting and harsh treatment from parents, for some unnatural excitement of the mind, dream, or fancy that they dream of seeing their guardian god coming to them in the form of a Bear, Wolf, The Sun, The Moon, a Tree &c, and directing them about their future conduct. Such dream no doubt has great effect during the life of its subject, and in his private worship all his songs are descriptive of some of the events which he saw in his dreams. He often repeats them and does not fail to attribute his success to the deity whose wonderful appearance had foretold his good fortune, or any mishap to his own bad conduct which incensed his guardian.

These deities are all subordinate agents of the great spirit; to whom, as the chief cause, prayers of gratitude of or supplication are directed.

Much of their unhappiness and misfortune is attributed to the evil spirits of which there are many. They are called Maatsēetseet (Those who are bad) Maunūtoowuk (Spirits), but are not distinguished by particular appellations. They have no doubt that good or bad conduct in this life has an effect upon their future happiness or misery, and they suppose that the punishment or reward commences as soon as life leaves the body. If they have led good lives in this world, their souls are transported to the land of the Great spirit in the South, where they find magnificent dwellings, beautiful streams and fertile lands. There they are employed in worshipping the great author of their existence, through whose means they are furnished with all necessary food, together with many luxuries, living eternally in the enjoyment of the same corporeal pleasures which constituted their happiness on earth, though more refined and not alloyed by pain. Those on the contrary who have led a wicked life, are met at death by some of the evil spirits, by whom they are tormented by different species of torture (among which is fire) eternally. Sometimes they are sent by them again to earth, where they roam about in perfect misery. They have an idea that the ghosts of their deceased friends appear to them in the night, particularly after a failure to offer the customary feast at the grave; and they immediately prepare to do what from neglect or disrespect had been left undone, when the ghost ceases the visits. When the ice is about to leave the rivers they make an offering of tobacco with a wooden bowl of parched corn, by placing it on the surface and telling their grandfather, as they call it, that they leave him a pipe to smoke and something to eat on his journey. They sometimes make this offering of tobacco to obtain a safe passage across the ice and for the same reason they throw it into the water when danger is apprehended. When they go to hunt, at the first encampment an offering of tobacco is made by burning, to the seven masters of the game, Mezinkhoaleekun. In former days much use was made of tobacco when going to war. Pipe says that when young he joined the war party of a chief who made such an offering to every stream which they passed, that when they killed any game, such parts as could not be carried were piled up and a piece of tobacco laid upon it, and that once meeting a large black snake the whole party was obliged to stop until the chief placed a little tobacco on the ground before him.

All offerings of tobacco are made to the particular deities of a place, as of a cave, a mountain, or a river, which are supposed to be their places of residence.

The grand national worship of the Delawares has been already alluded to, and I come now to a description of it. It is called Engōmween. There are three or four families in the nation whose duty it is by inheritance to prepare for and invite the nation to this assembly, and to whose care is committed every arrangement respecting it. Each family takes upon itself the performance of these duties once in three years; and as they do so in pretty regular succession, the worship is annual, or perhaps more frequent. The time and place of meeting is designated by this family, the principal male of which sends a messenger to the chief or head man of each village, who in his turn disseminates the information through the families of those under him. At the time appointed the nation, as well males as females assemble at a large lodge prepared for the purpose, where the females are placed in rear of the men. Here with grave and downcast looks they sit and receive from one of the old men an address upon the importance of a due observance of the ceremonies of the worship, and of abstinence from all unlawful pleasures during the continuance of them, among which any connection with women is counted a polluting sin. After describing at length the customs of their ancestors, among which this worship is placed in the foreground, the principal man of those who prepared the place of worship, having in his hand a small turtle shell containing a few gravel stones, gives it a sudden shake, and at the signal the worshippers all rise. He then commences a history of his early dream, repeating it in short sentences, in a natural tone of voice and being followed in the repetition of each sentence by all who are in the house.[13] At length he commences to sing his dream, being followed by the company as before, and relieved between the sentences by a chorus of singers who are seated apart from the other worshippers, and have a kind of tambourin composed of a deer skin stretched across four sticks, upon which they beat the time. The music is said to be agreeable and very soft. After this person has finished the tale of his dream, in which is described minutely every circumstance connected with the appearance of his tutelar Deity, as well as those events of his life, which being foretold, have of course come to pass, each person in the lodge takes him by the hand in a mystical manner and they all seat themselves. The men then smoke for a short time, preserving the utmost silence and gravity of deportment, during which occupation the speaker takes occasion to push the shell under his legs in a secret manner, to the next on his right, who declares his intention to speak by giving it a slight shake, or pushes it in the same secret way to the next. When one has accepted the turtle by the shake of accession, he remains in a state of apparent meditation for a few minutes, and then rising gives it another rattle, when, as in the preceding instance, he is joined by all the worshippers and the same ceremonies of repeating the dream, are performed. The worship is commenced at evening and continues until daybreak, when it ceases for the day during which time the worshippers remain in the lodge in perfect silence. Thus it is repeated from night to night six times, and at the closing of the last night they adjourn for an hour or two, and then finish the worship with the relation of the dream of some extraordinary personage, whose history has been preserved in tradition. They cease at noon of the last day. To discharge the menial services incident to the meeting of so large a body four servants are appointed, of whom two are males and two females. They sweep the council house at every interval of worship and perform any other duty required of them, for which they receive a compensation in wampum before the close of the meeting. To this stock of wampum when collected by the principal or leader of the assembly all contribute who have the mean. Besides these officers, an old man of the juggling class is employed to keep order in the assembly. It is supposed he can tell by going around the lodge whether any person has been polluted since the comencement of the worship by connection with the opposite sex. To such person he points a stick and if he be a man the male servants lead him out of the lodge, from which he is expelled during the remainder of the worship. If a woman the same service is performed by the female domestics. The old inquisitor is dressed in the skin of a bear, with a frightful mask on his face, and is said to be a terrific object, particularly to those guilty of a breach of the customs of the assembly. His attention is often roused by the complaints of some one while telling his dream, who will stop and pretending to find a difficulty in speaking will ascribe it to the improper conduct of one of the members. Upon such occasion the old man commences his examination and his scrutinizing eye points out the object (perhaps as innocent as himself) who is immediately removed, and the speaker continues.

During the intervals between the songs, or at least once every night, the principal rises from his seat and calls before him six or twelve (male) persons (generally to the latter number) from the worshippers. He then delivers to the male servants a quantity of wampum in strings, corresponding to the number of persons called. With these the servants precede the chosen, who go out of the lodge and with their faces turned to the east, seat themselves upon their hams and commence a kind of howl, which they repeat in the same tone twelve times. They then return to the lodge with great solemnity, and take their places as usual.—As a kind of relaxation from the severer duties of the worship, these chosen men are directed by the principal to scatter a quantity of wampum in grains, upon the ground within the lodge. This is for the benefit of the servants, who are obliged to stand upon one leg and take it up with the thumb and finger, a slow method, affording amusement to the spectators. But this only occurs at the close of the nights worship and would be considered improper at any other time. Dancing is sometimes practiced at these assemblages and besides the employment of relating their dreams they are frequently addressed by the old man in exhortations to preserve these customs in their purity, to prolong their own existence by continuing the meetings, and to adore the author, the G. Spirit.

They believe it of the utmost consequence to their children to subject them to hardships in their infancy and youth, and they practice what they profess until the child worn down by fatigue and starvation, undergoes a kind of mental derangement and fancies that he sees himself approached by an aged man who informs him that he is to become a mighty counsellor, or learns from a hunter with his arms covered with blood, that such is to be his profession, a war club, that he practice the art of war, or that by a belt of white wampum he was invested with the commission of mediator. It is easy to suppose that with such impressions, arising as well from the influence of custom as the actual derangement of his ideas, the subject of a dream would exert every act to fulfil the imagined prediction.

There is no juggling or other secret society among the Delawares, but individuals practice all the arts supposed to be in use among the jugglers of other nations which have organized societies. They believe in witches and wizzards and attribute their powers to the use of certain medecine, said to have been procured of the Nanticokes who had it from a naked infant found by them on the sea shore. In 1810, the prophet when preaching against the use of this medecine pointed out five or six men & women on white river as the possessors of it.[14] These persons protested their innocence and were put to the torture, where they were exhorted to save themselves by delivering the means of destruction which they possessed. Seeing no other prospect of escape from death, they professed a knowledge of the arts and promised compliance, but after release they were not able to produce the cause of the difficulty and they were by common consent condemned to death by burning.

Suicide is not uncommon among the Delawares. Mr. Conner knows of many instances of its having been committed, sometimes by shooting, but generally by eating the root of the may apple. It proceeds most frequently from excess of grief or from disappointment in love. Fifteen years since an Indian, a married man, became enamoured of a young woman and was about to take her to his house, but his wife made such resistance, and his mother reprimanded him so severely that distracted with disappointment he went secretly to the woods, ate of the fatal root, and died before assistance could be procured. They proceeded in due time to bury him, and while digging his grave the girl who had been the cause of his death sat at the side of the deceased body in an ecstacy of grief. At length she stole out of the company, procured some of the poisonous root and died at the grave in great agony. The two lovers were buried in the same grave.[15]

GENERAL MANNERS AND CUSTOMS

Their mode of salutation in meeting is not peculiar. They sometimes express a pleasure on seeing each other, at others the simple Anishee, (I am thankful,) is the only expression. They do not as with us, inquire after the health of their families, but of their business, route &c.

It is believed that shaking hands is an Indian custom, but before their knowledge of the whites they used the left hand. In the Engōmween, or worshipping assembly, where ancient customs are said to prevail altogether, they always use the left hand.[16]

This dance, (for it may be so called) and the Lēnkaun, or common dance, are the only dances which they claim as original among them. All others are said to be borrowed.

Great respect is paid to age and rank, and it is customary for the young men to present to the aged and infirm a portion of the products of the hunting season. In such cases the receiver makes a feast of the game to which he invites his aged companions, and there he distributes in moccasin patterns, the skins which composed a part of the present, always informing them of the name of him to whom they are indebted. This kind of generosity does not pass unrewarded for besides the grateful acknowledgements of the old men, it paves the way to an admission into the councils of the nation.

It is very common for them to visit each other for the purpose of serious debate on the affairs of the village or nation, or to relate anecdotes & fabulous tales of times gone by: and it is said that they will entertain each other a whole night with the ingenious story of a wolf, a raccoon, or of some great hunter, whose deeds have been handed down by their traditions. They always devote the evening to conversation and sometimes rise from their beds for that purpose.

They have no words equivalent to our habit of swearing, yet they manage to become as great blackguards, as any found among the whites. Both men & women are frequently very obscene in their conversation. They conceal as much as possible any strong feeling of love or affection to the opposite sex, but the exhibition of such feelings to the same sex is considered praise worthy. An indian returns to his home after a long absence with as much coolness as if he had not been separated from it. He enters his lodge with a word—"I have returned." His wife replies "Arnīshee, I am thankful"—But soon he commences a general conversa-sation upon the subject of the family, which upon the arrival of those who come to congratulate him, is extended to the affairs of the village or nation.

Notes

1. This is a transcript of a manuscript in the C. C. Trowbridge Papers in the Michigan Historical Collections of the University of Michigan, Ann Arbor, whose permission to publish it for the first time is gratefully acknowledged. There is a second manuscript in the same collection, essentially the same in content, entitled "Traditions of the Lenēē Lenāūpee or Delawares." The author of both documents, Charles C. Trowbridge, was engaged in 1823 by General Lewis Cass, governor of the Michigan Territory, to investigate the Indians. In the winter of 1823, Trowbridge visited the home of William Conner on the White River in Indiana, and during the ensuing three months obtained information from Delaware Indian informants, including the aged Captain Pipe, who came from Sandusky, Ohio, to converse with Trowbridge. Cf. James V. Campbell, "Biographical Sketch of Charles Christopher Trowbridge," *Michigan Pioneer and Historical Collections*, vol. 6, pp. 478–89 (1907 reprint, Lansing). This account was written long after the Delawares had been exposed to borrowings from other tribes as well as white influences, and it by no means characterizes their original culture.

2. Another form of Wapanachki, i.e., "people of the sunrise country."

3. This folklore may have originated after the Delawares were thrown into contact with the Wyandot in Ohio.

4. This may be a corrupt form of Atique, Atiga, etc., the Iroquois name for the village on the Allegheny River, which the Delawares knew as Kittanning.

5. The well-known Munsie town near New Castle, Pa.

6. A hero myth which is still remembered by some of the Oklahoma Delawares and, like the legends of King Arthur, became much exaggerated.

7. The concept of each of the three tribes having a war chief and a peace chief had apparently become institutionalized by the time the Delawares settled in Indiana, although as Trowbridge says they jointly shared certain civil authority.

8. See chap. 14 for an account of the burnings inspired by the Prophet.

9. Much confusion still exists about the ancient Delaware political structure, and the informant is probably referring to twelve clans as subdivisions of the three tribes.

10. There is no historical basis for this notion. The Delawares broke their ties with the Six Nations and considered themselves as men and warriors long before the Treaty of Greenville.

11. This incident is described in chap. 14.

12. In ancient times a man probably had as many wives as he was able to support. Monogamy was a concept introduced by Europeans.

13. If this description of the Big House Ceremony was obtained from Captain Pipe, it is doubtless a Munsie version.

14. The Prophet was, of course, Tecumseh's brother.

15. Loss of prestige among the men of his tribe, or shame due to personal failures, might, in extreme cases, also be a cause for self-destruction.

16. Mrs. Nora Thompson Dean remembers attending the Big House Ceremony as a child in Oklahoma, where one of the old Delawares, after reciting his vision, stood with his back to the centerpost and, with his left hand, shook hands with those who danced behind him.

Appendix 4

Voucher for Annuities Paid the Delawares in Missouri Territory on June 10, 1826 *

Delaware Agency James Fork of White River June 10, 1826. We the chiefs, councilmen & captains of the Delaware tribe of Indians do acknowledge that we have this day received from Richard Graham United States Indian Agent the sum of <u>Five Thousand</u> and <u>Three Hundred</u> Dollars the balance due us, after deducting the sum of Three Hundred Dollars paid to John Sample for the burning of his mill by order of the Secty of War, in full for the annuity due to us by the acts of appropriation of Congress May 1796, 1810, 1819 & 1822 in which our Salt Annuity is included [1] & we do hereby release the United States from any farther claims we have for annuity due for the present year—as witness our hands & seals this day & date above Written

In presence of	William Anderson [2]
John Campbell	Won-num-da-gum
Sub Indian Agt	Pe-che-na-ha-lous
James Wilson	Johnny Quick
James Pool	Poushe [Pooshies, the Cat]
Antoine Le claire	Na-qui-ti-ha-ta
	Capt. Killbuck
	Capt. Catchum
	Capt. Patterson
	Capt. Pipe
	Capt. Beaver

* Permission to reprint from the Richard Graham Papers, Missouri Historical Society, is gratefully acknowledged.

Notes

1. By Treaty of 1803 at Fort Wayne, the Delawares, Shawnee, Potawatomie, Miami, Eel River, Wea, Kickapoo, Piankashaw, and Kaskaskia
ceded certain lands to the United States, including the great salt spring
"on Saline Creek, which falls into the Ohio below the mouth of the
Wabash." Because the natives were being deprived of a source of salt,
the government agreed to deliver to them each year 150 bushels of salt
to be divided in such manner as the chiefs may determine. The Delaware
share was 30 bushels, but since it was expensive to ship, Agent John
Johnston settled $100 cash each year on the Delawares instead; see his
letter of October 22, 1821 to J. C. Calhoun, pp. 43–45, Richard C. Adams,
A *Delaware Indian Legend and the Story of Their Troubles*, Washington,
D.C., 1899.

2. The Richard Graham Papers also include a receipt dated June 14,
1826, bearing Anderson's mark and acknowledging he had received his
private annuity of $360 as agreed on in confidence at the Treaty of St.
Mary's in 1819.

Appendix 5

Letter from Caleb B. Smith, Secretary of the Interior,
to President Abraham Lincoln Relative to Delaware Lands

Department of the Interior,
Washington, April 30th 1861

To the President

The third article of the Treaty between the United States and the Delaware Indians, of May 30th 1860, provided that the residue of the lands of the Indians, after the tracts in severalty and those for the special objects therein named, should have been selected and set apart; should be sold, and that the Leavenworth, Pawnee, and Western R. R. Co. should have the preference and might purchase them within six months from the time they should be surveyed, at an appraisement to be made by Commissioners appointed by the Secretary of the Interior. It was also provided that the money resulting from such sale should be disposed of in the manner provided for by the 7th and 8th Articles of the Delaware treaty of May 6th 1854. The 7th and 8th Articles referred to provided that certain funds belonging to the Delawares, should from time to time be invested by the President of the United States in safe and profitable stocks &c.

The Senate of the United States amended this article of the Treaty, by providing that no patent should be issued to the R. R. Co. until twenty five miles of the R. Road from Leavenworth City should be completed and equipped, when a patent should issue for one half of the lands, and that a patent should issue for the other half when the remainder of the road should be completed and equipped; and that on failure of the Company to complete the road within a reasonable time, the land should be sold and the proceeds applied as before directed. This amendment has been agreed to by the Delawares.

All the lands have been surveyed and allotments made in accordance with the terms of the Treaty, and the remainder which is to be sold and the proceeds invested for the benefit of the Indians amounts to about 227,000 acres. This has been appraised by the Commissioners appointed for that purpose, at one dollar and twenty eight cents per acre, which will make the aggregate amount to be invested under the Treaty, the sum of $290,560.

The Rail Road Co. has the option to purchase the land at that price within six months from the time the survey is completed which is about accomplished.

The Directors of the R. Road Co. have filed in the Office of the Indian Bureau a memorial, alleging that in consequence of the general derangement of the business of the country they will be unable to pay for the lands within the time stipulated unless the lands can be used as a means of raising a portion of the capital necessary for the construction of the road. To enable them to carry out the object of the Treaty and secure to the Delawares, as well as to the country the benefit of the road they propose, that the money which they are required to pay for the lands, $290,560, shall be invested in Bonds of their Co. payable in ten years, with interest at the rate of six per cent, payable annually, to be secured by a mortgage on one hundred thousand acres of the land which the Co. has agreed to purchase under the provisions of the Treaty.

This proposition has been submitted to the Commissioner of Indian Affairs who has returned it to this Department with his approval and recommendation that it be accepted. As the proposed arrangement can be carried out only with your approval and under your direction, the object of this communication is to place before you the facts and to request your decision.

The proposed road is to extend from Leavenworth City to a point on the Kansas River opposite the town of Lawrence and thence to the Western line of the Delaware Reserve, a distance of about forty five miles. The construction of this road will be of great importance to the people of Kansas and also to the Delaware Indians, as it must greatly increase the value of their lands, through which it will be constructed, consisting of what is termed in the treaty the "diminished reserve," and containing one hundred and three thousand acres.

The object of the Treaty was two fold, first to secure a sale of the land for the benefit of the Indians, and second to secure to them the benefit of the increased value which would be given to their reserved lands by the construction of the Rail Road.

It is quite evident that unless the arrangement now proposed can be made, the road can not be constructed. In that event, under the terms of the Treaty, the Delaware lands, amounting to 227,000 acres, will be sold by the United States for the benefit of the Indians. Whatever may be the intrinsic value of the lands, the experience of past sales under similar circumstances, furnishes abundant evidence, that the usual combination of squatters to prevent competition at the sale, will prevent a sale for any thing above the minimum price of one dollar and twenty five cents per acre. The Indians will then receive this price for their lands, to be invested by the President in Stocks, while they will lose the benefit of the increased value of the lands which they retain, which would be created by the construction of the road.

On the other hand should the proposed arrangement be made, it will secure the completion of the road within a year or eighteen months, which will increase the value of the lands of the Indians and greatly benefit the State of Kansas. The accomplishment of these objects would fully justify the proposed investment if it shall be regarded as "safe and profitable."

The first point to be considered is, will the investment in these bonds be safe? The title to the whole 227,000 acres of the land is now in the United States. Should the proposed arrangement be carried out, the Rail Road Co. will pay to the United States for the benefit of the Indians, the appraised value of the lands. The United States will then with this money purchase from the Rail Road Co. an equal amount of their Bonds, payable in ten years with six per cent interest payable annually. To secure the prompt payment of the interest and the principal at the maturity of the bonds, the United States will take from the Rail Road Co. an agreement pledging all the interest of the Co. in one hundred thousand acres of the land. Upon the completion of twenty five miles of the road the United States will issue a patent to the Rail Road Co. for one half of the residue of the lands, sixty three thousand and five hundred acres; and upon the completion and equipment of the whole road, they will issue a patent for the remaining sixty three thousand and five hundred acres.

If the Rail Road Co. shall construct and equip the road within a reasonable time, they will acquire a title to one hundred and twenty seven thousand acres of the land. The title to the remaining one hundred thousand acres will continue in the United States as a security for the Bonds amounting to $290,560. Of course it will be impossible for the Rail Road Co. to lessen the security of the Bonds by selling or encumbering any portion of the lands thus pledged, as the title will remain in the United States. In order to determine then, whether the investment in the bonds will be safe, it is only necessary to ascertain what will be the value of the lands when the Rail Road shall be completed. These lands are regarded as among the best lands in the State of Kansas. It is estimated by competent judges, that as soon as the road will be completed they will readily sell for from ten to twenty dollars per acre. But we can hardly be mistaken in supposing that under any circumstances they will be worth at least five dollars per acre. This would make a fund of five hundred thousand dollars pledged as a security for the Bonds, amounting to less than three hundred thousand dollars. Should the Co. fail to construct the road they will not acquire a title to any portion of the lands.

Under these circumstances, I can not see how the investment can fail to be safe under any contingency. An investment at six per cent per annum is as profitable as it has been usual to make for the Indians and is as high a rate of interest as can be expected on permanent investment of so large sum. I see no reason to doubt then, that the proposed arrangement would constitute an investment in "safe and profitable stocks."

> Very Respectfully, Sir,
> Your Obt. Servant
> Caleb B. Smith
> Secretary of the Interior

Appendix 6

Letter from Attorneys for Delaware Indians to President
Abraham Lincoln et al, Relative to Railroads

Washington
June 4, 1861

To his Excellency the President of the United States, Hon The Secretary
of The Interior & Commissioner of Indian Affairs

The undersigned Attys for the Delaware Indians in the State of Kansas
would respectfully show to your Honors—That the appraisement of the
Lands made under the last Administration of that part of their Reserve
that was sold by Article of the Treaty of A.D. 1860 for the Leavenworth
and Pawnee Rail Road—is a fraud on the Indians of the most flagrant
character.

That said lands are now appraised at One $28/100$ Dolls per Acre when
they are in fact worth Ten Dolls per Acre and would readily Command
that price in ordinary times and would sell for Five Dolls or upwards
at this time.

2d That Said Treaty was a fraud in its execution, but it fairly carried
out the Indians desire no change—but in their name we protest against
said Rail Road Company obtaining any rights by virtue of said fraudulent
appraisement.

3d The Indians aforesaid have been by their late Agent kept in ignorance of the said appraisement and only discovered it within the last
month and we do on their behalf ask the appointment of appraisers for

said lands & ask one month to take testimony to prove the charges here
made.

> John P. Ushur and J. W. Wright
> Atts for Delaware [Indians]

Executive Mansion, May 13, 1861
I am not quite satisfied with the plan mentioned within; but I will
consent to it, if the papers be carefully worded to save all the points,
and particularly, with a provision for a forfeiture of the Companie's
right, if it fail in the prompt payment of interest; and for this reason I
wish to see the form of the mortgage, and of the Bonds, before I give my
official approval.

> A. Lincoln

Appendix 7

List of Delaware Indian Pupils in Attendance
at Baptist Mission School [Kansas Territory]
for the Quarter ending Sept. 30, 1858 [1]

	Age		Age
Armstrong, Arthur	14	Newcomb, Taylor	10
Armstrong, Edson	10	Newcomb, John	8
Bulletts, Simon	10	Parker, Job	11
Bulletts, John	8	Pechaqua, G. W.	12
Cummings, Andrew	11	Swanuc, Louise [2]	11
Everett, Solomon	12	Swanuc, James	5
Everett, Thomas	9	Smith, Nicodemus	11
Fall leaf, Cyrus	14	Sacondie, John [3]	9
Freddie Fallleaf	10	Sacondie, Jacob	7
Ferguson, George	6	Thomas, David	9
Haddon, Charles	9	Wilson, Edward	9
Harris, Edgar	9	Washington, William	12
Journeycake, Alex	8	Washington, Francis	8
Ketchum, Simon	9	Washington, Charlie	8
Ketchum, Abram	9	Washington, John	5
Ketchum, Best quality	7	Webb, Walter	10
Love, Samuel	14	Wolfe, John	10
Love, Harrison	13	Zeigler, Henry	9
Love, Solomon	12		
Love, John Franklin	8	Armstrong, H. E.	15
McErwin, Willie	7	Andrews, Elisabeth	13

	Age		Age
Bulletts, Laura	13	Ketchum, Jane	9
Bulletts, Lizzie	8	Ketchum, Barbara	7
Carlyle, Nancy	13	Marshall, Rosanna	9
Copeland, Sally Ann	7	Newcomb, Mary R.	5
Elliott, Lucinda	10	Perry, Nancy	9
Haff, Jane	11	Rogers, Rachel	12
Hendrick, Elvina	9	Rogers, Sophronia	6
Journeycake, Matilda	13	Sacondie, Mary	12
Journeycake, Polly	11	Swanuc, Dora	9
Journeycake, Lucy Jane	11	Thomas, Elisabeth	10
Ketchum, Nancy	11	Wilson, Clara	11

Boys   39
Girls 24
       ——
       63
Daily Average 55

In addition to the studies here indicated [Geography, Arithmetic, Reading, Writing, English Grammar] the Scriptures of the Old and New Testament are daily studied. The histories traced the warnings and promises noted for especial attention and the spirit inculcated. We endeavor to present the Bible as the Rule of Life, under every shade of circumstance.

We certify that the above is a correct report of the number, attendance and studies of the Baptist Mission School among the Delaware tribe of Indians.

[Miss] E. S. Morse, Teacher
J. G. Pratt, Sup't.

Notes

1. I am indebted to Mrs. Mary Smith Witcher for making available to me Microfilm M234 roll no. 275, Delaware Agency, National Archives of the United States from which the above is a transcript.

2. This name appears in such forms as Swannock, Suwannock, Shounack, and so forth and is the Delaware word for "white."

3. The usual form of the family name is given as Segondyne, Secondyan, or Secondine, which is translated as "as long as the building is."

Appendix 8

List of Delaware Indian Pupils in Attendance
at Baptist Mission School [Kansas Territory]
Delaware Reservation, Kansas, for the Six Months
ending December 31st, 1867 [1]

	Age		Age
Anderson, Daniel	12	Hawk, Willie	13
Armstrong, Fernandes	8	Hamilton, Henry	12
Bullett, George	13	Journeycake, Joseph	12
Buffalo, James	10	Journeycake, Isaac N.	8
Bascom, Doctor	11	Ketchum, Thomas	10
Brown, Starr	8	Newcomb, John	15
Compston, Willie	6	Newcomb, Cyrus	13
Clemens, Thomas	12	Newcomb, Thomas	12
Connor, Cyrus	9	Newcomb, Joseph	10
Connor, Willison A.	6	Nichols, John	11
Curleyhead, Albert	12	Randall, Frank	11
Elk-hair, Charlie	12	Smith, Tommie O.	6
Goodtraveller, J. W.	14	Swanuc, James	14
Goodtraveller, Horace	12	Sacondie, Simon	13
Griffey, J. W.	10	Swisher, Henry	6
Halfmoon, Edgar	15	Tanner, Charlie	6
Halfmoon, John	10	Washington, Edson	9
Halfmoon, Fielding	8	Washington, Albert	9
Honeywell, Ely	13	Washington, Ryland	7
Honeywell, Willie	6	Washington, Cyrus	5

	Age		Age
White Turkey, Otis	10	Journeycake, Adeline	15
White Turkey, Dutchman	9	Journeycake, Emeline	15
White Turkey, Harry	8	Journeycake, Anna E.	12
White Turkey, Cootyarkey	7	Journeycake, Cora L.	8
White Artie	11	Journeycake, Emma	10
Zeigler, John	5	Ketchum, Amanda	9
Zeigler, Charlie	14	Konkupots,[2] Mary Eliza	11
		Konkupots, Hannah	9
Armstrong, L. Maria	13	Konkupots, Rebecca	15
Armstrong, Lillie	8	Newcomb, Mary R.	13
Armstrong, Caroline	10	Love, Susie	6
Black Beaver, Lucy Jane	13	Randall, Mary	14
Curleyhead, Lottie	14	Pratt, Lavonia	14
Curleyhead, Carrie	10	Sacondie, Matilda	15
Davis, Melinda	14	Staggers, Mary Ellen	15
Fairfield, Amelia	11	Swisher, Mary F.	10
Goodtraveller, Charlie	14	Washington, Julia	14
Griffey, Hattie	10	Washington, Sarah	7
Honeywell, Susie	14	Williams, Julia A.	7
Hill, Elisabeth A.	10	Ketchum, Mary L.	20
Halfmoon, Lizzie	10	Ketchum, Jane	18

Boys	47
Girls	34
Total	81

Studies pursued were Reading, Writing, Arithmetic, Spelling, Defining, Composition and Bible Lessons

Text Books

Willson's Series as far as Third Reader

McGuffey's School and Family Charts

National School Tablets for Object teaching

Mitchel's Outline Maps and Colton's Geographical Cards

Globes Hemispheres Orrery

Ray's First and Second Arithmetics, Holbrook's Geometrical Forms & Solids for Object Teaching

We certify that the above is a correct statement of the number of Pupils in attendance at the Delaware School, Delaware Reservation Kansas for the Six Months ending December 31, 1867 [3]

Elisabeth S. Morse, Teacher

N. M. Pratt, Supt.

I certify on honor that I have carefully examined the above statement
of the number of Pupils in attendance at the Delaware School for the
Six Months ending December 31, 1867 inclusive and it is in my opinion
correct and just as set forth

John G. Pratt
United States Ind. Agent

Notes

1. Transcribed from the John G. Pratt Papers, Microfilm roll no. 6.

2. This is a family name among the Stockbridges (Mahican) usually
spelled Konkapot. Captain John Konkapot was a well-known Mahican
sachem in the early eighteenth century. Mary Eliza Konkupots listed
above was the grandmother of Mrs. Minnie Chamberlin of Avant, Oklahoma, and a daughter of Levi Konkapot, Jr., who was killed in the Civil
War.

3. There is another list on Roll no. 8 giving the names of 50 boys and
38 girls for a six-month period ending June 30, 1867. The peak attendance
at the school occurred during the period from June to December 1864
when there were 103 children in attendance; ibid., Roll no. 6.

Appendix 9

Delaware Indian Members, M Company,
6th Kansas Volunteer Cavalry
Delaware Council House, Sept. 7, 1864

These are the Following names of the Delaware tribe of Indians Members of M. Company 6th Kansas Volunteer Cavalry [1]

Sergt. 1. Wm. R. Ketchum
" 2. Benjamin Wright
Corp 3. Solomon Love
4. Joseph W. Love
5. Yellow Leaf
6. Thomas Wilson
7. Joseph Sarcoxie
8. John Fish
9. Jacob Linneas
10. John Hatt
11. Jacob Hill
12. John File
13. George Cummins
14. John Shawnee
15. Alex J. Conner
16. John Journeycake
17. John B. Pascal
18. Young Bobb
19. Young Jim
20. Benjamin Journeycake
21. Byan Washington
22. Samuel Wise
23. Philip Brokeknife
24. John Bill
25. John Capps
26. James Partridge

Note

1. This list in John G. Pratt's handwriting appears on Microfilm roll no. 6, John G. Pratt Papers. A letter from Dole to Pratt, dated Septem-

ber 20, 1864, and another from the Assistant Secretary of War to the Secretary of the Interior, May 29, 1865, indicates the above men were mustered in during May, June, and July of 1863 for three years military service. The Indians requested an earlier discharge, but the War Department rejected their request.

Appendix 10

List of Delawares on Reservation in Kansas
Who Decided to Become American Citizens [1]

No. of Families	Heads of Families	Age	No. Minor Children [2]
1.	Mary Jane Defries	24	2
2.	Frances C. Grinter	27	5
3.	Annie Grinter	45	4
4.	William Henry Grinter	25	0
5.	Rosanna Grinter	37	8
6.	Sally Honeywell	36	4
7.	George O. Collins	22	1
8.	Lewis Ketchum	—	—
	Elizabeth Z. Ketchum	31	7
9.	John W. Ketchum	24	0
10.	Mary E. Ketchum	21	0
11.	Sarah Ann Ketchum	41	0
12.	Ellen Swisher	24	4
13.	Melinda Wilcoxen	36	2
14.	Betsey Zeigler	54	1 (died Oct. 1867)
15.	Logan Zeigler	40	—
	Sophia Zeigler	32	2
16.	George Zeigler	24	1
17.	Mary Tiblow Stevenson	17	1
18.	Mary Ann Tiblow	43	5
19.	Nannie Pratt	24	3

Notes

1. Compiled by John G. Pratt according to provisions of 3d article of Treaty of July 1866: "It shall be the duty of the Secretary of the Interior to give each of all the adult Delaware Indians who have received their proportion of land in severalty an opportunity, free from all restraint, to elect whether they will dissolve their relations with their tribe and become citizens of the United States: and the lands of all such Indians as may elect so to become citizens, together with those of their minor children, held for them in severalty, shall be reserved from the sale hereinbefore provided for."

2. The names and ages of all of the minor children are given in the listing which appears on Microfilm roll no. 5 of the John G. Pratt Papers, but I have omitted their names in the above list, which is principally intended to show the heads of families.

Appendix 11

List of Delaware Indians Living on Anadarko Reservation—1876 [1]

Heads of families	Men	Women	Boys	Girls
Black Beaver	1	1	2	1
Joe Harry	2	4	1	3
Long horn	2	3	0	2
Strongman	1	0	0	0
Bull Wilson	1	0	0	0
Jack Williams	1	1	0	0
Bill Thomas	1	2	1	1
Jim Ned	1	1	0	1
Sam	1	2	1	1
Antonis	3	1	0	1
Jim Bob	2	1	0	1
Jim Bull	1	1	0	2
Red blanket	1	0	0	0
Mary Hunter	0	1	0	2
Opossum	2	3	0	0
Dick	1	1	1	0
Jack Harry	1	1	2	2
Betsy	0	2	0	0
Buck	1	0	0	0
Jack Hunter	1	0	0	0
Chinqua ["wild cat"]	1	1	1	0
Sarah	0	1	0	0
Jack Thomas	1	2	0	0
Total Delawares	26	29	9	19

[Also listed were the animals owned by each head of family, adding up to 323 horses, 10 mules, 249 cattle, and 218 hogs.]

Note

1. This document, a copy of which was kindly supplied me by Mrs. Belva Secondine, is in longhand, apparently a ledger page kept by one of the Indian agents. The original is in the Indian Archives Division, Oklahoma Historical Society.

Index

ABOUT THE AUTHOR

C. A. Weslager is the author of numerous articles and monographs and of thirteen books including *The Log Cabin in America, Delaware's Buried Past,* and *The English on the Delaware,* published by Rutgers University Press.

He was twice given the Award of Merit of the American Association for State and Local History and served as president of the Eastern States Archeological Federation and of the Archaeological Society of Delaware.

He is currently Visiting Professor of United States History at Brandywine College, Wilmington, Delaware.

The text of this book was set in Electra Linotype and printed by offset on P & S Special Book manufactured by P. H. Glatfelter Co., Spring Grove, Pa. Composed, printed and bound by Quinn & Boden Company, Inc., Rahway, N.J.

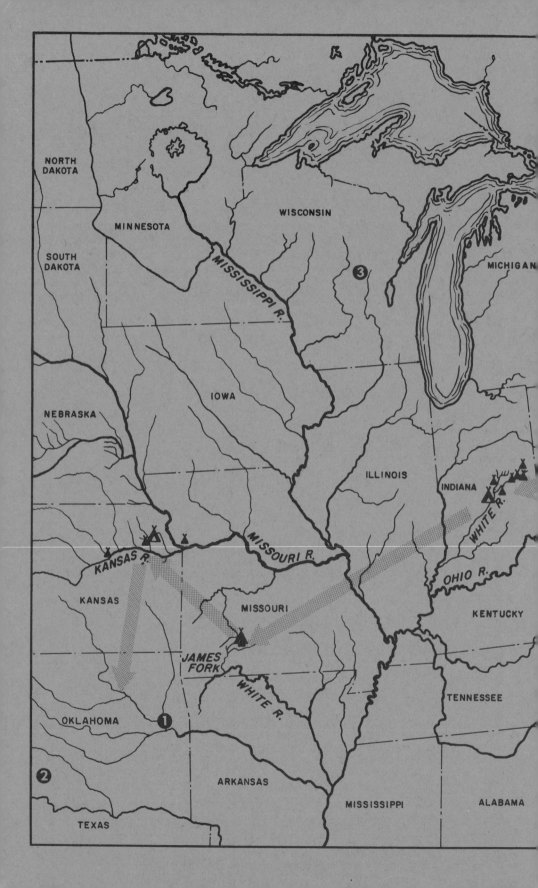